ECONOMICS OF TOURISM AND HOSPITALITY

This book offers students an accessible and applied introduction to microeconomics in tourism and hospitality through a comprehensive analysis of the market mechanism, demand and supply, firm behavior and strategy, and transaction and institution.

This book not only helps students to master core microeconomic theories that are essential for understanding the tourism and hospitality industry, but more importantly, it guides students to analyze consumer behavior and firm strategy specific to the industry. Throughout the book, readers are guided to develop an economic analysis of tourism and hospitality that progresses from economic intuition and graphical representation to mathematical quantification. Carefully corralled case studies showcase the applications of key microeconomic theories in solving a wide range of real-world problems, including Uber's surge pricing, Airbnb's supply adjustment, and McDonald's and Burger King vying for prime locations. This book is written in an accessible style, illustrated with exquisite diagrams, and enriched with a range of other features, such as chapter summaries, review questions, and further reading to aid readers' in-depth understanding.

By reading this book, students will be able to develop an economist's way of thinking, which will enable them to analyze tourism and hospitality businesses in a rigorous and critical manner. This book is essential reading for all tourism and hospitality students and teachers.

Yong Chen, Ph.D., is an Associate Professor at the Ecole hôtelière de Lausanne (EHL), Switzerland, where he lectures on the economics of tourism and hospitality. Prior to joining EHL in 2014, he was a Postdoctoral Fellow in the School of Hotel and Tourism Management at The Hong Kong Polytechnic University, where he also obtained his Ph.D. in 2012. Dr. Chen's research interests include tourist behavior, tourism demand, the sharing economy, and Chinese outbound tourism. Dr. Chen's research has been published in a diverse range of reputable journals, and his opinions have also appeared in CNN, CGTN, *South China Morning Post*, Sixth Tone, and EHL Hospitality Insights.

"This book represents a massive step forward in the understanding and teaching of tourism economics, being a pioneer in entirely focusing on the microeconomics behind tourism and hospitality. Students, teachers, and practitioners will appreciate the author's ability in effectively explaining real-world phenomena with rigorous theoretical analysis. It is a fascinating narrative of tourism and hospitality through the austere language of economics."

— Paolo Figini, Associate Professor of Economics, University of Bologna, Italy

"This book is a timely addition to the existing economics texts. The author has taken a balanced approach in integrating economic theories with tourism and hospitality practices. The coverage of the book is comprehensive and the contents are easily accessible by both undergraduate and postgraduate students studying tourism and hospitality programs. The book is also a very useful reference for academics who have research interests in tourist and firm behaviors."

— Haiyan Song, Professor of Tourism, The Hong Kong Polytechnic University, Hong Kong, China

"Professor Chen presents an insightful integration of modern microeconomic theory and the competitive dynamics of the tourism and hospitality industry. His analysis of the prevailing models and explanations are expertly framed and explicated using examples from a wide-array of industry segments and settings, and he contextualizes the implications in a cogent, comprehensive, and accessible manner that will appeal to students, scholars, and practitioners alike."

— J. Bruce Tracey, Professor of Management, Cornell University, USA

"This book introduces a theoretic overview of microeconomics and provides practical applications to the tourism and hospitality industries. This is a unique reference for students and industry practitioners in tourism and hospitality who are seeking an insight into rapidly changing global markets and customer behaviors. This book is clearly at the top of my recommended reading list."

— SooCheong (Shawn) Jang, Ph.D., Professor of Hospitality and Tourism Management, Purdue University, USA

ECONOMICS OF TOURISM AND HOSPITALITY

A Micro Approach

YONG CHEN

LONDON AND NEW YORK

First published 2021
by Routledge
2 Park Square, Milton Park, Abingdon, Oxon OX14 4RN

and by Routledge
605 Third Avenue, New York, NY 10158

Routledge is an imprint of the Taylor & Francis Group, an informa business

British Library Cataloguing-in-Publication Data
A catalogue record for this book is available from the British Library

Library of Congress Cataloging-in-Publication Data
Names: Chen, Yong (Tourism management scholar), author.
Title: Economics of tourism and hospitality : a micro approach / Yong Chen.
Description: Abingdon, Oxon ; New York, NY : Routledge, 2021. | Includes bibliographical references and index.
Identifiers: LCCN 2020047707 (print) | LCCN 2020047708 (ebook)
Subjects: LCSH: Hospitality industry. | Tourism. | Microeconomics.
Classification: LCC TX911 .C488 2021 (print) | LCC TX911 (ebook) | DDC 338.4/791—dc23
LC record available at https://lccn.loc.gov/2020047707
LC ebook record available at https://lccn.loc.gov/2020047708

ISBN: 978-0-367-90367-1 (hbk)
ISBN: 978-0-367-89735-2 (pbk)
ISBN: 978-1-003-02324-1 (ebk)

Typeset in Stone Serif, Avenir and Rockwell
by codeMantra

Access the Support Material: www.routledge.com/9780367897352

Dedicated to my students

Contents

Figures

Tables

Acronyms

ADR	average daily rate
AFC	average fixed cost
ATC	average total cost
AVC	average variable cost
BL	budget line
CPI	consumer price index
CR	concentration ratio
CS	consumer surplus
CTO	Caribbean Tourism Organization
DWL	deadweight loss
ERB	electronic reservation book
FAO	Food and Agriculture Organization of the United Nations
FC	fixed cost
GDP	gross domestic product
GDS	global distribution system
GVA	gross value added
HHI	Herfindahl-Hirschman Index
IPO	initial public offering
KFC	Kentucky Fried Chicken
LRAC	long-run average cost
MC	marginal cost
MR	marginal revenue
MRS	marginal rate of substitution
MRT	marginal rate of transformation
MU	marginal utility
NAICS	North American Industry Classification System
OECD	Organisation for Economic Co-operation and Development
OTA	online travel agency
PS	producer surplus
RevPAR	revenue per available room
SIC	Standard Industrial Classification
SIDS	small island developing state

SRAC	short-run average cost
SS	social surplus
STR	Smith Travel Research
TC	total cost
TCE	international tourist arrivals at collective tourism establishments
TF	international tourist arrivals at frontiers
THS	international tourist arrivals at hotels and similar establishments
TR	total revenue
UNWTO	World Tourism Organization (since 2005)
USCB	United States Census Bureau
USHG	Union Square Hospitality Group
VC	variable cost
WDI	World Development Indicators
WTO	World Tourism Organization (before 2005)
WTTC	World Travel & Tourism Council

Symbols

a	ask price, coefficient of quantity demanded or supplied
b	bid price, y-intercept of demand or supply curve
c	marginal cost, average cost
C	total cost
d	firm demand, firm demand curve
D	market demand, market demand curve
E	market equilibrium
F	firm, product of a firm
i	individual buyer, individual firm
I	consumer budget
j	individual seller, individual firm
K	capital
l	labor input of a firm, leisure
L	labor, Lerner index, length of street
N	number of firms, quantity of interactions
p	price set by a firm
P	market price
q	quantity demanded by a consumer, quantity supplied by a firm
Q	quantity demanded in the market, quantity supplied in the market
r	willingness to pay
R	firm revenue
s	willingness to sell, market share
S	market supply, market supply curve
t	time, transportation cost
T	time
U	utility, indifference curve
w	wage
Y	income
η	elasticity
λ	matching probability
π	firm profit

Preface

Perhaps nobody would deny the beauty of economics that by and large lies in its regularity and generality. Regularity represents the ethereal form in which economic models and theories are manifested. It demonstrates a great deal of precision, sophistication, and rigor, leaving no room for any misinterpretation or sophistry caused by the ignorance of economic assumptions. Such regularity is attributed to the mathematization of economic models which, ironically, is also the reason that economics has been criticized by many both in and outside the profession of economics for being insulated from explaining real-world phenomena. However, economists make no attempt to replicate the real world or the way it functions by developing economic models, nor would they claim to change the world, a mission that Karl Marx thinks is bestowed on philosophers. In fact, a scientific approach to explaining the real world is to know how to simplify its complexity in the first place, thereby distilling principles that can represent, rather than replicate, reality. This comes with the generality of economics, a set of general principles that are abstracted from one aspect of human behavior but are universally applicable. This is the first piece of information that this book aims to communicate to its readers besides the content per se.

The edifice of economics can be built little by little in one context and grounded on evidence piece by piece in another, but the context itself is not self-explanatory and needs to be interpreted. Tourism and hospitality are contexts, and thus need to be interpreted. There have been many attempts made and initiatives advocated by tourism pundits, surprisingly more in China than in other countries, to professionalize the study of tourism as a discipline. Many of them lament that the lack of a general theory of tourism, or a discipline for that matter, has encumbered tourism education and research which would otherwise be elevated to a status as widely admired as economics, for instance. I think it is the very opposite. Ignoring the contextual nature of tourism and hospitality would not only delude educators and researchers into thinking that the nonexistent general theory will be invented anyway, but would have also led young students who are passionate about studying tourism and hospitality astray from obtaining a genuine understanding of it. For tourism education and research, the key is to resort to a discipline, whatever it might be, for the discipline is *the* common language through which scholars with various academic training can converse scientifically with each other on subjects related to tourism and hospitality.

Economics is one of the disciplines. That said, I have no intention to downplay the significance of tourism and hospitality as a context that can help us better expound economic theories. On the contrary, tourism and hospitality education has rooted deeply in the industry context, beginning with serving the British leisure class in the late nineteenth century. This was also a pivotal time that resonated with the shift in research paradigm from classical economics to neoclassical economics. The context of tourism and hospitality is still pertinent today not only to running hospitality businesses but also to furnishing evidence for economics. Above all else, this context has tremendous implications for the study of behavioral economics because tourism consumption to some extent deviates from what rational choice theory would predict. For this reason, tourism and hospitality constitute the best context not only for us to apply economic theories but perhaps to generate economic theories that could benefit mainstream economics. Therefore, the present book explores this context from as far back as the 1840s when the first package tour was carried out in England to what is known as the sharing economy that has revolutionized world business since the 2000s. I hope this book can be an intriguing narrative of tourism and hospitality using the intriguing language of economics.

While the current book focuses on the application of microeconomic theories, it does not prescribe any course of action for operating businesses in tourism and hospitality. It is a positive economics text that aims to explain microeconomic foundations of tourism consumption, production, and transaction. What this book does convey is my belief in the principle of the free market and competition that can eventually lead to economic efficiency in tourism and hospitality. Tourism consumption and production are completely private economic activities except in those countries where the national economy depends heavily on tourism, and hence governmental intervention could be justified. However, this exception should not be seen as a norm in developing the tourism economy. The norm is that the industry is highly competitive, and the only way for businesses in tourism and hospitality to survive is through market competition, and to thrive is through constantly providing better goods and services to consumers at lower costs. This is where the well-being of both consumers and firms lies.

Lausanne, Switzerland
September 13, 2020

Instruction to readers

This book has primarily been written for students and teachers who study and teach the microeconomics of tourism and hospitality. If you are a student majoring in tourism and hospitality, this book provides you with a microeconomic analysis of the tourism and hospitality industry, including application of the market mechanism, analysis of tourism demand and supply, firm behavior and strategy as well as transaction and institution in tourism and hospitality. If you major in economics or other business disciplines, this book is a reference for you to understand where microeconomics and the tourism and hospitality industry meet and how to apply microeconomic theories in the industry. If you are an undergraduate, a perquisite for this book is rudimental microeconomics knowledge; even though this book expounds basic microeconomic theories in great detail, it does so in an analytical way. If you are a master's student, this book can help you sharpen your analytical skills of using economics to explain real-world problems. If you are a teacher wishing to adopt this book or take the approach of this book in your teaching, I provide detailed teaching notes, analytical diagrams as well as data and statistics in the industry, which can be tailored and integrated in your own teaching. These materials are available for download at www.routledge.com/9780367897352.

Throughout this book I underscore the linkage between the *context* and the *concept* in analyzing economics of tourism and hospitality. The context is industry evidence, or anything related to an economic problem or phenomenon in the tourism and hospitality industry. The concept is economic concept on which economic models and theories are developed in the first place. This book synthesizes core microeconomic theories that are required for undergraduates and master's students to develop an analytical understanding of the industry of tourism and hospitality. This book focuses on economic analysis of tourism and hospitality that progresses from economic intuition, graphical representation to mathematical inference. The analysis is structured in five modules. Module 1 lays down the empirical and theoretical foundations of economic analysis in which the market mechanism is articulated. Then, the analysis bifurcates between demand theory in Module 2 and supply theory in Module 3, on which firm behavior and strategy are grounded and expounded in Module 4. I conclude the book by touching on transaction and institution in Module 5 which resonate with the key empirical and theoretical issues outlined in Module 1. Each module concludes with a case-study chapter that applies theories in the module to an industry case except for Module 4, in which two case-study chapters are designed.

From a pedagogical point of view, I recommend allocating between 35 and 40 teaching hours for the whole book. Each of the 12 theoretical chapters is suggested as a 2- or 2.5-hour lecture; and each of the six case-study chapters can take 1 or 1.5 hours to complete. I provide two types of questions which enable students not only to grasp the content of each theoretical chapter but also to apply the concepts and models in each chapter. First are "review questions" designed for the 12 theoretical chapters. There are 10 multiple-choice questions for each chapter, aiming at testing students' understanding of key economic concepts, models, and theories. These questions can be assigned to students as homework or facilitated by instructors during or after class. I do not design chapter review questions for the six case-study chapters because these chapters focus on applications instead of introducing new concepts or theories. Second are "problem solving" questions designed for each chapter that aim to test students' competencies in applying economic theories into industry practices. Problem solving questions are open-ended, and can thus be used in tutorials, if any. Solutions are available for download at www.routledge.com/9780367897352.

This book is also a useful reference for practitioners or readers with an industry background either in tourism, hospitality, or in other industries that render goods and services to tourists. If you are the reader I'm referring to, you can simply disregard the analytical part of the book without compromising your understanding of the economic aspect of tourism and hospitality. While you can also disregard chapter review questions, problem solving questions might be of interest to you, because these questions pertain either to the industry practice or to the economic phenomena that might have long baffled you as a practitioner. That said, I have no intention to prescribe a course of action despite the fact that Modules 4 and 5 are exclusively dedicated to explaining firm behavior and strategy in tourism and hospitality. Economics, after all, differs fundamentally from action-oriented business subjects. It is grounded on a certain degree of abstraction which, in my opinion, is a cornerstone in learning and teaching economics. For this reason, I intentionally do not evade abstractions in this book despite the fact that abstraction is usually unpalatable to many.

Acknowledgments

This book would not have been possible without the trust and encouragement of Dr. Fabien Fresnel and Dr. Prashant Das as well as the support from Lydia Kessell, Emma Travis, and Cathy Hurren. First of all, I truly appreciated the trust and encouragement from my former dean Dr. Fresnel at the Ecole hôtelière de Lausanne (EHL), who assigned the teaching of tourism economics to me as far back as 2014 and had full confidence in my ability to elevate the academic standard of the course to what it is today. His trust and encouragement unexpectedly led to the publication of this book. I'm grateful to my colleague and friend, Dr. Das, because he was the one who incessantly prodded me into developing my ideas of teaching economics of tourism and hospitality into a book which could benefit students and teachers far beyond EHL. He also introduced me with great enthusiasm to Miss Travis, senior editor of *Tourism, Hospitality, and Events* at Routledge, who introduced me to my editor Miss Kessell and then to production editor Miss Hurren. I wish to express my great gratitude to Miss Kessell and Miss Hurren for their professional editing advice as well as for pardoning my interminable delays for the submission of the book.

I would like to thank my colleagues in the economics department of EHL. Dr. Claudio Sfreddo has influenced me unobtrusively yet deeply in my teaching. He exemplifies what an excellent teacher should be and what teaching excellence might look like. His influence on me took root in this book. Dr. Giuliano Bianchi, with whom I have concluded a few economics projects, made me immersed in the world of economics even through talking over the lunch table. Dr. Isabella Blengini, with whom I have been co-teaching tourism economics and later hospitality economics since 2015, helped me delve into teaching economics of tourism and hospitality from an economist's point of view. Dr. Mondher Sahli, my former colleague, provided me with valuable insights into the industry from a European's perspective. I would also like to thank Dr. Luciano Lopez and Dr. Benjamin Tissot-Daguette, whose vigorousness and agility keep inspiring me day after day. I would like to thank my deans Dr. Inès Blal and Dr. Reza Etemad-Sajadi for providing me with tremendous opportunities and academic freedom which allowed me to experiment with new ideas in my teaching and research.

I wish to thank the following people who furnished me with the data, statistics, and pictures, as well as study results, which fleshed out the empirical part of this book. Prof. Bruce Tracey and his colleagues from Cornell University inspired me to interpret the tourism and hospitality industry from the dimensions of breadth and depth in Chapter 1. Yang Li and Laura Delgado Álvarez at the World Tourism Organization granted me the permission to use the international tourism data in Chapter 1.

Dr. Jonathan Hall and Dr. Cory Kendrick both from Uber and Dr. Chris Nosko from the University of Chicago developed an excellent case study of Uber on which Chapter 3 was based. Prof. Haiyan Song from The Hong Kong Polytechnic University, Dr. Liesbeth Colen from the European Commission, and Prof. Johan Swinnen from the University of Leuven shared their study results in Chapter 5. Jenny Moran at the Record Office for Leicestershire, Leicester and Rutland granted me the permission to use a series of travel brochures of Thomas Cook in Chapter 6. Prof. Steven S. Cuellar at Sonoma State University shared his study results in Chapter 7. Steve Hood from STR, Prof. Hangjun Yang from the University of International Business and Economics of China, and my colleague Dr. Cindy Heo provided the data in Chapters 10 and 11. Prof. Raphael Thomadsen from Washington University in St. Louis shared his study results in Chapter 15. Prof. Roland Schegg from HES-SO Valais-Wallis and Cindy Estis Green from Kalibri Labs provided the data in Chapter 16. Doug Nathman and Edward T. Rose from Trefis provided a rich dataset of OpenTable in Chapter 18. I'd like to thank all the folks whose study results have been cited in this book but are not acknowledged above.

Judit Varga copyedited the book, and her suggestions brought clarity which I truly appreciated. My academic assistant Isabelle Campiche, also an EHL graduate and student in my class, helped me proofread the book at the final stage and provided me with valuable suggestions. My colleagues Andrew Brenner and Lorence Demian Marienthal provided me with various writing tips not only for writing up this book but also for other projects. Last but not least, I express my gratitude to my undergraduate students at EHL, Guilin Tourism University, China, and the École d'Hôtellerie et de Tourisme Paul Dubrule, Cambodia, and to my EMBA students at EHL and China Europe International Business School (CEIBS), whose inputs motivated me to improve the teaching of economics in tourism and hospitality. My influence on them, if any, is a principle which has been constantly underscored in my class, practiced by myself, and manifested in this book: the deeper we delve into the rudiments of economic theories, the more capable we shall be to unleash the power of economics in explaining real-world phenomena. This principle applied in Adam Smith's time is the same as it applies today, and it applies to human behavior in general the same as it applies to tourism and hospitality in particular. Of course, the power and beauty of economics is credited to all economists whose ideas were cited, expounded, and applied in this book.

Yong Chen
Lausanne, Switzerland
September 13, 2020

MODULE 1

The market

1 Economic approach to tourism and hospitality

We begin the economic analysis of tourism and hospitality by, first and foremost, providing an economic description of the industry from both demand and supply sides. On the one hand, we regard modern tourism as an economic phenomenon dating back to Thomas Cook's tour operating business in England in the 1840s. On the other, the legitimation of tourism in the national economy depends on its contribution to gross domestic product (GDP), among others. The economic approach to tourism and hospitality allows us to elicit the demand and supply forces that drive the tourist economy and are subject to economic analysis. The economic description of tourism and hospitality is not only set up for this book, but applies to the tourism and hospitality industry as a whole insofar as the economic aspect of the industry is concerned. Throughout the book we shall adhere to the economic description outlined in this chapter, and analyze the key components of the industry for both demand and supply.

AFTER STUDYING THIS CHAPTER, YOU SHOULD BE ABLE TO:

- Understand what makes up modern tourism and hospitality;
- Describe the supply side of tourism and hospitality, referred to as the breadth and depth of the industry;
- Describe the demand side of tourism and hospitality, namely the tourist and the tourist economy; and
- Appreciate the economic significance of tourism at both national and international levels.

1.1 Tourism and hospitality

1.1.1 The making of modern tourism

The making of modern tourism was, above anything else, an entrepreneurial endeavor. It began in England on July 5th, 1841 when Thomas Cook (1808–1892) chartered a train taking some 500 people on a one-day excursion between Leicester and Loughborough, two towns in central England merely eleven miles apart. Prior to his foray into what became known as the tourist business, Thomas Cook had been a preacher and social activist devoting his lifetime to the temperance movement prevailing in England in the second half of the nineteenth century for promoting complete abstinence from alcohol consumption. As a matter of fact, this excursion by and large was not only a byproduct of the temperance movement, but his later tourism business also had a more or less religious bent. It was not until 1845 that Thomas Cook inaugurated commercial package tours from Leicester to Liverpool and started to make profits from tourism.[1] In 1841 he founded Thomas Cook & Son in Leicester, a travel company specializing in the tour operating business, which to a large extent shaped the tourism industry in England and presaged mass tourism across Europe and North America. Over the decades in his tourism operation, Thomas Cook not only contracted with individual service providers, such as railway companies and hotels, to arrange package tours, but he himself would also escort tourists on their trips to Europe and beyond.

By today's standard the first package tour executed in 1841 was barely modern in terms of demand and supply. First of all, since the tourists were temperance activists, their travel had little bearing on the kind of leisure or recreation that underpins tourism in modern times. Second, the number of tourists was small and thus insufficient to entice suppliers in the majority of hospitality sectors such as accommodation and catering at the destination to deploy resources in producing goods and services for tourists. However, a series of these tours in the 1840s was a necessary prelude to modern tourism, because for the first time in history travel activities were commercialized in the form of package tours and institutionalized through the founding of tour operators. These revolutionary changes eventually allowed mass tourism to flourish in the late nineteenth and early twentieth centuries. The tour operating business did not only make tourism along with all sorts of hospitality products and services accessible and affordable to the burgeoning British leisure class, but it also unleashed the potential of tourism consumption far beyond Europe. For instance, in 1851, Thomas Cook was capable of organizing a whopping 150,000 visitors to attend the Great Exhibition in London.[2] During 1872–1873 he organized and escorted the first round-the-world tour, which took 222 days to complete and covered more than 29,000 miles.[3]

There is no doubt that massive human movement across England and beyond would not have been possible without the railroad revolution. By 1850 the United Kingdom already had 6,500 miles of railway line in operation, adding more than 500 miles per year in the decades that followed.[4] By the late nineteenth century, certain railway companies in England even started to operate package tours by themselves and competed with Thomas Cook. Above anything else, tour by train was not only a predominant travel mode but the very definition of tourism in the late nineteenth and early twentieth centuries. The technology brought about tremendous opportunities for tourism and hospitality businesses to flourish in England as it did for the whole economy as well. Yet the role that package tours had played in shaping the modern tourism industry was by no means in the shadow of the railroad revolution.

The business of package tours manifests the economic principle of mass and standardized production. As Thomas Cook put it:

> [t]he major cost of each train trip was the coaling and the 'steaming up,' so the idea was to pack it with people... I now see no reason why a hundred may not travel together as easily as a dozen.[5]

This principle is practiced by today's tour operating enterprises as well, including online travel agencies (OTAs). This business model would also mirror the mass production of automobiles by Henry Ford in the United States in the 1910s and 1920s through the assembly line in producing the Model T.

1.1.2 The essence of hospitality

Long before the nineteenth century when the word *tourism* entered the English language, a couple of synonyms, such as travel and hospitality, had been widely used to refer to one aspect of tourism or another. Nevertheless, these words are inadequate to capture the meaning of tourism even after tourism becomes mainstream in society. In modern connotations tourism is far beyond the displacement of people from their usual environment to an alien destination for subsistence, but instead it has a hedonic and utilitarian pursuit of well-being which can partially be fulfilled by travel. By no means is hospitality merely about offering food, shelter, and benevolence to friends at home or practicing the doctrine of Christianity that accommodates the needy and strangers in churches.[6] Because tourism in modern times encompasses recreational and hedonic experiences on the demand side, hospitality is accordingly morphed into a sophisticated business on the supply side. The business of hospitality aims to elevate various human needs and wants far beyond subsistence and material gratification in the pre-tourism era. Regardless of the context in which specific hospitality products and services are delivered, at the heart of hospitality is the amicable relationship between hosts as hospitality providers and guests as the receivers.

In common parlance, tourism suggests that anyone could be a stranger sometime and somewhere as long as he or she is exposed to an alien environment. This was the case for the first cohort of tourists traveling from Leicester to Loughborough who would desperately crave hospitality services and warmth rendered by their hosts in Loughborough. The separation between tourists' place of residence and a destination creates curiosity for tourists on the one hand, and on the other brings about uncertainty and insecurity. Since tourists are vulnerable to numerous adverse events and mishaps that may occur at a destination both geographically and culturally distant from their usual environment, they would crave safety and security more than they do at home. There is no question that today's hospitality industry needs to build up the amicable host–guest relationship that has been rooted deeply not only in the Christian doctrine of serving the needy but also in human nature at large. Nurturing such a relationship has opened up tremendous business opportunities for enterprises at destinations to proactively meet various needs of tourists. Therefore, we have seen miscellaneous hospitality products and services in the marketplace, ranging from shelter and accommodation provided by hotels, strength and energy restoration at restaurants to numerous amenities handed to tourists on a platter by today's splendid tourism and hospitality industries.

1.1.3 Tourism versus hospitality

When it comes to the analysis of tourism and hospitality, a predicament is how to distinguish between the words *tourism* and *hospitality* as they are sometimes used interchangeably both in the industry and in academia. Some distinctions have been made by academics attempting to exhaust all tourism- and hospitality-related businesses in the market, aiming to piece together a holistic picture of the tourism and/or hospitality industries. The fact is that travel-, tourism-, and hospitality-related sectors are not only fragmented with regard to their distinct functionalities but are also evolving as new businesses burgeon to meet the needs of tourists as well as locals. As far as supply is concerned, the tourism industry itself cannot be sustained in its own right because it is, by nature, a combination of a wide range of sectors, primarily hotels, airlines, restaurants, and so on. Hence tourism cannot be decoupled from hospitality. At the same time, however, many hospitality establishments, such as guest houses, inns, and taverns to name a few, long predated what became known as modern tourism in the mid-nineteenth century. As an economic phenomenon in the nineteenth century, tourism was restricted, if not exclusively, to recreational travel. Therefore, on the supply side, hospitality can be largely independent of recreational travel and mass tourism. However, as tourist demand expands, so does the supply of hospitality, and hence they become inseparable.

1.2 Breadth and depth of tourism and hospitality

There are many definitions of the tourism and/or hospitality industries based on the disciplinary perspective that one holds or the purpose of classification between tourism and hospitality. In fact, it would not be possible to propose *the* definition of the tourism and/or hospitality industries that suits various practical needs and theoretical explanations of the tourism phenomenon. A meaningful and feasible approach is to adopt *a* definition that is consistent with the generally accepted industry belief of what ought to be incorporated in tourism and hospitality and meanwhile serves the purpose of economic analysis. On the practical side, the tourism industry is not a single industry entity but a conglomerate of various travel-, tourism-, and hospitality-related sectors, such as hotels, restaurants, airlines, casinos, and so on. Insofar as economic analysis is concerned, we need to articulate the demand and supply sides of the industry. Because no such product as tourism really exists, the supply of tourism by which it can be compared with agriculture and manufacturing becomes elusive and undefinable. Perhaps not so perplexing is to explain tourism from the demand side. After all, each of these sectors mentioned above meets at least one aspect of tourist needs. This allows us to turn to the mechanism by which these sectors are organized to bridge the chasm between demand and supply that are geographically isolated in tourism.

In this book we subscribe to a definition proposed by Bill Carroll and his colleagues in their online course "Introduction to Global Hospitality Management" delivered on edX in 2015. Their approach aims to link the demand and supply of the whole industry through travel intermediaries, and thus the industry can be addressed on two dimensions, *breadth* and *depth*. We refer to this definition as the breadth-depth framework of the tourism industry (Figure 1.1). The breadth dimension addresses the supply side of the industry, which by and large incorporates all industrial sectors primarily at destinations that provide goods and services directly to tourists. In general, the breadth dimension summarizes all sectors related to either tourism, hospitality, or travel. Obviously, a majority of these sectors are hospitality sectors located at destinations. The depth dimension describes the linkage between demand and supply through travel intermediaries. Thus, the tourism industry is built up from one layer, namely suppliers, on another, namely various travel intermediaries that facilitate transactions between suppliers in all these sectors and tourists as end consumers. The breadth-depth framework not only integrates travel-, tourism-, and hospitality-related sectors on the supply side but also articulates the relationship between demand and supply.

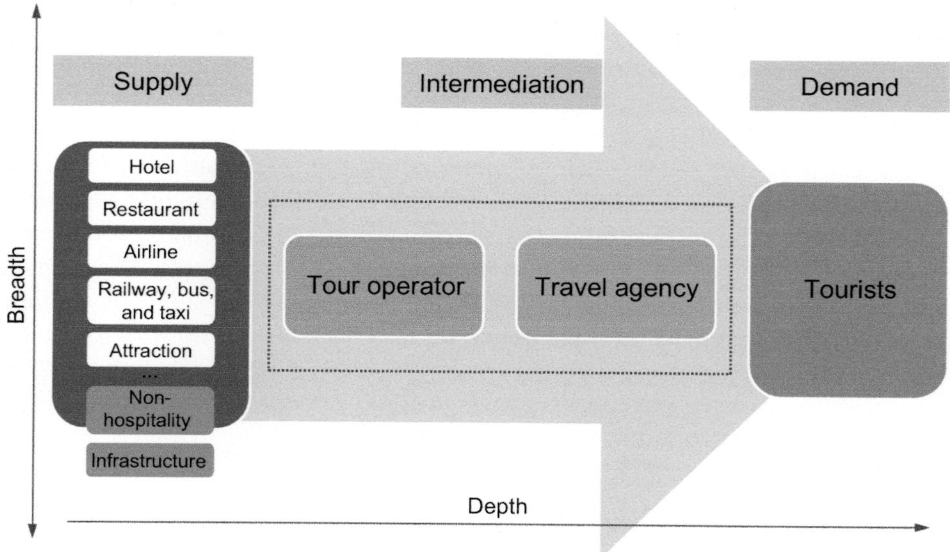

Figure 1.1
Breadth and depth of the tourism and hospitality industry

Note: This framework is produced based on the ideas of Bill Carroll, Jan deRoos, Cathy Enz, and Bruce Tracey in their 2015 online course "Introduction to Global Hospitality Management" on edX.

1.2.1 Breadth of the tourism industry

The breadth of the tourism industry addresses the wide scope of supply, ranging from hotels, restaurants, airlines, casinos to various destination attractions that render a plurality of products, services, and experiences to tourists. Besides conventional hospitality supply, the breadth of the industry may encompass infrastructure and other amenities that are not hospitality-oriented or do not serve tourists. However, they facilitate tourists' travel activity and for this reason also earn revenues from tourist expenditure at destinations. Therefore, the breadth of the industry is grounded on the fact that tourist needs are broad and heterogeneous. In addition to being met by conventional hospitality supply, these needs are met by peripheral infrastructure and public services, such as airports, highways, and consumer information. As a matter of fact, high-quality infrastructure and public services are instrumental in boosting tourism demand in the first place through attracting suppliers to produce in tourism and hospitality. From a practical point of view, tourist spending on peripheral services is counted as tourism receipts by destination countries, despite the fact that such expenditure is irrelevant to conventional tourism or hospitality products and services. Since peripheral businesses earn tourist dollars through facilitating tourism consumption, they are included in the tourist economy as far as the demand side of tourism is concerned.

The breadth of the industry also suggests that the scope of supply is extensive and dynamic. The supply of tourism and hospitality keeps expanding as new hospitality businesses or a hybrid of incumbent tourism or hospitality businesses emerge. For instance, a startup called NapCity in Germany provides sleep capsules at airports for travelers who have missed their flight or are waiting during long layovers.[7] These sleep capsules cannot be classified in the hotel sector nor in other incumbent lodging facilities, but they address unsatisfied accommodation needs of travelers in the market in the same way as other accommodation facilities. Another example is the Cleveland Clinic in the United States which integrates hospitality into health care to increase patient experience and well-being.[8] This example could herald a hybrid hospitality–hospital solution in the near future that combines hospitals and hotels for those who need professional medical care while at the same time craving impeccable hospitality services during their recuperation. Thus, the scope of hospitality supply is expanded despite the fact that many of these businesses may have little to do with tourism on the demand side. Moreover, sharing economy businesses, such as Airbnb and Uber, which rely on massive grassroots suppliers instead of traditional enterprises, are not conventional hospitality, but they are important alternatives to hotels and taxis, respectively, thereby expanding the supply of tourism and hospitality.

1.2.2 Depth of the tourism industry

The depth of the tourism industry addresses the organization of travel-, tourism-, and hospitality-related sectors downstream to bridge the gap between tourism demand and supply through travel intermediaries. Since tourism and hospitality supply at destinations is geographically separated from demand in source markets, it is travel intermediaries, including tour operators and travel agencies, that channel tourists from their home to destinations and even to specific hospitality suppliers. This is accomplished through travel intermediaries furnishing tourists with market information such as price among others. In the 1840s it was Thomas Cook who institutionalized the relationship between tourism demand and supply through his tour operating enterprise. On the one hand, it is travel intermediaries that operate and produce package tours through contracting with various hospitality businesses either at destinations, in source markets, or from a third country. On the other hand, they establish retailing outlets, known as travel agencies, to promote and sell package tours in source markets, thereby expanding the demand side of the industry. Tourists can reduce tremendous costs in information search and market transaction when purchasing tourism products from travel intermediaries instead of contacting service providers separately.

The intermediating role of travel agencies cannot be underestimated in institutionalizing the consumption and production of tourism. The advent of modern tourism was marked by Thomas Cook because of the establishment of tour operators, which render travel intermediaries indispensable in the mass production and consumption of tourism in the late nineteenth and early twentieth centuries. Yet this is not to say that the intersection of tourism demand and supply did not exist prior to Thomas Cook's tour operating business. The intersection, if any, would have occurred not only sporadically but also on a small scale without the engagement of tour operators. Historical evidence has shown that recreational tours prior to Thomas Cook were largely a privilege of the nobility and aristocrats because of the exorbitant prices of transportation and inconvenience in traveling. For instance, the Grand Tour in Europe was popularized among British aristocrats in the late seventeenth and early eighteenth centuries but never made its way to working classes, let alone became mainstream. The impediment to the mass consumption of tourism was less about social or political reasons but more about economic constraints. Costs impeded tourism consumption from trickling down from the elite to the masses. The costs were not only people's expenditure on goods and services at destinations but more importantly all expenses related to communication and transactions between tourists on one side and various suppliers on the other.

1.2.3 Supply expansion in tourism and hospitality

Given the tourism industry described in the breadth-depth framework, the expansion of the tourism industry can be attributed to structural changes on both breadth and depth dimensions. On the breadth dimension, the tourism industry has been growing through widening the supply scope to address various needs of tourists. It has also been evolving over time with incumbent sectors or products being supplanted by better alternatives. Historically, the breadth of the tourism industry was expanded as soon as air travel supplanted railways in the 1960s, which paved the way for mass tourism at a global level. As a consequence, British seaside tours via train were partly replaced by Mediterranean vacations via air travel in the second half of the twentieth century. While the accommodation sector has been relatively stable and less affected by technological advancement, its scope has been expanding when accommodation sharing businesses entered the market around 2008. Instead of relying on enterprises such as hotels, Airbnb creates accommodation supply through millions of grassroots hosts renting out their spare apartments or rooms. In city tours alike, Uber creates more affordable and convenient transportation services by reorganizing and redeploying resources that have already existed for tourism uses.

On the depth dimension, the contribution of Thomas Cook did not only lie with the use of railways to make destinations accessible but with the invention of package tours to make tourism more affordable than ever. The business model of package tours reduces costs associated with trading tourism products and services between tourists and various service providers that are geographically distant. The costs would be astronomical at a time when modern communication technologies such as telephones had not been widely used to transmit information in business until the early twentieth century. This can also explain why the tourism and hospitality industry has been a trailblazer to embrace technological innovations in the second half of the twentieth century. In particular, structural changes occurred in the airline industry in the 1970s when the global distribution system (GDS) and computerized booking made their debut. This further facilitated the transactions between airlines, travel intermediaries, and tourists by reducing transaction costs, particularly concerning information search. The same holds true for the advent of online travel agencies (OTAs) via the Internet in the 1990s. In recent decades sharing economy enterprises, such as Airbnb and Uber, have not only furnished tourists with alternative tourism products and services but more fundamentally established a new institutional arrangement to expand market transactions.

1.3 The tourist and the tourist economy

1.3.1 Tourism and the tourist

Now we turn to the demand side of the tourism and hospitality industry by centering on end consumers in the market. Since hospitality supply long predated modern tourism, the demand side of hospitality does not necessarily entail tourists as consumers. In fact, in developed economies local residents make up a substantial proportion of demand for hospitality services, particularly for restaurants, bars and pubs, to name a few. Nevertheless, tourists constitute the principal demand for all sorts of hospitality products and services in modern tourism era, especially for countries in which tourism makes up a large proportion of GDP. Some hospitality supply, such as hotels, is set up solely for serving tourists, and its growth is largely fueled by tourist demand from outside of destinations. Despite the fact that local residents' expenditure at a restaurant, for instance, or for domestic travel as a whole is indistinguishable from tourist expenditure in the same regard, the two expenditures bifurcate when it comes to assessing their contribution to GDP. As far as a destination country or economy is concerned, local residents' expenditure in hospitality sectors within the country is part of domestic consumption while tourist expenditure is part of exports of the country. In other words, international tourism is part of international trade.

Therefore, distinguishing tourists from local residents and identifying who is a tourist helps trace where tourism demand is originated as well as the extent to which tourism contributes to the national economy. As a matter of fact, defining the *tourist* would have been as difficult as defining the tourism industry because the purposes of definitions vary from one to another. Again, as far as economic analysis is concerned, we need to ensure that a definition should help us to quantify the number of tourists as end consumers of tourism products and services. On the other hand, it must be consistent as much as possible with the consensus among practitioners and policy makers with regard to what the tourism industry should incorporate. The United Nations Statistical Commission approved provisional guidelines on the statistics of international tourism as early as 1976. Yet it was not until 1993 that a statistical definition of tourism was officially adopted based on the recommendations of the World Tourism Organization (UNWTO).[9] According to this definition, tourism "comprises the activities of persons traveling to and staying in places outside their usual environment for not more than 12 consecutive months for leisure, business or other purposes not related to the exercise of an activity remunerated from within the place visited."[10] While this definition seems to define tourism, it does draw a line between who is and is not a tourist in relation to the nature and magnitude of a person's activity performed at a destination.

This definition stipulates three quantifiable criteria specific to tourism and tourist: distance, temporality, and consumption. In the first place, the distance criterion sets a boundary whereby tourism can be distinguished from excursions or other leisure activities that are undertaken in a person's usual environment, or staycation for short. Obviously, it makes little sense to set a universal threshold that can apply to all distance situations. A distance of 50 miles might be sufficient for Swiss people to separate their place of residence from a destination but is perhaps insufficient for most Chinese and Americans living in a metropolis to do so. In Thomas Cook's time, a distance of eleven miles was sufficient to set a person's usual environment in Leicester apart from the destination Loughborough. It is certainly not possible nowadays due to a drastic reduction in travel time that would make the two places within a person's usual environment. The usual environment also suggests places that are geographically distant but highly frequented by people. For instance, if a person commutes hundreds of miles between his home and workplace, his travel is not tourism because his workplace would be seen as his usual environment. However, the distance criterion becomes less confusing as far as international tourism is concerned. Other things being equal, citizens crossing national borders would be naturally regarded as international tourists. By and large tourism involves the displacement of people to a destination that is geographically and socially distant from their usual environment in the first place.

Second, on the time dimension tourism is a temporary activity undertaken by a person at a destination whereby we can exclude permanent population displacement, such as migrants, immigrants, refugees, and so on. While the time criterion is less ambiguous than the distance criterion, the 12-month length of stay in many countries or regions could sufficiently entitle a person to obtain a residential permit from the place he visited. For instance, foreign travelers who have been permitted to stay in Hong Kong for more than six months are required to register for an identity card and therefore are no longer regarded as tourists during their visit. In this aspect, the UNWTO states that "from a tourism standpoint any person who moves to another place in the same or in another country and intends to stay there for more than one year is immediately assimilated with the residents of that place."[11] Thus, the 12-month period can take into account almost all different situations pertaining to tourism. Third, tourism is exclusively associated with people's consumption at a destination, and therefore disqualifies any production activities undertaken by the displaced persons at the destination. That is, tourism excludes any work at an occupation remunerated from a destination that a person visits. This suggests that tourism makes a contribution to the destination economy through tourist consumption at a destination in the first place.

As long as the three criteria are met, tourism does not have to be leisure- or recreation-oriented. Thus, the UNWTO's framework of tourism statistics encompasses visit purposes ranging from holiday, visiting friends and relatives, business to religion (Figure 1.2).[12] The definition of tourism does not opine on exhausting all travel purposes that people may have. From a statistical point of view, it aims to elicit the most representative and vast majority of travelers whose activities are most likely to be leisure- or recreation-oriented and therefore economically significant to the destination economy. Tourism consumption can be associated with travelers from outside a destination, regardless of whether the destination is a town, city, or a country. Thus, tourism can be seen as displaced consumption if we take an economic point of view while ignoring the experiential and hedonic nature of tourism. On the one hand, the statistical definition

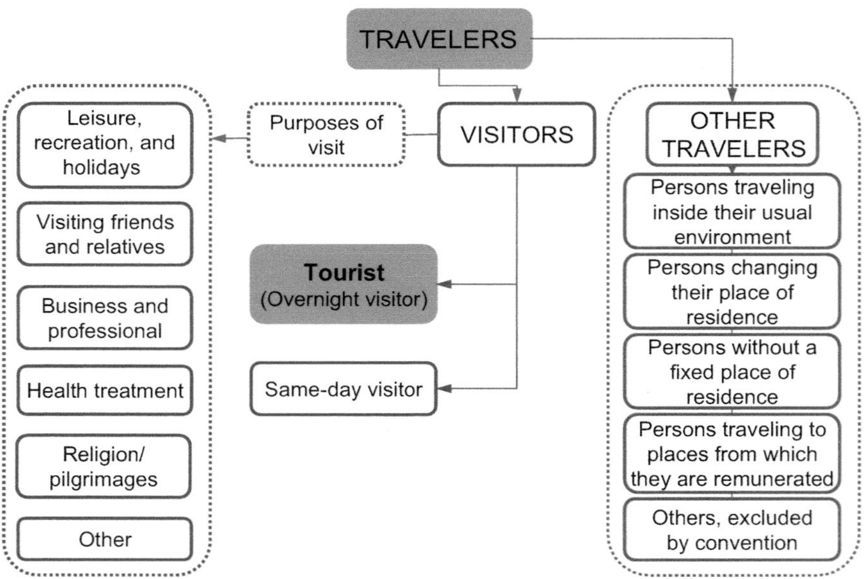

Figure 1.2
UNWTO classification of the purposes of visit

Source: WTO (1995). Concepts, Definitions and Classifications for Tourism Statistics. Madrid, Spain: UNWTO, p. 22. Reproduced from the UNWTO.

provides a yardstick to quantify tourism demand, with which tourism contribution to GDP is associated. On the other hand, it could overestimate the tourist economy by incorporating business travel or other forms of flows of people with no regard to recreation-based consumption. For instance, the flow of businesspersons between two trading partners could be substantial, but their activity may have little to do with recreational tourism. In this case, the effect of tourism on the national economy will be overstated.

1.3.2 Tourism consumption

On the supply side, the outputs in the tourism industry can be assessed by referring to the amount of goods and services produced in tourism- and hospitality-related sectors in a certain period of time. For instance, these outputs are measured by occupancy in the hotel sector, the number of meals sold in the restaurant sector, and passenger miles or loading factor in the airline sector, and so on. In addition to these specific measures, these outputs differ from one another in terms of the production process and technology that are adopted in producing these goods and services. There is no such universal measure that can be applied to all sectors because tourism product as a single entity does not exist. The tourism product is, in principle, an amalgamation of a variety of goods and services produced both in the hospitality and non-hospitality sectors so long as they are purchased by tourists. In other words, if these products were purchased by local residents, the output would have nothing to do with the tourist economy. Therefore, tourism depends much on who the end consumers are rather than what goods and services are consumed. Thus, tourism consumption can be estimated by aggregating the market values of all final goods and services consumed by tourists in all sectors of an economy, but such an aggregation is practically difficult, if not impossible.

As long as we can identify tourists and obtain information about how much they spend at a destination, the size of the tourist economy can be measured by tourist expenditure. Tourism can be decoupled from other economic activity at a destination by examining consumption from tourists. In order to assess tourist expenditure we need to know the number of visits made by tourists at the destination, referred to as tourist arrivals, and how much they spend on each visit. Total tourist expenditure is tourist arrivals multiplied by the expenditures per visit at the destination. Since a tourist may make multiple trips to the same destination in a given period of time, tourist arrivals would usually outpace the sheer number of tourists. Other things being equal, as tourist arrivals increase, so do goods and services sold for tourism consumption. In situations where tourist activity at a destination is not so connected to the destination economy, tourist arrivals may not correlate with tourist expenditures. For instance, natural destinations with beautiful beaches and mountains would entice tourists to come in droves, yet very little expenditure would be made because these resources are not transacted in the market. Once tourists are accommodated by their friends and relatives at a destination, they would also have little contact with commercial supply at the destination. Thus, the positive relationship between tourist arrivals and expenditure would become negligible.

As far as international tourism is concerned, an outflow of citizens from country *A* to country *B* is referred to as outbound tourism for *A* but inbound tourism for *B*. When using tourist arrivals or tourist expenditure we address only one side of tourism that corresponds to either inbound or outbound tourism. For country *B* as the destination, tourist arrivals are the size of inbound tourism, which can be generated from country *A* or from other countries. For country *A*, its tourist arrivals in country *B* are referred to as tourist departures from a source market's perspective. By the same token, tourist expenditures of citizens from country *A* are tourism receipts obtained by country *B* from a destination's point of view. While tourism receipts are more economically meaningful for a destination, the data are hard to collect because the goods and services that tourists purchase are heterogeneous and largely untraceable. International tourism organizations such as the UNWTO and national tourism authorities uniformly collect data on both tourist arrivals and tourism receipts in order to provide a holistic measure of destination performance (Table 1.1). It could be easy for most countries to collect data of tourist arrivals through immigration control at their frontiers, yet this is difficult for many European countries where foreigners can cross national borders freely. Instead, tourist arrivals are collected at accommodation establishments, primarily hotels, and sometimes hotel nights are used as a proxy to tourist arrivals. Data of tourist expenditure are usually collected through surveys administered to tourists whereby total expenditure can be estimated.

Table 1.1 International tourist arrivals and tourism receipts in Western Europe

Countries		International tourist arrivals			International tourism receipts		
	Series	(1,000)		Share (%)	(USD million)		Share (%)
		2017	2018	2018	2017	2018	2018
Austria	TCE	29,460	30,816	4.3	20,460	22,979	4.0
Belgium	TCE	8,358	9,154	1.3	12,485	13,474	2.4
France	TF	86,918	89,400	12.6	60,681	67,370	11.8
Germany	TCE	37,452	38,881	5.5	39,823	42,977	7.5
Liechtenstein	TCE	79	85	0.0	—	—	—
Luxembourg	TCE	1,046	1,018	0.1	4,552	4,990	0.9
Monaco	THS	355	347	0.0	—	—	—
Netherlands	TCE	17,924	19,014	2.7	16,643	18,641	3.3
Switzerland	TF	11,133	11,715	1.7	16,274	17,042	3.0

Note: Share (%) is the market share of each country in Europe. TCE = International tourist arrivals at collective tourism establishments, TF = International tourist arrivals at frontiers (overnight visitors, i.e., excluding same-day visitors), THS = International tourist arrivals at hotels and similar establishments, — = Figure or data not (yet) available.

Source: UNWTO (2019). International Tourism Highlights 2019, p. 18.

1.3.3 Global tourism growth and distribution

The use of tourist arrivals to measure the amount of tourism consumption is not perfect but feasible in practice. This measure allows us not only to track the trend of tourism growth over time but also to compare tourism performance across countries or regions in a certain period of time. According to the UNTWO, international tourist arrivals increased from 25.2 million in 1950, for which the data are available, to 1.4 billion as of 2018 (Figure 1.3). While a robust growth has occurred since 2000, in the meantime, global tourism was hindered by a couple of grave political and economic impediments, particularly the 9/11 terrorist attacks in 2001 and the 2007–08 global financial crisis. At the regional level, tourism growth has been uneven in terms of both tourist arrivals and tourism receipts. Europe is the largest destination region, accounting for 51% of tourist arrivals and 39% of tourism receipts in 2018, followed by Asia and the Pacific with 25% and 30%, respectively, the Americas with 15% and 23%, and Africa and the Middle East each accounting for less than 5% on both indicators.[13] According to a UNWTO forecast in 2011, Asia and the Pacific would become the fastest growing region reaching 535 million tourist arrivals by 2030 and the world tourist arrivals would reach 1.8 billion.[14] Unfortunately, the unprecedented coronavirus outbreak will inevitably impede tourism growth in the region and worldwide.

In Asia and the Pacific where outbound tourism growth has been the fastest over the past two decades, Japan and China are the two largest source markets. Japanese outbound tourism grew slowly before the 1980s, then soared between the 1980s and 1990s which hit 15.3 million in tourist arrivals in the mid-1990s before stagnating ever since.[15] Chinese outbound tourism took off in the mid-2000s, yet China did not become a major player in the global tourism market until it displaced Japan in terms of tourist departures in 2002 and tourist expenditures in 2009 (Figures 1.4–1.5). China has become the world's largest source market in terms of tourist departures since 2012 and expenditure since 2014

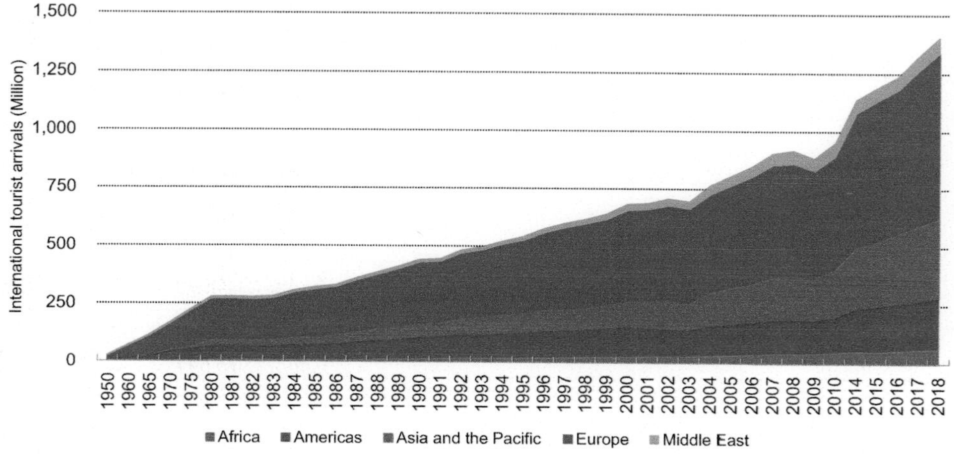

Figure 1.3
Global tourism growth and distribution (1950–2018)

Note: The time interval is not even due to a lack of data in some years. Data were retrieved from Our World in Data.

Source: UNWTO Tourism Barometer.

(Figures 1.4 and 1.5). As of 2018, Chinese outbound tourist departures amounted to 149.7 million and expenditure totaled US$277.3 billion, making up a respective 9.6% and 17.6% of global tourism.[16] Not only the sheer size but also the exponential growth of Chinese outbound tourism is staggering when compared with major source markets, such as the United States, Germany, the United Kingdom, and France (Figures 1.4 and 1.5).

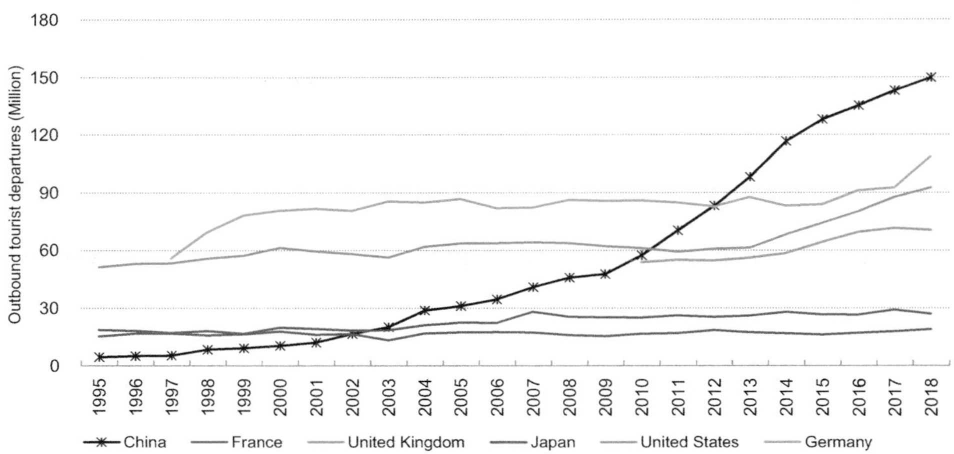

Figure 1.4
Chinese outbound tourist departures in comparison

Note: China only includes Mainland China.

Source: World Bank Open Data.

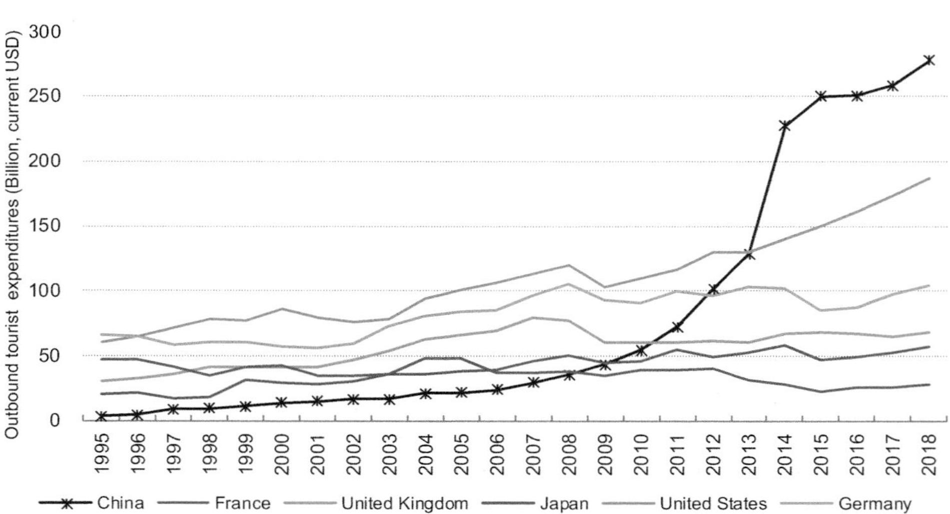

Figure 1.5
Chinese outbound tourist expenditures in comparison

Note: China only includes Mainland China. Outbound tourist expenditures include tourist spending on passenger transportation between home countries and destinations and spending on travel items at destinations.

Source: World Bank Open Data.

With Chinese tourists flooding the streets of overseas destinations, the Chinese tourism boom hit the headlines of international media. For instance, *The Economist* zeroed in on Chinese outbound consumption in 2014 and discussed its consequence on the balance of payments of China over the past two decades.[17]

1.4 Economic significance of tourism

The economic significance of tourism is attributed to tourism receipts that a destination country earns from inbound tourism in the first place. In fact, inbound tourism is an export of services of a destination country. The UNWTO statistics show that international tourism receipts amounted to US$1.7 trillion in 2018, accounting for 7% of global exports and 29% of services exports.[18] There are two caveats worth noting in relation to tourism receipts in the UNWTO statistics. First, the US$1.7 trillion is international tourism receipts, and thus does not include the market value of goods and services that tourists purchased in their home country, or domestic tourism receipts. Second, both international and domestic tourism receipts are direct expenditure of tourists with no regard to the subsequent impacts of tourism on the national economy. Hence tourism receipts are called the direct effects of tourism. By taking into account both international and domestic tourism, the World Travel & Tourism Council (WTTC) estimates that the direct effect of tourism on the global economy was US$2.8 trillion in 2018, suggesting that US$1.1 trillion, or 39.3%, was attributed to domestic tourism receipts by referring to the UNWTO statistics (Figure 1.6). According to the WTTC's estimation, the US$2.8 trillion accounted for slightly over one-third of the total contribution of tourism,

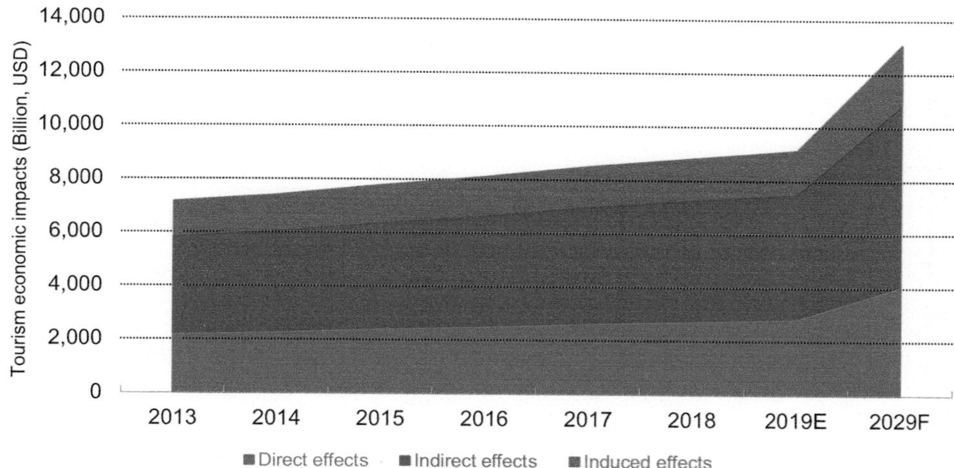

Figure 1.6
Direct, indirect, and induced effects of tourism

Note: Economic impacts were in real prices of 2018. Economic impacts include both international and domestic tourism. Direct effects include visitor exports, domestic expenditure, and purchases by tourism providers (including imported goods). 2019E is the estimate and 2029F is the forecast.

Source: WTTC (2019). Travel and Tourism Economic Impact 2019, pp. 8–10.

which was US$8.8 trillion in 2018, equivalent to 10% of world GDP (Figure 1.6). In other words, two-thirds of tourism contribution is not directly linked to tourism receipts, which is thus called the indirect and induced effects of tourism.

First of all, as tourist expenditures circulate in the national economy, they stimulate further production in upstream industries, including agriculture, manufacturing, and other service industries that sell goods and services to firms that directly serve tourists. The gross value added (GVA) from production in these upstream industries is known as the indirect effects of tourism. The indirect effects totaled US$4.5 trillion globally in 2018, accounting for slightly over 50% of total tourism contribution (Figure 1.6). Second, local residents employed in tourism and the upstream industries would earn more income from tourism, thereby stimulating their domestic consumption. The gross value added from domestic consumption of households is called the induced effects, which were US$1.5 trillion in 2018, or 17% of the total contribution of tourism. Despite the importance of tourism receipts, total tourism contribution relies heavily on indirect effects. According to the WTTC, the indirect effects of tourism have been equivalent to the sum of the direct and induced effects since the estimation was available in 2013. While the total tourism contribution is forecast by the WTTC to reach US$13 trillion by 2029, the shares of the three effects would remain quite stable with one-half attributed to the indirect effects (Figure 1.6).

At the national level, inbound tourism accounts for a disproportionately larger share in total exports of small island developing states (SIDS) than of developed countries. Figure 1.7 shows that international tourism receipts account for 30% to nearly 80% of total exports in six small island developing states in contrast to less than 20% of exports in nine developed and developing countries. Inbound tourism averaged 70.6% of total exports over the period 1995–2018 of the Bahamas, an island country in the

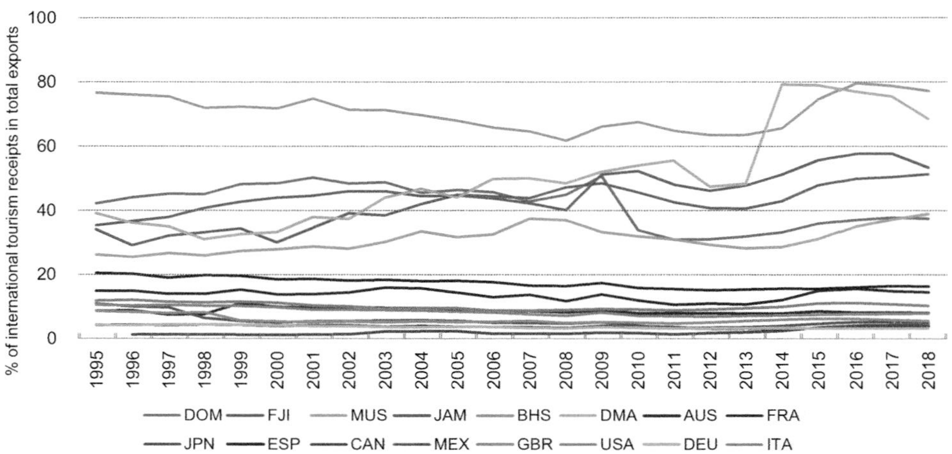

Figure 1.7
Share of international tourism receipts in total exports

Note: DOM = Dominican Republic, FJI = Fiji, MUS = Mauritius, JAM = Jamaica, BHS = Bahamas, DMA = Dominica, AUS = Australia, FRA = France, JPN = Japan, ESP = Spain, CAN = Canada, MEX = Mexico, GBR = United Kingdom, USA = United States, DEU = Germany, ITA = Italy.

Source: World Bank Open Data.

Caribbean with a population of only 390 thousand. The Bahamas depends heavily on inbound tourism to grow its economy largely due to its small domestic market. Large developing countries such as Mexico rely less on inbound tourism, which made up an average of 5.6% of its total exports over the same period. Spain would be one of the very few developed economies in which international tourism receipts made up nearly 20% of total exports. A majority of developed economies actually have inbound tourism representing less than 10% of total exports. In fact, this pattern will also hold when the proportion of inbound tourism in GDP is considered. Small island developing states lack the potential to grow their domestic tourism and other economic activities within the borders, and inbound tourism thus also makes up a substantially large share of their GDP.

In order to further articulate tourism contribution to GDP that differs drastically between small developing economies and developed economies, we zero in on the member states of the Organisation for Economic Co-operation and Development (OECD). Most OECD countries are developed economies, contributing substantially to the world economy. In OECD statistics, the direct effects of tourism are referred to as tourism direct GDP, which is the portion of GDP generated by all industries within a country that are directly associated with visitors. Thus, tourism direct GDP incorporates both inbound and domestic tourism receipts, which is consistent with the methodology used by the WTTC. Figure 1.8 shows the direct effects of tourism in the ten largest OECD economies based on their GDP in 2019. In general, the direct effects of tourism constitute less than 5% of GDP in a majority of developed economies, and this proportion has been fairly constant. Spain is the only developed country whose tourism direct GDP on average exceeded 10% over the period 2008–2017, followed by France's 7.4% in 2010–2018, and Italy's 5.8% in 2010 and 2015. Tourism direct GDP made up a share of 2–4% in the GDP of the United Kingdom, the United States, and Australia, and less than 2% in Canada and Japan in the same time period.

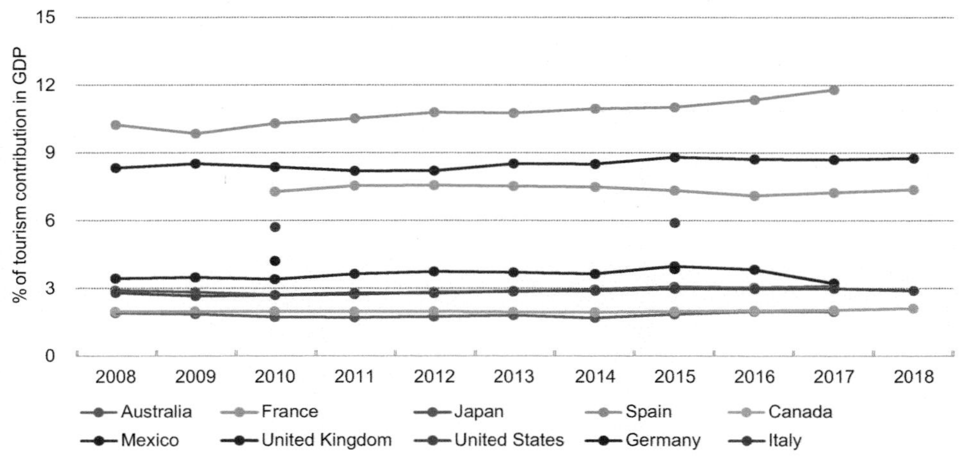

Figure 1.8
Share of tourism direct GDP in selected OECD countries

Note: Tourism direct GDP is the share of tourism contribution in GDP or GVA, depending on data availability. Data for Germany and Italy were only available for 2010 and 2015.

Source: OECD Data.

Summary

1. Modern tourism can be traced back to Thomas Cook's tour operating business in the 1840s because travel activities were for the first time in history institutionalized through the establishment of travel intermediaries. The business model of package tours made tourism accessible and affordable in Europe and beyond.
2. The essence of hospitality is to establish and nurture the host–guest relationship through offering goods, services, and warmth to the needy, strangers, and, in modern times, to tourists. While these goods and services do not entail tourists as the only consumers, the success of the hospitality businesses depends primarily on tourists.
3. The two words, tourism and hospitality, are sometimes used interchangeably in the industry and academia. However, hospitality businesses predated modern tourism and can be independent of tourist demand as they also accommodate local residents.
4. The breadth of the tourism and hospitality industry suggests the wide scope of supply, including but not limited to hotels, restaurants, airlines, cruise lines, and so on. The depth of the industry underscores the pivotal role of travel intermediaries in bridging the gap between demand and supply that are geographically separated in tourism.
5. The UNWTO defines tourism using three quantifiable criteria: distance, temporality, and consumption. This definition was proposed primarily for statistical purposes, and therefore provides a benchmark for measuring tourism consumption.
6. Tourist arrival and tourist expenditure are two indicators to measure the tourism performance of a destination. Tourist arrivals are the number of visits made by tourists at the destination in a given period of time, and tourist expenditures are the market value of all goods and services consumed by tourists at the destination.
7. Inbound and outbound tourism describe the flow of tourists from one country to another. The use of tourist arrivals takes the perspective of a destination, which corresponds to tourist departures from the perspective of a source market. Accordingly, tourist expenditures correspond to tourism receipts earned by a destination.
8. At the global level tourist arrivals reached 1.4 billion in 2018. While robust growth occurred after 2000, global tourism has been hindered by a couple of grave political and economic impediments over the past two decades. At the regional level Europe is the largest destination region in terms of both tourist arrivals and tourism receipts.
9. The total contribution of tourism includes the direct, indirect, and induced effects of tourism. The direct effects are the direct expenditure of tourists; the indirect effects are the gross value added in upstream industries of tourism, and the induced effects are the consumption of households whose income is generated from tourism.
10. In general, inbound tourism makes up a larger proportion of total exports in small island developing states (SIDS) than in developed countries. In general, tourism direct GDP in developed economies is less than 10%.

REVIEW QUESTIONS

Each question has four options, and there is only one correct answer to each question.

1. We regard the modern tourism industry dating back to the 1840s as a European phenomenon, or strictly speaking an English phenomenon. What would be the reason?
   A) The package tour business was pioneered in England.
   B) The package tour business made leisure travel affordable to the masses in Europe.
   C) The package tour business was invented by English entrepreneur Thomas Cook.
   D) All of the above.
2. Which of the following is correct regarding hospitality and/or the hospitality sector?
   A) Hospitality had not existed until modern tourism burgeoned in the 1840s.
   B) Hospitality values the amicable host–guest relationship.
   C) The hospitality sector is synonymous with the hotel sector.
   D) The hospitality sector only serves tourists.
3. Which of the following firms is (was) on the breadth dimension of the tourism and hospitality industry?
   A) British Airways
   B) TripAdvisor
   C) Booking.com
   D) Thomas Cook AG
4. Which of the following is INCORRECT in describing the tourism and hospitality industry?
   A) The breadth of the industry suggests the broad scope of supply.
   B) The depth of the industry suggests the levels of intermediaries.
   C) The breadth of the industry suggests that tourism demand is diverse.
   D) The depth of the industry suggests that tourism supply is diverse.
5. According to the definition of tourism proposed by the World Tourism Organization (UNWTO), which of the following does NOT qualify as an international tourist?
   A) A person studying in a foreign country returning home within twelve months.
   B) A person spending a holiday in a foreign country for three consecutive weeks.
   C) A person attending a conference in a foreign country returning home in two weeks.
   D) A person working as a receptionist in a hotel in a foreign country for three months.

6. Which of the following is NOT a measure of inbound tourism performance in Switzerland in a given year?
   A) Number of international tourist arrivals in Switzerland.
   B) Expenditure from international tourists in Switzerland.
   C) Hotel nights spent by international tourists in Switzerland.
   D) GDP per capita of Swiss citizens.
7. Which of the following can be best regarded as the output of international tourism in Switzerland?
   A) 1,000 skiing season passes sold in Saint Moritz, Switzerland in December.
   B) 1,000 Big Mac meals sold in Lausanne, Switzerland on Swiss National Day.
   C) 1,000 Swiss citizens took a two-day trip in Toulouse, France.
   D) 1,000 hotel nights in Davos, Switzerland sold to a Chinese delegation.
8. In which of the following scenarios are tourist arrivals positively correlated with tourist expenditures?
   A) Tourists taking a one-day trip to Disney World.
   B) Tourists taking a backpacking trip and camping in a natural destination.
   C) Tourists taking a trip while staying in their friends' houses.
   D) Tourists taking a holiday trip to an open beach with no peripheral services.
9. Chinese outbound tourist expenditures increased by 7.6% in 2018 compared to 2017, whereas tourist departures increased by only 4.7% over the same period. Other things being equal, which of the following is correct?
   A) Expenditure per visit overseas increased.
   B) Expenditure per visit overseas decreased.
   C) Expenditure per visit overseas remained the same.
   D) None of the above.
10. Which of the following may be the reason that tourism's total contribution to a country's GDP is larger than tourist direct expenditure within the country?
   A) The indirect effect of tourism on the country's economy is positive.
   B) The induced effect of tourism on the country's economy is positive.
   C) The country's economy is advanced and diversified.
   D) All of the above.

Problem solving

1. Danny Meyer, a famed American restaurateur, writes in his book *Setting the Table: The Transforming Power of Hospitality in Business* that "[h]ospitality is present when something happens for you. It is absent when something happens to you; these two prepositions *for* and *to* express it all." What do you think is the overriding goal of hospitality by referring to his interpretation of hospitality?
2. Referring to the breadth-depth framework of the tourism and hospitality industry outlined in Figure 1.1, on which dimension(s) would you put Airbnb and Uber, and on what grounds?
3. Tourism usually makes up a much smaller proportion of the GDP of developed countries compared to developing countries and in particular small island

developing states. However, the indirect and induced effects of tourism are much greater in developed countries than in small island developing states. What would be the reasons?

Solutions to all review questions and problem solving tasks are included in the Support Material for this book, which can be accessed at www.routledge.com/9780367897352.

Notes

1 For a detailed account of the history of Thomas Cook, please refer to Hamilton (2012).
2 Story of Leicester. Leicester—the birthplace of popular tourism. Retrieved on August 27, 2020 from https://www.storyofleicester.info/city-stories/thomas-cooks-leicester/
3 *CNN*. Thomas Cook: A history of one of the world's oldest travel firms. September 23, 2019.
4 Baxter (1866), p. 553.
5 Hamilton (2012), Kindle edition, the penultimate paragraph in Chapter 10.
6 Pohl (1999) provides a detailed account of the origin of hospitality that roots in Christianity.
7 *Bloomberg*. Airport sleep pods are here for stranded passengers. September 13, 2017.
8 *Forbes*. Hospitals and hospitality: What customer service and patient experience can teach your business? April 9, 2017.
9 The World Tourism Organization changed its acronym in English from WTO to UNWTO in 2005 in order to distinguish it from the World Trade Organization (WTO).
10 WTO (1995). Concepts, Definitions and Classifications for Tourism Statistics. Madrid, Spain: UNWTO, p. 21.
11 WTO (1995). Concepts, Definitions and Classifications for Tourism Statistics. Madrid, Spain: UNWTO, p. 24.
12 WTO (1995). Concepts, Definitions and Classifications for Tourism Statistics. Madrid, Spain: UNWTO, p. 22.
13 UNWTO (2019). International Tourism Highlights 2019. Madrid, Spain: UNWTO, p. 6.
14 UNWTO (2011). Tourism Towards 2030: Global Overview. Madrid, Spain: UNWTO, p. 15.
15 World Bank Open Data.
16 World Bank Open Data.
17 *The Economist*. Chinese tourists: Coming to a beach near you. April 19, 2014. *The Economist*. China's current-account surplus has vanished. March 14, 2019.
18 UNWTO (2019). International Tourism Highlights 2019. Madrid, Spain: UNWTO, p. 8.

Bibliography

Baxter, R. D. (1866). Railway extension and its results. *Journal of the Statistical Society of London, 29*(4), 549–595.

Hamilton, J. (2012). *Thomas Cook: The holiday-maker*. Kindle edition.

Pohl, C. D. (1999). *Making room: Recovering hospitality as a Christian tradition*. Cambridge, UK: Wm. B. Eerdmans Publishing Company.

2 Demand, supply, and the market

After describing the tourism and hospitality industry in the breadth-depth framework in Chapter 1, we proceed to introduce the key analytical frameworks and models of microeconomics that can explain demand and supply in tourism and hospitality. First, we briefly explain how economists model a specific phenomenon in the real world through economic intuition, diagrammatic representation to mathematical quantification. The conclusion from one phenomenon is generalized to various phenomena to obtain universal principles that are the constituents of economic models. Second, we explain the laws of demand and supply as two key universal principles that dictate consumer behavior and firm behavior. Third, we explain equilibrium analysis and market efficiency that are grounded on the laws of demand and supply. We conclude this chapter by proposing two models of tourism growth based on equilibrium analysis. The two models enable us to assess both the size of the tourism market and the market price of tourism at a destination.

AFTER STUDYING THIS CHAPTER, YOU SHOULD BE ABLE TO:

- Understand how economists theorize a phenomenon;
- Explain the laws of demand and supply, market equilibrium, and market efficiency;
- Explain tourism demand and supply using the push–pull framework and apply it to demand and supply analysis; and
- Understand and apply two tourism growth models that address inbound and outbound tourism, respectively.

2.1 Economic thinking

The phenomenon of tourism has long been discussed in a multidisciplinary framework in which almost all social sciences, primarily economics, sociology, and geography, have attempted to explain tourism from their own disciplinary angles.[1] This multidisciplinary approach has been a feature of tourism research since the 1970s when a handful of academic journals were founded and dedicated to the study of tourism.[2] As far as economics is concerned, tourists are nothing but consumers on the demand side and firms, regardless of which tourism or hospitality sector they operate in, are producers of goods and services for tourism consumption. Therefore, tourism activity is no different from any other economic activity. Economic analysis of tourism aims to explain the demand for and supply of goods and services that are directly associated with tourists. By doing this we can articulate how the market works to balance demand and supply. The principle of the market applies to tourism the same way as it applies to demand for and supply of any other goods and services. Besides this objective, the methodology used by economics to explain tourism or any other economic activity is different from other disciplines. Economic thinking begins with forming an economic intuition about a phenomenon, and then progresses from a diagrammatic representation of a model that can explain the phenomenon to mathematical inference.

First of all, economic intuition enables us to approach a phenomenon in the first place even if we lack any formal training in the profession of economics. For instance, it is not difficult for a layman to comprehend the relationship between the price of a good and the amount purchased by consumers. For instance, when the price of burgers rises, he knows that consumers would buy fewer burgers while firms would produce more.[3] However, such an intuition could also be fallacious because it is based on one single observation in a specific context that has no economic theory to back it up. We can proceed to make as many observations in different contexts as possible, allowing us to verify the relationships between the market price of a good and the amounts that consumers would purchase and firms would produce. Second, if we plot, for example, the market price of burgers, P, on the y-axis and the amount purchased by consumers, Q, on the x-axis, we would obtain a downward-sloping curve that manifests a negative relationship between the two variables (Figure 2.1a). Likewise, plotting the relationship between the market price of burgers, P, and the amount that firms produce, Q, we end

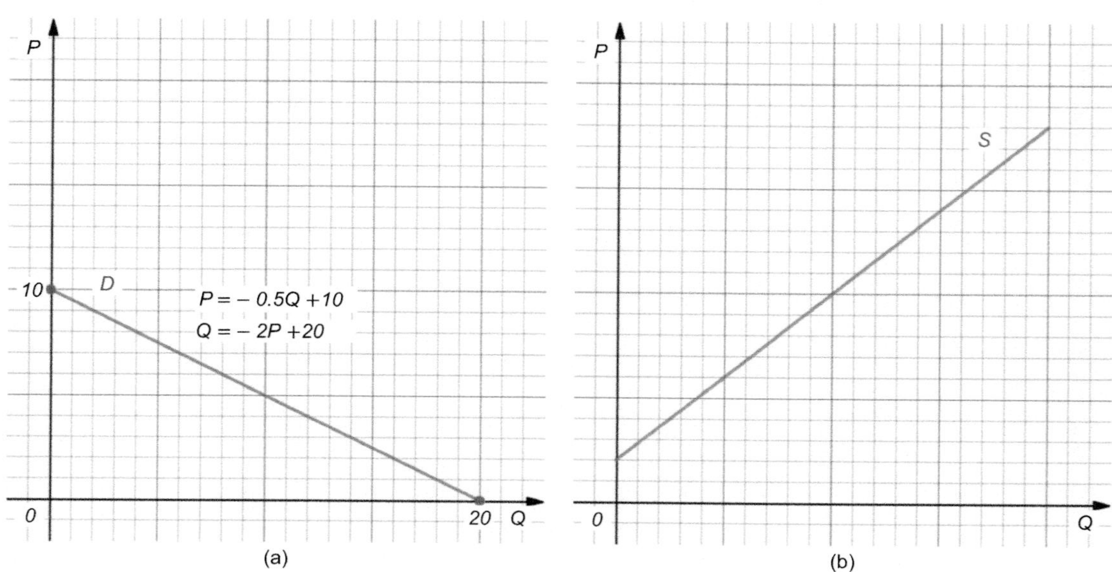

Figure 2.1
Demand and supply curves

up with an upward-sloping curve that exhibits a positive relationship between the two variables (Figure 2.1b).

The graphic representation in Figure 2.1a reveals the fundamental nature of the relationship between the price of a good and the quantity of the good purchased by consumers in various contexts. Third, as our inquiry progresses from grasping the nature of the relationship between price and quantity to quantifying its strength, mathematical thinking weighs in. Assume that the relationship between the market price of burgers and the quantity of burgers purchased is linear, and that the x-intercept stands for 20 burgers and the y-intercept stands for 10 dollars (Figure 2.1a). The two intercepts suggest in theory: when the market price is zero, the maximum quantity purchased by consumers would be 20 burgers; when the market price is \$10 per burger, the minimum quantity purchased by consumers would be zero. Thus, we can write out the function of the curve such that the market price (P) of burgers is a function of the quantity purchased (Q) by consumers:

$$P = -0.5Q + 10, \tag{2.1}$$

or the quantity of burgers purchased (Q) is a function of the market price (P):

$$Q = -2P + 20. \tag{2.2}$$

These two functions are mathematically equivalent but differ in their economic meanings. The difference lies in which of the two variables is considered the dependent variable and which the independent variable. Function (2.1) suggests that the market price of burgers is a function of the quantity purchased, suggesting how and to what extent the market price is determined by the amount of burgers consumers purchase. Hence this function predicts the value that consumers would attach to burgers with varying quantities. Function (2.1) further reveals that if consumers purchase one additional burger, the market price would fall by 0.5 dollars, meaning that one additional burger is worth 0.5 dollars less than the preceding one. On the other hand, function (2.2) suggests that the quantity of burgers purchased is a function of the market price, suggesting that the quantity of burgers purchased is determined by the market price. Hence this function predicts the number of burgers consumers would purchase with varying prices in the market. Function (2.2) further reveals that when the market price of burgers increases by 1 dollar, consumers would purchase two fewer burgers.

2.2 Equilibrium analysis

2.2.1 Laws of demand and supply

The burger case above can be generalized to all markets in which an inverse relationship can be drawn between the price of a good and the quantity demanded.

This relationship is referred to as the law of demand, manifested by the downward-sloping curve known as the demand curve, as shown in Figure 2.1a. We shall derive and address the demand curve in greater detail in Chapter 4. The convention of economic analysis that plots the market price P on the y-axis and the quantity demanded Q on the x-axis relates to a debate on economic thought in history. This debate dates from classical economists Adam Smith (1723–1790) and Karl Marx (1818–1883) all the way to neoclassical economists,[4] in particular marginalists in the 1870s, on how price, or the value of a good, is determined. Classical economists argued that the value of a good was determined by the production cost, whereby its market price was determined. Neoclassical economists argued that the value of a good is determined by consumers' willingness to pay, which in turn depends on the amount of the good that a consumer possesses. The more of the good he owns, the less he is willing to pay to acquire more, suggesting that the good becomes less valuable as the consumer possesses more. This is known as the law of diminishing marginal utility, which explains why the price of a good decreases as the quantity demanded increases. It thus provides the theoretical underpinning for the downward-sloping demand curve.

If we regard the quantity demanded as the dependent variable, the law of demand explains how the quantity of a good demanded is determined by its market price. It states that the amount of a good that a consumer purchases is inversely related to the market price of the good. According to the law of diminishing marginal utility, which we shall cover in Chapter 4, an additional unit of the good is associated with a lower value, and thus only when the price falls is the consumer willing to increase his purchase. When the price of the good increases, the quantity demanded falls, indicating that the scarcity of the good makes it highly valuable to the consumer. In both interpretations above, the demand curve essentially describes a systematic coordination between all possible quantities of the good that the consumer demands and his corresponding willingness to pay at each quantity.

In parallel on firms' side, there exists a positive relationship between the quantity of burgers that firms would produce and the market price of burgers. This relationship is known as the law of supply, represented by the upward-sloping curve in Figure 2.1b, called the supply curve. If we look at what determines the quantity supplied on the supply curve, it becomes clear that only when the price of burgers increases are firms willing to produce and sell more burgers. That is, an increase in quantity supplied necessitates an increase in market price, which thus provides economic incentives for firms to increase production in a perfectly competitive market, which we shall cover in Chapters 8 and 9. As we shall see in detail in Chapter 8, the supply curve is the upward-sloping portion of the marginal cost curve of a firm, underpinned by the law of diminishing marginal returns. This means that the more the firm produces, the more cost it would incur for each additional unit of the output, and hence the higher the price it needs to claim for profit maximization. Given a certain output of burgers, since producing one extra burger is associated with a higher cost than producing the preceding one, the economic return of the extra burger to the firm diminishes. In other words, only if the market price increases are firms willing to produce more burgers.

2.2.2 Market equilibrium

Note that the price variable—either on the demand curve or on the supply curve—is not the market price at which burgers are transacted between consumers and firms. On the one hand, the price variable denotes consumers' willingness to pay for a good that changes negatively with the quantity demanded of the good, and on the other hand, it denotes firms' willingness to sell the good that changes positively with the quantity supplied. Juxtaposing the demand curve and the supply curve in the same quadrant enables us to examine the interactions between demand and supply, whereby the market price of the good is determined. Only when consumers' willingness to pay equals firms' willingness to sell can the market price be determined (P_0), and so the quantities demanded by consumers and supplied by firms (Q_0) are determined in the market (Figure 2.2). This equalization is called the market equilibrium (E), which is a stationary state where demand and supply balance, holding other factors that may affect demand and supply constant. Thus P_0 is called the equilibrium price of the good and Q_0 is the equilibrium quantity, which are the price and quantity of the good traded in the market, respectively. In market equilibrium neither consumers nor firms have incentives to change their behavior, which therefore enables us to examine the price and the quantity of the good traded in the market.

In the history of economic thought, the notion of market equilibrium resolved the dispute on what determines the value of a good. What determines price, and how, had been a persistent dispute between classical and neoclassical economists until the late

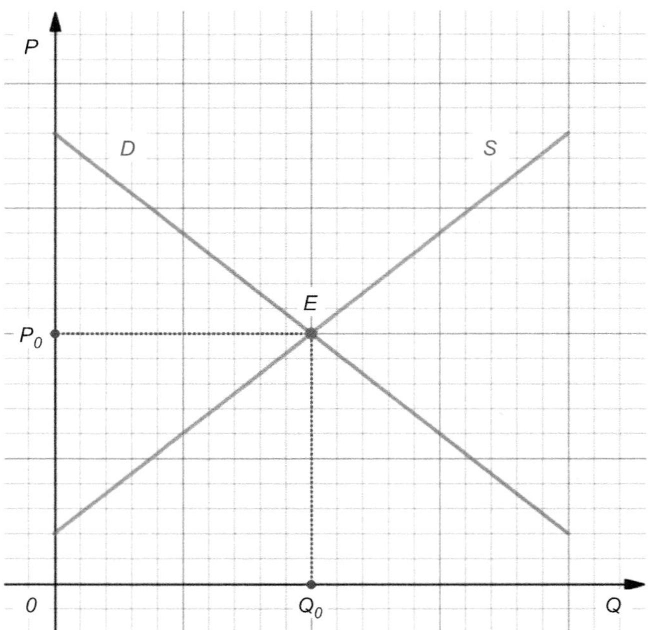

Figure 2.2
Demand, supply, and market equilibrium

nineteenth century when the idea of marginal utility was propounded. On the one hand, the labor theory of value pioneered by Adam Smith and Karl Marx argues that price is determined by the cost of producing a good, or by the supply curve. On the other hand, marginalists believe in marginal utility of the good, or the demand curve, that determines its price. In his magnum opus *Principles of Economics* (1890) British economist Alfred Marshall (1842–1924) formulated equilibrium analysis for the first time and metaphorically elucidated the mechanism by which price is determined. By analogy he states that a single blade of a pair of scissors, metaphorically referring to either the demand or supply in the market, cannot cut off a piece of paper, but both blades can by working together, referring to the coordination of demand and supply. By the same token, only when demand and supply balance can the price of a good be determined in the market. Marshall's equilibrium analysis eventually ended a century-long debate between classical economists and marginalists on price determination.

The laws of demand and supply assume that all factors other than price that may influence demand and supply do not change or, if they do, are isolated from economic analysis. This assumption is known as *ceteris paribus*, meaning other things being equal or being held constant. In the analysis of the properties of the demand and supply curves, the assumption *ceteris paribus* is implicitly stressed such that all factors that affect demand and/or supply other than price are constant. Thus, we can single out the most prominent relationship between price and quantity demanded/supplied in market transaction. The laws of demand and supply cannot be manifested or validated without isolating other supposedly relevant factors from economic analysis in the first place. On the one hand, the assumption *ceteris paribus* allows us to simplify complex economic phenomena whereby economic analysis can be carried out. On the other hand, it is an imperative in economic reasoning that aims to capture the most important and fundamental factor dictating consumer behavior and firm behavior. That said, the other factors are by no means disregarded or ruled out in economic analysis. On the contrary, economists are well aware of the limitations of their models, which may not work if a factor incorporated in *ceteris paribus* is not held constant.

2.2.3 Demand and supply versus quantity demanded and supplied

If, for instance, consumers' income increases, their willingness to pay for a good would increase accordingly, *ceteris paribus*. In this case, *ceteris paribus* means all factors, including the price of the good, other than consumer income being constant. Regardless of the price of the good, consumer demand increases with income, represented by a rightward shift in the demand curve from D_0 to D_1 as shown in Figure 2.3a. Note that a shift in the demand curve means that the new demand curve D_1 is parallel to the initial demand curve D_0. At any given price the quantity demanded increases by the same amount, $Q_1' - Q_0$, and hence we say that the demand increases by $Q_1' - Q_0$, which is the magnitude of the shift attributed to the increase in income (Figure 2.3a). We now see that the new demand curve D_1 and the supply curve S_0 intersect in a new market equilibrium E_1. Since the increase in income does not alter supply, the rightward shift

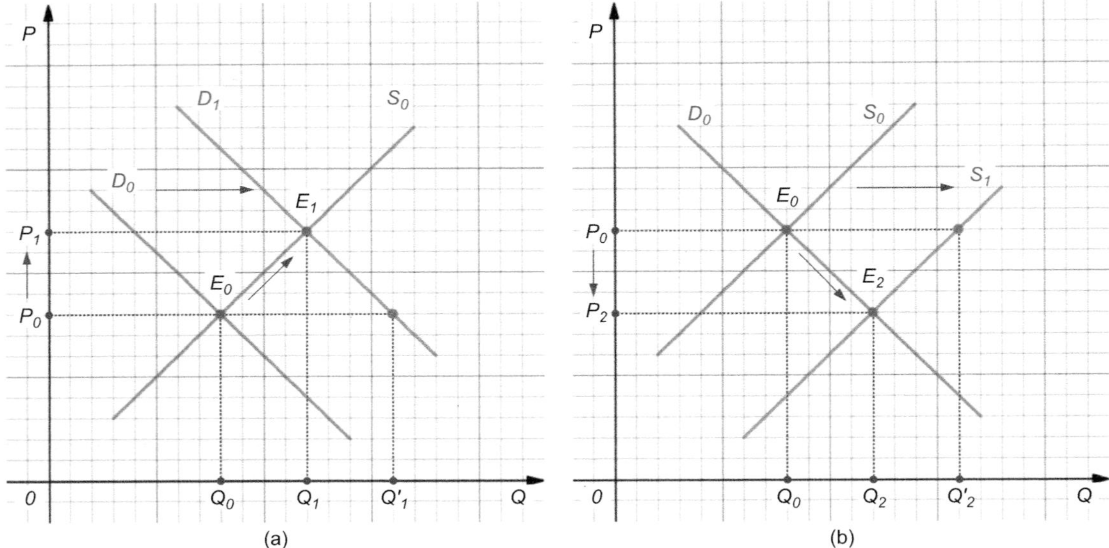

Figure 2.3
Shifts in demand and supply curves

in the demand curve actuates an upward movement of the market equilibrium from E_0 to E_1 along the supply curve S_0, ending up with an increase in equilibrium price from P_0 to P_1 and an increase in equilibrium quantity from Q_0 to Q_1 (Figure 2.3a). In the new market equilibrium E_1, consumers are willing and able to purchase more due to their higher income, and firms are willing and able to sell more due to the higher equilibrium price that is caused by the increase in demand.

Note that the upward movement of the market equilibrium E_0 along the supply curve S_0 is caused by the higher equilibrium price P_1 which, in turn, is caused by the increase in demand. Distinguishing between a change in demand and a change in quantity demanded is vital because they represent two mechanisms by which the amount of demand can be altered. Quantity demanded is a certain amount of demand that corresponds to a specific value of a demand determinant such as price. On the demand curve for example, a change in quantity demanded means a different x-coordinate on the demand curve that corresponds to a different price as the y-coordinate. Since a given demand curve describes a systematic coordination of all quantities demanded with their corresponding prices, a change in demand means that the whole coordination is no longer held due to the effects of factors other than price. All factors other than the price of a good can thus disrupt the initial price–quantity coordination dictated by the initial demand curve, thereby causing the demand curve to shift either leftward, suggesting that demand decreases, or rightward, suggesting that demand increases. Given the demand curve, any change in quantity demanded is solely due to the change in price, other things being equal.

The same is true for distinguishing between a change in supply and a change in quantity supplied by firms. By the same token, all factors other than the price of a good, such as technology advancement in production, severe droughts, natural disasters, and so on, will break down the initial price–quantity coordination that describes all possible quantities supplied with their corresponding prices on the supply curve. Hence a change in supply can be manifested as a leftward shift in the supply curve, suggesting a decrease in supply, or a rightward shift in the supply curve, suggesting an increase in supply. For example, technology advancement can increase supply by lowering costs and increasing production efficiency of firms. Figure 2.3b shows that the supply curve S_0 shifts rightward to S_1, indicating an increase in supply, other things being equal. Holding the price constant at P_0, we are able to quantify that the supply increases by $Q_2' - Q_0$, which is attributed to the effect of technology advancement on supply in the market (Figure 2.3b). Since demand does not change, there exists a downward movement of the market equilibrium from E_0 to E_2 along the initial demand curve D_0, ending up with a decrease of $P_0 - P_2$ in equilibrium price and an increase of $Q_2 - Q_0$ in equilibrium quantity (Figure 2.3b).

2.3 Economic surplus and market efficiency

2.3.1 Consumer surplus, producer surplus, and social surplus

A consumer whose willingness to pay is higher than the market price obtains consumer surplus, which is the consumer's willingness to pay less the market price. Thus, the higher the consumer's willingness to pay, the more the consumer surplus; and the lower the market price, the more the consumer surplus as well, other things being equal. Aggregating the consumer surplus of all consumers in the market we obtain total consumer surplus, denoted by the area beneath the demand curve D and above the equilibrium price P_0 bounded by zero and the equilibrium quantity Q_0 (Figure 2.4). In fact, consumers do not really claim such surplus because consumers' willingness to pay is subjective. Consumer surplus can thus be regarded as a kind of gratification that consumers obtain when purchasing at a price lower than what they value. By the same token, a firm whose willingness to sell is lower than the market price obtains producer surplus, which is the market price less the firm's willingness to sell. Thus, the lower the firm's willingness to sell, the more the producer surplus; and the higher the market price, the more the producer surplus as well, other things being equal. Aggregating the producer surplus of all firms in the market we obtain total producer surplus, denoted by the area beneath the equilibrium price P_0 and above the supply curve S bounded also by zero and the equilibrium quantity Q_0 (Figure 2.4). Different from consumer surplus, producer surplus is the economic profit that firms obtain by selling at a price higher than their marginal costs.

The sum of consumer surplus and producer surplus is social surplus, which is the total welfare obtained by both consumers and firms as a whole in the market. Social surplus is denoted by the area between the demand curve and the supply curve bounded by zero and the equilibrium quantity (Figure 2.4). Social surplus can be seen as the economic pie produced both by consumers and firms in voluntary transactions with each other in the free market. In market equilibrium the economic pie is the largest because any single consumer or firm who is willing and able to trade with each other can fulfil

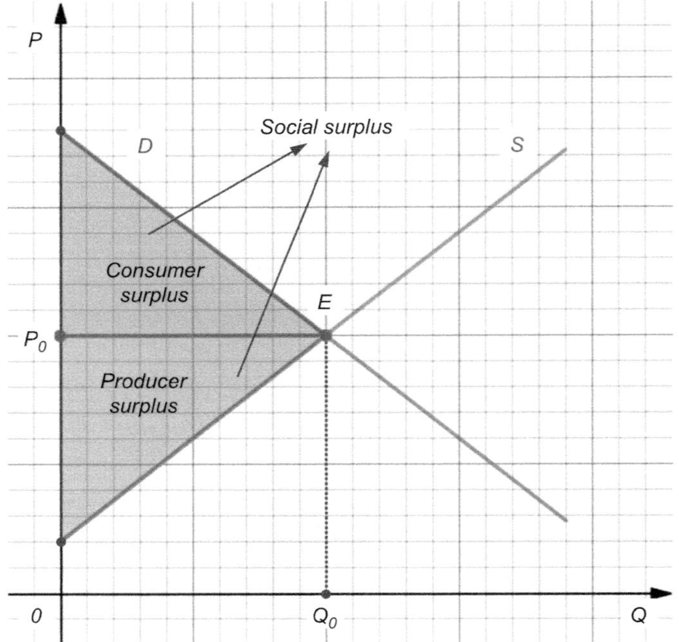

Figure 2.4
Consumer surplus, producer surplus, and social surplus

their transaction precisely at equilibrium price. On the one hand, market equilibrium is the outcome from voluntary transactions between consumers and firms in the free market based on their willingness to pay and sell. On the other hand, equilibrium price reflects that the last voluntary transaction is fulfilled in the market when a consumer's willingness to pay is equal to a firm's willingness to sell. Therefore, equilibrium quantity is the largest amount of transactions that the free market can accomplish. Hence only in market equilibrium can social surplus be maximized.

2.3.2 Price controls and deadweight loss

Given the demand and supply curves in Figure 2.4, consumer surplus and producer surplus that are determined in market equilibrium cannot be changed without changing price. In other words, if the market price deviates from equilibrium price, consumer surplus, producer surplus, and social surplus will be affected. The most notable cause for the market price to deviate from equilibrium price is government intervention through price controls. Price controls are referred to as government mandate of the price of a good in the market that deviates from the equilibrium price of the good. The rationale for price controls is that governments tend to believe the price would be too low or too high if left to be determined in the free market. As a result, the equilibrium price would hurt consumers or firms. Depending on whether the manipulated price is lower or higher than equilibrium price, price controls can further be classified as price ceilings and price floors. A price ceiling is the price of a good capped by government, through regulation or legislation, at a level lower than the equilibrium price of the good. Conversely, a price floor is the price of a good fixed by government at a level higher than the equilibrium price of the good.

One notable example of price ceilings is rent control by government, which prevents landlords from raising rents to the level dictated in market equilibrium. With rent control, governments intend that low-income households will be able to afford flats. Suppose that a rent in a housing market is mandated by the government at P_1 which by definition is lower than P_0 in market equilibrium (Figure 2.5a). Since the low rent entices tenants to rent more and/or larger flats, the quantity of flats demanded would increase from Q_0 to Q_1' along the demand curve. However, the low rent discourages landlords from renting out flats, thereby decreasing the quantity supplied from Q_0 to Q_1. When the rent is set at P_1, the quantity supplied Q_1 is smaller than the quantity demanded Q_1', ending up with a shortage of rental housing in the market denoted by $Q_1' - Q_1$. In fact, the same number of tenants and landlords, denoted by $Q_0 - Q_1$, who would both otherwise be willing to rent in and out at the equilibrium price P_0 cannot transact with each other under the rent control, leading to what is called deadweight loss. The deadweight loss in this case is denoted by the area between the demand curve and the supply curve bounded by the quantities Q_1 and Q_0 as shown in Figure 2.5a. Due to the deadweight loss, the volume of market transaction shrinks from Q_0 to Q_1, and hence both tenants and landlords are worse off.

One typical example of price floors is minimum wages mandated by government. If a wage, which is the price of labor, is left to employers and employees to determine in a free market, the government may believe that the market wage would be too low and thus hurt workers. Note that in the labor market employers are on the demand side for purchasing labor while employees are on the supply side for supplying labor.

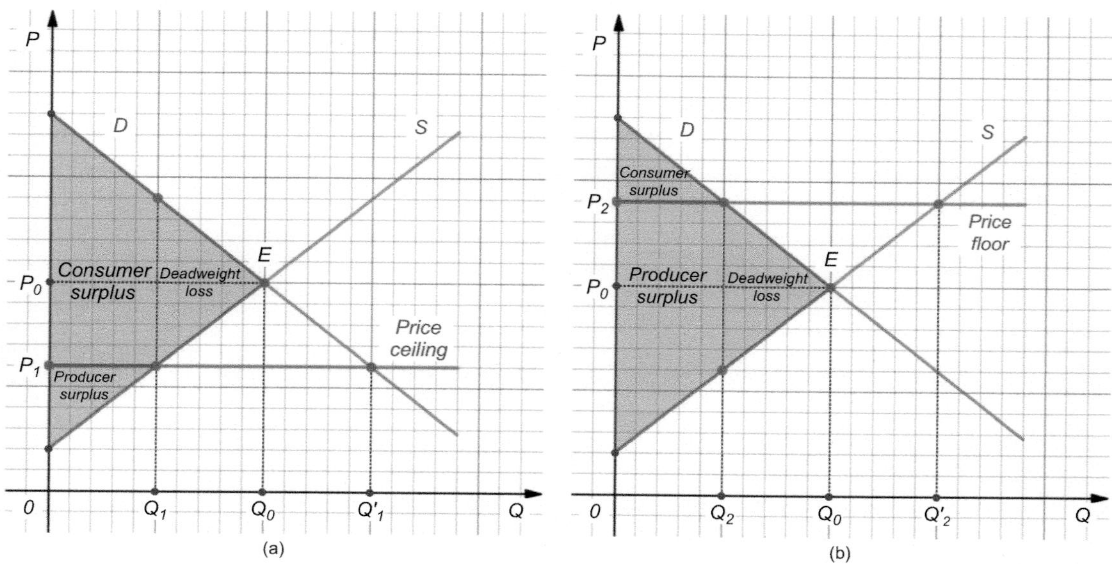

Figure 2.5
Price ceiling, price floor, and deadweight loss

Suppose that the minimum wage P_2 is mandated in the labor market, which by definition is higher than the equilibrium price of labor denoted by P_0 (Figure 2.5b). Given the high wage P_2, the number of people in the labor force seeking jobs would increase from Q_0 to Q_2' along the supply curve. Nevertheless, the number of employers willing to hire workers would decrease from Q_0 to Q_2 along the demand curve. Ultimately, the quantity of labor supplied by employees Q_2' would be greater than the quantity of labor demanded by employers Q_2, resulting in a surplus of labor supply in the market denoted by $Q_2' - Q_2$. This is because the same number of employers and employees, $Q_0 - Q_2$, who would both otherwise be willing to trade for labor at the equilibrium price P_0 cannot transact with each other. Thus, the volume of market transaction shrinks from Q_0 to Q_2, resulting in the deadweight loss, denoted by the area between the demand curve and the supply curve bounded by the quantities Q_2 and Q_0 (Figure 2.5b).[5]

2.3.3 Market efficiency

In the analysis of price controls above, the area between the demand and supply curves from zero to the equilibrium quantity Q_0 is divided into three portions, represented by consumer surplus, producer surplus, and deadweight loss (Figure 2.5). In the case of price ceilings (Figure 2.5a), producer surplus decreases due to the market price being lower than the equilibrium price, while consumer surplus could be greater or smaller than, or equal to, what is previously determined in the market equilibrium. In the case of price floors (Figure 2.5b), consumer surplus decreases due to the market price being higher than the equilibrium price, while producer surplus could be greater or smaller than, or equal to, what is previously determined in the market equilibrium. In both cases though, social surplus unambiguously shrinks due to the occurrence of the deadweight loss. As long as the market price deviates, for whatever reason, from equilibrium price in the free market, deadweight loss would arise. The occurrence of deadweight loss suggests that the market is no longer perfectly efficient in maximizing social surplus. This is because deadweight loss would otherwise be recouped if the price of a good were left for the free market to determine. When deadweight loss is zero, social surplus is maximized and thus the market ends up being perfectly efficient. This can only be achieved in the free market through voluntary trade between consumers and firms.

2.4 Determinants of demand and supply

2.4.1 Push factors versus pull factors

In what follows we first explore the determinants of tourism demand and supply, then apply equilibrium analysis to analyze the tourism market. Since tourism involves the flow of people from their usual environment, known as the source market, to a destination far afield, the determinants of tourism demand and supply pertain to

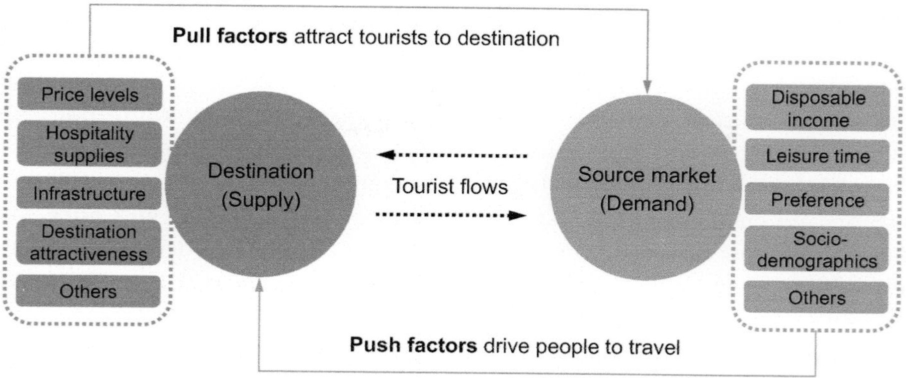

Figure 2.6
Push and pull factors in the tourism market

where tourists come from and where they travel to, and back and forth. On the one hand, factors which drive people to depart from their usual environment generate tourism demand in the first place, regardless of where they may travel to thereafter (Figure 2.6). Such factors as disposable income and leisure time available to people in the source market are referred to as push factors, suggesting that they stimulate people's craving for tourism. Of course, push factors can have negative impacts in the sense that they may preclude travel. Besides income and time, major push factors include a wide range of social and economic variables that are pertinent to tourists themselves or to the source market, from tourists' educational background and age to the population of the source market as a whole. On the other hand, factors which tempt tourists to, or preclude them from, a destination are referred to as pull factors (Figure 2.6). It is pull factors that draw tourists to a particular destination to satisfy their wanderlust. Pull factors, such as the abundance of hospitality supply and the attractiveness of a destination as a whole, are pertinent to the destination.

The push–pull framework in Figure 2.6 implies that tourism demand and supply are geographically separated, and are dictated by factors specific to the source market and to the destination. Note that the price level should not be interpreted as the market price of tourism but the living cost at the destination. The price factor helps tourists develop an expectation of the expensiveness of a destination in general, and thus affects their destination choice. The lower the price level at a destination, the more likely tourists will travel there, other things being equal. Many factors that affect tourism demand do not fall into this classification. For instance, tourism demand is affected by the transportation cost between a source market and a destination. Yet the transportation cost depends on the distance between the two, and thus it is neither a push nor a pull factor. Similarly, exchange rate is an important factor affecting tourism demand between two countries; yet it cannot be properly accounted for by the push–pull framework because exchange rate depends on the currencies of both countries. Also, hospitality supply does not have to be provided at destinations, a case where one takes a flight owned by a third country while traveling between the source market and the destination. Neither is the availability of the flight service a push nor a pull factor, but it is instrumental in determining tourism demand from a source market for a destination.

In economic analysis of tourism, push factors, by and large, dictate the nature and size of tourism demand and how the demand changes, while pull factors dictate the nature and size of tourism supply and how the supply changes. It is the interplay of push and pull factors that determines the market equilibrium in tourism and enables us to assess the size of the tourism market and price. When the determinants of tourism demand and supply change, the demand and supply curves shift accordingly, ending up with a set of new market equilibria. As the demand curve shifts, the initial relationship between tourists' willingness to pay and the quantity of tourism demanded is altered, and hence the demand is changed. Figure 2.7a shows the changes in tourism demand caused by the determinants of tourism demand. Given the supply, a change in tourism demand disrupts the initial market equilibrium E_0, indicated by a movement of the market equilibrium either downward or upward along the supply curve (Figure 2.7a). By the same token, when the supply changes, the previous relationship between firms' willingness to sell and the quantity supplied is altered. Figure 2.7b shows the changes in tourism supply that are caused by various determinants of tourism supply mentioned above. Given the demand, a change in tourism supply also disrupts the initial market equilibrium E_0, indicated by a movement of the market equilibrium either downward or upward along the demand curve (Figure 2.7b).

There are factors that can change both tourism demand and supply (Figure 2.8). For instance, a severe earthquake at a destination may not only destroy hotel properties, thereby decreasing hotel supply, but, at the same time, also spark tourists' fear of

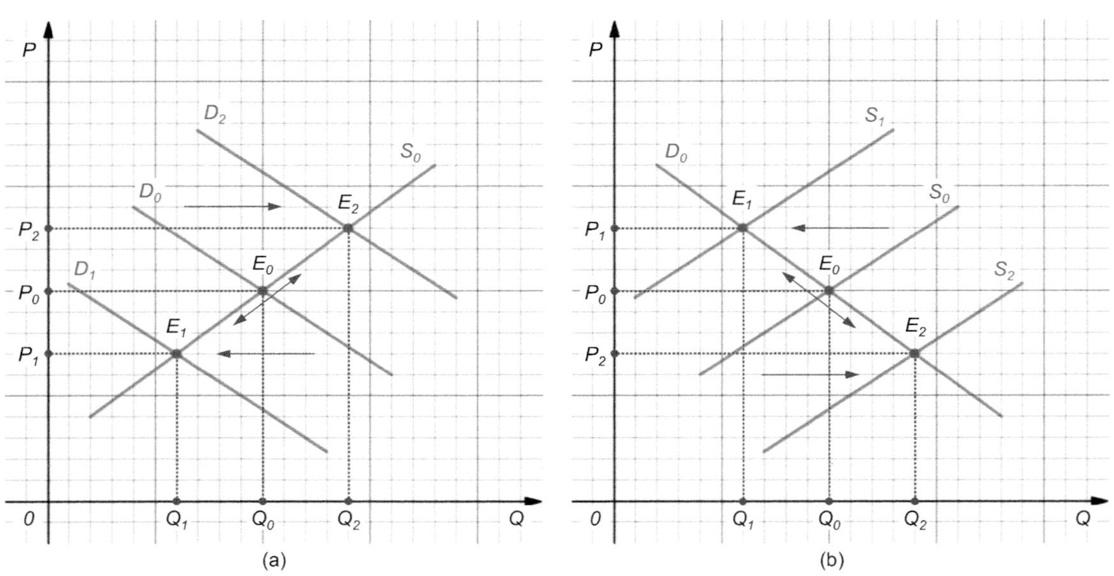

Figure 2.7
Changes in either demand or supply

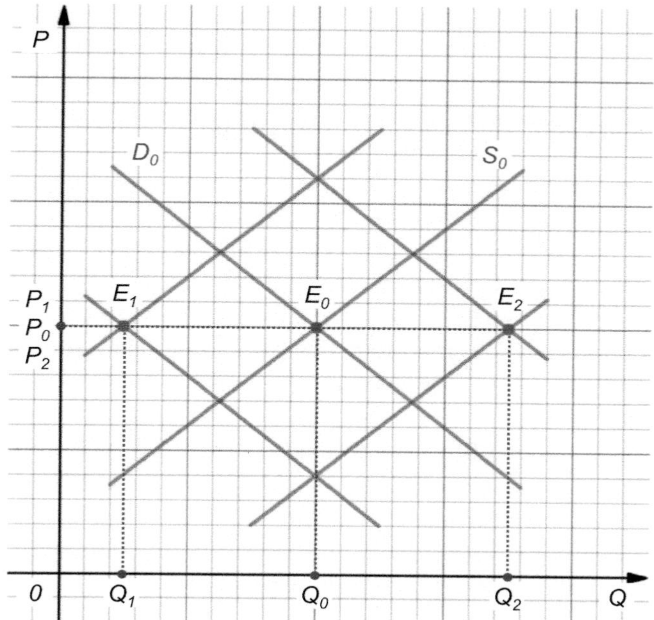

Figure 2.8
Changes in both demand and supply

traveling there and thus decreases hotel demand. Therefore, both demand and supply curves shift to the left, ending up with the market equilibrium changing from E_0 to E_1, suggesting a contraction in the tourism market (Figure 2.8). On the other hand, the widespread use of mobile payment may not only increase tourism demand due to its convenience to consumers but can also encourage firms to increase supply in various hospitality sectors, as it saves time and transaction costs. This would result in rightward shifts in both the demand and supply curves, and thus the market equilibrium changes from E_0 to E_2, leading to an expansion in the tourism market (Figure 2.8). The new market equilibria in these two cases suggest that the changes in equilibrium quantity are determinate yet the equilibrium prices can either be lower or higher than, or equal to, the initial equilibrium price P_0, depending on the extent to which the demand changes relative to the change in supply or vice versa.

2.4.2 Demand drives supply

When evaluating the market outcome, we must be aware that market equilibrium is in fact a snapshot of a market at a certain time when demand equals supply. What we have examined above is the static market equilibrium, with no regard to when it may change and for how long the change might be sustained. Since demand, supply, or both could change over time due to various factors, the change in market equilibrium can be associated with time. This allows us to track the dynamics of market equilibrium by comparing two or more equilibria in different periods of time. As a matter of fact, there exist a set of equilibria contingent on time as long as the factors that cause the demand and/or supply to change correlate with time. In general, the change in demand is much faster than the change in supply. Tourism demand in particular might even be volatile due to instantaneous changes in a wide range of demand determinants of tourism. For instance, unexpected heavy rain in a city could immediately create a demand spike in the taxicab market while having no impact on the supply. By contrast it would take a substantial amount of time to change the supply not only of taxicabs but also of other hospitality goods and services in the market. As far as the push–pull framework is concerned, it is also likely that push factors may change first to influence tourism demand in the source market, which is succeeded by pull factors that affect supply at the destination, or the other way around. Detecting the sequence of the change in demand and supply enables us to examine the mechanisms by which the tourism market is formed.

Note that push and pull factors may not be equally important in stimulating tourism demand as a whole. Push factors are indispensable in stimulating outbound tourism, while pull factors are crucial for destinations to build up supply capacity, thereby attracting inbound tourism. Depending on whether push or pull factors change first, the market equilibrium in tourism can be explained by two different models shown below. One is that demand drives supply, suggesting that push factors are instrumental in generating tourism demand in the first place, which in turn leads to a subsequent adjustment of supply at the destination. Suppose that the initial market equilibrium for tourism is E_0 at a destination, as shown in Figure 2.9. If the income of prospective tourists increases in a source market, the demand curve for tourism will shift rightward from D_0 to D_1, ending up with the new market equilibrium E_1. Thus, both tourist arrivals and the market price of tourism at the destination increase. In the long run though, E_1 is not stable because the increased tourism demand D_1, exemplified by the influx of tourists at the destination, could gradually entice suppliers to increase and customize the supply to the source market where the tourism demand originated. Such supply adjustment would eventually lead to a rightward shift in the supply curve from S_0 to S_1, ending up with another market equilibrium E_2 in the subsequent period of tourism development (Figure 2.9).

In Figure 2.9 the market equilibrium E_2 suggests that the size of the tourism market increases substantially from Q_0 to Q_2, while the price of tourism at the destination is indeterminate. The new equilibrium price P_2 could be either higher or lower than, or equal to, the initial equilibrium price P_0, depending on the increase in supply relative to the increase in demand (Figure 2.9). If the rightward shift in the supply curve is greater than that in the demand curve, the new equilibrium price P_2 will be driven down and thus be below the initial equilibrium price P_0, suggesting that the destination will become cheaper. If otherwise, the new market price P_2 will be pushed up and be above the initial equilibrium price P_0, suggesting that the destination will become more expensive. If the rightward shifts in both the demand and supply curves happen to be equal, the market price will remain unchanged at P_0 (Figure 2.9). In practice, since it takes time for a destination to adjust supply, while demand can

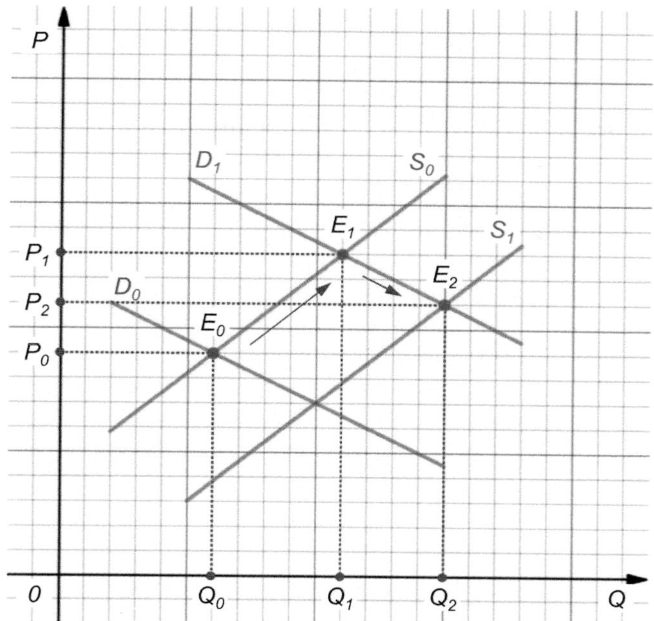

Figure 2.9
Demand drives supply

readily change in the short run, price fluctuations around the initial equilibrium price P_0 will often occur.

This model can explain the staggering growth of Chinese outbound tourism over the past two decades, which we documented in Figures 1.4 and 1.5 in Chapter 1. Underlying the Chinese tourism boom is the enormous size and vitality of the Chinese economy that has grown at an annual rate of 9.4% on average over the past four decades.[6] This has created a massive middle class amounting to 225 million households in 2016, with an average annual income of US$11,500–43,000.[7] The burgeoning middle-class consumers are shifting the Chinese economy from production-oriented to consumption-oriented, and by 2030 private consumption is expected to reach nearly 50% of China's GDP.[8] On the other hand, the demand boom from Chinese tourists has been enticing suppliers not only to increase supply capacity but also to adjust the supply toward serving Chinese tourists. For instance, hotels such as Shangri-La and Jin Jiang Hotels Group expanded and relocated supply to Europe and North America presumably due to the influx of Chinese tourists to these destinations over the past decade.[9] Enterprises across major European cities are also luring Chinese consumers through customizing their products and services. Not only are retail stores being staffed with Chinese-speaking salespersons, but a wide range of tourism firms are also practicing China-specific hospitality, ranging from providing hot drinking water in hotels to accepting UnionPay and Alipay for those who are used to paying with their smartphones at home.[10]

2.4.3 Supply creates demand

The second model is known as supply creates demand,[11] suggesting that pull factors are imperative for stimulating tourism demand in the first place. Suppose that the initial market equilibrium of tourism at a destination is E_0 (Figure 2.10). Suppose, for example, that there is an increase in infrastructure investment at the destination, stimulating the supply. This is represented by a rightward shift in the supply curve from S_0 to S_1, ending up with a new market equilibrium E_1 (Figure 2.10). Note that E_1 is not stable, because the supply abundance would make the destination appealing to tourists, thereby boosting tourism demand in subsequent periods. This is represented by a rightward shift in the demand curve from D_0 to D_1, resulting in another market equilibrium E_2 (Figure 2.10). Thus, tourist arrivals increase substantially from Q_0 to Q_2, yet the market price of tourism P_2 depends on the increase in demand relative to the increase in supply. If the rightward shift in the demand curve is greater than that in the supply curve, the new equilibrium price P_2 will be pushed up and be higher than P_0. If the rightward shift in the demand curve is smaller than that in the supply curve, P_2 will be lower than P_0. If both shifts happen to be equal, the equilibrium price will remain at P_0. Since tourism supply cannot be easily adjusted to the change in tourism demand, a destination would suffer a massive glut and a price plunge once negative demand shocks occur.

This model sheds light on the lack of supply that hampers tourism development in many developing countries. The sluggish tourism growth in Africa and the Middle East noted in Chapter 1 can partially be accounted for by this model. A number of studies

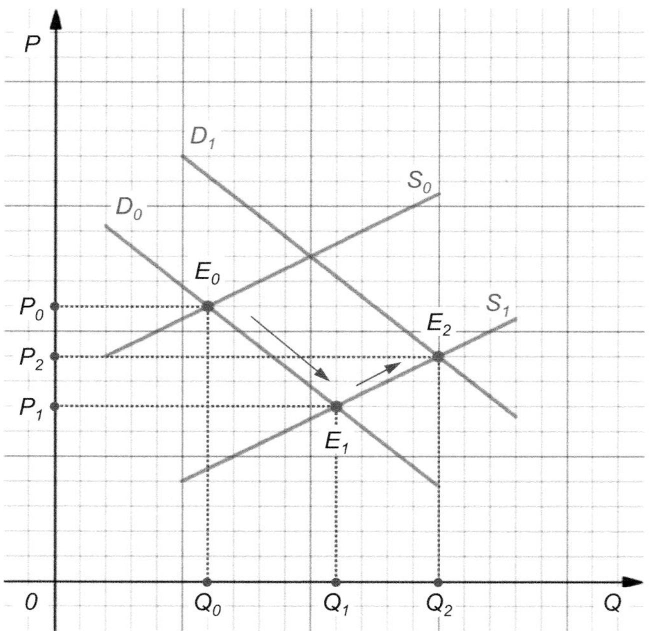

Figure 2.10
Supply creates demand

have found that tourism demand in African countries in particular is determined by various pull factors, such as political stability, tourism infrastructure, as well as economic development in general.[12] These studies have concluded that a destination needs to achieve a minimum threshold of social and economic development before tourism demand can be generated.[13] Probably no destination has yet to evidence this model better than Dubai. Back in 2000 the Dubai government started to transform the economy from petroleum to services, including tourism, through enormous investment in infrastructure as well as in tourism and hospitality facilities. Since 2010 Dubai has become one of the fastest growing cities in the world and is known for its marvelous infrastructure and supply, including the tallest skyscrapers, the largest shopping mall and the most luxurious hotel, the fourth largest airline, as well as the largest retail and entertainment theme park under construction. The development of the infrastructure and hospitality supply furnishes tourists with a great deal of convenience and value, making Dubai the world's fourth largest destination city in terms of tourist arrivals and top of the list in terms of tourist expenditure per visitor over the past decade or so.[14]

Summary

1. Economists approach a phenomenon in three ways, progressively from economic intuition, diagrammatic representation to mathematical inference. The objective is to elevate human understanding from a specific context to general principles.
2. The market is dictated by the laws of demand and supply. The law of demand suggests an inverse relationship between price and quantity demanded, *ceteris paribus*, which is represented by the demand curve. The law of supply is manifested as the supply curve, suggesting a positive relationship between price and quantity supplied.
3. The interactions between demand and supply result in the market equilibrium, at which demand equals supply. In market equilibrium neither consumers nor firms have incentives to change their behavior. Thus we are able to observe and assess the market outcome.
4. A change in demand is manifested as a shift in the demand curve and hence the initial price–quantity coordination is altered. A change in quantity demanded is due to the change in the price of a good insofar as we examine the demand curve, which is manifested as a point movement along the demand curve.
5. Likewise, a change in supply is manifested as a shift in the supply curve and hence the initial price–quantity coordination is altered on the supply curve. A change in quantity supplied is due to the change in the price of a good insofar as we examine the supply curve, which is manifested as a point movement along the supply curve.
6. Consumer surplus is a consumer's willingness to pay less the market price, and producer surplus is the market price less a firm's willingness to sell. Social surplus is the sum of consumer surplus and producer surplus, which indicates the welfare of society as a whole, obtained from market transactions.

7. Price controls are government interventions in the free market through mandating a market price, which deviates from equilibrium price. Price controls include price ceilings, in which the market price is lower than equilibrium price, and price floors, in which the market price is higher than equilibrium price.
8. Deadweight loss arises when price controls intervene in the free market. Social surplus decreases as long as deadweight loss arises. Social surplus maximizes when deadweight loss is zero, and then the market becomes perfectly efficient.
9. Push factors are the determinants of tourism demand specific to source markets, while pull factors are the determinants of tourism supply specific to destinations. Push factors drive people to leave their usual environment while pull factors attract tourists to certain destinations. The effects of push and pull factors can also be negative.
10. The model that demand drives supply suggests that push factors affect tourism demand in the first place, succeeded by supply adjustment at the destination. The model that supply creates demand suggests that pull factors affect tourism supply in the first place, followed by a change in demand in subsequent periods.

REVIEW QUESTIONS

Each question has four options, and there is only one correct answer to each question.

1. Which of the following is correct regarding how economists approach and analyze an economic problem or phenomenon?
   A) By economic intuition.
   B) By diagrammatic illustration.
   C) By mathematical inference.
   D) All of the above.
2. Which of the following is correct regarding the law of demand?
   A) It suggests a positive relationship between price and quantity demanded.
   B) It suggests a negative relationship between price and quantity supplied.
   C) It suggests consumers' willingness to pay that decreases with quantity.
   D) It suggests firms' willingness to sell that decreases with quantity.
3. According to the United Kingdom Office for National Statistics, foreigners made more than 4 million trips to the UK in July 2017, an increase of 6% compared to July 2016. Also, tourist expenditure amounted to £2.8 billion, a record high in a single month since 1961 for which the data are available. The stellar growth in tourism was in part due to depreciation of the pound by nearly 20% since 2016. How would the pound's depreciation have affected inbound tourism in the UK in the short run?
   A) The depreciated pound shifted the demand curve to the left.
   B) The depreciated pound shifted the demand curve to the right.

C) The depreciated pound led to a movement upward along the demand curve.
D) The depreciated pound led to a movement downward along the demand curve.

4. The hurricanes in 2016 devastated Florida in the United States by bringing floods, tearing down homes and properties, as well as causing fatalities. The graph below shows that the demand for and supply of tourism in Florida are D_0 and S_0, respectively, before the hurricanes. Which of the following is correct regarding the impact of the hurricanes on the tourism market in Florida?

A) Demand decreased by $Q_m - Q_j$
B) Supply decreased by $Q_m - Q_l$
C) Equilibrium quantity decreased by $Q_m - Q_l$
D) Equilibrium price decreased by $P_l - P_n$

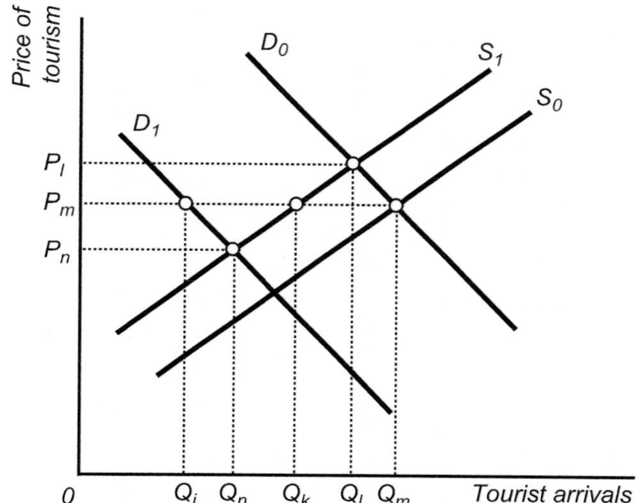

5. Suppose that Catherine bought two pieces of the same handmade necklace sold for $20 each in Bangkok. If she was willing to pay $40 for the first and only $25 for the second, what would be her consumer surplus?

A) $20
B) $25
C) $40
D) $65

6. The graph below shows the demand curve (*D*) and the supply curve (*S*) in the market for aviation services between two cities. What would be the social surplus if airlines were mandated by the government to sell each ticket at $200?

A) a + b
B) a + b + c
C) a + b + d
D) a + b + c + d + e

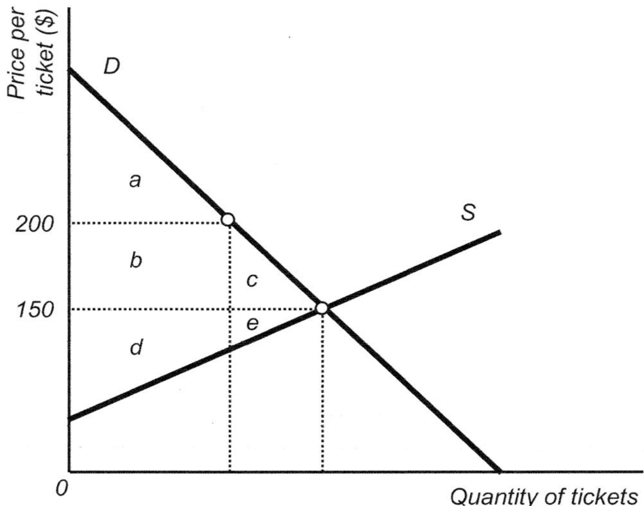

7. Given the information and the graph in Question 6 above, which of the following is correct?
   A) The market price would be $150 per ticket.
   B) The equilibrium price would be $200 per ticket.
   C) The price ceiling would be at $150 per ticket.
   D) The price floor would be at $200 per ticket.
8. Which of the following is correct regarding push and pull factors in affecting tourism demand and supply?
   A) Push factors have only positive effects on tourism demand.
   B) Pull factors have only negative effects on tourism demand.
   C) Push factors suggest the change in demand for tourism.
   D) Pull factors suggest the change in the price of tourism.
9. According to a recent report in the *Wall Street Journal*, Japan is learning from China about how people pay without cash in order to better serve Chinese tourists. This adjustment is brought about by an influx of Chinese tourists in Japan who expect to pay with a smartphone just like they do at home. In fact, the boom of Chinese outbound tourism, with Japan as one of the popular destinations, started as early as the 2000s due to the increased disposable income of Chinese people. Suppose that the market equilibrium *a* indicates the Chinese tourism market in Japan prior to the 2000s as shown in the graph below. Which of the following can best indicate the market equilibrium nowadays?
   A) *a*
   B) *b*
   C) *c*
   D) *d*

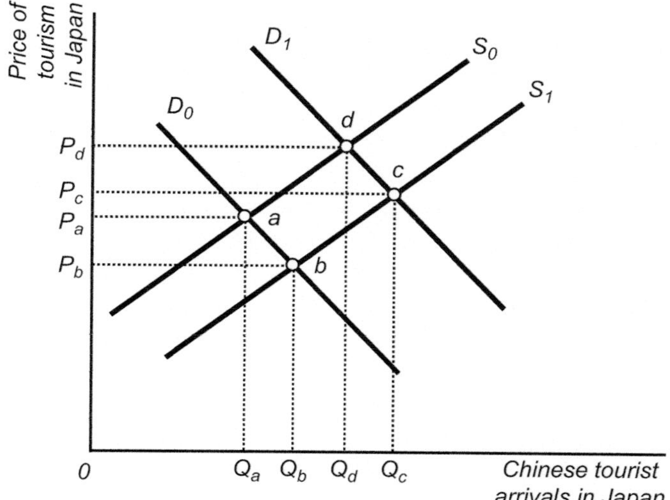

10. Which of the following conditions suggests that the market is perfectly efficient in production?

A) Producer surplus is maximized.
B) Consumer surplus is maximized.
C) Deadweight loss is zero.
D) Price controls are implemented.

Problem solving

1. It was widely reported in China in April 2020 that some restaurants were seemingly coerced into apologizing for having raised their prices during the subsiding period of the coronavirus outbreak.[15] The apologies came immediately after widespread outrage from consumers who believed that raising prices was inappropriate and unethical. What or who should determine the price in the restaurant industry? Given the fact that the virus outbreak was subsiding and demand started to bounce back, would you be able to justify the view that raising prices would actually help both consumers and restaurants?

2. International tourism by and large is impeded by regulations of destination countries through visa restrictions. Since foreigners have to apply for a visitor visa in advance in order to travel to and around a destination country, the destination government can dictate the quota of visitor visas issued to citizens from a particular country for various reasons besides tourism. Suppose that a destination country implements a certain quota of visitor visas, and therefore foreigners cannot travel as freely as they wish to the country. What would be the impact of the visa quota on the tourism market in the destination country? Do a graphical analysis to illustrate your answer.

3. Over the past quarter-century since the 1994 genocide, Rwanda's economy has flourished. Much of the economic miracle can be attributed to Paul Kagame, the president who steered Rwanda through a long period of reconciliation to emerge as one of the safest places in Africa. Not only has the development of infrastructure such as airports been seen in recent decades, but tourism and hospitality supply is also expanding. According to *Bloomberg*, Marriott and Radisson Blu have opened 200-plus-room hotels, and multiple carriers flying into Kigali International Airport make travel to and around this tiny landlocked country easier and more convenient than ever.[16] All of these factors have led to a tourism boom in Rwanda: international tourist arrivals increased from 494 thousand in 2006 to 932 thousand in 2016, and international tourism receipts increased from US$4 million to US$528 million in current prices over the period 1995–2018.[17] Explain the pattern of tourism growth in Rwanda.

Solutions to all review questions and problem solving tasks are included in the Support Material for this book, which can be accessed at www.routledge.com/9780367897352.

Notes

1 For a detailed account of the multidisciplinary nature of tourism studies, see Jafari and Ritchie (1981).

2 For instance, two of the most prestigious journals in the area: *Annals of Tourism Research* was founded in 1973 and the *Journal of Travel Research* was founded in 1968.

3 In describing an economic agent throughout this book, *he* and *she* are interchangeable unless indicated otherwise. To make the discussion concise, we use *he* in a neutral sense in this book, which can be equally replaced by *she* unless indicated otherwise.

4 The term "neoclassical economics" was proposed by Thorstein Veblen (1857–1929) to distinguish it from what is known as classical economics, or political economy, represented by Adam Smith (1723–1790), Jean-Baptiste Say (1767–1832), and David Ricardo (1772–1823) among others in the late eighteenth and mid-nineteenth centuries. By the 1870s a notable paradigm shift arose in economic studies from classical economics to neoclassical economics, led by Léon Walras (1834–1910), William Stanley Jevons (1835–1882), and Carl Menger (1840–1921). Neoclassical economists built their theories on utility and consumption instead of cost and production as classical economists did. On the other hand, neoclassical economics is distinguished from institutional economics that emerged in the late nineteenth and early twentieth centuries, which treats transaction as the unit of economic analysis. Besides the paradigm shift, neoclassical economics resorts to mathematics in building economic models to mimic the methodology of natural sciences, particularly physics.

5 As far as empirical studies are concerned, the impact of minimum wages could be ambiguous. Please refer to Card and Krueger (1994, 1995) for some empirical evidence.

6 World Bank Open Data. Accessed on August 11, 2020.

7 *The Economist*. Special report on China's middle class. July 9, 2016.

8 *The Economist*. The Chinese consumer in 2030. November 2, 2016.

9 *South China Morning Post*. Shangri-La sets sights on global expansion. July 28, 2008. *The Financial Times*. China budget hotel brands eye overseas expansion. February 7, 2017.

10 *People's Daily* Online. Hot water revolution: How Chinese tourists are changing the world. May 22, 2018. *The Wall Street Journal*. Smartphone-wielding Chinese tourists challenge cash's reign. March 3, 2019.

11 This phrase is different from, and has nothing to do with, Say's law that states that one's supply to meet the demand of others creates his own demand for others' production in the economy.

12 Please refer to Naudé and Saayman (2005) for details.

13 Please refer to Eugenio-Martin, Martín-Morales, and Sinclair (2008) for details.

14 Mastercard. Global Destination City Index, 2015–2019.

15 *Global Times*. Chinese chain restaurant Xibei apologizes for price hike after Haidilao. April 11, 2020. *South China Morning Post*. Coronavirus: China's consumers push back against price increases as firms seek to offset Covid-19 impact. April 18, 2020.

16 *Bloomberg*. How Rwanda became the unlikeliest tourism destination in Africa. September 28, 2017.

17 World Bank Open Data, accessed on August 11, 2020. The consumer price index (CPI) in Rwanda over the same period was approximately 6% on a yearly average. Adjusted by inflation, the growth of international tourism receipts in Rwanda was still remarkable.

Bibliography

Boulding, K. E. (1945). The concept of economic surplus. *American Economic Review, 35*(5), 851–869.

Card, D., & Krueger, A. B. (1994). Minimum wages and employment: A case study of the fast-food industry in New Jersey and Pennsylvania. *American Economic Review, 84*(4), 772–793.

Card, D., & Krueger, A. B. (1995). Time-series minimum-wage studies: A meta-analysis. *American Economic Review, 85*(2), 238–243.

Currie, J. M., Murphy, J. A., & Schmitz, A. (1971). The concept of economic surplus and its use in economic analysis. *Economic Journal, 81*(324), 741–799.

Eugenio-Martin, J. L., Martín-Morales, N., & Sinclair, M. T. (2008). The role of economic development in tourism demand. *Tourism Economics, 14*(4), 673–690.

Friedman, M. (1953). The methodology of positive economics. *Essays in positive economics*. Chicago, IL: University of Chicago Press.

Jafari, J., & Ritchie, J. B. (1981). Toward a framework for tourism education: Problems and prospects. *Annals of Tourism Research, 8*(1), 13–34.

Jenkin, F. (1872). On the principles which regulate the incidence of taxes. *Proceedings of the Royal Society of Edinburgh, 7*, 618–631.

Jevons, W. S. (1866). Brief account of a general mathematical theory of political economy. *Journal of the Royal Statistical Society, 29*, 282–287.

Marshall, A. (1890). *Principles of economics*. Peter Groenewegen, 2013. Reprint.

Naudé, W. A., & Saayman, A. (2005). Determinants of tourist arrivals in Africa: A panel data regression analysis. *Tourism Economics, 11*(3), 365–391.

3 Uber's surge pricing and market efficiency[1]

This chapter analyzes Uber's surge pricing, a pricing strategy widely used by Uber and other tech companies. From a practical point of view, Uber's ride-hailing service is part of tourism and hospitality supply but differs from other services as far as the capability of Uber to detect and measure demand is concerned. From a theoretical point of view, Uber's surge pricing is grounded on equilibrium analysis. To grasp the essence of Uber's surge pricing it is crucial for us to understand the peculiarity of demand for and supply of Uber rides. For Uber, demand, above anything else, lies at the heart of its pricing strategy because of the volatility of consumer demand for its services. We apply equilibrium analysis and demand theories to analyze Uber's surge pricing as well as to compare the market efficiencies with and without surge pricing. We highlight the central role of the price signal in improving market efficiency in the free market.

AFTER STUDYING THIS CHAPTER, YOU SHOULD BE ABLE TO:

- Explain the causes of demand surge for Uber rides with regard to time, place, and consumers;
- Analyze the economic mechanism of Uber's surge pricing and the consequence of its failure;
- Analyze the economic surplus of Uber's surge pricing and evaluate the market efficiency; and
- Outline the implications of Uber's surge pricing in economic analysis as well as for businesses in the digital era.

3.1 What is a surge in demand?

Consumer demand for a wide range of products and services in tourism and hospitality is volatile not only because they are by and large not essential consumption but also because there are alternatives in the market that consumers can turn to. The volatility of demand for tourism and hospitality products suggests that a change in demand could be local and ephemeral, meaning that demand fluctuates instantaneously from place to place and from one period of time to another. On the one hand, surges or plunges in demand occur due to demand shocks somewhere and sometime; on the other hand, they would even out very soon prior to being noticed by firms. Demand surges are exemplified by Uber, a ridesharing company founded in the United States in 2009, with its pricing strategy known as surge pricing. One outstanding example is that Uber was reported to jack up its prices fourfold amid a hostage crisis in Sydney, Australia in December 2014.[2] This price hike was notoriously criticized by the public, who accused Uber of taking advantage of those who were needing immediate ride services during the crisis. The widespread outrage eventually led the public in some countries to boycott Uber.

To economists a surge in demand, for whatever reason, is nothing but an increase in demand whereby new market forces kick in to turn the market around to reach a new equilibrium. In a free market where riders and drivers transact voluntarily with each other on Uber, the market will end up in equilibrium. This does not only apply to a demand surge but also to a demand plunge, which suggests an abrupt decrease in demand. Yet different from an increase in supply that may take time to arise, a demand surge in economic jargon is an almost instantaneous, yet substantial, rightward shift in the demand curve. Due to its local and ephemeral nature, supply can neither be readily adjusted to match the demand nor would it be necessary for supply to adjust at all because the surge would vanish very soon after. Since demand surge alters the market equilibrium due to the rightward shift in the demand curve while supply remains unchanged, the market price will increase, leading to a price surge, other things being equal. As tempting a strategy as it seems, surge pricing does not make inroads into conventional enterprises which are incapable of detecting where and when demand will surge and measuring the magnitude of a demand surge, if any.

3.2 How does surge pricing work?

3.2.1 Riders, drivers, and surge multipliers

When opening the Uber app to make a ride request, you would probably see a number such as 4.5× and the like on the interface (Figure 3.1a). These numbers are called surge multipliers, suggesting that Uber is implementing surge pricing on the ride you are ready to book. Under surge pricing, be aware that the rate you are billed is equal to the surge multiplier times the normal rate, which is what you would otherwise be charged if there was no demand surge. These new rates, usually higher than the normal rate, are called surge prices. On the rider's app, a surge price is accompanied by a short message from Uber: "Demand is off the charts! Fares have increased to get more Ubers on the road." As a justification for surge pricing from Uber's perspective though, this message indeed implies, to some extent, why and how surge pricing actually works, which we shall discuss shortly. If you choose not to accept the surge price, Uber will remind you on the app to check out updated rates later on, as the surge period will end anyway, and the rate will be set back to normal.

On the other hand, drivers can also see surge multipliers on their app but in a different and more sophisticated way (Figure 3.1b). Not only can drivers see all surge

Figure 3.1
Interfaces of Uber app for riders and drivers

multipliers that are currently being implemented in a city but they can also see the corresponding location where a particular surge multiplier is being executed. These multipliers are subject to change due to the change in demand as well as in supply of drivers. Figure 3.1b shows the Uber app of a driver in Lausanne, Switzerland for demonstration purposes. The information that the driver can obtain from his app is that surge multipliers in the city are now a factor between 1 and 4.5. In the central part of Lausanne, the rate is still around the normal rate with a multiplier equal to 1.1, while in other parts of the city he is entitled to charge a rate up to 4.5 times the normal rate, say at Lausanne-Gare. Depending on how far away he is from the districts where surge prices are being implemented, he not only knows where he should head to pick up riders but also understands whether to accept a ride request or not.

3.2.2 Surge pricing works

Uber's surge pricing was addressed in great detail by Hall, Kendrick, and Nosko (2015) in a case study in New York City. This case featured a quasi-natural experiment with real-world data from Uber, which enable us to compare the market outcomes with and without surge pricing. Uber's surge pricing was executed due to a concert given by American singer Ariana Grande at Madison Square Garden in New York City on the night of March 21, 2015. Figure 3.2 shows three curves plotted from the data collected by the Uber algorithm in the vicinity of Madison Square Garden from 7:30 p.m. on March 21 to 2 a.m. the following day. The blue curve at the top denotes that the number of prospective riders opening the Uber app skyrocketed to over 400% between 10:30 p.m. and 11:30 p.m. against the baseline, and then leveled off soon after. The red curve denotes the number of requests made by riders in the same area, which saw an increase of around 150% during the same period. The green curve denotes the number of drivers either available to accept a request, en route to pick up a rider, or on a trip with a rider in the same area. Similar to the red curve, the green curve experienced a moderate increase of around 180% over the same period. It is worth noting that the discrepancy between the red and green curves in the surge period is not as substantial as the discrepancies between both of them and the blue curve (Figure 3.2).

Suppose that Figure 3.3 shows the market for Uber rides at Madison Square Garden in the pre-surge period, denoted by the demand curve D_0, supply curve S_0, and the market equilibrium E_0. Thus, the normal rate is represented by the equilibrium price P_0, and the number of requests made by riders and served by drivers is the equilibrium quantity Q_0. The surge in demand between 10:30 p.m. and 11:30 p.m. shifts the demand curve rightward from D_0 to D_1 by a magnitude of $Q_2 - Q_0$, resulting in a new market equilibrium E_1. Thus, Uber raises the rate from P_0 to the new equilibrium price P_1, meaning that a surge multiplier, P_1 / P_0, is executed and shown on both riders' and drivers' apps. It is the new equilibrium price P_1 that incentivizes drivers to increase the quantity supplied from Q_0 to Q_1, dictated by a movement of the market equilibrium upward from E_0 to E_1 along the supply curve. Given the surge price P_1 which is higher than the normal rate P_0, the number of requests made by riders ends up at Q_1, indicated by a movement from point F to the new market equilibrium E_1 along the new demand curve D_1. That is, the number of riders opening the app yet making no request is $Q_2 - Q_1$, due to the surge price P_1. In the surge period the number of ride requests that Uber accomplishes increases by $Q_1 - Q_0$.

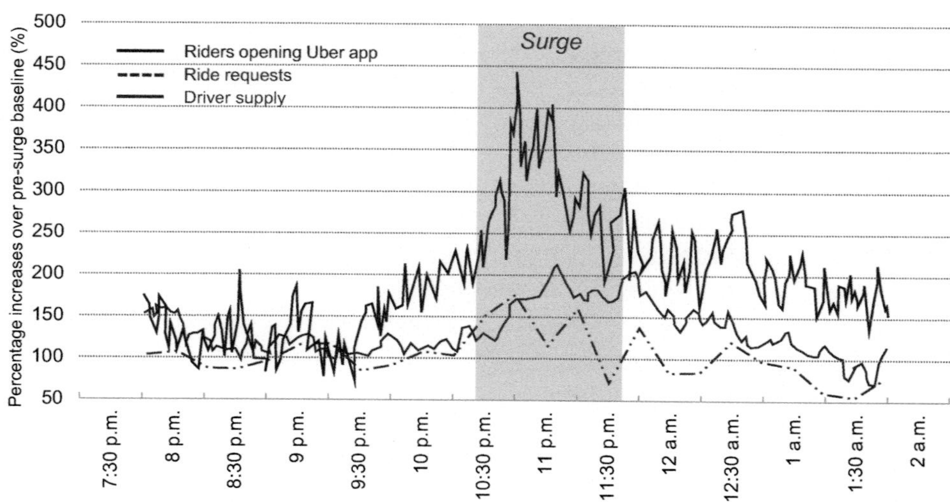

Figure 3.2
Uber ride requests and driver supply in the surge period

Note: Prospective riders opening the Uber app were recorded every minute from 7:30 p.m. to 2 a.m. Ride requests are the total requests recorded in every 15-minute interval. Driver supply is the number of UberX drivers either open and ready to accept a request, en route to pick up a rider, or on a trip with a rider. All the values are normalized to a pre-surge baseline between 9 p.m. and 9:30 p.m. Surge period was the time during which the surge multiplier exceeded one. All the data were collected for a restricted geospatial bounding box containing Madison Square Garden, roughly five avenues long and 15 streets wide.

Source: Reproduced from Hall et al. (2015).

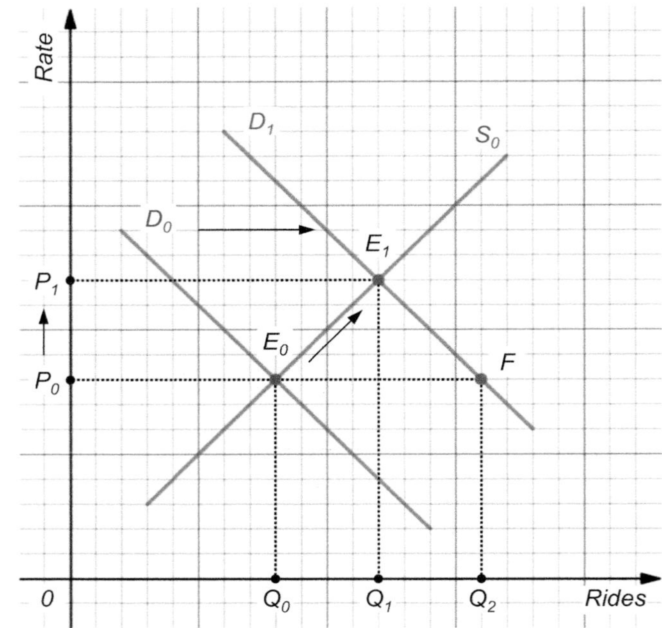

Figure 3.3
Uber's surge pricing works

Note that Ariana Grande's show at Madison Square Garden did not change Uber supply, which is the number of drivers registered on Uber or available in the city. The demand surge was due to the fact that the show amassed attendees who were eager to leave right after the show. They therefore had a greater willingness to pay at that time. It could also be because some attendees who usually do not take Uber decided to do so on this occasion. Regardless of whatever motivation riders may have, not only is Uber able to detect when and where demand surges but it can also assess the magnitude of the surge, in other words, the extent to which the demand shifts from D_0 to D_1 in the above analysis. Such information is obtained by detecting the number of prospective riders opening the app in the surge period, Q_2, against the number of requests made in the pre-surge period, Q_0. A rider's decision to open the app, which reveals his willingness to use Uber, is based on his prior knowledge about the normal rate. If the normal rate were implemented in the surge period, those prospective riders opening the app would proceed to make a request, and thus the number of requests made by riders in the surge period would also be Q_2. Conditional on the normal rate P_0, in this case the demand surged by $Q_2 - Q_0$.

3.2.3 Surge pricing fails

Similar to the demand surge caused by Ariana Grande's show, the celebration of New Year's Eve in New York City on December 31, 2014 caused a surge in demand for Uber rides near Madison Square Garden from 12:45 p.m. to 4 a.m. the following day (Figure 3.4).[3] We could enumerate many differences between this case and the preceding one in terms of the size of the two surges, how long they lasted, the baseline demand and supply, and so on. What makes these two cases comparable is that Uber's surge pricing algorithm broke down for around 26 minutes from 1:24 a.m. to 1:50 a.m. amid the surge period. This technical glitch might have made Uber unable to charge a certain surge price because the algorithm failed to detect and measure the demand surge in the 26-minute spell. Even if the demand surge had been detected and a surge price executed, this glitch might have made Uber unable to publish the new rate in the form of surge multiplier on both riders' and drivers' apps. Thus, the surge multiplier remained at 1 in the 26-minute spell as shown in Figure 3.4. As a result, riders and drivers could only see the normal rate on their apps and thus act on it accordingly.

Figure 3.5 shows the market for Uber rides in the pre-surge period as usual, denoted by the demand curve D_0 and the supply curve S_0. The market equilibrium E_0 manifests the equilibrium price P_0, which is the normal rate, and the equilibrium quantity Q_0, which is the number of requests made by riders and served by drivers in the pre-surge period. As the celebration of New Year's Eve was ending and people started to head home, the demand curve for Uber rides shifts rightward from D_0 to D_1, indicating that the number of prospective riders opening the app and ready to make a request increases by $Q_2 - Q_0$. Due to the glitch, the normal rate P_0 shown on the app is also the price at which riders make their requests in the surge period. Hence the number of requests eventually made by riders is Q_2 instead of Q_1 in the preceding case. Given the fact that the normal rate P_0 is also observable to drivers, there are no incentives for them to increase the quantity supplied beyond Q_0 by driving around the city. Thus, a shortage of supply, or an excess of demand, arises in the market, denoted by $Q_2 - Q_0$, which is the number of requests made by riders but not served by drivers. It is the new equilibrium price P_1 that would otherwise bring the demand and supply into balance through actuating both riders and drivers in the surge period.

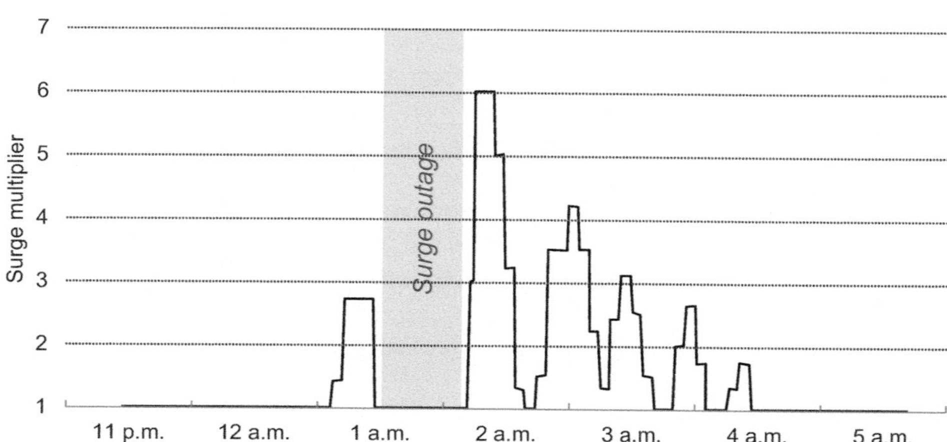

Figure 3.4
Surge multiplier and surge outage

Note: The surge multiplier was recorded for a given minute over the course of New Year's Eve for UberX vehicles within the same geospatial bounding box noted in Figure 3.2. Surge outage was the time during which Uber's surge pricing algorithm broke down.

Source: Reproduced from Hall et al. (2015).

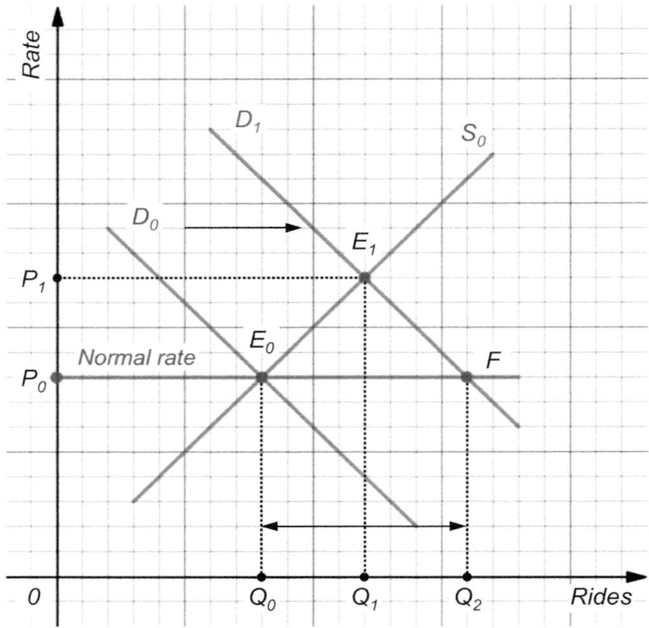

Figure 3.5
Uber's surge pricing fails

3.3 Welfare analysis of surge pricing

As far as consumers are concerned, the Uber outrage in Sydney or elsewhere may delude us into believing that surge pricing is a bad thing or at least immoral. Riders seem to be ripped off by Uber due to the exorbitant rates charged in the surge period. This myth prevails among those who criticize Uber's surge pricing while having little knowledge about why surge pricing occurs in the first place. The fallacy that surge pricing renders riders worse off is no different in principle than claiming that rent controls will help tenants and minimum wages will help workers, which we analyzed in Chapter 2. Though these claims may be tempting in justifying government regulation or consumer protection in one way or another, they are not only theoretically flawed, but also contradict empirical evidence. As a matter of fact, what we would obtain from wishing Uber to scrap surge pricing does not square with what we actually get in the market. The same thing occurs if we wish for rent controls to protect tenants and minimum wages to protect workers: we would end up with the very opposite in the market.

3.3.1 Economic surplus

When demand surges, the absence of a surge price acts the same way as a price ceiling that hampers a price from reaching a new market equilibrium. Figure 3.6 shows that if Uber were not able to implement a surge price or, for whatever reason, the surge price were not observable to riders and drivers on their apps, the market price would be capped at the normal rate P_0. As the demand increases from D_0 to D_1 in the surge period while the supply remains unchanged, the corresponding rate will be the new equilibrium price P_1 dictated by the new market equilibrium E_1. Because the normal rate P_0 is the price signal in the market, the quantity demanded by riders, which is the number of requests, increases from Q_0 to Q_2, while the quantity supplied by drivers, which is the number of requests served by drivers, will still be Q_0. This ends up with a shortage of supply from drivers, $Q_2 - Q_0$, which would otherwise be eradicated if the market price P_0 were freed up to reach the new equilibrium price P_1. Under the normal rate P_0, the number of drivers, $Q_1 - Q_0$, who would otherwise be willing to supply at P_1 have no incentives to do so. In practice, these drivers may either remain idle or head elsewhere for better business opportunities. On the demand side, the same number of riders, $Q_1 - Q_0$, whose requests would otherwise be served if the market price were at P_1, cannot get a ride at all. Hence deadweight loss arises.

Figure 3.6 shows that the deadweight loss is manifested on both demand and supply sides. In the surge period with the normal rate P_0, consumer surplus is the area between the demand curve D_1 and the normal rate P_0 bounded by zero and Q_0 on the x-axis. Compared to the pre-surge period, consumer surplus increases because the demand surges, other things being equal. However, those riders, denoted by $Q_1 - Q_0$, are worse off because they would otherwise be served by Uber if the rate increased to the new equilibrium price P_1. Obviously, those riders, denoted by Q_0, who are lucky enough to be served have their consumer surplus increase in the absence of the surge price. The problem is that social surplus in the surge period as a whole shrinks due to the deadweight loss, which would otherwise be eradicated if the surge price P_1 were

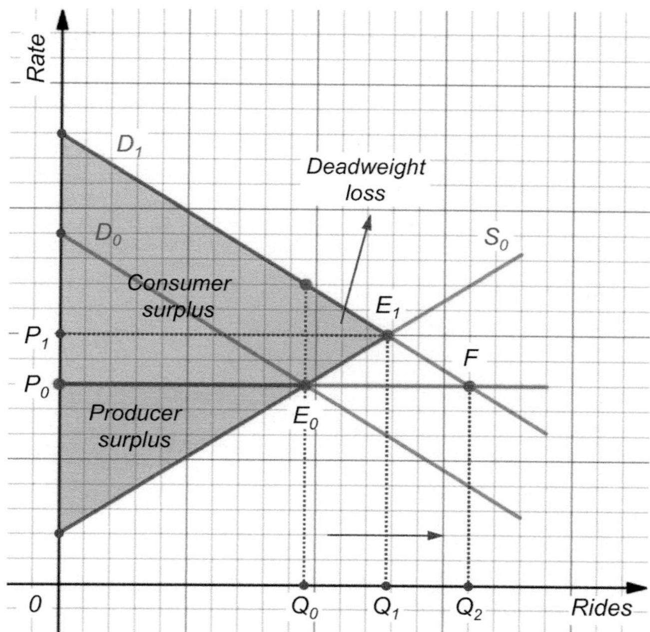

Figure 3.6
Economic surplus in the failure of surge pricing

executed. Hence the market is not perfectly efficient. Note that the social surplus is unevenly distributed between riders and drivers as shown in Figure 3.6. Because the normal rate P_0 is lower than the equilibrium price P_1 in the surge period, the drivers, Q_0, who can accept the normal rate P_0 in the surge period, are worse off compared to the same number of riders who get the ride. The market as a whole suffers nonetheless.

3.3.2 Empirical evidence

Using three metrics—the number of requests, riders' wait time, and completion rate—we can assess the welfare that surge pricing brings about in the market. The number of requests is recorded within every 15-minute interval, which is the quantity of rides demanded but may not necessarily be equal to the quantity supplied by drivers. Riders' wait time is the average time in minutes for a driver to arrive and pick up a rider after a request is accepted. Completion rate is the ratio of served requests to total requests made within every 15-minute interval. To simplify the discussion that follows, as well as to make the two cases comparable without loss of generality, we assume that both cases have the same demand in the pre-surge period and the same size of demand surge.[4] Figures 3.7 and 3.8 show that amid the two surge periods ride requests increased by 66.7% at Ariana Grande's show and by 300% on New Year's Eve against their respective pre-surge baselines.[5] Such a striking discrepancy between the two cases was due to the fact that the surge price acted as a disincentive for riders to make requests at Ariana Grande's show. That is, it ends up reducing the number of requests that are actually made by riders. We illustrated in Figures 3.3 and 3.5 above that the number of requests increases by $(Q_1 - Q_0)/Q_0$ with the surge price in effect and by $(Q_2 - Q_0)/Q_0$ without it. Since $Q_1 < Q_2$, then $(Q_1 - Q_0)/Q_0 < (Q_2 - Q_0)/Q_0$, which conforms to the empirical evidence.

Other things being equal, riders' wait time is a reliable indicator not only of the size of the shortage of supply but also of consumer surplus. It is the absence of the surge price that creates the shortage of supply $Q_2 - Q_0$ (Figure 3.5). The greater the shortage, the longer a rider has to wait for a driver to come, provided that his request is accepted.

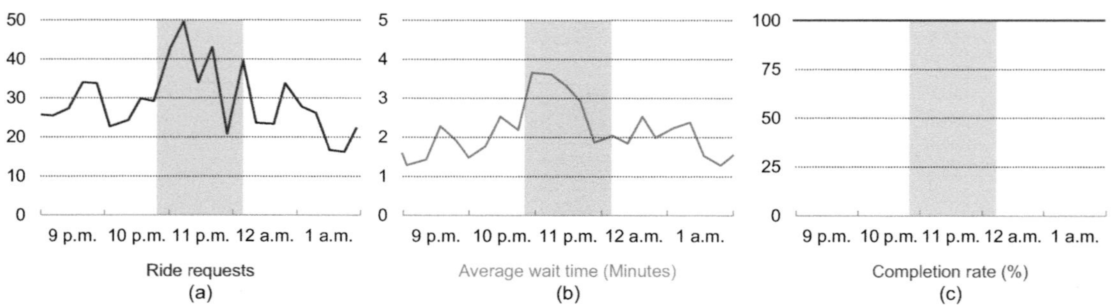

Figure 3.7
Market outcome with surge pricing

Note: For the definition of ride requests, see note in Figure 3.2. Average wait time is the average time for a driver to arrive in every 15-minute interval. Completion rate is the number of completed trips divided by the sum of completed trips and unfulfilled trips within every 15-minute interval. The blue boxes indicate the same surge period as in Figure 3.2, other things being the same.

Source: Reproduced from Hall et al. (2015).

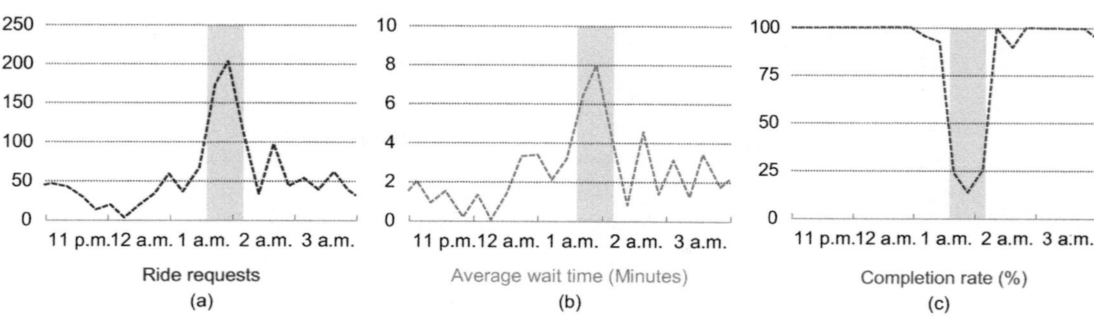

Figure 3.8
Market outcome without surge pricing

Note: For the definitions of ride requests, average wait time, and completion rate, see note in Figure 3.7. The red boxes indicate the same surge outage as in Figure 3.4, other things being the same.

Source: Reproduced from Hall et al. (2015).

Only in the market equilibrium where demand equals supply can riders' wait time be minimized. Evidence shows that riders' average wait time was 3.5 minutes in the presence of the surge price (Figure 3.7) versus 8 minutes in its absence (Figure 3.8). When the demand surges, the new equilibrium price, or the surge price, reduces the number of requests by discouraging riders from making requests on the one hand and incentivizing drivers to accept requests on the other. Eventually, the quantity demanded equals the quantity supplied, and hence a 100% completion rate can be achieved, denoted by Q_1 / Q_1 (Figure 3.3). Yet in the absence of the surge price, the completion rate is Q_0 / Q_2 ($Q_0 < Q_2$), which is strictly smaller than 100% (Figure 3.5). If surge pricing does not function, the greater the demand surge the lower the completion rate. Evidence shows that the completion rate dropped from 100% with the surge price (Figure 3.7) to merely 20% without it (Figure 3.8). Low completion rates could, in part, be attributed to the fact that a long wait time makes either riders, drivers, or both renege on some ongoing deals, and thus the requests end up not being served.

3.4 Information, price signal, and market efficiency

3.4.1 *Surge multiplier as the price signal*

So long as demand surges, surge multiplier is greater than 1 because the new equilibrium price is higher than the initial one. If demand plummets for whatever reason, surge multiplier is less than 1.[6] Note that the use of multiplier in surge pricing is not the same as the use of economic multipliers in macroeconomics—say the Keynesian multiplier, in which one factor leads to a multiplier effect on another through some sort of economic mechanism. When it comes to surge multiplier for Uber rides, surge price, which is the new equilibrium price, is not caused by, but benchmarked against, the normal rate. Thus, surge multiplier is simply the ratio of the new equilibrium price in the surge period to the initial equilibrium price in the pre-surge period, P_1 / P_0, as shown in Figure 3.3. In essence, surge multiplier is the magnitude of a demand surge reflected in the discrepancy between the new equilibrium price P_1 and the initial equilibrium price P_0 conditional on the same supply curve. In other words, if we know the supply function and the surge multiplier P_1 / P_0, we can also calculate the ratio of the new equilibrium quantity to the initial equilibrium quantity, Q_1 / Q_0, and vice versa in Figure 3.3.

Therefore, surge pricing should not be interpreted as Uber's manipulation of market price. On the contrary, it is Uber's agile response on the supply side to an instantaneous shock in demand and, for that matter, to the dynamic interaction between demand and supply. The surge multiplier is, in essence, the price signal that guides self-interested market participants, namely riders and drivers, to act in accordance with the laws of demand and supply in the free market. Thanks to technology, not only can the price signal disseminate more efficiently in the market, but firms like Uber can also avail themselves of such information to zero in on particular market participants at particular times and places. Compared to conventional price signals that take time to disseminate among consumers and firms, surge multiplier is instantaneously observable to both riders and drivers on their Uber apps, and can thus unleash the power of the price mechanism in allocating scarce resources in the free market. With regard to price, surge multiplier makes visible the invisible hand metaphorically referred to by Adam Smith.

3.4.2 "The use of knowledge in society"

Far back in 1945 Friedrich Hayek (1899–1992) critiques the efficacy of the centrally planned economy precisely on the ground that no centralized authority, such as a government or dictator, can acquire all the knowledge of economic activity that is incomplete, dispersed, and individualized in the market. The knowledge includes information of all kinds, particularly price and demand, that guides consumers and firms to make decisions on what to buy and sell, from whom, how many, at what price, and so on. To economists after all, consumers are nothing more than a set of demand curves, which differ from one another and vary by who they are, at what time and place. The volatility of demand in tourism and hospitality suggests that demand is subject to surge, plunge, or oscillation due to a wide range of factors known or unknown in the market. Since demand surge occurs and vanishes quickly, detecting when and where demand is surging becomes instrumental in pricing. Nevertheless, it takes time for supply to adjust, and supply shocks hardly occur in the short run, not to mention in hours or minutes.

Detecting consumer demand in a timely manner had not been possible until the advent of the Internet and mobile technologies. Powered by sophisticated machine learning algorithms, firms can not only detect and measure consumer demand precisely and instantaneously, they are also able to predict demand with high accuracies. No wonder Uber, along with other tech firms such as Google and Amazon, is the pioneer of surge pricing, or dynamic pricing as it is called elsewhere. Equipped by the technology, these enterprises have not only amassed an enormous trove of consumer data but also avail themselves of the data which consumers cannot assemble individually.

Garnering massive amounts of consumer data, which seemed impossible decades ago, has now become a reality. What Uber does with surge pricing has little bearing on the innovation of transportation services, but it has everything to do with harnessing the price mechanism to enable voluntary transactions between riders and drivers in an unfettered market. Rather than invalidating Hayek's assertion, Uber's surge pricing epitomizes the price mechanism as the best way to assemble and exchange all market information which eventually leads to market efficiency.

Summary

1. A surge in demand is an instantaneous and substantial increase in consumer demand due to factors that cause a positive demand shock. A demand surge leads to a rightward shift in the demand curve, ending up with a new market equilibrium.
2. Many factors can lead to a surge in demand, particularly some spectacular or unexpected events, such as a concert, festival or even a terrorist crisis. The phenomenon of demand surge suggests the volatility of demand.
3. A surge price is a new equilibrium price at which the surged demand meets the initial supply, suggesting that the market equilibrium moves upward along the supply curve. Surge pricing is the pricing strategy that manifests the new equilibrium price in the form of the surge multiplier, which is observable to both riders and drivers.
4. The surge multiplier is the ratio of the new equilibrium price in the surge period to the initial equilibrium price in the pre-surge period. It suggests the extent to which the new equilibrium price increases against the initial one. In essence, the surge multiplier is a price signal that guides the behavior of both consumers and firms in the market.
5. As long as demand surges, the absence of surge price is nothing more than a price ceiling in the market. Since the market price is prevented from reaching a new market equilibrium, a shortage of supply arises, and hence deadweight loss will occur. Thus, social surplus shrinks and the market deviates from perfect efficiency.
6. The occurrence of deadweight loss is evidenced by a substantial increase in riders' wait time and the fall in the completion rate of ride requests in the market. Also, the number of ride requests is greater without the surge price than it is with the surge price because riders' decisions are based on the initial, lower equilibrium price.
7. The key to implementing a surge price is to detect and measure the change in consumer demand accurately and instantaneously. This is why surge pricing is pervasive among tech firms such as Uber and had not been possible until the advent of the Internet and mobile technologies.
8. Surge pricing implies that the free market is the best way to organize economic activity through the invisible hand of the price signal. The surge multiplier is in essence the price signal that assembles and exchanges all market information which will eventually lead to market efficiency.

Problem solving

1. Suppose that n is the market equilibrium for Uber rides in a market prior to a demand surge as shown in the graph below. Given the possible changes in demand and/or supply as indicated in the graph, what would be the number of prospective riders opening the Uber app ready to make a ride request, and what would be the rate charged by Uber during the surge period? What would be the surge multiplier shown on the Uber app for riders and drivers?

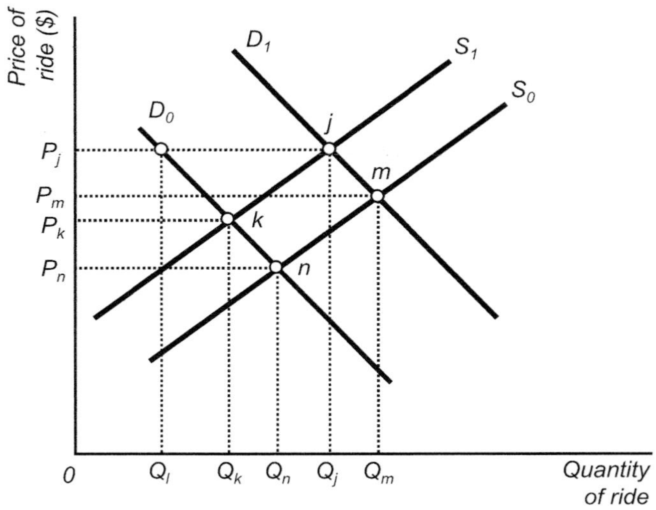

2. Suppose that the demand for and supply of Uber rides in Madison Square Garden are both linear, and the slope of the supply curve is 1/40. In the pre-surge period between 7:30 p.m. and 9:30 p.m. on March 21, 2015, suppose that the number of ride requests served by Uber was 800 at a rate of $25 per ride on average. Uber then detected that 3,200 prospective riders were opening their Uber app and ready to make a request between 10:30 p.m. and 11:30 p.m., and thus the Uber algorithm set a price at $60 per ride, which was observable to both riders and drivers. How many ride requests would Uber have successfully served in the surge period? What would be the completion rate in the surge period?
3. Suppose that amid a surge period between 2 a.m. and 4 a.m. in New York City on January 1st, 2015, Uber charged a certain rate, ending up with a 100% completion rate. Uber then detected that the demand was decreasing substantially between 4 a.m. and 7 a.m. Should Uber keep the rate or lower the rate? If Uber decided to maintain the previous rate, analyze the economic surplus in the market for Uber rides between 4 a.m. and 7 a.m.

Solutions to all review questions and problem solving tasks are included in the Support Material for this book, which can be accessed at www.routledge.com/9780367897352.

Notes

1 The empirical data and evidence in this chapter are based on Hall, Kendrick, and Nosko (2015).
2 *The Financial Times*. Uber drives into Sydney hostage controversy. December 15, 2014.
3 Note that this demand surge was applicable to New York City as a whole. However, the data were only collected for the vicinity of Madison Square Garden in order to make this case and Ariana Grande's show comparable.
4 Obviously, the demands in the pre-surge period could be different in these two cases, and the magnitudes of the two demand surges could also be different.
5 For the same reason, our primary concern is the size of the demand surge against the pre-surge baseline rather than the absolute demand during the surge period.
6 The word "surge" literally means that demand increases. However, as long as demand plunges, or the market encounters a negative demand shock, surge multiplier will be less than 1.

Bibliography

Hall, J., Kendrick, C., & Nosko, C. (2015). The effects of Uber's surge pricing: A case study. Retrieved on June 30, 2020 from https://eng.uber.com/research/the-effects-of-ubers-surge-pricing-a-case-study/

Hayek, F. A. (1945). The use of knowledge in society. *American Economic Review*, *35*(4), 519–530.

MODULE 2

Demand

4 Consumer choice and demand

This chapter delves into consumer theory which explains the law of demand in equilibrium analysis addressed in Chapter 2. We first raise the issue of the economic problem that builds upon three axioms of the economic aspect of human behavior, namely scarcity, tradeoff, and optimization. The economic problem manifested on the demand side is consumer maximization of utility and on the supply side is firm maximization of profit, which we shall address in Modules 3 and 4. As far as consumption is concerned, the consumer is assumed to be insatiable and is thus willing to consume the largest quantity of goods he prefers. Yet how much the consumer is able to purchase depends on his budget. Therefore, consumer optimization is jointly determined by consumer preference and budget constraint, from which we can derive the demand curve of the consumer. Based on consumer optimization, we analyze the work–leisure tradeoff as the microeconomic foundation for understanding the demand for leisure and tourism.

AFTER STUDYING THIS CHAPTER, YOU SHOULD BE ABLE TO:

- **Understand the constituents of the economic problem and the difference between economics and other disciplines of human behavior;**
- **Understand and explain utility, the indifference curve, and the budget constraint of the consumer;**
- **Analyze consumer optimization imposed by the indifference curve and the budget constraint; and**
- **Analyze the work–leisure tradeoff of the consumer, the substitution effect, and the income effect of a price change.**

4.1 The economic problem

A tenet of economic analysis of human behavior is that individuals make decisions to maximize their well-being under the constraint of scarce resources. Only when scarcity is taken into account can human decisions become an economic problem and be subject to economic analysis. On the consumer's side, scarcity is manifested in two aspects. One is that the resources that the consumer possesses and can thus deploy in meeting his needs are scarce, suggesting that what to purchase and how much the consumer can purchase are constrained by his budget. Hence he has to economize on the use of the resources. If the resources were infinitely abundant, such economization would be nonsense. The other aspect is that he needs to make tradeoffs when deciding the allocation of the scarce resources between alternative uses. For instance, he needs to decide to consume between one more unit of one good and fewer of the other or between more in the present and less in the future, or vice versa. Whatever the decision eventually made by the consumer, it reflects the value of one good relative to the other or the value of present consumption relative to the value of future consumption. If such tradeoffs did not exist, there would be no economic problem whatsoever.

Therefore, on the one hand, economics is set apart from various disciplines that also deal with how people behave and make decisions—to name a few, praxeology, psychology, and sociology. In these disciplines, scarcity, among other things, has no bearing on explaining human behavior with regard to tradeoff and optimization. As a matter of fact, economics conceptualizes a world in which each individual acts as a utility maximizer in consumption and a profit maximizer in production. Given the constraints the consumer faces, he is deemed to be completely rational in decision making, and his decisions will lead to consistent and robust outcomes. The economic man, as he is called by economists, is an abstract and atomistic representative of all human beings whose human characteristics such as emotions and irrationality are regarded as irrelevant to his economic decision-making and are therefore assumed away in economic analysis. Economic decisions are made as if the economic man constantly calculated tradeoffs, and found unambiguous and optimal solutions to his problems. Despite sounding unrealistic, rationality is the very foundation of economic theory. From an epistemological point view, the complex of human behavior cannot be comprehended and modeled if human beings are not reduced to the economic man.

The economic problem and economic behavior are by no means limited to the economy as the names may suggest, nor do they necessarily entail a market transaction in which the monetary value of a good is underscored. British economist Lionel Robbins (1898–1984) asserts that "[economics] does not attempt to pick out certain *kinds* of behaviour, but focuses attention on a particular *aspect* of behaviour, the form imposed by the influence of scarcity."[1] Therefore, any human behavior subject to the aspect of scarcity falls into the scope of economic analysis in which a tradeoff has to be made. For instance, an economic problem arises for the consumer when choosing between staying at home to watch a movie and going out for a jog, or deciding whether to cook at home or dine out. In these cases market transaction is either nonexistent or implicit. Nevertheless, insofar as a tradeoff arises due to the scarcity of one's limited time that needs to be allocated between watching a movie and jogging or due to one's finite budget that needs to be allocated between cooking at home and dining out, economic problems surface. How to trade off the two depends on which one brings about more utility to the consumer. The same precepts equally apply to producers on the supply side of economic behavior, which we shall address in detail in Modules 3 and 4.

4.2 Utility, preference, and indifference curve

4.2.1 Utility and diminishing marginal utility

We begin by exploring why the consumer acts regarding what to purchase and how much he can purchase. A consumer decision rests on the ultimate goal of maximizing well-being through the means of consumption. The well-being of the consumer is utility, which is the amount of gratification, satisfaction, or pleasure he obtains from consuming goods. For instance, eating a burger relieves his hunger, and drinking a can of cola quenches his thirst. Put differently, utility can be deemed as the absence of uneasiness, dissatisfaction, or pain, which would otherwise arise if his various wants were not satiated. The origin of the concept of utility can be traced back to English philosopher Jeremy Bentham (1747–1832), who asserts that pain and pleasure are the only two sovereign masters placed by nature to govern mankind. He argues that pain and pleasure point out what we *ought to* do and determine what we *shall* do, from which we derive the standard of right and wrong and the chain of causes and effects.[2] In his words, human behavior is subject to pain and pleasure, and every effort we can make to throw off our subjection will only serve to demonstrate and confirm it.[3] The ultimate goal of human decision is to maximize utility, which is the amount of pleasure net of pain.

As a subjective measure of well-being, the utility obtained from a good might be different from one person to another, and also varies by the amount of the good. Consider a consumer eating burgers to satiate his hunger. Figure 4.1 shows that the total utility that the consumer obtains usually increases as he eats more burgers,

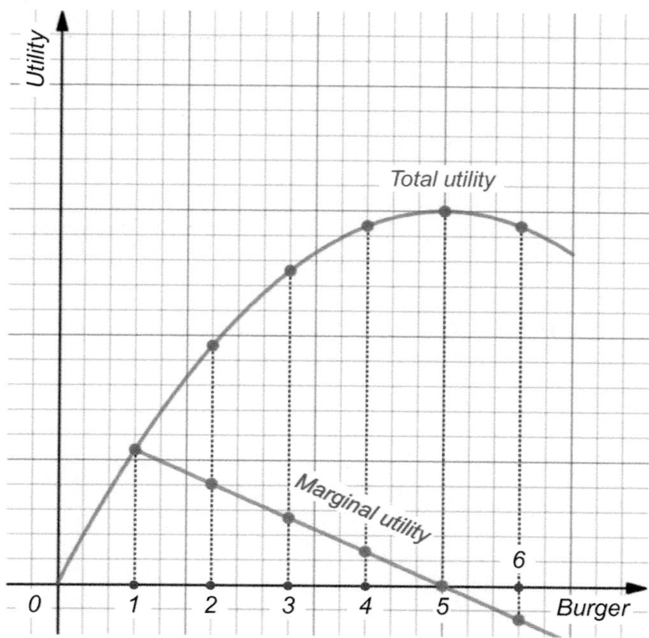

Figure 4.1
Total utility and diminishing marginal utility

other things being equal. Intuitively, the level of utility obtained from the first burger is the largest, as it reduces his hunger to the largest extent. When he continues to eat the second and the third burger, the additional utility he obtains from the second is arguably less than that of the first, and the additional utility from the third is less than that of the second, and so on, because he becomes less and less hungry as he eats more and more burgers. Such an incremental change in total utility (U) with respect to the quantity of a good (q) consumed is called marginal utility (MU):

$$MU = \frac{\Delta U}{\Delta q}. \tag{4.1}$$

Due to the decrease in marginal utility as the quantity of burgers increases, the consumer stops eating the fifth if the fifth brings zero utility as shown in Figure 4.1. By then his hunger is completely satiated and his total utility is maximized. Thus, total utility usually increases as the number of burgers increases, but it always increases at a decreasing rate, which is known as the law of diminishing marginal utility. If he continued, the sixth burger could bring about disutility because eating too much would make him uncomfortable and even do harm to his health. Hence the marginal utility could be negative. Figure 4.1 illustrates a negative relationship between the marginal utility and the quantity of burgers consumed.

The law of diminishing marginal utility reflects the value of a good to the consumer that diminishes as its quantity increases. It thus suggests a tradeoff between alternative uses of the good, more urgent versus less urgent uses. For instance, staples such as rice in southern China and wheat in the North used to be seriously deficient in rural China before the late 1970s. Peasants had no choice but to economize every particle of rice or wheat to eke out a living for the whole family. Usually, the elderly and children were the priority in a household to whom food was rationed first. As food production has substantially increased ever since due to the economic reforms and transition to the market economy, it has become commonplace that peasants start using leftovers and even extra food to feed poultry and livestock, such as chickens, ducks, and pigs, among others. Such food rearing is more common in wealthier rural areas such as the East and South than in poorer areas such as the West and inland. As food production increases, the more urgent use of food for people is relegated to the less urgent use for feeding poultry and livestock, suggesting that the marginal utility of food to people diminishes as food becomes abundant in society.

4.2.2 Consumption bundle and preference relation

As marginal utility decreases for one good, the consumer will divert some of his budget to another of which he has a little amount and, therefore, will generate more utility for him. He therefore needs to allocate his budget to a set of mutually exclusive goods which will maximize his total utility. For expository simplicity, we can always consider two mutually exclusive goods in consumption, such as burgers versus cola, or one good versus everything else. On the one hand, due to diminishing marginal utility,

the consumer would increase his consumption of cola when having more burgers brings about less and less utility. As cola enters into consumer choice with a small quantity, it brings about the largest amount of utility as opposed to burgers, which are relatively abundant. As the consumer drinks more cola, burgers become more valuable to him because their scarcity generates more utility. If the marginal utility of a good is always positive, he would always prefer more of that good in order to continuously increase his total utility if the quantity of the other good is held constant. When the consumer makes decisions in favor of one consumption bundle of the two goods over the other bundle with varying quantities, consumer preference arises.

Consider burgers and cola in two bundles, bundle A with 1 burger and 3 cola drinks and bundle B with 3 burgers and 1 cola drink. If the consumer thinks bundle A is at least as much preferred as bundle B, he is said to have a weak preference for bundle A, denoted as $A \succeq B$. If he strictly prefers A to B, he is said to have a strong preference for bundle A, denoted as $A \succ B$. If he is equally satisfied with bundles A and B, he is said to be indifferent between A and B, denoted as $A \sim B$. Given bundle C with 2 burgers and 2 cola drinks, if $C \succeq B$ and $B \succeq A$, then we have $C \succeq A$. This rule is referred to as transitivity in the consumer preference relation. Given the fourth bundle D with 3 burgers and 3 cola drinks, the consumer would always prefer D because it contains either more burgers or more cola or more both compared to bundles A, B and C, respectively. This concludes the non-satiation assumption in the consumer preference relation, meaning that the consumer strictly prefers a larger quantity of a good available, other things being equal. Last but not least, given a finite number of bundles of two goods in a consumption set X, say the above four bundles A, B, C, and $D \in X$, the consumer is completely certain about the preference relations among all these bundles, which is referred to as the completeness assumption of consumer preference. This assumption suggests that the consumer can always figure out the optimal bundle that will maximize his utility.

4.2.3 Indifference curve

We can compare the utility of different consumption bundles of two goods by ranking consumer preference. Hence utility is revealed by consumer preference. Figure 4.2a shows a downward-sloping curve convex to the origin, U_1, which represents different bundles of burgers and cola drinks on the x- and y-axis, respectively. This curve is called the indifference curve of the consumer because he, as assumed, is indifferent between any two bundles of the two goods that lie on U_1. For instance, he is indifferent between bundle A with 4 burgers and 15 cola drinks and bundle B with 5 burgers and 12 cola drinks because both bundles are on the same indifference curve. Likewise, he prefers bundle A as much as bundles C, D, E, F and so on, as all are on U_1. As he increases the quantity of one good holding the other constant or increases both, his indifference curve shifts outward to a higher level U_2 which is parallel to U_1 (Figure 4.2a). Indifference curve U_2 represents a higher level of utility as any bundle on U_2 contains a larger quantity of one good holding the other constant. By the same token, indifference curve U_3 represents a higher level of utility than U_2 because any bundle on U_3 contains a larger quantity of one good holding the other

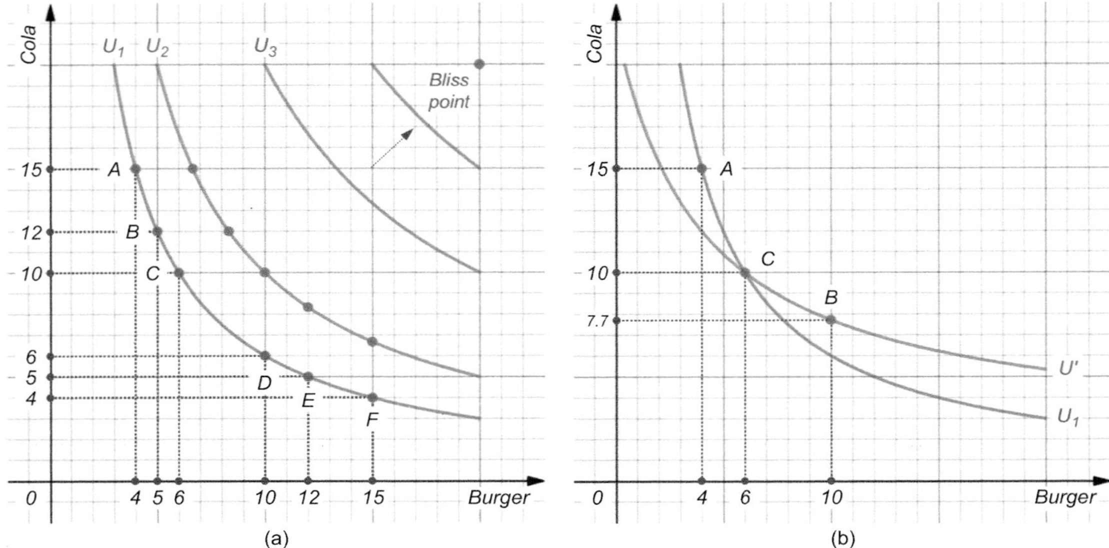

Figure 4.2
Indifference curves

constant as well. Other things being equal, the consumer always aims to climb to a higher indifference curve until he reaches what is called the bliss point at which the highest state of satisfaction is fulfilled without limits.

Assuming that the quantities of the two goods on the two axes are infinitely divisible, we can imagine that numerous indifference curves would exist between any two indifference curves we mentioned above. Nonetheless, no two indifference curves cross, meaning that they are always parallel to each other. Suppose that the two indifference curves U_1 and U' intersect at point C (Figure 4.2b). This would suggest that consumption bundle A on U_1 is indifferent from bundle C, which is indifferent from B on U'. Hence, we would conclude that bundle A is indifferent from bundle B because of the transitivity of consumer preference. Yet this conclusion contradicts the assumption that U_1 and U' are two different indifference curves and thus bundles A and B are by no means indifferent. In addition, all indifference curves are downward-sloping and convex to the origin. The slope of an indifference curve suggests the rate at which the consumer is willing to trade one unit of one good for the other while maintaining the same level of utility determined by the indifference curve. This is known as the marginal rate of substitution (MRS) at which he forgoes one unit of burgers on the x-axis in order to obtain certain units of cola on the y-axis while holding his utility constant:

$$MRS = \frac{\Delta y}{\Delta x} = -\frac{MU_x}{MU_y}, \tag{4.2}$$

where Δx and Δy are the changes in the quantities of burgers and cola, respectively, and MU_x and MU_y denote the marginal utilities of burgers and cola, respectively. Consider the consumer switching from bundle A to bundle B on indifference curve

U_1 (Figure 4.2a). He is willing to forgo 3 cola drinks to consume 1 more burger while maintaining the same level of utility. This means that from bundle A to bundle B, 1 burger is preferred at least as much as 3 cola drinks, meaning that he would substitute 1 burger for 3 cola drinks, hence $MRS = -3$. If he moves from bundle D to bundle E, he is willing to forgo 1 cola drink for 2 burgers while still maintaining the same level of utility, and hence $MRS = -1/2$. If he moves further from bundle E to bundle F, he is only willing to forgo 1 cola drink if he obtains 3 burgers, and thus $MRS = -1/3$. As he has more burgers, he is only willing to forgo an increasingly smaller quantity of cola drinks for one burger, a phenomenon known as the diminishing marginal rate of substitution. Diminishing marginal rate of substitution suggests that the slope of an indifference curve is negative and decreasing. This is due to the fact that the marginal utility of a good decreases when it becomes abundant but increases when it is scarce.

There are two exceptions to the diminishing marginal rate of substitution. One is the constant marginal rate of substitution. Figure 4.3a shows a set of linear indifference curves, where the marginal rates of substitution are constant. When the consumer switches between any two bundles of burgers and cola on indifference curve U_1, he will consistently substitute 1 burger for 1 cola drink, $MRS = -1$, irrespective of the quantities of the two goods he has. These two goods are thus called perfect substitutes. While there is little empirical evidence for perfect substitutes, the theoretical exploration helps us better understand consumer choice in relation to preference. The other is the zero marginal rate of substitution. Figure 4.3b shows a set of perpendicular indifference curves to the origin. To maintain the same level of utility, say on U_1', requires a minimum quantity of either burgers or cola, which is 3 units, regardless of the quantity of the other (Figure 4.3b). Hence, the marginal rate of substitution is $MRS = 0$ and $MRS = \infty$. This means that the utility of the consumer is determined only by the good with a smaller quantity on the same indifference curve. Since these two goods

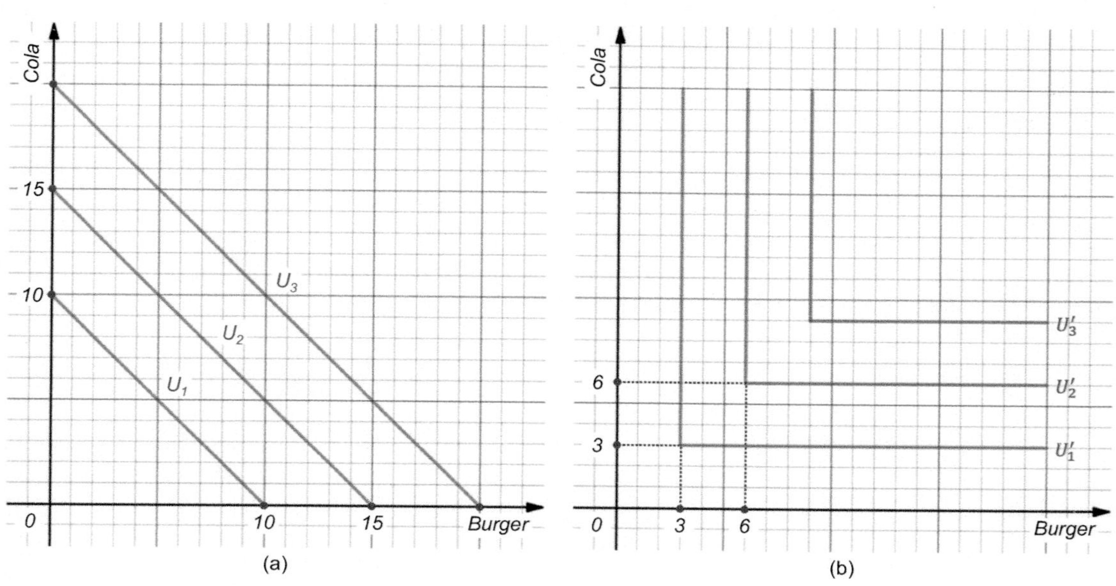

Figure 4.3
Indifference curve, perfect substitutes, and perfect complements

cannot be substituted for each other at all, they are called perfect complements. Thus, consumer utility cannot be changed unless the quantities of both goods are changed.

4.3 Budget constraint and consumer optimization

4.3.1 Budget line

While the consumer is willing to consume on the highest indifference curve, the bliss point is unreachable due to the scarcity of the resource. The extent to which he is able to maximize his utility is constrained by the amount of income he has, known as budget, denoted by I. An implicit assumption worth noting is that the consumer spends all his budget available, thereby ruling out the possibility that he chooses a lower level of utility while saving part of his income. Thus, the quantities of the two goods, burgers and cola, which he is able to consume depend on their respective prices in the market. Suppose that burgers and cola drinks are sold at p_x and p_y each, respectively. If budget I is spent entirely on burgers, he ends up buying the maximum quantity of burgers q_x; if it is spent entirely on cola, he ends up buying the maximum quantity of cola drinks q_y. He can also split budget I in arbitrary proportions between the two goods, ending up purchasing all bundles of burgers and cola, which is called the budget constraint. Given the prices of burgers and cola, the budget constraint manifests all bundles of burgers and cola with varying quantities he can afford by exhausting his budget I :

$$I = p_x x + p_y y, \tag{4.3}$$

where p_x and p_y denote the prices of burgers and cola drinks, and x and y denote their quantities, respectively. Graphically, the budget constraint is a downward-sloping straight line with the x-intercept at I / p_x and the y-intercept at I / p_y, known as the budget line (Figure 4.4a). The budget line shows all different consumption bundles of burgers and cola drinks the consumer is able to purchase by spending all his budget. The budget line demarcates between what he is able to consume yet unwilling to and what he is willing to consume yet unable to. All bundles of the two goods beneath the budget line are attainable, yet he is unwilling to choose; whereas all bundles above the budget line are unattainable, though he is willing to choose. As a utility maximizer, the consumer thus only chooses the bundles precisely on the budget line.

We rewrite function (4.3) such that the quantity of cola on the y-axis, denoted by y, is a function of the quantity of burgers on the x-axis, denoted by x:

$$y = -\frac{p_x}{p_y} x + \frac{I}{p_y}. \tag{4.4}$$

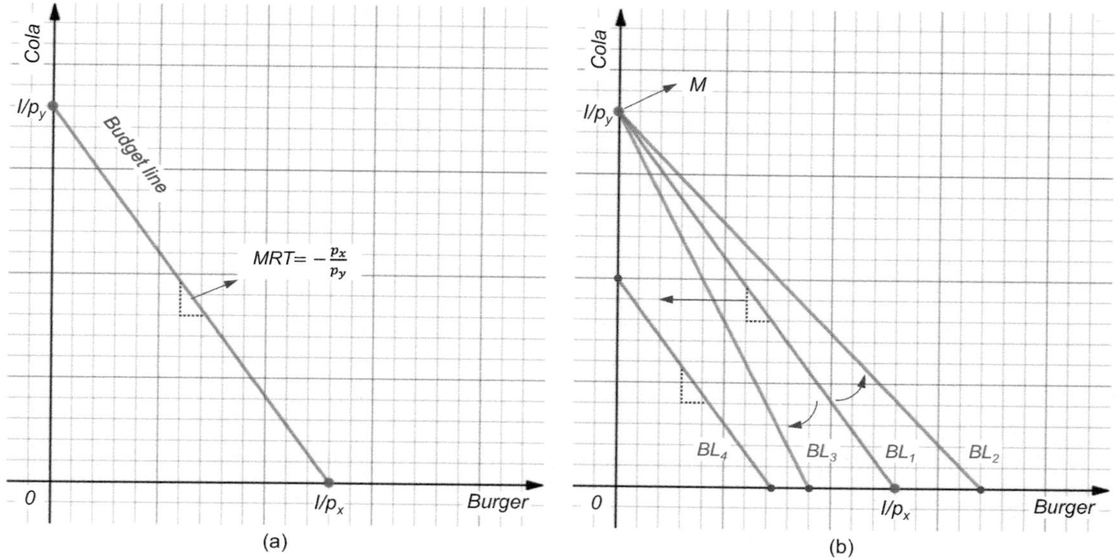

Figure 4.4
Budget line and marginal rate of transformation

Function (4.4) articulates that the slope of the budget line is the coefficient of $x, -p_x / p_y$, and the y-intercept is I / p_y (Figure 4.4a). The slope of the budget line turns out to be the negative ratio of the prices of the two goods, burgers and cola, denoted on the x- and y-axis, respectively. This slope is referred to as the marginal rate of transformation (*MRT*) between the two goods:

$$MRT = -\frac{p_x}{p_y}. \quad (4.5)$$

The marginal rate of transformation suggests that as the consumer purchases each unit of burgers he needs to decrease a constant quantity of cola, which is p_x / p_y, constrained by his budget. If the price of one good changes in the market, the budget line is altered, hence the marginal rate of transformation. Suppose that the price of burgers increases. Then the same budget enables the consumer to purchase fewer burgers with still the same amount of cola, and hence the budget line BL_1 pivots around point M inward, ending up with a new budget line BL_3 (Figure 4.4b). Conversely, if the price of burgers decreases, the budget line pivots outward around point M, ending up with another new budget line BL_2 (Figure 4.4b). On the other hand, if the price of cola changes, the same budget enables the consumer to purchase either more or less cola with still the same amount of burgers. Note that a change in the price of either burgers or cola does not alter the budget itself but only the quantity of one good the consumer can afford relative to the other, that is, the marginal rate of transformation between the two goods. Given the prices of the two goods, a change in consumer income will shift the budget line, thereby changing the quantities of both goods which

the consumer can afford with the new budget. Figure 4.4b shows that the budget line BL_1 shifts leftward to BL_4 due to a decrease in income. Thus, a change in income leads to a change in the budget while the marginal rate of transformation remains the same.

4.3.2 Consumer optimization

The problem of consumer optimization is what bundle of two goods the consumer will choose to maximize his utility under the budget constraint. On the one hand, the consumer is insatiable as assumed, and is thus *willing to* consume as many of the two goods as possible to achieve the highest level of utility. On the other hand, the amounts of the two goods he is *able to* purchase are constrained by his budget. This optimization problem is synonymous with what bundle of the two goods will minimize his budget if he aims for a certain level of utility. Due to the budget constraint, the consumer simply cannot reach the bliss point. Thus, only after the budget constraint is taken into account can consumer choice become an economic problem. Consumer optimization thus necessitates both economization of the budget and tradeoffs between the two goods when their prices change. This means that the optimal bundle of the two goods is jointly determined by the consumer's indifference curves and budget line. Figure 4.5 shows the consumer's budget line BL and indifference curves U_1, U_2, and U_3, representing a low, mediate, and high level of utility, respectively. The optimal bundle of the two goods that the consumer chooses is point A, 10 burgers and 6 cola drinks, at which the budget line BL is tangent to the indifference curve U_2.

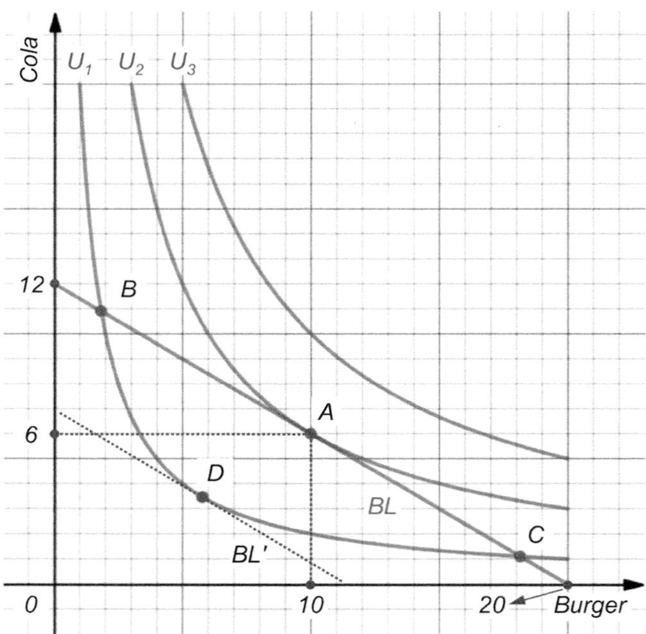

Figure 4.5
Budget line, indifference curve, and consumer optimization

Due to the properties of the budget line and indifference curve, consumer optimization is always manifested as the consumption bundle at which the budget line is tangent to an indifference curve. The optimal bundle of the two goods is unique. While indifference curve U_3 represents a higher level of utility than U_2, it is unattainable under the consumer's budget (Figure 4.5). Despite the indifference curve U_1 being attainable, the consumer will not choose the bundle denoted by either point B or C on U_1 because U_1 represents a lower level of utility than U_2. In fact, to achieve the same level of utility as denoted by point B or C, the consumer does not have to exhaust his budget. To illustrate this idea, imagine shifting the budget line inward until it is tangent to the indifference curve U_1 at point D (Figure 4.5). Since points D and B are on the same indifference curve, the consumer can obtain the same utility by choosing point D, yet with a smaller budget denoted by the hypothetical budget line *BL'*. As long as the budget line cuts off an indifference curve in question, it can always be tangent to a higher indifference curve which, together with the budget line, determines the optimal bundle of the two goods.

4.3.3 Equalization of marginal utility per dollar

As analyzed above in Figure 4.5, the optimal bundle of the two goods that the consumer chooses is the tangency point of the budget line and the indifference curve. Therefore, at the optimal bundle the slopes of the budget line and the indifference curve are equal, suggesting that the marginal rate of transformation in formula (4.5) is equal to the marginal rate of substitution in formula (4.2). Thus, we have

$$\frac{p_x}{p_y} = \frac{MU_x}{MU_y}. \tag{4.6}$$

Rearranging equation (4.6), we see that the marginal utility of one good given its market price, known as the marginal utility of the good per dollar, is equal to the marginal utility of the other good per dollar in the optimal bundle:

$$\frac{MU_x}{p_x} = \frac{MU_y}{p_y}. \tag{4.7}$$

The marginal utility of a good per dollar suggests that the marginal utility of the good is adjusted by its price in the market, other things being equal. It provides another perspective of assessing consumer optimization. That is, the optimal bundle of two goods that the consumer chooses is determined when their marginal utilities per dollar are equal. In Figure 4.5 above, only at the optimal bundle are the marginal utilities per dollar of burgers and cola drinks equal. Intuitively, given the prices of burgers and cola, if at some point the marginal utility of burgers per dollar is higher than that of cola, the consumer will be willing to spend the next dollar on burgers in order to increase his total utility. On the other hand, as he possesses more burgers, the marginal utility of burgers will decrease due to the law of diminishing marginal utility, and hence the marginal utility of burgers per dollar diminishes. As the consumer consumes more burgers, he will afford less cola. Thus, the marginal utility of cola increases, and hence the marginal utility of cola per dollar increases, given the price of cola. Eventually the marginal utilities of both goods per dollar will be equal through him constantly trading off one for the other, and vice versa, ending up with the consumer equilibrium in choosing between various bundles of the two goods.

4.4 Derivation of the demand curve

4.4.1 Consumer optimization and the demand curve

Consumer optimization provides the basis for deriving the demand curve of the consumer for a good. Figure 4.6a shows that the consumer has a certain budget allocated between burgers on the x-axis and cola on the y-axis. We know that the optimal bundle is point A at which the budget line BL_1 is tangent to indifference curve U_4. Now let the price of burgers increase from p_1 to p_2, p_3, p_4, and so on ($p_1 < p_2 < p_3 < p_4$), other things being equal. Thus the budget line pivots inward around point M, ending up with a set of corresponding budget lines BL_2, BL_3, BL_4, and so on. The optimal bundles that the consumer chooses will be the tangencies of the budget lines and the lower indifference curves, U_3, U_2, U_1, and so on. As a result, the optimal quantity of burgers decreases from 10 (q_1) to 7.5 (q_2), 5 (q_3), 2.5 (q_4), and so on. Figure 4.6b shows a negative relationship between the price of burgers and the optimal quantity of burgers purchased, which is the quantity demanded, other things being equal. Hence we obtain the demand curve of the consumer for burgers that passes through points D, C, B, A, and so on (Figure 4.6b). If the market price of burgers

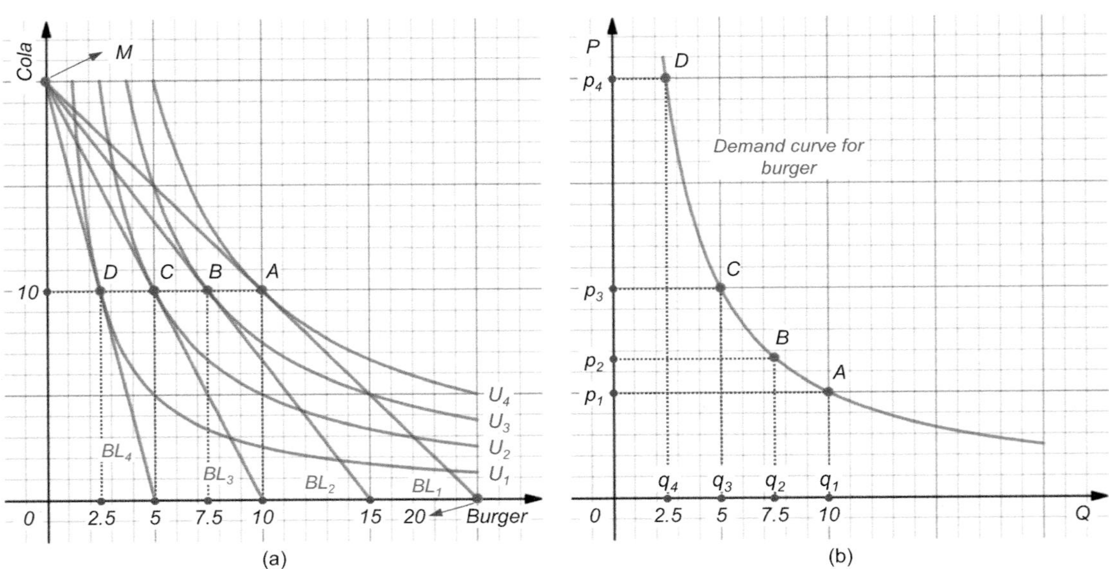

Figure 4.6
Consumer optimization and the demand curve

decreases, the budget line will pivot outward around point M. The tangencies of the budget lines and the higher indifference curves suggest that the consumption of burgers increases as the price of burgers decreases, exhibited on the same demand curve.

4.4.2 Properties of the demand curve

By the same token, we can derive the demand curve for any other good that the consumer chooses while holding the price of everything else constant. Since the derivation of the demand curve is grounded on consumer optimization, each quantity demanded is the optimal amount of a good that maximizes the consumer's utility under the budget constraint while holding everything else constant. The quantity demanded of the good varies only by its price in the market, which is exogenous to consumer choice. The consumer cannot alter the price of the good but has to accept it as given when choosing how much to consume. On the other hand, the market price of the good represents the consumer's willingness to pay for varying quantities of the good on the x-axis. In theory we can assume that the market price of a good changes continuously, and therefore the quantity demanded is also continuous, ending up with a differentiable demand curve. The overriding property of the demand curve is that the quantity of a good demanded is monotonically decreasing with its price. Hence the demand curve is downward-sloping and exhibits the law of diminishing marginal utility. There are a couple of exceptions, though, mainly for theoretical expositions in which the demand curve is horizontal or even upward-sloping, which we shall address in later chapters.

4.4.3 Demand functions

The mathematical representation of the demand curve and of the law of demand is called the demand function. Recall that we implicitly introduced the demand functions in functions (2.1) and (2.2) in Chapter 2 to provide a mathematical representation of the relationship between the price of a good and the quantity purchased by consumers in the market, other things being equal. Here we proceed to generalize the demand function by examining its theoretical foundation articulated above. For expository simplicity, assuming that the demand curve for burgers in Figure 4.6b is linear without loss of generality, we can write price (p) on the y-axis as a function of the quantity demanded (q), denoted on the x-axis as

$$p = aq + b, \tag{4.8}$$

where a and b are two parameters that define the properties of the function. Since function (4.8) suggests that price p is a function of quantity demanded q, it is called the inverse demand function, as opposed to the conventional demand function in which q is a function of p. Parameter a is the slope of the demand curve, and hence $a < 0$. It measures the nature and strength of the effect of quantity demanded on price, suggesting that price will change by a units due to a change of 1 unit in the quantity demanded q. It is thus the marginal change in price with respect to the quantity demanded. Parameter b describes the effects of all factors combined other than the quantity on price, which is the y-intercept of the demand curve. Regardless of the change in quantity, the effects of the other factors on price are constant and are thus captured by b. In deriving the demand curve we hold all these factors constant while letting the price of the good in question change. Hence the demand curve is entirely determined by the two parameters whereby we can distinguish between different demand curves.

From the inverse demand function (4.8), we can readily write out the conventional demand function in which quantity demanded (q) is a function of price (p):

$$q = \frac{1}{a}p - \frac{b}{a}, \tag{4.9}$$

where $1/a$ is the marginal change in demand with respect to price, and $-b/a$ is the x-intercept of the demand curve. The inverse and conventional demand functions are mathematically equivalent as they describe the same demand curve. We usually prefer to use the inverse demand function as it enables us to reconcile the graphical representation of the demand curve, in which price is on the y-axis while quantity demanded is on the x-axis, and the mathematical representation, in which the dependent variable is on the y-axis while the independent variable is on the x-axis. Hence, as long as we know the inverse demand function, we can readily know the slope of the demand curve through the parameter a and the y-intercept from the parameter b. Given any two price–quantity coordinates on the demand curve in Figure 4.6b, say A (q_1, p_1) and B (q_2, p_2), and assuming that the demand curve is linear, we can estimate the demand function by solving a and b in a system of two linear equations below:

$$\begin{cases} p_1 = aq_1 + b, \\ p_2 = aq_2 + b. \end{cases} \tag{4.10}$$

4.5 The work–leisure tradeoff

4.5.1 Substitution effect

The analysis of consumer optimization allows us to examine consumer choice between work and leisure under the constraint of time. This is known as the work–leisure tradeoff in modeling the supply of labor. It also explains tourism consumption because tourism is constrained by the amount of leisure time the consumer has, besides his income. Given a certain amount of time available to the consumer, there is a tradeoff between work, which generates income, and leisure, which generates satisfaction and pleasure. As opposed to leisure, work is a laborious activity but the source of income. Suppose that the consumer has T hours of time to spend on work and leisure, the amount of time spent on work is L and on leisure is l. Hence $T = L + l$, which constitutes his time constraint. Assuming that the hourly wage is w, Figure 4.7 shows the consumer's maximum income, wT, on the y-axis if he spends all his time on work and his maximum leisure time, T, on the x-axis if otherwise. This ends up with his budget line defined by T and wage w. Suppose that his indifference curve describing his preference for work and leisure is U_1. Figure 4.7 shows that his optimal bundle of work and leisure ends up at point A, at which budget line BL_1 is tangent to the indifference curve U_1. Thus, the consumer ends up spending l_0 hours on leisure and $T-l_0$ hours on work, generating an income of $w(T-l_0)$.

Now suppose that his wage increases from w to w' ($w' > w$), other things being equal. Then the budget line BL_1 pivots outward around point T, ending up with a new budget line BL_2 intercepting the y-axis at $w'T$. Hence the optimal bundle of work and leisure he chooses will be point B, l_1 hours of leisure and $T-l_1$ hours of work, at which the budget line BL_2 is tangent to indifference curve U_2. The change from point A to point B suggests that the consumption of leisure decreases from l_0 to l_1, which is referred to as total effect of the wage increase. Intuitively, when wages increase the consumer could be enticed to work longer hours to earn more income or to work less to enjoy more leisure. For the latter choice, the increased wage enables him to work less while maintaining the same income as before. To illustrate this idea, draw an imaginary budget line parallel to the new budget line BL_2 while tangent to the initial indifference curve U_1 at point S. Thus the optimal bundle of work and leisure is at point S, which denotes l_2 hours of leisure and $T-l_2$ hours of work, ensuring that his utility is maintained the same as before after his wage increases to w'. There thus exists a movement upward from point A to point S along the initial indifference curve U_1, meaning that the wage

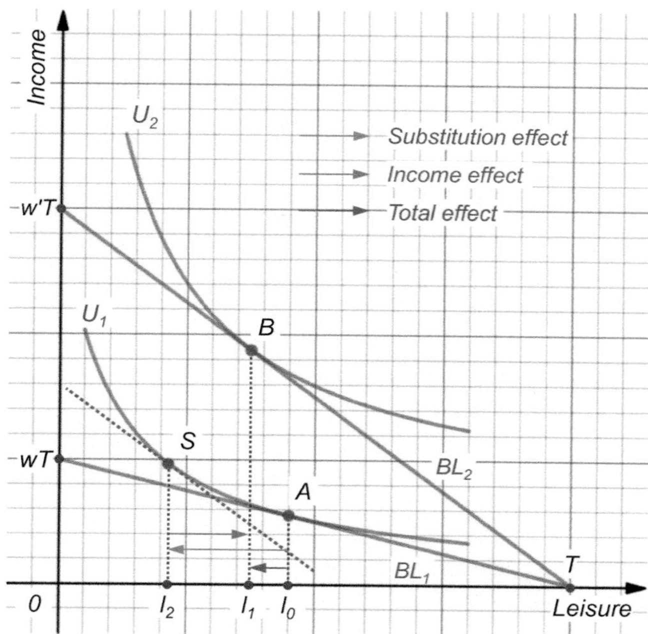

Figure 4.7
Substitution effect and income effect

increase entices the consumer to substitute work for leisure, ending up with a decrease of $l_0 - l_2$ hours in leisure consumption. This is known as the substitution effect of the wage increase, for the wage increase renders work more desirable.

4.5.2 Income effect

Since the imaginary budget line is parallel to the new budget line BL_2, they have the same marginal rate of transformation. The imaginary budget line in the above analysis allows us to discount the new budget to a level at which the initial utility is maintained while taking into account the wage increase. Hence the increase of leisure consumption of $l_1 - l_2$ hours from point S to point B is entirely due to the increase in income (Figure 4.7). This is known as the income effect of the wage increase, because the marginal rate of substitution is held constant. The total effect is the sum of the substitution effect and the income effect, and thus we have $(l_2 - l_0) + (l_1 - l_2) = l_1 - l_0$, which is exactly the decrease of $l_0 - l_1$ hours in leisure consumption mentioned above. As far as this analysis is concerned, the wage increase leads to both the substitution effect and the income effect, which act in opposite directions. On the one hand, the wage increase makes work more tempting and hence reduces leisure consumption, which is captured by the substitution effect. On the other hand, the wage increase boosts the consumption of leisure due to the income effect. Thus, the extent to which the consumption of leisure increases depends on whether and by how much the income effect outstrips the substitution effect. It is thus also plausible that the wage increase leads to an increase in leisure consumption as long as the income effect is greater than the substitution effect.

Note that throughout the analysis we have assumed implicitly that the consumption of leisure increases with income, other things being equal. Hence the wage increase does lead to an increase in leisure consumption illustrated by the positive income effect. In this case, leisure is referred to as a normal good. A vast majority of goods in the marketplace are normal goods, suggesting a positive relationship between the consumption of these goods and income, other things being equal. Yet some goods are known as inferior goods for which the relationship between the consumption and income is negative. For many consumers inferior goods presumably include fast food, such as McDonald's and instant noodles, to name two. As household income increases, the consumption of fast food would fall, other things being equal. If leisure were an inferior good, the wage increase would result in a decrease in leisure consumption, holding the substitution effect constant, as the income effect became negative. Hence, rather than offsetting the substitution effect on leisure consumption, the negative income effect reinforces the substitution effect, thereby exacerbating the decrease in leisure consumption.

4.5.3 Opportunity cost of leisure

In Figure 4.7, when the wage increases by $w' - w$, the total effect is a decrease of $l_0 - l_1$ hours in leisure consumption, corresponding to an increase of the same amount of work hours, which generates an additional income of $w'(l_0 - l_1)$. This means that the consumer forgoes $l_0 - l_1$ hours of leisure to obtain an income of $w'(l_0 - l_1)$ by working

$l_0 - l_1$ hours more. In other words, he has to give up an income of $w'(l_0 - l_1)$ which would otherwise have been obtained from work if he chooses to enjoy $l_0 - l_1$ hours of leisure. The amount of income he forgoes in order to enjoy leisure is defined as the opportunity cost of leisure. Thus, the opportunity cost of $l_0 - l_1$ hours of leisure is $w'(l_0 - l_1)$ when the wage is w'. The concept of opportunity cost is grounded on the fact that the consumer always faces a tradeoff in spending time between work and leisure or in choosing between one course of action and another. Obviously, the opportunity cost of leisure increases as wages increase in the labor market, which means that the consumer has to forgo more wage earnings in order to enjoy the same amount of leisure. The increased opportunity cost of leisure deters the consumer from consuming leisure, other things being equal. Likewise, the opportunity cost of work is the satisfaction and pleasure he forgoes which would otherwise be obtained from leisure. Insofar as the consumer has a strong preference for leisure, the opportunity cost of work increases.

If leisure is a normal good, the substitution and income effects will act in opposite directions, and hence leisure consumption could increase, decrease, or even remain unchanged when income increases. This is one of the reasons that empirical evidence suggests an ambiguous relationship between income and leisure consumption. Figure 4.8 shows that less than 20% of respondents in the Philippines, Pakistan, Yemen, and Morocco believe leisure is very important in their life, in contrast to nearly 60% of those in Ecuador, Mexico, and Chile, despite the fact their GDP per capita is roughly the same, lower than US$10,000. When income is low, so is the opportunity cost of leisure. Ecuadorians, Mexicans, and Chileans trade off work for leisure because the substitution effect outstrips the income effect. If the income effect dominates the substitution effect, a lower income would be associated with less importance being

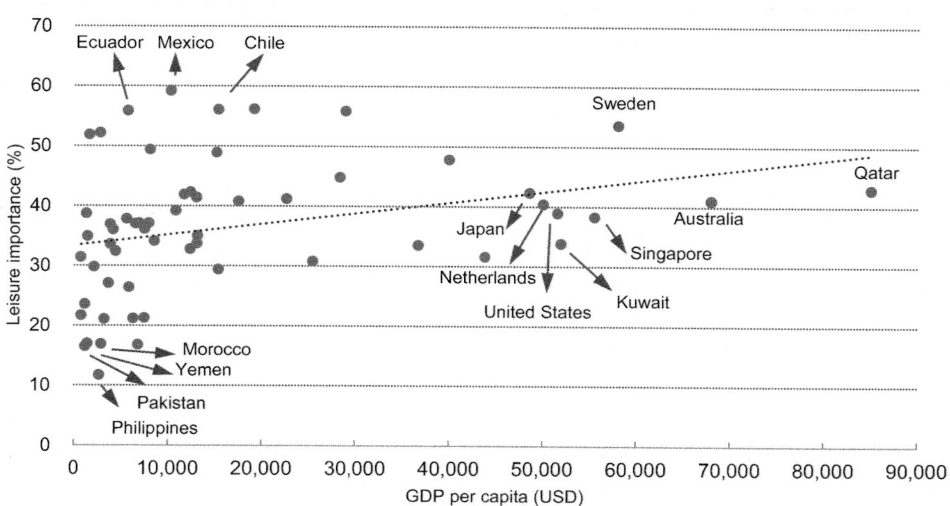

Figure 4.8
GDP per capita and leisure preference across countries

Note: The data points contain 58 countries/regions. Leisure importance is measured as the percentage of respondents who believed that leisure is "very important" in their life over the period 2010–2014. GDP per capita was in current U.S. dollars of 2012, which corresponded to the survey period of leisure importance.

Source: World Values Survey 6 (2010–2014) and World Bank Database.

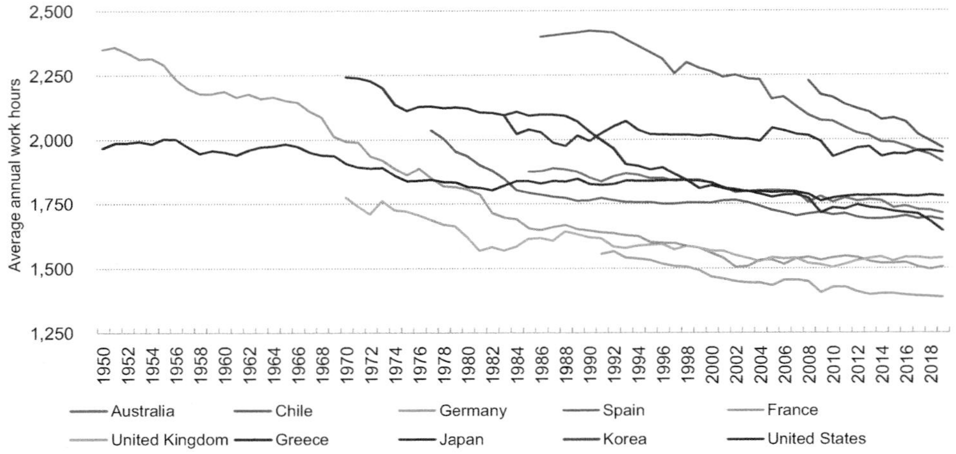

Figure 4.9
Decrease in work hours in developed countries

Note: Average annual work hours are the total number of hours actually worked per year divided by the average number of people in employment per year.

Source: OECD Data.

placed on leisure, which can explain why Filipinos, Pakistanis, and so on tend to belittle leisure in their life. It is interesting to note that Ecuadorians, Mexicans, and Chileans value leisure even more than do their counterparts in high-income countries such as Sweden, Australia, and Qatar whose GDP per capita is six to eight times higher. For many developed countries, the income effect presumably dominates the substitution effect, and thus drives leisure consumption as well, even though leisure is expensive.

If we focus on high-income countries, such as the OECD countries, annual work hours per worker have consistently declined since the 1970s—the period from which data are available for most countries (Figure 4.9). On average, work hours declined from around 2,000 hours per worker per year in 1970 to approximately 1,700 hours in 2019. This suggests that leisure time has increased by the same amount over the past five decades. While the increase in income pushes up the opportunity cost of leisure, the income effect would be more pronounced than the substitution effect, thereby boosting leisure consumption in these affluent societies. Yet the income effect is presumably higher in continental European countries, such as Germany and France, where work hours have decreased more sharply, and lower in Anglo-Saxon countries, such as Britain, the United States, and Australia, where work hours have decreased less. Such a difference might also be due to their different preferences, namely that continental European countries value leisure more than Anglo-Saxon countries do. Worth noting is Japan which, on the one hand, economically resembles Western developed countries and, on the other, is culturally distinct from them. The pattern of leisure consumption in Japan lies between that of continental European and of Anglo-Saxon countries. The income effect increases Japanese consumption of leisure while the substitution effect is also robust and thus decreases their consumption of leisure simultaneously.

Summary

1. The economic problem is characterized by the optimization of human behavior that involves trading off alternative uses of scarce resources. "[Economics] does not attempt to pick out certain *kinds* of behaviour, but focuses attention on a particular *aspect* of behaviour, the form imposed by the influence of scarcity."
2. Utility is the satisfaction, gratification, and pleasure that consumers obtain from consuming goods. The more they consume, the more utility they can obtain. However, the larger the quantity of a good the less utility is obtained from an extra unit of the good, which is known as the law of diminishing marginal utility.
3. An indifference curve depicts all consumption bundles of two goods in various quantities that generate the same level of utility to the consumer. That is, the consumer is indifferent between any two bundles of the two goods on the same indifference curve. The higher the indifference curve, the more utility it represents. The slope of the indifference curve represents the marginal rate of substitution between the two goods.
4. A budget constraint depicts all consumption bundles of two goods that the consumer is able to afford, given their prices, by exhausting all his income. A budget line is a graphical representation of the budget constraint, and its slope represents the marginal rate of transformation between the two goods.
5. Consumer optimization is the optimal bundle that the consumer can afford while representing the highest level of utility. Graphically, it is the tangency of the budget line and the indifference curve at which the marginal rate of substitution equals the marginal rate of transformation between the two goods.
6. From consumer optimization we can drive the demand curve for a good while holding the price of everything else constant. Thus, each point on the demand curve represents consumer optimization of the quantity demanded as the price of the good in question varies. The mathematical representation of the demand curve is the demand function.
7. The work–leisure tradeoff provides the fundamental explanation for the demand for tourism, as it articulates the two constraints of tourism: income and time. Given the certain amount of time the consumer has, he needs to trade off work, which generates income, and leisure, which generates utility.
8. A wage increase in the labor market leads to the substitution effect, suggesting that the consumer would substitute work for leisure because the opportunity cost of leisure increases. Hence the demand for tourism, and leisure generally, decreases.
9. In the meantime, a wage increase in the market leads to the income effect, suggesting that the consumer would demand more for leisure. Hence leisure is a normal good. If the relationship between income and consumption is negative, a good is an inferior good, and hence the income effect is negative.
10. The opportunity cost of leisure is the wage income that is forgone due to trading off work for leisure. As income increases, the opportunity cost of leisure increases. Yet the demand for leisure depends on the sum of the substitution effect and the income effect.

REVIEW QUESTIONS

Each question has four options, and there is only one correct answer to each question.

1. British economist Lionel Robbins defines economics as "the science which studies human behaviour as a relationship between ends and scarce means which have alternative uses." Which of the following is INCORRECT regarding the economic problem in human behavior?
   A) Humans face scarcity.
   B) Humans make tradeoffs.
   C) Humans aim to maximize utility.
   D) Humans can reach the bliss point.
2. Which of the following does NOT provide evidence for the law of diminishing marginal utility?
   A) First-time visitors are usually more excited than repeat visitors.
   B) Consumers usually enjoy the first hamburger more than the second.
   C) Peasants use leftovers and extra food to feed poultry and livestock.
   D) People purchase lottery tickets when the odds of winning increase.
3. Suppose that a consumer prefers bundle *A* (3 burgers and 2 cola drinks) to bundle *B* (2 burgers and 2 cola drinks) but is indifferent between bundle *A* and bundle *C* (3 burgers and 1 cola drink). Given bundle *D* (2 burgers and 1 cola drink) and bundle *E* (1 burger and 2 cola drinks), which of the following is correct regarding his preference relation?
   A) $B \succ C$
   B) $B \sim D$
   C) $D \sim E$
   D) $E \succ C$
4. The figure below shows Fiona's budget line *BL* and preferences for cola and burgers represented by indifference curves U_1, U_2, and U_3. At which point of the bundle is her marginal rate of substitution greater than the marginal rate of transformation?
   A) Point *a*
   B) Point *b*
   C) Point *c*
   D) Point *d*

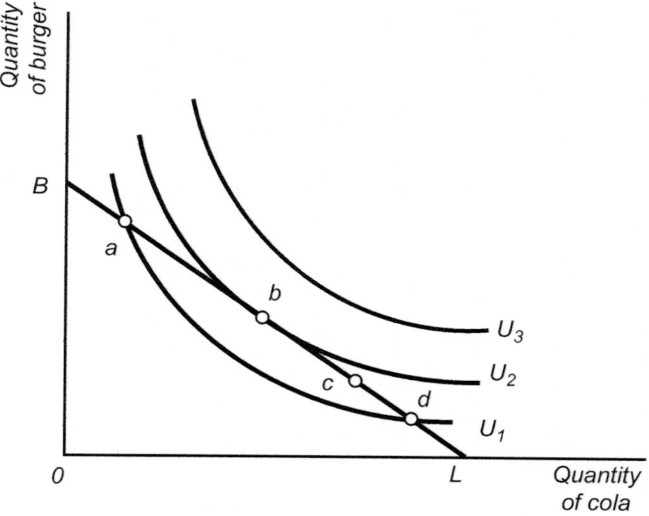

5. The graph below shows that Bryan's initial budget line is BL_0 for going skiing and watching movies. The budget line BL_0 first pivots outward around point *A* to a new budget line BL_1, which further pivots outward around point *B* to another new budget line BL_2. Suppose that his income does not change, other things being equal. Which of the following is correct?
   A) The price of movies first decreased, then the price of skiing increased.
   B) The price of movies first decreased, then the price of skiing decreased.
   C) The price of skiing first decreased, then the price of movies increased.
   D) The price of skiing first decreased, then the price of movies decreased.

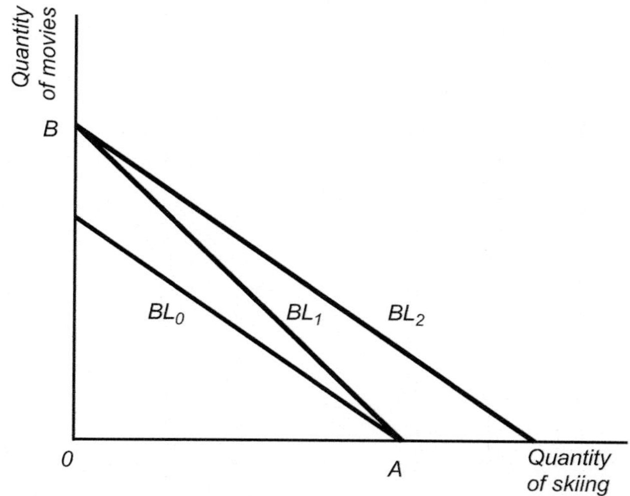

6. The graph below shows four linear indifference curves of a consumer, U_1, U_2, U_3, and U_4, for consuming two goods X and Y and his budget line BL (dotted line). Which of the following bundles would be chosen by the consumer?
   A) Bundle A
   B) Bundle B
   C) Bundle C
   D) Bundle D

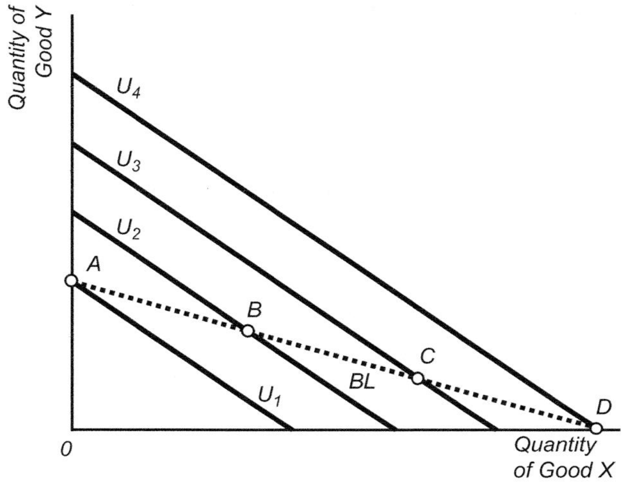

7. Rita's demand for instant noodles declines whereas her demand for sushi increases as her salary increases, other things being equal. Which of the following is correct?
   A) Instant noodles could be an inferior good.
   B) Instant noodles could be a normal good.
   C) Instant noodles and sushi could be substitutes.
   D) Instant noodles and sushi could be complements.
8. Suppose that the demand curve for a one-day metro ticket in Paris is linear. According to market research, if the price decreased by \$0.2 per ticket, the number of tickets sold would increase by 40 per day. If the prevailing price in the market is \$10 per ticket, and daily sales are 800 tickets, what is the inverse demand function?
   A) $Q = -200P + 2800$
   B) $Q = 200P + 2800$
   C) $P = -0.005Q + 14$
   D) $P = 0.005Q + 14$
9. Suppose that the graph below shows a consumer's preference for work and leisure, represented by indifference curves U_1 and U_2. His initial budget line is BL_1, which pivots inward to BL_2 due to a decrease in his hourly wage. Suppose that the dotted line is parallel to BL_2. What would be the substitution effect of the wage decrease on his leisure consumption?
   A) His leisure time would increase by 5 hours.
   B) His leisure time would increase by 3 hours.

C) His leisure time would decrease by 5 hours.
D) His leisure time would decrease by 3 hours.

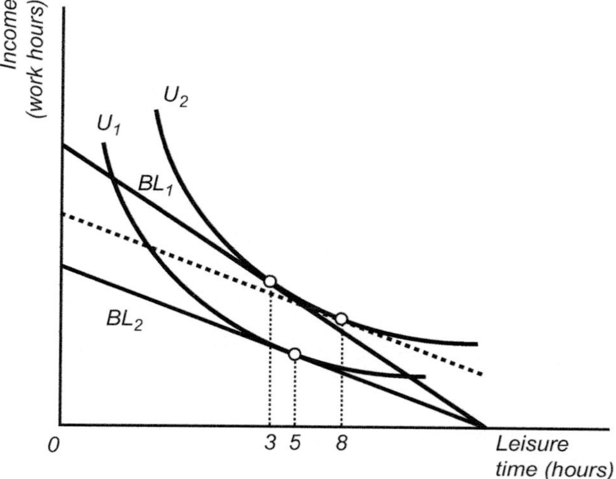

10. Which of the following adages/proverbs can best illuminate the concept of opportunity cost?
A) "No pain, no gain."
B) "One bad apple spoils the barrel."
C) "There's no such thing as a free lunch."
D) "He who chases two rabbits catches neither."

Problem solving

1. Governments have basically adopted two policies to stimulate consumption, including tourism consumption, amid the coronavirus pandemic in 2020. One is that the government dispenses a certain amount of cash to citizens who can use the money as they wish. For instance, the Hong Kong government initiated what is called the "Cash Payout Scheme" in June, which disbursed HK$10,000, equivalent to US$1,300, to each Hong Kong permanent resident aged 18 or above.[4] The other is to offer a tourist voucher worth a certain amount of money that can only be spent for tourism consumption, such as hotels, restaurants, and tourist attractions. Sometimes tourist vouchers can only be used at specific times. For instance, the European Commission proposed a tourist voucher scheme in July to stimulate consumption.[5] Prague is implementing a tourist voucher scheme called "In Prague As At Home," which entitles each tourist to redeem $17 for every hotel night up to four nights or for expenditure on tourist attractions in the city.[6] Suppose that the government can choose to use either a cash or tourist voucher scheme to disburse the same amount of money to the citizens. Analyze the impacts of the two schemes on tourism consumption, respectively.

2. Suppose that Luciano has a budget of $1,200 to spend on skiing in St. Moritz and a spa in Lausanne. The figure below shows his preference for skiing and spa represented by indifference curves U_1 and U_2. If the price of the spa remains unchanged at CHF 200 per hour while the price of skiing decreases, what will be the income and substitution effects of the price change of skiing (the dotted line is parallel to budget line BL_2)? If the demand curve for Luciano's skiing is linear, what is his demand function for skiing?

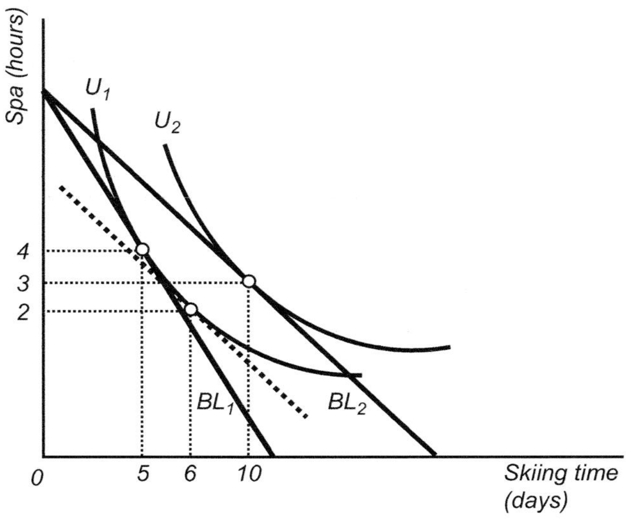

3. Refer to Figure 4.8 and suppose that two citizens in Ecuador and the Philippines each win a lottery of US$50,000. How would their budget lines change after the winning of the lottery? How would the lottery winning affect their choice of work and consumption of leisure? Elaborate the implications of your answers for tourism demand.

Solutions to all review questions and problem solving tasks are included in the Support Material for this book, which can be accessed at www.routledge.com/9780367897352.

Notes

1 See Robbins (1935), pp. 16–17. Words are italicized in the original text.

2 See Bentham (1789), p. i.

3 See Bentham (1789), p. i.

4 The Government of the Hong Kong Special Administrative Region. Accessed on August 12, 2020 from https://www.cashpayout.gov.hk/eng/index.html.

5 The European Commission. European Commission partners with tourism industry and leading European businesses to boost patronage voucher schemes across the EU. July 8, 2020.

6 *The New York Times*. Visa waivers, vouchers, flight discounts and other travel lures. July 20, 2020.

Bibliography

Bentham, J. (1789). *An introduction to the principles of morals and legislation*. Printed in the year 1780, and now first published. London, UK: Printed for T. Payne, and Son, at the Mews Gate.

Ohanian, L., & Raffo, A. (2012). Aggregate hours worked in OECD countries: New measurement and implications for business cycles. *Journal of Monetary Economics, 59*(1), 40–56.

Ohanian, L., Raffo, A., & Rogerson, R. (2008). Long-term changes in labor supply and taxes: Evidence from OECD countries, 1956–2004. *Journal of Monetary Economics, 55*(8), 1353–1362.

Robbins, L. (1935). *An essay on the nature and significance of economic science* (2nd ed.). London, UK: Macmillan and Co., Limited.

5 Elasticity of consumer demand

This chapter extends consumer theory and demand in Chapter 4 to further assess the responsiveness of demand to major determinants of demand, particularly the price of a good, consumer income, and the price of a related good in the market. To this end we compare the marginal demand and the elasticity of demand in quantifying the responsiveness of demand to a demand determinant. First, we focus on calculating the price elasticity of demand and illustrating the differences between arc elasticity, midpoint elasticity, and point elasticity of demand. Second, we go on to interpret the elasticity of demand based on the nature and magnitude of the effect of a demand determinant. Third, we interpret three major elasticities of demand with respect to the price of a good, consumer income, and the price of a related good by drawing evidence from the industry. We conclude by articulating the relationship between the price elasticity of demand and firm revenue.

AFTER STUDYING THIS CHAPTER, YOU SHOULD BE ABLE TO:

- **Understand the responsiveness of demand by examining the marginal demand and the elasticity of demand;**
- **Calculate arc elasticity, midpoint elasticity, and point elasticity of demand with respect to a demand determinant;**
- **Interpret three major elasticities of demand, the price elasticity, the income elasticity, and the cross-price elasticity of demand; and**
- **Analyze the effect of price elasticity of demand on firm revenue with regard to linear demand.**

5.1 The responsiveness of demand

We have seen that a number of factors affect consumer demand, among which are the price of a good in question, the income of consumers, and the price of a related good. These factors are instrumental in explaining consumption and deriving the demand curve. In addition to examining whether a demand determinant has a positive or negative effect, we need to measure the extent to which the demand determinant affects consumer demand while holding other variables constant. That is, we measure both the nature and the magnitude of the responsiveness of demand to a change in the demand determinant in question, say price. In the first place we can use the marginal demand to assess the effect of a demand determinant on the quantity demanded for a good. Suppose that the price of a good increases from P_1 to P_2 ($P_1 < P_2$), and correspondingly the quantity demanded decreases from Q_1 to Q_2 ($Q_1 > Q_2$), other things being equal. By definition the marginal demand for the good with respect to its price is the change in the quantity demanded Q divided by the change in the price P:

$$\frac{\Delta Q}{\Delta P} = \frac{Q_2 - Q_1}{P_2 - P_1}. \tag{5.1}$$

Marginal demand measures the incremental change in the quantity demanded of a good due to a change in the price of the good, and thus assesses the extent to which demand responds to a price change. Graphically, the marginal demand $\Delta Q / \Delta P$ is the reciprocal of the slope of the demand curve between point A (Q_1, P_1) and point B (Q_2, P_2) as shown in Figure 5.1. If the demand curve is linear, the marginal demand will be constant, which is the reciprocal of the slope of the demand curve as a whole. Therefore, from the slope of the demand curve, we can readily obtain the marginal demand with respect to price. For the linear inverse demand function $P = aQ + b$ in function (4.8), demonstrated in Chapter 4,[1] we know that parameter a is the slope of the demand curve, and thus $1/a$ is the marginal demand with respect to price. We can therefore evaluate demand responsiveness with respect to price by assessing the slope of the demand curve.

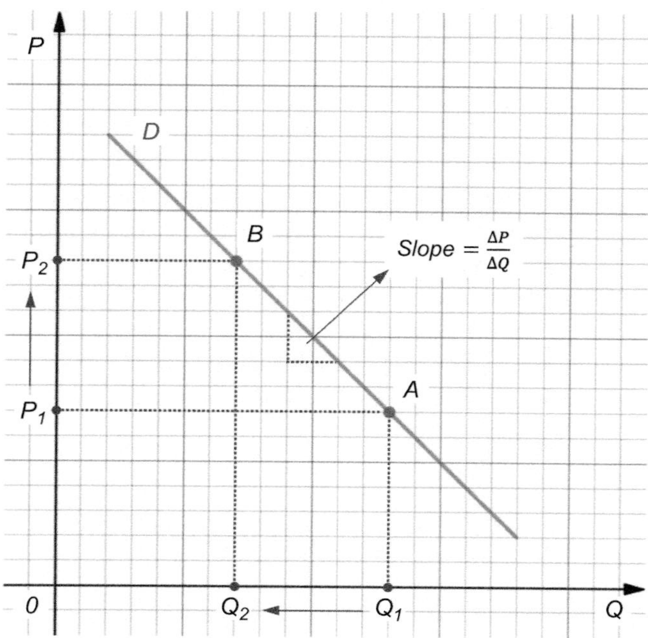

Figure 5.1
Marginal demand with respect to price

For instance, if the price of a bottle of wine increases from \$10 (P_1) to \$12 (P_2), the quantity demanded decreases from 200 bottles (Q_1) to 150 bottles (Q_2) accordingly, other things being equal. Thus, the marginal demand for the wine with respect to price is

$$\frac{\Delta Q}{\Delta P} = \frac{Q_2 - Q_1}{P_2 - P_1} = \frac{(150-200)\ bottles}{(12-10)\ dollars} = -25\ bottles/dollar. \quad (5.2)$$

This means that when the price of the wine increases by \$1 per bottle, the quantity demanded for the wine falls by 25 bottles; conversely, if the price decreases by \$1 per bottle, the quantity demanded will increase by 25 bottles. On the one hand, marginal demand indicates the nature of the relationship between price and quantity demanded with reference to the sign of $\Delta Q / \Delta P$, which is negative. Hence the quantity demanded changes in the opposite direction to price. On the other hand, it quantifies the magnitude of the price effect on the quantity demanded with reference to absolute value $|\Delta Q / \Delta P|$. Marginal demand can thus differ in nature and magnitude depending on which demand determinant is concerned.

Suppose that there is an infinitesimal change in price. That is, the increase from P_1 to P_2 is infinitely small, $\Delta P \to 0$, leading to the quantity of a good demanded $Q(P)$ decreasing from Q_1 to Q_2 by $Q(P+\Delta P)-Q(P)$. If the demand curve is differentiable between point A (Q_1, P_1) and point B (Q_2, P_2), the marginal demand for the good with respect to price can ultimately be expressed as the derivative of the quantity demanded with respect to price:

$$\frac{\Delta Q}{\Delta P} = \frac{Q_2 - Q_1}{P_2 - P_1} = \lim_{\Delta P \to 0} \frac{Q(P+\Delta P)-Q(P)}{\Delta P} = \frac{dQ}{dP}. \quad (5.3)$$

The arithmetic case above of the wine demand in formula (5.2) cannot be applied in formula (5.3), because the price change of \$2 is not an infinitesimal change. Besides, we have no information about the demand function for the wine, and thus cannot assess how the demand would change if there was an infinitesimal change in price. For this reason, we are not able to calculate the derivative of demand with respect to price at a certain point of the demand curve, and hence we cannot ascertain the marginal demand with respect to price at a particular point, say A (Q_1, P_1). While an infinitesimal change in price or in any other demand determinants may sound unrealistic in real-world markets, it does help us develop a deeper understanding of the instantaneous responsiveness of demand with respect to a demand determinant, which we shall address shortly in this chapter.

5.2 Defining and calculating elasticity

In general, marginal demand measures the responsiveness of demand with respect to a demand determinant quite well. Yet it has a drawback when it comes to drawing comparisons between the demands for two different goods, or even for the same good if the measurements of the variables are different. As indicated in formula (5.2), the marginal demand is associated with the units of measurement of the demand determinant and the quantity demanded. In formula (5.2), the marginal demand for the wine is a decrease of 25 bottles with an increase of 1 dollar in price. Consider converting the dollar into cents to measure the same price change, then the marginal demand for the wine will be a decrease of 0.25 bottles with respect to an increase of 1 cent in price. As a matter of fact, the responsiveness of demand with respect to price in the two scenarios is equivalent, provided that we take no account of the measurement of price. If both the quantity demanded and the price are measured differently from one good to another, it would become even more challenging to compare the marginal demand with respect to a demand determinant, say price, between two goods. British economist Alfred Marshall (1842–1924) developed the concept of elasticity to standardize the responsiveness of demand to a demand determinant that is independent of measurement units, thereby making the responsiveness of demand comparable across different goods.

5.2.1 Arc elasticity

Instead of assessing the marginal demand that is based on absolute changes in quantity demanded and in a demand determinant, we can calculate the proportional changes in the quantity demanded and in the demand determinant. Consider price as a demand determinant which increases from P_1 to P_2, leading to the quantity demanded decreasing from Q_1 to Q_2. The proportional change in price is the change in price divided by the initial value of price, $(P_2 - P_1)/P_1$, which is the percentage change in price. Likewise, the proportional change in quantity demanded is $(Q_2 - Q_1)/Q_1$, which is the percentage change in the quantity demanded caused by the price change. Then, the price elasticity of demand is defined as the responsiveness of quantity demanded with respect to price in terms of percentage changes in the two variables. Thus, the price elasticity of demand, η_P, is calculated as the ratio of the percentage change in quantity demanded to the percentage change in price:

$$\eta_P = \frac{(Q_2 - Q_1)/Q_1}{(P_2 - P_1)/P_1}. \qquad (5.4)$$

The definition in formula (5.4) is referred to as arc elasticity of demand with respect to price. It is called arc elasticity because formula (5.4) in fact assesses the responsiveness of demand between two given points, or in a certain interval, of a demand curve without regard to the exact shape of the demand curve. In the aforementioned example of the wine, when the price increases from \$10 (P_1) to \$12 (P_2) and the quantity demanded decreases from 200 bottles (Q_1) to 150 bottles (Q_2), the price elasticity of demand for the wine is

$$\eta_P = \frac{(150 - 200)\ \textit{bottles}}{200\ \textit{bottles}} \bigg/ \frac{(12 - 10)\ \textit{dollars}}{10\ \textit{dollars}} = -\frac{1/4}{1/5} = -1.25. \qquad (5.5)$$

We interpret the price elasticity of demand for the wine in formula (5.5) as follows: when the price of the wine increases by 1%, the quantity demanded for the wine will decrease by 1.25%; or conversely, when the price decreases by 1%, the quantity demanded for the wine will increase by 1.25%, other things being equal. In calculating percentage changes, the units of measurement of two variables are cancelled out, and hence elasticity is unit-free. Compared to marginal demand, the elasticity of demand is independent of the units of quantity demanded and the demand determinant. Therefore, the responsiveness of demand with respect to a demand determinant is standardized across different measurements.

We further rearrange formula (5.4) to articulate the relationship between marginal demand and the price elasticity of demand:

$$\eta_P = \frac{(Q_2 - Q_1)/Q_1}{(P_2 - P_1)/P_1} = \frac{Q_2 - Q_1}{P_2 - P_1}\frac{P_1}{Q_1} = \frac{\Delta Q}{\Delta P}\frac{P_1}{Q_1}. \tag{5.6}$$

We can see that the price elasticity of demand is the marginal demand $\Delta Q / \Delta P$ multiplied by the ratio of the initial price P_1 to the initial quantity demanded Q_1. This means that if we know the marginal demand at point A (Q_1, P_1) on the demand curve, and the values of Q_1 and P_1, we can calculate the price elasticity of demand (Figure 5.1). If we know the price elasticity of demand η_P and the values of Q_1 and P_1, we can readily obtain the marginal demand as well.

Further consider the two points, A (Q_1, P_1) and B (Q_2, P_2), on the demand curve in Figure 5.1. If the price decreases from P_2 to P_1, the price change in absolute value, $|P_1 - P_2|$, will be equal to $|P_2 - P_1|$ for which the price increases from P_1 to P_2. Correspondingly, the change in quantity demanded in absolute value $|Q_1 - Q_2|$ is equal to $|Q_2 - Q_1|$. This suggests that the marginal demand with respect to price is the same, no matter whether the price increases or decreases in the interval $[P_1, P_2]$. However, the percentage change in price does depend on whether the price increases from P_1 to P_2 : $|P_2 - P_1| / P_1$ or decreases from P_2 to P_1 : $|P_1 - P_2| / P_2$, because the denominators are different. This difference also applies to the percentage changes in quantity demanded, which are $|Q_2 - Q_1| / Q_1$ when the quantity demanded decreases from Q_1 to Q_2, and $|Q_1 - Q_2| / Q_2$ when the quantity demanded increases from Q_2 to Q_1. In the wine example above, if the price of the wine instead decreases from \$12 (P_2) to \$10 (P_1), and correspondingly the quantity demanded increases from 150 bottles (Q_2) to 200 bottles (Q_1), the price elasticity of demand for the wine will be

$$\eta_P = \frac{(200 - 150)\ bottles}{150\ bottles} \bigg/ \frac{(10 - 12)\ dollars}{12\ dollars} = -\frac{1/3}{1/6} = -2. \tag{5.7}$$

The price elasticity of demand for the wine in formula (5.7) suggests that when the price of the wine decreases by 1%, the quantity demanded for the wine will increase by 2%; or when the price increases by 1%, the quantity demanded will decrease by 2%. Obviously, the price elasticities of demand for the wine between the two points A (Q_1, P_1) and B (Q_2, P_2) are different contingent on whether the price increases or

decreases. Since the denominators of the percentage changes in price and quantity demanded vary with the direction of the price change, the price elasticities of demand in the same interval vary accordingly.

5.2.2 Midpoint elasticity

In order to remove the effect of the change in the base values of variables when assessing elasticity in a certain interval, we can calculate what is called midpoint elasticity of demand by using the means of the interval as the base values for calculating percentage changes. Thus, the percentage change in price at the midpoint is the change in price divided by the mean of the two price points, that is, $(P_1 + P_2)/2$. Likewise, the percentage change in quantity demanded at the midpoint is the change in quantity demanded divided by the mean of the two corresponding quantities, that is, $(Q_1 + Q_2)/2$. Thus the midpoint price elasticity of demand, η_P^M, between the two points $A\ (Q_1, P_1)$ and $B\ (Q_2, P_2)$ is given as

$$\eta_P^M = \frac{(Q_2 - Q_1)/\frac{1}{2}(Q_1 + Q_2)}{(P_2 - P_1)/\frac{1}{2}(P_1 + P_2)} = \frac{\Delta Q}{\Delta P}\frac{P_1 + P_2}{Q_1 + Q_2}. \quad (5.8)$$

Regardless of the direction of the price change, the midpoint price elasticity of demand is always identical in the interval because the denominators of price and quantity demanded are fixed at their means. Referring to the wine example, we can calculate the midpoint price elasticity of demand for the wine as

$$\eta_P^M = \frac{(150 - 200)\ bottles}{(12 - 10)\ dollars} \times \frac{22\ dollars}{350\ bottles} = -\frac{11}{7} \approx -1.57. \quad (5.9)$$

Conditional on the same interval between points $A\ (Q_1, P_1)$ and $B\ (Q_2, P_2)$ on the demand curve (Figure 5.1), the price elasticities of demand in formulas (5.5), (5.7), and (5.9) are slightly different from each other. This is simply because the base values of the two variables that are used for standardization are different. As shown in Figure 5.2, the greater the interval between the two points $A\ (Q_1, P_1)$ and $B\ (Q_2, P_2)$ on the demand curve D_1, the more the midpoint M deviates from the two bounds of the interval, and the more the midpoint elasticity of demand diverges from the arc elasticities in both directions of the price change. Conversely, the smaller the interval, the more the arc elasticities in both directions converge to the midpoint elasticity.

5.2.3 Point elasticity

If the interval is infinitely small, then the two points $A\ (Q_1, P_1)$ and $B\ (Q_2, P_2)$ will converge to the midpoint M on the demand curve D_1 (Figure 5.2). We thus obtain what is called point elasticity of demand, defined as the percentage change in quantity demanded with respect to an infinitesimal change in price at a certain point of the demand curve. In other words, the point elasticity, η_P^P, is the limit of the ratio of the percentage change in quantity demanded to the percentage change in price insofar as the price change approaches zero:

$$\eta_P^P = \lim_{\Delta P \to 0} \frac{(Q_2 - Q_1)/\frac{1}{2}(Q_1 + Q_2)}{(P_2 - P_1)/\frac{1}{2}(P_1 + P_2)} = \frac{dQ/Q}{dP/P} = \frac{dQ}{dP}\frac{P}{Q}. \quad (5.10)$$

As formula (5.10) shows, the point elasticity of demand is the limit of the arc elasticity between the two points $A\ (Q_1, P_1)$ and $B\ (Q_2, P_2)$ as the interval approaches zero. Thus, the point elasticity of demand with respect to price is the derivative of demand with respect to price, which is the marginal demand multiplied by the price–quantity ratio at a certain point of the demand curve. If we know the demand function, we can calculate the price elasticity of demand at any single point on the demand curve, provided that the demand function is differentiable. Figure 5.2 shows that the other two demand curves D_2 and D_3 also cross the two points $A\ (Q_1, P_1)$ and $B\ (Q_2, P_2)$, and thus the arc and midpoint price elasticities of demand calculated in formulas (5.5), (5.7), and (5.9) will be identical for all three demand curves. Nevertheless, their point price elasticities at either point A or point B will vary because the slopes of the three demand curves, namely the marginal demands, are different from one another. It is the point price elasticity that captures the instantaneous responsiveness of demand to a change in price. To calculate the point elasticity though, we need to know the demand function.

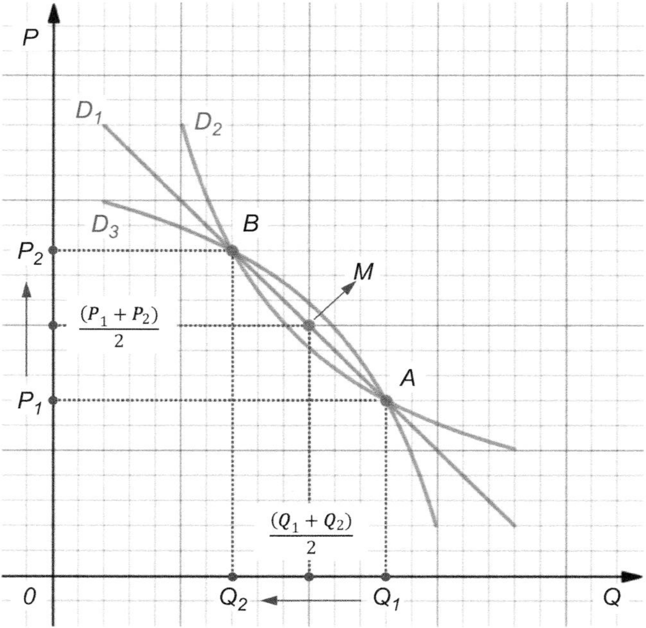

Figure 5.2
Arc elasticity, midpoint elasticity, and point elasticity

5.3 Interpretation of elasticity

5.3.1 Nature of the effect

Since the elasticity of demand cancels out the units of measurement, it standardizes the responsiveness of demand to a change in a demand determinant regardless of how demand and the demand determinant are measured. Like marginal demand, the elasticity of demand suggests, in the first place, the nature of the relationship between demand and the demand determinant in question, indicated by the sign of elasticity. A positive elasticity of demand suggests that quantity demanded changes in the same direction as the demand determinant, while a negative elasticity suggests that both variables change in opposite directions. For instance, the price elasticity of demand is always negative, with very few exceptions,[2] suggesting that the quantity demanded increases as price decreases, or the quantity demanded decreases as price increases, other things being equal. The negative price elasticity of demand is a manifestation of the law of demand. If income is a demand determinant, we know that the income elasticity of demand for normal goods is positive, because an increase in consumer income leads to an increase in demand, other things being equal. The income elasticity of demand is negative for inferior goods for which the income effect is negative. By the same token, we can explore the nature of the relationship between demand and a wide range of demand determinants besides price and income.

5.3.2 Magnitude of the effect

The absolute value of elasticity of demand suggests the magnitude of the responsiveness of demand to a demand determinant, which is the strength of the relationship between demand and the demand determinant. If the absolute value of elasticity is less than 1, the demand is referred to as inelastic with respect to the demand determinant. That is, a 1% change in the demand determinant will lead to a less than 1% change in the quantity demanded. If it is greater than 1, the demand is elastic, meaning that a 1% change in the demand determinant will lead to a greater than 1% change in the quantity demanded. If it is equal to 1, the demand is referred to as unit elastic, and hence the percentage changes in demand and the demand determinant are the same. Unit elasticity is taken as a threshold in judging demand responsiveness, for it suggests that demand responds at exactly the same magnitude as the change in the demand determinant. If the percentage change in demand is greater than the percentage change in the demand determinant, the elasticity of demand will be greater than 1 in absolute value, suggesting that demand is more responsive to the change in the demand determinant, hence elastic. If the percentage change in demand is smaller than the percentage change in the demand determinant, the elasticity of demand will be less than 1 in absolute value, and hence demand is less responsive to the change in the determinant and is inelastic.

Note that the sign of elasticity tells us nothing about the magnitude of the effect of a demand determinant on demand. Insofar as elasticities are compared by magnitude, we examine the absolute values because the signs are irrelevant to the magnitude.

Consider the price elasticity of demand. On the one hand, the price elasticity must be negative, dictated by the law of demand, and on the other hand, the magnitude of the price effect on demand varies across different demands. If the price elasticity of demand is zero, it makes no sense to discuss either the nature or the magnitude of the price effect, because demand simply does not respond to price at all. In other words, the marginal demand is also zero. While a zero price elasticity is improbable in practice, it suggests in theory that the demand is perfectly inelastic, exhibited by a vertical demand curve with the x-intercept at a certain quantity Q_0 (Figure 5.3a). Then, the demand is constant at the quantity Q_0 regardless of the change in price, other things being equal. If the price elasticity of demand is infinite, the demand is perfectly elastic, meaning that demand vanishes as long as price changes. Therefore, the demand curve is horizontal with the y-intercept at the price P_0 (Figure 5.3b). Only at this price can the demand exist. While perfectly elastic and inelastic demands are impractical, they are theoretically indispensable in economic analysis, which we shall address in later chapters.

5.4 Major elasticities of demand

Since elasticity is a standardized and unit-free measure of demand responsiveness, it enables us to assess the nature and magnitude of the effect of a demand determinant on demand across different goods or markets. Among the important determinants of demand are the price of a good in question, the income of consumers, and the price of a related good, because they are instrumental in constructing consumer theory addressed in Chapter 4. In what follows we focus on the responsiveness of the market demand with respect to each of the three demand determinants. This gives rise to

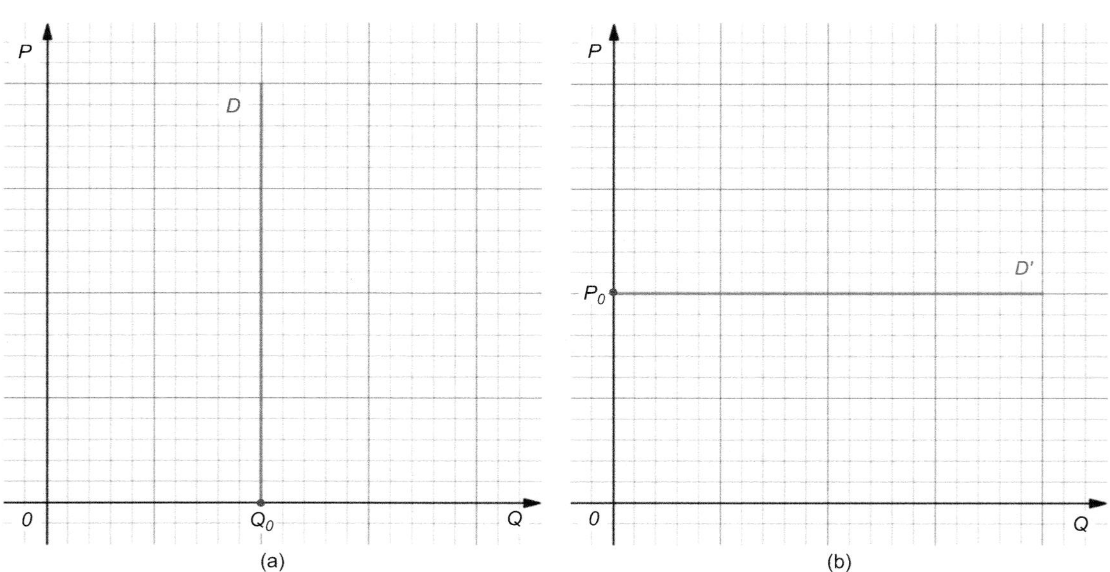

Figure 5.3
Perfectly inelastic and perfectly elastic demand

the price elasticity of demand, the income elasticity of demand, and the cross-price elasticity of demand, respectively.

5.4.1 Price elasticity of demand

As stated above in great detail, the price elasticity of demand assesses the responsiveness of demand with respect to the price of a good. It reveals the properties of different goods in consumer demand. Since the formulas and calculations of the price elasticity of demand are presented in the preceding sections, in this section we focus on articulating the implications of the price elasticity of demand. Table 5.1 shows the price elasticities of demand for a wide range of goods and services in the U.S. market. Demand for tourism products and services is usually elastic: to name a few, restaurant meals (2.30), long-run airline travel (2.40), and long-run foreign travel (4.00). Demand for everyday necessities, such as salt (0.10), matches (0.10), toothpicks (0.10), short-run airline travel (0.10), and so on, is inelastic. Thus, a 1% change in price will lead to a greater than 1% change in quantity demanded for tourism products and services but a less than 1% change in quantity demanded for everyday necessities. We know that all price elasticities of demand are negative except when indicated otherwise, so there is always an inverse relationship between price and quantity demanded. Therefore, the sign of the price elasticity of demand is often omitted when it comes to comparing the size of the price effect on demand, unless indicated otherwise.

As illustrated above, the price elasticity of demand varies in the interval of price change and depends also on calculation methods. Yet Table 5.1 implies that the price elasticity of demand for each product is constant, independent of the interval of a price change. To compare the price elasticity of demand across products, there are two implicit assumptions worth noting. They help to remove the distortion of the price interval, thereby making the price elasticity of demand constant or approximately constant for a given good. One is that the price change of a good in practice usually hovers around the initial market price instead of oscillating between two polar prices, and therefore the price interval is very small. Thus, the price elasticity of demand for the good more or less reflects the point elasticity of demand no matter whether the price increases or decreases. The second assumption is that the whole demand curve has a constant elasticity regardless of the change in price, which can be manifested by nonlinear demand.[3] Since the extent to which price changes may vary from one product to another, which in turn could affect the price elasticity of demand, comparing elasticities across products would make more sense if demand elasticity did not change substantially with the price change per se but reflected the property of the demand in general.

In general, the demand for international tourism is elastic, suggesting that international tourism demand is highly responsive to price changes. Yet the price elasticity of tourism demand for a particular destination may vary across different source markets. Table 5.2 shows that Indonesians' demand for tourism in Hong Kong is highly elastic (2.89) while Malaysians' demand is highly inelastic (0.21). Specifically, when the price of tourism increases (decreases) by 1% in Hong Kong, Indonesians' demand would decrease (increase) by 2.89%, while Malaysians' would decrease (increase) by merely 0.21% for the same destination. The price elasticity of tourism demand also reveals the nature of tourism on the supply side if we examine the same source market. That is, the price elasticity of demand from the same source market may vary across destinations. For instance, Chinese demand for long-haul destinations such as Switzerland is presumably more elastic than for short-haul destinations such as Thailand. One explanation would be that long-haul travel is expensive, and thus the price–quantity ratio is greater conditional on the same marginal demand. If we regard destinations as products, the price elasticity of demand for tourism reveals the nature of different destinations, which resembles the nature of different goods and services in Table 5.1.

5.4.2 Income elasticity of demand

In principle we can define the elasticity of demand with respect to any demand determinant the same way as we define the price elasticity of demand. If we focus on

Table 5.1 Price elasticities of demand for various goods and services

Price elasticity	Goods and services
0.10	Salt / Matches / Toothpicks / Airline travel, short-run / Residential natural gas, short-run
0.20	Gasoline, short-run / Automobiles, long-run
0.25	Coffee
0.40	Legal services, short-run
0.45	Tobacco products, short-run
0.50	Residential natural gas, long-run / Fish (cod) consumed at home
0.60	Physician services / Taxi, short-run
0.70	Gasoline, long-run
0.90	Movies / Shellfish, consumed at home / Tires, short-run
1.10	Oysters consumed at home / Private education
1.20	Housing, owner occupied, long-run / Tires, long-run / Radio and television receivers
1.2–1.5	Automobiles, short-run
2.30	Restaurant meals
2.40	Airline travel, long-run
2.80	Fresh green peas
4.00	Foreign travel, long-run / Chevrolet automobiles
4.60	Fresh tomatoes

Note: Since the price elasticity of demand is always negative, we usually omit the negative sign when reporting the price elasticity of demand.

Source: Anderson, McLellan, Overton, and Wolfram (1997), p. 60.

Table 5.2 Elasticities of tourism demand for Hong Kong

Country/region	Price elasticity	Income elasticity	Cross-price elasticity
Australia	0.583	—	0.552
Canada	1.012	3.322	—
China (Mainland)	0.402	1.521	1.248
France	0.436	2.616	0.663
Germany	1.389	3.620	—
Indonesia	2.885	1.484	—
India	1.059	1.459	1.209
Japan	—	2.530	—
Korea	—	1.704	—
Malaysia	0.206	1.020	—
Philippines	—	—	1.657
Singapore	1.223	1.316	—
Taiwan	1.729	2.140	—
Thailand	0.911	0.944	—
United Kingdom	0.492	2.096	0.643
United States	1.004	1.499	0.463

Note: The negative signs of the price elasticity of demand are omitted. The destination related to Hong Kong for which the cross-price elasticity of demand is calculated is Singapore; — = Statistics are not available or are statistically insignificant.

Source: Song, Wong, and Chon (2003), p. 445.

the responsiveness of demand with respect to consumer income, other things being equal, we can define the income elasticity of demand as the responsiveness of quantity demanded with respect to consumer income. Suppose that consumer income changes from Y_1 to Y_2, and correspondingly the quantity of a good demanded changes from Q_1 to Q_2. Other things being equal, the income elasticity of demand, η_Y, for the good is given by the ratio of the percentage change in quantity demanded to the percentage change in consumer income:

$$\eta_Y = \frac{(Q_2 - Q_1)/Q_1}{(Y_2 - Y_1)/Y_1}. \tag{5.11}$$

Similar to the other two ways of calculating the price elasticity above, we can calculate the midpoint income elasticity of demand using formula (5.8) and the point income elasticity of demand using formula (5.10) by simply replacing price P with income Y. Note that in the formulas for calculating the income elasticity we assume that the change in quantity demanded is due to the change in consumer income, other things being equal.

The income elasticity of demand allows us to further classify goods beyond normal goods versus inferior goods, which we addressed in Chapter 4. Obviously, the income elasticity of demand for normal goods is positive, denoted by curves I_1, I_2, and I_3 in Figure 5.4. Very few goods are inferior goods with a negative income effect, and hence a negative income elasticity, I_4. Note that the distinction between normal goods and inferior goods is due to the nature of the relationship between demand and income with no regard to the magnitude of the income effect. Normal goods can be further classified as necessities and luxury goods based on the size of the income effect. The income elasticity of necessities is between 0 and 1, suggesting that a 1% increase (decrease) in income will lead to a less than 1% increase (decrease) in quantity demanded, denoted by I_2, other things being equal. The income elasticity of luxuries is greater than 1, suggesting that a 1% increase (decrease) in income will lead to a greater than 1% increase (decrease) in demand, denoted by I_3. Hence the income effect on demand is greater for luxury goods than for necessities. Note that necessity, luxury, and inferior goods are defined by the income effect while holding the price constant, despite the fact that necessities and inferior goods could be inexpensive and luxuries prohibitive.

Tourism products and services usually have positive income elasticities, and hence are normal goods. Long-haul international travel and overseas holidays are usually luxury goods, meaning that their income elasticity is greater than 1, and the income effect is positive and large. Table 5.2 shows that the income elasticity of demand for international tourism in Hong Kong varies by source market, and therefore reveals the nature of different source markets. It is also plausible that some tourism products and services may become inferior goods under certain circumstances. In economic

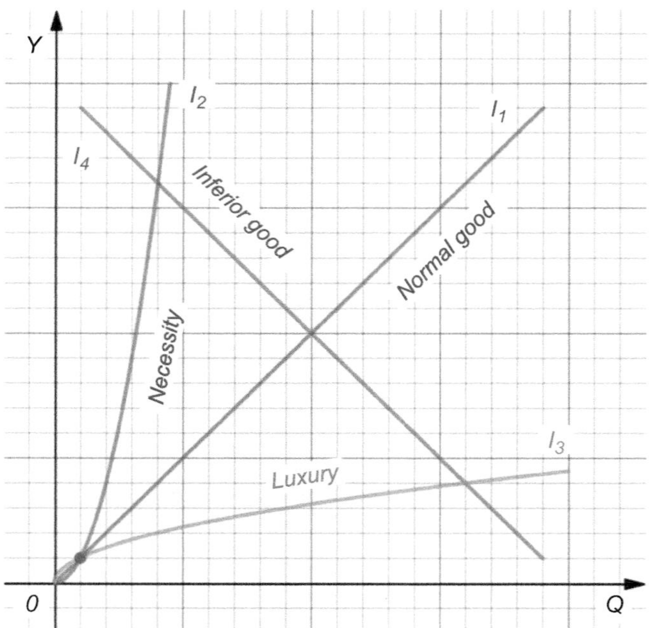

Figure 5.4
Income elasticity of demand

hardship, people are probably loath to reduce their tourism consumption completely, and instead may substitute domestic tourism for international tourism, other things being equal. Such behavioral change results in a negative relationship between income and quantity demanded for domestic tourism, relegating domestic tourism to an inferior good. This also means that international tourism is usually a luxury good, for which the demand will be unleashed once consumer income increases.

For a given good though, the relationship between income and demand may vary by the income levels of consumers. That is, the income effect of demand for a good, or the income elasticity of demand, is not constant across different income brackets. A study on beer consumption over the period 1961–2012 shows an inverted *U*-shaped relationship between income and beer consumption in high-income countries, such as Germany, Belgium, the United Kingdom, and the United States (Figure 5.5). As income increases in these countries, beer consumption first increases, yet further income growth leads to a decrease in beer consumption. On the other hand, there exists a positive relationship between income and beer consumption in low- and middle-income countries, such as Brazil, Russia, and China (Figure 5.5). This study concludes that GDP per capita of US$27,000 could be a threshold that alters the nature of the income elasticity of demand for beer. Since GDP per capita in low- and middle-income countries is below this threshold, an increase in income boosts consumer demand for beer, suggesting that beer is a normal good in developing countries. However, since GDP per capita in high-income countries has far exceeded this threshold, further income growth leads to a decrease in consumer demand for beer, and hence beer morphs into an inferior good. This conclusion implies that beer could become an inferior good when consumer income in developing countries enters a higher income bracket.

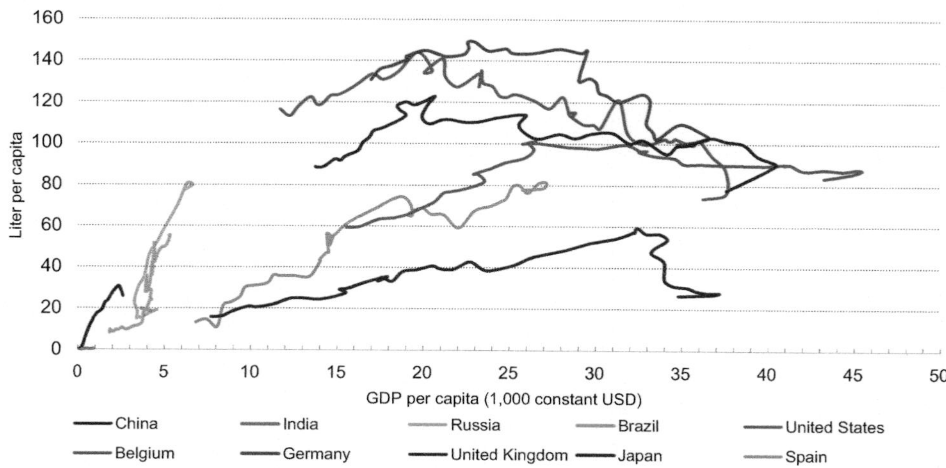

Figure 5.5
Income distribution and beer consumption (1961–2012)

Note: Beer consumption is measured as liters of beer consumed per person per year; data from the Food and Agriculture Organization of the United Nations (FAO). GDP per capita is in constant U.S. dollars; data from the World Development Indicators (WDI) (2013).

Source: Reproduced from Colen and Swinnen (2016), p. 192.

5.4.3 Cross-price elasticity of demand

When examining the responsiveness of demand for one good with respect to the price of another, other things being equal, we obtain what is called the cross-price elasticity of demand. Underlying the cross-price elasticity of demand is the assumption that two goods A and B are related in one way or another in consumer consumption, and therefore the price change of one good will affect the quantity demanded of the other. This is the substitution effect of a price change addressed in Chapter 4. The cross-price elasticity of demand thus measures the relationship of the two goods in consumer demand. Similar to the calculation of price elasticity and income elasticity, the cross-price elasticity of demand is given by the ratio of the percentage change in the quantity demanded for good A (Q^A) to the percentage change in the price of good B (P^B), or vice versa. Suppose that the price of B changes from P_1^B to P_2^B, and the quantity demanded of A changes from Q_1^A to Q_2^A accordingly. Other things being equal, the cross-price elasticity of demand, $\eta_{A,B}$, for good A with respect to the price of good B is expressed as

$$\eta_{A,B} = \frac{\left(Q_2^A - Q_1^A\right)/Q_1^A}{\left(P_2^B - P_1^B\right)/P_1^B}. \quad (5.12)$$

Consider two products, hotels and Airbnb. We are interested to know whether, and the extent to which, the price of Airbnb affects hotel demand. Suppose that the price of Airbnb increases in the market, and thus by the law of demand there must be a decrease in quantity demanded for Airbnb in the first place. Other things being equal, the demand for hotels could increase, decrease, or remain unchanged due to the decrease in Airbnb demand. If we observe that hotel demand increases in the market, other things being equal, this is because consumers are substituting hotels for Airbnb, and hence hotels and Airbnb are substitutes (Figure 5.6). Therefore, there exists a positive relationship between the price of Airbnb and hotel demand, hence a positive cross-price elasticity of demand for hotels, with respect to the price of Airbnb. If, on the other hand, hotel demand decreases, other things being equal, we can infer that consumers regard hotels and Airbnb as complements in their consumption (Figure 5.6). Thus, there is a negative relationship between the price of Airbnb and hotel demand, and hence a negative cross-price elasticity of demand for hotels. If hotel demand does not change at all, hotels and Airbnb are independent in consumption, ending up with a zero cross-price elasticity of demand.

Therefore, depending on whether the cross-price elasticity of demand is positive or negative, we can ascertain whether two related goods are substitutes or complements (Figure 5.7). This suggests that the distinction between substitutes and complements rests on the nature of the relationship between the price of one good and the demand for the other. Furthermore, the cross-price elasticity of demand in absolute value quantifies the degree to which two goods are substitutable or complementary with each other in consumption. The greater the cross-price elasticity in absolute value, the more substitutable or complementary the two goods are, and the smaller the cross-price elasticity the less substitutable or complementary they are. If we regard destinations

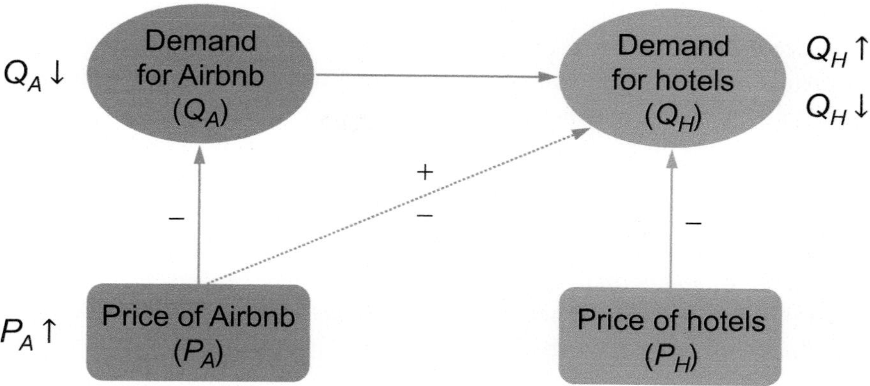

Figure 5.6
Cross-price elasticity of demand

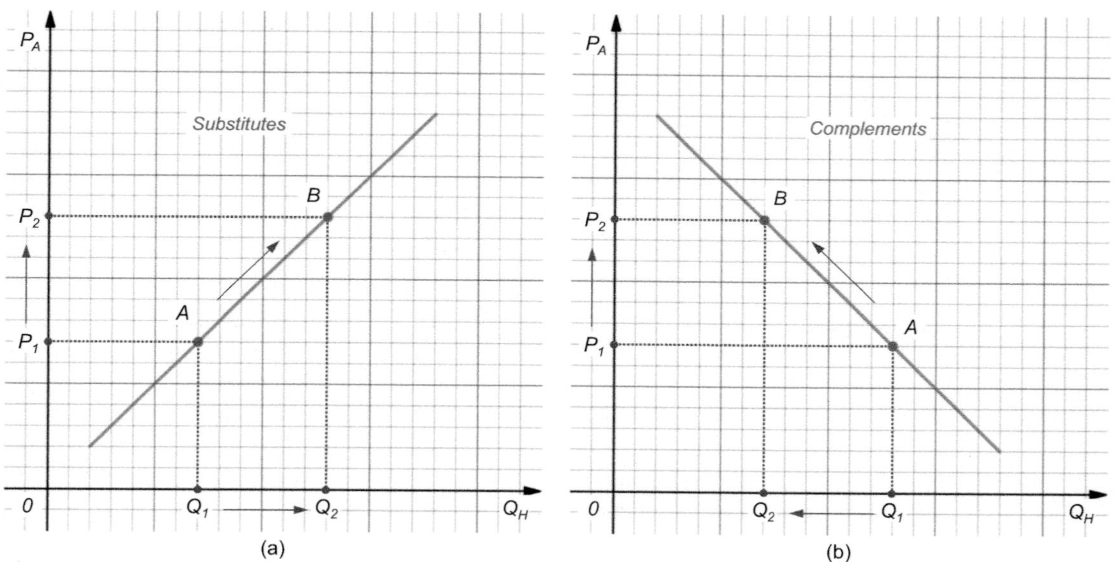

Figure 5.7
Substitutes, complements, and cross-price elasticity

Note: P_A is the price of Airbnb, and Q_H is the quantity demanded for hotels.

as products, Hong Kong and Singapore are likely to be substitutes for some tourists, such as Australians, Mainland Chinese, and French, as shown in Table 5.2. An increase in the price of tourism in one destination could boost demand for the other, due to the similar attractions and culture in the two cities. However, Hong Kong and Macau might be complements for Mainland Chinese because an increase in price in one city could decrease the demand for the other, due to their distinct attraction endowments.

As far as the tourism and hospitality industry is concerned, the breadth of the industry we outlined in Chapter 1 suggests that a wide range of sectors from hotels, restaurants, airlines to attractions are complements. Thus, the demand in one sector is inversely correlated with the prices of goods and services in other sectors, meaning that a price decrease in one sector can boost consumer demand in other sectors. The fundamental reason is that tourist consumption is heterogeneous, which entails a combination of various goods and services to create experiences. The degree of the complementarity between different sectors indicates the extent to which these sectors are interdependent in tourist consumption as well as in the tourist economy as a whole. On the other hand, goods and services supplied by different firms within the same sector are presumably substitutes, and thus the demand for a good is positively associated with the price of an alternative good in the same sector. The degree of substitutability between different firms in the same sector indicates the level of competition or rivalry among these firms, which we shall address in detail in Chapters 9 and 10.

5.5 Price elasticity and firm revenue

5.5.1 Price elasticity of linear demand

The immediate application of the price elasticity of demand is about understanding how firm revenue changes with price when a firm faces varying price elasticities. Before we analyze the relationship between firm revenue and price elasticity, we need to articulate how the price elasticity of demand may vary along a given demand curve. For expository simplicity, we focus on the linear demand curve. Figure 5.8 exhibits a linear demand curve for a good with the x- and y-intercepts at 20 and 15, respectively. When the price of the good changes, using formula (5.8) we can calculate the midpoint price elasticities between points A and B, C and M, M and D, E and F, and so on, along the demand curve. As we move downward from point A to point F along the demand curve, the price elasticity decreases, and thus the demand becomes increasingly less elastic. Moreover, using formula (5.10) we can calculate the price elasticity at the midpoint M of the demand curve, which is –1.[4] Since the midpoint M is unit elastic, we may conclude that the upper half of the linear demand is presumably elastic, while the lower half is inelastic.

The above presumption that the midpoint separates the linear demand curve into the elastic portion above it and the inelastic portion below it can be proved and generalized to any linear demand. To prove it, referring to the linear inverse demand function (4.8) in Chapter 4, $P = aQ + b$, we can calculate the point price elasticity of demand using formula (5.10):

$$\eta_P = \frac{dQ}{dP}\frac{P}{Q} = \frac{1}{a}\frac{P}{Q}, \tag{5.13}$$

where $1/a$ is the marginal demand, which is the reciprocal of the slope of the linear demand curve, and P/Q is the ratio of the price of the good to the quantity demanded. On the one hand, since the slope of the linear demand curve is constant, the marginal demand is constant. On the other hand, the price–quantity ratio, P/Q, changes as we

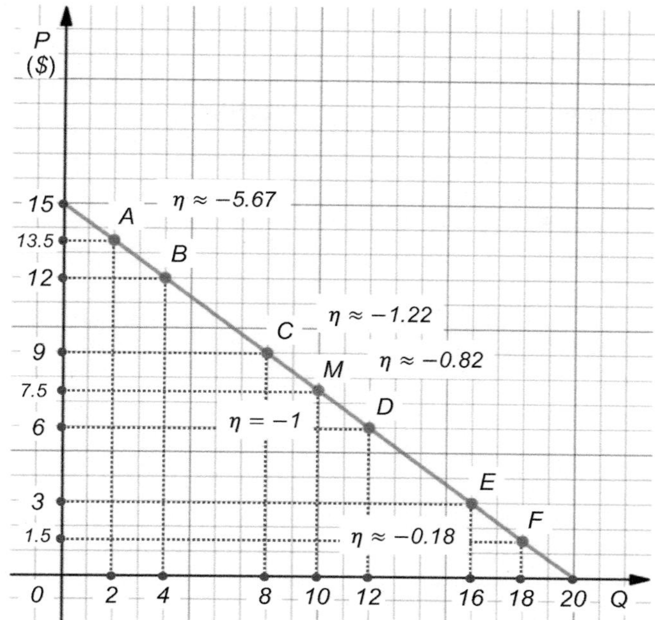

Figure 5.8
Price elasticity and linear demand

move along the linear demand curve, and therefore the point price elasticity of demand varies. As exemplified by Figure 5.8, the linear demand is more responsive to a price change when moving upward along the demand curve, because the price–quantity ratio increases as price increases and quantity demanded decreases. Thus, the higher the price the more elastic the demand. When moving downward along the demand curve, price decreases whereas quantity demanded increases. Thus, as the price–quantity ratio decreases, so does the price elasticity. Hence the lower the price on the demand curve the less elastic the demand. Given the linear demand function in Figure 5.9, we can obtain the abscissa and ordinate of the midpoint M, $Q_M = -b/2a$ and $P_M = b/2$, and therefore the price elasticity at the midpoint M can be calculated from formula (5.13):

$$\eta_M = \frac{1}{a}\frac{P_M}{Q_M} = \frac{1}{a}\left(\frac{b/2}{-b/2a}\right) = -1. \tag{5.14}$$

5.5.2 Price elasticity and firm revenue

On the one hand, if a firm faces an elastic demand, cutting price will lead to a disproportionately greater increase in quantity demanded, thus increasing firm revenue. For instance, in Figure 5.8, if the firm cuts price from \$13.5 to \$12, total revenue will increase from \$27 = \$13.5 × 2 to \$48 = \$12 × 4. On the other hand, if the demand is inelastic, raising price leads to a disproportionately smaller decrease in quantity demanded, thus also increasing firm revenue. In Figure 5.8, when raising the price from \$1.5 to \$3, total revenue will increase from $\$27=\$1.5\times18$ to $\$48=\$16\times3$. Since the demand curve is negatively sloped, the firm needs to trade off between charging a higher price and selling a greater quantity to increase total revenue. This decision depends entirely on the price elasticity of demand, other things being equal. To articulate the relationship between the price elasticity of demand and firm revenue, we introduce total revenue (R) function of the firm, which by definition is a product of the price (p) of a good and the quantity demanded (q):[5]

$$R=pq. \tag{5.15}$$

Intuitively, we know that the firm cannot raise or cut prices constantly to increase revenue due to the tradeoff between a higher price and a greater quantity. Behind this intuition is that increasing revenue entails cutting price in the elastic portion of the demand curve or raising price in the inelastic portion. Therefore, there must exist a tipping point on the linear demand curve at which either raising or cutting price only leads to a decrease in revenue monotonically. Hence the tipping point exhibits the revenue-maximizing price and quantity demanded. While there are economic solutions to identify this tipping point which we shall address in later chapters, a geometric solution is immediately available that requires no further economic reasoning. That is, in the triangle bounded by the demand curve and the two axes in Figure 5.9 we need to identify an inscribed rectangle whose area is maximized. Since the inscribed rectangle denotes total revenue based on the demand curve, the maximal inscribed rectangle represents the maximized total revenue.

To locate the total revenue rectangle, suppose that point M (q,p) is an arbitrary point on the linear demand curve $p=aq+b$ in Figure 5.9. Then the area of the inscribed rectangle is

$$R=pq=(aq+b)q=aq^2+bq. \tag{5.16}$$

Function (5.16) is a univariate quadratic function of q. Since $a<0$, total revenue R has a maximum, which is obtained by setting the derivative of R with respect to q to zero:

$$\frac{dR}{dq}=\frac{d\left(aq^2+bq\right)}{dq}=2aq+b=0. \tag{5.17}$$

Solving equation (5.17) we obtain $q=-b/2a$ first, and then $p=b/2$ from the inverse demand function introduced above. We thus proved that point M $(-b/2a,b/2)$ at which total revenue is maximized is indeed the midpoint of the linear demand curve (Figure 5.9). If the price is raised above $b/2$, the quantity demanded will decrease

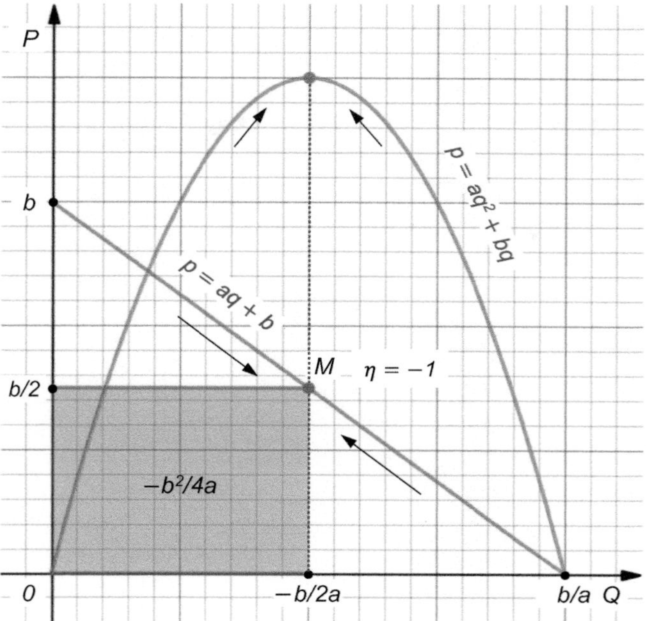

Figure 5.9
Price elasticity of demand and firm revenue

disproportionately more than the increase in price because the upper half of the demand curve is increasingly elastic, and hence total revenue decreases. If the price is cut to below $b/2$, the quantity demanded will increase disproportionately less than the decrease in price because the lower half of the demand curve is increasingly inelastic, and hence total revenue also falls.

Figure 5.9 shows that the curve of total revenue function (5.16) is a downward-opening parabola ($a < 0$). Thus, as the quantity demanded increases from zero, total revenue first increases until it reaches the vertex at which the demand becomes unit elastic, and then decreases as the quantity demanded continues to increase. As long as the price elasticity of demand is greater than 1, that is, the demand is elastic, the firm can continuously lower price to sell a disproportionately larger quantity, thus increasing revenue. As long as the price elasticity is smaller than 1, that is, the demand is inelastic, the firm can raise price which is associated with a disproportionately smaller decrease in quantity, thus also increasing revenue. Only when the percentage change in quantity demanded is equal to the percentage change in price, namely that demand is unit elastic, can total revenue be maximized. As far as linear demand is concerned, total revenue is maximized at the midpoint of the demand curve:

$$R = pq = \frac{b}{2}\left(\frac{-b}{2a}\right) = -\frac{b^2}{4a}. \quad (5.18)$$

Summary

1. The responsiveness of demand can be assessed using marginal demand and demand elasticity. Marginal demand is the change in the quantity demanded of a good divided by the change in a demand determinant. Elasticity of demand is the percentage change in the quantity demanded divided by the percentage change in the demand determinant.
2. Elasticity of demand is a unit-free measure of demand responsiveness, because the calculation of percentage changes cancels out measurement units. Elasticity of demand can be calculated in three ways: arc elasticity, midpoint elasticity, and point elasticity.
3. Elasticity of demand with respect to a demand determinant suggests the nature of the relationship between the two variables indicated by the sign of elasticity and the size of the effect of the demand determinant indicated by the absolute value of elasticity. When comparing the size of elasticity, we ignore the sign of elasticity.
4. When the percentage change in demand is greater than the percentage change in the demand determinant, elasticity is greater than 1, and hence demand is elastic. When percentage change in demand is smaller than the percentage change in the demand determinant, elasticity is smaller than 1, and hence demand is inelastic. When the two percentage changes are equal, demand is unit elastic.
5. The price elasticity of demand is the percentage change in quantity demanded divided by the percentage change in the price of a good. The demand for tourism products and services in general is elastic.
6. The income elasticity of demand is the percentage change in quantity demanded divided by the percentage change in consumer income. Using income elasticity we can distinguish between inferior goods and normal goods, and further divide normal goods into necessities and luxuries. Tourism products and services in general are luxuries.
7. The cross-price elasticity of demand is the percentage change in the quantity demanded of a good divided by the percentage change in the price of a related good. Using cross-price elasticity we can assess whether the two goods are substitutes or complements.
8. The price elasticity of demand decreases monotonically when moving downward along the linear demand curve and increases when moving upward. Separated by the midpoint of the linear demand curve at which demand is unit elastic, the upper half of the demand curve is elastic while the lower half is inelastic.
9. There is a tradeoff between charging a higher price and selling a larger quantity, dictated by the law of demand. There exists a unique pair of price–quantity coordinates on the linear demand curve, which is the midpoint, at which the firm maximizes total revenue.
10. When demand is elastic, cutting price ends up increasing revenue; when demand is inelastic, raising price ends up increasing revenue as well. Total revenue is maximized at the midpoint of the linear demand curve because the demand is unit elastic.

REVIEW QUESTIONS

Each question has four options, and there is only one correct answer to each question.

1. If the price elasticity of demand for McDonald's Big Mac is 0.8, which of the following is correct?
   A) If price decreased by \$1, the quantity demanded would increase by 0.8 units.
   B) If price increased by \$0.8, the quantity demanded would decrease by 1 unit.
   C) If price decreased by 1%, the quantity demanded would increase by 0.8%.
   D) If price increased by 0.8%, the quantity demanded would decrease by 1%.
2. Suppose that the price elasticity of demand for a movie is constant at 1.5, and 5,000 tickets are sold per week at a certain price per ticket. If the price of the movie ticket increased by 20%, what would be the number of tickets sold each week?
   A) 2,500
   B) 3,500
   C) 4,000
   D) 4,500
3. If we know the arc elasticity of two points on a demand curve is 1.5, which of the following is correct regarding the midpoint elasticity of the two points?
   A) The midpoint elasticity must be greater than 1.5.
   B) The midpoint elasticity must be smaller than 1.5.
   C) The midpoint elasticity must be equal to 1.5.
   D) None of the above.
4. Suppose that the price elasticity of demand for coffee is 0.5 and for movies is 0.9. Which of the following is correct?
   A) The demand for coffee is more elastic than for movies.
   B) The demand for coffee is inelastic while for movies is elastic.
   C) The price elasticity of coffee is greater than that of movies.
   D) The price elasticity of coffee is smaller than that of movies.
5. Suppose that the market demand for a good is perfectly elastic. If supply increased by 200 units, other things being equal, what would be the change in the equilibrium quantity?
   A) Increased by less than 200 units.
   B) Increased by more than 200 units.
   C) Increased by exact 200 units.
   D) All of the above.
6. The figure below shows that the relationships between consumers' income and their demand for goods X_1, X_2, and X_3 are represented by three straight lines from

the origin, I_1, I_2, and I_3, respectively. Note that I_1 is a 45-degree ray. Other things being equal, which of the following is correct?

A) X_1 is a normal good.
B) X_2 is a necessity.
C) X_3 is a luxury.
D) All of the above.

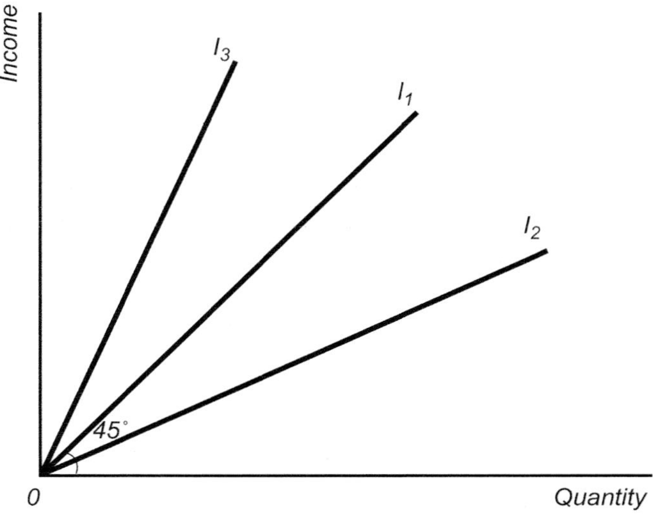

7. Suppose we observed in Paris in a certain period of time that the relationship between the admission fee of the Louvre and visits to the Eiffel Tower is positive, other things being equal. Which of the following is correct regarding the two attractions?
   A) They are substitutes.
   B) They are complements.
   C) Both are normal goods.
   D) Both are luxury goods.
8. Suppose that the demands of leisure travelers (D_L) and business travelers (D_B) for airline tickets from Geneva to Paris are both linear, as shown in the graph below. In order to maximize revenue, how much should the airline charge leisure and business travelers, respectively?
   A) \$100; \$200
   B) \$200; \$300
   C) \$100; \$300
   D) \$200; \$400

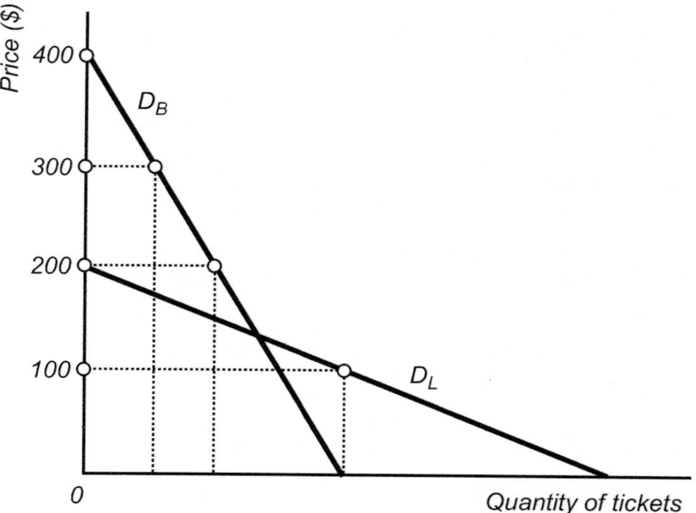

9. Based on a research report about the coffee market, a manager of a coffee shop decides to increase the price of a type of coffee in order to increase revenue. What information would the research report have provided to the manager?
   A) The coffee must be a normal good.
   B) The coffee must be an inferior good.
   C) The demand for the coffee must be elastic.
   D) The demand for the coffee must be inelastic.
10. Suppose that a firm faces a linear demand curve. If the firm increases the price of its product from \$10 to \$15 per unit, the quantity demanded would decrease by 50%. At which price (p) would total revenue be maximized?
   A) $p = \$10$
   B) $\$10 < p < \$15$
   C) $p = \$15$
   D) $p > \$15$

Problem solving

1. Many countries charge a tourist tax, which is an amount of money that visitors need to pay to enter or leave a destination country or for certain consumptions in the country. The tax revenue is usually used to finance the construction and maintenance of tourism infrastructure as well as to protect natural resources. The tourist tax is levied in two ways. One is the so-called arrival or departure tax, levied on tourists upon arrival in or before departure from a destination country. For instance, each international visitor entering New Zealand will have to pay 35 New Zealand

dollars (US$23.94); each international visitor leaving Japan needs to pay 1,000 yen (US$9.25).[6] The other one is city tax levied on visitors for certain consumptions at a destination. For instance, the canton of Basel-Stadt in Switzerland charges 4 Swiss francs (US$4.42) per visitor per night in accommodation establishments.[7] Suppose that tourists would have to pay the same amount of either an arrival or departure tax or a city tax. Other things being equal, explain why the city tax might be superior to the arrival or departure tax from a destination's point of view.

2. There is a conjecture in economics known as the Alchian-Allen theorem, named after American economists Armen A. Alchian (1914–2013) and William R. Allen (1924–). The theorem would imply that "Australians drink higher-quality Californian wine [more] than Californians, and vice-versa, because it is only worth the transportation costs for the most expensive wine."[8] Suppose that there are two wines, *A* and *B*, produced in California and shipped to supermarkets in Sydney where they are sold at $35 and $55 per bottle, respectively. Now suppose that the shipping cost increases by $5 per bottle which applies to both wines. Thus, the supermarkets add the shipping cost to the prices of the two wines accordingly. If consumers in Sydney could choose either one and their income does not change, how would you explain why wine *B* would be shipped out for Australians while wine *A* would be retained in California for local consumption?
3. Suppose that British Airways decides to offer a 10% discount on a scheduled flight between London and Geneva. According to market research, British Airways knows that its customers can be divided into two segments: Segment *A*, customers booking the ticket online; and Segment *B*, customers booking offline (e.g., booking via travel agencies). Moreover, these two segments differ in their likely responses to the price discount, represented by the number of tickets that would be bought with and without the discount as shown in the table below. Assuming that both segments were charged the same price before the discount, other things being equal, to which segment(s) should the discount be offered?

With and without the 10% discount	Segment A	Segment B
Tickets would be bought without the discount	15,000	15,500
Tickets would be bought with the discount	17,000	16,500

Solutions to all review questions and problem solving tasks are included in the Support Material for this book, which can be accessed at www.routledge.com/9780367897352.

Notes

1 Note that the inverse demand function (4.8) introduced in Chapter 4 is the demand function of an individual consumer. In this chapter we focus on the demand function of all consumers in the market, namely the market demand function. Therefore, we use market demand Q and price P to replace q and p for the individual consumer in the function, other things being equal.

2 Giffen goods and Veblen goods are two exceptions. Please refer to Chapter 6 for an explanation of Veblen goods. We will not discuss Giffen goods in this book.
3 Nonlinear demand is beyond the scope of this book.
4 To apply formula (5.10), we need to know the marginal demand dQ / dP first. For linear demand, the marginal demand is constant, which is the reciprocal of the slope of the linear demand curve $dP / dQ = -3 / 4$. Thus, the elasticity at the midpoint M in Figure 5.8 is $\eta = (dQ / dP)(P / Q) = (-4 / 3) \times (7.5 / 10) = -1$.
5 We use q and p here to label quantity and price, respectively, because we address one individual firm instead of the quantity and the price in the market.
6 *Insider.* 41 countries around the world that charge a tourist tax. February 27, 2019.
7 Basel Tourism. City tax. Retrieved on August 28, 2020 from https://www.basel.com/en/City-tax.
8 *The Financial Times*. Dear economist. November 24, 2006.

Bibliography

Allen, R. G. D., & Lerner, A. P. (1934). The concept of arc elasticity of demand. *Review of Economic Studies, 1*(3), 226–230.
Anderson, P. L., McLellan, R., Overton, J. P., & Wolfram, G. (1997). *The universal tuition tax credit: A proposal to advance parental choice in education*. Midland, MI: Mackinac Center for Public Policy.
Colen, L., & Swinnen, J. (2016). Economic growth, globalisation and beer consumption. *Journal of Agricultural Economics, 67*(1), 186–207.
Lerner, A. P. (1933). The diagrammatical representation of elasticity of demand. *Review of Economic Studies, 1*(1), 39–44.
Marshall, A. (1890). *Principles of economics*. Peter Groenewegen, 2013. Reprint.
Song, H., Wong, K. K., & Chon, K. K. (2003). Modelling and forecasting the demand for Hong Kong tourism. *International Journal of Hospitality Management, 22*(4), 435–451.

6 Network effects in market demand

This chapter extends consumer demand discussed in Chapters 4 and 5 that is primarily examined on an individual basis to market demand. In particular, we analyze the non-additivity of market demand in which the market demand is not equal to the aggregation of demands over individual consumers. This is due to network effects in consumer behavior leading individual demand to be interdependent rather than independent. We focus on analyzing the influence of three network effects, namely the bandwagon effect, the snob effect, and the Veblen effect, on market demand. Based on the demand curves for the bandwagon, snob and Veblen good, we distinguish between the functional and nonfunctional demand of consumers. Because of nonfunctional demand, individual consumption morphs into a social activity, which sheds light on articulating the social benefits of tourism consumption. We conclude this chapter with a discussion on consumer information and belief whereby the network effects are transmitted from one consumer to another.

AFTER STUDYING THIS CHAPTER, YOU SHOULD BE ABLE TO:

- Understand the influence of network effects on market demand and the non-additivity of market demand;
- Analyze three network effects, namely the bandwagon effect, the snob effect, and the Veblen effect, and derive the associated demand curves;
- Understand and analyze the functional demand and nonfunctional demand associated with the three network effects; and
- Understand the importance of consumer information and belief in the construction of the demand curves associated with the three network effects.

6.1 Individual demand versus market demand

Consumer theory which we have discussed heretofore is grounded, implicitly, on the assumption that one individual's consumption or demand is independent of the demand of another. This means that a consumer bases his decision of what and how much of a good to purchase on the inherent quality of the good with no regard to peer influence. This assumption is the cornerstone in neoclassical economic models that aims to simplify the complex reality. Yet some neoclassical economists in the nineteenth century, including Alfred Marshall, were well aware that consumption has its social connotation, and hence each consumer's demand is interdependent in a society. American economist Thorstein Veblen (1857–1929), among others, formally asserts that the value of a good will increase beyond its immanent quality insofar as consumption becomes a means for people to flaunt wealth and impress others. This was the phenomenon of conspicuous consumption in the late nineteenth century when consumption morphed more or less into a social activity. If one consumer's demand for a good depends, in part, on the demand of others, it follows that, other things being equal, the consumer's demand for the good is subject to change due to peer influence. Therefore, the market demand for the good will behave differently from the one in the absence of peer influence.

6.1.1 Additivity in market demand

In deriving the demand curve in Chapter 4 we focused on consumer optimization by examining the demand of only one consumer in the market. If all consumers make their decisions independently on how much to purchase based on the market price of a good, other things being equal, we can simply aggregate the demands of all individual consumers to derive the market demand for the good. The market demand thus suggests the relationship between the price of the good in the market and the aggregate quantity demanded over all consumers in the market. For expository convenience, consider a market with two consumers, 1 and 2, whose demands for a good are denoted as d_1 and d_2, respectively, if they make their decisions independently. Figure 6.1 shows that the market demand is simply a summation of the two individual demands, $D = d_1 + d_2$, at each corresponding price of the good. Obviously, we can extend the two-consumer market to the n-consumer market ($n > 2$) in the same vein. Assuming that each consumer has the same demand d, the market demand will be $D = nd$, which describes the relationship between the price of the good and the aggregate quantity demanded over the n consumers in the market.

An implicit assumption underlying the summation of individual demands to derive the market demand is that one consumer has no influence on the other in his consumption, and vice versa. On the one hand, the addition of individual demand to construct market demand takes root in the methodology of neoclassical economics, in which each consumer is deemed as a separate and atomistic agent acting to maximize his utility directly from a good he consumes. Since demand is individualistic, market demand is simply an addition of all individual demands in the market. Such an additive market demand can simplify the model of collective behavior because it takes no account of peer influence which would complicate economic analysis. In the above aggregation (Figure 6.1), consumers 1 and 2 have two different demands which are linear as assumed, the market demand curve is kinked at point K, suggesting that the market demand starts diverting from the linear form due to the aggregation but it is always determinate and predictable from the individual demands. On the other hand,

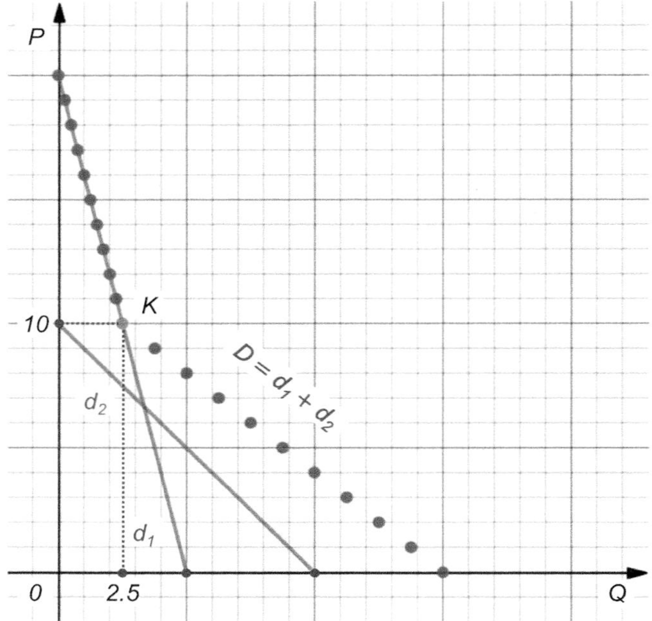

Figure 6.1
Additivity in market demand

if peer influence is pervasive in consumption, the nature of the market demand will be altered. Individual consumers will adjust their demand based on their expectation of the market demand, and hence individual demand depends in part on the market demand.

6.1.2 Demand interdependence and non-additivity

There are situations where one consumer's demand depends in part on the demand of another, and then the summation of individual demands to derive the market demand will not apply. In the above case suppose that consumer 2 knows accurately that the quantity demanded by consumer 1 will be 2.5 units when price is $10. He thus increases his demand from zero, which he would demand independently, to 1 unit owing to the influence of consumer 1 (Figure 6.1). Thus, the additional unit demanded of consumer 2 is not due to the good per se but consumer 1's demand. Hence consumer 2's demand is a function of not only the price of the good but also consumer 1's demand. Other things being equal, when the price is $10, the market demand ends up with 3.5 units instead of 2.5 units. Thus, the market demand will not equal the sum of the demands of consumers 1 and 2 when they behave interdependently. Then the market demand is referred to as non-additive. The same logic holds true for consumer 1 whose demand can be influenced by consumer 2's, and is thus in part a function of consumer 2's demand. Note that the peer influence of the two consumers can also be negative, and hence the market demand will be smaller than the sum of their respective demands.

Suppose that d_1^a and d_2^a are the demands of consumers 1 and 2, respectively, if they base their decisions on the expectation that the market demand will end up at a units. Thus, d_1^a and d_2^a describe the relationships between their respective willingness to pay and the quantity demanded by taking into account the market demand a. Now we aggregate d_1^a and d_2^a at each price to obtain the market demand $D^a = d_1^a + d_2^a$, which is conditional on a units. If both consumers expect the market demand to be b units ($a < b$), they will adjust their demand accordingly based on b, denoted as d_1^b and d_2^b, respectively. In this case, the market demand becomes $D^b = d_1^b + d_2^b$ conditional on b units. If the change in the market demand did not affect individual demand, namely that a and b have no impact on their demand at all, we would have $d_1^a = d_1^b = d_1$ for consumer 1 and $d_2^a = d_2^b = d_2$ for consumer 2. Hence $D^a = D^b = D$ in which consumer expectation of the market demand is irrelevant. However, if the change in the market demand affected individual demand, we would have $d_1^a < d_1^b$ or $d_1^a > d_1^b$ for consumer 1 and $d_2^a < d_2^b$ or $d_2^a > d_2^b$ for consumer 2 at each price, depending on whether the market demand affected individual demand positively or negatively, and hence $D^a \neq D^b \neq D$. The discrepancy between D^a and D^b is thus accounted for by the change in the market demand, $b-a$, which is independent of the price of the good.

To illustrate this idea, suppose that consumer demand is positively affected by the market demand expected by consumers. Figure 6.2 shows that by holding the price constant at p_0, the market demand will increase from D^a to D^b, and hence D^b is parallel to D^a to its right. If consumers expect the market demand to be c units ($a < b < c$), the market demand curve will shift rightward to D^c conditional on c units. Nevertheless, the marginal demand with respect to price across the three market demands D^a, D^b, and D^c is the same as it describes the same consumers responding to a certain price change

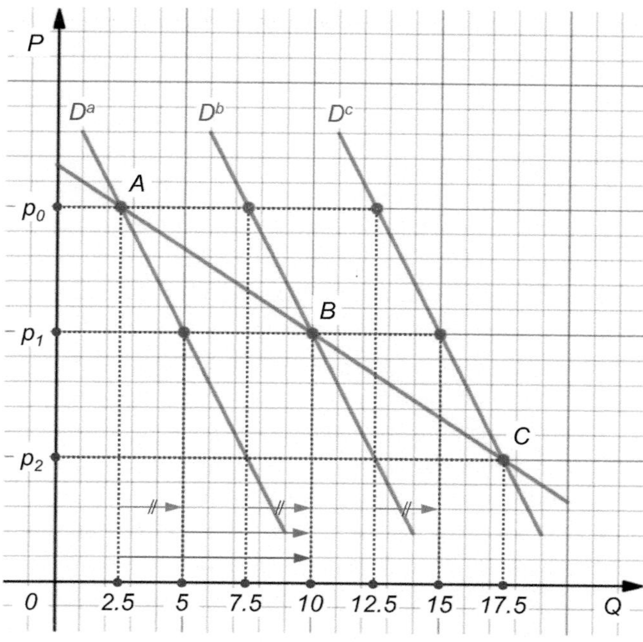

Figure 6.2
Non-additivity in market demand

in the market, other things being equal. For instance, if we let the price fall from p_0 to p_1 in Figure 6.2, the marginal demand increases by 2.5 units on D^a, which is the same as on D^b and D^c. Yet by taking into account the increase in the market demand from a to b, the same decrease in price from p_0 to p_1 corresponds to an increase of 7.5 units from point A to point B (Figure 6.2), which consists of a marginal demand with respect to price, 2.5 units, and an increase of 5 units owing to consumers' positive response to the change in the market demand from a to b. If we further lower the price from p_1 to p_2 (Figure 6.2), the quantity demanded will end up with 17.5 units on D^c by factoring in the increase in the market demand from b to c at the same time.

6.1.3 Network externality and network effects

Demand interdependence illustrated above occurs because consumers can obtain a type of utility generated from their fellows' consumption of a good that is beyond the immanent utility of the good per se. For instance, consumers may gravitate to one restaurant bustling with guests yet are lukewarm about another nearby offering exactly the same cuisine yet with empty seats. Since the inherent quality of the cuisines and, for this matter, of all other ancillary services rendered by the two restaurants can be seen as the same, both restaurants would presumably obtain the same popularity among consumers if consumers only valued the cuisines. As far as peer influence is concerned, one explanation for the seemingly irrational consumption is that the bustling restaurant, due to guest crowds sitting inside or lining up outside, generates additional utility for prospective consumers to patronize. Such utility could include, but is not limited to, a kind of gratification when one's taste conforms to others' beyond the cuisine per se. Other things being equal, the more the guests sitting in or waiting in the line, the more utility consumers can obtain and the greater the market demand. Thus, each consumer's utility depends not only on the cuisine he himself consumes but also on others who are consuming it or are about to consume.

The restaurant example suggests that there exists an externality in consumption. An externality can be a benefit that a consumer generates to others through his consumption, but he is not reimbursed for the benefit by the beneficiaries. It can also be a cost that the consumer brings about to others but does not compensate those who are affected by his behavior. Insofar as externality is associated with the number of consumers in the market or the quantity of a good demanded, it is referred to as network externality. Network externality in demand suggests that an individual's demand is influenced by the demand of others, and the more the consumers the larger the peer influence, or the network effects.[1] American economist Harvey Leibenstein (1922–1994) was the first to formulate the idea of network effects in consumer demand. He classifies three types of network effects depending on their directions and the underlying causes. A positive network effect, also known as the bandwagon effect, suggests that a consumer's demand changes in the same direction as the demand of others. By contrast, a negative network effect, also known as the snob effect, suggests that a consumer's demand changes in the opposite direction to the demand of others. Consumers also respond to the value of a good placed by others who may or may not be the consumers of the good themselves, which is known as the Veblen effect named after Thorstein Veblen.

6.2 Network effects and market demand

6.2.1 Bandwagon effect

The bandwagon effect is a metaphor of the positive network effect, suggesting that spectators are inclined to jump on a bandwagon in a parade to conform to others' behavior, or to keep up with the Joneses. Suppose that the initial demand curve D^a is the market demand when consumers anticipate perfectly that the quantity demanded of a good in the market will end up as a (Figure 6.3). Assuming that one consumer buys only one unit of the good, a is also the number of consumers in the market, or the consumer base. Hence the demand curve D^a describes the relationship between the price of the good and the quantity demanded in the market by taking into account the consumer base a. However, only one point exists on the demand curve D^a that manifests the market price and the quantity at which the good is demanded, which is the equilibrium demand. Given consumers' perfect anticipation of the consumer base a, the equilibrium demand E^a is determined such that the quantity demanded in the market ends up being equal to consumers' anticipation of a (Figure 6.3). On the other hand, if consumers anticipate that market demand will be greater, say b ($a < b$), the market demand curve will shift rightward from D^a to D^b, suggesting that the market demand increases due to the increase in consumer base from a to b. Likewise, the equilibrium on the demand curve D^b ends up being E^b, which is determined such that the quantity demanded in the market is equal to consumers' perfect anticipation of the market demand to be b.

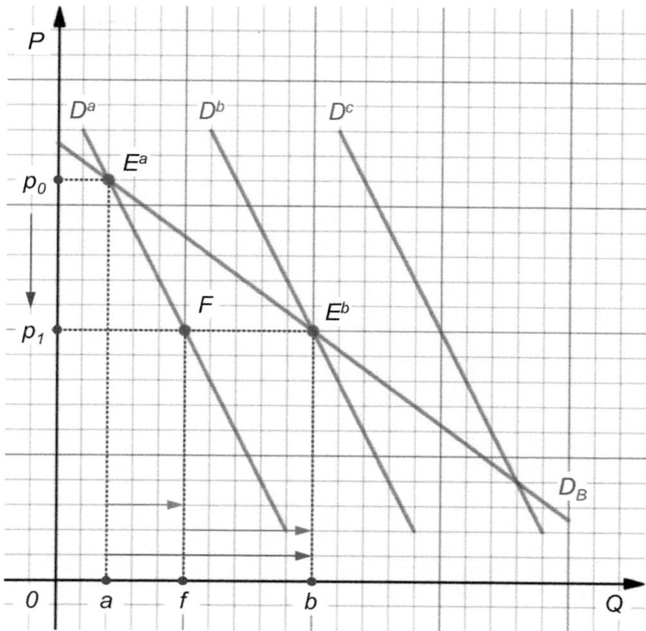

Figure 6.3
Demand for the bandwagon good

We therefore obtain the demand curve for the bandwagon good, D_B, by connecting the equilibrium demands E^a (a, p_0) and E^b (b, p_1) as opposed to the initial demand curve D^a (Figure 6.3). If consumers anticipate that the market demand will end up at c $(a < b < c)$, D_B will also cross the demand curve D^c, and so on (Figure 6.3). If the price falls from p_0 to p_1, the quantity demanded increases from a to b along the bandwagon demand curve D_B, which is referred to as total price effect. The total price effect is composed of two sub-effects. First, holding the consumer base constant at a, the quantity demanded increases from a to f, exhibiting a movement downward from the equilibrium demand E^a to point F along D^a. The increase of $f - a$ is solely caused by the price change of $p_1 - p_0$, and hence is called the pure price effect. Second, holding the price constant at p_1, the quantity demanded further increases from f to b due to a rightward shift in the demand curve from D^a to D^b. The increase of $b - f$ is due to the increase in consumer base from a to b that generates the bandwagon effect, and hence is called the bandwagon effect. Compared to the initial demand curve D^a, the bandwagon demand curve D_B is more elastic. A price decrease leads both to a pure price effect and a bandwagon effect that act in the same direction, thereby reinforcing each other in affecting market demand. Hence, market demand becomes more responsive to price changes.

Bandwagon effects in tourism were evidenced vividly by Thomas Cook's first package tour mentioned in Chapter 1. Figure 6.4 shows what this tour could look like as a scene. Not only were the pioneer tourists beaming with extraordinary excitement and jubilation on the train rally between Leicester and Loughborough, but the spectators were as excited as the tourists, hoping to embark on the same trip that featured the train as the iconic transport in industrial England. It is not surprising that these spectators would sooner or later become tourists, not least because of the influence of the pioneers who made recreational tours socially desirable. It turns out that one person joining the tour would entice others to join, thereby making the tour even more appealing

Figure 6.4
First package tour in England in 1841

Source: Thomas Cook Archives at the Record Office for Leicestershire, Leicester and Rutland.

to the masses. Had the first package tour been taken unobtrusively with no regard to the peer influence, Thomas Cook could not have amassed thousands upon thousands of people joining his tour groups in a very short period of time. As a matter of fact, Thomas Cook himself had proactively been creating such bandwagon through various marketing and advertising campaigns before the tour. The tourism boom in the late nineteenth century was in part due to the fact that temperance activists as the first batch of tourists were emulated by the leisure class who in turn were emulated by the masses in performing recreational travel. This eventually led to the popularization of package tours across Europe in the late nineteenth and early twentieth centuries.

6.2.2 Snob effect

In contrast to the bandwagon effect, the snob effect suggests that consumers' demand increases (decreases) in the market as the demand of others decreases (increases). It metaphorically suggests that some people are inclined to search for exclusiveness or disconfirm from others, and are thus called snobs. Still suppose that the demand curve for a good is D^a if consumers anticipate perfectly that the market demand will end up at a (Figure 6.5). Thus, the equilibrium demand E^a is manifested such that the quantity demanded in the market is equal to consumers' anticipation of the market demand a, which corresponds to the price p_0 at which the good is demanded. If consumers anticipate that the market demand will be greater, say b ($a < b$), the market demand curve will shift leftward from D^a to D^b (Figure 6.5). This suggests that the market demand for the snob good, by definition, decreases as the consumer base increases

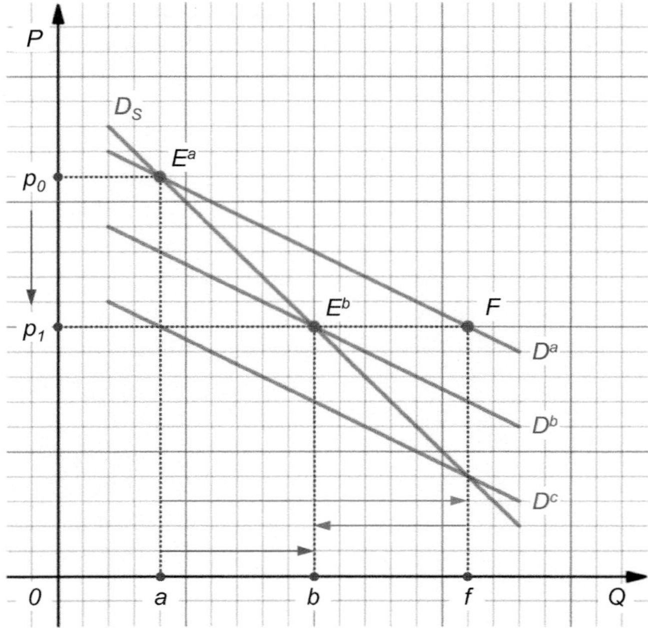

Figure 6.5
Demand for the snob good

from a to b, and therefore is in opposition to the bandwagon effect. On the demand curve D^b, the new equilibrium demand ends up at E^b, at which the quantity demanded in the market ends up matching consumers' anticipation of the market demand at b. By the same token, we can derive the demand curve for the snob good, denoted as D_S, which passes through the two equilibrium demands E^a (a, p_0) and E^b (b, p_1) as opposed to the initial demand curve D^a which has no change in consumer base.

If the price falls from p_o to p_1, the quantity demanded for the snob good increases from a to b along the snob demand curve D_S, which is referred to as total price effect (Figure 6.5). Likewise, a total price effect can be decomposed into a pure price effect and a snob effect. First, holding the consumer base constant at a, the pure price effect is manifested as an increase in the quantity demanded from a to f, denoted by a movement downward from the equilibrium demand E^a to point F along D^a. Second, holding the price constant at p_1, the snob effect is manifested as a decrease in the quantity demanded from f to b, due to the increase in consumer base from a to b which renders the good less socially desirable. Therefore, the size of the snob effect is the magnitude of the shift in the market demand curve from D^a to D^b. The total price effect, $b-a$, is the sum of the pure price effect $f-a$ and the snob effect $b-f$. Compared with the initial demand curve D^a with no change in consumer base, the snob demand curve D_S becomes less elastic. This property is due to the fact that the pure price effect is, in part, offset by the snob effect that exercises in the opposite direction. Since a price decrease leads to disproportionately less of an increase in quantity demanded than it otherwise would, the demand for a snob good becomes less responsive to price changes.

Snob effects can explain the lifecycle of tourist destinations, specifically why a destination may lose its popularity at a certain stage and be superseded by new ones. Figure 6.6 shows the travel brochures published by Thomas Cook & Son, which featured different destinations or travel modes between the 1900s and 1950s. By the time vacationists were flooding streets across England, presumably some, especially the well-heeled leisure class, might no longer be interested in traveling around England and instead ventured to Scotland, Switzerland, and Italy. Figure 6.6a shows that Thomas Cook was promoting a European continental tour and steamer sailing in 1902. Thus, vacationing in the continent might have become a new bandwagon in the early 1900s while touring England presumably ended up being a snob effect. Figure 6.6b shows that the continental vacation might have lost its popularity to tropical destinations in Africa and South America in the 1920s, and thus became a snob effect at least for some European tourists. By the 1950s train travel, which used to be a bandwagon in the nineteenth century, might have morphed into a snob effect after being supplanted by air travel as shown in Figure 6.6c. In the meantime, seaside excursions in England gave way to long-haul trips to the Mediterranean which was within arm's reach by flight. Thus, the rise and fall of destinations is driven in sequence by the bandwagon and snob effects.

6.2.3 Veblen effect

The idea of Veblen goods was propounded by Thorstein Veblen to address a type of unconventional consumption practiced by the burgeoning British leisure class in the late nineteenth century. This consumption, known as conspicuous consumption,

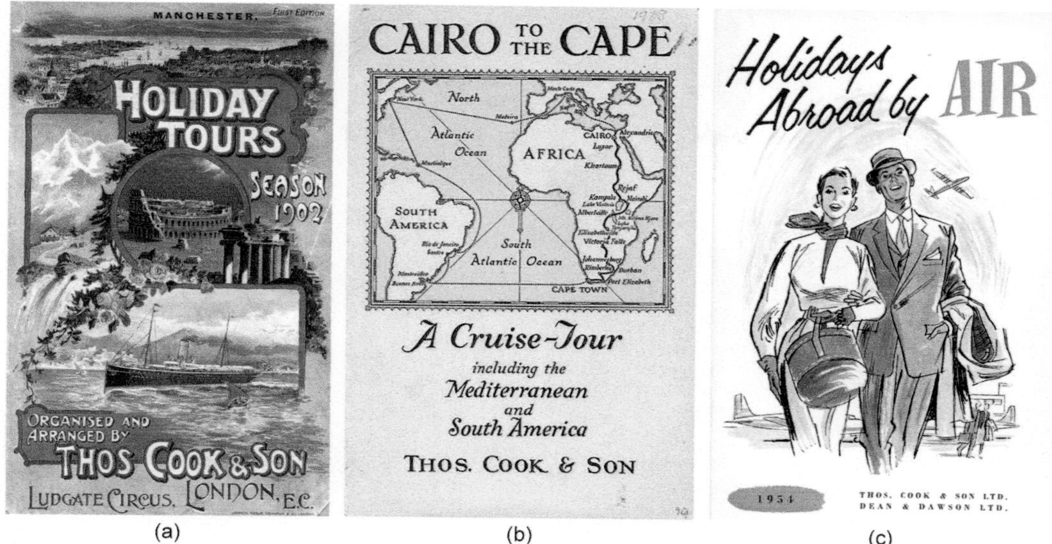

(a) (b) (c)

Figure 6.6
Travel brochure archives from Thomas Cook & Son

Source: Thomas Cook Archives at the Record Office for Leicestershire, Leicester and Rutland.

seemingly contradicts what rational behavior models predict. That is, the demand for Veblen goods may, due to peer influence, increase as price rises, *ceteris paribus*. Veblen goods have two distinct yet mutually dependent features. On the one hand, Veblen goods are, or are believed to be, prohibitive: an indication of expensiveness that consumers think other people would attach to the goods. On the other hand, Veblen goods are futile, which refers to their inappreciable functionality to consumers. Among the most notable Veblen goods were, as Veblen himself exemplified, high heels in the late nineteenth century. In the first place, the expensiveness of high heels singles out the upper class who are consumers from the working class who are not. In the second place, high heels signify that the upper class are liberated from the drudgery that the working class routinely perform, as the shoes encumber people in performing chores and work. Therefore, high heels are futile in terms of functionality as shoes but are socially desired by consumers to create social distinctions (Figure 6.7). Insofar as social benefits dominate over the functionality, high heels as shoes become inappreciable.

Suppose that the initial demand curve for a Veblen good is D^1 on the condition that consumers believe that the good has a conspicuous price p_1^C, which is the expensiveness of the good perceived by others (Figure 6.8). Hence the demand curve D^1 depicts the relationship between the market price of the good and the quantity demanded under the conspicuous price p_1^C. If consumers have perfect knowledge of the price, the conspicuous price will converge to the market price at which the good is demanded. There exists a unique point on D^1 at which the market price p_1 ends up being equal to the conspicuous price p_1^C, whereby the quantity demanded in the market is determined. This point is the equilibrium demand E^1 for the Veblen good under the conspicuous price p_1^C (Figure 6.8). The reason is that if p_1 is different from p_1^C,

Figure 6.7
Women dressed extravagantly in Victorian England

Source: James Tissot. The Gallery of HMS 'Calcutta' (Portsmouth), 1876, Tate, London.

consumers will always adjust the quantity demanded to a point on the demand curve D^1 at which $p_1 = p_1^C$. As the conspicuous price increases from p_1^C to p_2^C ($p_1^C < p_2^C$), by definition the demand curve will shift rightward from D^1 to D^2 (Figure 6.8), indicating that the market demand increases because the good becomes more conspicuous and entices consumers. By the same token, the equilibrium demand E^2 is determined such that the market price p_2 equals the conspicuous price p_2^C, a higher level of expensiveness. Thus, the demand curve D^2 depicts the relationship between the market price and the quantity demanded when the good is perceived to have the conspicuous price of p_2^C. If consumers believe that the good is even more expensive and conspicuous, the demand curve will further shift rightward from D^2 to D^3 and so on (Figure 6.8).

We can derive the demand curve for the Veblen good, D_V, by connecting the equilibrium demands E^1 (q_1, p_1) and E^2 (q_V, p_2) as opposed to D^1 with no change in conspicuous price (Figure 6.8). If the market price increases from p_1 to p_2, the quantity demanded for the Veblen good increases from q_1 to q_V along D_V, which is referred to as total price effect. The total price effect consists of a pure price effect and a Veblen effect. First, conditional on the conspicuous price p_1^C, the quantity demanded decreases from q_1 to q_2 along D^1 due to the increase in the market price from p_1 to p_2, suggesting the pure price effect. Second, holding the market price constant at p_2, the quantity demanded increases from q_2 to q_V due to the increase in the conspicuous price from p_1^C to p_2^C, suggesting the Veblen effect. The conspicuous price is the principal reason for consumers to increase demand, and hence the Veblen effect is different from the bandwagon and snob effects by its cause. Counterintuitively, a price increase leads to an increase in the

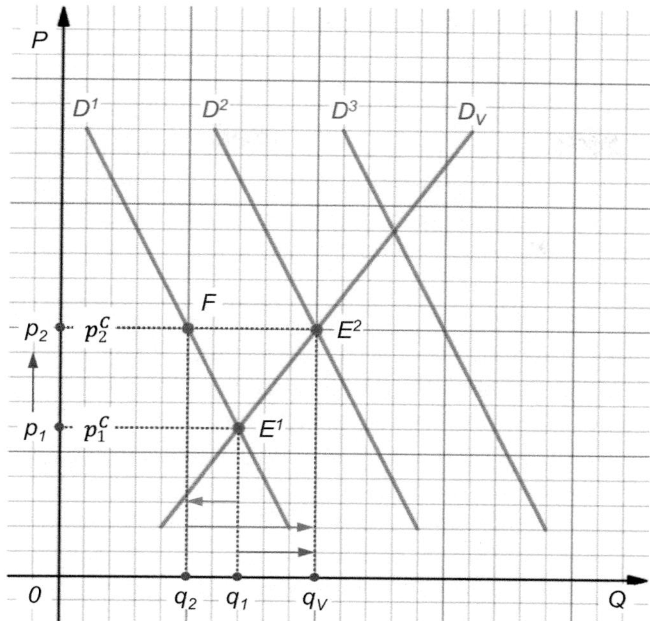

Figure 6.8
Demand for the Veblen good

quantity demanded for Veblen goods, because the Veblen effect usually outstrips the pure price effect that acts in the opposite direction. Therefore, Veblen goods, above anything else, are canonically featured by an upward-sloping demand curve[2] in contrast to the demands for bandwagon and snob goods. Note that the Veblen demand curve can still slope downward insofar as the Veblen effect is smaller than the pure price effect.

The consumption of the upper class and nobilities in Victorian England was featured by the procuring of sophisticated goods which have inexpensive alternatives. For instance, tableware was made of silver and exquisite porcelain, opulent lace was used in dresses, and high heels were favored by ladies, all of which became a means for the upper class to flaunt wealth and manifest their superior social status. As a matter of fact, the functionality of these articles was of little difference from inexpensive alternatives used by the masses. Leisure was also one notable example of the Veblen goods at that time. On the one hand, for laborers or wage workers leisure is unproductive labor and is thus futile as opposed to work. On the other hand, those who can afford to squander time on leisure achieve a high social status by distinguishing themselves from the working class. Thus, for the upper class the social benefits of leisure outstrip the income generated from the same amount of work time. Nowadays extravagant foreign travel can also be seen as a Veblen good due to its expensiveness and futility as opposed to work or anything useful. Veblen goods do not in any way opine on the absolute futility but on the fact that the pronounced Veblen effect renders their functionality negligible. In fact, any good could have some sort of Veblen effect as long as its conspicuous price positively affects the consumption of the good in the market.

6.3 Nonfunctional demand and utility

6.3.1 Functional demand versus nonfunctional demand

The reason that network effects exist in consumer demand rests on the fact that consumer utility of a good depends on the demand of other consumers in one way or another in addition to the good per se. This gives rise to the classification of functional demand and nonfunctional demand in the market. Functional demand is consumer demand for a good that is attributed to the intrinsic functionality of the good, which brings about functional utility to consumers. For instance, a burger is consumed because it relieves the consumer's hunger, and so is a cola to quench his thirst, both exemplifying the immanent utility of the goods to the consumer. Thus, functional demand for a good exists on its own right without depending on the presence of other people consuming the good in a social context. The orthodox theory of consumer demand that we addressed in Chapters 4 and 5 is constructed exclusively on functional demand. By contrast, nonfunctional demand is consumer demand for a good that is attributed to factors other than its intrinsic functionality. Probably the most important source of nonfunctional demand is the three network effects discussed above. As far as a network effect is concerned, nonfunctional demand suggests that consumption is no longer individualistic but morphs into a social activity in which one individual's consumption of a good becomes the reason for others to consume the good.

Both for bandwagon and snob goods, nonfunctional demand arises due to the change in consumer base that endows the goods with a social benefit beyond their functionality. For Veblen goods, nonfunctional demand is associated with the conspicuous price of the goods which in turn is due to the fact that consumption is a social activity. In other words, conspicuous price would not matter at all if consumption itself were individualistic with no regard to how one's consumption is judged by others. Suppose that the initial demand for a bandwagon good, snob good, and Veblen good is the same, denoted by D^0 in Figure 6.9. We can readily derive their corresponding demand curves D_B, D_S, and D_V against the initial demand D^0. For all three goods, as the price decreases from p_0 to p_1, the quantity demanded will increase from q_0 to q_1 along D^0, suggesting that the same functional demand for the three goods is accounted for by the same pure price effect (Figure 6.9). For the bandwagon good, the nonfunctional demand increases from q_1 to q_B, which is accounted for by the bandwagon effect, because the increased consumer base renders the good more socially desirable. For the snob good, the nonfunctional demand decreases from q_1 to q_S which is accounted for by the snob effect in the sense that the increased consumer base renders the good less socially desirable.

Similarly to the snob good, the nonfunctional demand for the Veblen good also decreases, but from q_1 to q_V ($q_V < q_0 < q_S$). There are two differences concerning nonfunctional demand for the Veblen good and for the snob good. First, the change in the nonfunctional demand for the Veblen good is due to the change in conspicuous price instead of the change in consumer base. That is, nonfunctional demand decreases for the Veblen good because the good becomes less conspicuous. Second, the decrease in the nonfunctional demand for the Veblen good usually overtakes the

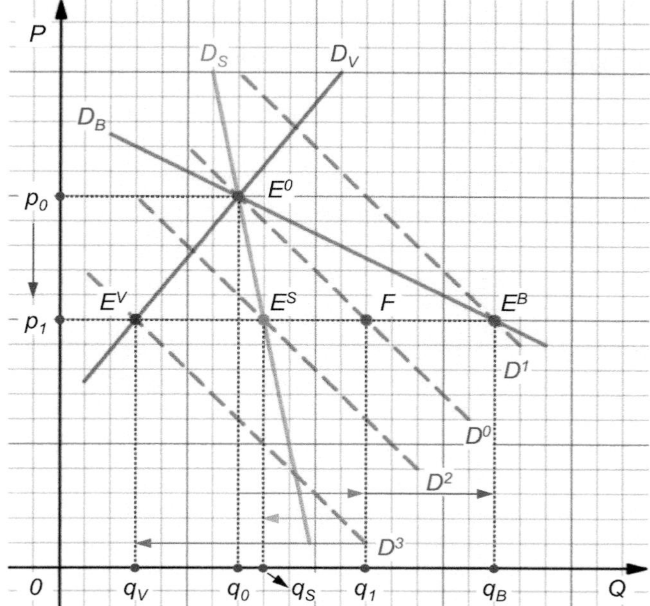

Figure 6.9
Network effects and nonfunctional demand

functional demand that changes in the opposite direction, thereby altering the nature of the demand curve for the Veblen good. Hence the demand curve for the Veblen good has a positive slope while for the snob good has a negative slope to conform to the law of demand. While for Veblen goods nonfunctional demand does not have to be greater than functional demand, the canonical model of the upward-sloping demand curve underscores the futility of Veblen goods. This means that functional demand for Veblen goods becomes insignificant to consumers as opposed to nonfunctional demand. However, this does not mean that Veblen goods have no functional utility but means that functional utility is inappreciable relative to the enormous nonfunctional utility. Thus, in Figure 6.9 the total quantity demanded, $q_V - q_0$, is entirely accounted for by the nonfunctional demand, and hence the Veblen good becomes futile.

6.3.2 Functional utility versus nonfunctional utility

In the preindustrial era travel had various functional utilities which do not necessarily rely on the presence of others in undertaking travel activities. Historically, travel took a wide range of forms from exploration, pilgrimage to commerce and trade before modern tourism emerged in England. While these travel activities might be undertaken collectively, many, if not all, of them were for subsistence on an individual basis or wealth accumulation for states, and thus suggest the functional utility of travel per se. This type of travel was particularly exemplified by the epic journey of Venetian merchant Marco Polo (1254–1324) along the Silk Road from Venice, Italy to China in the late thirteenth century. In the industrial era the functional utility of travel for subsistence and mercantilism gave way to recreational travel that aimed at increasing the well-being of individuals. The utilitarianism revolution in nineteenth-century England underscored the consumption of intangible experiences, such as leisure and pastime, in improving one's well-being. Recreational travel soon became mainstream in Europe as people were flocking to seasides and springs for various health purposes.[3] During this period recreationists would take short periods of regular travel to escape from industrial-world routines, hoping to better reunite with society. In the 1950s, retreat through camping played an important role in American society in rejuvenating people's energy and aspiration in order to improve their work efficiency.

From an industrialist's point of view, leisure and tourism may be deemed as having no functionality at all as opposed to work during the Industrial Revolution. This is because leisure was unproductive labor, an ideology that prevailed in the industrial society in which the value of labor lies at production. This ideology by and large formed the basis of the work–leisure tradeoff addressed in Chapter 4. Therefore, notwithstanding enormous wealth accumulation in England in the nineteenth century, for laborers working long hours was both economically and socially legitimized. To the working class as argued by Veblen, leisure was futile because the time spent on leisure would otherwise be devoted to production for generating economic benefits. The ideology that deems leisure time wasteful also prevailed in countries in the twentieth century which had undergone dramatic economic growth. For instance, leisure and tourism had no social and political legitimacy in China before the 1980s for they were deemed unproductive. By the time people started to value leisure and tourism as opposed to work, leisure consumption and the tourism industry at large were burgeoning in Chinese society. The consumption of tourism is no different from other commodities that generate functional utility in the form of experiential satisfaction and pleasure on an individual basis.

In the meantime, leisure or tourism has long been legitimized in the upper class. Spending time on leisure and tourism suggests that the elites are liberated from the working class and thus can afford to squander time and money on expensive articles that are deemed futile to the working class. Hence nonfunctional utility overrides functional utility in the consumption of leisure and tourism. The existence of nonfunctional utility explains why people are obsessed with spending extravagantly on luxuries, including overseas vacations, that seem not to live up to their intrinsic functionality. The consumption of luxuries is usually driven by their nonfunctional utility to consumers, exemplified by the fact that luxuries can reinforce a recognition of consumers' high social status among the masses. Thus, consumption becomes social and public instead of individualistic and private, visible and conspicuous instead of unobtrusive and discreet, for the sake of impressing others. Flaunting one's wealth to impress others and be distinguished from others becomes the ultimate goal of luxury consumption, which renders the functional utility of luxuries insignificant. While material items, such as sumptuous handbags, jewelry, and limos, are effective in parading one's wealth, extravagant experiences, such as lavish holidays, would create new social distinctions nowadays when these experiences are being propagated on social networks.

6.4 Consumer belief and information cues

In analyzing the bandwagon and snob effects we assumed that consumers can accurately anticipate the aggregate quantity demanded in the market upon which their own demand is adjusted. In analyzing the Veblen effect, we assumed that consumers know the conspicuous price of a good that others would attach to it, through which they can also adjust their own demand. Therefore, market demand reflects not only the price effect but also various network effects. The information of consumer base or conspicuous price is the prerequisite for network effects to exercise on consumers. While such information is by no means perfect in the marketplace, there are various information cues that could indicate consumer base or conspicuous price in the market. For instance, bandwagon goods tend to be heavily advertised because advertising signals that there is a considerable number of consumers expecting the goods. Hence individual demand which would otherwise be mute could be stimulated by advertising because the goods appear in high demand. It is not unusual to see diners lining up in droves at a restaurant, which could signal that the restaurant has been popular for a while and therefore entices followers to come. On the other hand, the existence of the bandwagon effect can explain why restaurants prefer keeping diners waiting in the line rather than simply raising prices to divert them. The imminent risk of raising prices is the loss of the information cue and hence the nonfunctional demand.

For snob goods, the information of a highly selective consumer base is conveyed through providing customers with limited editions, memberships, or VIP cards. For instance, it is not uncommon that the luxury industry from time to time rolls out limited editions of sports cars, watches, and the like to underscore the exclusiveness of their products and services. These limited editions signify that consumers are restricted in order to provide a sense of exclusiveness to generate nonfunctional demand from their target customers while weeding out less valuable ones. Providing VIP cards and other privileged access to goods and services is a widespread practice in businesses where the direct observation of fellow consumers' behavior is difficult. For instance, memberships and VIP cards are pervasive in luxury hotel and airline businesses as opposed to the restaurant industry, because hotel and airline demand is less obtrusive than the frequent patronage of restaurants. This is one of the reasons that customized services are usually furnished by hotels and airlines to lure customers who demand exclusiveness. Contrary to bandwagon goods for which advertising is crucial, snob goods are not publicly advertised on mass media because this would backfire and mislead prospective consumers into thinking that the goods are commonplace and pedestrian.

For Veblen goods consumer belief is manifested such that consumers think others would think of them as having paid a prohibitive price for the goods. This is how conspicuous price really comes about and influences the demand of those who would be the consumers of the goods. Thus, nonfunctional utility is derived from how the goods demanded by a consumer are viewed by others. The prohibitive prices of Veblen goods are certainly information cues which help to construct consumers' belief in the expensiveness of the goods, and hence generate nonfunctional demand. For instance, a study shows that consumers tend to underrate a wine once they are told the wine is inexpensive, and thus their demand for the wine is presumably conspicuous.[4] Yet the expensiveness of Veblen goods does not have to be associated with the market price all the time. As long as the conspicuous price of a good roots deep in people's belief, consumers will increase nonfunctional demand anyway because the expensiveness has been well acknowledged by others. This can explain why price discounts, if any, are not advertised for Veblen goods as much as they are for grocery necessities: on the contrary, a price raise is usually followed by a blaze of publicity to increase the conspicuousness of the goods among consumers.

Summary

1. When individual demand is independent of one another, market demand is the summation of the demand over all individuals. When individual demand is interdependent, market demand could be smaller or greater than the aggregation of the demand of all consumers. Hence market demand is non-additive.
2. The non-additivity of market demand can be attributed to demand interdependence in which one's demand is affected either positively or negatively by the demand of others. Therefore, consumer demand is not only a function of the price of a good but also of the demand of others for the good.
3. The bandwagon effect is a positive network effect, suggesting that the quantity of a good demanded by a consumer is positively associated with the number of others in the market. The demand curve for the bandwagon good is more elastic compared to the initial demand curve without taking account of the change in consumer base.
4. The snob effect is a negative network effect, suggesting that the quantity of a good demanded by a consumer is negatively associated with the number of other consumers in the market. The demand curve for the snob good is less elastic compared to the initial demand curve without taking account of the change in consumer base.
5. The Veblen effect is a network effect caused by the conspicuous price of a good. The demand for the Veblen good is determined by both the market price of the good and the conspicuous price perceived by others. The demand curve for the Veblen good usually slopes upward.
6. For the three goods a change in quantity demanded can be decomposed into a pure price effect and a network effect. The Bandwagon effect works in the same direction while the snob effect works in the opposite direction as the pure price effect. The Veblen effect usually outstrips the pure price effect that works in the opposite direction.
7. Consumer demand can be classified into functional demand and nonfunctional demand. Functional demand is the demand for a good that is attributed to the intrinsic functionality of the good which brings about functional utility.
8. For bandwagon and snob goods, nonfunctional demand is due to the change in consumer base that endows the goods with nonfunctional utility. For Veblen goods, nonfunctional demand is caused by the conspicuous price of the goods which in turn generates nonfunctional utility.

9. Like many other commodities, leisure and tourism have various functional utilities which do not necessarily rely on the presence of others. On the other hand, leisure and tourism are becoming increasingly social and extravagant in order to create social distinction.
10. In practice there are many information cues through which consumes can anticipate the market demand and thereby adjust their own demand. These information cues are manifested differently across the bandwagon, snob, and Veblen effects.

REVIEW QUESTIONS

Each question has four options, and there is only one correct answer to each question.

1. Suppose that a market consists of two consumers. If the two consumers made their decisions independently, their quantity demanded for a good would be 20 and 30, respectively, at a certain price. If one consumer's demand affects the other's, which of the following is correct regarding the quantity demanded in the market (Q)?
   A) $Q = 50$
   B) $Q \neq 50$
   C) $Q < 50$
   D) $Q > 50$
2. Which of the following is correct regarding the three network effects?
   A) The bandwagon effect is a negative network effect only if price increases.
   B) The snob effect is a positive network effect only if price decreases.
   C) The Veblen effect is a negative network effect only if income increases.
   D) None of the above.
3. Which of the following is correct regarding the market demand for the three goods?
   A) The market demand becomes less elastic for bandwagon goods.
   B) The market demand becomes more elastic for snob goods.
   C) The market demand becomes inelastic for Veblen goods.
   D) None of the above.
4. In the late nineteenth century leisure was probably a Veblen good among the so-called leisure class in England. Which of the following is correct?
   A) Spending time on leisure would become individualistic.
   B) Spending time on leisure would become obtrusive.
   C) Spending time on leisure would have no nonfunctional utility.
   D) Spending time on leisure would have no functional utility.
5. Suppose that the demand for Airbnb in Paris has a snob effect. When the room rate is \$90, Airbnb can sell 150 room nights per day, indicated by the demand curve D_0 in the graph below. When Airbnb cuts the room rate from \$90 to

$70 which stimulates the snob effect, what will be the snob effect on the demand for Airbnb?

A) An increase of 450 room nights.
B) A decrease of 400 room nights.
C) An increase of 300 room nights.
D) A decrease of 150 room nights.

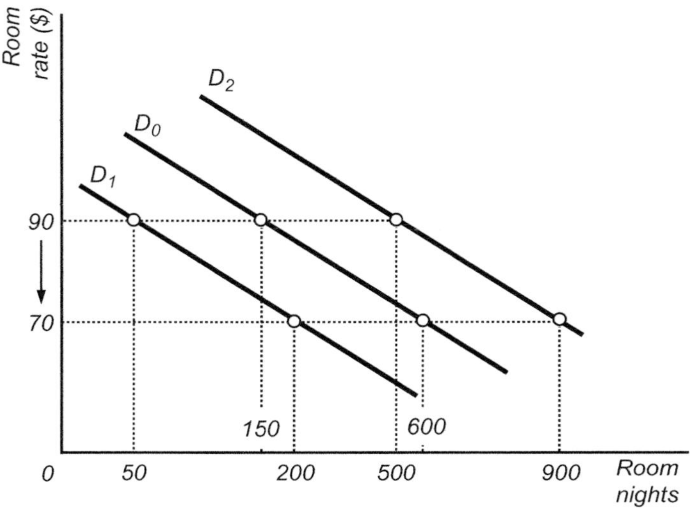

6. Which of the following is correct regarding the underlying reasons for the three network effects?
   A) Bandwagon effects are caused by a change in consumer preference.
   B) Snob effects are caused by a change in consumer income.
   C) Veblen effects are caused by a change in functional utility.
   D) None of the above.
7. Suppose that the demand for a French cuisine has a bandwagon effect. When the price is $50 per meal, the restaurant can sell 1,200 meals per week, indicated by the demand curve D_0 in the graph below. When the restaurant raises the price from $50 to $80 which triggers the bandwagon effect, what will be the demand curve for the French cuisine?
   A) The straight line passing through points E_1 and F_2.
   B) The straight line passing through points E_1 and F_3.
   C) The straight line passing through points E_2 and F_1.
   D) The straight line passing through points E_3 and F_2.

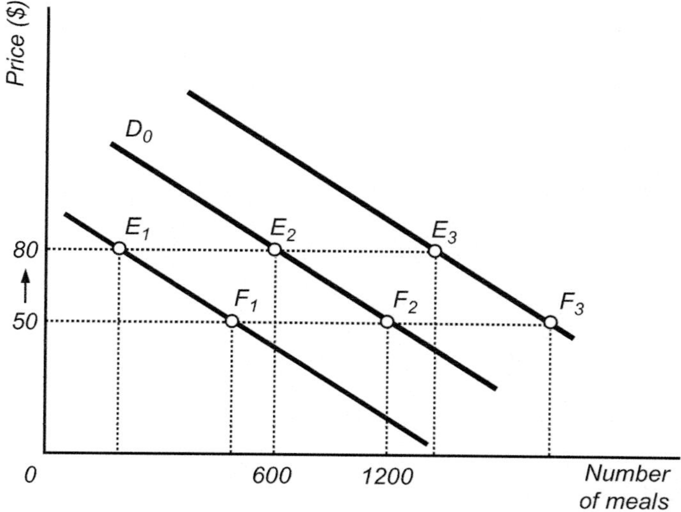

8. Suppose that a type of coffee sold at Starbucks has a Veblen effect. Which of the following explains the positive slope of the demand curve for the coffee?
   A) Functional demand is smaller than nonfunctional demand.
   B) Functional demand is greater than nonfunctional demand.
   C) Functional demand is equal to nonfunctional demand.
   D) None of the above.
9. Nobel Prize-winning economist Gary Becker writes in a research article that "Stephen Hawking's *A Brief History of Time* was on the *New York Times* best-seller list for over 100 weeks and sold more than 1.1 million hardcover copies. Yet I doubt if 1 percent of those who bought the book could understand it. Its main value to purchasers has been as a display on coffee tables and as a source of pride in conversations at parties." What kind of utility does Becker underscore about Hawking's book?
   A) Functional utility
   B) Nonfunctional utility
   C) Marginal utility
   D) Total utility
10. "See You Again," a song recorded by American rapper Wiz Khalifa and singer Charlie Puth, has hit 4.67 billion views and garnered 29 million likes since its release on YouTube in April 2015. It is now the fourth most viewed video on YouTube. Which of the following effects can best describe the popularity of the song?
   A) Veblen effect
   B) Bandwagon effect
   C) Snob effect
   D) Income effect

Problem solving

1. Economist Gary Becker mentioned in a research article that he used to be baffled by the pricing behavior of restaurants:

   > A popular seafood restaurant in Palo Alto, California, does not take reservations, and every day it has long queues for tables during prime hours. Almost directly across the street is another seafood restaurant with comparable food, slightly higher prices, and similar service and other amenities. Yet this restaurant has many empty seats most of the time. Why doesn't the popular restaurant raise prices, which would reduce the queue for seats but expand profits?[5]

   Explain why the popular restaurant doesn't raise prices.

2. Suppose that a French wine has a snob effect. When the price of the wine is \$20 per bottle, the quantity demanded ends up being 3,000 bottles in the market. If the price increased by \$5, the functional demand for the wine would decrease by 500 bottles, but the nonfunctional demand would increase by 50 bottles. Assuming that the demand curve for the wine is linear, what would be the price elasticity of demand if the price further increased by \$5?
3. According to a McKinsey report in 2019, China's luxury spending could increase to 168 billion euros in 2025, up from 105 billion euros in 2018, accounting for 40% of the global luxury spending.[6] About 70% of Chinese consumers who demand luxuries, ranging from fashion, jewelry, prestige cosmetics to artwork and extravagant holidays, will shop overseas through outbound travel.[7] By contrast, Elizabeth Currid-Halkett observes that a type of inconspicuous consumption, which she dubs as aspirational consumption, has been burgeoning in the United States since the 1990s.[8] The so-called American aspirational class is defined by their cultural capital, such as elite educational background, rather than material wealth, and their consumption is discreet and unobtrusive. For instance, they eat free-range chicken and heirloom tomatoes, wear organic cotton shirts and TOMS shoes, and prefer a free New Yorker magazine tote bag to a \$10,000 Hermès bag.[9] How would you explain the shift from conspicuous consumption to aspirational consumption? What network effect does aspirational consumption imply?

Solutions to all review questions and problem solving tasks are included in the Support Material for this book, which can be accessed at www.routledge.com/9780367897352.

Notes

1 We use "network externality" and "network effect" interchangeably in the chapter. In general, when referring to a specific network externality, we use network effect to better illustrate the direction of the externality.

2 Giffen goods also feature an upward-sloping demand curve, but for a different reason.

3 See Zuelow (2015).

4 See Peterson (2014), p. 76.

5 Becker (1991), p. 1109.

6 *McKinsey*. How young Chinese consumers are reshaping global luxury. April 25, 2019.

7 *McKinsey Quarterly*. The Chinese luxury consumer. August 12, 2019.

8 Currid-Halkett, E. (2017). *The sum of small things: A theory of the aspirational class*. Princeton, NJ: Princeton University Press.

9 *MarketWatch*. How a free canvas tote became a bigger status symbol than a $10,000 Hermès bag. September 9, 2017.

Bibliography

Becker, G. S. (1991). A note on restaurant pricing and other examples of social influences on price. *Journal of Political Economy, 99*(5), 1109–1116.

Leibenstein, H. (1950). Bandwagon, snob, and Veblen effects in the theory of consumers' demand. *Quarterly Journal of Economics, 64*(2), 183–207.

Morgenstern, O. (1948). Demand theory reconsidered. *Quarterly Journal of Economics, 62*(2), 165–201.

Peterson, K. (2014). The snob effect of red wine: Estimating consumer bias in experimental blind wine tastings. *The American Economist, 59*(1), 76–89.

Pigou, A. C. (1913). The interdependence of different sources of demand and supply in a market. *Economic Journal, 23*(89), 19–24.

Veblen, T. (1899). *The theory of the leisure class: An economic study of institutions*. New York, NY: The Macmillan Company.

Zuelow, E. (2015). *A history of modern tourism*. London, UK: Macmillan Education.

7 Demand for Pinot Noir versus Merlot

The Sideways effect[1]

This chapter concludes the module with an analysis of what is known as the Sideways effect on wine consumption triggered by the namesake movie in 2004. The Sideways effect is generated due to the leading actor of the movie who was portrayed as a Pinot Noir fan praising Pinot Noir earnestly while belittling Merlot in many memorable scenes of the movie. Along with the success of the movie, not only did the public demonstrate a great deal of interest in wine consumption but they also developed a strong preference for Pinot Noir over Merlot. We aim to analyze the Sideways effect on the demand for the two wines by drawing evidence from the wine market in the U.S. In particular, we illustrate the economic mechanism whereby the Sideways effect is manifested in wine consumption. In addition, this case study sheds light on the role of consumer knowledge of wine in mediating the Sideways effect on wine demand as wine consumption is knowledge intensive.

AFTER STUDYING THIS CHAPTER, YOU SHOULD BE ABLE TO:

- Understand the reason behind the changes in the demand for Pinot Noir and Merlot in relation to the movie;
- Understand how consumer preference and the demand for Pinot Noir and Merlot are affected by the movie;
- Quantify the Sideways effect on the demand for Pinot Noir and for Merlot from both empirical and theoretical perspectives; and
- Understand why the Sideways effect may vary by the knowledge of wine that consumers possess.

7.1 Sideways and the wines

Sideways was a 2004 American dramedy film which featured two men reaching middle age, Miles Raymond, a depressed writer, and Jack Cole, a past-his-prime actor, taking a week-long road trip to Santa Barbara County wine country in California. In addition to its boffo box office in the United States, the movie received widespread acclaim after its release in October 2004, which was strengthened after it won the Best Adapted Screenplay among the five Academy Award nominations in 2005. Throughout the film Miles Raymond starring Paul Giamatti, who was portrayed as a Pinot Noir fan, earnestly admires Pinot Noir while denigrating Merlot in various memorable scenes. Unexpectedly, his predilections caused what is known as the "Sideways" effect on wine consumption across the U.S. According to the *New York Times*, "Pinot Noir, the wine exalted so poetically in the movie, has enjoyed a burst of sales nationwide while Merlot, so memorably derided by Miles, is faltering, at least among those who have seen the movie."[2] This also led many wineries to promote their wine as well as to lure tourists to participate in wine tourism in California where many scenes of the movie were shot. The Sideways effect was propagated by mass media through their interminable coverage of not only the movie but also of the effect of the movie on wine demand.

In order to examine the size of the Sideways effect on Pinot Noir and Merlot, we select two other red wines, Cabernet Sauvignon and Syrah, in a control group that are similar to Pinot Noir and Merlot in consumer demand but were not featured in the movie. Hence the demand for Cabernet Sauvignon and Syrah was not affected by the movie, having no Sideways effect. It follows that any changes in the demand for Pinot Noir and Merlot that deviate from the change in the demand for the control group can be attributed to the Sideways effect. If the demand patterns of all three groups of wine were similar prior to the release of the movie but differed substantially from each other thereafter, we can speculate that the movie could have some sort of effect on the demand for Pinot Noir and Merlot. If the Sideways effect did not exist at all, the changes in the demand for Pinot Noir and Merlot would be similar before and after the movie release on the one hand, and on the other would follow the same change pattern of the control group. We index the sales volumes of the three groups of wine in 1999 to be zero in order to standardize the changes in demand in the whole study period that covered the release time of the movie and the possible duration of the Sideways effect. Hence the change in demand since 1999 is interpreted as the relative growth rate of the three groups (Figure 7.1).

Figure 7.1 shows that the changes in the demand for the three groups of wine were very similar prior to 2004 when the movie was released while diverging substantially between Pinot Noir and the other two groups ever since. The demand for Pinot Noir grew by nearly 60% between 2004 and 2005 in contrast to negligible growths in the demand for both Merlot and the control group. Despite the structural change in demand occurring after 2004, particularly for Pinot Noir, this change could also be due to factors other than the movie that affected the demand for Pinot Noir. Namely, there might be other factors coinciding with the post-2004 period that caused the demand for Pinot Noir to surge. The other factors were more likely to be product- or consumer-specific

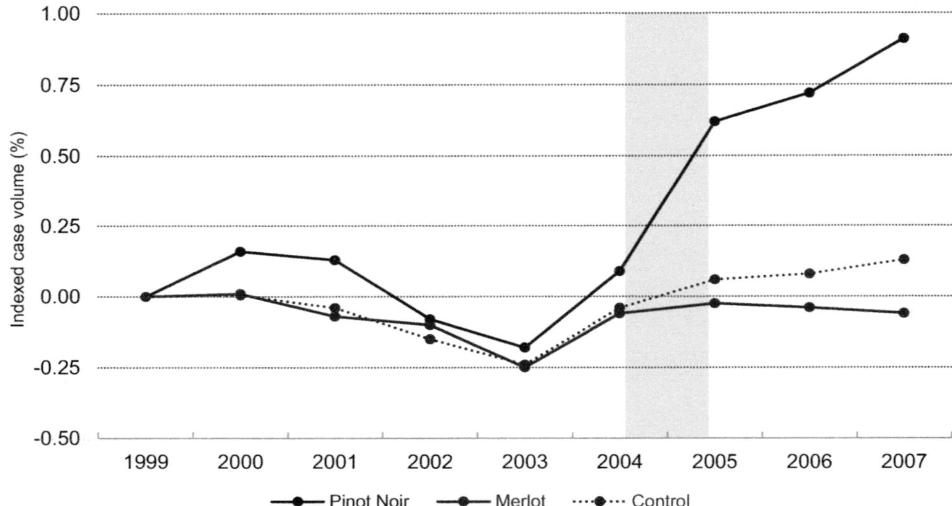

Figure 7.1
Indexed case volume of the wines sold

Note: Annual case volume of the wines is indexed to zero in 1999, and thus the graph shows the relative growth rate of sales volume of each wine group after 1999. The shaded red box indicates the release time of the movie from October 2004 to May 2005.

Source: Reproduced from Cuellar et al. (2009), p. 4.

for Pinot Noir, because any macroeconomic variables, such as income, that affect the demand for Pinot Noir would also affect the demand for other wines. Also, because the structural change in demand for Pinot Noir was sustained in a short period of time, the change in consumer preference for Pinot Noir was more likely to be caused by the movie. Not only did the movie feature Pinot Noir extensively, but it also praised the wine enthusiastically. This may have changed consumer preference as indicated by the anecdotal evidence mentioned above. We aim to measure the Sideways effect on the demand for Pinot Noir and Merlot from both empirical and theoretical perspectives.

7.2 *Sideways* on wine consumption

7.2.1 *Standardization and comparisons*

Since factors other than the movie could also affect the demand for the wines in the study period, the fluctuations in demand cannot be entirely attributed to the movie. During and after the movie release, other factors might have mingled with the Sideways effect, and hence we need to isolate the effects of these other factors. Since the control group, by definition, was not affected by *Sideways*, all the changes in the demand for the control group were accounted for by the other factors which might vary coincidentally before and after the movie release but were irrelevant to the movie. In this regard, we use the ratios of the demand for Pinot Noir and Merlot to the demand for the control group to quantify the changes in the demand for Pinot Noir and Merlot that were caused by *Sideways*. If the Pinot–control ratio increases during and after the movie release, we can conclude that the Sideways effect on the demand for Pinot Noir is positive; if the Merlot–control ratio decreases, the Sideways effect on Merlot is negative. If the Sideways effect did not exist, both the Pinot–control and Merlot–control ratios would remain unchanged despite the fact that their absolute demand may still change. This is because in the absence of the Sideways effect all the changes in the demand for Pinot Noir and Merlot are entirely accounted for by the other factors, which are the same as for the control group, ending up with the two ratios being zero.

7.2.2 The Sideways effect on quantity

Figure 7.2 shows that before 2004 both the Pinot–control and Merlot–control ratios were close to zero but changed drastically since. On the one hand, before 2004 the Merlot–control ratio was almost zero, indicating that the demand for Merlot and the control group follows exactly the same growth pattern. The other factors that explain the demand for the control group also precisely accounted for the change in the demand for Merlot. On the other hand, the Pinot–control ratio hovered around 10% between 1999 and 2004, suggesting that the demand for Pinot Noir is slightly different from the demand for the control group in this period. This means that the other factors that explain the demand for Pinot Noir are not exactly the same as those factors explaining the demand for the control group. In other words, the other factors that explain the changes in the demand for Merlot and the control group do not fully account for the change in the demand for Pinot Noir. Also, because the demand for Merlot resembles the demand for the control group while the demand for Pinot Noir behaves slightly differently, the Merlot–Pinot ratio before 2004 manifests a symmetric reverse of the Pinot–control ratio against the x-axis as shown in Figure 7.2. Conversely, the Merlot–Pinot ratio reflects the change in the demand for Pinot Noir since the demand for Merlot was no different from the demand for the control group prior to 2004.

Note that the Pinot–control ratio increased up to 55% in 2005 from only 10% prior to 2004. Such structural variation was also found in the Merlot–control ratio, which decreased by around 5% in 2005. In particular, the Merlot–control ratio continued decreasing from 5% in 2005 to 20% in 2008, a period during which the movie was supposed to exert its influence because of the Oscar acclaim. These structural changes in demand can thus be attributed to the Sideways effect, which is positive on the demand for Pinot Noir while negative on the demand for Merlot. In addition, we know that the positive effect is much stronger than the negative effect, evidenced by the Pinot–control ratio being substantially greater than the Merlot–control ratio in absolute value. Figure 7.2 shows different growth patterns in the demand before and after the period 2004–2005, during which the changes in the demand for both Pinot Noir and Merlot almost systematically diverged from the control group. This indicates that all the changes in the demand for Pinot Noir and Merlot were no longer entirely accounted for by the other factors but were, in part, explained by the movie. It is also possible that the substantial changes in the demand for Pinot Noir and Merlot after 2005 were due to the price changes of the two wines. That is, the increase in the quantity demanded for Pinot Noir is due to a price decrease while the decrease in the

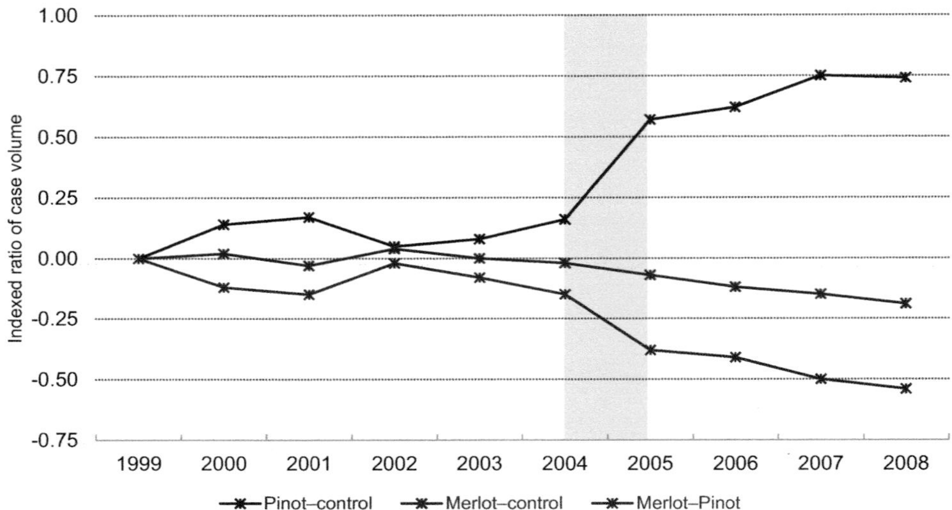

Figure 7.2
Indexed ratios of case volume of the wines sold

Note: Indexed ratio of case volume measures the growth rate of one wine group against that of the other in sales. The values are indexed to zero in 1999. The shaded red box indicates the release time of the movie from October 2004 to May 2005.

Source: Reproduced from Cuellar et al. (2009), p. 6.

demand for Merlot is due to a price hike. As we shall see below, this hypothesis is not supported by evidence in the market.

7.2.3 The Sideways effect on price

Figure 7.3 shows the price changes of the three groups of wine adjusted by the price level in 1999. The price change pattern of Merlot resembles that of the control group between 2002 and 2005. Not only did the price change of the two groups follow the same pattern, but the price discrepancies between the two were negligible. While there was a relatively greater divergence in the prices of Merlot and the control group before 2002, the price change patterns were also very similar. Only after 2005 did the price of Merlot start to diverge from the price of the control group. For whatever reason, the price of the control group gradually increased while the price of Merlot kept decreasing since 2005. This ended up causing an increasing divergence in the prices between the two groups, which could in part be attributed to the Sideways effect. While the price of Pinot Noir was substantially higher than the prices of Merlot and the control group in much of the study period, it gradually diverged from the price of the control group since 2004. Due to the price decrease of Merlot after 2005, the price divergence between Pinot Noir and Merlot intensified ever since. We can conclude that the price divergence of Pinot Noir and Merlot since 2004 was due to the positive effect of Sideways on the demand for Pinot Noir while the negative effect on the demand for Merlot.

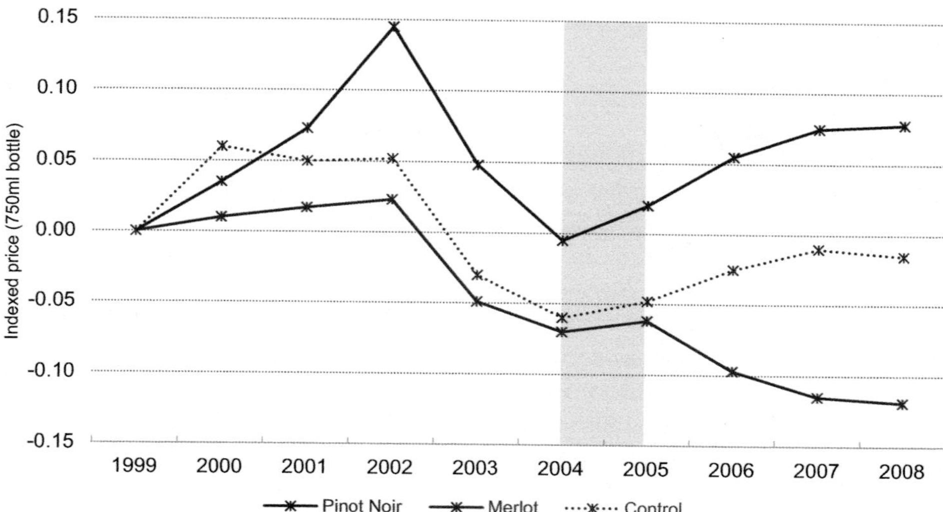

Figure 7.3
Indexed real prices of the wines

Note: The real prices of the wines are indexed to zero in 1999, and thus the graph shows the relative price change of each wine group after 1999. The shaded red box indicates the release time of the movie from October 2004 to May 2005.

Source: Reproduced from Cuellar et al. (2009), p. 8.

The change in the prices of Pinot Noir and Merlot could also be caused by the change in supply, other things being equal. That is, the price increase of Pinot Noir and the control group after 2004 was due to a decrease in supply while the price decrease of Merlot was due to an increase in supply. That said, we cannot reconcile the argument that the supply of Pinot Noir and the control group decreased while the supply of Merlot increased. The reason is that the supply of various vintages in the same region is subject to similar climate conditions in a given period of time, and hence the change in supply, if any, would occur uniformly to all wines. It is also hard to justify why the abrupt changes in the supply of the three groups of wine occurred around 2005. Assuming that the supply was constant before and after the movie release, we can attribute the price increase of Pinot Noir and the control group and the price decrease of Merlot to the changes in demand that were caused by the movie. This is evidenced by Cuellar et al.'s (2009) study that the Sideways effect is statistically significant in affecting the demand for Pinot Noir and Merlot in different ways. Therefore, at least part of the price changes of Pinot Noir and Merlot was accounted for by the Sideways effect in one way or another. Given the popularity of the movie, it would not be surprising that the price of the control group also increased. This is due to the positive Sideways effect on the demand for all wines but the demeaned Merlot. In other words, not only did the movie increase consumer demand for Pinot Noir but it also increased demand for other wines through raising consumer awareness of wine consumption.

7.3 Decomposing price and the Sideways effect

7.3.1 Change in price or quantity

To illustrate the Sideways effect on Pinot Noir and Merlot, let's select Cabernet Sauvignon in the control group as a benchmark whose demand is not affected by the movie. We assume that the changes in demand, if any, for the three wines are the same before and after the movie release without the Sideways effect. As long as the demand for Pinot Noir and Merlot changes after the movie release, and hence deviates from the demand for Cabernet Sauvignon, the deviations suggest the Sideways effect on the demand for the two wines under investigation. For simplicity, suppose that the three wines are sold at p_0 with the same sales volume of q_0 in the market before the movie release, denoted by the equilibrium E_0 (Figure 7.4a). If we observe in the market that the prices of the three wines all end up at p_1 ($p_0 < p_1$) after the movie release, and the quantities demanded for the three wines are q_C for Cabernet Sauvignon, q_N for Pinot Noir, and q_M for Merlot ($q_M < q_C < q_N$) as shown in Figure 7.4a, the Sideways effect on the demand for Pinot Noir is thus an increase of $q_N - q_C$ while on the demand for Merlot it is a decrease of $q_C - q_M$. The Sideways effect is indicated by the rightward shift in the demand curve from D_0 to D_N for Pinot Noir and by the leftward shift in the demand curve from D_0 to D_M for Merlot. In addition, the decrease of $q_0 - q_C$ in the demand for Cabernet Sauvignon is attributed to the pure price effect as the price increases from p_0 to p_1.

If we observe that the quantities demanded for the three wines all end up at q_1 ($q_0 < q_1$), and the corresponding prices are p_C for Cabernet Sauvignon, p_N for Pinot Noir, and p_M for Merlot ($p_M < p_C < p_N$) as shown in Figure 7.4b, then the Sideways effect

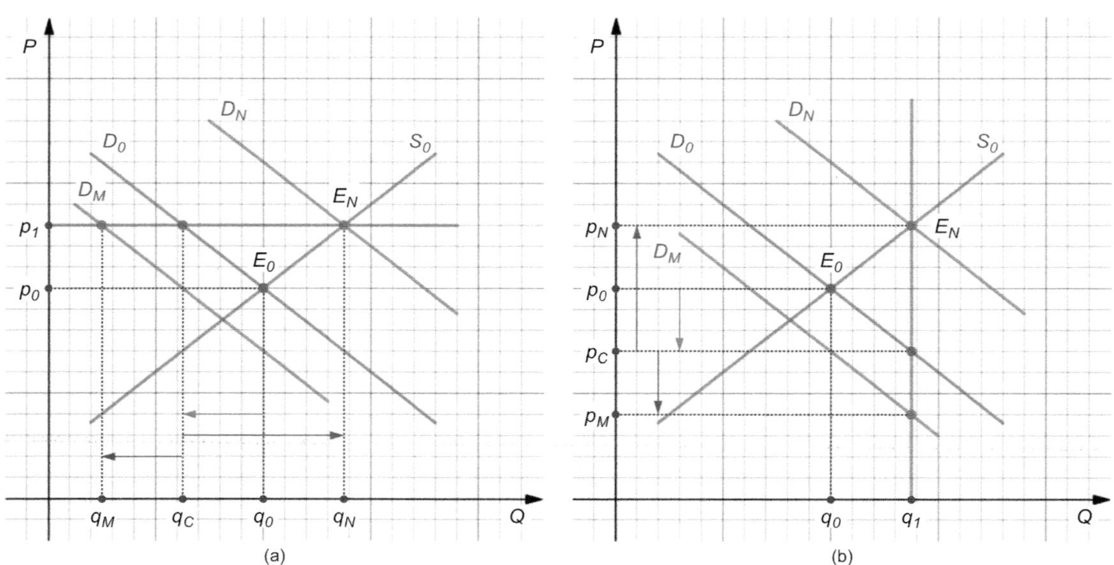

Figure 7.4
Sideways effect on quantity and price

leads to an increase of $p_N - p_C$ in the price of Pinot Noir but a decrease of $p_C - p_M$ in the price of Merlot. This means that if the Sideways effect did not exist, the demand for Pinot Noir and Merlot would be the same as the demand for Cabernet Sauvignon, ending up with $p_N = p_M = p_C$. Holding the quantity demanded constant, the price discrepancies between the two wines and Cabernet Sauvignon after the movie release are thus attributed to the Sideways effect. It is *Sideways* that increases the demand for Pinot Noir while decreasing the demand for Merlot, eventually leading to the price discrepancies. Note that the demand for Cabernet Sauvignon does not have to be the same as the demand for Pinot Noir and Merlot without the Sideways effect. If consumer demands are different across the three wines, we can refer to the relative changes in demand, namely the Pinot–control and Merlot–control ratios, before and after the movie release to measure the Sideways effect. If the Pinot–control ratio increases after the movie release, there exists a positive Sideways effect on Pinot Noir; if the Merlot–control ratio decreases, there exists a negative Sideways effect on Merlot. If the two ratios remain unchanged before and after the movie release, the Sideways effect does not exist.

7.3.2 Changes in both price and quantity

Given the same price of the three wines p_0 and the quantity demanded q_0 before the movie release, it is likely that both the prices and quantities demanded differ across the three wines after the movie release. Figure 7.5 shows that the price of Cabernet Sauvignon ends up at p_C and the quantity demanded at q_C denoted by point C on the demand curve D_0, while the price and quantity demanded of Pinot Noir are p_N and q_N denoted by point N and of Merlot are p_M and q_M denoted by point M. We can decompose the total price effect into the pure price effect and the Sideways effect by identifying the changes in demand for Pinot Noir and Merlot after the movie release. Given the demand curve D_0, the Sideways effect on the demand for Pinot Noir is represented by the rightward shift in the demand curve from D_0 to D_N that passes through point N. The Sideways effect on the demand for Merlot is represented by the leftward shift in the demand curve from D_0 to D_M that passes through point M. The Sideways effect on the demand for Pinot Noir is thus quantified by the magnitude of the rightward shift in the demand curve from D_0 to D_N while for Merlot it is the magnitude of the leftward shift from D_0 to D_M. Different from the two cases in Figure 7.4, the pure price effect varies across the three wines because their price changes are not the same before and after the movie release.

For simplicity, suppose that the demands for all three wines is linear. To measure the magnitude of the shifts we need to solve the demand function for D_0 in the first place. Given the linear inverse demand function $p = aq + b$, we can plug the values of point E_0 and point C on the demand curve D_0 into the demand function to obtain

$$\begin{cases} p_0 = aq_0 + b, \\ p_C = aq_C + b. \end{cases} \tag{7.1}$$

Solving equations (7.1) we obtain the parameters $a=(p_0-p_C)/(q_0-q_C)$ and $b=(p_Cq_0-p_0q_C)/(q_0-q_C)$. Thus, the inverse demand function for D_0 is

$$p=\frac{p_0-p_C}{q_0-q_C}q+\frac{p_Cq_0-p_0q_C}{q_0-q_C}. \tag{7.2}$$

Conditional on the price of Pinot Noir after the movie release, p_N, we can calculate the quantity that would otherwise be demanded for Cabernet Sauvignon assuming that its price is the same as p_N. This allows us to hold the price constant at p_N while measuring the magnitude of the shift in the demand curve from D_0 to D_N. With $p=p_N$ in function (7.2), we can readily obtain the quantity demanded for Cabernet Sauvignon q_1, and thus the Sideways effect on the demand for Pinot Noir is q_N-q_1 (Figure 7.5). By the same token, for Merlot if $p=p_M$ in function (7.2), we can obtain the quantity that would otherwise be demanded for Cabernet Sauvignon q_2, and thus the Sideways effect on the demand for Merlot is q_M-q_2. Figure 7.5 shows the positive Sideways effect on the demand for Pinot Noir and the negative Sideways effect on the demand for Merlot, which are represented by the shifts in the demand curve from D_0 to D_N and D_M, respectively. The pure price effect on the demand for Pinot Noir is the movement upward along the demand curve D_0 as the benchmark when its price increases from p_0 to p_N, ending up with a decrease of q_0-q_1 in the quantity demanded. For Merlot, the pure price effect is the movement downward along D_0 caused by the price decrease from p_0 to p_M, leading to an increase of q_2-q_0 in the quantity demanded.

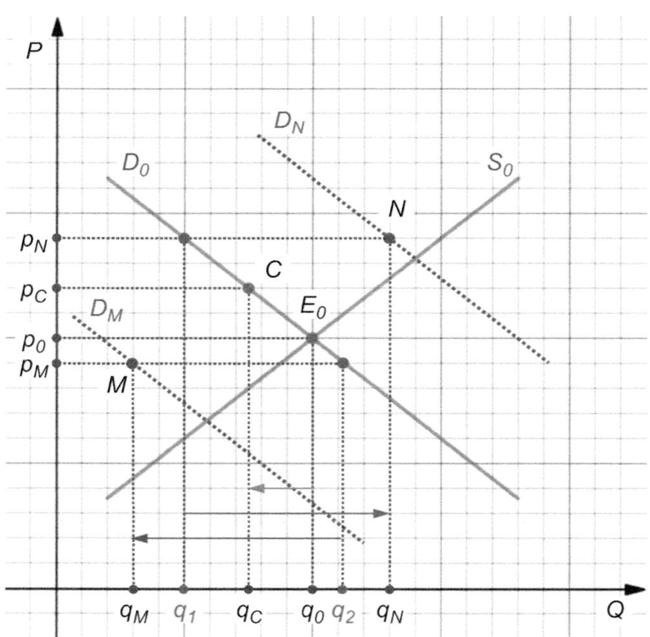

Figure 7.5
Sideways effect with varying prices and quantities

7.4 Consumer knowledge and the Sideways effect

7.4.1 Consumer knowledge and wine consumption

Different from other consumptions, wine consumption or appreciation requires consumers to accumulate a wide range of knowledge about wines from their intrinsic qualities such as aroma and flavor to the geography and climate in which grapes are harvested. Educated consumers such as Miles Raymond are certain about which wine they like or dislike, and hence have well-established preferences. Thus, the Sideways effect may vary depending on consumers' knowledge about wine. The movie in essence increases the awareness of wine consumption among the public, which obviously matters more to novice consumers but less to oenophiles in their purchase decisions. As far as wine consumption is concerned, the price of wine is a useful segmentation device that can reflect consumers' knowledge of wine. The reason for using price to segment consumers is that for most people with little wine knowledge, inexpensive wines would taste the same as expensive ones. Insofar as consumers are not able to tell the difference between the two, low-priced wines are purchased disproportionately more by novice consumers. Only well-informed consumers are able to discern different types of wines, and thus their preferences are less relevant to the price of wine. However, well-informed consumers usually have a good taste for fine wines, thus ending up purchasing high-priced wines disproportionately more than low-priced wines.

On the one hand, the Sideways effect, if any, would be more pronounced on the demand for low-priced wines because the movie first and foremost increases consumer knowledge of wine and Pinot Noir in particular, which oenophiles have already possessed. Hence the increase in demand for Pinot Noir and for wine in general is largely because the movie enticed novice consumers and the general public to consume wine. On the other hand, only after consumers have accumulated some wine knowledge can they be capable of weighing up, say, Pinot Noir versus Merlot and for this comparison to make more sense to them. Therefore, we can conjecture that the positive Sideways effect on Pinot Noir or even on the control group is more substantial in the low-priced segment while the negative Sideways effect on Merlot is more substantial in the high-priced segment. That is, despite the fact that the movie praised Pinot Noir while belittling Merlot, what matters to consumers in the low-priced segment is the publicity of wine consumption in general instead of a specific wine. We classify wine in three price categories, under \$10 per bottle (low-priced), \$10–\$20 per bottle (medium-priced), and \$20–\$40 per bottle (high-priced). We focus on the standard 750ml glass bottle in the study period, which accounts for approximately 84% of all wine purchases in the U.S.

7.4.2 Heterogeneity of the Sideways effect

Figures 7.6 and 7.7 show that Pinot Noir and Merlot exhibit different patterns of demand against the control group in the low- and medium-priced segments before 2004. In the low-priced segment, although the demand for Pinot Noir grew

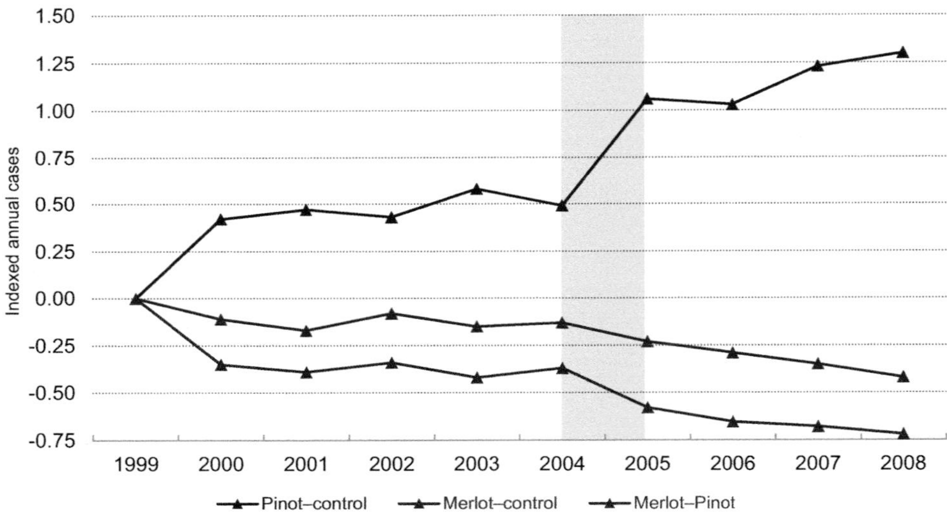

Figure 7.6
Indexed ratios of case volume sold: Low-priced

Note: Indexed ratio of case volume measures the growth rate of one wine group against that of the other in sales. The values are indexed to zero in 1999. The shaded red box indicates the release time of the movie from October 2004 to May 2005.

Source: Reproduced from Cuellar et al. (2009), p. 10.

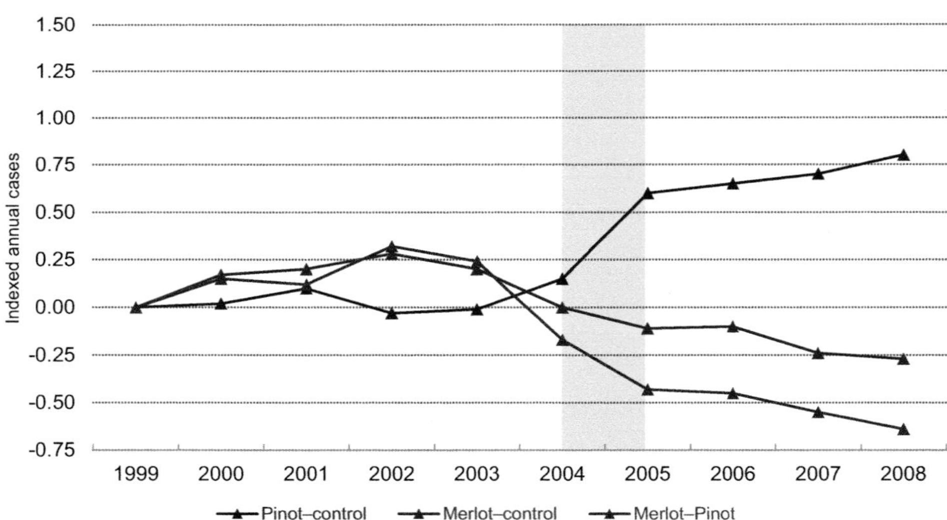

Figure 7.7
Indexed ratios of case volume sold: Medium-priced

Note: Indexed ratio of case volume measures the growth rate of one wine group against that of the other in sales. The values are indexed to zero in 1999. The shaded red box indicates the release time of the movie from October 2004 to May 2005.

Source: Reproduced from Cuellar et al. (2009), p. 12.

consistently faster and for Merlot grew slower than the control group, there were no structural changes in the demand for the two wines before 2004. This result reflects the intrinsic differences in the consumption of the two wines that are irrelevant to the Sideways effect. In the medium-priced segment, the changes in the demand for the two wines were quite similar before 2004, which perhaps suggests that consumers in this segment tend to regard Pinot Noir and Merlot alongside the control group as close substitutes. Nevertheless, striking structural changes in demand occurred for Pinot Noir and Merlot between 2004 and 2005. Pinot Noir in both segments experienced a surge in demand while Merlot experienced a noticeable decrease since 2004, during which the movie was released. In particular, the Merlot–Pinot ratio indicates that the decrease in demand for Merlot is more pronounced than indicated by the Merlot–control ratio. This suggests that there must be some common factors, coinciding with the movie, that led to the structural changes in the demand for the three wine groups. The directions of the structural changes are consistent with the positive Sideways effect on Pinot Noir while with the negative effect on Merlot. As we have conjectured, the positive Sideways effect on Pinot Noir is stronger in the low-priced segment than it is in the medium-priced segment; by contrast the negative Sideways effect on Merlot is weaker in the low-priced segment than it is in the medium-priced segment.

Interestingly, the demand changes for Pinot Noir and Merlot in the high-priced segment were more volatile than in the other two segments before 2004 (Figure 7.8). It is worth noting that the demand for Merlot outpaced the demand for Pinot Noir before 2004. This means that consumers in the high-priced segment do have well-established

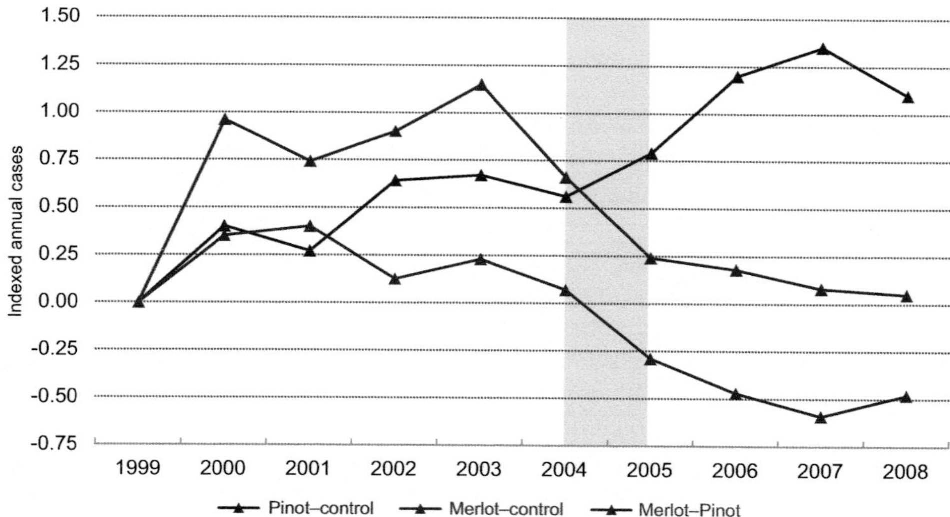

Figure 7.8
Indexed ratios of case volume sold: High-priced

Note: Indexed ratio of case volume measures the growth rate of one wine group against that of the other in sales. The values are indexed to zero in 1999. The shaded red box indicates the release time of the movie from October 2004 to May 2005.

Source: Reproduced from Cuellar et al. (2009), p. 12.

preferences for the two wines: some prefer Pinot Noir while others are obsessed with Merlot. Different consumer preferences for the two wines can explain why demand fluctuates substantially in the high-priced segment but not in the low- and medium-priced segments. Similarly to the low- and medium-priced segments, only after 2004 did the demand for Pinot Noir and Merlot start to experience structural changes. The demand for Pinot Noir surged but for Merlot plunged, suggesting a positive Sideways effect on Pinot Noir and a negative Sideways effect on Merlot. Despite the demand patterns for the two wines differing before 2004, the differences across the three segments tend to resemble each other after 2004, which can only be attributed to the release of the movie. Consistent with our conjecture, the negative Sideways effect on the demand for Merlot is much stronger in the high-priced segment than it is in the low- and medium-priced segments. Figure 7.8 shows that the Merlot–control ratio plunged drastically from 110% to less than 25% between 2003 and 2005. In addition, the Sideways effect in the high-priced segment seems short-lived as the effect started to wane after 2007.

Summary

1. The Sideways effect on wine consumption is triggered by the namesake movie in which the Pinot Noir fan praises Pinot Noir while denigrating Merlot. Alongside the success of the movie, consumers start to increase their demand for Pinot Noir while decreasing their demand for Merlot.
2. The structural changes in the demand for Pinot Noir and Merlot after 2004 are attributed to the Sideways effect, which is positive on the demand for Pinot Noir and negative on the demand for Merlot. The positive effect is stronger than the negative effect.
3. The price divergence of Pinot Noir and Merlot since 2004 is due to the positive effect of Sideways on the demand for Pinot Noir and the negative effect on the demand for Merlot. After the movie release, the price of Pinot Noir increased substantially while the price of Merlot decreased noticeably.
4. Holding the prices of the wines the same after the movie release, we can measure the size of the Sideways effect on the demand for Pinot Noir and Merlot. This is conducted by examining the magnitude of the shift in the demand curve of the control group. Holding the quantity demanded the same, we can measure the Sideways effect on price.
5. If both the prices and quantities demanded differ across the three wines after the movie release, we can decompose the total price effect into the pure price effect and the Sideways effect. This requires us to figure out the demand function for the control group.
6. The movie *Sideways* increases the awareness of wine consumption among the public, which matters more to novice consumers and less to oenophiles in their purchase decisions. For wine consumption, price is a useful segmentation device that can reflect consumers' knowledge of wine.
7. The positive Sideways effect on Pinot Noir is stronger in the low-priced segment than it is in the medium-priced segment; by contrast, the negative Sideways effect on Merlot is weaker in the low-priced segment than it is in the medium-priced segment.

8. The negative Sideways effect on the demand for Merlot is much stronger in the high-priced segment than it is in the low- and medium-priced segments. The Sideways effect on the demand for Pinot Noir in the high-priced segment seems short-lived.

Problem solving

1. Some people argue that the Sideways effect on the demand for Pinot Noir is a bandwagon effect while on the demand for Merlot is a snob effect. Others argue that the Sideways effect on the demand for both Pinot Noir and Merlot is a bandwagon effect. Comment on the two opinions.
2. In order to examine the Sideways effect on the demand for Pinot Noir and Merlot, we select a wine, *A*, as a benchmark whose demand is not affected by the movie because it was not featured in the movie. This means that we assume the demand for the three wines is the same if the Sideways effect does not exist. Suppose that all three wines were sold at $40 per bottle with the same sales volume of 2,000 bottles each in the market before the release of the movie. We also know that the sales of wine *A* increased to 2,500 bottles after the movie release due to a 10% decrease in its price, other things being equal. If we observe after the movie release that the prices of both Pinot Noir and Merlot decreased by 5% while the sales of Pinot Noir and Merlot increased to 2,750 bottles and 2,125 bottles, respectively, what would be the Sideways effect on the demand for Pinot Noir and Merlot, respectively? (Assume that the demands for the three wines are all linear.)
3. Explain why the Sideways effect would vary across different price ranges of Pinot Noir and Merlot. Which market segment has a greater nonfunctional demand relative to functional demand: the low-priced segment or the high-priced segment?

Solutions to all review questions and problem solving tasks are included in the Support Material for this book, which can be accessed at www.routledge.com/9780367897352.

Notes

1 The evidence in this chapter is from Cuellar et al. (2009). I thank Professor Steven S. Cuellar at the Department of Economics of Sonoma State University for granting me the permission to use his study results.
2 *The New York Times*. A film's boon to Pinot Noir. February 25, 2005.

Bibliography

Haeger, J. W., & Storchmann, K. (2006). Prices of American Pinot Noir wines: Climate, craftsmanship, critics. *Agricultural Economics*, *35*(1), 67–78.

Costanigro, M., McCluskey, J. J., & Mittelhammer, R. C. (2007). Segmenting the wine market based on price: Hedonic regression when different prices mean different products. *Journal of Agricultural Economics*, *58*(3), 454–466.

Cuellar, S. S., Karnowsky, D., & Acosta, F. (2009). The Sideways effect: A test for changes in the demand for Merlot and Pinot Noir wines. *Journal of Wine Economics*, *4*(2), 1–14.

MODULE 3

Supply

8 Firm production and cost

This chapter lays out a foundation for analyzing the theory of the firm by explaining the relationship between firm production and cost. Cost is the most important factor that firms need to take into account in deciding output. We begin by exploring the properties of the production function that are grounded on the distinction between capital and labor on the one hand and the coordination of the two inputs in production on the other. Given the prices of capital and labor, the expenditures on capital and labor inputs constitute fixed costs and variable costs, respectively. Based on the production function, we derive the variable cost curve which in turn gives rise to a family of cost curves that are associated with output, including the average variable cost, the average total cost, and marginal cost curves. Finally, we analyze firm production both in the short run in which fixed costs cannot be changed and the long run during which all costs become variable.

AFTER STUDYING THIS CHAPTER, YOU SHOULD BE ABLE TO:

- **Understand the production function and analyze the properties of the production function in relation to capital and labor inputs;**
- **Understand the distinction between fixed costs and variable costs as well as graph a family of cost curves that are associated with output;**
- **Analyze firm production in the short run, including breakeven analysis and optimization analysis; and**
- **Understand firm production in the long run, the long-run average cost, and the concept of economies of scale.**

8.1 Production function

The breadth of tourism and hospitality supply is characterized by various types of investments, some astronomically large and others negligible. An Airbus A380 aircraft costs US$445.6 million, Galaxy Hotel in Macau incurred an investment of US$2.1 billion in the first phase, Shanghai Disneyland amounted to US$5.5 billion in construction, and Dubailand, an entertainment complex slated to open in Dubai in 2020, would cost a whopping US$64.3 billion.[1] By contrast, it would take only hundreds of dollars to finance a rickshaw business, an iconic and traditional tourist transportation in India and many Southeast Asian countries. Some hospitality businesses necessitate an enormous investment prior to operation, while others would encounter escalating costs over the course of operation. Some hospitality businesses are touted by featuring low costs as a selling point, such as the so-called low-cost airlines and budget hotels, to name a few. Low-cost airlines such as easyJet and Ryanair may let you fly between two European cities for dozens of euros. The same amount of money would also let you be accommodated at 7 Days Inn, the largest budget hotel chain in China. For every business in the economy and in tourism and hospitality in particular, cost is instrumental in firm production and is under the control of firms.

8.1.1 Capital and labor

Regardless of which industry is concerned in the economy, firms need to purchase various inputs in the first place and turn them into outputs, thereby rendering products and services to consumers. At the heart of firm production is the relationship between the amount of inputs that a firm puts in production and the amount of outputs it can produce. We distinguish between two inputs, capital (K) and labor (L), which are ubiquitous and fundamental in firm production of all kinds. Capital includes everything from factory to machinery, which is invested by firms in advance before production starts and stays unchanged in a certain period of time. Thus, capital does not vary with the output along the spectrum of firm production. Labor, which can be exemplified by the number of employees or work hours, is incurred as long as production starts and continues. Thus, the more firms produce, the more the amount of labor they need. If a firm has invested a certain amount of capital prior to production, it needs to hire workers to work with the capital in order to initiate the production. Given a fixed amount of capital $(\bar{K})$, the maximum output that the firm can produce is a function of the quantity of labor (L):

$$q = f\left(L, \bar{K}\right) \tag{8.1}$$

Equation (8.1) is called the production function, which describes the relationship between the maximum output and the quantity of two inputs with capital being held constant. The idea of the production function was credited to German economist Johann Heinrich von Thünen (1783–1850) for expounding the mathematical foundations of marginal productivity theory. For simplicity we shall not specify the mathematical forms of the production function but instead illustrate its economic properties graphically. Figure 8.1 shows that the production function is S-shaped, depicting the relationship between the quantity of labor L on the x-axis and the quantity of output Q on the y-axis. The production function has three important properties that are manifested on different levels of labor input. When labor is at the minimum, increasing labor in production leads to an increase in output, and thus

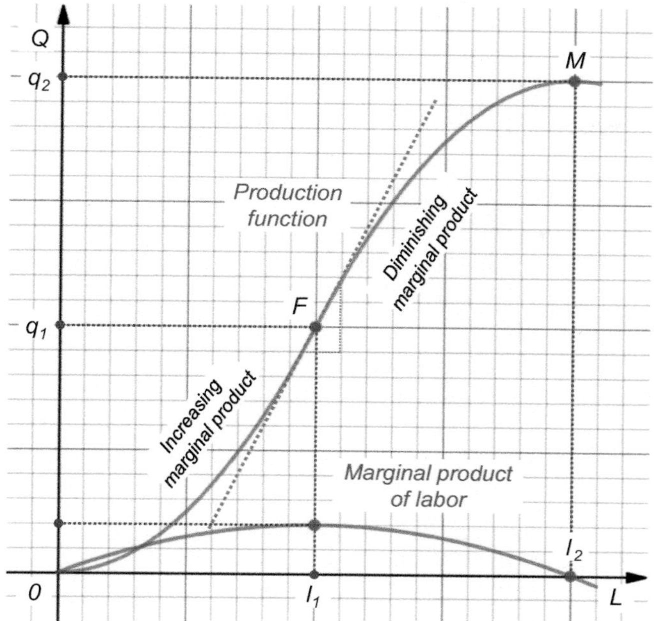

Figure 8.1
Production function and diminishing marginal product

the production function slopes upward. Figure 8.1 shows that when increasing labor input from 0 to l_1, not only does output increase from 0 to q_1, but the marginal product of labor, $\Delta q / \Delta l$, which is the change in output divided by the change in labor, also increases. This phenomenon is referred to as increasing marginal product of labor. The reason is that when labor is insufficient as opposed to capital, increasing labor gets close to an optimal combination between capital and labor in production and therefore accelerates output. Figure 8.1 shows that this optimal combination between capital and labor is point F on the production function at which the marginal product of labor is maximized.

To illustrate the idea of increasing marginal product, suppose that a restaurateur has invested a certain amount of capital, including leasing premises, furnishing the restaurant, purchasing equipment, and so on, prior to operation. To initiate operation, he needs to hire employees to produce meals, and suppose that he hires one employee at a time. If the first employee produces 50 meals per day, then the marginal product of labor is 50 meals. When the second employee is hired, the output increases from 50 to 120 meals per day, with the second employee adding 70 meals as the marginal product. When the third employee is in, the output further increases from 120 to 210 meals; the third employee contributes an additional 90 meals as the marginal product, and so on. Increasing marginal product occurs because the increase in labor input facilitates the division and specialization of labor, thereby boosting production efficiency of the restaurant. At the three-employee staffed restaurant the operation procedure can be divided such that one employee works as a chef, one as a server, and one as a cashier. If there were only one employee, he would have to handle, but is by no means specialized in, everything from cooking, serving to billing. Hence, the productivity of the restaurant as a whole is undermined without the division of labor.

8.1.2 Diminishing marginal product

As labor input reaches a modest level, say l_1 as assumed, increasing the quantity of labor would further increase output but at a decreasing rate. Thus, the production function continues to slope upward but increasingly flattens as production continues (Figure 8.1). This means that when labor increases from l_1 to l_2, the marginal product of labor actually falls, which is referred to as diminishing marginal product of labor (Figure 8.1). The diminishing marginal product of labor arises because capital, which is fixed by definition, starts to impose a constraint on production insofar as labor becomes abundant and even idle. In the case above when the restaurant is constrained by the premises and the capacity of the equipment, the more employees working at the restaurant, the more likely they would hinder each other in performing their own tasks and therefore production efficiency as a whole is undermined. Constrained by capital, increasing labor input beyond l_1 makes labor increasingly idle, whereby the combination between capital and labor starts to deviate from the optimum at point F, ending up decreasing production efficiency as a whole.

To illustrate the idea of diminishing marginal product of labor after l_1, now suppose that the restaurateur continues to hire the fourth employee. Then the output increases from 210 meals to 280 with an additional 70 meals being added. Hiring the fifth employee increases the output further from 280 meals to 330, and hence the fifth adds 50 meals, and so on, until the last employee, say the 10th, adds an additional one meal. While hiring more employees increases total output, each employee from the fourth onwards adds a decreasing number of meals compared to the preceding one. The diminishing marginal product of labor arises because capital becomes an obstacle to increasing production efficiency when labor is abundant. This could be exemplified such that the four-employee staffed restaurant may need two servers to take customer orders and deliver dishes in order to further increase output. However, the restaurant premises would become too crowded to accommodate four employees and make them work smoothly. Thus, all of them end up working less efficiently than they otherwise could. The scenario where labor becomes idle applies to other positions, such as chefs and cashiers, in which the capital constraint hinders employees from working as efficiently as they otherwise could, thereby impairing the productivity of the restaurant as a whole.

Further increasing labor beyond l_2, the production function starts to slope downward perpetually, and thus total output decreases (Figure 8.1). This is because the marginal product of labor becomes negative as soon as the labor input exceeds l_2. Thus l_2 is the quantity of labor input at which the marginal product of labor is zero, and hence total output is maximized at point M on the production function represented by q_2. In the restaurant case above, l_2 could be exemplified by the 11th employee who would add zero meals if he were hired, and the 12th would add negative units of meals, and so on. Due to the constraints of the restaurant premises and the equipment, the employees would obstruct each other in performing their work. The quantities of labor input l_1 and l_2 are the two thresholds beyond which the property of the production function alters. At l_1 the marginal product of labor is maximized as the optimal combination between capital and labor is achieved. Hence either increasing or decreasing the labor input from l_1 ends up reducing the marginal product. At l_2 the marginal product is minimized, and thus total output is maximized (Figure 8.1). As the labor input increases from zero to l_1, the production function slopes upward at an increasing rate, thereby accelerating the output. As the labor input continues to increase from l_1 to l_2 the production function slopes upward at a decreasing rate, thus decelerating the output.

8.2 Derivation of cost curves

8.2.1 Cost structure

Based on the two fundamental inputs in the production function, costs are defined as the expenditure on capital and labor given their respective prices. That is, costs are the quantity of inputs multiplied by their prices in the market. Consistent with the classification of capital and labor, costs consist of fixed costs (FC) and variable costs (VC). Fixed costs are the costs that do not vary with the amount of output, and are thus independent of how much a firm produces. Fixed costs are incurred prior to production, for example through a hotel investing in real estate, purchasing equipment, and training its staff, and so on, even though the hotel is not yet in operation. Variable costs, by contrast, vary with output, and are thus a function of the firm's output. For instance, to kick off the operation, a restaurateur needs to hire employees and purchase ingredients, giving rise to variable costs as long as meals are produced. Obviously, variable costs are zero if there is no meal produced at all. The more meals the restaurant produces, the more employees and ingredients it needs, and the higher the variable costs. If the restaurant shuts down, no variable costs will be incurred for there is no production, but fixed costs remain.

The distinction between fixed costs and variable costs is grounded on whether and the extent to which they can be changed in production in a certain period of time or at a finite production level. Fixed costs are invariant to output in a given period of time, and thus firms are said to be operating in the short run. As long as a firm is able to change its fixed costs in a given period of time, it is said to be operating in the long run in that period. Note that the short run and the long run, which we shall refer to from time to time in our analysis, are related to, but not defined on, time. There is no yardstick with regard to a certain spell of time in production by which we can demarcate between the short run and the long run. A couple of days may suggest the long run for a street-food vendor, because such a short spell could still enable him to set up one stall after another, thereby changing fixed costs of the vending business. Nevertheless, a couple of days is insufficient for a hotelier to erect new hotel premises, thereby changing fixed costs of the hotel business, and hence it indicates the short run. A few years may enable the hotelier to operate in the long run through expanding his hotel premises, yet it does not suffice for infrastructure providers to operate in the long run, because expanding infrastructure capacity, such as an airport, may take decades to accomplish.

The sum of fixed costs and variable costs is total cost, which is the total expenditure on inputs incurred to firms for the whole production. The proportion of fixed costs relative to that of variable costs, or vice versa, in total cost suggests cost structure. The breadth of tourism and hospitality supply, which we addressed in Chapter 1, can further be elucidated by referring to cost structures which vary across a wide range of tourism and hospitality sectors. Some hospitality businesses are intensive in fixed costs, i.e. capital intensive, meaning that fixed costs make up a large proportion relative to variable costs in total cost. For example, airlines, amusement parks, cruise lines, and so forth entail an enormous amount of capital investment in the first instance. Other hospitality businesses are intensive in variable costs, i.e. labor intensive, meaning that variable costs make up a relatively large proportion in total cost. For example, a restaurant business necessitates a laborious process from cooking, delivering to serving, thereby requiring considerable frontline staff, and hence considerable variable costs are incurred.

8.2.2 Cost concepts

Based on fixed costs and variable costs as well as their relationships to firm production, we can further derive a set of cost concepts that are associated with output. These derived cost concepts allow us to further explore how costs and cost structure change with the output of firms. To decide how much to produce a firm needs to understand how various costs would change with output in the first place. This means that cost imposes a constraint on firm production. From fixed costs, the average fixed cost (*AFC*) can be obtained through dividing fixed costs (*FC*) by output (q):

$$AFC = \frac{FC}{q}. \tag{8.2}$$

Thus, average fixed cost is fixed costs per unit of output when the output is q units, suggesting that fixed costs are evenly spread on the q units of the output. Since fixed costs are constant in the short run, the more a firm produces, the smaller the average fixed cost, and thus average fixed cost is monotonically decreasing with output. From variable costs, the average variable cost (*AVC*) can be obtained through dividing variable costs (*VC*) by output (q):

$$AVC = \frac{VC}{q}. \tag{8.3}$$

Similarly, average variable cost is the variable costs per unit of output when the output is q units. Note that variable costs are a function of output, and therefore the property of average variable cost is distinct from that of average fixed cost. We shall elaborate on the property of average variable cost shortly when it comes to graphing the average variable cost curve. From total cost, the average total cost (*ATC*) can be obtained through dividing total cost (*TC*) by output (*q*):

$$ATC = \frac{TC}{q}. \quad (8.4)$$

Likewise, average total cost is the total cost per unit of output when the output is *q* units, which is the unit total cost of production. Since variable costs are a function of output, total cost is also a function of output as it incorporates variable costs. Therefore, the property of average total cost is also distinct from that of the average fixed cost but resembles that of average variable cost. We can also write average total cost in formula (8.4) by further articulating average fixed cost and average variable cost:

$$ATC = \frac{TC}{q} = \frac{FC+VC}{q} = \frac{FC}{q} + \frac{VC}{q} = AFC + AVC. \quad (8.5)$$

Last but not least, marginal cost (*MC*) measures the change in total cost with respect to a change in output (*q*):

$$MC = \frac{\Delta TC}{\Delta q} = \frac{dTC}{dq}. \quad (8.6)$$

Formula (8.6) indicates that marginal cost measures the incremental change in total cost as output changes, and thus it is expressed as the derivative of total cost with respect to output. Marginal cost differs fundamentally from average total cost which is total cost spread on a given output. Despite the fact that both marginal cost and various average costs are associated with output, marginal cost is instrumental in firm production and affects the properties of other costs. Similarly, we can write marginal cost in formula (8.6) as the sum of marginal fixed cost and marginal variable cost by breaking down total cost into fixed costs and variable costs:

$$MC = \frac{\Delta TC}{\Delta q} = \frac{\Delta(FC+VC)}{\Delta q} = \frac{\Delta FC}{\Delta q} + \frac{\Delta VC}{\Delta q} = \frac{\Delta VC}{\Delta q}. \quad (8.7)$$

Since fixed costs, by definition, do not change with output in the short run, marginal fixed cost is zero. Thus, marginal cost is equal to marginal variable cost in the short run. That is, marginal cost depends entirely on variable costs. Intuitively, since variable costs change with output in the short run while fixed costs don't, the change in total cost is fully accounted for by the change in variable costs while independent of fixed costs.

8.2.3 Cost curves

Based on the algebraic expressions of the cost concepts above, we can proceed to graph their curves. On the one hand, cost curves enable us to better articulate their properties and behavior, and on the other hand, they allow us to better comprehend their relationships to output. In the first place, since costs are derived from the production function, we can write out the cost function as the inverse of the production function. It follows that we regard the quantity of output as the independent variable on the x-axis and the quantity of inputs as the dependent variable on the y-axis. Assuming that the prices of capital and labor are fixed, we know that the expenditures on the two inputs are costs, which depend entirely on their quantities in production. Given a predetermined amount of capital $\bar{K}$ in the production function, we can write variable costs (VC), denoted by the expenditure on labor inputs, as the inverse of the production function:

$$VC = f^{-1}(q). \tag{8.8}$$

Therefore, the variable cost curve can be readily obtained by swapping the x- and y-axis of the production function, whereby labor becomes the dependent variable and output the independent variable. Formula (8.8) suggests that the variable cost curve is the production function being flipped upward or downward against the 45-degree diagonal as shown in Figure 8.2a. By depicting the variable cost curve with the x- and y-axis denoting output and variable costs, respectively, in Figure 8.2b, we obtain the standard variable cost curve. Since the shapes of the variable cost curve and the production function are reversed, all the properties of the production function are shared by the variable cost curve but with reversed interpretations. Increasing marginal product of labor now suggests that increasing the output from 0 to q_1 leads

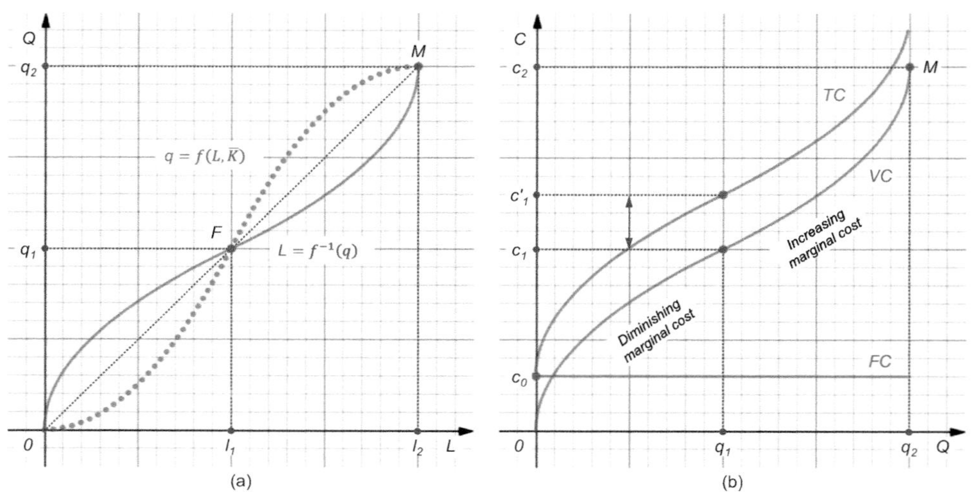

Figure 8.2
Production function and variable cost curve

to an increase in variable costs at a decreasing rate ($\Delta VC / \Delta q \downarrow$), which is referred to as diminishing marginal cost. Thus, the variable cost curve has a positive yet decreasing slope as the output increases from 0 to q_1. On the other hand, diminishing marginal product of labor suggests that increasing the output from q_1 to q_2 leads to an increase in variable costs at an increasing rate ($\Delta VC / \Delta q \uparrow$), a phenomenon referred to as increasing marginal cost. Thus, the variable cost curve has a positive yet increasing slope as the output increases from q_1 to q_2.

Based on the variable cost curve, we can easily derive the total cost curve. Since total cost (TC) is the sum of fixed costs and variable costs, $TC = FC + VC$, the total cost curve is obtained by simply shifting the variable cost curve upward for the size of fixed costs denoted by c_0 in Figure 8.2b. Thus, the total cost curve has a positive y-intercept equal to c_0, which is the size of fixed costs. Since the total cost curve and the variable cost curve have exactly the same shape, their slopes are identical at any given output. This conclusion confirms that marginal cost is actually the marginal variable cost as we derived mathematically in formula (8.7). All the properties of the variable cost curve, specifically diminishing and increasing marginal costs that occur in sequence as output increases, are equally possessed by the total cost curve.

Given the variable cost and total cost curves, we can graph the average variable cost (AVC) curve and the average total cost (ATC) curve. Since $AVC = VC / q$, average variable cost at any given output is the slope of the ray from the origin that cuts through the variable cost curve at point (q, VC) (Figure 8.3a). Thus, the average variable cost curve is composed of the slopes of all the rays from the origin that cut through the variable cost curve at all points (q, VC). As output increases, the slopes of these rays first decrease before starting to increase, suggesting that the average variable cost curve is U-shaped above the x-axis. Figure 8.3b shows that the average variable cost curve first slopes downward as output increases from zero until it reaches

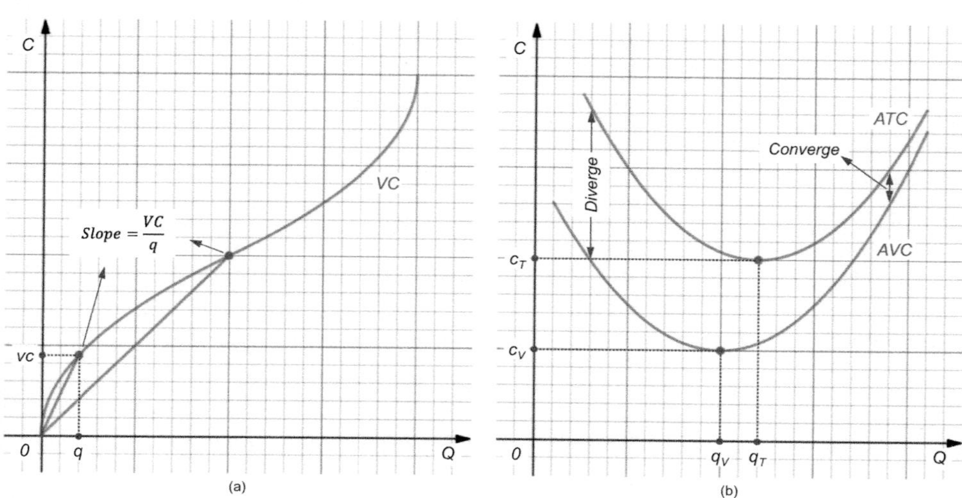

Figure 8.3
Variable cost curve and average cost curve

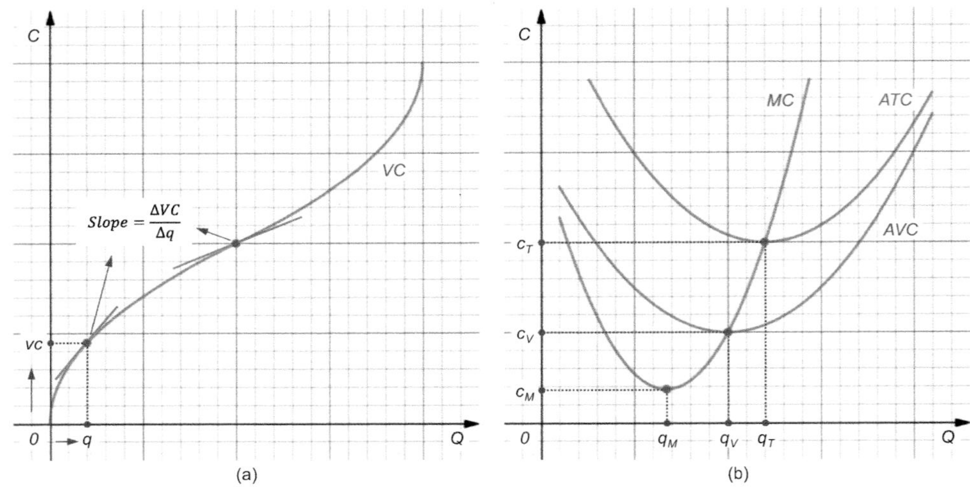

Figure 8.4
Variable cost curve and marginal cost curve

the minimum at output q_V, beyond which it starts to slope upward. By the same token, average total cost, $ATC = TC / q$, suggests that the average total cost curve is the slopes of all the rays from the origin that cut through the total cost curve at all points (q, TC). Thus, the average total cost curve is also *U*-shaped above the *x*-axis and thus has a minimum. The average total cost curve resembles the average variable cost curve but differs in two aspects. First, since $ATC = AFC + AVC$ and $AFC > 0$, the average total cost curve always lies above the average variable cost curve (Figure 8.3b). Second, since *AFC* is monotonically decreasing, the average total cost curve and the average variable cost curve diverge insofar as output approaches zero but converging as output approaches infinity (Figure 8.3b).

Since marginal cost $MC = \Delta VC / \Delta q$, the marginal cost curve is the slope of the variable cost curve (Figure 8.4a). As output increases, the slope of the variable cost curve first decreases and then increases. Hence the marginal cost curve is also *U*-shaped (Figure 8.4b). Due to diminishing marginal cost, both average variable cost and average total cost are driven down as output increases. Thus, output q_M at which marginal cost is minimized is smaller than both q_V at which average variable cost is minimized and q_T at which average total cost is minimized. If marginal cost were strictly lower than average variable cost, increasing output would continuously drive down average variable cost, contradicting the average variable cost curve being *U*-shaped. Marginal cost drives down average variable cost when $MC < AVC$ while pushing it up when $MC > AVC$, suggesting that the marginal cost curve intersects the average variable cost curve at the minimum of the latter. Likewise, marginal cost drives down average total cost when $MC < ATC$ while pushing it up when $MC > ATC$, suggesting that the marginal cost curve also cuts through the average total cost curve at the minimum of the latter. Note that q_V is strictly smaller than q_T because the average total cost curve lies above the average variable cost curve and marginal cost is strictly increasing from q_M. Hence we have $q_M < q_V < q_T$ (Figure 8.4b).

8.3 Cost and short-run production

8.3.1 Revenue, cost, and profit

We first analyze firm production in the short run under which fixed costs are constant by definition whereas variable costs vary as output changes. Due to the constraint of fixed costs, firms experience diminishing marginal cost and increasing marginal cost in sequence, which in turn affect the optimal output that they decide to produce. For expository convenience, we assume that the price of a good is given in the market, meaning that firms cannot change the price of the good. Thus, the price is a constant and exogenous to a firm's output decision of the good. This is a key characteristic of firms in perfect competition which we shall address in detail in Chapter 9. Let us follow this assumption for the time being in order to proceed with the analysis of firm production. Therefore, the firm's decision is solely on output whereby its total revenue, cost, and profit are determined, respectively. Given the market price ($\bar{P}$), the firm's total revenue (R) turns out to be a function of output (q) only:

$$R = \bar{P}q. \tag{8.9}$$

Specifically, total revenue R in formula (8.9) is a linear function of output q which increases at a constant rate of $\bar{P}$. Note that formula (8.9) is in contrast to the generic revenue function in equation (5.15) in Chapter 5 in which total revenue is a function of both the price and quantity of a good demanded in the market. Formula (8.9) suggests that the firm can obtain a constant revenue equal to $\bar{P}$ by selling each unit of the good. Therefore, the market price $\bar{P}$ is also the marginal revenue (MR), which by definition is the change in total revenue divided by the change in quantity of the good sold by the firm:

$$MR = \frac{\Delta R}{\Delta q} = \frac{dR}{dq} = \bar{P}. \tag{8.10}$$

Given total revenue in formula (8.9) and total cost, total profit (π) is obtained by subtracting total cost (C) from total revenue (R):

$$\pi = R - C. \tag{8.11}$$

Since the total revenue curve is linear while the total cost curve is nonlinear, total profit must be a nonlinear function of output. Given the total revenue and total cost curves, the profit curve can be obtained by plotting the residuals of total revenue subtracting total cost (Figure 8.5). We can identify three threshold values of output which suggest the key features of these residuals. First is the zero output at which total profit is negative, equal to the size of fixed costs, $\pi = -FC$. Second is the output

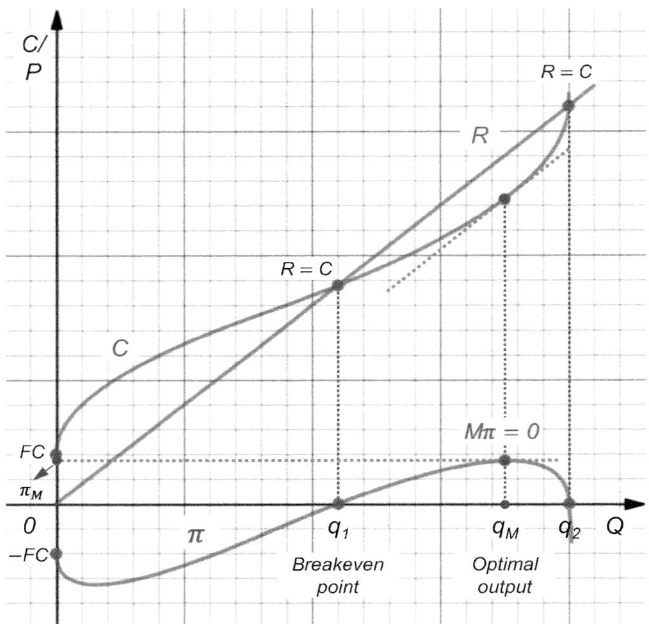

Figure 8.5
Revenue, cost, and profit curves

q_1 at which total revenue equals total cost, $R = C$, or profit $\pi = 0$. Third is the output q_2 at which total revenue also equals total cost, $R = C$, or profit $\pi = 0$. Thus, the profit curve consists of three portions separated by q_1 and q_2. The first portion is the output between zero and q_1 in which profit is negative and rising to zero as output increases. The second portion is the output between q_1 and q_2 in which profit is positive, first increasing from zero at q_1 then decreasing to zero at q_2. The third portion is a perpetually negative profit as output exceeds q_2, due to the nonlinear growth of total cost that will eventually overtake the linear growth of total revenue as output continues to increase.

8.3.2 Breakeven point

The profit curve allows us to identify the firm's breakeven point, which is defined as the output beyond which the firm starts to make positive profits. Figure 8.5 shows that the firm breaks even when producing q_1 at which total revenue equals total cost for the first time, namely profit $\pi = 0$. Since total revenue grows at constant rate $\overline{P}$ while total cost accelerates as the output increases beyond q_1, total cost will eventually catch up with, and then outpace, total revenue as the firm keeps producing. While the outputs q_1 and q_2 are mathematically equivalent to suggest a zero profit, q_2 is not the breakeven point because the firm will encounter negative profits perpetually when producing beyond q_2. Also, because total profit is maximized somewhere between q_1 and q_2, the firm will never produce q_2. If the market price increased, the total revenue curve would pivot upward around the origin, enabling the firm to produce less than q_1 to break even. If the market price decreased, the total revenue curve would pivot downward, and thus the firm needs to produce more than q_1 to break even.

8.3.3 Firm optimization

Similar to utility maximization for the consumer, the firm's ultimate goal is to maximize profit given the price of a good and the cost of production. Note that the breakeven point tells us nothing about the optimal output at which the firm maximizes profit. Optimal output is analogous to some sort of equilibrium in production in which the firm has no incentive either to increase or to decrease output. In Figure 8.5, the profit curve between the outputs q_1 and q_2 is hump-shaped, suggesting that profit is maximized between q_1 and q_2. To understand the behavior of total profit, we need to refer to the concept of marginal profit, which is the change in total profit divided by the change in output, that is, $M\pi = \Delta\pi / \Delta q$. As long as marginal profit is positive at a given output, increasing output by one additional unit leads to an increase in total profit; as long as marginal profit is negative, decreasing output by one additional unit also leads to an increase in total profit. Therefore, only when marginal profit is zero can total profit be maximized. If otherwise, the firm can either increase or decrease output in order to increase total profit. Graphically, the slope of a tangent line to the profit curve is the marginal profit of the firm at a given output. Insofar as the tangent line is horizontal suggesting that its slope is zero, the marginal profit is zero. Figure 8.5 shows that the optimal output is identified as q_M at which the straight line tangent to the hump-shaped portion of the profit curve is horizontal.

The firm's profit-maximizing condition that marginal profit is equal to zero $(M\pi = 0)$ is equivalent to the condition that marginal revenue is equal to marginal cost, $MR = MC$. The firm's total profit increases as long as $MR > MC$, or $M\pi > 0$, and decreases as long as $MR < MC$, or $M\pi < 0$. Only when $MR = MC$ can total profit be maximized. Thus optimal output q_M is also where the slopes of the total revenue curve and total cost curve equalize as they are the marginal revenue and marginal cost, respectively. Since the slope of the total revenue curve is constant $\left(MR = \overline{P}\right)$, the profit-maximizing condition $MR = MC$ entails that the tangent line to the total cost curve must be parallel to the total revenue curve (Figure 8.5). If the market price rises and hence marginal revenue increases, the equalization of marginal revenue and marginal cost entails a larger marginal cost which in turn requires increasing output. Thus, the new optimal output at which total profit is maximized will be greater than q_M. If the market price falls, the equalization of marginal revenue and marginal cost entails a smaller marginal cost which in turn entails decreasing output. Thus, the new profit-maximizing output will be smaller than the initial optimal output q_M.

8.4 Cost and long-run production

8.4.1 Long-run average cost

In the long run fixed costs are free to vary and thus a firm can choose different levels of fixed costs to maximize production efficiency with varying outputs. It is worth noting that fixed costs cannot be changed continuously the same way as variable costs. Let us return to the restaurant case. Suppose that the restaurant initially operates on a medium-sized premises which exemplifies a medium level of fixed costs. We know

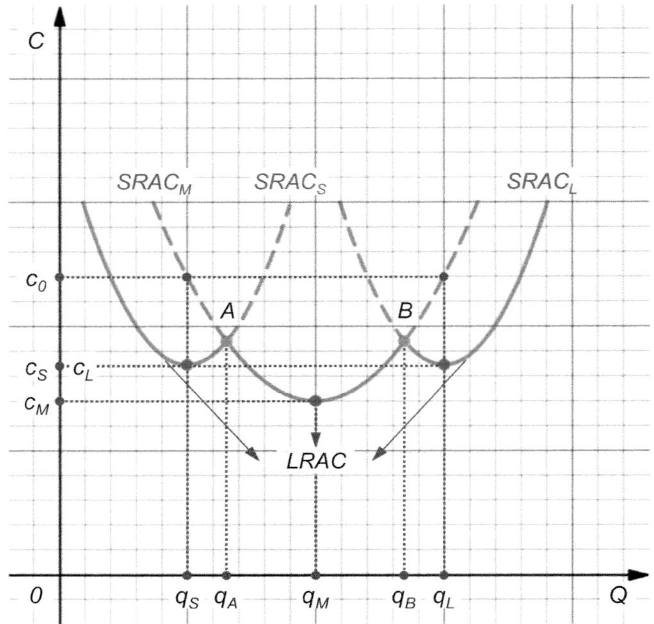

Figure 8.6
Long-run average cost curve

that average total cost in the short run, also referred to as the short-run average cost (*SRAC*), is *U*-shaped. Figure 8.6 shows the short-run average cost of the restaurant, $SRAC_M$, which corresponds to the medium level of fixed costs. Given $SRAC_M$, the restaurant's most efficient output is q_M at which its short-run average cost is minimized at c_M. Suppose now that the restaurant needs to produce a smaller quantity, say q_S ($q_S < q_M$), due to a decrease in demand or for whatever the reason. Then the short-run average cost will increase drastically from c_M to c_0. This is because the smaller output no longer enables the restaurant to reach an optimal combination between its fixed costs and the decreased variable costs. This means that a small level of fixed costs, exemplified by a small-sized premises, is entailed to produce q_S at which the short-run average cost, $SRAC_S$, can be minimized at c_S ($c_S < c_0$). By the same token, if the restaurant wants to produce a larger quantity, say q_L ($q_S < q_M < q_L$), it needs a large level of fixed costs whereby the short-run average cost, $SRAC_L$, can be brought down from c_0 to c_L ($c_L < c_0$).

Therefore, with varying outputs, only when fixed costs can be adjusted accordingly can average cost be minimized at different levels of output, and hence the restaurant can maximize production efficiency continuously. Suppose that the restaurant needs to vary its output from q_S, q_M to q_L. Then the best strategy would be to set up the small-, medium-, and large-sized premises accordingly which, though, is infeasible in the short run. Given the three levels of fixed costs illustrated above, insofar as output is smaller than q_A at which the short-run cost curves $SRAC_S$ and $SRAC_M$ intersect at point *A*, the best strategy is to use the small-sized premises as it incurs the lowest average cost. For the same reason, insofar as output is greater than

q_B at which the short-run cost curves $SRAC_M$ and $SRAC_L$ intersect at point B, the best strategy is to use the large-sized premises. When output is between q_A and q_B, operating on the medium-sized premises will be the best strategy. It follows that in the long run during which the restaurant can adjust fixed costs freely at the three levels, the average cost curve is composed of the solid portions of the three short-run average cost curves along the production range as indicated in Figure 8.6. This curve is referred to as the long-run average cost curve ($LRAC$), which describes the relationship between the lowest average cost and output insofar as all costs become variable.

8.4.2 Economies of scale

A different perspective on the role that the long-run average cost plays in firm production is to look at how the firm adjusts costs at the margins of a series of the short-run average cost curves. Figure 8.6 shows that only if producing q_A+1 units incurs a lower average cost on the medium-sized premises will the restaurateur be willing to increase fixed costs beyond the small level. Only if producing q_B+1 ends up with a lower average cost on the large-sized premises will the restaurateur be willing to further increase fixed costs beyond the medium level. Now suppose that the restaurant can change fixed costs continuously in theory. We will obtain a smooth long-run average cost curve as depicted in Figure 8.7. Since the long-run average cost is strictly lower than or at least equal to the short-run average costs, the long-run average cost curve is always the lower envelope of an infinite number of the short-run average cost curves (Figure 8.7). On the long-run average cost curve there exists a strictly negative relationship between the average cost and output in the production range from zero to q_E as shown in Figure 8.7, a phenomenon known as economies of scale. Due to economies of scale, the restaurant can enjoy increasingly lower average costs as long as it produces in large quantities until

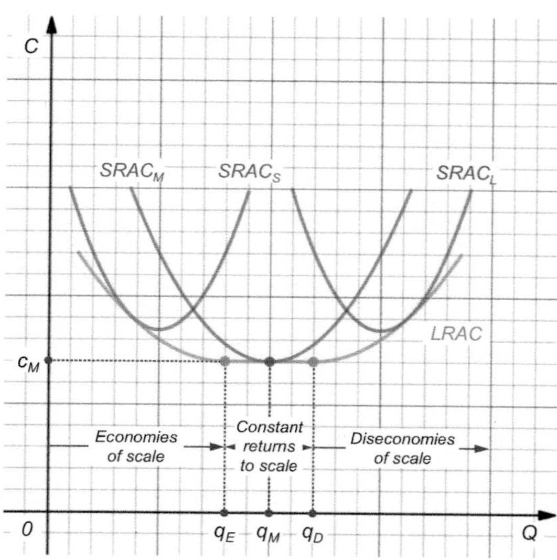

Figure 8.7
Long-run average cost and economies of scale

the output reaches q_E. Note that economies of scale occur in the long run and thus differ from diminishing marginal cost in the short run.

Not only can the long-run average cost be driven down as output increases, but the minimum of average costs can also be sustained in a certain range of production. This is illustrated in Figure 8.7 by assuming that the restaurant continues to expand the premises, eventually rendering the long-run average cost curve flat between q_E and q_D. This means that the long-run average cost is invariant insofar as the restaurant produces any output between q_E and q_D. This phenomenon is referred to as constant returns to scale. Constant returns to scale occur because relaxing the constraint of fixed costs in the long run can defer the increasing marginal cost that would otherwise arise in the short run. Nevertheless, as the level of fixed costs further expands, production efficiency could be undermined due to, for example, complicated coordination problems between different departments of a corporation as well as cumbersome bureaucracy in big corporations. This leads to an increase in average costs when the output exceeds q_D as shown in Figure 8.7, which is referred to as diseconomies of scale. The existence of diseconomies of scale implies, on the one hand, that firm size is by no means infinite but has its limits. On the other hand, there would be different sizes of firms in terms of output that coexist in the market in a certain period of time.

8.4.3 Why economies of scale arise

The phenomenon of economies of scale is not peculiar to firm production in the economic sphere but a universal law that holds in a wide range of scientific explorations. Economies of scale, in essence, suggest that outcome increases disproportionately more than the increase in input through some sort of mechanism. For instance, the mechanism by which economies of scale arise can be referred to, or is an analogy of, the square-cube law in geometry. Consider a 1×1 cm square. If we double the side length to 2 cm, we end up with an area of 4 cm^2, which is four times the area of the initial square. Similarly, consider a $1 \times 1 \times 1$ cm cube, doubling the edge length to 2 cm ends up with a surface area of 24 cm^2 and a volume of 8 cm^3, which are four times the surface area and eight times the volume of the initial cube, respectively. Therefore, the outcome, regardless of whether it is a surface area, volume, or production efficiency, increases disproportionately more than the increase in input. This means that there exists some sort of multiplier effect of input on the output.

As far as firm production is concerned, economies of scale are manifested such that the long-run average cost falls disproportionately more than the increase in total cost. Economies of scale are substantiated by the fact that big corporations are usually more productive than their smaller counterparts. This is because big corporations can not only increase labor inputs to match a large level of fixed costs but can also generate a high degree of labor division and specialization, ending up with high productivity as a whole. Increased specialization of labor accelerates accumulation of knowledge in specialized areas of production, which further explains why economies of scale occur in big corporations. Note that fixed costs need to be invested in the first place prior to production in order to achieve economies of scale, which implies that firms cannot change fixed costs incrementally the same way as they change variable costs. For instance, when an airline purchases a large aircraft, its fixed costs are increased discretely—aircraft by aircraft instead of, incrementally, seat by seat on the airplane—because an aircraft is indivisible after all. Hence the long-run production is synonymous with firm strategy, for it entails planning a certain level of fixed costs in advance as well as accurately forecasting that a huge increase in demand is around the corner. By contrast the short-run production is synonymous with firm operation, for it requires nothing more than altering variable costs incrementally when production proceeds.

Summary

1. The production function delineates the relationship between the quantities of two inputs, capital and labor, and the maximum output that a firm can produce. The production function slopes upward, suggesting that output increases with the quantity of labor when capital is fixed.
2. Increasing marginal product of labor suggests that output accelerates with labor when capital is relatively abundant. Diminishing marginal product of labor suggests that output decelerates with labor when capital eventually becomes a constraint.
3. Costs are the expenditure on the inputs of capital and labor in producing the maximum output given their respective prices in the market. Fixed costs do not vary with output while variable costs vary with output in the short run. The sum of fixed costs and variable costs is total cost.
4. Average fixed cost is per unit fixed costs of a certain output, and average variable cost is per unit variable costs of the output. Average total cost is per unit total cost of the output, which is the sum of average fixed cost and average variable cost. Marginal cost is the change in total cost with respect to a change in output.
5. The variable cost curve is the inverse of the production function. The total cost curve is obtained by shifting the variable cost curve upward by the size of fixed costs. The average variable cost curve and marginal cost curve are derived from the variable cost curve. The average total cost curve is derived from the total cost curve.
6. The average variable cost, average total cost, and marginal cost curves are all *U*-shaped. The average total cost curve always lies above the average variable cost curve, and they diverge as output decreases and converge as output increases.
7. Average variable cost and average total cost are minimized when the marginal cost curve crosses the average variable cost and average total cost curves, respectively. The output at which marginal cost is minimized is smaller than the output at which average variable cost is minimized, which is smaller than the output at which average total cost is minimized.
8. In the short run a firm breaks even at the output at which total revenue equals total cost and beyond which the firm starts marking positive profits. Optimal output is the output at which total profit is maximized, that is, marginal profit equals zero.

9. In the long run fixed costs are subject to change, and thus all costs become variable in production. In theory the long-run average cost curve is the lower envelope of an infinite number of short-run average cost curves.
10. The phenomenon that the long-run average cost is driven down disproportionately more than the increase in total cost is called economies of scale. Economies of scale arise because large corporations can create a high degree of labor division and specialization, ending up with high productivity as a whole.

REVIEW QUESTIONS

Each question has four options, and there is only one correct answer to each question.

1. Which of the following is correct regarding the production function in the short run?
   A) Total output is maximized when marginal product is maximized.
   B) Total output continues to increase as labor inputs increase.
   C) Increasing marginal returns are due to the increase in capital inputs.
   D) Diminishing marginal returns will always arise.
2. The figure below shows the production function of a restaurant selling cheeseburgers. How many employees have been hired by the restaurant before the marginal product of labor starts to diminish?
   A) 2
   B) 3
   C) 4
   D) 5

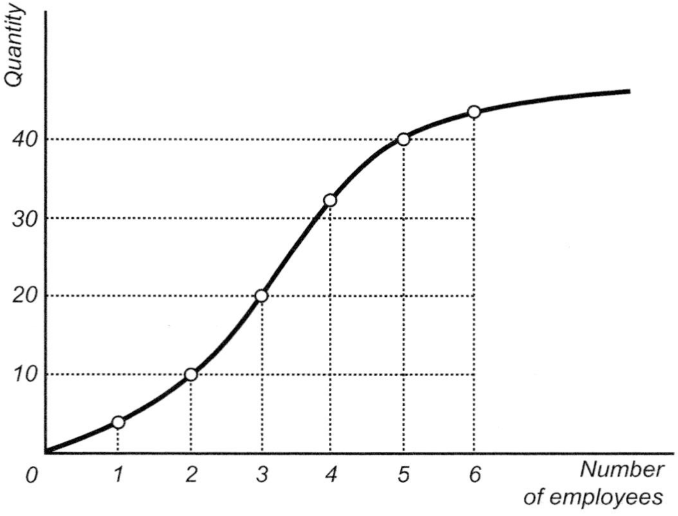

3. Which of the following is INCORRECT regarding the short run and the long run?
   A) In the short run, fixed costs cannot be changed.
   B) In the short run, the quantity of capital cannot be changed.
   C) In the long run, economies of scale could arise.
   D) In the long run, average variable cost is strictly decreasing.
4. Suppose that a restaurateur leases premises to sell burgers. He pays rents on a yearly basis at the beginning of each year and the rents totaled US$15,000 in 2019. If the rents were to increase by 10% in 2020, other things being equal, which of the following is correct?
   A) Fixed costs would increase by 10%.
   B) Variable costs would increase by 10%.
   C) Marginal cost would increase by 10%.
   D) Total cost would remain unchanged.
5. The table below shows some information on the output, the number of employees, and the total cost of a restaurant in producing bagels. What are the marginal cost and marginal product of labor, respectively, when the output increases from 6,000 bagels to 7,500?
   A) \$2; 75 bagels
   B) \$3; 75 bagels
   C) \$2; 125 bagels
   D) \$3; 125 bagels

Output (bagels per week)	Labor (employees per week)	Total costs (\$)
4,000	20	11,000
6,000	40	19,000
7,500	60	23,500
8,500	80	25,500
9,000	100	27,000

6. Bianchi's souvenir shop produces 50 handmade necklaces per week at a total cost of \$2,000, of which \$400 will be incurred anyway even if output is zero. If he increases output to 75 necklaces, his total cost will increase to \$2,500. If the output q is where Bianchi minimizes the average variable cost of the necklaces, which of the following is correct?
   A) $q < 50$
   B) $q = 50$
   C) $q = 75$
   D) $q > 75$

7. A firm's average variable cost is $10 per unit when producing a quantity of 500 units, which starts to increase monotonically as soon as output exceeds 500 units. Which of the following costs is minimized when producing 500 units?
   A) Marginal cost
   B) Average variable cost
   C) Average fixed cost
   D) Average total cost
8. The graph below shows the total cost (*TC*), total revenue (*TR*), and total profit (π) curves of a restaurant in the short run. Suppose that the restaurant sells meals at a given price in the market. If the total profit is zero at the outputs q_1 and q_3, and maximized at the output q_2, which of the following is correct?
   A) The restaurant's marginal profit is maximized at output q_2.
   B) The restaurant's marginal revenue is equal to zero at output q_3.
   C) The restaurant's marginal cost decreases when output increases from q_1 to q_2.
   D) The restaurant's marginal cost decreases when output increases from q_2 and q_3.

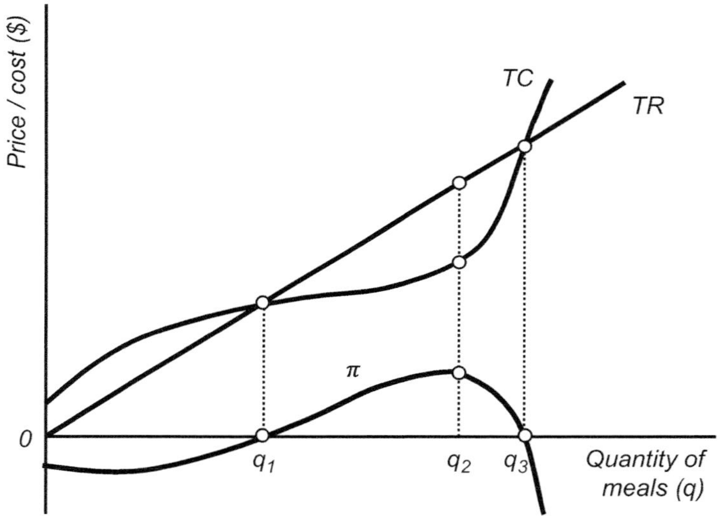

9. The figure below shows the average total cost curves of a firm operating on small and large premises, represented by ATC_S and ATC_L, respectively. If the firm chooses to operate on the large premises, which of the following is correct?
   A) The expected output must be greater than q_3.
   B) The expected output must be smaller than q_4.
   C) The expected output must be smaller than q_5.
   D) The expected output must be between q_3 and q_5.

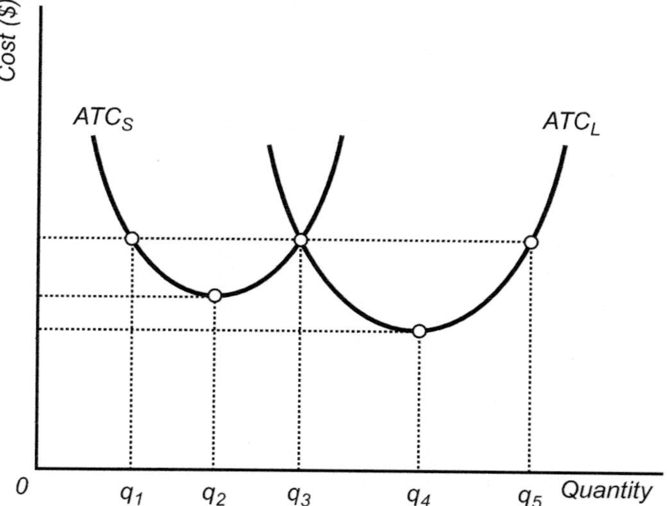

10. Which of the following is correct regarding the interpretation of economies of scale?
   A) Short-run average fixed cost falls as output increases.
   B) Short-run average total cost falls as output increases.
   C) Long-run average fixed cost falls as output increases.
   D) Long-run average total cost falls as output increases.

Problem solving

1. Due to the outbreak of the Covid-19 pandemic, many companies in the tourism and hospitality industry, such as AccorHotels and Disney World, are furloughing or even laying off their employees one after another, hoping to weather the crisis through cutting operating expenses.[2] British Airways was reported in early April to furlough 30,000 cabin crew and ground staff and have reached a deal with its 4,000 pilots for a 50% pay cut over two months.[3] Some argue that the salaries of both flight attendants and pilots are the variable costs of airlines because both are the expenditures on labor inputs in airline operation. What do you think? Would laying off pilots and cabin crew members affect the output of an airline differently? If so, what would be the differences?
2. There are two types of hotels in the market, full-service and limited-service hotels. Full-service hotels are by and large upscale and luxury hotels which provide a wide range of amenities, such as catering services and conference venues, besides accommodation, and are thus served by a large number of frontline staff. Rather

differently, limited-service hotels offer little more than accommodation, and sometimes guests need to check in/out by themselves because very few staff are hired.[4] In recent years, robot-staffed hotels have also emerged to continue reducing labor costs in hotel operation.[5] Suppose that a hotel real estate can be converted into a full-service or a limited-service hotel, and the variable costs of the full-service hotel are twice as much as that of the limited-service hotel. Other things being equal, if both hotels can sell their rooms at the same rate in the market, how would their room sales be different in the short run, and why? If they end up selling the same number of rooms, how would their room rates be different in the short run, and why?

3. Airlines use different types of aircraft to operate on different routes depending on the flight range and capacity of an aircraft. For instance, Lufthansa uses Bombardier CRJ900 (90 seats) in its subsidiary CityLine to serve regional destinations,[6] Airbus A320-200 (168 seats) to fly between Frankfurt and Dublin,[7] and Airbus A340–600 (297 seats)[8] to fly between Munich and New York City.[9] In the airline industry we use cost per available seat mile to measure the efficiency of the airline operation, which is calculated as an airline's total operating costs divided by the number of available seat miles on a route. One available seat mile is defined as one aircraft seat flown one mile, whether occupied or not.[10] For instance, Bombardier CRJ900 with 90 seats flying a distance of 100 miles generates 9,000 available seat miles. Explain the rationale behind Lufthansa's deployment of the three types of aircraft mentioned above.

Solutions to all review questions and problem solving tasks are included in the Support Material for this book, which can be accessed at www.routledge.com/9780367897352.

Notes

1 Airbus. Airbus 2018 price list press release. January 15, 2018. Galaxy Macau. Galaxy Macau overview. Retrieved on August 16, 2020. *The New York Times*. How China won the keys to Disney's magic kingdom. June 15, 2016. *Forbes*. How Dubai earned its wings in the theme park industry. December 31, 2018.

2 *The Financial Times*. Accor suspends dividend and cuts staff hours as coronavirus hits hotels. April 2, 2020. *The New York Times*. Disney World furloughing 43,000 workers. April 12, 2020.

3 *BBC*. Coronavirus: BA reaches deal to suspend thousands of workers. April 2, 2020.

4 Hospitality Technology. Lindner Hotels & Resorts rolls out self check-in. June 17, 2015.

5 TheGuardian.com. The Japan's robot hotel: A dinosaur at reception, a machine for room service. July 16, 2015.

6 Lufthansa. Bombardier CRJ900. Retrieved on August 29, 2020 from https://www.lufthansa.com/de/de/cr9.

7 Simple Flying. Lufthansa to offer A340 widebody flights on multiple European routes. May 9, 2019.

8 The 297 seats consist of eight in first class, 44 in business, 32 in premium economy, and 213 in economy. Source: Lufthansa.

9 Upgraded Points. The definitive guide to Lufthansa's direct routes from the U.S. July 6, 2020.

10 MIT Airline Data Project. Glossary. Retrieved on September 3, 2020 from http://web.mit.edu/airlinedata/www/Res_Glossary.html.

Bibliography

Cobb, C. W., & Douglas, P. H. (1928). A theory of production. *American Economic Review, 18*(1), 139–165.

Douglas, P. H. (1948). Are there laws of production? *American Economic Review, 38*(1), 1–41.

Gordon, D., & Vaughan, R. (2011). The historical role of the production function in economics and business. *American Journal of Business Education, 4*(4), 25–30.

Stigler, G. J. (1958). The economies of scale. *Journal of Law and Economics, 1*, 54–71.

9 Competition and market structure

This chapter continues to introduce the theory of the firm by explaining the market structure of an industry in which individual firms operate and compete with each other. Market structures impose exogenous constraints on firm behavior besides cost which is endogenous to firms. That is, market structure dictates the extent to which firms interact with each other in an industry, thereby affecting firm output, pricing, and product offering. We introduce the four market structures of perfect competition, monopolistic competition, oligopoly, and monopoly, in which firm interaction diminishes in succession and the market becomes less and less competitive. We first lay out perfect competition and monopoly as two extremes of market structure, and then discuss monopolistic competition and oligopoly lying between the two extremes. Building upon key features and assumptions of the four market structures, we analyze how firms behave in each of the four market structures and the limits of firm behavior.

AFTER STUDYING THIS CHAPTER, YOU SHOULD BE ABLE TO:

- Understand the concept of market structure and the constraint it imposes on firm behavior;
- Explain firm behavior in perfect competition and understand the derivation of the supply curve;
- Understand monopoly and analyze monopoly output and price;
- Understand firm behavior in monopolistic competition; and
- Understand firm behavior in oligopoly and the model of Bertrand competition.

9.1 Market structure in a nutshell

9.1.1 What is market structure

Economists use market structure to describe the interactions of a group of firms producing or selling the same or similar products to certain consumers. On the one hand, market structure discerns the scope of an industry that is made up of competing firms. On the other hand, it measures the degree to which these firms interact and compete with each other for acquiring consumers in a market whose boundary is demarcated. Market structure furnishes us with a second lens besides cost through which we can examine firm behavior externally, that is, how a firm would behave by taking into account the influences of others. As we shall discuss in this chapter and the following chapters, a firm's behavior, ranging from output, pricing to product differentiation, depends on the market structure in which it operates. Certain firm behavior can also alter the existing market structure through affecting firm performance, such as market share, revenue, and profit. Thus, besides imposing a constraint on firm behavior, market structure varies with the way a firm behaves.

A simplified yet useful approach to understanding the intensity of firm interaction in a market is to place the four market structures, namely perfect competition, monopolistic competition, oligopoly, and monopoly which we shall address in detail, on a spectrum that is defined, among other things, by the number of firms in the market (Figure 9.1). One extreme is that a market consists of numerous firms producing or selling homogeneous products, which gives rise to perfect competition, and the market is also referred to as perfectly competitive. Each firm in perfect competition makes up a negligible market share, and thus has an inappreciable influence on the market outcome. By contrast, the other three market structures are referred to as imperfect competition, for which the theoretical foundation was laid by American economist Edward Chamberlin (1899–1967) and British economist Joan Robinson (1903–1983) among others. Monopoly is the other extreme in which only one firm operates in the market. Between the two polar cases are monopolistic competition which tilts toward perfect competition and oligopoly toward monopoly. Monopolistic competition is distinguished from perfect competition in the sense that products are slightly differentiated from one firm to another, and thus product differentiation is the overriding feature of monopolistic competition. Oligopoly differs from monopoly in the sense that oligopoly has a few firms which are more or less comparable but no firm can dominate the market.

While firm numbers are not the only characteristic to classify market structures, they readily suggest that firm interaction and competition could intensify when more and

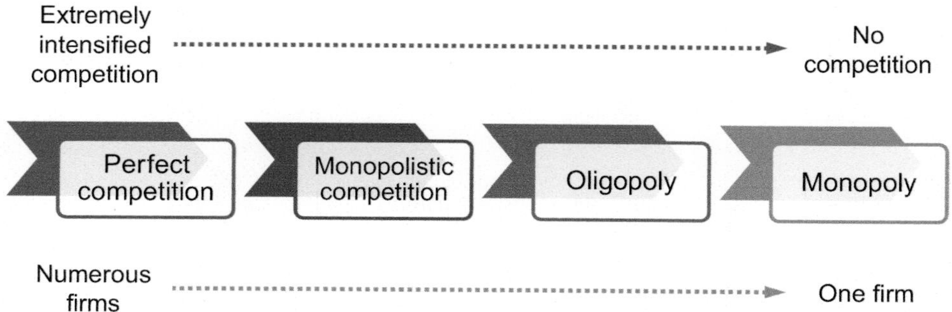

Figure 9.1
Firm number, competition, and market structure

more firms enter the market. Despite the fact that firm numbers and the intensity of interaction are not always positively correlated, examining this relationship is useful for us to approach market structure intuitively. Presumably firm interaction intensifies when a market structure transforms from monopoly, oligopoly, monopolistic competition to perfect competition. At the two extremes, monopoly entails no firm interaction at all because there is only one firm in the market while perfect competition suggests that firm interaction is omnipresent and perpetual in the market. The overriding objective to assess market structure is to understand the market power that a firm can exercise in different market structures. Obviously, a firm in monopoly, known as the monopolist, has tremendous market power, for it corners the whole market and can set price freely. A firm in perfect competition has no market power at all because the astronomical number of competitors would dilute its market power completely. Firms in oligopoly and monopolistic competition usually have some market power between that of the monopolist and of a firm in perfect competition.

Table 9.1 summarizes key characteristics of the four market structures. Perfect competition is the market in which firms produce or sell homogenous products, which in turn intensifies competition between them. Thus, in perfect competition the complexity of firm behavior is relegated to the decision of output only. For monopoly, product differentiation makes no sense as there is only one firm, and therefore the monopolist decides on price and output. As far as monopolistic competition is concerned, product differentiation gives rise to the market power of each firm, thereby setting it apart from perfect competition. Yet the market power of each firm is not as pronounced as the market power of a monopolist. In oligopoly firms can produce or sell either homogenous or differentiated products, with the former intensifying competition while the latter alleviates competition. Oligopolists compete strategically and extensively on output, price, and the extent to which their products can be differentiated. In perfect competition firms can enter and exit a market freely in the long run, which is not the case for monopoly though. It is precisely the entry and exit barriers that grant firms various degrees of market power in different market structures.

Table 9.1 Assumptions and characteristics of market structures

Characteristics	Perfect competition	Imperfect competition		
		Monopolistic competition	Oligopoly	Monopoly
Number of firms	Numerous	Considerable	Very few	One
Product	Homogenous	Slightly differentiated	Homogenous or slightly differentiated	No close substitutes
Firm's control over price	No	Limited	Considerable or no	Substantial
Barriers to entry and/or exit	No	Very low	Moderate	High
Market information	Complete	Incomplete	Incomplete	Incomplete

9.1.2 Market structures in tourism and hospitality

Market structure sheds light on understanding the breadth of tourism and hospitality supply outlined in Chapter 1. Different tourism and hospitality sectors are by and large featured by different market structures, suggesting that the degree of interactions of a group of competing firms varies from one sector to another and from one period of time to another in the same sector. For instance, the airline industry in the United States used to be dominated by very few large passenger carriers before the deregulation in the late 1970s. It became increasingly competitive as low-cost airlines entered the market ever since. Shortly after the 9/11 terrorist attacks in 2001, the airline industry weathered a barrage of bankruptcy, succeeded by mergers and acquisitions in the decade that followed. The U.S. airline industry has become more concentrated once again. By contrast, the European airline industry is relatively competitive, not only because of deregulation and the presence of low-cost airlines, but also because of the vast freedoms of air ratified by European countries. These freedoms grant an airline originated from one country in Europe the rights to carry passengers and cargo between two foreign countries in the European Union.

When it comes to tourist destinations, the most distinct tourist attractions would be historic sites and natural wonders, from China's Great Wall to Egypt's Pyramids, from Mount Fuji in Japan to Niagara Falls straddling the U.S.–Canada border. Since their uniqueness cannot be duplicated elsewhere, nor can it be supplanted by other alternatives, the uniqueness grants a privilege to the owner, may it be a person, corporation, or state, for reaping the proceeds generated from visitor attendance across the world. Such privilege would be consolidated as soon as these attractions make the list of the UNESCO World Heritage sites. There are no competitors locally or globally. Thus, historic sites and natural wonders, if managed by a firm or government agency to exercise the right of pricing, would be monopolies. In fact, many natural and cultural heritage sites are insulated from competition completely because their uniqueness, irreproducibility, as well as the accolade granted by UNESCO make the entry barriers insurmountable, thereby preventing any potential competitors from entering the market. On the one hand, the operators of these heritage attractions are enticed to jack up entrance fees that would infuriate visitors as widely reported.[1] On the other hand, these attractions are flooded with visitors, especially in peak seasons, a phenomenon that is no different from any other monopolies.[2]

9.2 Perfect competition

Perfect competition is the most restrictive market structure due to a number of assumptions that are imposed on firms. First of all, the market is composed of numerous firms and numerous consumers, and neither a firm nor a consumer is able to dominate the market. Second, firms have no entry and exit barriers, and thus firms can enter the market freely when the market price is high and exit when the market price is low. Third, all firms produce or sell homogenous products. Fourth, consumers have perfect information of transactions, and can thus immediately identify a firm which could have charged a different price than the market price. These assumptions are certainly not realistic, and thus cause perfect competition to deviate from any market one can think of in the real world. Nonetheless, perfect competition is, in essence, a theoretical benchmark of competition by which we can analyze monopolistic competition, oligopoly, and monopoly that are more realistic and pertinent to the real world. The model of perfect competition is aimed at illustrating the principle of the free market through simplifying, rather than replicating, the market in the real world. It typifies the methodology of economic analysis that leaves realistic yet less relevant details aside before the simplest case is well understood.

9.2.1 Market demand versus firm demand

One of the key assumptions of perfect competition is that there are numerous firms producing or selling an identical product demanded by numerous consumers in the market. As far as supply is concerned, the market outcome is a result of interactions of all firms combined, with each firm making up a negligible market share. Thus, no firm has any influence on the market as a whole. The market outcome is the result of all firms interacting and competing with each other but does not depend on the act of any single firm in the market. An analogy to perfect competition is perhaps Brownian motion in physics, in which the pattern of particle motion in a fluid is determined by all particles colliding with each other rather than by the motion of any single particle. In perfect competition the price of a product is determined by all consumers and all firms that interact with each other in the market (Figure 9.2a). In other words, the demand for and supply of the product that determine the market price, namely the equilibrium

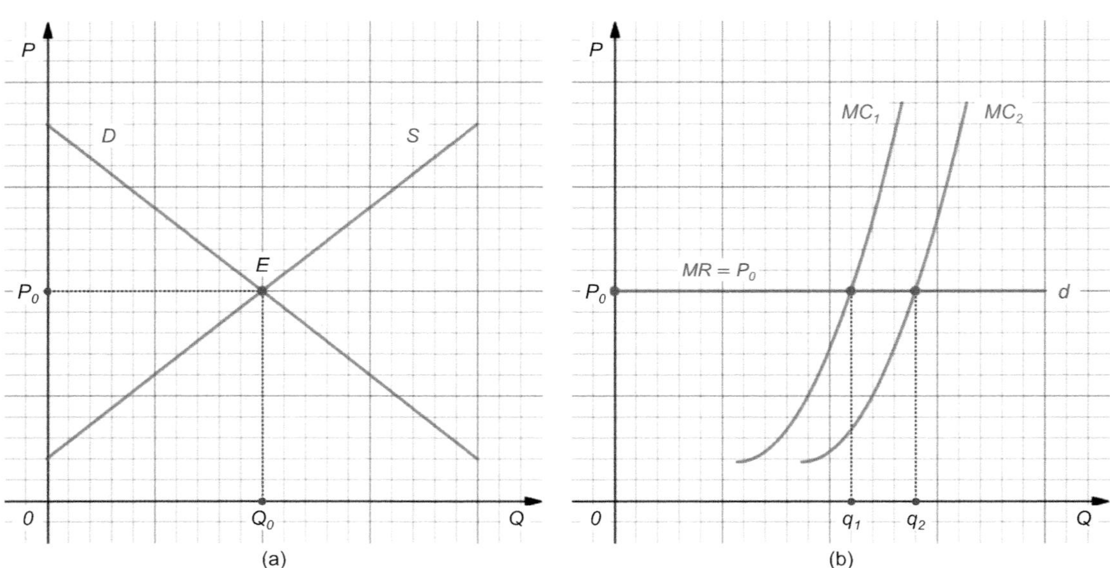

Figure 9.2
Market demand and firm demand in perfect competition

price, are the market demand that consists of the demands of all consumers and the market supply that consists of the supplies from all firms, respectively.

Since the market equilibrium is the result of numerous firms and consumers interacting with each other in the market, no single firm is able to sell the product at a price other than the equilibrium price. Suppose that a firm raised the price by an arbitrarily small amount; all of its consumers would instantaneously switch to its competitors, and thus its demand vanishes. If it lowered price by an arbitrarily small amount, the market as whole would not be affected due to its negligible market share. Therefore, in perfect competition the market price is exogenous to a firm's decision, which sets perfect competition apart from other market structures. As a result, each firm faces the same perfectly elastic demand, denoted by the horizontal demand curve d with the y-intercept at the equilibrium price P_0 (Figure 9.2b). On the one hand, taking the market price P_0 as given, each firm can choose to supply the maximum quantity of the product it is able to supply, and on the other hand the quantity it is willing to supply is constrained by its marginal cost. Figure 9.2b shows that two firms in perfect competition face the same perfectly elastic demand (d) with slightly different marginal costs, denoted by MC_1 and MC_2. We shall examine shortly in detail that the exact quantities supplied by the two firms are jointly determined by their demand and marginal cost curves.

9.2.2 Positive profit, zero profit, and shutdown

Since market prices are exogenous to individual firms in perfect competition, firm behavior is only a matter of output choice. As we demonstrated in Chapter 8 in which we assumed that the market price is given, a profit-maximizing firm produces the output at which marginal profit is zero, $M\pi = 0$, or marginal revenue (MR) equals marginal cost (MC), $MR = MC$. This is the case of firms in perfect competition in which the market price is given. Thus, a firm can sell any quantity at the market price P_0, thereby reaping a constant marginal revenue equal to P_0 (Figure 9.2b). That is, the perfectly elastic demand curve that each firm faces is its marginal revenue curve. Given the marginal revenue and marginal cost curves of a firm in the short run, the optimal output is the unique output at which marginal revenue equals marginal cost, or $MR = MC$ (Figure 9.2b). While consumers in perfect competition demand whatever quantity a firm is able and willing to supply at the market price P_0, the optimal output could differ from firm to firm by a reasonably small amount in the short run, because firms do not necessarily have the same marginal cost (Figure 9.2b). The lower the marginal cost, the more a firm is able and willing to supply at the optimum. That said, the market share of each firm would be more or less even in the long run because of the free entry and exit in the market.

A caveat to perfect competition in the short run is that profit maximization does not guarantee that a firm earns a positive profit in the market. It simply means that given the market price, the profit-maximizing output is the optimum despite the fact that the maximized profit might end up being zero or even negative. In situations where a zero or negative profit occurs, profit maximization suggests that the firm loses the least given the market price, other things being equal. The occurrence of zero or negative profits is because the market prices are too low to enable the firm to break even at the optimal output. Now we rewrite the profit function (8.11) introduced in Chapter 8 to single out the relationship between the market price (P) and the average total cost (ATC) of a firm:

$$\pi = R - C = Pq - qATC = (P - ATC)q. \tag{9.1}$$

It becomes evident that whether the firm can earn a positive profit or not depends on whether the market price is greater than the average total cost at the optimal output. As long as the market price is equal to or lower than the average total cost, the firm makes a zero or negative profit, respectively, despite the fact that the output q is optimal. To illustrate this idea we examine the relationship between firm profit (π), the average total cost (ATC), and marginal cost (MC) curves (Figure 9.3). If the market price of a good is P_1, the firm earns a positive profit, $\pi_1 = (P_1 - ATC_1)q_1$, because the market price is greater than the average total cost at the optimal output q_1. Figure 9.3 shows that the profit π_1 is obtained by subtracting the total cost $q_1 ATC_1$ from the total revenue $P_1 q_1$ at the optimal output q_1. If the market price happens to be P_2 ($P_2 < P_1$), which is tangent to the average total cost curve at its minimum that corresponds to the output q_2, we end up with the marginal revenue, marginal cost, and average total cost curves simultaneously intersecting at the optimal output q_2: $P_2 = MR = MC = ATC_2$. Thus, the firm earns a zero profit, or breaks even: $\pi_2 = (P_2 - ATC_2)q_2 = 0$. The optimal output q_2 is thus called the zero-profit condition of the firm. As long as the market price is below P_2, say P_3 ($P_3 < P_2 < P_1$), the firm earns a negative profit because the average total cost curve

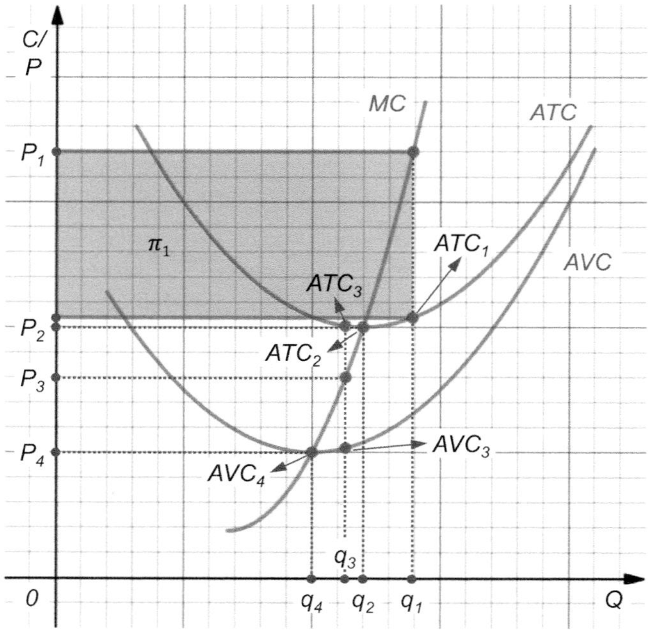

Figure 9.3
Positive profit, zero profit, and shutdown

at the optimal output q_3 is always above the market price of the good. We can calculate the negative profit, $\pi_3 = (P_3 - ATC_3)q_3 < 0$, which is equal to the total revenue P_3q_3 by subtracting the total cost q_3ATC_3 at the optimal output q_3 (Figure 9.3).

On the one hand, in perfect competition an incumbent firm is not able to earn a positive economic profit in the long run, because any positive economic profit will entice other firms to enter the market and consequently dissipate the profit in the market through competition. On the other hand, even if the economic profit is zero or negative in the short run, it is still economically viable for the firm to continue producing the outputs q_2 and q_3 as indicated in Figure 9.3, as long as the market price is still higher than the firm's average variable cost at the optimal output. To illustrate this idea we can further rewrite the profit function to single out the relationship between the market price (P), average variable cost (AVC), and fixed costs (FC):

$$\pi = R - C = Pq - qAVC - FC = (P - AVC)q - FC. \quad (9.2)$$

Since fixed costs are constant in the short run, they can be compensated with the amount of positive proceeds that the firm reaps, $(P - AVC)q$, as long as the market price is greater than the average variable cost at the optimal output q. Thus, it pays off for the firm to produce the output q despite the market price being lower than the average total cost. In Figure 9.3 above, when the market price is P_3, we have $AVC_3 < P_3 < ATC_3$ at the optimal output q_3, and therefore the firm can compensate $(P_3 - AVC_3)q_3 > 0$ for its fixed costs. If the market price happens to be P_4, the optimal output q_4 ends up with $P_4 = MR = MC = AVC_4$, and hence $P_4 - AVC_4 = 0$, and $\pi = -FC$ (Figure 9.3). Then there is no difference between producing q_4 and producing nothing, because the firm ends up with a negative profit equal to the amount of fixed costs regardless. Hence the firm shuts down, and the optimal output q_4 is called the shutdown point. If the market price continues to fall below P_4, the firm will never produce the supposedly optimal output at which $MR = MC$ and remains in shutdown. As long as the firm shuts down, output falls to zero and so do variable costs, but fixed costs remain unchanged in the short run. Only in the long run can fixed costs be changed through, for instance, liquidation or diversion to other alternative uses. By then the firm exits the market.

9.2.3 Derivation of the supply curve

From the analysis above we know that the marginal cost (MC) curve cuts through the average variable cost (AVC) and average total cost (ATC) curves at the shutdown point and the zero-profit point, respectively. These two points separate the marginal cost curve into three portions: the shutdown portion to the left of the shutdown point q_4, the negative-profit portion between the shutdown point q_4 and the zero-profit point q_2, and the positive-profit portion to the right of the zero-profit point q_2 (Figure 9.4). Only when the market price is greater than P_4 will the optimal output ensure that the average variable cost is lower than the market price, and thus the firm starts to produce. As long as the market price is greater than P_4, the optimal output will be always greater than q_4. This is

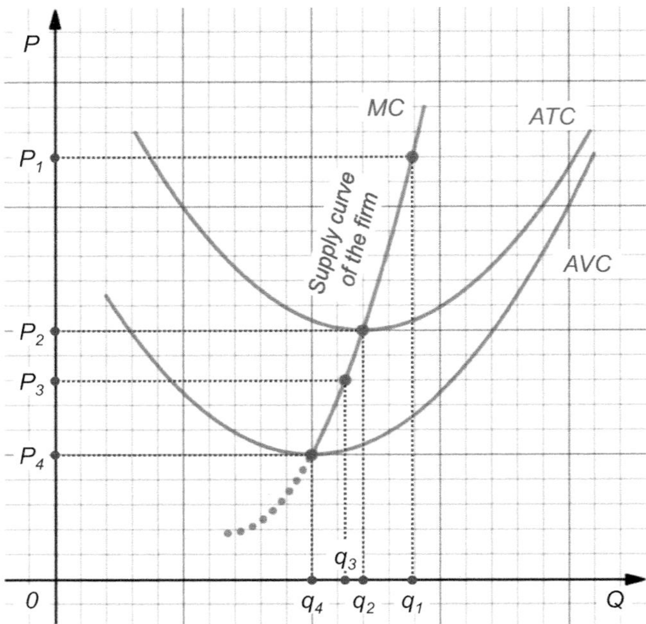

Figure 9.4
Marginal cost curve and the supply curve

because the portion of the marginal cost curve beyond q_4 is monotonically increasing. Therefore, as the market price increases above p_4, the optimal output will increase beyond q_4, suggesting a positive relationship between the market price and the optimal output of the firm. Hence the portion of the marginal cost curve above the shutdown point q_4 constitutes the supply curve of the firm (Figure 9.4). Like the downward-sloping demand curve underpinned by the law of diminishing marginal utility, the upward-sloping supply curve is grounded on the law of increasing marginal cost.

Since the market price is given in perfect competition, each point on the supply curve of the firm is the optimal output at which profit is maximized at the corresponding market price. This is the same logic in reasoning the demand curve on which each point on the demand curve is the optimal quantity of a good consumed by the consumer that maximizes his utility. Likewise, the upward-sloping supply curve is the diagrammatic representation of the law of supply, which can also be represented mathematically by the supply function. For expository simplicity, assuming that a firm's supply curve of a good is linear without loss of generality, the inverse supply function $p(q)$ is given as

$$p = aq + b, \tag{9.3}$$

where p is the market price of the good, q is the quantity supplied by the firm, and the two parameters a and b define the properties of the supply function. The inverse supply function (9.3) of the firm and the inverse demand function (4.8) of the consumer have the same mathematical form but different economic meanings. In the supply

function, the parameter a is the slope of the supply curve, and hence $a > 0$, and b is the y-intercept. From the inverse supply function in (9.3) we can also write out the conventional supply function $q(p)$ in which q is a function of p:

$$q = \frac{1}{a}p - \frac{b}{a}. \tag{9.4}$$

9.3 Monopoly

9.3.1 Downward-sloping demand curve

Since one firm represents the whole market in monopoly, the demand curve that a monopolist faces is the market demand curve. Thus, a monopolist faces a downward-sloping demand curve, which is the fundamental difference between monopolists and firms in perfect competition (Figure 9.5). This suggests that both the price and output are endogenous to a firm's decision in monopoly on the one hand, and on the other a monopolist faces a tradeoff between selling more at a lower price and selling less at a higher price. If the monopolist wants to sell more, it compromises on a higher price it could otherwise charge; if it wants to raise the price, it compromises on a larger quantity it could otherwise sell. This is the situation we analyzed in Chapter 5 for articulating the relationship between demand elasticity and firm revenue on the linear demand curve. Here we move one step further to address the profit-maximizing problem of the monopolist. Different from a firm in perfect competition that takes the price of

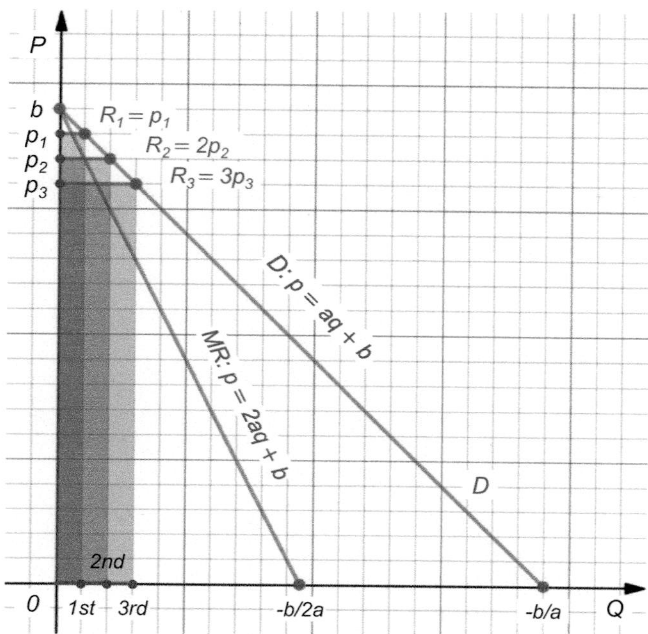

Figure 9.5
Marginal revenue and demand in monopoly

a good as given in the market, a monopolist is a price maker and can thus decide the price of its product. Therefore, there is no such supply curve in monopoly, namely that a quantity supplied in the market depends on the demand that a monopolist faces instead of the exogenous market price. In principle a monopolist can supply any quantity of a good insofar as consumers' willingness to pay is above its marginal cost.

9.3.2 Marginal revenue curve

Given the downward-sloping demand curve, on the one extreme a monopolist can charge the highest price which consumers are willing to pay, but will end up selling only one unit of a good. On the other extreme, the monopolist can sell the largest quantity, but has to charge the lowest price yet above its marginal cost. Figure 9.5 shows that if the monopolist sells one unit only, it can charge the highest price which is equal to consumers' willingness to pay for one unit, reaping a revenue equal to the price p_1. If it sells two units, it has to lower price to p_2 ($p_2 < p_1$) which is equal to consumers' willingness to pay for two units. Thus, the first unit, which was previously sold at a higher price (p_1), is discounted at the lower price (p_2) charged for two units. This ends up with the revenue reaped from the second unit not only smaller than the revenue from the first unit but also less than the average revenue for the two units. If the monopolist sells three units, both the first and the second units are discounted at a much lower price, p_3 ($p_3 < p_2 < p_1$), which is charged based on consumers' willingness to pay for three units. This ends up with the revenue reaped from the third unit being not only smaller than the revenue from the second unit but also less than the average revenue for the three units, and so on.

Therefore, any additional unit of sales always generates a revenue not only lower than the revenue from the preceding unit but also lower than consumers' willingness to pay for all units sold as a whole. Hence the marginal revenue (*MR*) curve slopes downward and is beneath the demand curve (Figure 9.5), a property that contrasts to the horizontal marginal revenue curve and also the demand curve that a firm faces in perfect competition. To further unravel the properties of the marginal revenue curve of a monopolist and its relationship with the demand curve, suppose the demand curve that the monopolist faces is linear, $p = aq + b$. Then total revenue will be $R = pq = aq^2 + bq$, which was discussed in function (5.16) in Chapter 5. Marginal revenue (*MR*) is obtained by differentiating total revenue *R* with respect to quantity demanded q:

$$MR = \frac{dR}{dq} = \frac{d\left(aq^2 + bq\right)}{dq} = 2aq + b. \tag{9.5}$$

Function (9.5) is a function of the marginal revenue for the linear demand, which is the same as equation (5.17) in Chapter 5. We now should be able to comprehend the economic meaning of equation (5.17), which is in fact the marginal revenue of the firm. A digression here is that total revenue is maximized when marginal revenue is zero, and thus the geometric solution in equation (5.17) is economically equivalent to $MR = 0$ for revenue maximization. Different from a firm in perfect competition that has a constant marginal revenue equal to the market price, a monopolist's marginal revenue is a linear

function of the quantity demanded provided that the demand function is linear. Figure 9.5 shows that the marginal revenue curve has the same y-intercept as the linear demand curve but half of the x-intercept of the linear demand curve. That is, the slope of the marginal revenue curve is twice the slope of the linear demand curve.

9.3.3 Output and price decision

Since a monopolist can decide both output and price, optimal output and price are determined when its profit is maximized. First, the profit-maximizing monopolist chooses the optimal output at which marginal revenue equals marginal cost, $MR = MC$. Second, the optimal price is determined based on consumers' willingness to pay at the optimal output, in other words, determined by the demand curve that the monopolist faces in the market. Figure 9.6 shows the demand curve D, marginal revenue (MR), marginal cost (MC), and average total cost (ATC) curves of a monopolist. To maximize profit the monopolist sets the optimal output q_M at which $MR = MC$. The optimal output q_M is referred to as the monopoly output. Based on consumers' willingness to pay at the output q_M, the monopolist sets the optimal price p_M equal to consumers' willingness to pay precisely for this quantity. The optimal price p_M is referred to as the monopoly price. Hence the monopoly output q_M and monopoly price p_M determine the maximized profit, $\pi = (p_M - c_M)q_M$, referred to as the monopoly profit (Figure 9.6). The monopoly profit is obtained by subtracting the total cost $c_M q_M$ from the total revenue $p_M q_M$ at the optimal output q_M.

Since the marginal revenue (MR) curve of a firm in perfect competition is also the demand curve the firm faces in the market, the profit-maximizing condition $MR = MC$

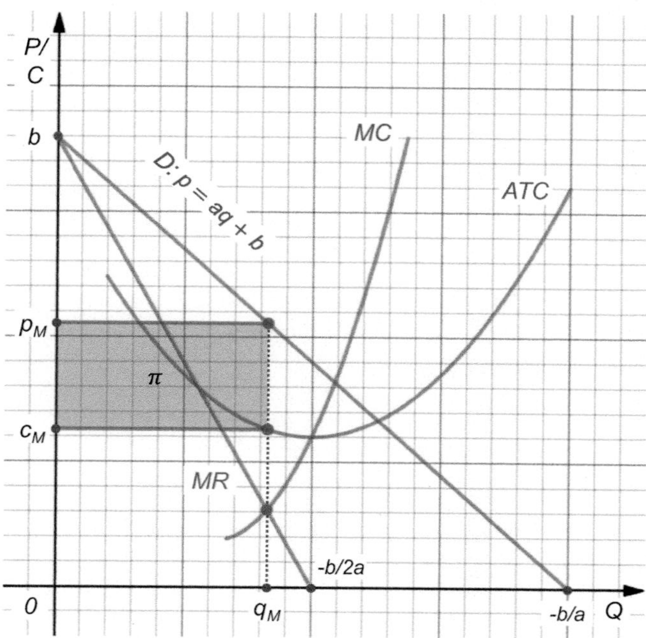

Figure 9.6
Profit maximization of monopoly

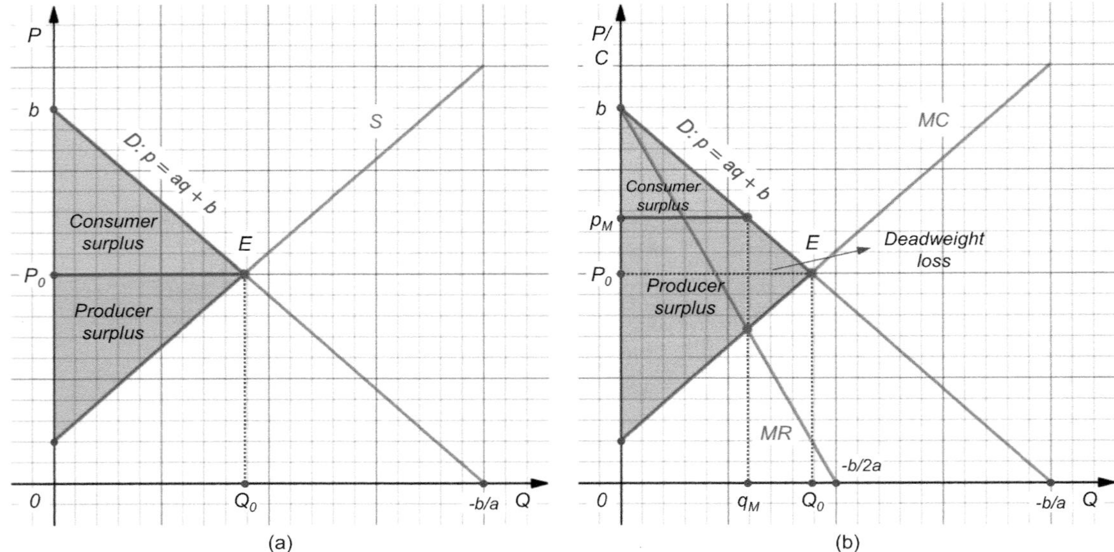

Figure 9.7
Outputs in perfect competition and monopoly

means that each firm produces an optimal output at which its demand curve and marginal cost curve intersect. In the market the equilibrium quantity is the output Q_0 and the equilibrium price is P_0 at which demand equals supply (Figure 9.7a). Now suppose that the market is controlled by a monopolist, other things being equal. Since the marginal revenue curve of the monopolist is beneath the demand curve, the optimal output q_M, at which the marginal revenue curve intersects the marginal cost curve, will be strictly smaller than the equilibrium quantity Q_0 in perfect competition (Figure 9.7b). Thus, the monopolist ends up underproducing the output relative to what would be produced in perfect competition. Reducing the output by $Q_0 - q_M$ enables the monopolist to charge the monopoly price p_M which is higher than the equilibrium price P_0 in perfect competition. The gap between what is socially optimal in perfect competition and what is optimal for the profit-maximizing monopolist creates deadweight loss (Figure 9.7b). The deadweight loss suggests that the monopolist is able, but not willing, to produce the amount of $Q_0 - q_M$ for which consumers are actually willing to pay. The occurrence of deadweight loss suggests that monopoly is detrimental to market efficiency.

9.4 Monopolistic competition

9.4.1 Product differentiation and demand

Monopolistic competition resembles perfect competition except for the assumption that products in the market are slightly differentiated from one firm to another. While such product differentiation is insufficient to grant a firm a monopoly status, it does render the demand curve that the firm faces slightly downward-sloping, but not as

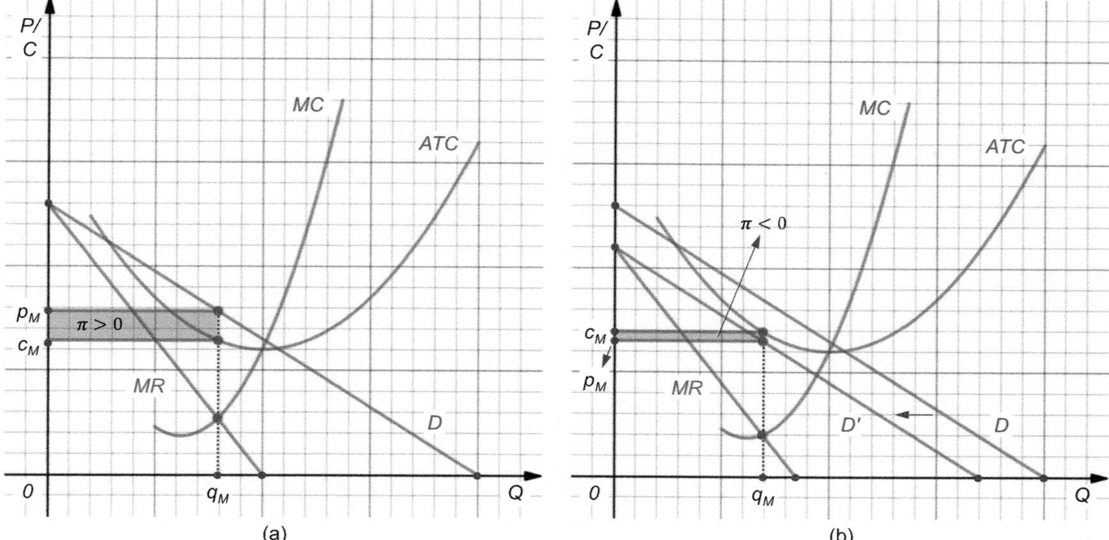

Figure 9.8
Output in the short run versus in the long run

steep as the demand curve that a monopolist faces. In other words, the demand curve that a firm faces in monopolistic competition is considerably, yet not perfectly, elastic (Figure 9.8a). In fact, depending on the extent to which products are differentiated in the market, theoretically the market can be transformed from perfect competition on the one extreme to monopoly on the other. If products were homogenous, the demand that each firm faces would become perfectly elastic, and the market would morph into perfect competition; if products were so differentiated that no other firm in the market could provide substitutes, each firm would become a monopolist in its own right. Above all else, the significance of monopolistic competition lies in the fact that it is probably the most pervasive market structure in the real world. As far as the tourism and hospitality industry is concerned, sectors that are characterized by monopolistic competition are primarily the restaurant and the hotel sectors.

A firm in monopolistic competition is entitled to have slight market power due to the fact that its product is slightly differentiated from its competitors'. On the one hand, it slightly differs from a firm in perfect competition which has no market power at all. On the other hand, it cannot drive its competitors out of the market because its product has many close substitutes provided by its competitors. Figure 9.8a shows that a firm in monopolistic competition faces a considerably elastic demand curve D, along with the downward-sloping marginal revenue curve MR. Similarly to a monopolist, the profit-maximizing firm needs to figure out the optimal output q_M at which marginal revenue equals marginal cost, $MR = MC$. Then the optimal price p_M is determined by consumers' willingness to pay for the output q_M. Because the demand curve is considerably elastic, the optimal price p_M will end up being only slightly above the firm's average total cost curve. Hence the firm's market power in deciding output and price is largely restricted in contrast to the market power of a monopolist addressed above. In the short run, because the price p_M is above the average total cost c_M at the optimal output q_M, the firm earns a positive economic profit, $\pi = (p_M - c_M)q_M$.

9.4.2 Monopolistic competition in the long run

In perfect competition firms can enter and exit the market freely in the long run, thereby driving down the economic profit to zero. Similarly, the entry and exit barriers are very low for firms in monopolistic competition, and therefore the positive economic profit, if any, not only retains incumbent firms but also entices new firms to enter the market. Hence the demand for the firm in question will shrink as more and more firms enter the market, leading to a leftward shift in the demand curve that the firm faces. Figure 9.8b shows that the demand curve that the firm faces shifts leftward from D to D' and lies below the average total cost curve. The firm now makes a negative economic profit despite still producing the optimal output q_M at which marginal revenue equals marginal cost and charging the price p_M equal to consumers' willingness to pay for the output q_M (Figure 9.8b). On the one hand, any positive economic profit entices firms to enter the market, leading the demand for the firm in question to shrink. On the other hand, as long as the economic profit is negative, firms start exiting the market, leading the demand for the firm in question to bounce back. Thus, in the long run the demand curve that the firm faces would enable it to earn a zero economic profit the same as firms in perfect competition.

In monopolistic competition firms with highly differentiated products would obtain a markup slightly above the market price, while firms with similar products suffer a price slightly lower than the market price. Note that the optimal output in monopolistic competition is still smaller than the output produced in perfect competition in which the demand curve intersects the supply curve (Figure 9.7a). This is because the demand curve that a firm in monopolistic competition faces is still downward-sloping despite being more elastic than the demand faced by a monopolist. Therefore, consumers' willingness to pay for the optimal output at which marginal revenue is equal to marginal cost is still greater than the marginal revenue of the firm (Figure 9.8). In other words, each firm in monopolistic competition charges a price above its marginal revenue and produces the optimal quantity that is smaller than the quantity at which the demand curve intersects the supply in perfect competition. Therefore, deadweight loss will also arise in monopolistic competition but much smaller than it is in monopoly.

9.5 Oligopoly

9.5.1 Strategic competition

Firm interaction lies at the heart of oligopolistic behavior, which makes oligopoly strikingly different from the other three market structures. The intensity of firm interaction in oligopoly is grounded on two key assumptions. First, the number of firms in oligopoly is very limited, and thus the action of one firm will be factored into the response of another, and vice versa. Hence oligopoly is distinguished from perfect competition and monopolistic competition in which the tit-for-tat strategy does not make sense among numerous firms. Second, no firm can dominate the market in oligopoly, and thus each firm's actions equally matter, thereby distinguishing oligopoly from monopoly. The interactions between firms in oligopoly are not only instrumental in determining the market outcome as a whole but are also endogenous in each other's behavior. Suppose that firms do not cooperate or collude in oligopoly: once a firm chooses a certain output, price, or even a certain product to manufacture, other firms will respond accordingly, which in turn is retaliated by the firm in question, and so on. For this reason, economists have developed sophisticated models, particularly game theory, to analyze oligopoly due to the fact that oligopolistic behavior itself is complicated, dynamic, and strategic.

9.5.2 Duopoly and Bertrand competition

While oligopolists can decide on output,[3] price, and the extent to which their products are differentiated from each other,[4] in this chapter we focus on how oligopolists set price. This is because pricing is among the most common phenomena observed in oligopoly. In what follows we analyze a special case of oligopoly that consists of only two firms, known as duopoly, and the two firms are called duopolists. Suppose that two duopolists produce a homogenous product with no output constraint. The duopolists' pricing problem is addressed by the model of Bertrand competition, named after French mathematician and economist Joseph Bertrand (1822–1900). In Bertrand competition we suppose that two duopolists F_1 and F_2 produce a homogenous good and incur a constant marginal cost, $c_1 = c_2 = c$. Since both have no output constraint, either one is capable of serving all the market demand. Consumer demand depends on the market price of the good, which will be the lower price, if the duopolists charge different prices. We assume that consumers have no preference for F_1 and F_2 if both charge the same price, and thus are indifferent between F_1 and F_2 when making a purchase.

Figure 9.9 shows that F_1 and F_2 face the same linear demand curve depicted symmetrically on the two sides of the y-axis for comparison. For expository simplicity without loss of generality, we assume that $c_1 = c_2 = 0$ for the moment. If F_1 and F_2 do not collude and set price independently, each would behave as a monopolist, producing the same monopoly output, $q_1 = q_2 = q_M$, at which marginal revenue equals marginal cost, and charging the same monopoly price, $p_1 = p_2 = p_M$. As long as the duopolists compete with each other, the monopoly price p_M is no longer stable because both have incentives to charge a price below p_M in order to acquire a larger market share, and hence more profits. Suppose that F_1 undercuts F_2 by an infinitesimal amount, $p_1 < p_2 = p_M$, so F_1 will take all the market. If F_2 acts the same way by undercutting F_1, F_2 will take all the market as well. As long as there is no collusion, F_1 and F_2 will undercut each other successively until their prices become equal to their marginal costs, $p_1 = p_2 = c$. Neither one has an incentive to raise price above or cut price below its marginal cost, because the firm that changes price will end up obtaining either a zero or negative profit, other things being equal. Nor is one willing to raise price above the monopoly price p_M, because this will lead the other to corner the market. Thus, the market equilibrium ends up with $p_1 = p_2 = c$, each serving 50% of the market.

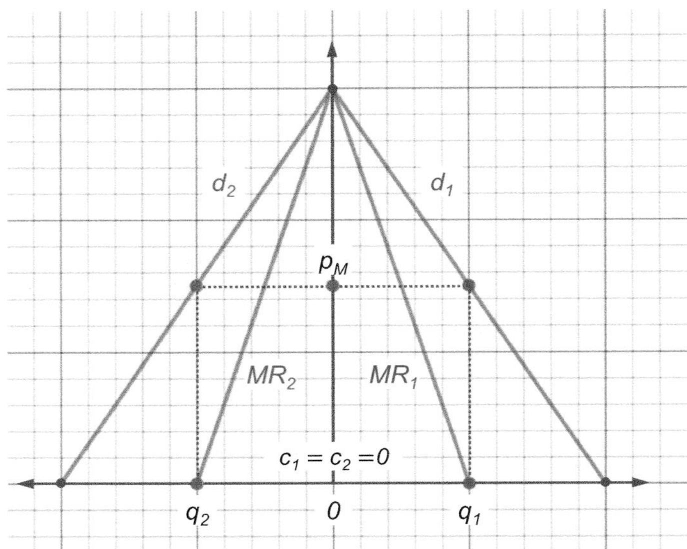

Figure 9.9
Firm demand in Bertrand competition

In Bertrand competition above the effects of output variation and product differentiation are assumed away, and therefore one firm's profit depends entirely on its price relative to the price of the other. As a result, price competition becomes the only firm behavior. Figure 9.10a shows that prices p_1 and p_2 charged by F_1 and F_2 are placed on the y- and x-axis, respectively. We first analyze that F_1's price p_1 responds to F_2's price p_2, meaning that p_1 is a function of p_2: $p_1(p_2)$. To begin with, when F_2 sets the monopoly price $p_2 = p_M$ by default, F_1's best response is to set p_1 lower than p_M by an arbitrarily small amount in order to corner the market. When F_2 retaliates by undercutting F_1, F_1's best response is still $p_1 < p_2$, and so on, until F_2 eventually sets its price equal to the marginal cost, $p_2 = c$. As long as F_2 sets $p_2 \leq c$, F_1 will stick to $p_1 = c$, which is F_1's dominant strategy, ending up with a zero profit. However, if F_2 raises price p_2 above the monopoly price p_M, F_1 will stick to $p_1 = p_M$ and thus corner the market, earning a monopoly profit. As Figure 9.10a shows, F_1's price response function, $p_1(p_2)$, is manifested differently in three intervals of F_2's price on the x-axis: when $p_2 \leq c$, $p_1(p_2)$ exhibits a horizontal line intercepting the y-axis at the marginal cost c; when $c < p_2 \leq p_M$, $p_1(p_2)$ is parallel to and slightly beneath the 45-degree ray from the origin, which indicates $p_1 < p_2$; when $p_2 > p_M$, $p_1(p_2)$ exhibits a horizontal line intercepting the y-axis at the monopoly price p_M.

Now we consider how F_2 would respond to F_1's price in Figure 9.10b. Given F_1's price p_1 on the y-axis, F_2 would actually respond exactly the same way on the x-axis as F_1 does on the y-axis. When F_1 sets the monopoly price $p_1 = p_M$, F_2's best response is to undercut F_1 by an infinitesimal amount in order to corner the market, $p_2 < p_1$. This strategy will be executed by F_2 until F_1 eventually sets the price p_1 equal to its marginal cost, $p_1 = c$. As long as F_1 sets price $p_1 \leq c$, F_2's best response will always be $p_2 = c$, earning a zero profit. However, if F_1 raises price above the monopoly price p_M, F_2 will not follow but stick to $p_2 = p_M$, obtaining a monopoly profit. In Figure 9.10b,

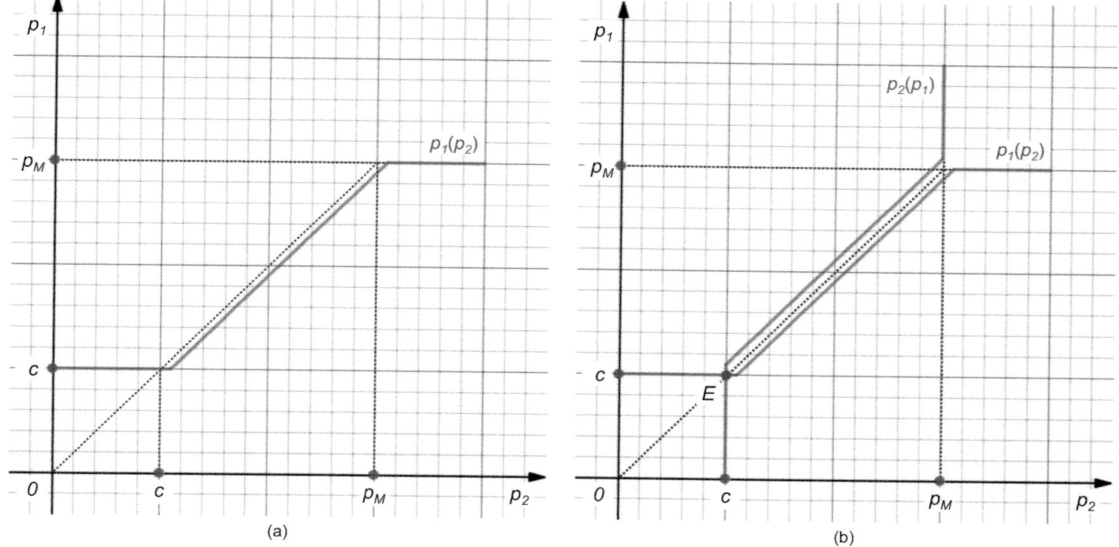

Figure 9.10
Price response in Bertrand competition

F_2's price response function, $p_2(p_1)$, is symmetric with F_1's against the 45-degree ray from the origin and has the same properties as $p_1(p_2)$ does evaluated on the y-axis. Depending on the interval of p_1, F_2's price response function, $p_2(p_1)$, is manifested differently: when $p_1 \le c$, $p_2(p_1)$ exhibits a vertical line intercepting the x-axis at the marginal cost c; when $c < p_1 \le p_M$, $p_2(p_1)$ is parallel to and slightly above the 45-degree ray from the origin; when $p_1 > p_M$, $p_2(p_1)$ is a vertical line intercepting the x-axis at the monopoly price p_M. Figure 9.10b shows that the price equilibrium is point E at which the two price response functions intersect. The market equilibrium suggests that Bertrand competition ends up with F_1 and F_2 charging the same price equal to their marginal costs, that is, $p_1 = p_2 = c$.

9.5.3 Market efficiency

In general, firms in imperfect competition will obtain market power which enables them to charge a price higher than their marginal costs. Nevertheless, profit-maximizing duopolists in Bertrand competition end up with the same market equilibrium as in perfect competition, namely that marginal revenue equals marginal cost equals the market price, $P = MR = MC$. On the one hand, both firms become price takers, and on the other, they charge the same price equal to their marginal costs, each earning a zero economic profit. Thus, Bertrand competition also suggests a case of perfectly competitive markets. While this conclusion has profound implications for analyzing oligopolistic behavior, it cannot be generalized to other oligopolies in which some or all of the assumptions in Bertrand competition are violated. Bertrand competition is grounded on very restrictive assumptions that are certainly not realistic in the real world. Above all else in Bertrand competition, the assumption that two firms are identical and symmetric is key to understanding their behavior in general and pricing in particular. It is the symmetry of the duopolists assumed in Bertrand competition that leads to the perfectly competitive market in oligopoly. Therefore, market efficiency depends more on competition intensity and less on firm numbers, other things being equal. As long as two firms are different in one way or another, say having different marginal costs or differentiated products, the market outcome will deviate from perfect efficiency which we shall analyze in later chapters.

Summary

1. Market structure describes the extent to which firms in an industry interact and compete with each other. Market structure is an exogenous constraint imposed by other firms on the firm in question and thus dictates its market power.
2. An expository approach to understating market structure is to examine the intensity of firm interaction caused by the number of firms operating in the market. Depending on interaction intensity, market structure is classified as perfect competition, monopolistic competition, oligopoly, and monopoly.
3. Perfect competition is characterized by numerous firms supplying homogenous products and facing numerous consumers in the market. Perfect competition is a theoretical benchmark by which we can analyze the other three market structures that are more realistic and pertinent to the real world.
4. Each firm in perfect competition faces a perfectly elastic demand. It accepts the market price as given and produces the output at which marginal revenue equals marginal cost. In the short run, depending on whether the market price is above or equal to the average total cost, the firm earns a positive or zero economic profit. If the market price is below the average variable cost, the firm shuts down with a zero output.
5. From perfect competition we derive the supply curve of a firm, which is the portion of the firm's marginal cost curve above the shutdown point. Similar to the demand curve, each point on the supply curve represents the optimal output of the firm given the market price and the marginal cost.
6. Monopoly by definition contains only one firm in the market. A monopolist faces a downward-sloping demand curve, and thus faces a tradeoff between setting a higher price and producing a larger quantity of output.
7. A monopolist sets price in two consecutive steps. First, it figures out the optimal output at which marginal revenue is equal to marginal cost for profit maximization. Second, it sets the price equal to consumers' willingness to pay at the optimal output. Output is underproduced in monopoly compared to the social optimum, leading to deadweight loss.
8. Since each firm in monopolistic competition produces a slightly different product from one another, it faces a slightly elastic demand curve, thereby obtaining slight market power. Monopolistic competition is pervasive in tourism and hospitality.
9. Oligopoly is featured by a few firms, but no single firm predominates over others. Thus, firms in oligopoly behave strategically and/or cooperatively in deciding

output, price, and the extent to which their products are differentiated from one another.

10. Duopoly is a special type of oligopoly with only two firms. In Bertrand competition duopolists compete on price and eventually drive price down to the marginal cost, ending up with perfect market efficiency the same as perfect competition.

REVIEW QUESTIONS

Each question has four options, and there is only one correct answer to each question.

1. Which of the following market structures suggests the least degree of competition among firms in a market?
   A) Perfect competition
   B) Monopolistic competition
   C) Oligopoly
   D) Monopoly
2. Which of the following grants natural and cultural wonders such as Mount Fuji in Japan and the Great Wall in China a monopoly status?
   A) Imperfect information
   B) Government regulation
   C) Exorbitant entrance fees
   D) Uniqueness and irreproducibility
3. Which of the following is correct regarding firms in perfect competition?
   A) Each firm faces a perfectly inelastic demand curve.
   B) Each firm obtains a marginal revenue equal to its marginal cost.
   C) Each firm earns a zero profit in the short run.
   D) Each firm can enter and exit the market freely.
4. If the market price is lower than the average total cost of a firm but above its average variable cost when the firm produces in perfect competition. Which of the following is correct in the short run?
   A) The firm would earn a positive profit.
   B) The firm would earn a negative profit.
   C) The firm would earn a zero profit.
   D) All of the above.
5. The figure below shows a firm's marginal cost (*MC*), average variable cost (*AVC*), and average total cost (*ATC*) curves in perfect competition. Which quantity of the output will NOT be produced by the firm?
   A) 20
   B) 40
   C) 70
   D) 90

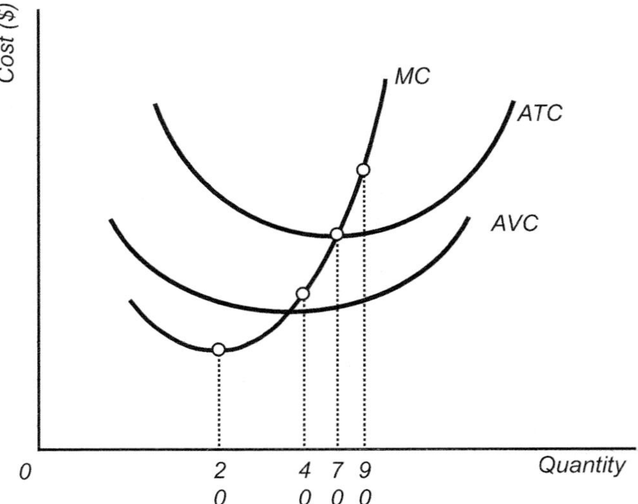

6. The figure below shows the demand curve that a monopolist faces in a market. What would be the marginal revenue obtained if the monopolist cuts price from p_1 to p_2?
   A) $b-c$
   B) $c-b$
   C) $a-b$
   D) $a-c$

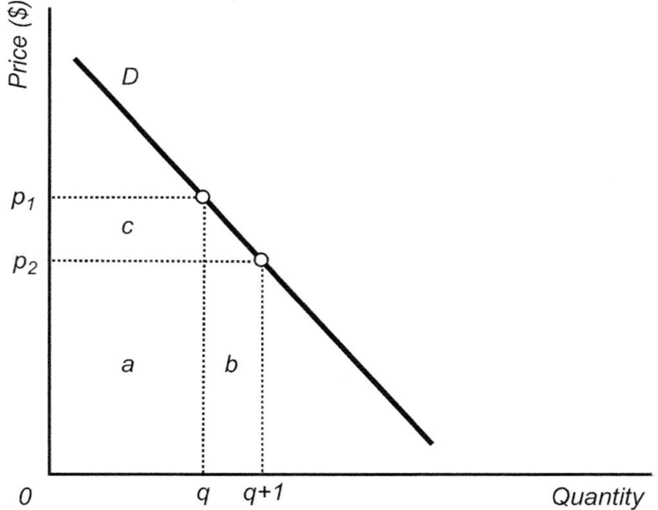

7. The figure below shows the demand curve (D) that a monopolist faces in the market and its marginal revenue (MR), marginal cost (MC), and average total cost (ATC) curves. Which of the following is correct?
   A) The monopolist sells 200 units for $10 per unit.
   B) The monopolist sells 200 units for $28 per unit.
   C) The monopolist sells 500 units for $20 per unit.
   D) The monopolist sells 500 units for $28 per unit.

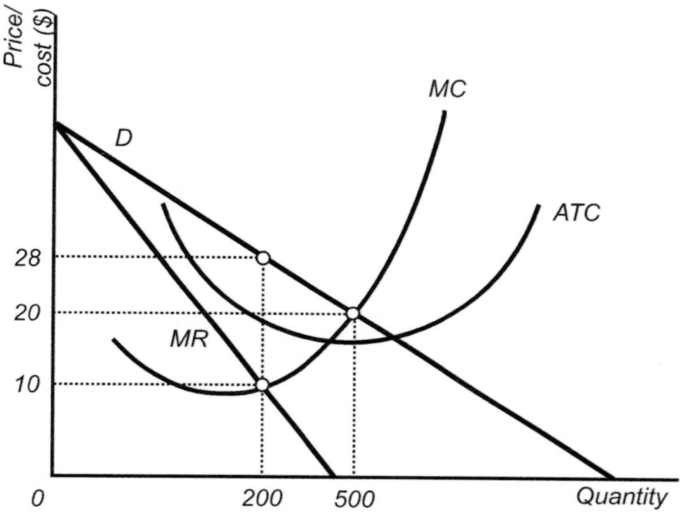

8. In which of the following market structures is product differentiation indispensable?
   A) Perfect competition
   B) Monopolistic competition
   C) Oligopoly
   D) Monopoly
9. Which of the following is correct regarding Bertrand competition?
   A) It explains firm behavior in monopolistic competition.
   B) Two firms each charge different prices in the market equilibrium.
   C) Two firms each earn a zero profit in the market equilibrium.
   D) Products sold by two firms are slightly differentiated.
10. If one firm charged a price slightly lower than the monopoly price in Bertrand competition, what would be the immediate response of the other firm?
   A) It would charge the monopoly price.
   B) It would charge a price equal to its marginal cost.
   C) It would charge the same price as its competitor's.
   D) It would charge a price slightly lower than its competitor's.

Problem solving

1. La Terrasse is one of many small coffee shops in Geneva selling a classic espresso coffee as its competitors do. Consumers have no preference for the coffee sold by different shops but make their purchase decisions exclusively on the price of the coffee in the market. Suppose that the demand function for the espresso in the market is $Q = -10P + 65$, where P is the price of the espresso per cup in dollars and Q is the number of cups in thousands. There were usually 40 thousand cups sold at $2.5 per cup every day in Geneva; however, some coffee shops cut their production or even shut down due to the coronavirus pandemic, leading to a decrease of 15 thousand cups sold each day in the market. The figure below shows various costs of La Terrasse associated with selling the espresso coffee. Other things being equal, how would the profit of La Terrasse change in the short run due to the coronavirus pandemic, and what would be its profit during the pandemic?

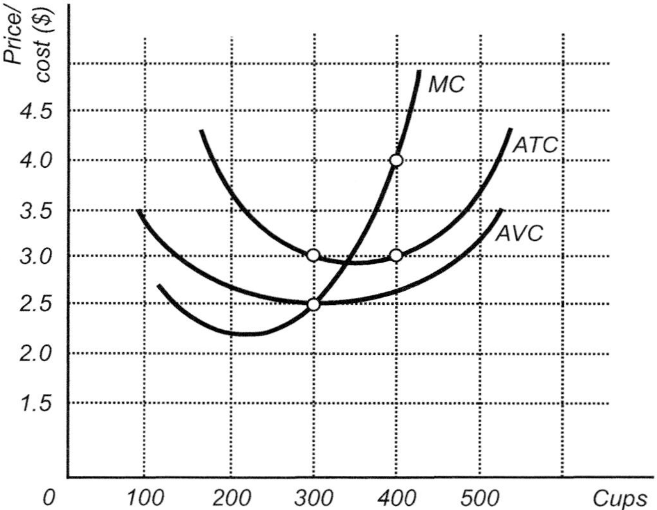

2. Suppose that there is a souvenir shop selling a unique handmade necklace in Ouchy, Lausanne, where the International Olympic Committee is headquartered. The table below shows the sales and output projected in one week at various prices that the shop could charge for the necklace. Suppose that the demand curve and the marginal cost curve are both linear. What would be the price of the necklace and the profit of the shop? If the demand increases by 78 necklaces in the following week, other things being equal, what would be the price of the necklace and the profit of the shop?

Price of the necklace ($)	Sales projected (quantity)	Output projected (quantity)
59	0	390
32	162	120
30	174	100
28	186	80
24	210	40
20	234	0

3. The Caribbean comprises more than 700 tropical islands which offer a standardized mass tourism product, beach tourism, also known as the "3S"s (sea, sun, and sand) tourism. Besides Cuba, Jamaica, Puerto Rico, and the Dominican Republic, the vast majority of the Caribbean countries or territories are small and not competitive in the tourism market. The Caribbean's share of world tourism in terms of tourist arrivals is projected to fall to 1.7% by 2030 from the current 2.1%.[5] One of the reasons is that beach tourism destinations are ubiquitous, distributed from Southeast Asia to the Mediterranean, and are by and large not differentiated from each other. In 1989 the Caribbean Tourism Organization (CTO) was founded, comprising 24 Dutch, English, Spanish, and French country members as well as a myriad of private sector allied members.[6] The CTO functions as a single tourism development agency representing the whole Caribbean, aiming to lead sustainable tourism in the region on the one hand and promote "One Sea, One Voice, One Caribbean" to the global market on the other. Explain how the market structure of beach tourism in the Caribbean would have changed after the foundation of the CTO. Examine whether the CTO can help to strengthen the competitiveness of the Caribbean in the global beach tourism market, and why.

Solutions to all review questions and problem solving tasks are included in the Support Material for this book, which can be accessed at www.routledge.com/9780367897352.

Notes

1 *China Daily*. Price hikes won't do heritage sites good. December 7, 2004. *CNN*. China: Too expensive for Chinese travelers? May 3, 2012.

2 *CGTN*. Tourist sites brought to standstill by 'Golden Week' tourist influx. October 3, 2018. *South China Moring Post*. China's scenic sites limit 'golden week' visitor numbers to cut crowds. October 3, 2019.

3 Output competition in duopoly was modeled by French mathematician and economist Antoine Augustin Cournot (1801–1877). Bertrand formulated his model of price competition as a response to the Cournot model.

4 We shall introduce in Chapter 14 the Hotelling model named after American economist Harold Hotelling (1895–1973) which addresses product differentiation in duopoly.

5 *TravelDailyNews*. Caribbean losing market share as competition in beach tourism heats up. September 2, 2014.

6 Caribbean Tourism Organization. About CTO. Accessed on September 6, 2020.

Bibliography

Chamberlin, E. H. (1949). *Theory of monopolistic competition: A re-orientation of the theory of value*. London, UK: Oxford University Press.

Edgeworth, F. Y. (1925). The pure theory of monopoly. *Papers Relating to Political Economy, 1*, 111–142.

Hall, R. L., & Hitch, C. J. (1939). Price theory and business behaviour. *Oxford Economic Papers, 2*(1), 12–45.

Harrod, R. F. (1934). Doctrines of imperfect competition. *Quarterly Journal of Economics, 48*(3), 442–470.

Robinson, J. (1933). *The economics of imperfect competition. London*, UK: Macmillan and Co., Limited, 1942.

Sweezy, P. M. (1939). Demand under conditions of oligopoly. *Journal of Political Economy, 47*(4), 568–573.

10 Market concentration and market power

This chapter extends the theoretical models of market structure in Chapter 9 to its measurement in practice. Beginning with the definition of a market or an industry, we point out that the boundary of a market or an industry, which is taken for granted in theory, is by no means clearly demarcated in practice. Thus, measuring market structure and firms' market power can be complicated when the boundary of a market is blurred due to changes in both supply and demand forces. We use the market concentration indices to measure market structure on the supply side and the Lerner index to assess the market power of firms on the demand side. Market concentration and market power cast light on understanding the complexity of the tourism industry as a whole, which is virtually composed of a wide range of complementary sectors. Hence the tourism industry does not reconcile the intrinsic nature of competition in an industry from an economic point of view.

AFTER STUDYING THIS CHAPTER, YOU SHOULD BE ABLE TO:

- **Understand the boundary of markets defined by product and location;**
- **Understand and calculate the market concentration indices, graph the Lorenz curve, and assess the degree of market concentration;**
- **Understand and explain the Lerner index in assessing the market power of firms and its relationship with demand elasticity; and**
- **Understand the differences between an industry and a sector in tourism and hospitality with regard to market concentration.**

10.1 Market definition and market boundary

10.1.1 Market boundary by product

Market structure as we have discussed so far is grounded on an implicit assumption that markets or industries[1] are clearly defined, and hence can be distinguished one from another. That is, we assume that we can discern the boundary of a market, and therefore are well aware not only of which firm is or is not included in the market but also of which product is or is not sold in the market. While the boundary of markets does not matter in the theoretical models of market structure, it matters in practice when it comes to assessing competition. By no means are market boundaries demarcated in practice, nor will they remain unchanged, because demand and supply forces can render the boundaries blurred. This situation is exacerbated in tourism and hospitality in particular, as we noted in Chapter 1: tourism cannot be defined properly on the supply side. A standalone product called *tourism* does not exist in the market either. Rather, tourism is a bundle of heterogeneous products and services provided by firms in all sorts of sectors that are more or less related to tourism, hospitality, travel, and so on. Even though we focus on one well-defined sector, say hotels, the prevalence of substitutes would make hotels unable to maintain their market status or exercise their market power as they otherwise could.

In the analysis of market structure, a market or an industry is supposed to consist of firms producing or selling homogenous or similar products. In tourism and hospitality there is no doubt that airlines and hotels operate in different markets because their products differ drastically in terms of functionality, and hence are not substitutes for each other. This issue becomes less clear though when it comes to airlines versus high-speed railway, for instance. The question is whether they should be regarded as belonging in two distinct markets or in the same market. Addressing this question is far more crucial than one might think because the market power of a firm would diminish if the boundary of a market were extended but increasing if the boundary were narrowed down. For instance, if we regard Coca-Cola as in the market for carbonated drinks, the company would make up over 50% of the market share (Figure 10.1). Coca-Cola's market share decreases to around 20% if it is assessed in the market for soft drinks, then to less than 10% in the market for bottled water (Figure 10.1). As the boundary of a market expands, firms that produce substitutes are included, and therefore the market power of incumbent firms is diluted, and hence the market becomes less concentrated. However, this does not mean that the boundary of a market can be arbitrarily demarcated. It

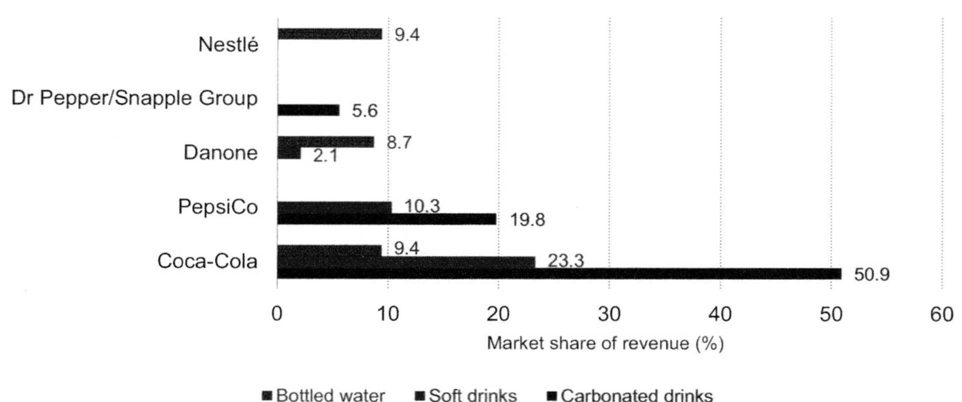

Figure 10.1
Product boundary and market share of firms

Note: The figures are market shares by firm revenue in 2016.

Source: Reproduced from *The Economist*. A unicorn apart: Among private tech firms, Airbnb has pursued a distinct strategy. May 27, 2017.

depends on the extent to which the demand for and/or supply of two or more products can be substituted, which we shall address shortly.

10.1.2 Market boundary by location

Besides the product dimension, the boundary of a market can be created by the location of operation or business, which is the geographic boundary of the market. The geographic boundary of a market suggests the extent to which firms in different locations can obtain market power, thereby influencing the market outcome. In tourism and hospitality, the market boundaries are not limited on the product dimension but are usually defined geographically. Whether and to what extent a firm can influence the market outcome depends on the geographic scope of its business. It perhaps makes little sense to regard hotels in New York City as in the same market as their counterparts in San Francisco, because their influences on each other are largely contained by the long distance between the two cities. Therefore, the market power of hotels in one city is regional, which may not change regardless of whether their counterparts in the other city are in presence or not. At the regional level though, hotels in one city constitute a particular market by themselves regardless of how their counterparts behave in the other city. Thus, it is the geographic boundaries that grant firms the market power even though there might be numerous firms elsewhere producing the same products.

Geographic boundaries can also limit competition between two tourist destinations which provide the same or very similar attractions or amenities. For example, Las Vegas and Macau are both casino destinations. As a matter of fact, many casinos in the two cities are owned and operated by the same corporations. However, casinos in the two cities are hardly competitors, nor are the two cities themselves competitors for attracting tourists, due to the geographic boundary that separates two consumer markets. The demand for casinos in Las Vegas is presumably from North and Central Americas while for Macau from South East Asia and Greater China. It is hard, if not impossible, for one city to surmount the geographic boundary, thereby exerting its influence on the other, because consumers would not compromise their geographic proximity, other things being equal. This ends up with the two cities being monopolists in their respective geographic regions. For instance, Macau reaped a revenue of US$1,354 per visitor from casinos in 2012, which is almost nine times more than Las Vegas did.[2] The striking discrepancy in revenue suggests that Macau and Las Vegas indeed belong to two distinct markets. Were Las Vegas and Macau located next to each other, competition would eradicate the discrepancy in their performance and the two casino markets would converge to one.

10.1.3 Market concentration and market power

Market structure is a theoretical assessment of the extent to which firms compete with each other in a market, thereby exerting their market power accordingly. Perfect competition suggests that competition between firms is extremely intensified while monopoly suggests no competition in the market at all. Between the two extremes are monopolistic competition and oligopoly, with varying degrees of competition between firms. Underlying market structure is the market power that a firm can exercise on its competitors. In practice, the number of firms in a market is a heuristic, but not a decisive, indicator of a certain market structure. This is because market power also depends on the degree of dominance of one or a few larger firms over the vast majority of smaller firms. As far as market power is concerned, monopoly does not entail only one firm in the market but whether a firm possesses considerable market power that renders all other firms, if any, almost insignificant in affecting the market outcome. Nor does a perfectly competitive market entail an astronomically large number of firms. A market could also be perfectly competitive with very few firms provided that each firm is equivalent in all aspects, and therefore no firm is able to dictate the market outcome such as the case illustrated by Bertrand competition.

Given a certain number of firms in an industry, market structure can be measured by the extent to which the market is controlled by large firms, which is referred to as market concentration or industry concentration. A systematic study on market concentration can date back to American economist Gardiner Means (1896–1988), who raised the concern of the escalating concentration in the U.S. economy in the 1920s. Means estimated that the largest 130 corporations at that time controlled over 80% of gross assets of all corporations traded regularly on the New York Stock Exchange.[3] His study was followed by many economists in the 1930s and the aftermath of World War II, who obtained an almost unanimous conclusion that the U.S. economy became increasingly concentrated. Above everything else, market concentration reflects structural changes in an industry or a market as well as the conduct of firms such as pricing. Monopoly is one extreme in which a market is controlled by one firm and hence is the most concentrated or, in other words, the least competitive. Perfect competition is the other extreme in which no firm can control a market, and the market is the least concentrated or the most competitive. Varying between the two extremes are oligopoly in which a few large firms control almost the whole market and monopolistic competition in which each firm takes a negligible market share.

10.2 Measuring market concentration

To measure market concentration we need to know the number of firms in an industry as well as the size distribution of firms, which is the market share of each firm. Other things being equal, a market or an industry would become more concentrated as the number of firms diminishes while less concentrated as the number of firms increases. Yet firm numbers are not a sufficient condition to assess the degree of market concentration. Large firm numbers in a market do not guarantee that the market will be less concentrated, because there may exist dominant firms that render the rest of other firms insignificant. On the other hand, given a certain number of firms in a market, the market would become less concentrated if each firm has a more even market share and more concentrated if their market shares are less even. Yet identifying every single firm and its market share is not necessary, not only because such information is usually unavailable but also because the primary concern of regulators is about large and influential firms. Precisely for this reason, market concentration can reveal the degree of oligopoly in an industry, that is, the extent to which the industry is controlled by a few dominant firms. In what follows we introduce three measures of market concentration which are based on the number of firms and their size distribution.

10.2.1 Four-firm concentration ratio

Among the most widely used measures of market concentration is the market concentration ratio (*CR*). It is computed by aggregating the market shares of a certain number of the largest firms in an industry to reveal the degree of concentration of the industry. The United States Census Bureau (USCB) has been publishing the concentration ratio measured by firm revenue since 1947. The USCB first published the concentration ratio for the manufacturing industry only, then extended it to nearly 900 industries and sectors in the U.S. economy. The most common market concentration ratio computed by the USCB is the so-called four-firm concentration ratio, or CR_4 for short. As the name suggests, it is computed by aggregating the market shares of the four largest firms in an industry:

$$CR_4 = \sum_{i}^{4} s_i, \tag{10.1}$$

where i indexes the ith largest firm in the industry ranked by market share, and s_i is the market share of the ith largest firm. The market share of each firm in an industry indicates the size distribution. If the size distribution is perfectly even, each firm's market share is equal. If otherwise, there are dominant firms with larger market shares versus small firms with smaller market shares. There are two issues concerning the market concentration ratio. First, we conventionally factor the four largest firms, instead of five or more, into the computation largely due to data availability. Probably before the 1950s,[4] the data of smaller firms were not disclosed by the USCB, and hence computing the CR_4 was not only an expediency but a norm. Now the USCB also publishes the concentration ratios aggregated for the largest 8, 20, and 50 firms, which are referred to as the CR_8, CR_{20}, and CR_{50}, respectively. These more sophisticated concentration ratios allow us to assess market concentration more precisely and fully as firms have been proliferating in almost all industries. Second, the USCB measures the market share of firms using firms' sales and revenue. Note that firm revenue is not the only dimension on which firm size can be assessed. Alongside firm revenue, the USCB collects information on annual payroll and the number of paid employees of each firm. This information can be used as a complement to assess firm size in an industry.

Figure 10.2 shows the four largest airlines, American, Delta, Southwest, and United, in terms of domestic revenue in the United Sates in 2019. They each accounted for 17.6%, 17.5%, 16.9%, and 14.9% of the market share, respectively. Thus, the four-firm concentration ratio (CR_4) of the U.S. airline industry in 2019 is obtained by aggregating the market shares of the four largest airlines:

$$CR_4 = 17.6\% + 17.5\% + 16.9\% + 14.9\% = 66.9\%. \tag{10.2}$$

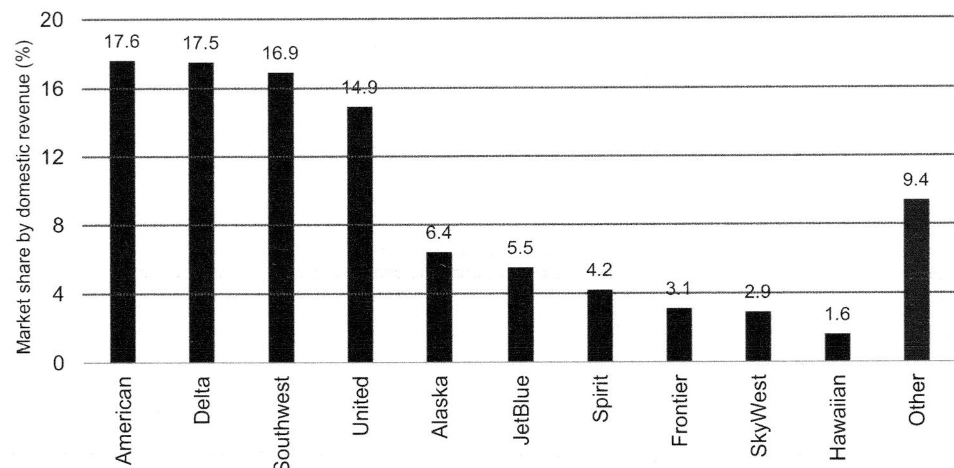

Figure 10.2
Domestic market share of U.S. airlines in 2019

Note: U.S. airline market share is measured as revenue passenger miles on domestic flights across the U.S. in 2019. The other category includes the sum of the market shares of unspecified U.S. airlines.

Source: Bureau of Transportation Statistics, U.S. Department of Transportation.

The information in Figure 10.2 also allows us to calculate the eight-firm concentration ratio (CR_8) by aggregating the market shares of the eight largest airlines:

$$CR_8 = 17.6\% + 17.5\% + 16.9 + 14.9 + \cdots + 3.1\% = 86.1\%. \qquad (10.3)$$

If the number of firms in an industry is equal to or smaller than four, obviously the $CR_4 = 100\%$; if otherwise, the CR_4 is certainly below 100%. Suppose that an industry contains a considerably large number of firms and the size distribution is perfectly even. Then the CR_4 will converge to zero. Perfect competition, by definition, suggests that the CR_4 is close to zero, and a CR_4 close to zero also suggests that a market is close to perfect competition. The CR_4 of monopoly is 100% as monopolists account for 100% of the market share, yet a CR_4 equal to 100% does not necessarily suggest monopoly. Consider an oligopoly with only four or fewer firms. The CR_4 of the oligopoly will be 100% regardless of the size distribution of firms. Hence the CR_4 takes values in [0,100%], with monopolistic competition and oligopoly having a CR_4 between 0 and 100%. Other things being equal, the greater the CR_4, the more concentrated or the least competitive an industry; the smaller the CR_4, the less concentrated or the more competitive an industry. Note that the market concentration ratio suggests no decisive delimitation between one market structure and another because market power arising from different market structures is not categorically defined.

From the latest concentration ratios published by the USCB in 2012, we can have a glance at the degrees of market concentration in ten major industries in the U.S. economy. Figure 10.3 shows that the three most concentrated industries are

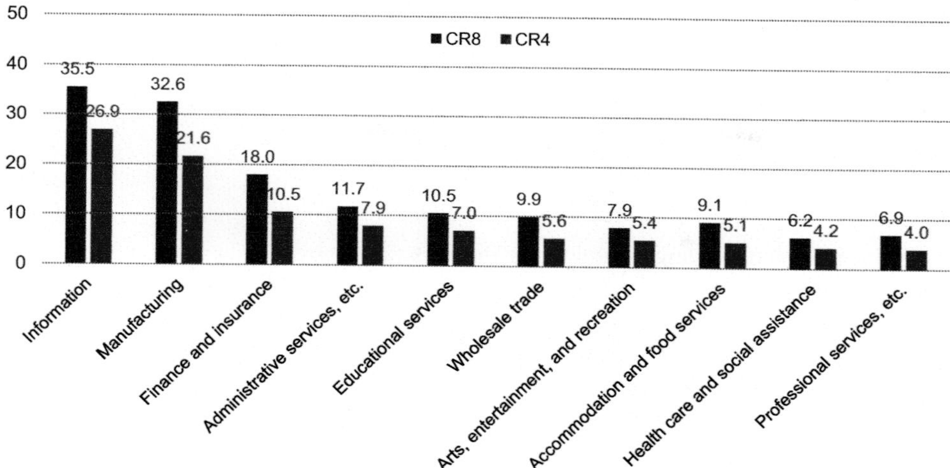

Figure 10.3
Market concentration in U.S. industries in 2012

Note: Market concentration ratio is based on the market share of firm revenue in each industry or sector. Since the USCB does not publish a single index of market concentration ratio for manufacturing, we computed the concentration ratios of manufacturing using the weighted averages of the concentration ratios of all 21 three-digit NAICS[5] manufacturing sectors. The weights are based on each sector's share in the total revenue of the manufacturing industry.

Source: USCB. Economic Census of the United States 2012.

information, manufacturing, and finance and insurance, whose CR_4s are 26.9%, 21.6%, and 10.5%, respectively. The manufacturing industry, which used to be the most predominant industry in much of the twentieth century, has been supplanted by the information industry. By contrast, service industries are exclusively less concentrated, with the CR_4 around 5%. Even though we refer to the CR_8, all service industries except educational services are still below 10%. However, the CR_8s for both information and manufacturing industries exceed 30%, which means that more than one-third of firm revenue in each of the two industries is controlled by the eight largest firms. It is evident that the increased concentration in the U.S. economy since the 1990s has by and large been driven by high degrees of market concentration in information, manufacturing, and finance and insurance, among others. Yet the increased proportions of service industries in the U.S. economy could mitigate the concentration.

10.2.2 Herfindahl-Hirschman Index

The second measure of market concentration is the Herfindahl-Hirschman Index (*HHI*), named after two economists American Orris Herfindahl (1918–1972) and German-born American Albert Hirschman (1915–2012). Hirschman and Herfindahl developed the index independently in 1945 and 1950, respectively. Similarly to the computation of the concentration ratio, the *HHI* also relies on the information of both the number of firms in an industry and their size distribution. The major difference between the two indices is that the *HHI* is computed by aggregating the squared market share for each firm in an industry:

$$HHI = \sum_{i}^{N} s_i^2, \quad (10.4)$$

where i indexes the ith largest firm in the industry ranked by market share, s_i is the market share of the ith largest firm, and N is the total number of firms. To compute the *HHI*, we usually factor the market share squared for up to 50 firms into calculation, which is also the methodology adopted by the USCB. If firm number is smaller than 50, all firms are taken into account. As more firms are entered in computation, the *HHI* becomes more representative and informative, especially when an industry has a large number of firms. In this aspect, the *HHI* is superior to the four-firm or eight-firm concentration ratio.

Let us compute the *HHI* of the U.S. airline industry based on the information in Figure 10.2. Note that we have no information on the exact number of airlines in the industry. We only know the ten largest airlines plus the other category which aggregates all other smaller airlines making up 9.4% of the market share. For illustrative purposes, we need to regard the other category as if it were one corporate entity to proceed with the computation.[6] This manipulation ends up with 11 airlines with the "other" category being the fifth largest (9.4%) and Hawaiian (1.6%) the smallest. Thus, the *HHI* of the U.S. airline industry is obtained by aggregating the market shares squared for all 11 airline entities. For convenience we disregard percentage symbols in the computation of the *HHI*:

$$HHI = 17.6^2 + 17.5^2 + \cdots + 2.9^2 + 1.6^2 = 1321.42. \quad (10.5)$$

Obviously, monopoly has the largest *HHI* equal to 10,000 because a monopolist accounts for 100% of the market share; perfect competition has the smallest *HHI* close to zero, because each firm's market share is close to zero. Monopolistic competition and oligopoly have an *HHI* between 0 and 10,000. Hence the *HHI* takes values in [0,10,000]. Other things being equal, the greater the *HHI*, the more concentrated or less competitive an industry; the smaller the *HHI*, the less concentrated or more competitive an industry. Similarly to the market concentration ratio, the *HHI* suggests no artificial line of demarcation between the four market structures but only the degree of market concentration. From a policy point of view, the U.S. Department of Justice and Federal Trade Commission, which are responsible for the enforcement of U.S. antitrust law, do suggest the cutoff values of the *HHI* in classifying markets: unconcentrated markets ($HHI < 1{,}500$), moderately concentrated markets ($1{,}500 \le HHI \le 2{,}500$), and highly concentrated markets ($HHI > 2{,}500$).[7]

Both the concentration ratio and the *HHI* measure the degree of market concentration yet from slightly different methodological points of view. The *CR* is easy to compute but may not be as accurate as the *HHI* especially when the size distribution is uneven. One advantage of computing the *HHI* is that it can reflect the market power of dominant

Table 10.1 CR_4 versus *HHI* in measuring market concentration

Industries	Scenario 1: Size distribution unknown	Scenario 2: Size distribution known: A: 25% each; B: 81% + 19×1%
Industry A: 4 firms	$CR_4 = 100\%$	$CR_4 = 100\%$
	$4 \times (100/4)^2 \leq HHI < 10{,}000$	$HHI = 4 \times 25^2 = 2{,}500$
Industry B: 20 firms	$CR_4 < 100\%$	$CR_4 = 84\%$
	$20 \times (100/20)^2 \leq HHI < 10{,}000$	$HHI = 81^2 + 19 \times 1 = 6{,}580$

firms in an industry in which the size distribution is uneven. Consider two industries, *A* and *B*, having 4 and 20 firms, respectively, as shown in Table 10.1. In scenario 1, suppose that we have no information about the size distribution of firms in the two industries. Obviously, industry *A*'s CR_4 is 100% whereas *B*'s is certainly smaller than 100% despite the exact CR_4 of industry *B* being unknown. This may mislead us to conclude that *A* is more concentrated than *B*, which may not be the case though. In scenario 2, suppose that each firm in *A* has the same market share of 25%, while the largest firm in *B* accounts for 81%, the remaining 19 firms each marking up 1%. Despite *A*'s CR_4 always being greater than *B*'s in both scenarios, industry *A*'s *HHI* is 2,500 whereas *B*'s is 6,580 in scenario 2, and hence *B* is more concentrated than *A*. As a matter of fact, in scenario 2 industry *A* is an oligopoly while *B*, despite having more firms, is a monopoly due to the dominant firm that makes up the lion's share of the market.

The USCB has published the *HHI* of 459 four-digit SIC manufacturing sectors since 1947, and the latest indices are available for 1992.[8] It is difficult to track changes in the *HHI* because the data were not consecutively collected in the period 1947–1992. Figure 10.4a shows the ten most concentrated sectors in manufacturing, denoted by the highest *HHI*s in the whole period ranging from 2,717 to 2,999. Among them are the four sectors pertaining to household consumption: greeting cards (2,922), chewing and smoking tobacco (2,894), household laundry equipment (2,855), and household refrigerators and freezers (2,745). By contrast, Figure 10.4b shows the ten least concentrated manufacturing sectors, with the *HHI*s ranging from 1 to 23. Interestingly, the ten least concentrated sectors are obscure to consumers and have no bearing on household consumption. This result may suggest that large consumer numbers entice firms to dominate in an industry and thereby leverage economies of scale. Figure 10.4 also shows that large firm numbers can dilute the market concentration. The largest firm number in the most concentrated sectors barely exceeds 200 while the smallest firm number in the least concentrated sectors easily surpasses a few thousand.

10.2.3 Lorenz curve

A relevant measure that resembles the idea of the market concentration ratio is the Lorenz curve developed by American economist Max Lorenz (1876–1959). Although

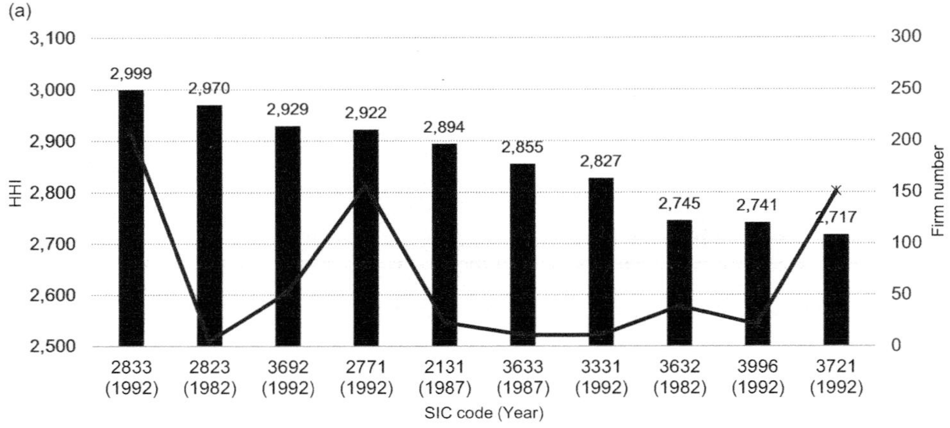

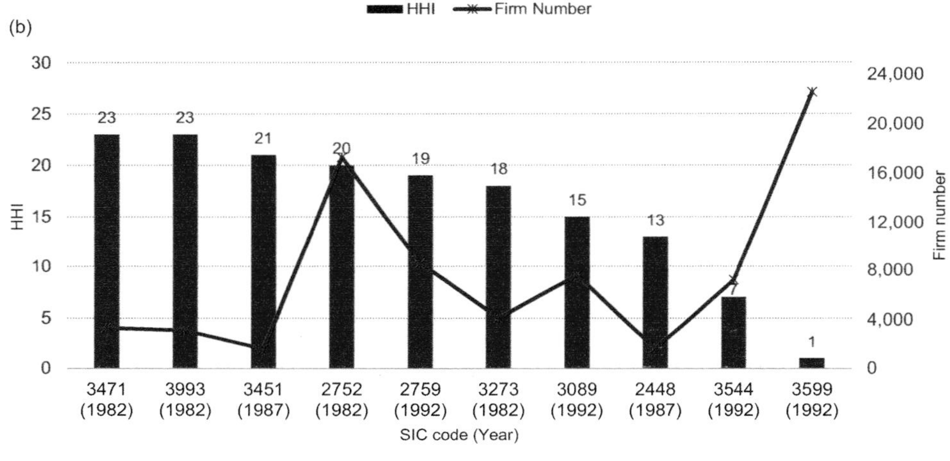

Figure 10.4 Market concentration in U.S. manufacturing

Note: The *HHI* is based on the market share of firm revenue in each industry or sector. Each figure in brackets on the horizontal axis is the year when an industry recorded the highest *HHI* in the period 1947–1992. Four-digit SIC codes: (a): 2833 = Medicinals and botanicals, 2823 = Cellulosic manmade fibers, 3692 = Primary batteries, dry and wet, 2771 = Greeting cards, 2131 = Chewing and smoking tobacco, 3633 = Household laundry equipment, 3331 = Primary copper, 3632 = Household refrigerators and freezers, 3996 = Hard surface floor coverings, not elsewhere classified (nec.), 3721 = Aircraft; (b): 3471 = Electroplating, plating, polishing, anodizing, and coloring, 3993 = Signs and advertising specialties, 3451 = Screw machine products, 2752 = Commercial printing, lithographic, 2759 = Commercial printing, nec., 3273 = Ready-mixed concrete, 3089 = Plastics products, nec., 2448 = Wood pallets and skids, 3544 = Special dies and tools, die sets, jigs and fixtures, and industrial molds, 3599 = Industrial and commercial machinery and equipment, nec.

Source: USCB. Economic Census Manufacturing Concentration Ratios (1947–1992).

the Lorenz curve was developed to measure income or wealth distribution, it is virtually a generic statistic that can be applied to any context in which the size distribution of subjects in a population is known. Instead of generating an index like the *CR* or *HHI*, the Lorenz curve depicts a holistic pattern of market concentration that takes into account the accumulative market share from the largest firm to the smallest firm in an industry. Given N firms ($N \geq 1$) in an industry and the size distribution, we rank all firms from the largest to the smallest on the x-axis and their cumulative market share on the y-axis (Figure 10.5). On the x-axis let the ith ($i = 1, 2, \ldots, N$) firm take value i / N in sequence, equal to the proportion of the i firm(s) in all N firms, and the corresponding value on the y-axis be the cumulative market share of all the i firms. Thus, each pair of coordinates indicates the proportion of the i firm(s) in all N firms that corresponds to their cumulative market share. When i takes value successively from 1, 2, ..., to N, all the coordinates constitute a curve bounded between zero and 100% on both x- and y-axis. This curve is known as the Lorenz curve (Figure 10.5).

If the size distribution is perfectly even, each firm makes up a proportion of $1 / N$ in both firm numbers and market share. We end up obtaining a 45-degree diagonal from the origin to the upper-right coordinates (100%, 100%). Given the firm number N, this diagonal is *the* Lorenz curve that suggests the least degree of concentration in an industry. In other words, the condition for an industry to be the least concentrated is that the size distribution of firms is perfectly even, other things being equal. Of course, the diagonal does not suffice for the conclusion that the industry is in perfect competition, because perfect competition entails numerous firms in the market in the first place, that is, N must be sufficiently large. As long as the size distribution is uneven in an industry, the Lorenz curve will bend outward above the diagonal regardless of the number of firms in the industry, and hence the industry becomes more concentrated. Given the firm number N, the more the Lorenz curve bends outward the more concentrated an industry is. The Lorenz curve of monopoly deviates the farthest away from the diagonal, ending up on the verges of the upper triangle in Figure 10.5. Hence the diagonal and the verges of the upper triangle set the lower and upper bounds of the Lorenz curve in which oligopoly and monopolistic competition can be positioned.

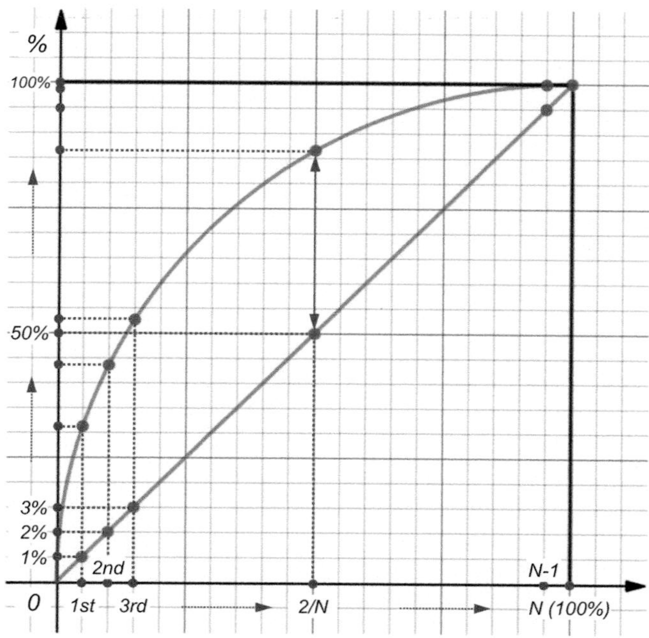

Figure 10.5
Lorenz curve and market concentration

Figure 10.6 portrays the Lorenz curves of the ten industries except manufacturing in the U.S. economy in 2012 which we assessed earlier in Figure 10.3. The manufacturing industry was excluded because the complete data of firm numbers and size distribution are not available. Since the data are only available for the largest 4, 8, 20, and 50 firms, we are not able to portray precisely the Lorenz curves over all firms in each industry. It turns out that all the nine Lorenz curves seem to cluster on the *y*-axis because even the 50 firms may account for a tiny fraction of hundreds of thousands of firms in each of these industries. Hence the exact shape of the Lorenz curve beyond 50 cannot be properly delineated, which is also why the Lorenz curves are not smooth either. Nevertheless, from Figure 10.6 we can still assess market concentration in the nine industries by examining the extent to which each of the Lorenz curves deviates from the 45-degree diagonal. The most concentrated industry is information, followed by finance and insurance, wholesale trade, all the way to health care and social assistance. It is worth noting that there are noticeable divergences in market concentration between the three most concentrated industries, yet the divergences in the service industries are inappreciable as their Lorenz curves tend to cluster all together.

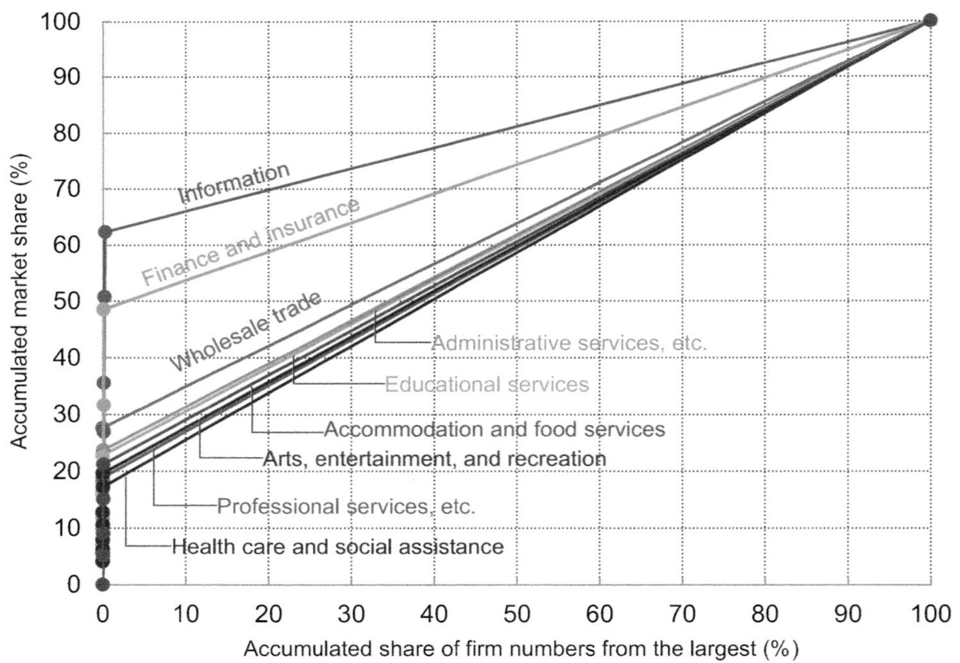

Figure 10.6
Lorenz curves of the U.S. industries

Note: Market share is measured as the market share of firm revenue in each industry or sector. Due to the lack of data for the market share from the 51st largest firm in each industry, we are not able to detect the exact shape of the whole Lorenz curve.

Source: USCB. Economic Census of the United States 2012.

10.3 Measuring market power

10.3.1 Lerner index and price elasticity of demand

The measures of market concentration we discussed above are the post hoc assessment of market structure because they are exclusively inferred from historical performance of firms. Besides, market concentration can be manifested on dimensions other than market share, such as pricing and product differentiation, among others. In Chapter 9 we noted that market structure is associated with the pricing power of firms in a market. Firms in a perfectly competitive market are price takers while monopolists are price makers. Thus, a different perspective of examining market concertation is to assess the extent to which firms can set their prices as well as how much the prices deviate from their marginal costs. This in turn relates to how consumers respond to the product of a firm, namely the demand elasticity that the firm faces in the market. If demand is considerably inelastic, the firm will have tremendous market power of raising price above the marginal cost while still being able to captivate consumers. If otherwise, the firm's pricing power will be restricted. This is the very idea behind the Lerner index developed by and named after Russian British economist Abba Lerner (1903–1982). The Lerner index is used to assess the market power of a firm and in particular the degree of monopoly in an industry. The Lerner index (L) is formulated as the ratio of the divergence between the price and the marginal cost of a product to the price:

$$L = \frac{p-c}{p}, \tag{10.6}$$

where p is the price of the product that a firm charges to maximize profit, and c is the marginal cost of the product. Thus, the divergence $p-c$ is the firm's markup for each unit of the product it sells. Assuming the marginal cost is constant, if the firm is able to charge a price far above its marginal cost, then the Lerner index will converge to 1 as the maximum. Hence $L=1$ indicates the greatest monopoly power a firm can possess in an industry, and the market is the most concentrated. If the price ends up being equal to the marginal cost, such as in perfect competition and Bertrand competition, we will have $L=0$. Therefore, the market is the least concentrated given firm numbers, and each firm has no market power.

Given marginal cost, a firm's markup, $p-c$, depends on the price it is able to charge which in turn depends on the demand elasticity it faces in the market. We proceed to articulate the relationship between the Lerner index and demand elasticity. Suppose that a firm has the inverse demand function denoted as $p(q)$ and its total cost is $c(q)$. We can specify the profit function (8.11) introduced in Chapter 8, $\pi = R-C$, as

$$\pi = p(q)q - c(q). \tag{10.7}$$

Function (10.7) suggests that profit is a function of quantity demanded and price, which in turn is a function of quantity demanded. Given the profit-maximization condition that marginal profit is equal to zero and letting the derivate of the profit π with respect to q be zero, we have

$$p'(q)q + p(q) - c'(q) = 0, \tag{10.8}$$

where $p'(q)$ is the derivative of price with respect to quantity demanded, and $c'(q)$ is the derivative of total cost with respect to quantity, which is marginal cost. Rearranging equation (10.8) and dividing both sides by $p(q)$, we obtain

$$\frac{p(q) - c'(q)}{p(q)} = -\frac{p'(q)q}{p(q)}, \tag{10.9}$$

where the left-hand side of equation (10.9) is the Lerner index in formula (10.6), and the right-hand side is the negative reciprocal of the price elasticity of demand. Thus, the Lerner index depends inversely on the price elasticity of demand, whereby the market power of a firm is attributed to demand forces. The economic intuition of the Lerner index is straightforward. In perfect competition each firm faces a perfectly elastic demand, and hence the reciprocal of price elasticity is zero, and so is the Lerner index. Thus, each firm obtains a marginal revenue equal to the market price of a good, and produces an output at which its marginal revenue is equal to marginal cost. For the same reason, the Lerner index is also zero in Bertrand competition, in which duopolists also face perfectly elastic demand. A monopolist ends up obtaining a greater markup and hence more market power when demand is less elastic but less market power when demand is more elastic. Given the marginal cost of a monopolist, if the price is extremely high, the markup will converge to the price, and hence the Lerner index converges to 1, at which demand is unit elastic. Therefore, the Lerner index takes values in $[0,1]$. The less elastic the demand, the greater the Lerner index, and the more concentrated a market; and the more elastic the demand, the smaller the Lerner index, and the less concentrated a market.

10.3.2 Lerner index and demand substitutability

As far as market concentration is concerned, the demand elasticity of a firm in question varies due to the availability of substitutes in a market. As long as a substitute is available to consumers, the demand that a firm faces will become more elastic, and hence the Lerner index diminishes, and the market becomes less concentrated. Thus, market concentration also depends on demand substitutability, which is the extent to which consumers are able and willing to substitute one good for another in two supposedly different markets. If demand substitutability between two goods is considerably high, the market boundary will be blurred or even vanish despite no structural changes on the supply side. If demand substitutability is substantially low, a market boundary may arise in the supposedly same market or industry. Table 10.2 shows a bunch of hotel brands in two classes, economy and luxury, in New York City. Obviously, the demand substitutability between any two hotels in each class is high while relatively low between classes. Thus, the market boundary arises between economy and luxury classes despite both being in the hotel industry. The demand that each hotel faces within its class tends to be more elastic than across classes. Therefore, the rate discrepancies are much smaller within a class than across classes as shown in Table 10.2. In other words, the market power of hotels within a class is restricted.

Since it is difficult to delimitate market boundaries on the supply side, especially in tourism and hospitality, what matters is how consumers respond to the product of a firm. The Lerner index enables us to examine the dynamic ramifications of a firm's pricing insofar as consumer demand is concerned. Since demand is dynamic and volatile compared to supply, the Lerner index reflects the market power of a firm when demand is subject to change in the short run due to the availability of substitutes among other things. A study in China's airline industry shows that the Lerner indices of the three major airlines, Air China, China Southern Airlines, and China Eastern Airlines, fluctuate considerably on a quarterly basis (Figure 10.7). In particular, the three airlines obtain more market power in the third quarter indicated by higher Lerner indices, probably because they are in high demand in summer seasons. Such

Table 10.2 Convergence and divergence of hotel rates

Classes	Hotel brands	Rate (US$)
Economy hotels		107.4
	Hotel Pennsylvania	121.0
	Hotel Marrakech	104.0
	Midtown West Hotel	107.0
	The Jane	80.0
	Manhattan Broadway Hotel	125.0
Luxury hotels		443.1
	Hyatt Centric Times Square	409.0
	Arlo NoMad	395.0
	Four Points by Sheraton	479.0
	Courtyard by Marriott	422.0
	Row NYC	423.0
	Gansevoort Meatpacking	505.0
	City Club Hotel	469.0

Source: Data were collected by the author on Booking.com in March 2018.

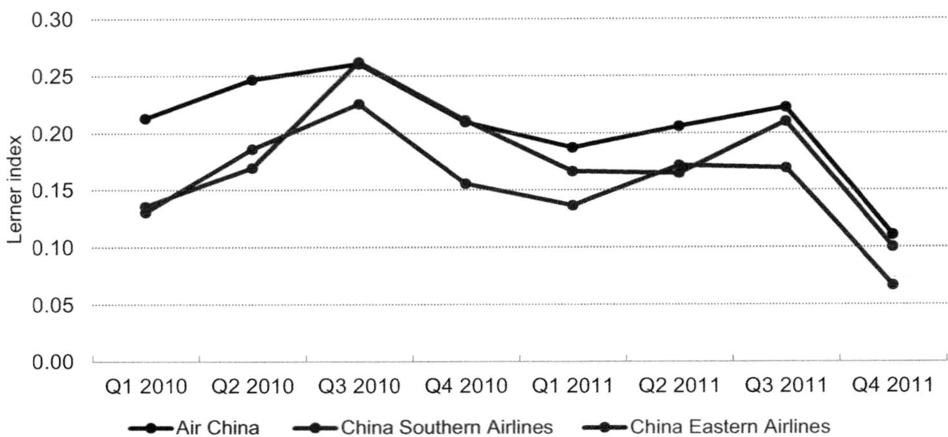

Figure 10.7
Lerner index of Chinese airlines

Source: Reproduced from Zhang et al. (2014), p. 6.

fluctuations cannot be attributed to structural changes on the supply side which are more likely to occur in the long run. Rather, it is the demand change in the short run that alters the price elasticity of demand that the airlines face, hence resulting in the short-run fluctuations in the Lerner index. The short-run change in demand is primarily due to demand seasonality of tourism in general as well as the extent to which consumers substitute rail travel for air travel in different seasons.

10.4 Industry versus sector

10.4.1 The complementary nature of the tourism industry

In public discourse and even in scientific research the tourism industry is deemed to encompass a wide range of travel-, tourism-, and hospitality-related sectors, primarily hotels, restaurants, casinos, airlines, railways, cruise lines, amusement parks, and so on. We can go down the line to enumerate many other peripheral sectors as long as they render products and services to tourists as the end consumers. Yet as far as market power and competition are concerned, the *tourism industry* is a misnomer because these sectors are not substitutes but complements. On the one hand, products and services in these sectors are clearly defined by their respective functionalities and production technologies. For instance, the cost structure and operation of an airline are by no means comparable to those of a hotel or restaurant, and so on. On the other hand, a firm in one sector cannot exercise its market power on a firm in another sector despite both accommodating the same consumers. Therefore, the tourism industry is not an *industry* in which firms are supposed to compete with one another but a combination of various complementary *sectors*. As a matter of expediency, we can replace the tourism industry with tourism industries or sectors in order to reconcile the contradiction between an industry that is defined by competition and the tourism industry that is virtually a conglomerate of different industrial sectors.

In various tourism and hospitality sectors, it is perhaps difficult for firms in one sector to supplant the production in another to respond to changes in a market. This is referred to as supply substitutability, suggesting the extent to which firms are able to substitute the production of one good for the production of another or to substitute the operation in one sector for the operation in another. For example, Starbucks would find it difficult to operate hotel businesses, thus substituting the provision of accommodation for the production of drinks is low. This in turn creates a market boundary between the accommodation and catering sectors. Nevertheless, it is easy for Starbucks to divert its resources from coffee production to tea production because the production of both goods shares similar technologies, operation processes, as well as a great deal of ingredients. Thus, the market boundary between coffee and tea could be blurred despite the fact that the demand substitutability between the two goods might be low. Therefore, the two markets would converge to one single market on the supply side, say the market for soft drinks, and become less concentrated than the two separate markets. Yet no matter how unsurmountable a market boundary is for firms in production, the market power of firms will be restrained as long as consumers can surmount the boundary in their consumption.

10.4.2 Market concentration in tourism and hospitality

In practice, the tourism- and hospitality-related sectors are scattered over a wide range of domains in the national economy, which makes analyzing market concentration in tourism and hospitality hard. As a matter of fact, measuring concentration in tourism as a whole is not necessary because the boundary of the tourism industry cannot be clearly demarcated on the supply side nor on the demand side. The USCB lists "accommodation and food services and drinking places" as one single sector with the NAICS code of 72, alongside other major industries such as manufacturing, information, and finance and insurance. This sector is arguably the most tourism- and/or hospitality-relevant as it encompasses hotels and restaurants among others. It is by no means inclusive. Firms in this sector totaled 662,489 and generated a revenue of US$708 billion in the U.S. in 2012, in contrast to 256,304 firms and a revenue of US$5.7 trillion in manufacturing.[9] Figure 10.8 shows that the accommodation sector is much more concentrated than the sector of food services and drinking places (referred to as the catering sector thereafter). The four-firm concentration ratio is 15.7% in the accommodation sector versus 6.3% in the catering sector. In addition, twenty largest firms control more than one-third of the revenue in the accommodation sector in contrast to 14.3% of the revenue in the catering sector.

The difference in market concentration between the accommodation and catering sectors is perhaps because the former has a more narrowly defined consumer market. The majority of consumers in the accommodation sector are tourists as opposed to both tourists and locals served by the catering sector. Table 10.3 shows that the

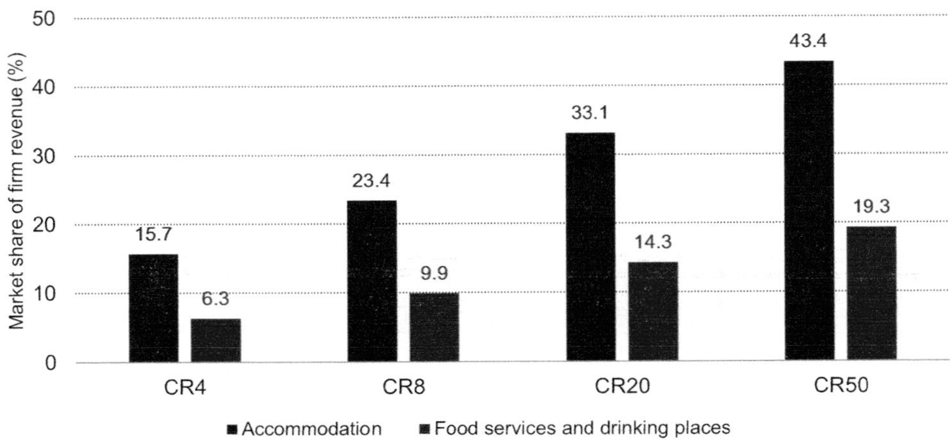

Figure 10.8
Concentration ratios in accommodation versus catering

Note: Market concentration ratio is based on the market share of firm revenue in each industry or sector. CR_{20} is the aggregate market share of the 20 largest firms, and CR_{50} is the aggregate market share of the 50 largest firms.

Source: USCB. Summary Statistics by Concentration of Largest Firms for the U.S. 2012.

Table 10.3 Accommodation versus catering

Sectors and NAICS codes	Concentration ratios				Number of establishments	Revenue (US$1,000)
	CR_4	CR_8	CR_{20}	CR_{50}		
Accommodation (721)	15.7	23.4	33.1	43.4	63,833	195,858,388
7211	16.2	24.2	34.1	44.8	54,289	189,672,313
7212	5.6	8.0	11.5	17.4	7,414	4,838,704
7213	21.0	28.2	38.9	48.6	2,130	1,347,371
Food services and drinking places (722)	6.3	9.9	14.3	19.3	598,656	512,280,210
7223	54.6	61.7	68.1	72.3	38,974	45,212,208
7224	2.5	3.6	5.6	8.2	41,774	19,725,909
7225	5.6	8.0	11.9	16.6	517,908	447,342,093

Note: Market concentration ratio is based on the market share of firm revenue in each industry or sector. CR_{20} is the aggregate market share of the 20 largest firms, and CR_{50} is the aggregate market share of the 50 largest firms. NAICS codes: 7211 = Traveler accommodation, 7212 = RV (recreational vehicle) parks and recreational camps, 7213 = Rooming and boarding houses, 7223 = Special food services, 7224 = Drinking places (alcoholic beverages), 7225 = Restaurants and other eating places. Included in traveler accommodation (7211) are 72111 = Hotels (except casino hotels) and motels, 72112 = Casino hotels, and 72119 = Other traveler accommodation.

Source: USCB. Summary Statistics by Concentration of Largest Firms for the U.S. 2012.

subsector traveler accommodation (7211), which exclusively serves tourists, accounts for 85% of firm numbers (63,833) and 97% of revenue (US$195.9 billion) in the accommodation sector. On the other hand, a plurality of restaurants, clubs and bars, and so on compete locally, and thus these businesses tend to scatter geographically. There are also a lot of substitutes in the catering sector, and hence the market concentration is mitigated. Within the accommodation sector are two subsectors, traveler accommodation (7211) and rooming and boarding houses (7213), which are quite concentrated as shown in Table 10.3. Only one subsector in the catering sector, the special food services sector (7223), is highly concentrated. Table 10.3 also shows that firm numbers have a considerable influence on market concentration. The catering sector has almost ten times more firms than does the accommodation sector. Firms in each subsector of the catering sector also far outnumber their counterparts in accommodation.

Summary

1. A market or an industry consists of firms producing the same or similar products that compete with each other. The boundary of a market is subject to change depending on the extent to which two products can be substituted for each other or two firms can exercise influence on each other.
2. Market concentration examines the extent to which a market or an industry is controlled by a few large firms. Different degrees of market concentration manifest different market structures and reflect the market power of firms.
3. Market concentration is commonly measured by the concentration ratio (*CR*), the Herfindahl-Hirschman Index (*HHI*), and the Lorenz curve. These measures are computed based on the number of firms in a market and the size distribution of firms.
4. The four-firm concentration ratio (CR_4) aggregates the market shares of the four largest firms in an industry. The CR_4 takes values from 0 to 100%, which correspond to the four market structures from perfect competition to monopoly.
5. The Herfindahl-Hirschman Index (*HHI*) aggregates the squared market shares of up to 50 firms in an industry. It takes values from 0 to 10,000, which correspond to the four market structures as well. When the size distribution of firms is considerably uneven, the *HHI* is superior to the CR_4 in assessing market concentration.
6. The Lorenz curve depicts market concentration by taking into account all firms in an industry. Other things being equal, the Lorenz curve denoted by the 45-degree diagonal suggests the least concentrated market. The more the Lorenz curve deviates from the 45-degree diagonal the more concentrated a market is.
7. The Lerner index measures the market power of a firm by assessing the extent to which the firm can charge a price above its marginal cost, which in turn depends on the demand elasticity that the firm faces in a market.
8. The Lerner index is the negative reciprocal of the price elasticity of demand. It takes values from 0 to 1, suggesting market structures from perfect competition to monopoly. Due to demand substitutability, the Lerner index varies with demand.

9. Since the tourism industry encompasses a wide range of complementary sectors pertinent to tourism and/or hospitality, the tourism industry is a misnomer. This is because competition does not exist between different sectors in tourism and hospitality.
10. As far as the United States is concerned, the accommodation sector is more concentrated than the catering sector in terms of concentration ratios. The catering sector has almost ten times more firms than does the accommodation sector, suggesting that large firm numbers would dilute market concentration.

REVIEW QUESTIONS

Each question has four options, and there is only one correct answer to each question.

1. Suppose that consumers have high demand substitutability between iced tea and cola, which are produced by Nestlé and Pepsi, respectively. Which of the following is correct?
   A) The prices of iced tea and cola in the market tend to converge.
   B) The market for soft drinks could become more concentrated.
   C) The product boundary between iced tea and cola can be demarcated.
   D) Nestlé and Pepsi can maintain their market power in their respective markets.
2. Which of the following is correct regarding the four-firm concentration ratio (CR_4) and the Herfindahl-Hirschman Index (HHI) of a market?
   A) $CR_4 = 100\%$ suggests that the market is monopoly
   B) $CR_4 = 100\%$ suggests that the market is oligopoly
   C) $HHI = 10{,}000$ suggests that the market is monopoly
   D) $HHI = 10{,}000$ suggests that the market is oligopoly
3. Suppose that there are 14 casinos in Macau. The four largest casinos earned a revenue of \$200, \$150, \$150, and \$100 (all in million), respectively, and the remaining ten casinos combined earned \$400 million in 2019. What was the four-firm concentration ratio (CR_4)?
   A) 20%
   B) 40%
   C) 60%
   D) 80%
4. Suppose that in the market for bottled water Evian accounts for 25% of the market share, followed by Coca-Cola 15%, Danone 10%, Henniez 10%, and 20 other small firms each accounting for 2%. What are the four-firm concentration ratio (CR_4) and the Herfindahl-Hirschman Index (HHI), respectively?
   A) 40%; 1130
   B) 60%; 1130

C) 40%; 2650
D) 60%; 2650

5. We use the Lorenz curve to measure the market concentration of four industries, *j*, *k*, *l*, and *m*. Suppose that four coordinates, *J*, *K*, *L* and *M*, are on the Lorenz curves of the four industries, *j*, *k*, *l*, and *m*, respectively, as shown in the graph below. Which industry is the most concentrated?
   A) *j*
   B) *k*
   C) *l*
   D) *m*

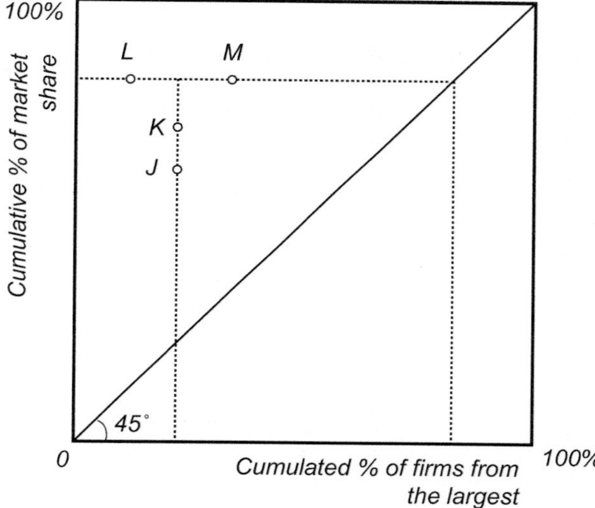

6. Suppose that there is a considerable but finite number of firms in the fast-food industry of a city, each having the same market share. If two of these firms merged, which of the following would be correct regarding the four-firm concentration ratio (CR_4) and the Herfindahl-Hirschman Index (*HHI*)?
   A) Both the CR_4 and the *HHI* would decrease.
   B) Both the CR_4 and the *HHI* would increase.
   C) The CR_4 would decrease while the *HHI* would increase.
   D) The CR_4 would increase while the *HHI* would decrease.
7. Suppose that a monopolist faces a linear demand curve $q = -2p + 100$ in the market, and its marginal cost is \$10 for producing a good. What is the Lerner index of the firm?
   A) 2/3
   B) 3/2
   C) 1
   D) 0

8. Which of the following is correct regarding the Lerner index?
   A) The Lerner index is equal to the price elasticity of demand a firm faces.
   B) The Lerner index is greater than zero for a firm in perfect competition.
   C) The Lerner index is greater than 1 for a firm in Bertrand competition.
   D) The Lerner index is equal to 1 if the marginal cost of a firm is zero.
9. Which of the following is correct regarding demand substitutability and supply substitutability between two goods in affecting market concentration?
   A) High demand substitutability increases market concentration.
   B) Low demand substitutability increases firm competition.
   C) High supply substitutability decreases firm competition.
   D) Low supply substitutability increases market concentration.
10. Which of the following is correct regarding the tourism industry in relation to market concentration?
    A) Firms in different sectors of the tourism industry are competitors.
    B) Products within each sector of the tourism industry are complements.
    C) Supply substitutability between sectors of the tourism industry is low.
    D) Demand substitutability between sectors of the tourism industry is high.

Problem solving

1. As of November 2016, Airbnb reported having over 3 million listings worldwide, which were nearly three times the room numbers of Marriott International after the acquisition of Starwood. Unlike the hotel industry in which descriptive attributes are drawn from fixed real estate, not all Airbnb listings are comparable to hotel rooms because listings differ by the type of properties and size, with availability constantly changing as hosts take their listings on and off Airbnb. According to STR's estimation, Airbnb supply comprises four types of listings: (1) units not

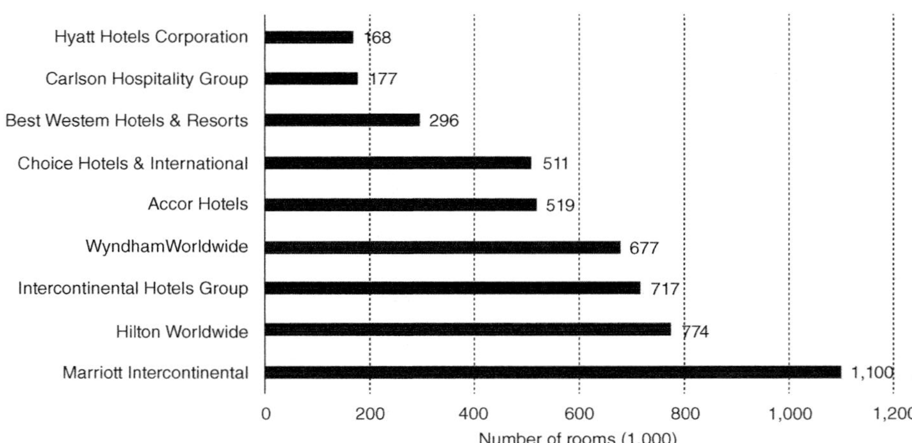

Note: The data indicate hotel room numbers in 2016.

Source: STR. Airbnb & Hotel Performance: An Analysis of Proprietary Data in 13 Global Markets. 2017, pp. 9–10.

available for rent, (2) shared rooms, (3) private rooms, and/or (4) units that can accommodate large groups (seven or more people), only 36% of which are effectively available and reasonably competitive with hotels.[10] Suppose that the hotel industry only consists of the nine largest hotel groups as shown in the figure above. Calculate the four-firm concentration ratio (CR_4) and the Herfindahl-Hirschman Index (HHI) of the hotel industry in terms of room numbers. How will the CR_4 and HHI change if Airbnb is taken into account? To measure the concentration of the hotel industry, why is it better to factor the 36% of, instead of all, Airbnb listings into calculations of the CR_4 and HHI?

2. Table 10.3 shows that the U.S. accommodation and catering sectors each have three subsectors with the four-digit SIC codes. Included in the accommodation sector are traveler accommodation (7211), RV (recreational vehicle) parks and recreational camps (7212), and rooming and boarding houses (7213); and included in the catering sector are special food services (7223), drinking places (alcoholic beverages) (7224), and restaurants and other eating places (7225). Given the information in the table, plot the Lorenz curves of the six subsectors. How would you interpret these Lorenz curves?
3. Suppose that Jiangnan Food is the only Chinese restaurant in Lausanne which sells a type of seafood hotpot. It faces a linear demand in the city which can be described by the demand function $q = -0.4p + 20$, where q is the quantity of the hotpot and p is the price of each hotpot. If the marginal cost of selling the hotpot is $5, what is the Lerner index for the restaurant (rounded to two decimal places)? Explain why the profit-maximizing price is on the elastic portion of the demand curve.

Solutions to all review questions and problem solving tasks are included in the Support Material for this book, which can be accessed at www.routledge.com/9780367897352.

Notes

1 We use "market" and "industry" interchangeably in this chapter. Whether market or industry is used depends on which one suits the context.
2 *Statista*. Macau makes ten times more revenue than Vegas per visitor. September 16, 2013.
3 Means (1931), pp. 12–13.
4 Adelman (1951).
5 NAICS is the acronym of the North American Industry Classification System (NAICS code). It is a classification system of industries and industrial sectors by the type of economic activity used in the U.S. in particular. NAICS replaced the Standard Industrial Classification (SIC) in 1997.
6 Ideally, we need to identify all the individual airlines and their market shares in the "other" category.
7 U.S. Department of Justice and the Federal Trade Commission (2010). Horizontal merger guidelines, p. 19.

8 The SIC is the Standard Industrial Classification established in the U.S. in 1937, which used to be the classification system of industries before being gradually replaced by the NAICS code in 1997.

9 USCB. Summary Statistics by Concentration of Largest Firms for the U.S. 2012.

10 STR. Airbnb & Hotel Performance: An Analysis of Proprietary Data in 13 Global Markets. 2017, pp. 9–10.

Bibliography

Adelman, M. A. (1951). The measurement of industrial concentration. *Review of Economics and Statistics*, 269–296.

Grullon, G., Larkin, Y., & Michaely, R. (2019). Are U.S. industries becoming more concentrated? *Review of Finance*, *23*(4), 697–743.

Lerner, A. P. (1934). The concept of monopoly and the measurement of monopoly power. *Review of Economic Studies*, *1*(3), 157–175.

Lorenz, M. O. (1905). Methods of measuring the concentration of wealth. *Publications of the American Statistical Association*, *9*(70), 209–219.

Means, G. C. (1931). The growth in the relative importance of the large corporation in American economic life. *American Economic Review*, 10–42.

Mueller, W. F., & Hamm, L. G. (1974). Trends in industrial market concentration, 1947 to 1970. *Review of Economics and Statistics*, 511–520.

Shepherd, W. G. (1982). Causes of increased competition in the U.S. economy, 1939–1980. *Review of Economics and Statistics*, 613–626.

Zhang, Q., Yang, H., Wang, Q., & Zhang, A. (2014). Market power and its determinants in the Chinese airline industry. *Transportation Research Part A: Policy and Practice*, *64*, 1–13.

11 Airbnb versus hotels in supply adjustment

This chapter concludes the module by applying cost and market structure theories to the supply of Airbnb and hotels in the lodging industry. We analyze the causes of the discrepancies between Airbnb and hotels in average daily rate (ADR) and occupancy. Empirical evidence has shown that Airbnb ADR and occupancy are almost constant on a monthly basis while hotel ADR and occupancy fluctuate substantially in the same period of time. In addition, there is a positive correlation between hotel ADR and occupancy in the short run while such correlation is inconclusive for Airbnb. Moreover, Airbnb ADR and occupancy are constantly lower than hotel ADR and occupancy in the same lodging market, and such discrepancies are more pronounced in peak seasons than in off-seasons. We attribute these discrepancies to the peculiar property Airbnb supply that can be readily adjusted through Airbnb hosts' listing behavior in response to demand seasonality whereas hotel supply is rigid in the short run.

AFTER STUDYING THIS CHAPTER, YOU SHOULD BE ABLE TO:

- **Understand and calculate key performance indicators in the lodging industry;**
- **Explain why Airbnb ADR and occupancy are stationary in contrast to the fluctuations of hotel ADR and occupancy;**
- **Explain why Airbnb ADR and occupancy are lower than hotel ADR and occupancy especially in peak seasons; and**
- **Understand market competition in the lodging industry and the impacts of Airbnb on hotel performance.**

11.1 Performance metrics in the lodging industry

11.1.1 Supply and demand

The lodging industry encompasses various temporary dwelling facilities to meet consumer needs for sleep and shelter among others. These facilities primarily include, but are not limited to, hotels, motels, hostels, and bed and breakfast accommodation. In a given period of time the supply in the lodging industry depends on the number of rooms available in all facilities, which can be referred to as supply capacity.[1] Supply capacity in the lodging industry is fixed in the short run because firms cannot expand their supply by erecting new properties nor are they able to liquidate the existing properties in the cycles of boom and bust. Holding supply capacity constant, the supply also depends on time, which is the maximum number of days available in a period of time. Thus, the supply in the lodging industry is supply capacity, which is the number of rooms available in all facilities, multiplied by the number of days available in a given period of time. In practice we use room days or room nights to measure supply stock in the lodging industry in a certain period of time.

Suppose that we need to measure the supply stock of a hotel on a monthly basis. Then room days available is the supply capacity of the hotel times the number of days in each month. For instance, a hotel with 100 rooms has a supply stock of 3,100 room days in January, 2,800 in February, 3,100 in March, and so on (Table 11.1). The discrepancy in supply stock between months is due entirely to the fact that different months may have different days available, such as 31 days in January versus 28 or 29 days in February. Other things being equal, hoteliers would make all hotel rooms available every single day in a given period of time, and thus the number of available days exhausts the maximum length of that period of time. In the short run, the difference, if any, in the supply stock of two hotels in a certain period of time is entirely due to their different supply capacities because the number of days available is the same for all lodging facilities in the market. As far as the lodging industry as a whole is concerned, supply stock is also fixed in the short run in a given period of time because supply capacity cannot be changed unless lodging firms operate in the long run.

The number of room days sold in a given period of time is room numbers sold multiplied by the number of days sold for each room. Note that the number of room days sold, in economic jargon, is the equilibrium quantity of room days. A certain number of room days sold in a given period of time is manifested in each of the three scenarios: a certain number of rooms unanimously sold for the whole period, all rooms sold on particular days in the period, or a mixture of the two scenarios in one way or another. Of interest in economic analysis is the total number of room days sold by

Table 11.1 Monthly hotel room days available and sold

Month	Room days available	Room days sold	Room revenue (US$)	Occupancy (%)	ADR (US$)	RevPAR (US$)
Jan 2015	3,100	2,345	198,765	75.6	84.8	64.1
Feb 2015	2,800	2,002	175,432	71.5	87.6	62.7
Mar 2015	3,100	1,776	175,012	57.3	98.5	56.5
Apr 2015	3,000	2,468	234,567	82.3	95.0	78.2
May 2015	3,100	2,987	312,345	96.4	104.6	100.8

Source: STR. Certification in Hotel Industry Analytics: Flipped Class Version 2016, slides 56–57.

a lodging firm or in the market regardless of which room is sold and on which day. Obviously, room days sold is constrained by room days available in a hotel or in a market as a whole, whereas the maximum room days that can be sold is equal to the maximum room days available in a given period of time. For instance, Table 11.1 shows that the number of room days sold by the 100-room hotel was 2,345 in January 2015, which was 755 short of the maximum room days available, and 2,002 in February, which was 798 short of the maximum room days available, and so on. On the one hand, the maximum room days sold cannot exceed room days available in a given period of time; on the other, the exact room days sold is also determined by demand.

11.1.2 Occupancy, ADR, and RevPAR

Since supply capacity may differ drastically from one hotel to another and from one lodging sector to another, it makes little sense to compare market performance across either hotels or lodging sectors on the basis of the absolute number of room days sold. Other things being equal, a large hotel would sell more room days simply because it has a large supply capacity. Taking into account the variation in supply capacity of different hotels, we use occupancy as a standardized measure of room days sold by adjusting room days available that may vary across hotels or lodging sectors. Occupancy is given as the ratio of room days sold to room days available at a hotel or in the whole market:

$$Occupancy = \frac{Room\ days\ sold}{Room\ days\ available} \times 100\%. \quad (11.1)$$

Using formula (11.1) we can calculate the occupancy of each month for the aforementioned hotel as shown in Table 11.1. Since occupancy is room days sold adjusted by room days available, it enables us to standardize the absolute equilibrium quantity and therefore draw comparisons across hotels or lodging sectors with different supply capacities. Since supply stock is fixed in the short run, occupancy precisely corresponds to the number of room days sold in the market. Given occupancy, we can immediately obtain the number of room days sold as well:

$$Room\ days\ sold = Occupancy \times Room\ days\ available. \quad (11.2)$$

Since a hotel may charge different rates for the same room on different days or charge slightly different rates for different rooms on the same day, we average the rates for different rooms on different days to obtain the rate per room per day. The average room rate is called average daily rate (ADR) in the lodging industry. Suppose that rate variations exist for a certain number of rooms sold on different days in a given period of time for a hotel. Then the ADR of the hotel can be expressed in a generic form:

$$ADR = \frac{1}{qt} \sum_{i=1}^{q} \sum_{j=1}^{t} p_{ij}, \quad (11.3)$$

where i indicates room, j indicates day on which a room is sold, q is the number of rooms sold, and t is the number of days sold. Thus, the product qt is the number of room days sold, or the equilibrium quantity in the market. Intuitively, ADR can be regarded as the rate of a representative room on a representative day sold by the hotel in the market. Given room revenue and room days sold or occupancy, ADR can also be obtained by room revenue divided by room days sold:

$$ADR = \frac{Room\ revenue}{Room\ days\ sold} = \frac{Room\ revenue}{Occupancy \times Room\ days\ available}. \qquad (11.4)$$

In Table 11.1 we calculate the ADR of each month for the aforementioned hotel using formula (11.4). Averaging ADR for all hotels in the market, we obtain ADR in the market. In perfect competition, a hotel cannot set its daily rate other than the ADR in the market, and hence the market ADR is also the marginal revenue of the hotel. The hotel can only decide its occupancy at which its marginal revenue is equal to marginal cost. Given room revenue and occupancy of a hotel, we can calculate the revenue per available room (RevPAR), which is defined as room revenue divided by room days available:

$$RevPAR = \frac{Room\ revenue}{Room\ days\ available} = ADR \times Occupancy. \qquad (11.5)$$

Table 11.1 shows the RevPAR of each month calculated using formula (11.5). Since room days available are always greater than or equal to room days sold, RevPAR never exceeds ADR. Since room revenue is equal to ADR multiplied by room days sold, RevPAR is actually the product of ADR and occupancy as shown in formula (11.5). In perfect competition in which ADR is given, RevPAR and occupancy are positively correlated. In monopoly, since a hotel can decide both its daily rate and occupancy for profit maximization, there exists a unique RevPAR determined by the optimal occupancy and daily rate.

11.2 Discrepancy in market performance

11.2.1 Airbnb ADR and occupancy are stationary

Consider the hotel sector and Airbnb in Paris in 2014 for which we have the data. On the one hand, Figure 11.1a shows that hotel ADR fluctuates considerably on a monthly basis throughout the year, and the discrepancy between the lowest hotel ADR (147.9 euros in February) and the highest (216.2 euros in June) amounts to nearly 70 euros. Usually February and August of the year see the lowest ADR, slightly below 150 euros, whereas June, September, and October see the highest, above 200 euros. Figure 11.1b shows that hotels also record the lowest occupancy of 66% in February and the highest of above 85% in June, September, and October. In addition, there is a noticeably positive correlation between hotel ADR and hotel occupancy (Figure 11.1).

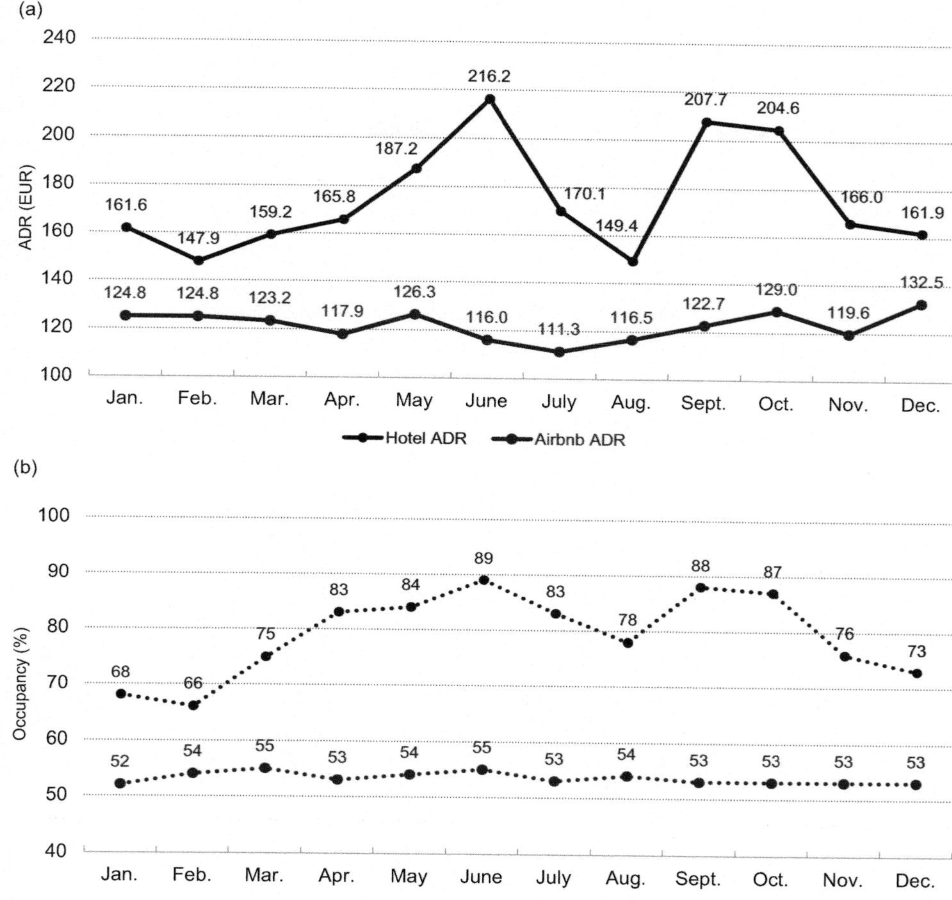

Figure 11.1
ADR and occupancy of Airbnb versus hotels in Paris

Source: Cindy Yoonjoung Heo, Inès Blal, and Miju Choi. What is happening in Paris? Airbnb, Hotels and Parisian. Presentation slides 21–22. Ecole hôtelière de Lausanne, May 15, 2017.

On the other hand, Figure 11.1a shows that Airbnb ADR is almost stationary on a monthly basis, hovering around 120 euros in the same city and over the same period of time. Figure 11.1b shows that Airbnb occupancy is surprisingly stable, which is around 53% throughout the whole year. Given the extremely small variations in Airbnb ADR and occupancy, the correlation between Airbnb ADR and occupancy is inconclusive.

11.2.2 Airbnb ADR and occupancy are lower

In addition, Figure 11.1 shows that both the ADR and occupancy of Airbnb are constantly lower than those of hotels in Paris in 2014. It is worth noting that such discrepancies between Airbnb and hotels are not peculiar to Paris nor are they only manifested on a monthly basis in a particular year. A report from Smith Travel Research (STR) shows that Airbnb ADR in U.S. cities is by and large lower than hotel ADR, and on average, hotel ADR is 10% higher than Airbnb ADR for all seven cities (Figure 11.2a). New Orleans is an exception where Airbnb ADR is slightly higher than hotel ADR. The discrepancy in the U.S. cities is not as pronounced as observed in Paris perhaps because the 12-month moving average statistics smooth the discrepancies in peak seasons. On the other hand, Airbnb occupancy is also constantly lower than hotel occupancy across the seven U.S. cities examined in the report on a 12-month moving average (Figure 11.2b). The largest discrepancy is found in Miami where hotel occupancy is 46.6 percentage points higher than Airbnb occupancy on the 12-month moving average, and the smallest discrepancy of 28.2 percentage points is detected in Los Angeles during the same period. On average, hotel occupancy is 32.8 percentage points higher than Airbnb occupancy across the U.S. cities in Figure 11.2b.

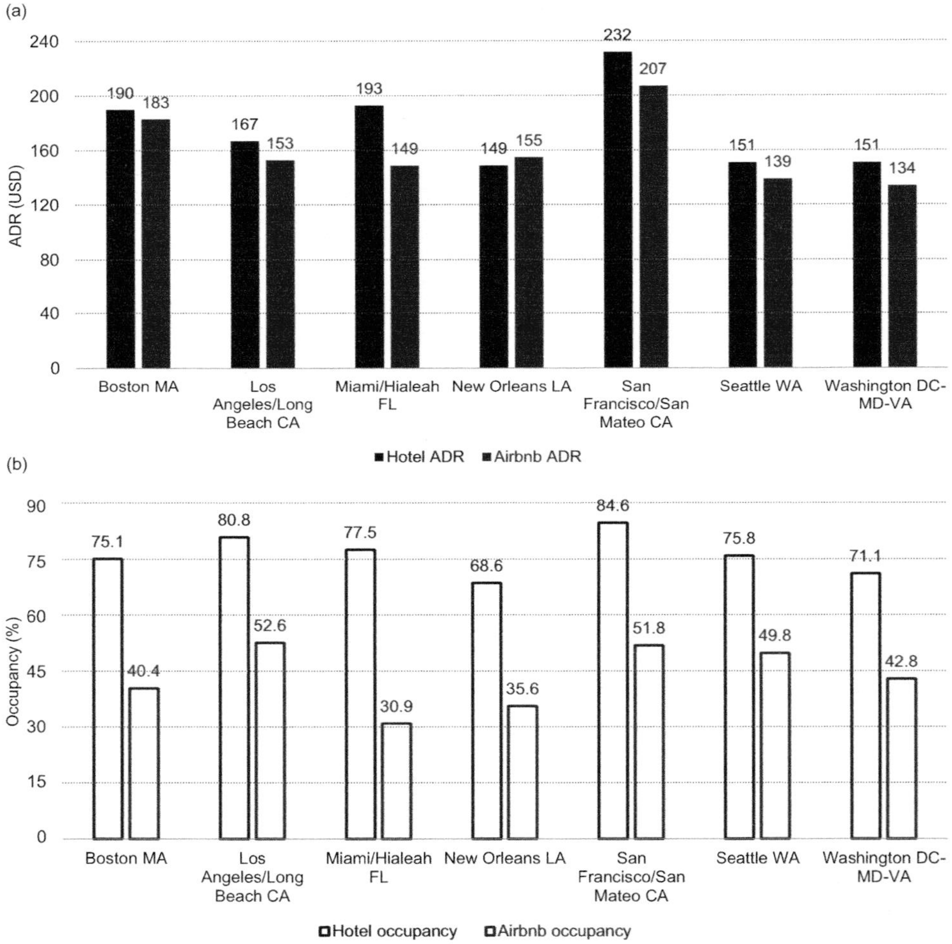

(a)

ADR (USD)	Hotel ADR	Airbnb ADR
Boston MA	190	183
Los Angeles/Long Beach CA	167	153
Miami/Hialeah FL	193	149
New Orleans LA	149	155
San Francisco/San Mateo CA	232	207
Seattle WA	151	139
Washington DC-MD-VA	151	134

(b)

Occupancy (%)	Hotel occupancy	Airbnb occupancy
Boston MA	75.1	40.4
Los Angeles/Long Beach CA	80.8	52.6
Miami/Hialeah FL	77.5	30.9
New Orleans LA	68.6	35.6
San Francisco/San Mateo CA	84.6	51.8
Seattle WA	75.8	49.8
Washington DC-MD-VA	71.1	42.8

Figure 11.2

ADR and occupancy of Airbnb versus hotels across U.S. cities

Note: Hotel ADR and occupancy are measured as the 12-month moving average ending July 2016.

Source: STR. Airbnb & Hotel Performance: An Analysis of Proprietary Data in 13 Global Markets 2017, p. 19.

As far as the U.S. market is concerned, Airbnb ADR is also constantly lower than hotel ADR on a weekly basis based on the 12-monthly moving average data in 2016 as shown in Figure 11.3a. The discrepancy is much more pronounced during weekdays than on weekends.[2] On average, hotel ADR is US$20, or nearly 13%, higher than Airbnb ADR during the whole week. Figure 11.3b shows that the discrepancy in occupancy of hotels and Airbnb is substantial throughout the week. On average, hotel occupancy is as much as 32 percentage points higher than Airbnb occupancy. We have so far presented compelling and consistent evidence shown in Figures 11.1–11.3. On the one hand, Airbnb ADR and occupancy are considerably stationary over time in contrast to hotel ADR and occupancy; on the other hand, Airbnb ADR and occupancy are constantly lower than those of hotels across different cities and over time. One of the reasons is perhaps that Airbnb and hotels target different consumer markets, which could explain

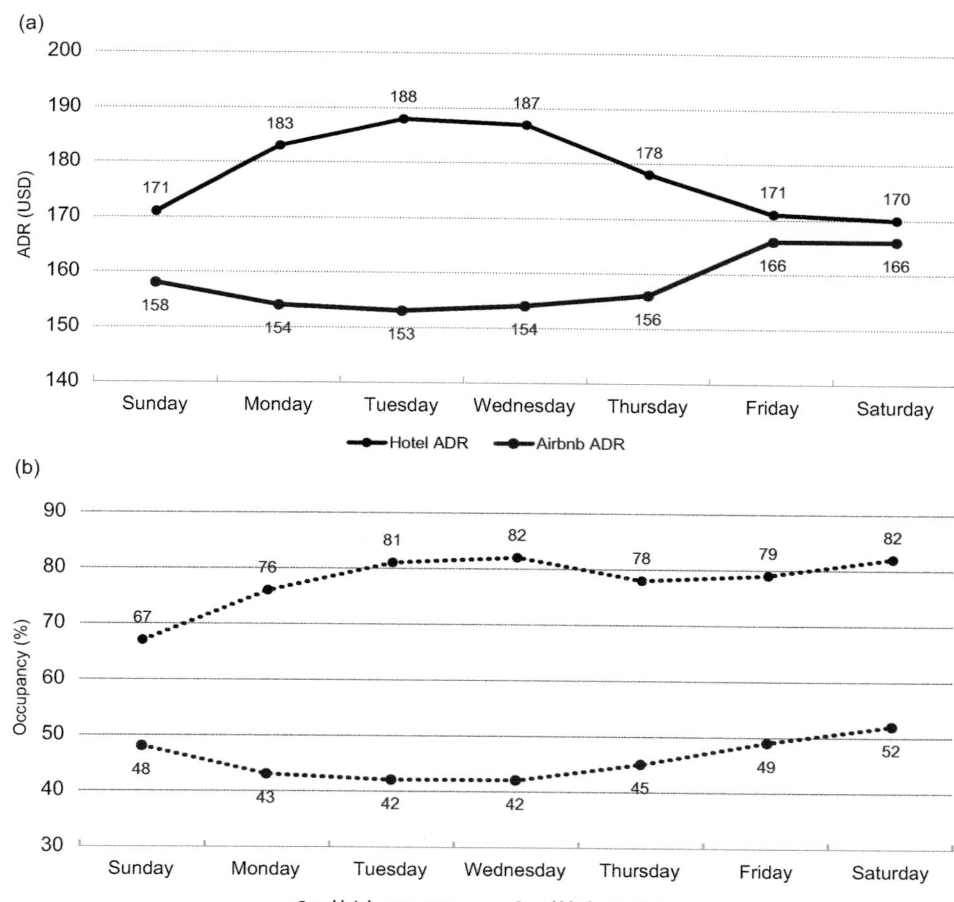

Figure 11.3
ADR and occupancy of Airbnb versus hotels by day of week

Note: Hotel ADR and occupancy are measured as the 12-month moving average ending July 2016.

Source: STR. Airbnb & Hotel Performance: An Analysis of Proprietary Data in 13 Global Markets 2017, pp. 11–12.

why Airbnb ADR and occupancy are lower than hotel ADR and occupancy but cannot explain why the former are invariant over time. The fundamental reason, as we shall demonstrate, lies in the supply of Airbnb. Even though Airbnb and hotels face the same consumer demand, the discrepancies in their ADR and occupancy may still persist.

11.3 Demand seasonality and supply adjustment

11.3.1 Supply adjustment

To explain the performance differences between Airbnb and hotels in terms of ADR and occupancy, we need to articulate the nature of their supply as well as the causes for the supply to change. As we explained above, the supply stock of hotels and of other conventional lodging sectors in the short run depends entirely on supply capacity $(\overline{q})$ in a given period of time (t_0). Thus, room days available, Q_H^S, is constant in the short run:

$$Q_H^S = \overline{q}t_0. \tag{11.6}$$

In the long run hotel supply can be changed through hotels entering or exiting the market and/or incumbent hotels increasing or decreasing investment in a given period of time. That is, hotel supply is changed due to the change in hotel capacity denoted as q. Therefore, we can denote the number of room days available in the long run, Q_H^L, in a given period of time (t_0) as

$$Q_H^L = qt_0. \tag{11.7}$$

Note that in the long run the supply stock of hotels Q_H^L changes not because of time per se, but because a sufficiently long period of time would enable hotels to adjust their supply capacity through erecting or reducing hotel properties. Hotel supply remains unchanged in the short run because supply capacity is fixed after all. Take the U.S. hotel industry for example. Figure 11.4a shows that the monthly growth rates of hotel supply are remarkably stable, which were 2% in 2019 and around 1.4% on average over the period 2008–2019. Nevertheless, a longer period of times does enable the hotel industry to adjust supply. As far as the yearly data are considered over the same period, the annual growth rates of hotel supply fluctuate substantially as shown in Figure 11.4b. The highest growth rate was 2.8% in 2009, which dropped substantially to merely 0.3% in 2012 before gradually bouncing up to 2% in 2019. If we extend the study horizon as far back as to 1990, we are able to see some sort of a business cycle in hotel supply that oscillates between 0 and 4% on yearly growth and recurs approximately every ten years in the U.S. market.[3] This business cycle suggests that it

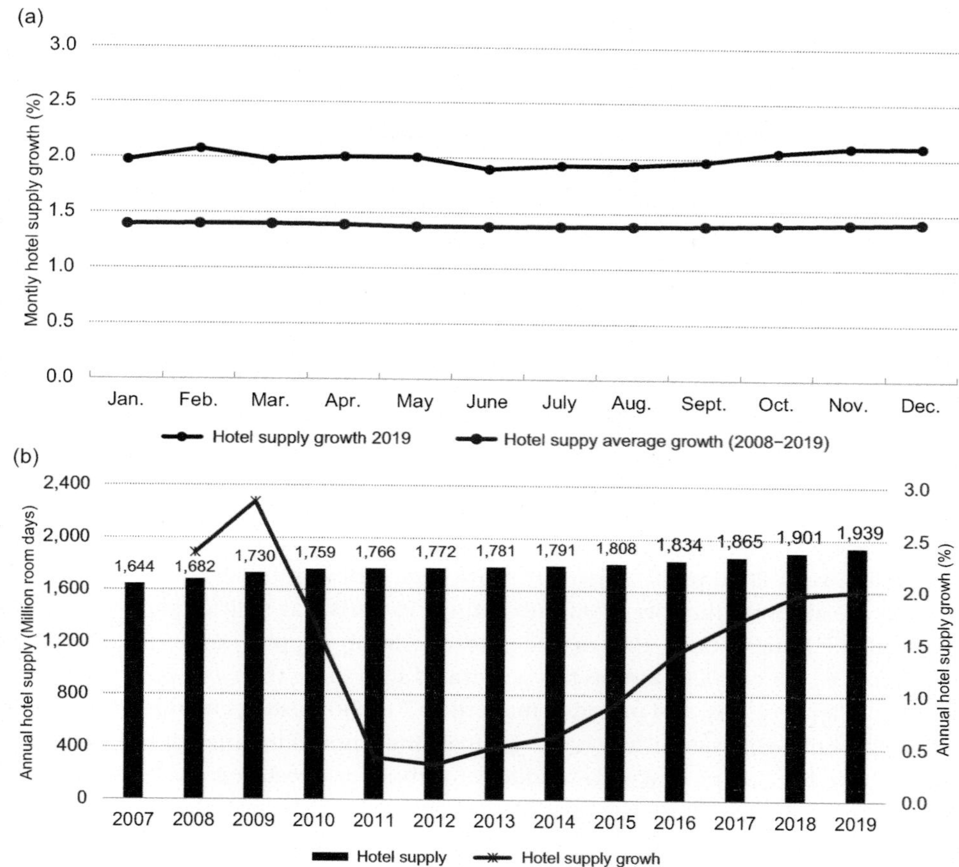

Figure 11.4
Monthly and annual growth of hotel supply in the U.S.

Note: STR defines hotel supply as room days available in a specified time period.

Source: STR. The United States Trend Report (2007–2020).

may take a decade for the whole hotel industry to change its fixed costs and investment as flexibly as possible.

However, the mechanism by which hotel supply changes does not apply to Airbnb. As an alternative use of spare rooms or a living space, Airbnb hosts can decide not only the number of rooms listed but also the number of days available in a given period of time on Airbnb. On the one hand, the supply capacity of Airbnb can be adjusted as hosts list or delist their spare rooms on Airbnb. This does not mean that hosts can list as many rooms as they wish, because rooms for Airbnb use are constrained by all residential room stock in a city in a given period of time. This situation is similar to hotel supply which cannot be changed in the short run either. Yet rooms at the disposal of Airbnb hosts are a minuscule fraction of all room stock available, and hosts usually do not have to build new apartments exclusively for rent on Airbnb. Therefore, the supply capacity of Airbnb is not only flexible but to some extent unlimited in contrast to hotel supply. On the other hand, it is not necessary or economically viable for Airbnb hosts to exhaust all days available in a given period of time as hoteliers would, because certain days in the period could be more profitable than others. At the market level, Airbnb supply, Q_A, varies not only due to the entry and/or exit of hosts (q) but also because incumbent hosts may change the number of listing days (t) in a given period of time:

$$Q_A = qt. \tag{11.8}$$

Hence it would be more appropriate to regard Airbnb supply as if Airbnb hosts were always operating in the long run in a given period of time irrespective of how long that period might be. Evidence has shown that Airbnb supply is considerably volatile, contrasting drastically to hotel supply. Figure 11.5 shows that Airbnb listings experienced an average growth rate of 231.3% in contrast to 9.7% in the supply of hotel rooms in Paris from 2010 to 2015. The annual growth of Airbnb supply peaked at 436.4% from 2010 to 2011 while the lowest growth was 98.1% from 2014 to 2015. While the absolute number of Airbnb listings in Paris was still far smaller than the number of hotel rooms, the growth rate of Airbnb supply was remarkably more pronounced. As of 2020, Airbnb has penetrated into more than 100,000 cities in 220 countries and regions, and provided more than 7 million listings worldwide,[4] a record no single hotel chain in history has ever envisioned, not to mention achieving it. This could have led Brian Chesky, co-founder of Airbnb, to tweet in early 2014: "Marriott wants to add 30,000 rooms this year. We will add that in the next 2 weeks".

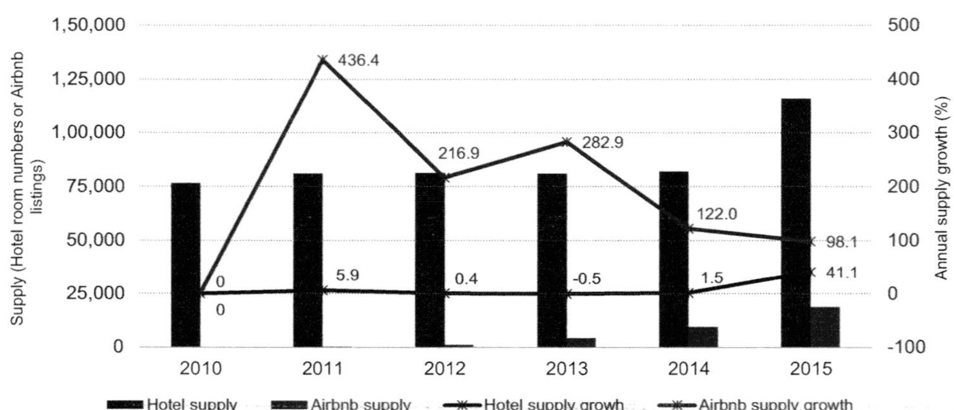

Figure 11.5
Supply growth of Airbnb versus hotels in Paris

Note: Hotel supply is measured as the number of hotel rooms and Airbnb supply is measured as the number of listings in Paris in a specified time period between 2010 and 2015.

Source: Heo, Blal, and Choi (2019), p. 80.

11.3.2 Demand seasonality and market equilibrium

Suppose that Airbnb and hotels target the same consumers and operate independently in their respective markets. Thus, their market performances can solely be attributed to their supply. The market equilibrium in the lodging industry varies in the short run because of the demand seasonality of tourism. In fact, demand seasonality would be more pronounced for Airbnb than for hotels because Airbnb presumably accommodates more leisure travelers whose demand is seasonal. For simplicity, suppose that one year can be divided into off-, shoulder, and peak seasons, suggesting the lowest, moderate, and highest demand, represented by three parallel demand curves D_1, D_0, and D_2, respectively (Figure 11.6). Since hotel supply S_0 is invariant across the three seasons in the short run, the changes in demand in the three seasons end up with three market equilibria, E_1 in off-season, E_0 in shoulder season, and E_2 in peak season, on the same supply curve S_0. On the one hand, because hotel supply remains unchanged, the number of room days sold, namely the equilibrium quantities Q_1, Q_0, and Q_2, is perfectly correlated with hotel occupancies in the three seasons. On the other hand, there exists a decisively positive correlation between hotel occupancy and equilibrium price, namely ADR.

The positive correlation between occupancy and ADR in the hotel industry is due to the fact that hotel supply cannot be adjusted in the short run. What is adjusted in the hotel industry in the short run is the number of room days supplied, or occupancy, due to the change in demand. Therefore, not only is hotel occupancy strongly correlated with hotel demand, but hotel ADR is also determined by demand as far as in the short run.

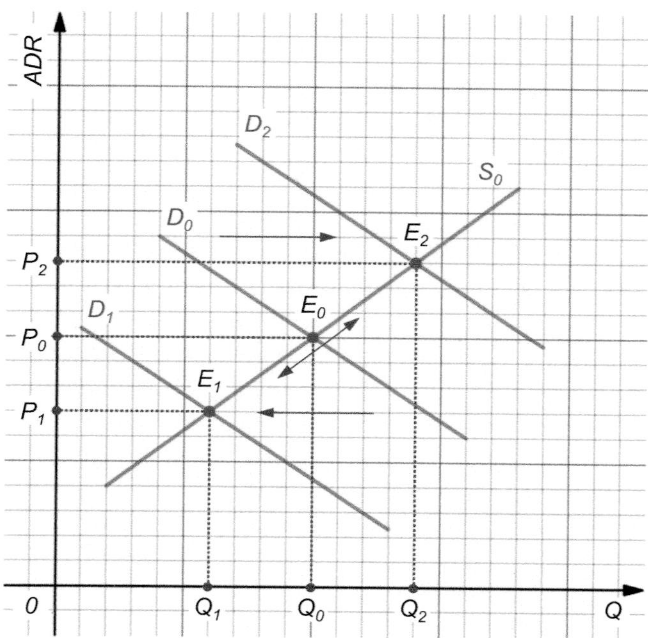

Figure 11.6
Demand seasonality and hotel ADR and occupancy

Since a hotel cannot change its supply in the short run, and the hotel industry as a whole is highly competitive, a higher ADR in peak seasons entails a higher marginal cost to equalize for profit maximization, which in turn is associated with a higher occupancy of the hotel. In off-seasons, a lower ADR entails a lower marginal cost to equalize for profit maximization, hence a lower occupancy. Thus, the correlation between hotel occupancy and ADR is strong and positive in the short run. The positive correlation between hotel occupancy and ADR is robust not only on a monthly basis that reflects the seasonality of tourism demand but on a yearly basis that may suggest the impacts of other demand shocks, such as economic crises and pandemics. No matter whether and how demand changes, hotel supply does not change in the short run.

However, Airbnb supply responds swiftly to demand seasonality. As illustrated, Airbnb supply can be adjusted on both supply capacity and the length of a listing period. Since demand seasonality is a cyclical change on a yearly basis and hence is predictable, Airbnb hosts would not only list more rooms but also extend the listing period when anticipating robust demand in peak seasons, while delisting rooms or shortening the listing period in off-seasons. Suppose that the demands for Airbnb in off-, shoulder, and peak seasons are the same as for hotels, denoted by the three parallel demand curves D_1, D_0, and D_2, respectively (Figure 11.7). As demand increases in peak season (D_2), Airbnb supply will increase accordingly through new hosts entering the market and/or incumbent hosts extending the listing period. Thus, the supply curve shifts rightward from S_0 to S_2, ending up with the market equilibrium E_2' in peak season. As demand shrinks in off-season (D_1), Airbnb supply will decrease through incumbent hosts shortening the listing period or exiting the market. Thus, the supply curve shifts leftward from S_0 to S_1, ending up with the market equilibrium E_1' in off-season. Since both the demand and supply change in the same direction, the equilibrium quantities, Q_1', Q_0', and Q_2', vary substantially across the three seasons while the equilibrium prices, P_1', P_0', and P_2', barely change.

Figure 11.7 shows that Airbnb ADR, indicated by the equilibrium price, is almost stationary across the three seasons. The extent to which Airbnb ADR deviates from P_0' in shoulder season depends on the change in supply relative to the change in demand, or vice versa. If the change in supply is the same as the change in demand in the three seasons, Airbnb ADR will stay the same, and hence $P_1' = P_2' = P_0'$. However, the number of room days sold on Airbnb increases substantially from off- (Q_1'), shoulder (Q_0') to peak season (Q_2') compared to hotels because Airbnb supply also increases with the demand. Note that the equilibrium quantity does not reflect Airbnb occupancy as it does for hotels. This is because a change in the equilibrium quantity is caused by changes in both demand for and supply of Airbnb. While the number of room days sold in peak season, Q_2', is large, it does not indicate a high occupancy of Airbnb because supply also increases in peak season. Similarly, the number of room days sold in off-season, Q_1', is small, but it does not indicate a low occupancy because Airbnb supply decreases simultaneously. Hence Airbnb occupancy may remain unchanged across the three seasons. We are not able to ascertain the relationship between Airbnb occupancy and room days sold on Airbnb unless we know the exact supply of Airbnb in different seasons. This means that occupancy is not a reliable proxy for the equilibrium quantity of Airbnb, nor are Airbnb occupancy and hotel occupancy comparable in assessing their equilibrium quantities.

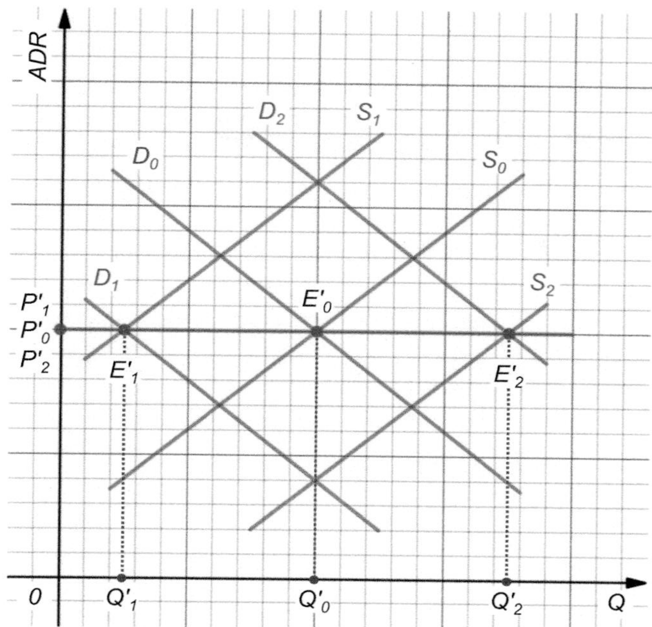

Figure 11.7
Demand seasonality and Airbnb ADR and occupancy

11.3.3 Cost and host behavior of Airbnb

The above analysis also sheds light on the observation that Airbnb ADR is constantly lower than hotel ADR in a certain period of time as shown in Figures 11.1a, 11.2a, and 11.3a. Suppose that Airbnb and hotels have the same supply in shoulder season and face the same demand that changes in the same way across the three seasons as shown in Figures 11.6 and 11.7. We assume that Airbnb and hotels have the same ADR in shoulder season as a benchmark,[5] $P_0 = P_0'$, which is determined by the market equilibria, $E_0 = E_0'$. Obviously, hotel ADR will outstrip Airbnb ADR as demand increases in peak season but will be below Airbnb ADR as demand decreases in off-season. Evidence in Paris in Figure 11.1a only partially supports this prediction as hotel ADR exceeds Airbnb ADR throughout the year, but more substantially in peak season than in off-season. One of the reasons that Airbnb ADR is lower than hotel ADR in off-season is that the marginal cost in the hotel industry is higher than that of Airbnb, ending up with a higher supply curve in the first place. As a matter of fact, the hotel industry incorporates not only economy hotels, which are by and large comparable to Airbnb, but also luxury hotels whose marginal cost is certainly higher than Airbnb's. Hence the marginal cost of the hotel industry as a whole is higher than the marginal cost of Airbnb. Therefore, even if demand seasonality is ruled out, hotel ADR may still be higher than Airbnb ADR as long as the two sectors are independent.

Another explanation for the lower Airbnb ADR pertains to how Airbnb supply is adjusted in off-season versus in peak season. Assume that Airbnb ADR and hotel

ADR are the same in shoulder season as a benchmark, and hence $P_0 = P_0'$ as shown in Figures 11.6 and 11.7. We postulate that Airbnb hosts are enticed to increase supply when facing demand spikes in peak seasons yet are reluctant to reduce supply when facing inadequate demand in off-seasons. If hosts are reluctant to cut supply when demand decreases in off-seasons, the decrease in Airbnb supply will be disproportionately less than the decrease in demand. Therefore, on the one hand, Airbnb ADR will be lower in off-season than in shoulder season. On the other hand, despite the postulate suggesting that Airbnb ADR will still be higher than hotel ADR in off-season, the discrepancy will become negligible. This explanation conforms to the observation of Airbnb's constantly lower occupancy as well, due to the fact that Airbnb supply is more sensitive to an increase in demand in peak seasons but less sensitive to a decrease in demand in off-seasons. In practice, this theory may suggest that Airbnb hosts are more willing to enter the market or extend the listing period in peak seasons but less willing to exit the market or shorten the listing period in off-seasons.[6] It is worth noting that the Paris evidence in Figure 11.1a may not be applicable to other markets.

11.4 Competition in the lodging industry

Throughout the current analysis we have treated Airbnb and hotels as if they operated independently in their respective markets in order to rule out the substitution between the two on the demand side. Obviously, if Airbnb and hotels are substitutes, and consumers can readily substitute one for the other, neither Airbnb nor hotels would be able to raise prices above the ADR determined in the whole lodging market that incorporates both. Hence no discrepancy would exist between Airbnb ADR and hotel ADR. Yet empirical evidence has suggested otherwise. Not only is Airbnb ADR lower than hotel ADR in almost all cities, including Paris, for which we have the data, but the discrepancy is also more pronounced in peak seasons than in off-seasons and on weekdays than on weekends. This means that competition between Airbnb and hotels, if any, is restricted to the extent that hotels still maintain market power in general and in particular periods of time. As we have pointed out, this could be because Airbnb only competes with economy hotels rather than luxury hotels, suggesting that consumer demands for Airbnb and for luxury hotels are different.

Recent studies have shown that the hotel industry, especially the economy hotel sector, is negatively affected by Airbnb. According to HVS, Airbnb could have caused a loss of US$451 million in room revenues in the conventional lodging industry in New York City during the fiscal year of August 2015.[7] A study found that hotel revenue is driven down by 8–10% on average in Austin, the United States due to the high penetration rate of Airbnb in the city, and economy hotels are affected most.[8] On the other hand, Airbnb claims that the lodging industry as a whole is a beneficiary of the presence of Airbnb, because it increases the tourism economic pie that generates demand for other hospitality businesses including hotels as well. An Airbnb study in France found that around 23% of Airbnb guests said that they would not have gone on a trip, and 66% would not have stayed in a hotel if Airbnb had not been an option.[9] According to this study, Airbnb guests spend 600 euros per person per visit in Paris that include 475 euros on non-accommodation items. This adds up to a contribution of 2.5 billion euros to the local economy by taking into account the direct, indirect, and induced effects of the expenditures of all Airbnb guests in Paris.[10]

Interestingly, many hoteliers do not regard Airbnb as a threat or subscribe to the positive impact of Airbnb on the hotel industry. When interviewed by the *New York Times* in 2015, Steve Joyce, chief executive of Choice Hotels International, said that his hotel brands have not seen any impact from Airbnb, and Kerry Ranson, chairman of the InterContinental Hotels Group Owners Association, also mentioned that he does not see Airbnb as a threat or a competitor.[11] Hilton CEO Christopher Nassetta expressed a similar view that Airbnb is not a major threat to his company's business, but added that the impact of Airbnb, if at all, is perhaps heterogeneous across hotel segments.[12] There are perhaps two reasons why hoteliers may have overlooked the impact of Airbnb on the hotel industry. First, since Airbnb usually competes with economy hotels, it would not be surprising if the performance of upscale and luxury hotels is still robust despite the presence of Airbnb in the market. Second, it is because the substitution and complementary effects of Airbnb on hotels may have canceled each other out. On the one hand, Airbnb could decrease hotel demand by luring away hotel guests, and thus drive down hotel ADR and occupancy. On the other hand, it could increase hotel demand by expanding the economic pie of tourism, and thus push up hotel ADR and occupancy. If both effects happen to equalize, the market equilibrium of the hotel industry will remain the same, and so will hotel ADR and occupancy.

Summary

1. The number of room days available in a given period of time indicates the supply of the lodging industry, which depends on supply capacity. The number of room days sold in a given period of time is the equilibrium quantity in the market.
2. Average daily rate (ADR) is room revenue divided by room days sold, which is the average market price of room days. Occupancy is room days sold divided by room days available in a given period of time. Occupancy enables us to compare room days sold across different hotel capacities.
3. Revenue per available room (RevPAR) is room revenue divided by room days available in a given period of time. Hence, RevPAR depends entirely on ADR and occupancy. RevPAR can also be expressed as the product of ADR and occupancy.
4. In the short run hotel supply is fixed whereas Airbnb supply can be changed due to the entry/exit of Airbnb hosts and/or changes in the length of the listing period. This difference lies in the fact that Airbnb supply is generated from the alternative use of spare rooms or apartments.
5. Airbnb ADR and occupancy are almost constant in contrast to hotel ADR and occupancy. The reason is that Airbnb supply changes in the same direction as demand through hosts entering/exiting the market or extending/shortening the listing period.

6. There are two explanations for Airbnb ADR and occupancy that are lower than hotel ADR and occupancy. It could be that the marginal cost in the hotel industry is higher than that of Airbnb, ending up with a higher supply curve in the hotel industry in the first place. It could be that Airbnb hosts are reluctant to adjust supply in off-seasons.
7. A change in the equilibrium quantity of Airbnb can be attributed to changes in both demand and supply in the same direction. Airbnb occupancy may end up being unchanged. In contrast to hotels for which occupancy and room days sold are perfectly correlated, a higher Airbnb occupancy does not indicate that more room days are sold on Airbnb.
8. It is possible that Airbnb affects the hotel industry both positively and negatively. Hotel ADR and occupancy will remain unchanged if the two forces cancel each other out. Hoteliers do not see the impact of Airbnb because the substitution and commentary effects of Airbnb offset each other.

Problem solving

1. Suppose that luxury, midscale, and economy hotels differ in their fixed costs, with luxury hotels having the largest fixed costs due to their huge capital investment in hotel real estate, followed by midscale and economy hotels. Suppose that the operation of a luxury, midscale, and economy hotel incurs the same variable costs. We know that the ADRs in the three hotel segments are different: luxury hotels are $400 per room per night, upscale hotels are $200 per room per night, and economy hotels are $100 per room per night. Suppose that each of the three hotel segments is close to perfect competition, and they are not competitors of each other. Other things being equal, which hotel segment will have the highest occupancy and which will have the lowest occupancy in the short run?
2. The figure below shows the demand and supply growths of Airbnb in 13 cities. Airbnb demand and supply by and large grow at the same pace, and the difference, if any, is not substantial. What might be the reasons? Specifically, the demand growth is only 3 percentage points greater than the supply growth in New Orleans LA but as much as 23 percentage points greater in Greater Barcelona. What could be the reasons for the striking difference between the two cities? How do the discrepancies between demand and supply growth affect Airbnb ADR and occupancy in the two cities?
3. Berkshire Hathaway is a financial conglomerate headquartered in Omaha in the U.S. state of Nebraska. The annual shareholder meeting of Berkshire Hathaway has been held in Omaha since 1980, drawing some 40,000 attendees including Warren Buffett each year, which is equivalent to nearly 10% of the city's population. During the meeting, Omaha's few hotels would jack up prices to as much as $400 a night besides imposing three-day minimum stays for the one-day meeting.[13] However, the hotels' heyday is numbered. According to *The Economist,* in the three weeks before the 2015 meeting, 1,750 Omaha residents added new properties

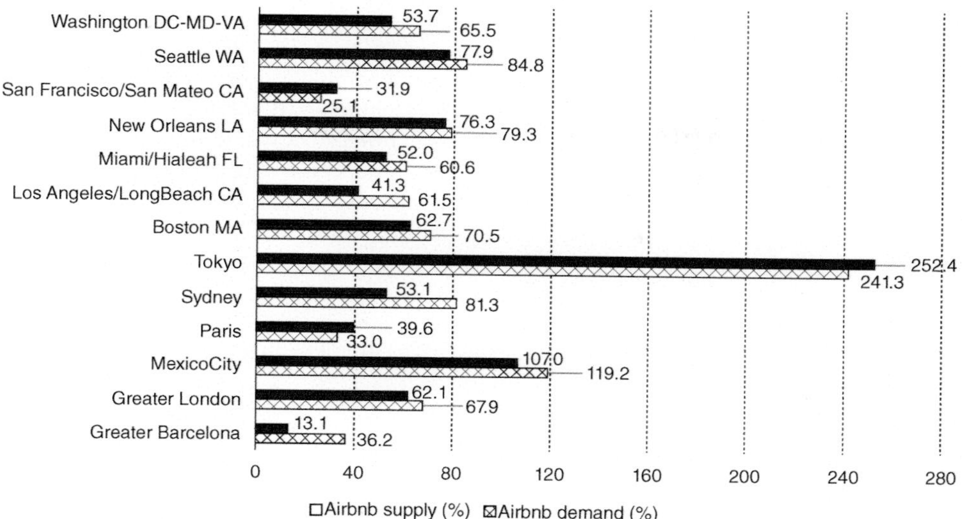

Note: Supply and demand growths are measured as the 12-month moving average ending July 2016.

Source: STR. Airbnb & Hotel Performance: An Analysis of Proprietary Data in 13 Global Markets 2017, p. 17.

on Airbnb, the equivalent of three of the city's biggest hotel, Omaha Hilton. This led Airbnb listings in the city increase to 5,000, of which 76% were booked at an average rate of $209 on May 1st, 2015. In addition, Airbnb hosts charged 60% more during the meeting than in days before and after in contrast to a price hike of more than 200% by hotels.[14] Explain the differences in market performance between Airbnb and hotels in Omaha during the meeting and in other periods of time.

Solutions to all review questions and problem solving tasks are included in the Support Material for this book, which can be accessed at www.routledge.com/9780367897352.

Notes

1 For a better exposition of supply in the lodging industry, we use and distinguish between two terminologies, "supply capacity" and "supply stock". Supply capacity refers only to the number of rooms available in the lodging industry in a given period of time. Hence it measures the physical capacity of the industry that depends on the amount of fixed costs. Supply stock takes into account time and thus refers to the number of room days available in a given period of time, which is supply capacity multiplied by the number of days available. As far as the hotel sector is concerned, supply stock and supply capacity are perfectly correlated. Yet for Airbnb supply which we shall illustrate in this chapter, supply stock is not necessarily aligned with supply capacity.

2 In the lodging industry weekdays are regarded as commencing on Sunday and ending on Thursday while weekends incorporate Friday and Saturday.

3 *The Economist*. Life is suite: Hotel chains are thriving, for now, thanks to innovation and a bit of luck. August 6, 2015.

4 Airbnb. About us. Retrieved on August 22, 2020 from https://news.airbnb.com/about-us/.
5 This assumption is instrumental in the analysis that follows. If off-season were used as a benchmark, hotel ADR would be constantly higher than Airbnb ADR in the short run. If peak season were used as a benchmark, hotel ADR would be constantly lower than Airbnb ADR. In fact, the selection of benchmarks is a matter of empirical congruency, which may be different from one city to another.
6 This conjecture is substantiated by Barron, Kung, and Proserpio (2020). They note that Airbnb hosts often neglect to delist their properties despite an easy cancelling solution available on Airbnb. This has created what they call "stale vacancies" that seem available for rent but are actually not.
7 HVS. Airbnb and impacts on the New York City lodging market and economy. October 27, 2015.
8 Zervas, Proserpio, and Byers (2017), p. 687.
9 Airbnb. Airbnb economic impacts in France. Retrieved on August 17, 2020 from https://blog.atairbnb.com/airbnb-economic-impacts-in-france/.
10 See Note 9.
11 *The New York Times*. Airbnb grows to a million rooms, and hotel rivals are quiet, for now. May 12, 2015.
12 *CNN*. Hilton: We're not scared of Airbnb. October 28, 2015.
13 *The Economist*. Buffett's revenge. January 7, 2016.
14 *The Economist*. Buffett's revenge. January 7, 2016.

Bibliography

Barron, K., Kung, E., & Proserpio, D. (2020). The effect of home-sharing on house prices and rents: Evidence from Airbnb. *Marketing Science*. Online: October 2, 2020. https://doi.org/10.1287/mksc.2020.1227

Heo, C. Y., Blal, I., & Choi, M. (2019). What is happening in Paris? Airbnb, hotels, and the Parisian market: A case study. *Tourism Management, 70*, 78–88.

Zervas, G., Proserpio, D., & Byers, J. W. (2017). The rise of the sharing economy: Estimating the impact of Airbnb on the hotel industry. *Journal of Marketing Research, 54*(5), 687–705.

MODULE 4

Firm behavior and strategy

12 Monopoly and price discrimination

This chapter addresses price discrimination in which a firm with monopoly power charges more than one price for the same product for reasons other than the difference in cost. Price discrimination is in contrast to monopoly pricing addressed in Chapter 9. In price discrimination consumers are charged different prices for the same product under different conditions, leading to the coexistence of different prices for the same product in the market. Depending on whether to price discriminate on consumers or on the quantity of sales, price discrimination is specified as first-degree price discrimination, second-degree price discrimination, and third-degree price discrimination. Firms price discriminate because price discrimination increases producer surplus as opposed to monopoly pricing, yet whether and to what extent a firm is able to price discriminate depends on the extent to which it knows consumer demand. We conclude this chapter by drawing the relevance of price discrimination to market efficiency.

AFTER STUDYING THIS CHAPTER, YOU SHOULD BE ABLE TO:

- Understand the concept of price discrimination and the difference between price discrimination and monopoly pricing;
- Explain the economic rationales behind price discriminating on consumers and on the quantity of sales, respectively;
- Analyze third-degree, second-degree, and first-degree price discrimination and the corresponding economic surplus; and
- Evaluate price discrimination versus monopoly pricing with regard to market efficiency.

12.1 Price discrimination versus uniform pricing

12.1.1 Uniform pricing of a monopolist

We have discussed that a monopolist faces a downward-sloping demand curve, and therefore confronts a tradeoff between increasing output and raising price for profit maximization. Since increasing output is at the expense of reducing price while raising price is at the expense of cutting output, the profit-maximizing monopolist needs to figure out the optimal coordinates of output and price dictated by the demand curve. In the analysis in Chapter 9 we have shown that the optimal output–price coordinates are obtained in two steps. First, the monopolist chooses the optimal quantity of output at which its marginal revenue equals marginal cost for profit maximization. Second, it sets price equal to consumers' willingness to pay for the optimal quantity of output. The optimal price of a product derived from the standard monopoly pricing is known as the uniform price, because it is charged uniformly regardless of who purchases the product and irrespective of the quantity of purchase. Thus, there is only one price that exhibits for each product in the marketplace.

12.1.2 What is price discrimination

Instead of charging a uniform price, a monopolist can charge different prices for the same product for reasons other than the difference in cost. Such multiple pricing is known as price discrimination. There are two basic approaches to price discrimination. One approach is to price discriminate on consumers, meaning that the firm charges different prices for the same good to different consumers. For instance, movie theaters usually provide students with a discount, suggesting that they charge students a lower price as opposed to a standard price to other audience. The other is to price discriminate on the quantity of sales for the good, meaning that the firm charges different prices for different quantities of the good. For instance, ice cream vendors usually sell the second ice cream cone at a lower price than the first one if consumers agree to buy two. From these two approaches we can derive what is referred to as third-degree, second-degree, and first-degree price discrimination, distinguished by British economist Arthur Pigou (1877–1959). Third-degree price discrimination is to discriminate on consumer segments, i.e. that a firm charges different prices to different consumer segments.[1] Second-degree price discrimination is to discriminate on sale blocks,[2] meaning that the firm charges different prices on different sale blocks. First-degree price discrimination is to discriminate on individual consumers, that is, the firm charges each individual consumer a different price.

Price discrimination is grounded on the fact that consumers' willingness to pay for a good varies in one way or another. On the one hand, consumers in the market have different demands for the good, meaning that the elasticities of their demand for the good differ from each other. On the other hand, one consumer's willingness to pay also varies by different quantities of the good he purchases. That is, he is willing to pay a higher price for a smaller quantity but a lower price for a larger quantity, which is dictated by the law of diminishing marginal utility. Thus, not only can different prices of a good be charged to different consumers with different demand elasticities, but they can also be charged on different quantities of the good purchased by the same consumer. The word *degree* indicates the amount of information on demand that a firm needs to acquire in order to implement a certain degree of price discrimination. We shall start with third-degree price discrimination, followed by second-degree and first-degree price discrimination, because the firm needs to acquire more and more information about consumer demand to implement them. In other words, implementing first-degree price discrimination requires the maximum amount of information of demand, followed by second-degree and third-degree. Hence third-degree price discrimination prevails in the marketplace, followed by second-degree and first-degree price discrimination.

12.2 Third-degree price discrimination

12.2.1 Demand heterogeneity by consumer segment

When booking a flight, you would probably find that the airfare you paid in the same class for the same route on the same day is different from what is paid by others on the same flight. Obviously, such price differences are not due to the difference in cost because you fly the same class and are served with the same onboard amenities as others. Figure 12.1 shows that the tickets are priced differently depending on a consumer's booking window, which is a period of time between a booking date and a departure date of a flight. Consider economy class in Figure 12.1: Booking window ranges from one day, namely booking and departing on the same day, to 90 days, that is, a booking is made 90 days before the departure date. You would be charged only $100 if you book the flight 90 days before departure, while as much as $351 if you book the same flight in the same class 21 days before departure. Such price discrepancies based on booking windows can also be seen in business class and first class. Note that price discrepancies between economy, business, and first classes are not due to price discrimination because seats in different classes are not the same product.

For simplicity, we consider two prices in economy class, $100 with a 90-day booking window and $351 with a 21-day booking window. The airline does not charge

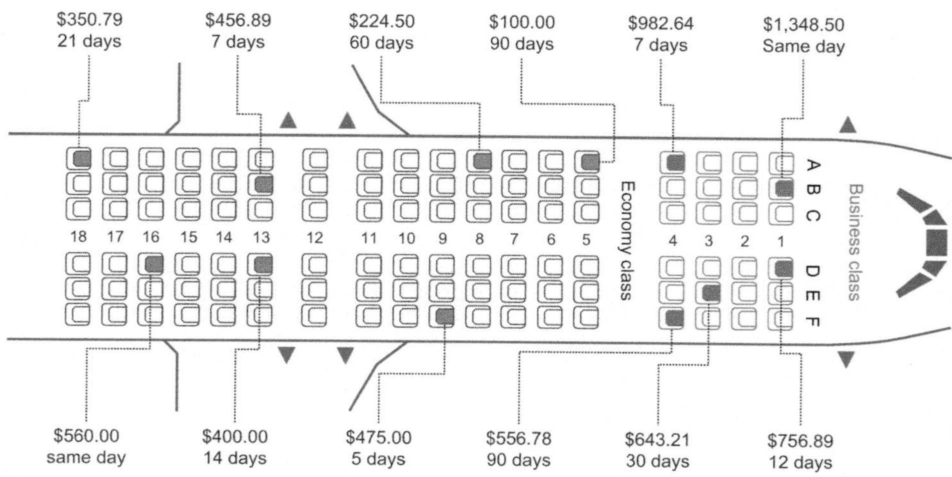

Figure 12.1
Airline pricing and booking window

a uniform price because price discrimination is superior, provided that there exist two consumer segments with heterogeneous willingness to pay that is correlated with the booking window. Consumers having a long booking window are more likely to have a lower willingness to pay, meaning that their demand is more elastic, and thus are charged for \$100 per ticket. Consumers having a short booking window are more likely to have a higher willingness to pay, meaning that their demand is less elastic, and thus are charged for \$351 for the same ticket. Intuitively, leisure travelers fall into the first segment whose schedule is flexible, and thus their demand is more elastic. Business travelers fall into the second segment whose schedule is not only rigid, but the airfare is usually footed by their employers. Hence business travelers' demand is less elastic. If we plot the market demand curve by pooling consumers from the two segments, we will find that the demand curve exhibits some sort of discontinuity that changes abruptly from one segment to the other.

12.2.2 Pricing on consumer segments

Suppose that an airline sells in two consumer segments, business and leisure markets, which have different demand curves. For expository simplicity, we assume that the demand curves of business and leisure segments are both linear, and the marginal cost of the tickets is constant, equal to the average variable cost of \$50 per ticket. We further assume that the demand curve of business travelers is D_1 with the x-intercept at 500 and y-intercept at 650 (Figure 12.2a). This information allows us to derive the demand function for calculation purposes.

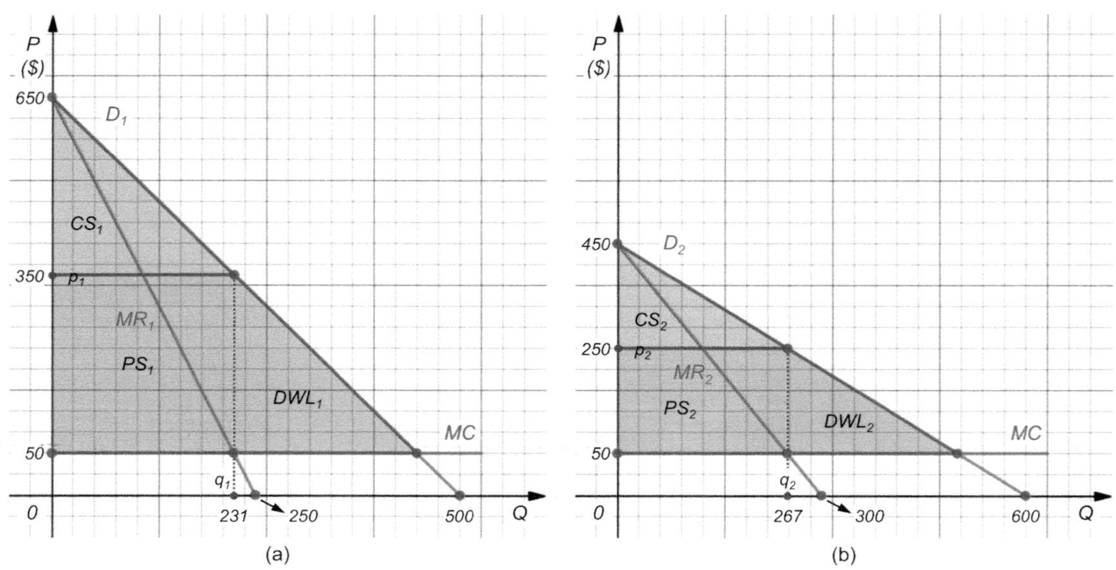

Figure 12.2
Third-degree price discrimination

Given the linear inverse demand function $p = aq + b$ and the two intercepts specified in Figure 12.2a, we can obtain the inverse demand function of business travelers by solving a system of two linear equations:

$$\begin{cases} 650 = b, \\ 0 = 500a + b. \end{cases} \quad (12.1)$$

We obtain the parameters $a = -1.3$ and $b = 650$, and therefore the inverse demand function of business travelers is

$$p = -1.3q + 650. \quad (12.2)$$

Based on the inverse demand function, we can write out the marginal revenue (MR) function of the airline in the business segment by referring to the relationship between the linear demand function and the marginal revenue function addressed in Chapter 9:

$$p = -2.6q + 650. \quad (12.3)$$

To maximize profit, the airline first decides the optimal quantity of sales, $q_1 = 231$, at which marginal revenue equals marginal cost, $MR_1 = MC = \$50$ (Figure 12.2a).[3] Second, the airline sets the monopoly price $p_1 = \$350$, equal to business travelers' willingness to pay for purchasing 231 tickets in the market (Figure 12.2a). This is the optimal price that the airline charges, which brings about producer surplus equal to $\$69,300 = (350 - 50) \times 231$, denoted by the area PS_1, consumer surplus equal to $\$34,650 = 0.5 \times (650 - 350) \times 231$, denoted by CS_1, and deadweight loss denoted by the area DWL_1. The occurrence of the deadweight loss is twofold. On the supply side, the airline is able, but not willing, to sell any quantity beyond 231 despite consumers' willingness to pay at a larger quantity being above its marginal cost of \$50. It is not willing to sell more than 231 tickets at a lower price, because any quantity other than 231 tickets does not maximize its producer surplus. On the demand side, despite there being consumers in the market who are willing to pay a price between \$50 and \$350, they will not be able to get any additional tickets because the airline is not willing to sell more than 231 tickets.

Note that the remaining consumers who are willing to pay a price below \$350 belong to a categorically distinct segment, which is the leisure segment. Thus, their demand cannot be described by the demand curve of business travelers. This means that if the airline were to charge a monopoly price in the leisure segment, the price would be different from \$350 charged in the business segment. Suppose that the airline is able to separate leisure travelers from business travelers, and charges a different price in the leisure segment. This pricing strategy would end up with two prices coexisting in the two consumer segments for the same product, suggesting that the airline implements third-degree price discrimination. For simplicity, suppose that the demand curve of leisure travelers is D_2, which has an x-intercept at 600 and y-intercept at 450, other things being equal (Figure 12.2b). By the same token, we can figure out the optimal quantity and price of the tickets sold to leisure travelers. First, we obtain the inverse demand function of leisure travelers by solving the linear equations:

$$\begin{cases} 450 = b, \\ 0 = 600a + b. \end{cases} \tag{12.4}$$

Solving equations (12.4) we obtain $a = -0.75$ and $b = 450$, and thus the inverse demand function of leisure travelers is

$$p = -0.75q + 450. \tag{12.5}$$

Second, from equation (12.5) we obtain the marginal revenue function in the leisure segment:

$$p = -1.5q + 450. \tag{12.6}$$

Let marginal revenue be equal to marginal cost, $MR = MC = \$50$, for profit maximization. First, the airline figures out the optimal quantity of the tickets sold in the leisure segment $q_2 = 267$, at which the marginal revenue equals marginal cost. Second, it sets the monopoly price $p_2 = \$250$, which is equal to leisure travelers' willingness to pay for purchasing 267 tickets in the market (Figure 12.2b). From the leisure segment the airline obtains additional producer surplus equal to $\$53,400 = (250 - 50) \times 267$, denoted by the area PS_2. This also leads leisure travelers to obtain consumer surplus equal to $\$26,700 = 0.5 \times (450 - 250) \times 267$, denoted by CS_2.

In the case above third-degree price discrimination is executed such that the airline sells a total of 498 tickets at two monopoly prices simultaneously in two market segments: 231 tickets sold at \$350 per ticket in the business segment and 267 tickets sold at \$250 per ticket in the leisure segment. The airline's producer surplus amounts to \$122,700, which is the sum of the producer surplus of \$69,300 in the business segment and of \$53,400 in the leisure segment (Figure 12.2). Not only does the producer surplus increase through price discrimination, but the consumer surplus also increases because those who are willing to pay a price lower than \$350 but higher than \$250 obtain consumer surplus in the leisure segment. Thus, the deadweight loss decreases, and market efficiency improves. Note that third-degree price discrimination also applies to situations where there exist more than two consumer segments as long as their demands are different. As a matter of fact, there do exist a number of consumer segments in the airline market, revealed by numerous prices associated with different booking windows (Figure 12.1). Thus, different monopoly prices would be charged

according to different consumer segments, provided that the airline is able to discern these segments and measure consumers' willingness to pay respectively.

12.2.3 Discontinuity in market demand

Third-degree price discrimination implies that segmenting a market based on consumers' willingness to pay is key. Whether a market can be segmented depends fundamentally on whether discontinuities exist in market demand, that is, whether consumer demands in two or more segments are categorically different from one another in terms of the price elasticity of demand. If discontinuities exist, the demands of consumer segments cannot be accounted for by the same demand function. The existence of discontinuities in market demand is the necessary condition for third-degree price discrimination to work. Put differently, if market demand is continuous and homogenous, arbitrarily segmenting a market on whatever attribute that describes the market in one way or another does not lead to third-degree price discrimination, because such market demand entails a uniform price to all consumers in the market. If discontinuities exist, the sufficient condition for third-degree price discrimination is that the less elastic consumer segment entails a higher price and the more elastic segment entails a lower price. Therefore, there will be different prices that coexist in different consumer segments for the same product, and the price variation is not due to cost difference, if any.

Discontinuities in market demand can be revealed by consumer attributes or behavioral patterns on which a market can be segmented. Such market segmentation is the very foundation for third-degree price discrimination to work. In order for third-degree price discrimination to work, firms also need to prevent arbitrage, an opportunistic behavior that consumers buy low in one segment and sell high in another. For instance, if a leisure traveler buying at $250 per ticket can sell to a business traveler for $300, both are better off as the leisure traveler makes a profit of $50 per ticket and the business traveler saves $50. Once arbitrage occurs, third-degree price discrimination collapses because arbitrage will eventually make the two prices converge to the uniform price of $300 per ticket. Thus, the airline is no longer able to charge a high price in the business segment. Obviously, arbitrage never occurs in the airline market because one's ticket is accompanied with his identity, and thus is futile to someone else. On other occasions where students are provided with a price discount to watch a movie, they are required to present their student card for the sake of preventing arbitrage from happening.

12.3 Second-degree price discrimination

12.3.1 Block selling and diminishing marginal utility

Second-degree price discrimination is to discriminate on sale blocks, meaning that firms charge an additional quantity of a product for a discounted price after a certain quantity is sold for a standard price. When implementing second-degree price discrimination, a firm charges a standard price (p_1) for a certain quantity (q_1) of a product that constitutes a sale block, then a lower price p_2 ($p_2 < p_1$) for any additional quantity of the product sold, say q_2, and so on. In the simplest case the firm will sell a total of $q_1 + q_2$ units of the product with two different prices p_1 and p_2, respectively, for the two sale blocks. For example, if you buy one ice cream cone at Laura Secord, you are charged $2, but you only need to pay an extra of $1 for the second one. In other words, if you buy two, you only need to pay $3 instead of $4. Why wouldn't Laura Secord simply charge an average price of $1.5 per cone regardless of whether consumers buy one cone or two? And if a consumer buys two, Laura Secord ends up reaping $3 as well. Furthermore, given the fact that the first cone is sold for $2, why wouldn't Laura Secord simply charge the second one for the same price? That is, how would Laura Secord determine the price for the first cone, the second, and so on? Note that this example is not the best to illustrate second-degree price discrimination, because selling ice cream cones one by one, strictly speaking, is not block selling.

We start with a profit-maximizing firm that first determines the optimal quantity of sales q_1 at which marginal revenue equals marginal cost, and then sets the price p_1 equal to consumers' willingness to pay at q_1. After the monopoly profit is captured by selling the first block with q_1, the firm proceeds to sell an additional quantity q_2 in the second block, as long as consumers' willingness to pay is still above its marginal cost for a total quantity of $q_1 + q_2$. Obviously, second-degree price discrimination increases producer surplus compared to the uniform pricing because the firm can sell an additional quantity after having obtained the monopoly profit. On the demand side, consumers will increase purchase only if the subsequent quantity q_2 in the second block is sold at a lower price, as each unit in the second block brings about less utility than the utility generated by each unit in the first block. Due to the law of diminishing marginal utility, a consumer's willingness to pay declines as he possesses or consumes more of a product. We shall demonstrate below, from a social perspective, that second-degree price discrimination is also superior to the uniform price because it reduces deadweight loss and hence increases social surplus.

12.3.2 Pricing on sale blocks

Suppose that the airline we mentioned earlier sells tickets to one customer, say a company, which normally makes a purchase up to hundreds of tickets for its employees. For expositional simplicity, suppose that the airline faces the same linear demand curve as for business travelers above, other things being equal (Figure 12.3). This demand curve now delineates the company's willingness to pay which varies by different quantities of the tickets it would purchase. The more tickets the company buys the lower its willingness to pay due to diminishing marginal utility. As we demonstrated above, under uniform pricing the optimal quantity of sales is 231 tickets at which the marginal revenue equals marginal cost for profit maximization. Thus, the optimal price is set at $350 per ticket, which is determined by the company's willingness to pay when the quantity demanded is 231 tickets. The airline ends up selling 231 tickets each at $350 to the company, maximizing producer surplus equal to $\$69{,}300 = (350 - 50) \times 231$, denoted by the area PS_1 (Figure 12.3).

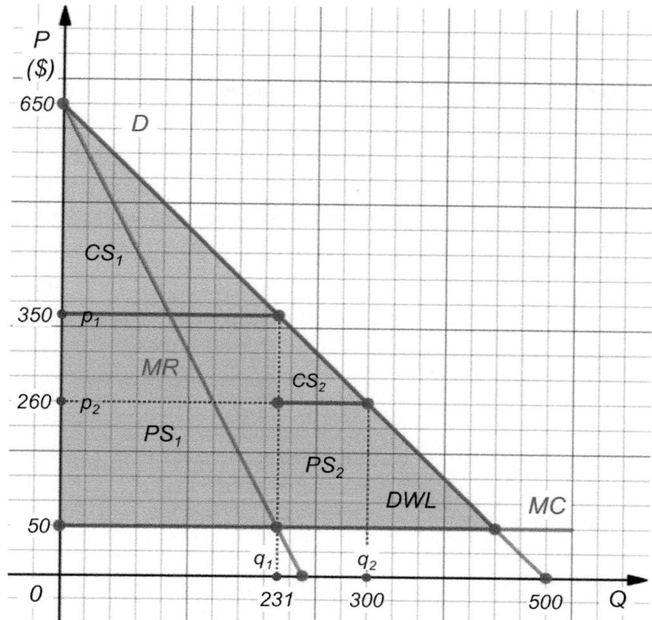

Figure 12.3
Second-degree price discrimination

After capturing the monopoly profit under the uniform price, the airline is also able and willing to sell additional tickets at a lower price, provided that it knows precisely how the company would respond afterwards. For instance, it could sell an additional 69 tickets each at \$260, which is equal to the company's willingness to pay for a total of 300 tickets (Figure 12.3). This pricing strategy is manifested such that the airline sells 300 tickets in two blocks: 231 tickets at \$350 per ticket in the first block, which are the monopoly quantity and price, respectively, and an additional 69 tickets at \$260 per ticket in the second block. This exemplifies second-degree price discrimination under which only after the first block is sold will the airline be able and willing to lower price for the second block, and so on. It is not in the interest of the airline to sell 300 tickets at \$260 per ticket once for all, because its producer surplus would always be smaller than that from selling 231 tickets at \$350 each in monopoly pricing. On the demand side, only if the airline lowers price to \$260 per ticket will the company be willing to buy an additional 69 tickets based on its demand curve, ending up with a total purchase of 300 tickets. Therefore, there exist two prices for the same product on two sale blocks charged successively to the same customer, which is a case of second-degree price discrimination.

12.3.3 Welfare analysis

In second-degree price discrimination not only does producer surplus increase by \$14,490 = (260 – 50) × 69, denoted by area PS_2, but consumer surplus also increases by \$3,105 = 0.5 × (350 – 260) × 69, denoted by area CS_2 (Figure 12.3). For each additional sale block, the area below the demand curve and above the price of the block, represents the increase in consumer surplus. Hence social surplus increases and deadweight loss decreases. This is because selling an additional block at a lower price increases both the quantity demanded and the quantity supplied insofar as the price is above the marginal cost of the firm. Starting with the first block that captures the monopoly profit under uniform pricing, second-degree price discrimination can proceed by selling as many blocks as possible until the consumer's willingness to pay for the total quantity of all blocks combined is equal to the firm's marginal cost. Therefore, both producer surplus and consumer surplus increase in second-degree price discrimination, which is the same as in third-degree price discrimination. However, the difference between the two is that second-degree price discrimination increases sales to the same consumer sequentially, conditional on the same demand curve, instead of to different consumer segments which are associated with two or more demand curves simultaneously.

Nevertheless, second-degree price discrimination cannot eradicate deadweight loss even though the airline can sell all blocks attainable in theory. This is because in the airline case the last ticket cannot be sold regardless of how sale blocks are created. To illustrate this idea, suppose that the airline continuously sells in blocks until the last ticket for which the company's willingness to pay is infinitesimally greater than the marginal cost of the tickets. Assume that the maximum number of tickets the airline is *able to* sell is 461, at which the company's willingness to pay is right above the marginal cost of the tickets.[4] If the 461st ticket is incorporated in the last sale block, the 460th must be in the same block. According to the law of demand, the company is willing to pay a higher price for purchasing 460 tickets than for purchasing 461 tickets. Yet in second-degree price

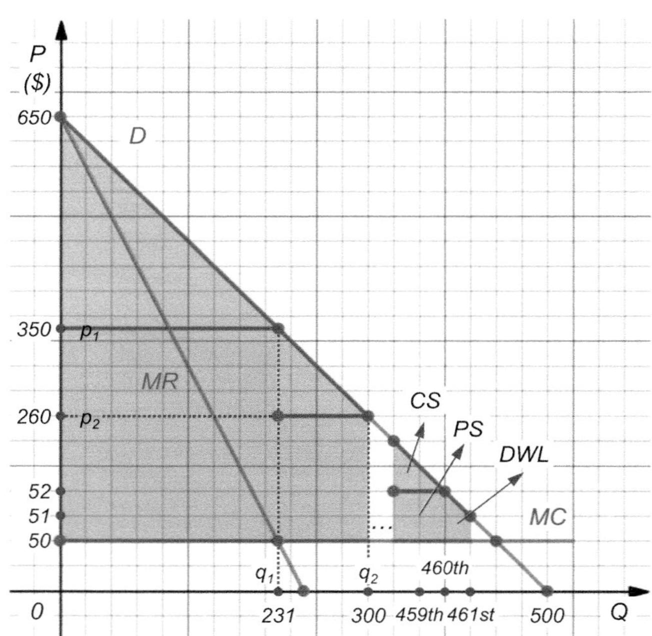

Figure 12.4
Deadweight loss in second-degree price discrimination

discrimination the 460th will be sold at the same price as the 461st. This ends up with an infinitesimal amount of producer surplus not only from selling the 461st ticket but also from selling the 460th and all preceding tickets, if any, in the same block, which is not in the interest of the airline. Since the smallest sale block must contain two tickets, the 461st cannot be sustained as one sale block, and thus, in theory, ends up being unsold.[5] Assuming that the demand is continuous and the ticket is divisible, deadweight loss will eventually arise, represented by the area enclosed by the demand curve and the marginal cost curve bounded by the 460th and 461st tickets (Figure 12.4). In practice, this is a loss in the market for not being able to trade the last ticket despite the fact that the trade will make both the company and the airline better off.

12.4 First-degree price discrimination

12.4.1 Pricing on individuals

First-degree price discrimination states that firms charge different prices to different consumers in the market. Suppose that the airline in the previous case can identify all consumers in the market and knows each individual consumer's willingness to pay. Assume that there are 461 consumers in the market whose willingness to pay differs from one another, and the lowest is slightly above or equal to the airline's marginal cost. The airline can rank the 461 consumers based on their willingness to pay, starting from the first consumer who is willing to pay the highest price of $650, followed by the second at $649, the third at $648, and so on, all the way to the last, or the 461st, who is willing to pay, say $51, which is right above the marginal cost of $50. If we plot all the 461 consumers' willingness to pay and the quantity demanded accumulated for all consumers in the market, we obtain the market demand curve (Figure 12.5). First-degree price discrimination is executed when the airline charges each consumer a price equal to his willingness to pay, ending up selling 461 tickets at 461 distinct prices to all 461 consumers in the market. That is, the first consumer is charged exactly the same price as he is willing to pay, and so is the second, the third, and so on.

It is evident that first-degree price discrimination can be regarded as a combination of second-degree and third-degree price discrimination. It resembles third-degree price discrimination if each individual consumer is seen as a distinct consumer segment, or a single-consumer segment. It follows that the airline charges different prices based on the willingness to pay of each single-consumer segment. It also resembles second-degree price discrimination if each ticket is seen as one block, or a single-ticket block. It then follows that the first block containing the first ticket only is sold at the highest price, followed by the second, the third, and so on, until the last block containing only the last ticket is sold slightly above the marginal cost. Obviously, a combination of second-degree and third-degree price discrimination does not make up a first-degree price discrimination. This is because third-degree price discrimination by definition deals with each consumer segment which must contain more than one consumer, and second-degree price discrimination deals with each sale block which must contain more than one unit of a product.

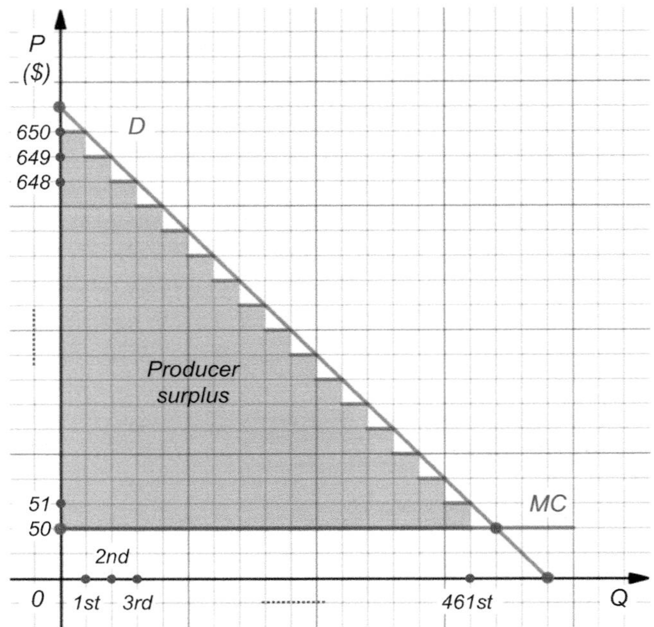

Figure 12.5
First-degree price discrimination

12.4.2 Social optimum and market efficiency

In the airline case above, on the one hand, since each consumer is charged exactly what he is willing to pay for the ticket in first-degree price discrimination, he obtains a zero consumer surplus. Hence first-degree price discrimination results in zero consumer surplus in the market as a whole. On the other hand, producer surplus is maximized for each ticket sold, because the price that the airline charges for each ticket is each consumer's willingness to pay. Thus, producer surplus in the market is maximized, equal to $\$138{,}300 = 0.5 \times (650 - 50) \times 461$ as indicated in Figure 12.5. Since the airline is able and willing to sell all tickets to all consumers whose willingness to pay is higher than its marginal cost, deadweight loss becomes zero, and thus social surplus is maximized. The market turns out to be perfectly efficient in terms of production, and for this reason first-degree price discrimination is also called perfect price discrimination. As a matter of fact, the airline obtains all economic surplus in the market, i.e. all consumer surplus and deadweight loss which would otherwise arise under uniform pricing are transformed into producer surplus.

While price discrimination is originated from imperfect competition, particularly monopoly, first-degree price discrimination ends up with the quantity produced by a monopolist being the same as the quantity produced by firms in perfect competition. Figure 12.6 shows that the quantity Q_0 produced by all firms in perfect competition is equal to Q_0', which is produced by the monopolist in first-degree price discrimination, other things being equal. The reason is that the monopolist in first-degree price discrimination produces on the same condition as firms do in perfect competition.

In perfect competition each firm faces the same demand curve, which is also the curve of its marginal revenue equal to the market price P_0. Thus, each firm produces an optimal output at which the marginal revenue equals the marginal cost equals the market price, $P_0 = MR = MC$, for profit maximization (Figure 12.6a). In first-degree price discrimination, since the monopolist's marginal revenue curve converges to its demand curve, the optimal output Q_0' is also determined when the marginal revenue equals the marginal cost equals the price that the firm charges, $P = MR = MC$ (Figure 12.6b). The difference though is that in first-degree price discrimination the market price P is not a constant but a function of the quantity Q in which each unit of the good is priced differently for different consumers.[6]

12.4.3 An example of first-degree price discrimination

First-degree price discrimination is the most difficult one to implement because it requires a firm to identify each individual consumer as well as his willingness to pay. Thus, first-degree price discrimination is not as common as second-degree and third-degree price discrimination in the real world. When it comes to acquiring information on consumer demand, auction is one example in which individual consumers reveal their willingness to pay through bidding. Yet auction in general has nothing to do with price discrimination because there always exists only one price charged to the highest bidder. A special type of auction provided by Swiss Air for selling its class-upgrade services is a telling example of first-degree price discrimination.[7] After you booked an economy class ticket, Swiss Air may send you an email a couple of weeks before your departure, furnishing you with an opportunity to bid for an upgrade to business class. For an economy ticket from Zurich to Hong Kong in April 2016 for

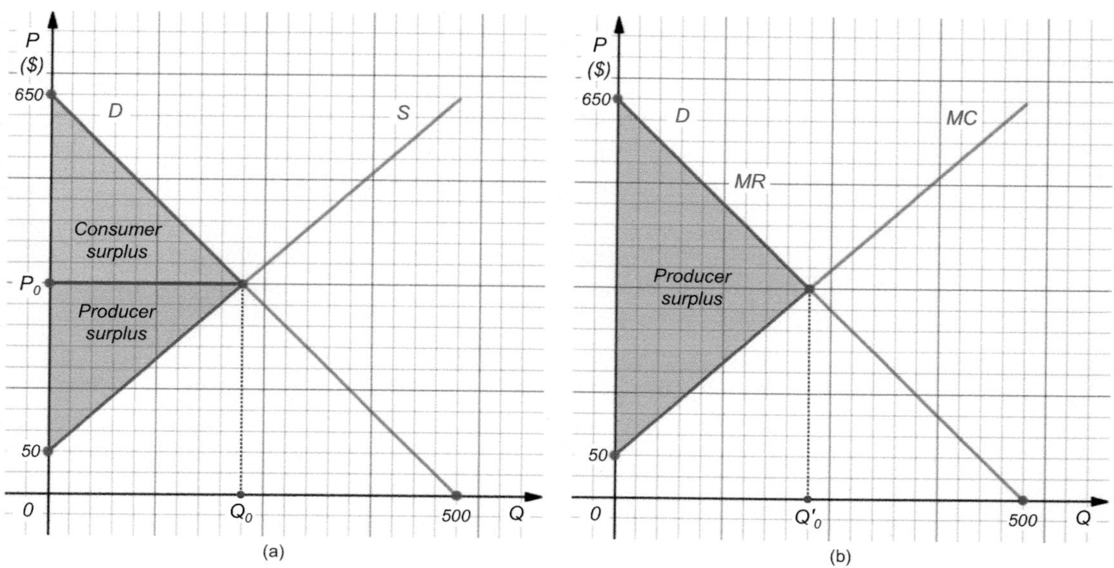

Figure 12.6
Perfect competition and first-degree price discrimination

instance, Swiss Air would allow you to bid any price between 30 francs and 200 francs for your route depending on, as it states explicitly, how much the upgrade is worth to you. You would then be notified whether your bid had been successful or not within 48 hours before departure. Why wouldn't Swiss Air simply charge a uniform price for the upgrade services?

Different from an auction in which anyone can see anybody else's bidding price to bid against one another, Swiss Air aims to entice all consumers to reveal their willingness to pay privately and independently through the upgrade bargain. For simplicity, we can assume that all consumers bid different prices without loss of generality. By gathering all consumers' willingness to pay, Swiss Air is able to rank all prices between 30 francs and 200 francs bid by the consumers who are interested in the upgrade services. In other words, Swiss Air obtains the demand function for the upgrade services in the market. Obviously, the marginal cost of the upgrade services is below 30 francs, and the highest price a consumer is willing to pay is 200 francs. The information on the price range can be obtained through market research or the airline's historical data of consumer demand. The allocation of the upgrade services proceeds such that the highest bidder is charged for 200 francs and gets the first upgrade service, followed by the second-highest bidder changed for 199 francs, and so on, until the last bidding 30 francs gets the last upgrade service. First-degree price discrimination enables Swiss Air to maximize its producer surplus from each consumer in the market, and hence the entire economic surplus accrues to Swiss Air as the producer surplus.

12.5 Market imperfection, information, and price discrimination

12.5.1 Price discrimination and market efficiency

Market imperfection is the prerequisite for price discrimination. Price discrimination does not exist in perfect competition because all firms face the same perfectly elastic demand, and thus price is exogenous to firm decision. While price discrimination is usually discussed with regard to monopoly, monopoly is a sufficient but not a necessary condition for a firm to price discriminate. Price discrimination is feasible as long as a firm has some degree of market power which enables it to set prices other than the market price. Therefore, firms in monopolistic competition and oligopoly can also price discriminate under certain circumstances. While a monopolist sells the optimal quantity at which its marginal revenue equals marginal cost and charges the uniform price for profit maximization, the optimal quantity is not optimal for society as a whole. Through second-degree or third-degree price discrimination, not only does a price-discriminating monopolist increase producer surplus beyond what is obtained under the uniform price, but it can also increase consumer surplus, ending up increasing social surplus and reducing deadweight loss.

Because the marginal revenue curve overlaps the demand curve in first-degree price discrimination, the optimal quantity at which a firm maximizes profit equals the social optimum. In all price discrimination other than first-degree, the marginal revenue curve of a firm is always beneath the demand curve, and thus the optimal quantity at which marginal revenue equals marginal cost is always smaller than the social optimum at which the demand curve intersects the marginal cost curve. Compared to uniform pricing, both third-degree and second-degree price discrimination improve market efficiency through reducing deadweight loss. Only in first-degree price discrimination where the marginal revenue curve and the demand curve overlap can the optimal quantity for the firm be equal to the social optimum in the market. Hence social surplus is maximized, the same as in perfect competition. The maximized social surplus in perfect competition, though, is shared by both consumers in the form of consumer surplus and by firms in the form of producer surplus. In first-degree price discrimination, the maximized social surplus solely accrues to the firm as producer surplus. Hence first-degree price discrimination brings about production efficiency but not allocation efficiency whereas perfect competition achieves both.

12.5.2 Information acquisition about demand

Price discrimination requires a firm to know consumers' willingness to pay with varying degrees of detail, ranging from the price elasticity of demand to the whole demand curve. Firms can know the demand curve through two mechanisms, signaling and screening. Signaling suggests that consumers' intrinsic characteristics, such as age, gender, and other socio-demographics, can serve as signals of their willingness to pay. For instance, seniors and youngsters usually have lower willingness to pay, meaning that their demand is more elastic, and are therefore provided with price discounts for movie tickets and transport passes, for instance.[8] It is reported that women's razors are priced as much as 40% higher than the identical male counterparts at CVS Pharmacy in the United States,[9] because females' demand for razors is less elastic while males' is more elastic. According to a study from the New York City Department of Consumer Affairs, shampoo and conditioner marketed to women are priced on average 48% more than those marketed to men, women's jeans 10% more than men's, and girls' bikes and scooters 6% more than boys'.[10] Not only can consumer characteristics, particularly socio-demographics, function as signals of the elasticity of demand, but consumer behavior can also be a signal. In the case of pricing airline tickets above, travelers' willingness to pay is associated with and revealed by their behavioral patterns such as booking windows.

Firms also design various devices, such as coloring a product or providing coupons in the market, to elicit consumers' willingness to pay. These are the proactive actions known as screening that firms take to compel consumers to reveal their willingness to pay. While gender is a signal that could distinguish between females' willingness to pay and males', firms could offer two colors of the same razor, blue and pink, whereby consumers are actuated to sort themselves into two segments. Since blue is regarded as masculine, tempting males who have a lower willingness to pay, and pink as feminine, tempting females who have a higher willingness to pay, pink razors are usually more expensive than blue ones in the market.[11] Note that gender is a signal in its own right while using blue and pink to sort consumers is screening. Another example is the provision of coupons by which firms can sort consumers into two segments, coupon users and non-coupon users. Since a coupon entitles consumers to a price discount, coupon users are, in fact, charged a lower price than non-coupon users. Since it takes time to garner coupons and one has to remember bringing a coupon when patronizing a shop, for coupon users a lower price overrides the convenience in their purchase decision. Therefore, coupon users usually have a lower willingness to pay than non-coupon users.

Depending on the extent to which a firm knows about consumer demand, it can implement third-degree, second-degree, and first-degree price discrimination successively. Third-degree price discrimination aims at pricing consumer segments based on categorically different demands, and hence discerning different elasticities of demand suffices. Since second-degree price discrimination aims at pricing sale blocks in sequence based on the same demand curve, the firm needs to know and quantify different portions of the demand curve associated with different sale blocks. The more the sale blocks, the subtler each portion of the demand, and the more information the firm needs about the demand curve. To implement first-degree price discrimination the firm needs to know each individual consumer's willingness to pay in the market or, if there is only one consumer, his willingness to pay at different quantities of purchase. Thus, the firm needs to figure out the demand function, thereby discerning the willingness to pay of the consumer(s) precisely at each quantity of purchase.

12.5.3 Economic discrimination versus social discrimination

Price discrimination in economic behavior is not discrimination of any kind in social behavior with regard to age, gender, race, or any other observable attributes that could lead to prejudices against an individual or a certain group of people. The reason is that price discrimination is fundamentally grounded on the differences in consumers' willingness to pay which may or may not be related to and revealed by the observable personal attributes. That is, the value that consumers place on a product differs from one another or varies by the quantity of purchase. For instance, the case above that females are charged a higher price for a razor while males a lower price is not because of gender per se, but because of consumers' different willingness to pay that happens to be associated with gender. Suppose that both males and females have the same willingness to pay, say \$5 for the razor, in which gender becomes irrelevant to signal their willingness to pay. Then a profit-maximizing firm will charge both the same price, and price discrimination will not occur at all. Yet social discrimination would arise in one way or another if the firm charged two different prices, say \$5 for males while either \$4 or \$6 for females. Due to social discrimination, the firm ends up either losing \$1 or failing to sell to females regardless of one believing whether males are being discriminated against or females.

If males and females have different willingness to pay, say \$4 and \$6, respectively, ironically social discrimination arises as long as the firm charges whatever the same price, say the average \$5, regardless of one believing whether males are being discriminated against or females. Such social discrimination ends up with the firm selling to females only while losing business from males, and precisely for this reason, males are worse off. Note that price discrimination occurs in this case only when the firm sells to males at or slightly below $4 and to females at or slightly below $6, which are entirely attributed to their different willingness to pay instead of their gender. Due to price discrimination, not only does the firm capture all businesses but all the consumers, regardless of gender, are also better off because they are able and willing to purchase the product they value. Thus, not only is price discrimination economically viable to firms, but it is also beneficial to consumers as a whole. However, social discrimination, regardless of whatever personal attribute it is based on, hurts consumers the same way as it hurts firms. Social discrimination is detrimental to social welfare, because what people are discriminated against on has no relevance whatsoever to their valuation of a product.

Summary

1. Profit-maximizing monopolists usually charge one uniform price, known as monopoly price, regardless of who purchases the product and irrespective of the quantity of purchase. Thus, there is only one price for each product in the market.
2. Price discrimination states that a firm charges more than one price for the same product for reasons other than the difference in cost. Firms have two basic approaches to price discrimination: on consumers in the market and, for the same consumer, on the quantity of purchase.
3. From the two basic approaches we classify first-degree, second-degree, and third-degree price discrimination. In price discrimination there is more than one price for the same product manifested in the market at which the product is transacted.
4. Third-degree price discrimination is to price discriminate on consumer segments in terms of demand elasticities. A high price is charged in a segment with less elastic demand and a low price in a segment with more elastic demand.
5. To implement third-degree price discrimination, a firm needs to identify consumers' elasticity of demand that is categorically different from one segment to another. There exist discontinuities in consumers' willingness to pay in the whole market.
6. Second-degree price discrimination is to price discriminate on the quantity of sales conditional on the same consumer or the same market. It is executed such that the first block is sold at the monopoly price, followed by the second block at a lower price equal to the consumer's willingness to pay for the sum of the two blocks, and so on.
7. To implement second-degree price discrimination, a firm needs to know different portions of the demand curve of the consumer or the market that are associated with different sale blocks. Thus, it can set the prices of the product equal to the consumer's willingness to pay at different quantities of sales.

8. First-degree price discrimination is also called perfect price discrimination in which each consumer is charged a distinct price equal to his willingness to pay. The prerequisite for implementing first-degree price discrimination is to know the entire demand curve and identify each consumer in the market.
9. Firms can use signaling and screening to obtain information on consumer demand. Signaling suggests that consumers' willingness to pay is revealed by their intrinsic characteristics or behavior. Screening suggests that firms can design devices to elicit consumers' willingness to pay.
10. Price discrimination improves market efficiency by reducing deadweight loss. In third-degree and second-degree price discrimination, the decrease in deadweight loss is converted into both producer surplus and consumer surplus. In first-degree price discrimination, deadweight loss is zero and all economic surplus accrues to the firm.

REVIEW QUESTIONS

Each question has four options, and there is only one correct answer to each question.

1. Suppose that females' willingness to pay for a good is \$5 per unit and males' willingness to pay is \$7 per unit. Assuming that each consumer only buys one unit of the good, which of the following is related to price discrimination?
   A) Both males and females are charged \$5 per unit.
   B) Both males and females are charged \$7 per unit.
   C) Males are charged \$5 per unit while females \$7 per unit.
   D) Females are charged \$5 per unit while males \$7 per unit.
2. Figure 12.1 in this chapter shows the prices of seats in both business and economy classes with various booking windows on an airplane for the same route on the same day. Which of the following is INCORRECT?
   A) Price differences between the two classes are due to price discrimination.
   B) Price differences in business class are due to price discrimination.
   C) Price differences in economy class are due to price discrimination.
   D) The airline cannot be in a perfectly competitive market.
3. Suppose that a fast food restaurant has two types of consumers, millennials and baby boomers. From a survey the restaurant has obtained consumers' willingness to pay for a cheeseburger as shown in the table below. If the marginal cost of the cheeseburgers is \$4, what will be the prices charged for millennials and baby boomers, respectively?
   A) \$6; \$8
   B) \$8; \$6
   C) \$4; \$4
   D) \$8; \$8

Price of cheeseburgers	Millennials	Baby boomers
$4	500	400
$6	400	200
$8	180	180
$10	50	0
$12	0	0

4. Suppose that a fine-dining restaurant is able to implement a type of price discrimination on the same group of consumers by charging two prices, $30 and $50, for a meal as shown in the graph below. Which of the following is correct?
   A) 300 meals are sold out at $30 per meal.
   B) 400 meals are sold out at $30 per meal.
   C) 200 meals are sold out at $50 per meal.
   D) 300 meals are sold out at $50 per meal.

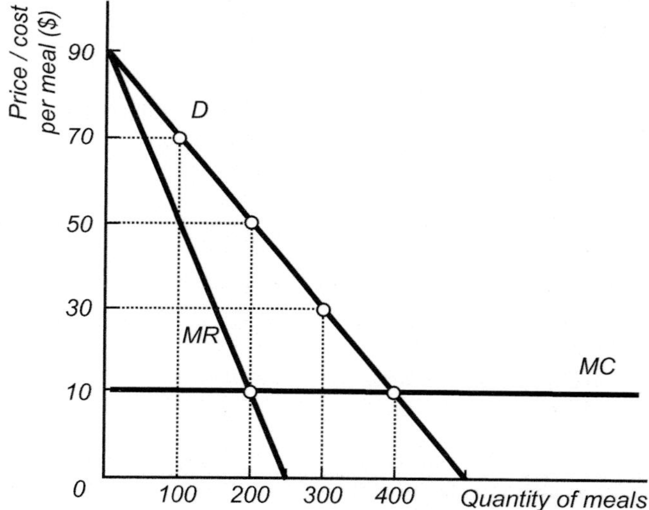

5. Suppose that Ryanair is the only airline operating between two cities. The figure below shows the linear demand curve (*D*) that Ryanair faces in the market, along with its marginal revenue (*MR*) and constant marginal cost (*MC*) curves. If Ryanair is able and willing to sell a ticket at any price between $200 and $500, what will the consumer surplus be?
   A) $0
   B) $2,250
   C) $4,500
   D) $9,000

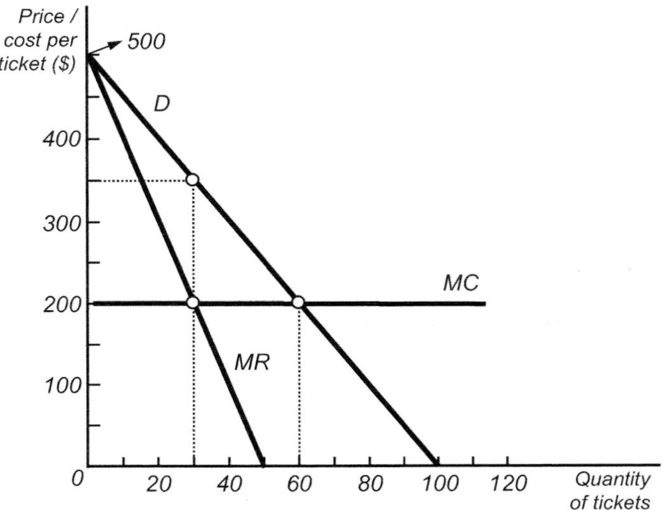

6. Suppose that the price scheme of a daily pass at Disney World is as follows: a one-day pass is sold for $98.79; if you pay an extra $90.65 you can buy a two-day pass; if you pay another extra $83.29 you can buy a three-day pass. For a fourth-day pass, you'll pay an extra of only $18.91 besides what you pay for the three-day pass. From the fifth day up to the tenth, you'll pay an extra of around $10.65 per day. Which of the following is correct?
   A) The marginal cost of the daily pass is below $10.65 per ticket per day.
   B) Consumers' willingness to pay for the third day is below $83.29.
   C) Producer surplus is maximized when Disney World sells the three-day pass.
   D) Consumer surplus is maximized when consumers buy the three-day pass.
7. Which of the following is correct regarding signaling and screening in price discrimination?
   A) Colors of razors are signals of consumer demand.
   B) Booking windows of flights are a screening device.
   C) Coupons of restaurants are a signal of consumer demand.
   D) Bidding for airlines' upgrade services is a screening device.
8. Compared to the uniform pricing of a monopoly, which of the following is correct regarding price discrimination in relation to economic surplus?
   A) Third-degree price dissemination decreases consumer surplus.
   B) Second-degree price discrimination maximizes social surplus.
   C) First-degree price discrimination maximizes producer surplus.
   D) All of the above.
9. In order for a firm to implement first-degree price discrimination, what kind of information is indispensable for the firm to acquire?
   A) Demand elasticities of different consumer segments.
   B) Consumers' socio-demographics, such as gender and age.
   C) Consumers' willingness to pay on different sale blocks.
   D) Consumer identity and each consumer's willingness to pay.

10. Which of the following is correct regarding first-degree price discrimination implemented by a firm?

A) The marginal cost of the firm has to be constant.
B) The demand curve that the firm faces needs to be linear.
C) The price that the firm charges is equal to its marginal cost.
D) The marginal revenue curve of the firm is the demand curve.

Problem solving

1. Boccalino is the only pizza hut in the city selling a type of pizza at a marginal cost of $3 each. In order to attract consumers and increase sales, it decides to dispense coupons which offer consumers a certain price discount as long as they use a coupon to buy the pizza. After conducting a market survey, Boccalino is well aware of the demand of consumers who may use the coupon and of those who may not. The figure below shows the linear demand curves of consumers without using coupons (D_1) and those using coupons (D_2). Suppose that consumers can only use one coupon to buy one pizza, and they have countless coupons at their disposal. What will be the discount stated on the coupon?

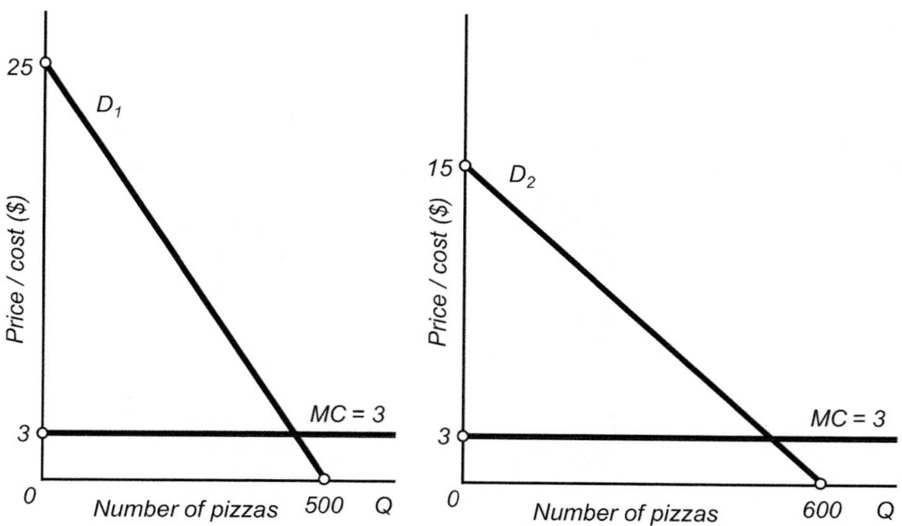

2. Boats Rental Ouchy is a recreational boating company adjacent to the port of Ouchy in Lausanne. It offers boating services which do not require sailors to have a license, and hence are popular among tourists as well as locals. As the company advertises on its website, it will "let you sail on the waves of Lake Geneva to sunbathe along the coast."[12] The company offers two types of pedal boats, 4-seat and 5-seat ones, which can accommodate a maximum of four and five riders, respectively. The table below shows the prices of boating based on seat capacity and the length of sailing. Suppose that consumer demands for the two boat types are different but both are linear, regardless of the sailing time. If the marginal cost of a ride is CHF 0.05 per minute for both types of boats, what will be the prices for a ride of 75 minutes on the two boat types?

Boat types	30 minutes	60 minutes
4-seat pedal boat	CHF 17	CHF 25
5-seat pedal boat	CHF 20	CHF 28

Note: CHF 1 is equivalent to US$1.

Source: Boats Rental Ouchy.

3. After you booked an economy class ticket from Swiss Air, you would probably receive an email from the airline, asking you to bid for an upgrade to business class. You're allowed to bid any price between $40 and $200 for your route, and you will find out 48 hours before departure whether your bid has been successful or not. Suppose that the demand (*D*) curve for the upgrade services is linear, along with the linear marginal cost (*MC*) curve, shown in the graph below. If Swiss Air can sell all the upgrade services on this route, what will the producer surplus be?

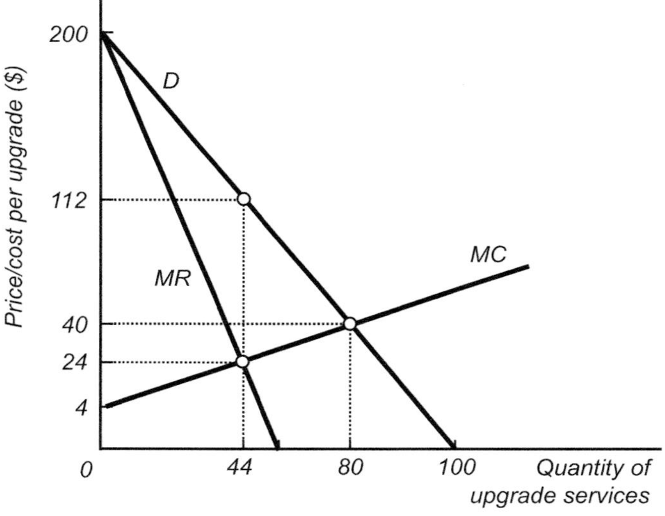

Solutions to all review questions and problem solving tasks are included in the Support Material for this book, which can be accessed at www.routledge.com/9780367897352.

Notes

1 We regard the smallest size of a consumer segment as having two consumers.
2 We regard the smallest size of a sale block as having two units of a product.
3 All the numbers in the calculations are rounded to the nearest integers unless indicated otherwise.

4 Plugging $p = 50$, which is the marginal cost of \$50, into the inverse demand function (12.2), we obtain $q \approx 461.5$ at which the company's willingness to pay is equal to the marginal cost of the tickets. Thus, the maximum number of tickets that the airline is able to sell is 461, which is the nearest integer for the number of tickets that indicates the company's willingness to pay being right above the marginal cost of the tickets.

5 As long as there is one sale block that contains at least two units of a good sold by a firm, the firm still executes second-degree price discrimination despite the fact that it sells the remaining quantity individually. This thus distinguishes from first-degree price discrimination in which all quantities of the good are sold individually. In second-degree price discrimination, we do not assume that some units are sold individually because this implies that the firm knows the demand function and can thus implement first-degree price discrimination.

6 To be inclusive, first-degree price discrimination incorporates two scenarios in which the quantity of a good is interpreted differently. One scenario addresses a market that consists of a certain number of consumers with different willingness to pay. In this scenario each consumer buys one unit of the good, and thus all consumers' willingness to pay from the highest to the lowest forms the market demand. First-degree price discrimination follows that each consumer is charged a different price, which is equivalent to each unit of the good being priced differently. This is the case we analyzed in this chapter. The other scenario addresses one consumer only, who buys a certain quantity of the good. The consumer's willingness to pay that varies from buying the first unit of the good to buying the last unit forms his demand. In this case first-degree price discrimination follows that each unit of the good is priced differently and sold to the consumer due to diminishing marginal utility.

7 SWISS. Bid upgrade. Retrieved on August 17, 2020 from https://www.swiss.com/ch/en/book/swiss-choice/swiss-upgrade-bargain.

8 Swiss Federal Railways (SBB) provides youngsters aged below 26 with a 15% discount on the Swiss Travel Pass with the same validity.

9 Buzzworthy. It's official: Being a woman is more expensive than being a man. Here's why. August 2, 2016.

10 U.S. News. The pink tax: Why women's products often cost more. February 17, 2016.

11 This case should not be mistakenly interpreted as product differentiation, because both colors of the razors are supposed to be sold at the same price insofar as product differentiation is concerned. The blue and pink are symmetric in product differentiation on color. Please refer to Chapter 14 for the theory of product differentiation.

12 Boats Rental Ouchy. Welcome. Retrieved on August 25, 2020 from http://www.bateaux-location-ouchy.ch/en/.

Bibliography

Phlips, L. (1988). Price discrimination: A survey of the theory. *Journal of Economic Surveys, 2*(2), 135–167.

Pigou, A. C. (1929). *The economics of welfare* (3rd ed.). London, UK: Macmillan.

Robinson, J. (1933). *The economics of imperfect competition*. London, UK: Macmillan and Co., Limited, 1942.

13 Starbucks pricing

Tall, Grande, and Venti

This chapter applies the theory of price discrimination in Chapter 12 to analyze Starbucks pricing. Starbucks's pricing strategy features the seemingly obfuscated relationship between three sizes of the receptacle for a drink, namely Tall, Grande, and Venti, and their price tags on the menu. Drawing upon the theory of price discrimination, we demonstrate that Starbucks implements either second-degree or third-degree price discrimination depending on how the price tags on the menu are interpreted. However, we demonstrate that second-degree price discrimination is more theoretically convincing and practically feasible than third-degree price discrimination in Starbucks pricing. Regardless of whether it is second-degree or third-degree price discrimination, there are three distinct prices coexisting on the menu but concealed by the price tags of the three sizes. If Starbucks were to offer one single size of the receptacle, we would be able to calculate the optimal size. This sheds light on why the optimal size is the smallest size in Starbucks's size portfolio.

AFTER STUDYING THIS CHAPTER, YOU SHOULD BE ABLE TO:

- Analyze second-degree price discrimination in Starbucks pricing based on the relationship between the receptacle size and the price tag;
- Calculate the optimal size and price of a drink if Starbucks were to offer one single size of the receptacle;
- Analyze third-degree price discrimination in Starbucks pricing by interpreting the receptacle size as a screening device; and
- Understand why second-degree price discrimination is superior to third-degree price discrimination in Starbucks pricing.

13.1 Receptacle size and price tag

Starbucks usually sells its drinks in three sizes of a receptacle, a Tall with 12 fluid ounces, Grande 16 ounces, and Venti 20 ounces. Figure 13.1 shows a standard Starbucks menu which you may see when patronizing a Starbucks shop. On the menu both hot and

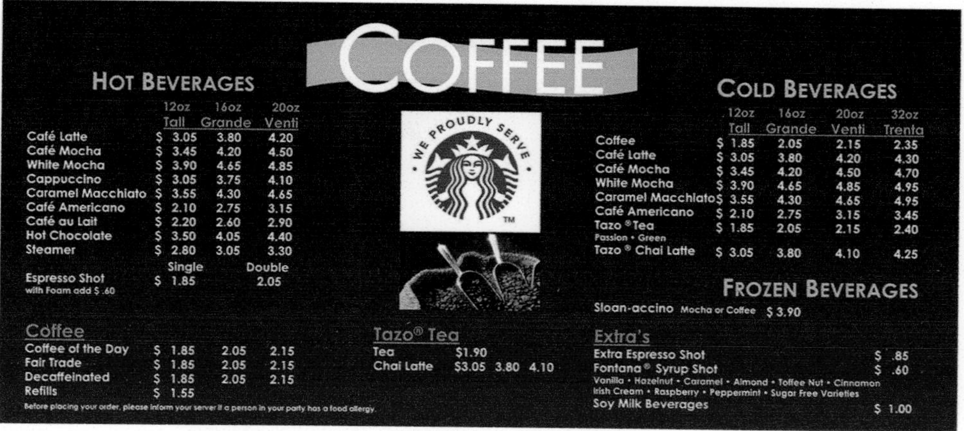

Figure 13.1
Starbucks coffee menu

Source: Starbucks.

cold beverages are exclusively served with the three receptacle sizes. If we look at one single size, say Tall (12 ounces) in the hot beverage category, we can find that Café Latte is sold for $3.05 per cup, Café Mocha $3.45, and so on, all the way to the cheapest one of the Steamer for $2.80. Such price variations are by and large due to different costs associated with producing and preparing the different beverages. If we focus on the same product, say Café Latte in the hot beverage category, a Tall is sold for $3.05, a Grande $3.80, and a Venti $4.20. Since the product is the same, such price variations cannot be explained by the differences in costs, nor, as we shall illustrate below, can they be explained by the increase in price proportional to the increase in the size of the receptacle. If the latter were the case, the unit price of Café Latte or of any other drinks in the three sizes would be the same. If so, there will be no need whatsoever for Starbucks to offer the three sizes but just one single size.

Throughout the analysis we take Café Latte in the hot beverage category as an example. To articulate the relationship between the price and size of Café Latte that is concealed in the price tags on the menu, we need to calculate the unit price of each size as well as to examine how the price tag changes with the receptacle size. Table 13.1 shows that by size a Grande is 33.3% larger than a Tall, and a Venti is 25% larger than a Grande, whereas the price of a Grande is 24.6% higher than a Tall, and of a Venti is 10.5% higher than a Grande. In other words, the increase in price is disproportionately smaller than the increase in size, and hence Venti is the cheapest per ounce, followed by Grande and Tall. This conclusion can also be confirmed by referring to the unit prices of Café Latte in the three sizes. Café Latte is sold for $0.254 per ounce in Tall, $0.238 per ounce in Grande, and $0.210 per ounce in Venti (Table 13.1). We shall illustrate shortly that the three unit prices may or may not be the prices for which the three sizes of Café Latte are actually sold, as they depend on whether Starbucks implements third-degree price discrimination or second-degree price discrimination. Yet no matter how Starbucks's price discriminates, the compelling evidence is that three different prices coexist on the menu in relation to the receptacle size for the same product.

Table 13.1 Comparison of size and price of Café Latte

Measures	Tall	Grande	Venti
Volume (ounce)	12	16	20
% change in volume		33.3%	25.0%
Price tag ($)	$3.05	$3.80	$4.20
% change in price		24.6%	10.5%
Unit price ($)	$0.254	$0.238	$0.210

13.2 Second-degree price discrimination

13.2.1 How does it work?

First of all, we argue for second-degree price discrimination because it is not only more theoretically convincing but also practically feasible than third-degree, which we shall explain in detail later. As illustrated in Table 13.1, there is an inverse relationship between the unit price of Café Latte and the size of the receptacle, which represents the quantity of Café Latte demanded in ounces. The more you buy the less you pay, which alludes to second-degree price discrimination. Table 13.2 shows that by size a Grande is composed of a Tall and an additional 4 ounces, and a Venti is composed of a Grande and an additional 4 ounces, in which the Grande is further composed of a Tall and an additional 4 ounces. By price a Grande $3.80 is made up of a Tall $3.05 plus $0.75, and a Venti $4.20 is made up of a Grande $3.80 plus $0.40, in which the Grande is further made up of a Tall $3.05 and $0.75. Hence selling a Grande with 16 ounces for $3.80 is as if Starbucks sold a Tall (12 ounces) for $3.05 and an additional 4 ounces for $0.187 per ounce. Furthermore, selling a Venti with 20 ounces for $4.20 is as if Starbucks sold a Grande (16 ounces) for $3.80 and an additional 4 ounces for $0.100 per ounce, in which the Grande were further sold as a Tall (12 ounces) for $3.05 and an additional 4 ounces for $0.187 per ounce.

Therefore, a Grande is sold in two blocks, a Tall of 12 ounces $0.254 per ounce in the first block and an additional 4 ounces $0.187 per ounce in the second block. A Venti is sold in three blocks, a Tall of 12 ounces $0.254 per ounce in the first block, an additional 4 ounces $0.187 per ounce in the second block, and another additional 4 ounces $0.100 per ounce in the third block. To illustrate the above ideas graphically, suppose that Starbucks faces an identical linear demand for Café Latte no matter whether it offers three sizes, two sizes, or one single size,[1] and assume that the marginal cost of Café Latte is $0.05 per ounce (Figure 13.2).[2] As a matter of fact, we can infer from the menu that the marginal cost must be below $0.100 because the last additional 4 ounces in Venti is sold precisely for $0.100 per ounce. Figure 13.2 shows the producer surplus of selling a Tall, a Grande, and a Venti, denoted by the areas t, $t+g$, and $t+g+v$, respectively. With the Tall as a benchmark, selling a Grande does not only increase producer surplus by the area g, but also consumer surplus by the area g_c, thereby

Table 13.2 Compositions of size and price of Café Latte

Size and price	Tall	Grande	Venti
Size composition (ounce)	12	16 = 12 + 4	20 = 16+ 4 = 12 + 4 + 4
Price composition ($)	$3.05	$3.80 = $3.05 + $0.75	$4.20 = $3.80 + $0.40 = $3.05 + $0.75 + $0.40
Unit price ($)	$0.254 = $3.05/12	$0.254 = $3.05/12 $0.187 = $0.75/4	$0.254 = $3.05/12 $0.187 = $0.75/4 $0.100 = $0.40/4

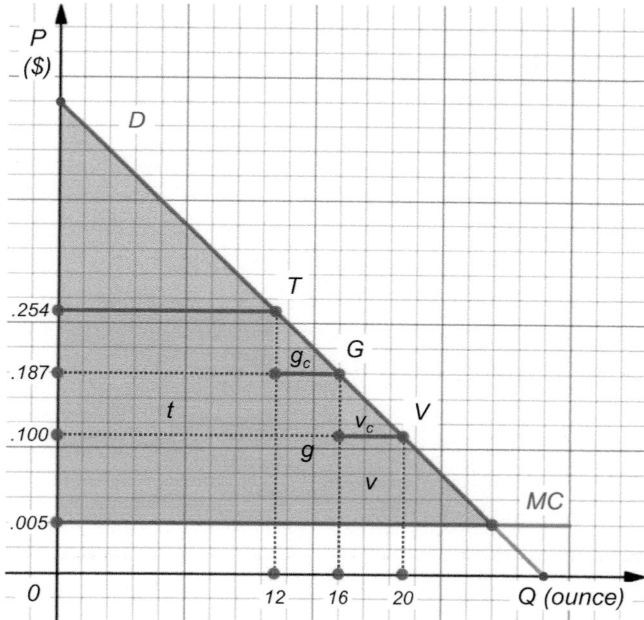

Figure 13.2
Unit prices of Tall, Grande, and Venti

increasing social surplus. Likewise, selling a Venti further increases producer surplus by the area v and consumer surplus by the area v_c, ending up increasing social surplus further (Figure 13.2).

Given the fact that a Tall is sold at $0.254 per ounce, totaling $3.05 on the menu, we may wonder why a Grande is not sold the same way as the Tall, namely $0.238 per ounce, totaling $3.80 as exhibited on the menu. This would be plausible if and only if Tall did not exist on the menu, that is, only Grande and Venti would go on sale. Only by excluding Tall from the menu could we justify that a Venti with 20 ounces for $4.20 is composed of a Grande (16 ounces) sold for $3.80 in the first block, or $0.238 per ounce, and an additional 4 ounces sold for $0.100 per ounce in the second block (Figure 13.3a).

However, this justification is erroneous simply because of the existence of Tall. If a Grande were sold for $0.238 per ounce, a Tall must be sold for a higher price which, as the menu reveals, is $0.254 per ounce. It follows that a Grande will not be sold for $0.238 per ounce because Starbucks will be better off selling 12 ounces out of 16 ounces for $0.254 per ounce, and the remaining 4 ounces for a price lower than $0.254 per ounce. Note that the remaining 4 ounces cannot be sold for $0.238 per ounce, because this ends up with the unit price of a Grande being higher than $0.238, and hence the price will be higher than $3.80, contradicting the price tag on the menu. Either way contradiction will arise. Given the fact that a Grande is sold for $3.80 per cup, the additional 4 ounces are sold for $0.187 per ounce as illustrated in Figure 13.2.

By the same token, a Venti could be sold for a uniform price of $0.210 per ounce if and only if Tall and Grande did not exist on the menu, that is, only Venti would be sold (Figure 13.3b). Since Tall and Grande are sold on the menu, it is infeasible to sell a Venti for $0.254 per ounce, which is the unit price of a Tall, or, if Tall did not exist, for $0.238 per ounce, the unit price of a Grande. This is because the law of demand will be violated otherwise, and there would exist a uniform price of Café Latte irrespective of size. The fact is that a Tall is sold for $0.254 per ounce for 12 ounces, totaling $3.05 in the first place, whereby a Grande is sold in two blocks, a Tall for $0.254 per ounce in the first block and an additional 4 ounces for $0.187 per ounce in the second block; a Venti is sold in three blocks, a Tall for $0.254 per ounce in the first block, an additional 4 ounces for $0.187 per ounce in the second block, and another additional 4 ounces for $0.100 per ounce in the third block (Figure 13.2). Hence the three prices coexist in the market, though implicitly, for which Café Latte is sold, which are $0.254 per ounce for 12 ounces in the first block, $0.187 per ounce for 4 ounces in the second block, and $0.100 per ounce for 4 ounces in the third block.

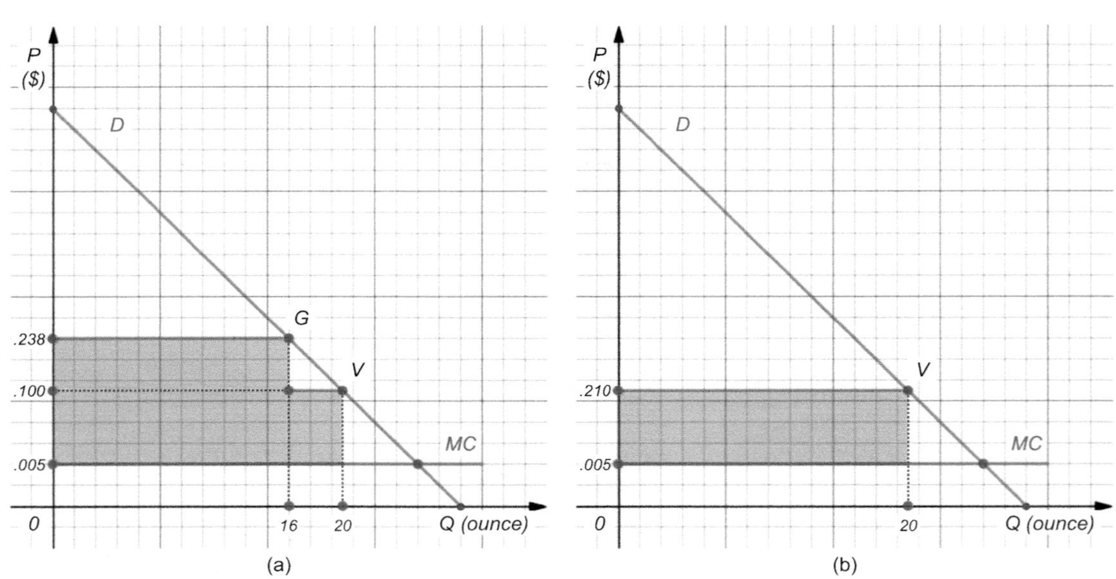

Figure 13.3
Unit prices of Grande and Venti

13.2.2 Why the Tall is the optimal single size

Alternatively, Starbucks could sell Café Latte in one single size only as other coffee shops would do to simplify business operation. In this case, price discrimination will not occur as only one price is exhibited on the menu. If there were only one single size, what would be the size and the price for a cup of Café Latte? This single size is actually the optimal quantity of Café Latte that allows Starbucks as a monopolist to maximize profit. Given the information we elicited from the menu, we can figure out, approximately, the demand function of consumers for Café Latte, thereby identifying the optimal size and price. To simply the analysis, we assume that the inverse demand function for Café Latte is linear without loss of generality: $p = aq + b$. The relationship between the price and size in Tall and Grande suffices to specify the demand function by solving the parameters a and b. On the demand curve in Figure 13.2 we can identify point T (12, 0.254), manifested by Tall, and point G (16, 0.187), manifested by Grande. The two points are sufficient to determine the linear demand function for Café Latte by satisfying a system of two linear equations:

$$\begin{cases} 0.254 = 12a + b, \\ 0.187 = 16a + b. \end{cases} \tag{13.1}$$

Solving equations (13.1) we obtain the parameters $a = -0.01675$ and $b = 0.455$. Thus we obtain the inverse demand function of consumers for Café Latte:

$$p = -0.01675q + 0.455. \tag{13.2}$$

From the demand function (13.2) we obtain the marginal revenue function, which has the same parameter b but twice the parameter a as the linear inverse demand function:

$$p = -0.0335q + 0.455. \tag{13.3}$$

We have assumed that the marginal cost $MC = \$0.05$, which is reasonable and realistic according to the price and size information of Café Latte on the menu. Now let the marginal revenue be equal to the marginal cost $MR = MC = \$0.05$ to solve q in the marginal revenue function (13.3). We obtain the optimal quantity $q = 12$ ounces,[3] which is the optimal size for the single size. Plugging $q = 12$ into the inverse demand function (13.2), we obtain the monopoly price $p = \$0.254$, which is consumers' willingness to pay each ounce for 12 ounces. The optimal size turns out to be the size of Tall and sold at \$0.254 per ounce, ending up with the price tag of \$3.05 per cup on the menu (Figure 13.4). It is not accidental but essential that the optimal size is the smallest size, Tall, in the size portfolio of Starbucks that contains Grande and Venti. Only if the smallest size secures the monopoly profit in the first place will Starbucks be willing to sell larger sizes, such as Grande, Venti, and so on.

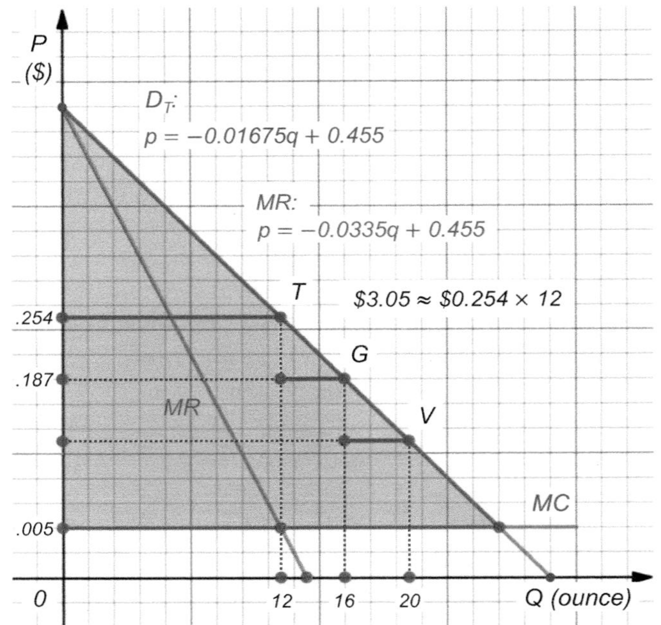

Figure 13.4
Optimal size and price of Tall

Note that the demand for Café Latte is actually nonlinear because point V (20, 0.100), manifested by Venti, is not on the linear demand curve we derived (Figure 13.4). In fact, we are not able to figure out the demand function from the menu if the demand is not linear. However, the linear demand function models consumers' demand for Café Latte quite well as far as the menu in Figure 13.1 is concerned. The analysis of second-degree price discrimination holds even if the demand is nonlinear. There is no doubt that the size of Tall is instrumental in creating the size portfolio of Starbucks. As illustrated in second-degree price discrimination in Chapter 12, the size of the first block must be the optimal quantity by which a firm captures the monopoly profit as a prerequisite, and then the second block, the third block, and so on are sold in sequence. If the first block contained any quantity other than the optimal, selling an additional block would deviate from profit maximization. In the three-size portfolio, as long as the optimal quantity is designated as the smallest size Tall, Starbucks secures the monopoly profit regardless of whether a consumer purchases a Tall, Grande, or Venti. If a consumer buys a Grande or Venti instead, Starbucks will further increase its producer surplus beyond the monopoly profit because all larger sizes contain a Tall.

13.2.3 Optimal sizes and prices for Grande and Venti

Given the optimal single size (Tall) derived above, if Starbucks continues to add a larger receptacle, say Grande, to create a two-size portfolio, there will still be an optimization problem about the second size and price. The key is to identify the optimal size of the second block, together with Tall, to make up the second size. In what follows we focus on illustrating the principle of this optimization while omitting the calculation. Figure 13.5 shows the optimal size of the first block (q_1), which is the size of Tall derived above. Then, the optimal size of the second block is determined by the additional quantity that maximizes profit in the second block. We can identify the optimal second size, q_2, at which the marginal revenue equals marginal cost, $MR_2 = MC = c$, by leaving the first block aside for the moment (Figure 13.5). And the optimal price for the second block ends up at p_2, which is consumers' willingness to pay for q_2. Note that the optimal size of the second block is $q_2 - q_1$, and hence the price of a Grande is $p_1 q_1 + p_2 (q_2 - q_1)$. If Starbucks adds Venti, by the same token the optimal size of the third block is determined by the additional quantity, q_3, that maximizes profit in the third block by leaving the first two blocks aside (Figure 13.5). Then, the optimal size of the third block will be $q_3 - q_2$, and sold at p_3, which is consumers' willingness to pay for q_3. Thus the price of a Venti ends up with $p_1 q_1 + p_2 (q_2 - q_1) + p_3 (q_3 - q_2)$.

Of course, the results of this theoretical analysis may slightly differ from the three sizes of Café Latte on the Starbucks menu. One reason is that the demand curve of consumers is nonlinear, and hence the discrepancy between the theoretical results and the price tags on the menu would arise. Another reason is that Starbucks may not focus on figuring out the optimal sizes for a Grande and Venti in practice. In theory, second-degree price discrimination can continue by incorporating as many sizes as possible until the unit price in the last block is equal to the marginal cost of the drink. Based on the demand function of consumers for Café Latte and the marginal cost of the drink, we

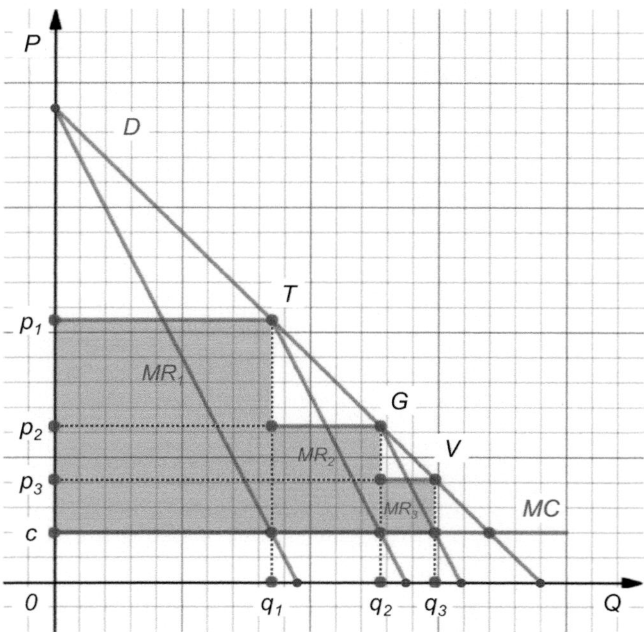

Figure 13.5
Optimal sizes and prices of Grande and Venti

can also calculate the optimal size of the last block attainable as well as the price of the last block, and hence figure out the largest size that Starbucks can sell. While in theory both producer surplus and consumer surplus will increase as more sizes are added in the size portfolio, in practice expanding the size portfolio will compromise the operation efficiency of Starbucks. As the size portfolio expands, on the one hand it will become difficult for Starbucks to obtain more information about the demand and to manage the size portfolio properly, and on the other, consumers might not be sophisticated enough to distinguish between various sizes and their corresponding value.

13.3 Third-degree price discrimination

13.3.1 How does it work?

A different approach to explaining Starbucks pricing involves applying third-degree price discrimination. This explanation is as theoretically sound as second-degree price discrimination, but might not be as feasible in practice. Third-degree price discrimination can be justified if and only if three conditions are articulated and held true. First of all, three different prices must be the unit prices of the three sizes, namely \$0.254 per ounce for a Tall, \$0.238 per ounce for a Grande, and \$0.210 per ounce for a Venti, rather than \$0.254, \$0.187, and \$0.100 per ounce for the three blocks, 12 ounces, 4 ounces, and 4 ounces, respectively. Second, the three prices coexist because there exist three consumer segments whose demands are categorically different from each other in terms of demand elasticity. One segment exclusively buys Tall referred to as Tall consumers, one buying Grande referred to as Grande consumers, and one buying Venti referred to as Venti consumers. That is, there exist two discontinuities in the market demand for Café Latte which separate consumers' willingness to pay into three levels. Starbucks designs the three sizes of the receptacle whereby consumers can sort themselves into the three segments correspondingly. In other words, the size of the receptacle is a screening device. Third, the three prices must be the three monopoly prices charged in the three segments for profit maximization.

For simplicity, suppose that the demands of the three consumers segments, Tall (D_T), Grande (D_G), and Venti (D_V), for Café Latte are linear, other things being equal. First of all, we have already figured out the optimal size and price for Tall as shown in Figure 13.4 above. In third-degree price discrimination, a Tall of 12 ounces at \$0.254 per ounce is supposed to be sold to Tall consumers, which maximizes profit. By the same token, Figure 13.6a shows that the optimal size for a Grande is 16 ounces at which the marginal revenue equals marginal cost, $MR_G = MC = \$0.05$. Hence a Grande is sold independently at \$0.238 per ounce for 16 ounces, ending up with a price of $\$3.80 \approx \$0.238 \times 16$, to Grande consumers. Figure 13.6b shows that the optimal size for a Venti is 20 ounces at which the marginal revenue equals marginal cost, $MR_V = MC = \$0.05$. Hence a Venti is also sold independently yet at \$0.210 per ounce for 20 ounces, ending up with a price of $\$4.20 = \$0.210 \times 20$, to Venti consumers. Note that the three sizes are completely independent in third-degree price discrimination, because the demands of the three consumer segments are distinct and independent in the first place.

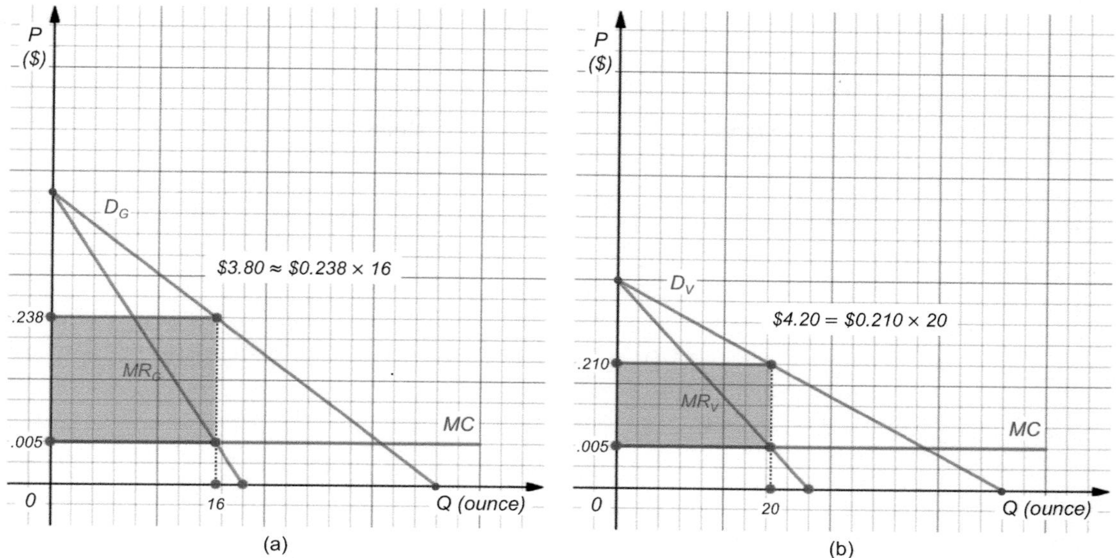

Figure 13.6
Receptacle size and pricing on consumer segments

13.3.2 Nonfunctional utility and elasticity of demand

As third-degree price discrimination shows, Tall consumers are charged the highest price, $0.254 per ounce of Café Latte, followed by Grande consumers at $0.238 per ounce, and Venti consumers at $0.210 per ounce. We may wonder why Tall consumers are charged the highest price whereas Venti consumers are charged the lowest price. In other words, we need to justify why the demand of Tall consumers is the least elastic among the three. This question suggests the fundamental difference between third-degree and second-degree price discrimination. That is, third-degree price discrimination requires consumer demand to vary by consumer segment while second-degree price discrimination is grounded on the same demand whereby consumers' willingness to pay varies by the quantity of purchase. Comparing Starbucks with other coffee shops, we may readily realize that many consumers gravitate to Starbucks not only for the functional utility of coffee as a beverage but also for the nonfunctional utility that Starbucks creates for socialization. In practice, consumers make use of the premises of Starbucks for various social activities, such as study and work, far beyond sipping their coffee. In this sense, Starbucks creates nonfunctional utility for consumers in addition to the functional utility of coffee as a beverage. In fact, Starbucks is dedicated to creating a servicescape by setting up socially friendly layouts, sofas, and ambient lighting, all of which facilitate people socialize while savoring their coffee at the same time.

If a consumer values the nonfunctional utility of Café Latte more than its functional utility as a beverage, he would be more likely to buy a Tall while less likely to buy a Grande or Venti. This is because the nonfunctional utility, which is obtained through occupying, or justifying, a seat at Starbucks as a prerequisite, only depends on whether a cup of coffee is purchased or not. The nonfunctional utility is invariant no matter whether the consumer buys a Tall, Grande, Venti, or any other size available. If the price of Café Latte decreased, he would increase his demand to purchase a larger size, but by disproportionately less than the decrease in price. The reason is that he values the nonfunctional utility, which does not change with the size of Café Latte. If the price increased, he would certainly reduce his demand by disproportionately more than the increase in price, ending up purchasing a much smaller size if available. In the latter case though, since the smallest size is fixed as Tall, he cannot reduce his demand freely and ends up buying Tall. Therefore, the consumer's demand in both cases ends up being less responsive to price changes, and is thus less elastic. This conclusion, of course, can be generalized to the whole Tall segment.

13.3.3 Elasticity of demand across sizes

In contrast to Tall consumers, assume that Venti consumers only value the functional utility of Café Latte for expository simplicity. This does not mean that Café Latte in Venti has no nonfunctional utility but it would have the least amount against its functional utility. Thus, we can quantify the nonfunctional demand of the three consumer segments for Café Latte relative to the functional demand. Figure 13.7 shows the demand curve of Venti consumers, D_V, as a benchmark against which the demand curves of Grande and Tall consumers can be derived. Suppose that the price falls from p_1 to p_2. Then Venti consumers will increase their demand from q_1 to q_2, with $q_2 - q_1$ suggesting the increase in the functional demand for Café Latte. Grande consumers will also increase their demand from q_1, say, to q_G ($q_G < q_2$), because they do not value the functional utility as much as Venti consumers do. Thus, the demand curve of Grande consumers, D_G, exhibits a straight line passing through points A and G, with $q_2 - q_G$ suggesting the nonfunctional demand on the condition that Venti consumers have no nonfunctional demand as assumed (Figure 13.7).[4] Likewise, Tall consumers will also increase their demand from q_1, say, to q_T ($q_T < q_G < q_2$), because they do not value the functional utility as much as Grande consumers do. Thus, the demand curve of Tall consumers, D_T, is a straight line passing through points A and T, with $q_2 - q_T$ suggesting the nonfunctional demand on the conditions that Venti consumers have no nonfunctional demand and Grande consumers have less of it than Tall consumers (Figure 13.7).

Based on the analysis in Figure 13.7, we are able to isolate and compare the effects of the price change from p_1 to p_2 on the quantity demanded for Café Latte in the three consumer segments, assuming that Venti consumers have no nonfunctional demand. Table 13.3 summarizes total quantities demanded for Café Latte in the three consumer segments caused by the price decrease of $p_1 - p_2$: $q_2 - q_1$ for Venti consumers, $q_G - q_1$ for Grande consumers, and $q_T - q_1$ for Tall consumers.

Given the demand of Venti consumers (D_V) as a benchmark, we can readily know from Figure 13.7 that the demand of Grande consumers (D_G) is less elastic than D_V, and the demand of Tall consumers (D_T) is the least elastic. We can also calculate

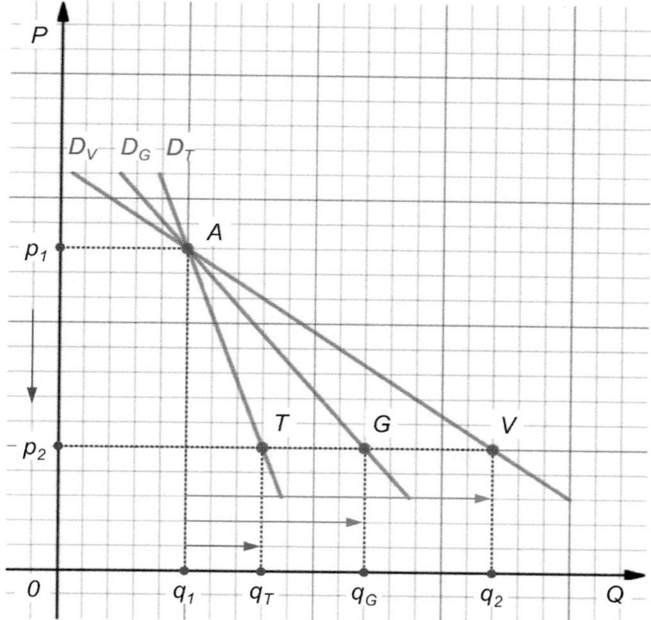

Figure 13.7
Nonfunctional demand and price elasticity of demand

Table 13.3 Comparison of functional and nonfunctional demand

	Functional demand	Nonfunctional demand
Venti	$q_2 - q_1$	0
Grande	$q_G - q_1$	$q_2 - q_G$
Tall	$q_T - q_1$	$q_2 - q_T$

the price elasticities of demand for Tall (η_T), Grande (η_G), and Venti (η_V) consumers, respectively:

$$\eta_T = \frac{(q_T - q_1)/q_1}{(p_2 - p_1)/p_1}, \quad \eta_G = \frac{(q_G - q_1)/q_1}{(p_2 - p_1)/p_1}, \quad \eta_V = \frac{(q_2 - q_1)/q_1}{(p_2 - p_1)/p_1}. \qquad (13.4)$$

Since the quantities demanded $q_T < q_G < q_2$, we conclude $\eta_T < \eta_G < \eta_V$ when the price of Café Latte decreases from p_1 to p_2. The relationship of the demand elasticities in the three consumer segments eventually justifies third-degree price discrimination. That is, the highest price, \$0.254 per ounce, is charged for Tall consumers whose demand is the least elastic (η_T), the lowest price, \$0.210 per ounce, is charged for Venti consumers whose demand is the most elastic (η_V), and the moderate price, \$0.238 per ounce, is charged for Grande consumers whose elasticity of demand (η_G) is in between the two.

13.4 Rationality versus irrationality

After stepping into a Starbucks shop and seeing the menu, you would probably not bother to do the tedious calculations in Table 13.1. Instead, you pick up a Tall, because it appears the cheapest to you based on the three price tags on the menu. If this were how some consumers really behave based on their heuristics, Tall would captivate consumers whose demand is more, instead of less, elastic and who would otherwise buy Grande or Venti. This irrational behavior will end up with the preponderance of Tall in consumer choice as a whole. Yet this does no harm whatsoever to Starbucks insofar as second-degree price discrimination is concerned, because the size of Tall generates the monopoly profit for Starbucks in the first place. Nonetheless, such irrational choice would make third-degree price discrimination economically inviable in practice as we implied earlier. It cannot reconcile the contradiction that Tall, which is supposed to be purchased by consumers whose demand is the least elastic, ends up in the hands of those whose demand is the most elastic. This means that third-degree price discrimination that uses the receptacle size to sort consumers into multiple segments works perfectly in theory but may fail in practice. It fails as long as consumers' willingness to pay in the three segments does not match, due to the delusion of the price tags on the menu, with the prices they are supposed to be charged by Starbucks for profit maximization.

As a matter of fact, when consumers were asked why a Tall is preferred to a Grande or Venti, they would probably say without hesitation that Tall is, or at least appears, the cheapest among the three—an illusion created by the price tags on the menu. Since the price tags are themselves explicit and conveniently observable on the menu, they are immediately used by consumers as a heuristic tool in decision making. Unexpectedly, the use of the price tags will lead to consumers' irrational decision in an economic sense, namely that those who are willing to pay a low price ironically end up paying a high price, which contradicts what rational choice theory predicts. Nevertheless, such illusion does not invalidate second-degree price discrimination in practice, and hence is inconsequential to Starbucks pricing. Even if consumers overwhelmingly favored Tall, as their experience accumulates they would eventually find out that Grande is worth more than Tall, and Venti is worth more than Grande. If one does not need to consume a Grande or Venti, he ends up buying a Tall. No matter what size consumers purchase, Starbucks secures the monopoly profit anyway because the optimal size is designated as the smallest size in the size portfolio.

Summary

1. The relationship between the three sizes of receptacle, Tall, Grande, and Venti, and the corresponding price tags for the same drink suggests three prices coexisting in the market. Starbucks implements second-degree price discrimination *or* third-degree price discrimination depending on the interpretation of the three prices.

2. In second-degree price discrimination, a Tall of Café Latte is sold for 12 ounces \$0.254 per ounce, a Grande is sold for 12 ounces \$0.254 per ounce in the first block and an additional 4 ounces \$0.187 per ounce in the second block, and a Venti is sold for 12 ounces \$0.254 per ounce in the first block, an additional 4 ounces \$0.187 per ounce in the second block, and another additional 4 ounces \$0.100 per ounce in the third block.
3. If Starbucks were to offer one single size of Café Latte, the optimal size would be 12 ounces, which is the size of Tall in the three-size portfolio. Regardless of what size Starbucks would continue to sell, the smallest size must be 12 ounces because it secures the monopoly profit in the first place.
4. Third-degree price discrimination is grounded on the assumption that the three sizes of the receptacle are used to sort consumers into three segments whose demand elasticities are categorically different. This means that there are three independent consumer segments who would buy Tall, Grande, and Venti, respectively.
5. In third-degree price discrimination, Café Latte is sold such that Tall consumers are charged \$0.254 per ounce for purchasing 12 ounces, Grande consumers \$0.238 per ounce for 16 ounces, and Venti consumers \$0.210 per ounce for 20 ounces. These three prices are the monopoly prices in the three consumer segments.
6. In third-degree price discrimination, Tall consumers are charged the highest price (\$0.254 per ounce), followed by Grande (\$0.238 per ounce), and Venti consumers (\$0.210 per ounce) because their demand elasticities satisfy $\eta_T < \eta_G < \eta_V$.
7. In third-degree price discrimination, the demand elasticities satisfy $\eta_T < \eta_G < \eta_V$ because the functional demand relative to the nonfunctional demand for the drink is the smallest for Tall consumers, followed by Grande, and Venti consumers.
8. In Starbucks pricing second-degree price discrimination is more convincing and practically feasible than third-degree price discrimination because Starbucks secures the monopoly profit in the first place regardless of which size consumers will purchase.

Problem solving

1. Starbucks normally offers multiple sizes of receptacle for the drinks it sells. Consider Café Mocha: Tall (12 ounces) sold at \$3.45, Grande (16 ounces) at \$4.20, and Venti (20 ounces) at \$4.55. Suppose that Starbucks faces an identical linear demand curve for Café Mocha no matter whether it offers three sizes or one single size. Assume that the marginal cost associated with the receptacle and Café Mocha is zero for simplicity. If Starbucks decides to offer one single size only for Café Mocha, what would the optimal size (round to the nearest integer) and price (round to two decimal places) be?
2. Starbucks rolled out the largest size of its drinks ever in the United States in January 2011.[5] The size is called the Trenta, which means "Thirty" in Italian. A Trenta carries 31 ounces in one cup, which is 7 ounces more than a Venti, available only for iced drinks in the United States. We know that the three smaller sizes and the corresponding price tags on the menu for Iced Coffee are Tall (12 ounces) sold at \$1.95, Grande (16 ounces) at \$2.45, and Venti (24 ounces) at \$2.95. Assume that

the marginal cost of Iced Coffee is $0.05 per ounce, other things being equal. If Starbucks implements second-degree price discrimination, what will the price range be for Trenta?

3. In the question above, suppose that Starbucks uses the four sizes of receptacle to sort consumers of Iced Coffee into four market segments and thus implements third-degree price discrimination. Suppose that consumers obtain the same amount of nonfunctional utility as long as they purchase a cup of Iced Coffee no matter what size. What would be the price elasticity of demand for Iced Coffee in Trenta?

Solutions to all review questions and problem solving tasks are included in the Support Material for this book, which can be accessed at www.routledge.com/9780367897352.

Notes

1 This assumption is indispensable for us to rule out the possibility of third-degree price discrimination for the moment.

2 Actually, the maximum marginal cost of Café Latte can be estimated from the Starbucks menu. The marginal cost must be lower than the average price of the third block in Venti, which is $0.100 per ounce. Hence the assumption of the marginal cost being $0.05 per ounce is fairly reasonable.

3 We round $q = 12.09$ to the nearest integer. This result suggests that the assumptions of the linear demand curve for Café Latte and the marginal cost of $0.05 per ounce perfectly fit the Starbucks menu.

4 Here, the amount of nonfunctional demand is quantified as being relative to the size of functional demand. Since the nonfunctional utility is the same regardless of the size of receptacle, the nonfunctional demand of the three consumer segments that is derived from the nonfunctional utility can only be compared in relative terms, namely adjusted by the size of the functional demand.

5 *Reuters*. Starbucks 31-oz "Trenta" cup size set for US debut. January 16, 2011.

Bibliography

Leibenstein, H. (1950). Bandwagon, snob, and Veblen effects in the theory of consumers' demand. *Quarterly Journal of Economics, 64*(2), 183–207.

Thaler, R. H. (2015). *Misbehaving: The making of behavioral economics*. New York, NY: W. W. Norton & Company.

14 Duopoly and product differentiation

This chapter addresses the issue of firms differentiating products in response to competition in duopoly. First, we lay out the definitions of horizontal versus vertical product differentiation. It follows that if two duopolists offer two products that are identical in all aspects other than the location of the firms, the products are differentiated on location as long as they locate differently on a linear street. Second, drawing upon the Hotelling model, we analyze the equilibrium of product differentiation in which the duopolists end up locating halfway along the street and charging the same price equal to their marginal costs. Third, given maximum product differentiation in which the duopolists locate at both ends of the street, they end up charging the same price above their marginal costs. Finally, we illustrate that the source of product differentiation is consumer preference. We conclude this chapter by illustrating market efficiency in product differentiation whereby Hotelling competition differs from Bertrand competition.

AFTER STUDYING THIS CHAPTER, YOU SHOULD BE ABLE TO:

- Understand horizontal product differentiation and vertical product differentiation as well as their relationships with consumer preference;
- Analyze market equilibrium when two duopolists compete on location and explain the principle of minimum product differentiation;
- Analyze the market price of the products when the duopolists execute maximum product differentiation; and
- Explain the relationships between product differentiation, consumer preference, and market efficiency in the Hotelling model.

14.1 Horizontal versus vertical product differentiation

We proceed to analyze the third type of firm behavior, product differentiation, in addition to output decision for firms in perfect competition and price discrimination of monopolists. Obviously, product differentiation does not exist in perfect competition in which products are assumed to be identical for all firms, nor in monopoly in which there is no need for a monopolist to differentiate its product. Only in monopolistic competition or oligopoly would firms turn their attention to differentiating their products in one way or another, thereby diverting competition from price. Product differentiation is the overriding difference between monopolistic competition and perfect competition. While it is not necessary for firms in oligopoly to differentiate their products, product differentiation lies at the heart of oligopolistic behavior besides price competition. We shall focus on duopoly and analyze how duopolists compete on the extent to which their products can be differentiated in the market, which will in turn affect their pricing behavior. Therefore, product differentiation is an extension of Bertrand competition in which duopolists are assumed to produce homogenous products.

Product differentiation consists of horizontal product differentiation and vertical product differentiation. Given two products, *A* and *B*, sold for the same price as assumed, they are horizontally differentiated if consumers have no consensus on which one is preferred. Some consumers would always prefer *A* while others always prefer *B*. On the same price condition, they are vertically differentiated if all consumers have a consensus on which one is preferred, meaning that all consumers would unanimously prefer either product *A* or product *B*. For example, if economy classes on Swiss Air (Swiss economy) and British Airways (BA economy) are sold for the same price, some consumers probably prefer Swiss economy while others prefer BA economy. Hence the classification of Swiss economy and BA economy is horizontal product differentiation on airline brand, other things being equal (Figure 14.1). If the economy and business classes on Swiss Air are sold for the same price, all consumers will prefer the business class to the economy class. Hence the classification of Swiss economy and Swiss business is vertical product differentiation on service standard, other things being equal (Figure 14.1), so also is the classification of BA economy and BA

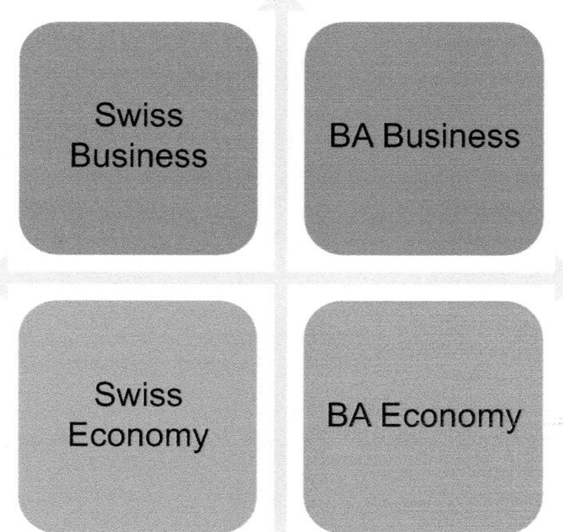

Figure 14.1
Horizontal versus vertical product differentiation

business under the same price condition. Therefore, horizontal product differentiation manifests the relative consumer preference while vertical product differentiation manifests the absolute consumer preference.

Hotels are classified on two dimensions, class and chain, among others. Hotel class stipulates different levels of service standard whereas hotel chain is synonymous with hotel brand. According to the classification of STR, there are six classes in the hotel industry, ranging from economy, midscale, upper midscale, upscale, upper upscale to luxury. Assuming that hotel rooms across all six classes are sold for the same price, obviously all consumers will prefer, in sequence, luxury to upper upscale to upscale, all the way to economy. Hence the classification of hotels on the dimension of class is vertical product differentiation. Under each of the six classes are various hotel chains. For instance, luxury class incorporates hotel chains such as Marriott, Ritz-Carlton, Four Seasons, and Shangri-La, to name a few. Assuming that their hotel rooms are sold for the same price, some consumers will prefer Marriott to Ritz-Carlton, some will prefer Ritz-Carlton to Four Seasons, and some may prefer Four Seasons to Shangri-La, and so on. Hence in the same class the classification of hotels on chain is horizontal product differentiation. Included in economy class are hotel chains such as Super 8, Days Inn, and Motel 6, to name a few. Consumers may have no consensus on which one is preferred if hotel rooms of all chains in economy class are sold for the same price, which also exemplifies horizontal product differentiation.

When two products are differentiated on more than one attribute, identifying which product is preferred becomes complicated, if not impossible. For instance, if hotel rooms in Marriott and Super 8 are sold for the same price, consumer preference will become obscure. Identifying which one is preferred requires knowing consumer preferences for both class and chain as well as the extent to which consumers will compromise one versus the other. As a matter of fact, products can be differentiated on a wide range of attributes that constitute a multi-characteristic differentiation space. For expository simplicity though, we assume that two products are identical on all attributes except the dominant one on which firms aim to differentiate. That is, we assume that products are differentiated on one attribute at a time instead of on multiple attributes simultaneously. In practice, firms differentiate their products progressively on one attribute by another, ending up with a variety of products in the marketplace. Thus, a wide array of heterogeneous products which we see in the marketplace are not a concurrent exhibition of different products but the ramifications of product differentiation that progresses on one attribute by another over time.

14.2 Minimum product differentiation

The theory of product differentiation was developed by American economist Harold Hotelling (1895–1973), and is thus known as the Hotelling model or Hotelling competition. Hotelling competition is similar to Bertrand competition in many aspects except for product differentiation, which is absent in Bertrand competition but lies at the heart of Hotelling competition. The Hotelling model explains product differentiation on the attribute of location that two firms would choose to sell their products. It addresses

two basic questions in competition for product offerings. First, we assume that two products sold by two firms, namely duopolists, are identical in all aspects but location. Insofar as the two firms choose different locations for their businesses, their products are automatically differentiated on the attribute of location. If both products are sold for the same price, how will the two firms choose their locations, thereby differentiating their products on location? Second, if their locations are given and different from each other, that is, the two products are differentiated to some extent on location, how will the two firms set price? Note that location choice involves changing fixed costs, and hence it is in the long run, while price decision is in the short run. We shall illustrate below the market equilibrium of location and price when the two firms compete with each other on location in order to maximize their profits.

14.2.1 Assumptions of the model

To make the Hotelling model work we need to lay out a set of assumptions in the first place, and their implications will be discussed as our analysis proceeds. Suppose that two firms F_1 and F_2 sell an identical product[1] along a fixed-length street of L miles ($L > 0$) (Figure 14.2a). Then the products sold by F_1 and F_2 will be differentiated on location as long as they choose different locations to sell and consumers have preference for location. Thus, location becomes *the* only attribute on which the two products can be differentiated. We further assume that both firms have the same

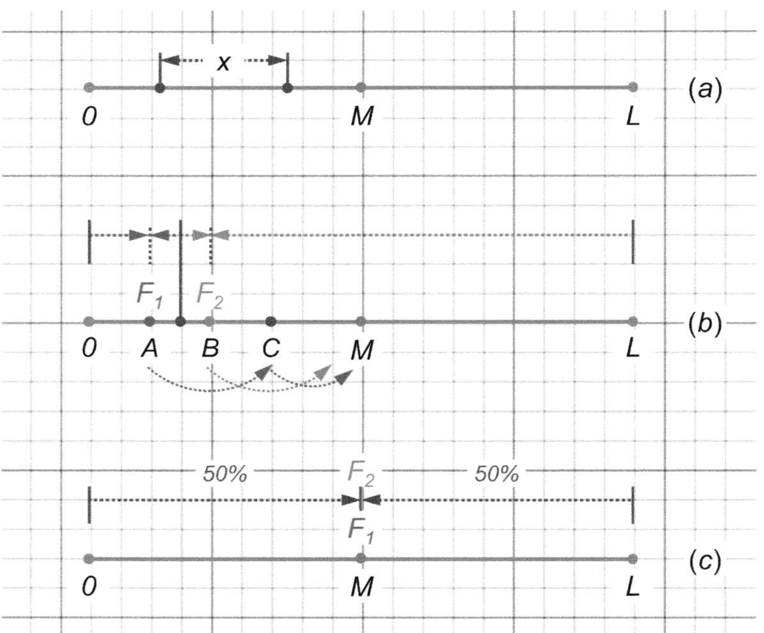

Figure 14.2
Location equilibrium and minimum product differentiation

marginal cost, $c_1 = c_2 = c$, and have no constraint of production capacity. Thus, either firm is capable of serving all demand in the market. On the demand side, we assume that a continuum of consumers are uniformly distributed along the street.[2] This means that any arbitrary length of the street, say x miles $(0 \le x \le L)$, regardless of where, contains the proportion of consumers equal to x/L (Figure 14.2a). Assuming that each consumer incurs an identical transportation cost of t per mile $(t > 0)$, each consumer will prefer the location that is proximate to him, other things being equal. We assume that each consumer has the same willingness to pay higher than or equal to the prices of the two products, and buys one unit of the products. Thus, the total quantity of the two products demanded in the market will be equal to the number of consumers.

Suppose that firms F_1 and F_2 charge an identical price, $p_1 = p_2 = p > c$, for the moment, and assume that they do not change their prices when choosing their locations afterwards. Where should the two firms locate and thus differentiate their products on location? Obviously, the optimal locations entail that F_1 and F_2 maximize their profits π_1 and π_2, respectively:

$$\pi_1 = (p - c)q_1, \tag{14.1}$$

$$\pi_2 = (p - c)q_2, \tag{14.2}$$

where $p_1 = p_2 = p$ and $c_1 = c_2 = c$ are given, q_1 is the quantity sold by F_1, and q_2 is the quantity sold by F_2. Hence $q = q_1 + q_2$ is the total quantity of the two products sold in the market, equal to the number of consumers in the market, which is given as well. Therefore, we actually have only one variable in equations (14.1) and (14.2), q_1 or q_2. The optimization problem is, in fact, that each firm maximizes its own market share, namely F_1 maximizing q_1 and F_2 maximizing q_2. As we shall illustrate, the market share of one firm depends entirely on its location along the street against the other's location. Thus, the profit-maximizing problem in the Hotelling model is translated into the problem of location choice. This in turn suggests product differentiation executed by F_1 and F_2 on location as long as they end up choosing different locations.

14.2.2 Location choice and price competition

In the first stage, suppose that F_1 chooses to locate at an arbitrary point A to the left of the center M (Figure 14.2b). Given F_1's location, the best location for F_2 is to the right of F_1 but as close to F_1 as possible, which is denoted by point B. This location enables F_2 to acquire all the consumers to its right and also half of the consumers divided equidistantly between them, leaving F_1 all the consumers to its left plus the other half between them (Figure 14.2b). It is worth noting that it is in the best interest of F_2

to narrow down the distance between point *A* and point *B* as much as possible, yet never to locate back to back with F_1. This allows F_2 to maximize the market share to its right while leaving as little as possible to share with F_1. In fact, as long as F_1 locates to the left, regardless of where, of the center *M*, F_2's current location will always generate more than 50% of the market share, leaving F_1 less than 50%. Of course, F_1 can relocate given F_2's location. In the second stage, F_1 will act the same way as F_2 did by locating to the right of F_2 but as close to F_2 as possible, denoted by point *C*. This relocation allows F_1 to maximize the market share to its right while sharing as little market share as possible with F_2. Thus, F_1 ends up acquiring more than 50% of the market share, leaving F_2 less than 50%. Note that neither firm will choose to locate side by side with the other, because it would otherwise be able to obtain more than 50% of the market share.

The game of location choice illustrated above will continue until one firm eventually ends up locating halfway along the street, denoted by point *M* (Figure 14.2c). Suppose that F_1 locates halfway along the street first (Figure 14.2c). Given the central location of F_1, it is not difficult to conclude that F_1 will invariably end up acquiring more than 50% of the market share regardless of where F_2 chooses to locate except in the center the same as F_1. Actually, only if F_2 chooses to locate in the center can F_2 acquire 50% of the market share, which is the maximum for F_2 given F_1's location in the center. Nevertheless, F_2 would acquire more than 50% of the market share in the center if F_1 chose to divert from the center, regardless of where F_1 would locate afterwards. The same holds true for F_1 to locate in the center side by side with F_2 if F_2 occupies the center in the first place. As long as both are in the center of the street back to back, there is no incentive for either one to divert from the center. If so, the one which relocates away from the center ends up obtaining less than 50% of the market share. Because F_1 and F_2 cannot change their prices as assumed, they will not only end up locating back to back in the center but will also stick to the central location. Hence the central location of the street is their equilibrium location in the market (Figure 14.2c).

Now let's assume that both firms can change their prices in the equilibrium location. As a matter of fact, as long as F_1 and F_2 locate back to back in the center of the street, one firm's immediate interest is to undercut the other to increase market share (Figure 14.2c). If F_1 undercuts F_2 by an infinitesimal amount ($p_1 < p_2$), F_1 will take the whole market. Of course, F_2 can retaliate by acting exactly the same way as F_1 did in order to corner the market. Such price competition will continue until one firm cuts the price to the marginal cost, which pushes the other also to lower price to the marginal cost, and hence $p_1 = p_2 = c$. As long as $p_1 = p_2 = c$, there is no incentive for either firm to divert price from the marginal cost, which is the same conclusion we derived in Bertrand competition in Chapter 9. Therefore, $p_1 = p_2 = c$ is the equilibrium price under which each firm ends up obtaining 50% of the market share but zero profits. In fact, even if we allow F_1 and F_2 to compete on location and price simultaneously, they will also end up locating in the center of the street and charging prices $p_1 = p_2 = c$, the same equilibrium location and price we derived in the two successive stages. This is because any discrepancy between the two firms in location and/or in price will give one firm an advantage over the other, which in turn will cause the other to retaliate until both reach the equilibrium.

14.2.3 Law of minimum product differentiation

The equilibrium location, where firms F_1 and F_2 locate back to back in the center of the street, is referred to as the law of minimum product differentiation. That is, the two products are not differentiated at all in equilibrium. Thus, the two products sold by F_1 and F_2 are not differentiated on location nor, as assumed, on all other attributes, and hence they end up being completely identical. In minimum product differentiation, each consumer, regardless of where he is along the street, will randomize over the two firms to patronize. That is, consumers have no preference whatsoever on location when both firms locate back to back in the center of the street. Given the same price, minimum product differentiation will also arise as long as the two firms choose to locate at the same place, regardless of where. This will also lead consumers to randomly choose either of them to patronize. As long as F_1 and F_2 locate differently, their products are horizontally differentiated to some extent, whereby consumers closer to F_1 will always prefer F_1 and those closer to F_2 will always prefer F_2. Only the consumer locating equidistantly between F_1 and F_2 will have no preference, and thus will randomly choose either F_1 or F_2 to patronize. Nonetheless, all locations other than the center of the street are not stable and thus are not in market equilibrium.

Since the two products are not differentiated when both firms locate back to back in the center, the two firms will divert to price competition, eventually driving price down to their marginal costs. If the two products are not differentiated, neither firm is able to obtain market power that would enable it to charge a price higher than marginal cost. If we disregard consumer preference, Hotelling competition will be no different from Bertrand competition, in which the two products are assumed to be identical, and hence price competition is the only firm behavior, leading to $p_1 = p_2 = c$ as well. Also, both the Hotelling model and Bertrand model end up with the same market outcome as in perfect competition, in which firms make zero profits in the short run. The difference in Hotelling competition though is that minimum product differentiation is optimal for duopolists but not socially optimal as far as consumers are concerned. The reason is that Hotelling competition is grounded on consumer preference, yet consumer preference is not satisfied when F_1 and F_2 locate back to back in the center of the street. As long as consumer preference exists due to positive transportation costs, the social optimum entails providing differentiated rather than homogenous products.

14.3 Maximum product differentiation

14.3.1 What is maximum product differentiation

Based on the same assumptions, we proceed to address the second question in the Hotelling model. Given different locations of the two firms, how would they set price? This is a question of how the prices of two differentiated products are determined. For expository simplicity, suppose that firms F_1 and F_2 locate at the two ends of the street, and assume that they do not change their locations throughout

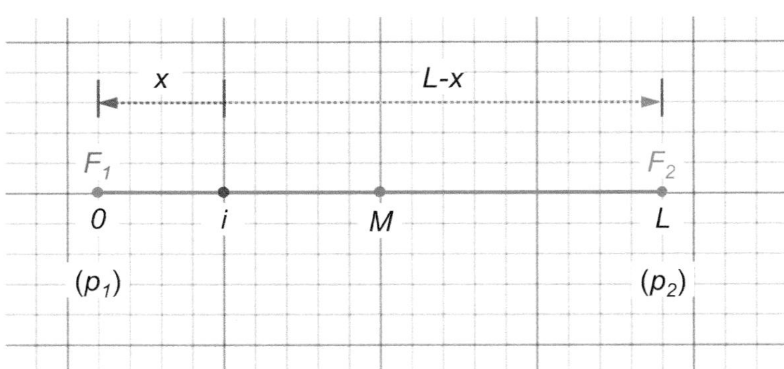

Figure 14.3
Maximum product differentiation and pricing

competition (Figure 14.3). Assuming that both firms charge the same price, $p_1 = p_2 > c$, F_1 and F_2 each will end up acquiring 50% of the market share, the same as in minimum product differentiation. It is noteworthy that the 50% of the market share of F_1 is from all the consumers between F_1 and the center of the street while of F_2 it is from all the consumers between F_2 and the center of the street. That is, separated by the center of the street, all the consumers to the left of the center prefer F_1 while all the consumers to the right prefer F_2. Therefore, consumers do have a preference yet have no consensus on which one is preferred. That is, horizontal product differentiation on location arises when F_1 and F_2 locate differently. Since the two ends of the street represent the longest distance between any two arbitrary locations along the street, F_1 and F_2 execute maximum product differentiation on location by locating at the two ends.

Obviously, now one firm would immediately consider lowering the price of its product in order to increase its market share, provided that the other does not change price. If one firm, say F_1, undercuts the other, F_2, by an arbitrarily small amount, obviously F_1 will obtain more than 50% of the market share by luring some consumers to the right of the center who would otherwise prefer F_2. Likewise, F_2 can retaliate by undercutting F_1 to increase its market share beyond 50% through tempting the consumers of F_1. Depending on how much p_1 changes relative to p_2, or vice versa, any arbitrary consumer, i, regardless of where he is along the street, will swing back and forth in choosing between F_1 and F_2 (Figure 14.3). If p_1 is sufficiently lower than p_2, F_1 is even able to corner the whole market, and the same holds true for F_2 if p_2 is sufficiently lower than p_1. As long as F_1 and F_2 no longer have incentives to alter their prices, or no matter what prices they charge they would not be able to increase their market shares further, the market equilibrium on price is reached.

14.3.2 Equilibrium price in maximum product differentiation

On the demand side the price equilibrium implies that any arbitrary consumer i is indifferent in choosing between F_1 and F_2 under certain p_1 and p_2. Suppose that consumer i locates a distance of x miles away from F_1 ($0 \le x \le L$) (Figure 14.3). Then he can be anywhere along the street depending on the value of x, and can thus represent any single consumer along the street. Suppose that consumer i's willingness to pay is r, and $r \ge p_1$, p_2 as we assumed earlier. Thus, all consumers in the market will choose either F_1 or F_2 to patronize, and the total quantity demanded can be represented by the length of the street L. If consumer i as the marginal consumer is indifferent between F_1 and F_2, it follows that all the consumers locating between firm F_1 and consumer i will certainly prefer F_1, and the remaining consumers will prefer F_2 (Figure 14.3). This means that x denotes the quantity demanded for F_1, $q_1 = x$, and thus $L - x$ is the quantity demanded for F_2, $q_2 = L - x$, given the prices p_1 and p_2. Since consumer i is indifferent between F_1 and F_2, his consumer surplus is the same regardless of whether he purchases from F_1 or F_2. Note that consumer i's surplus is his willingness to pay, subtracting the sum of the price of the firm he chooses and the transportation cost that he incurs to reach that firm. Denoting consumer i's surplus when he makes a purchase from F_1 as CS_1 and from F_2 as CS_2, we have

$$CS_1 = r - (p_1 + tx), \tag{14.3}$$

$$CS_2 = r - \left[p_2 + t(L - x)\right], \tag{14.4}$$

where both the length of the street L and the average transportation cost t are constants. As we explained above, the price equilibrium is determined when consumer i is indifferent between F_1 and F_2 given their prices. Therefore, consumer i's surplus obtained from F_1 and F_2 must be equal. Let $CS_1 = CS_2$, we obtain consumers' demand function for F_1 by solving x:

$$x = \frac{p_2 - p_1}{2t} + \frac{L}{2}. \tag{14.5}$$

Equation (14.5) suggests that consumers' demand function for F_1 is a function of its price p_1 given F_2's price p_2. Given F_1's demand x, consumers' demand function for F_2 is simply $L - x$, which is all the remaining consumers in the market:

$$L - x = \frac{p_1 - p_2}{2t} + \frac{L}{2}. \tag{14.6}$$

Equation (14.6) suggests that consumers' demand function for F_2 is its price p_2 given F_1's price p_1. Since the length of the street L and the average transportation cost t are two constants, consumers' demands for F_1 and F_2 depend entirely on their prices p_1 and p_2. Given one firm's price, consumers' demand for the other firm will depend entirely on the price it charges, and vice versa. After specifying F_1's demand, $q_1 = x$, in equation (14.5) and F_2's demand, $q_2 = L - x$, in equation (14.6), we can further specify F_1's profit function in equation (14.1) and F_2's in equation (14.2), respectively:

$$\pi_1 = (p_1 - c)q_1 = (p_1 - c)\left(\frac{p_2 - p_1}{2t} + \frac{L}{2}\right), \tag{14.7}$$

$$\pi_2 = (p_2 - c)q_2 = (p_2 - c)\left(\frac{p_1 - p_2}{2t} + \frac{L}{2}\right). \tag{14.8}$$

Since the marginal cost c is also a constant, the two firms' profits π_1 and π_2 also depend entirely on p_1 and p_2, respectively. Equation (14.7) suggests that given F_2's price p_2, F_1's profit π_1 depends entirely on its price p_1; and equation (14.8) suggests that given F_1's price p_1, F_2's profit π_2 depends entirely on its price p_2. Note that in the Hotelling model a change in quantity demanded is due ultimately to a price change, and therefore the profit ends up being a function of price instead of quantity demanded. Thus, the profit-maximizing condition for F_1 is that its marginal profit $M\pi_1$ with respect to p_1 is zero. For F_1, we differentiate the profit π_1 with respect to price p_1, and let the marginal profit be zero:

$$\frac{\partial \pi_1}{\partial p_1} = \left(\frac{p_2 - p_1}{2t} + \frac{L}{2}\right) - \frac{p_1 - c}{2t} = 0. \tag{14.9}$$

Rearranging equation (14.9) we obtain p_1 as a function of p_2:

$$p_1 = \frac{p_2 + Lt + c}{2}. \tag{14.10}$$

Likewise, the profit-maximizing condition for F_2 is that its marginal profit $M\pi_2$ with respect to p_2 is equal to zero. We differentiate the profit π_2 with respect to price p_2, and let the marginal profit be zero:

$$\frac{\partial \pi_2}{\partial p_2} = \left(\frac{p_1 - p_2}{2t} + \frac{L}{2}\right) - \frac{p_2 - c}{2t} = 0. \tag{14.11}$$

Rearranging equation (14.11) we obtain p_2 as a function of p_1:

$$p_2 = \frac{p_1 + Lt + c}{2}. \tag{14.12}$$

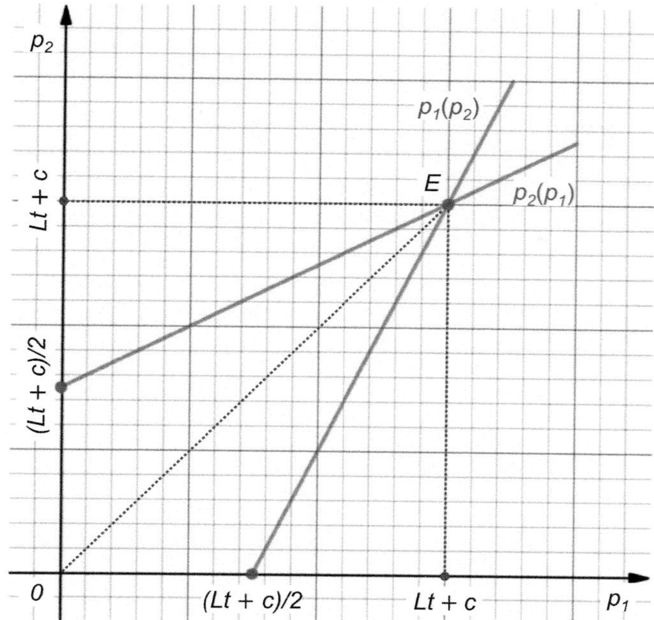

Figure 14.4
Price responses in maximum product differentiation

From equations (14.10) and (14.12) we know that the only variable that one firm can manipulate is its own price, which depends entirely on the price of the other. Hence the two functions are referred to as the price response functions of the two firms engaging in price competition. Because F_1 and F_2 are symmetric, meaning that both are equally interchangeable, their price response functions have the same structure: both are linear with the same slope, $1/2$, and the same intercept, $(Lt+c)/2$, contingent on whether p_1 or p_2 is seen as the independent variable. Figure 14.4 depicts the two price response functions (14.10) and (14.12), with p_1 on the x-axis and p_2 on the y-axis. We can see that p_2 increases by a rate of 1/2 of p_1, and vice versa, until both curves intersect at point E $(Lt + c,\ Lt + c)$, at which the price equilibrium is determined. As long as $p_1 = p_2 = Lt+c$, F_1 and F_2 cannot charge prices other than $Lt+c$ to increase their profits, nor do they have any incentive to do so.

Mathematically we can also solve the two equations, $p_1(p_2)$ in equation (14.10) and $p_2(p_1)$ in equation (14.12), by plugging one into the other. Thus, we obtain

$$p_1 = p_2 = Lt+c. \tag{14.13}$$

When firms F_1 and F_2 locate at the two ends of the street executing maximum product differentiation, they end up charging the same price also as in minimum product

differentiation but each obtaining the same markup $p-c=Lt>0$. Therefore, product differentiation endows both firms with market power as long as consumers have a preference on location that entails product differentiation. Intuitively, this conclusion can be extended to cases where F_1 and F_2 choose any different locations other than the two ends of the street. This means that F_1 and F_2 execute some, but not the maximum, degree of product differentiation on location. On the one hand, each firm will invariably end up charging a price above its marginal cost, but the markup will be smaller than Lt obtained in maximum product differentiation. On the other hand, the two firms' prices in market equilibrium will not be the same unless their locations are symmetric along the street, which means that they are equidistant from the two ends of the street or toward the center.

14.3.3 Sources of firm profit

From the analysis above we conclude that the markup $p-c=Lt$ obtained by firms F_1 and F_2 depends entirely on the two constants, the length of the street L and the average transportation cost t. Other things being equal, the larger the L, the greater the markup that both firms will obtain, and the larger the t, the greater the markup that both firms will obtain as well. Given the equilibrium price $p_1 = p_2 = Lt + c$ in equation (14.13) we can calculate the maximized profits of F_1 and F_2, respectively, by referring to equations (14.7) and (14.8):

$$\pi_1 = \pi_2 = \frac{1}{2}L^2 t. \tag{14.14}$$

Equation (14.14) suggests that total profit in the market is $L^2 t$, which is split between F_1 and F_2. Given maximum product differentiation, we find that not only the equilibrium price but also total profit $L^2 t$ depends on the length of the street L and the average transportation cost t. The larger the L, the greater the total profit; and the larger the t, the greater the total profit as well, and hence the greater the profit each firm shares. This conclusion is not difficult to comprehend as we have illustrated above that firm profit in the Hotelling model depends on the market share of each firm which in turn depends on their prices p_1 and p_2, given their locations. In market equilibrium, p_1 and p_2 depend on L and t as we illustrated above, and so does firm profit. Equation (14.14) also suggests that holding the length of the street L constant, total profit grows linearly with the average transportation cost t; holding t constant, total profit grows quadratically with L. Nevertheless, as long as F_1 and F_2 do not collude, as assumed, to form a monopoly or collaboratively execute maximum product differentiation by locating at the two ends of the street, maximum product differentiation is unstable. In order to obtain a larger market share, F_1 and F_2 will eventually relocate until they end up locating back to back halfway along the street, and hence the law of minimum product differentiation still holds.

14.4 Consumer preference and product differentiation

14.4.1 Dispersion of consumer preference

In maximum product differentiation in which F_1 and F_2 locate at the two ends of the street, the equilibrium price depends entirely on the length of the street L and the average transportation cost t, and so does firm profit. In essence, L measures the extent to which consumer preferences on location are dispersed in the market, other things being equal. The longer the L, the more dispersed the consumer preferences, meaning that consumer preferences increasingly spread on location. If $L = 0$, there will be no dispersion of consumer preference at all, a case where consumer preferences converge to a point. Hence, no consumer preference can be created on location. We end up with $p_1 = p_2 = c$, and $\pi_1 = \pi_2 = 0$, the same conclusion as in minimum product differentiation in which F_1 and F_2 locate back to back halfway along the street with positive L and t. This means that despite F_1 and F_2 locating at the two ends of the street or differently, their products cannot be differentiated on location anymore, because consumer preference on location disappears in the first place when $L = 0$. Therefore, F_1 and F_2 are homogenous in all aspects, and consumers are indifferent between the two. If L is infinite, consumer preferences will infinitely spread on location. Hence any two different locations for F_1 and F_2 along the street suggest that their products are extremely differentiated.

Suppose that along a 4-mile long street ($L = 4$) are five consumers, i_1, i_2, i_3, i_4, and i_5, uniformly distributed. Each consumer incurs the same transportation cost of \$1 per mile ($t = 1$). For convenience, the five consumers' locations are also denoted by their respective identities (Figure 14.5a). Thus, any two consumers are 1 mile away as the

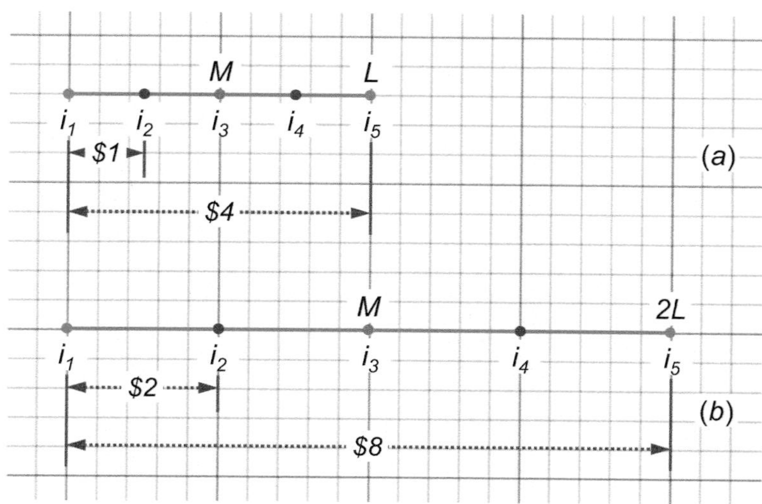

Figure 14.5
Dispersion of consumer preference

minimum, namely the distance between any two neighboring consumers, and 4 miles away as the maximum, namely the distance between consumers i_1 and i_5 at the two ends. For example, to make consumer i_1 indifferent between locations i_1 and i_5, \$4 needs to be compensated to him by a firm locating at i_5, other things being equal. This means that his own location, i_1, is worth \$4 against location i_5. To enumerate, his preference for location i_1 is worth \$3 against i_4, \$2 against i_3, and \$1 against i_2. Thus, the maximum dispersion of consumer preference between locations i_1 and i_5 is valued at \$4, and the minimum dispersion between any two neighboring locations is valued at \$1. If we double the length of the street from 4 miles to 8 miles, consumer i_1's preference for his own location, i_1, is worth \$8 against i_5 (Figure 14.5b). Hence the maximum dispersion of consumer preference is doubled, and so are the minimum dispersion and any other degrees of dispersion. Thus, consumer preference becomes more dispersed as L lengthens. When $L = 0$, there will be no dispersion of consumer preference at all, hence no consumer preference on location.

14.4.2 Intensity of consumer preference

Now let the average transportation cost t change while holding L constant, other things being equal. Suppose that t increases from \$1 per mile to \$2 per mile, and then to \$10 per mile, along the 4-mile long street. Then consumer i_1's preference for location i_1 against the neighboring location i_2 is now worth \$2 and \$10, respectively, as the minimum dispersion of consumer preference (Figure 14.6). As t increases, consumer i_1's preference for location i_1 is worth more against i_2, meaning that his preference for his own location i_1 intensifies. Thus, t measures the degree to which consumer preference for a given location intensifies. If $t = 0$, consumer i_1 will have no preference whatsoever for his own location over all other locations, and hence he is indifferent among all locations. This is because it costs him nothing to travel to whatever location he wants along the street, and hence his own location is worthless against any other locations. Thus, there is no intensity in consumer preference on location. This applies to all other consumers as well. Since no consumer preference

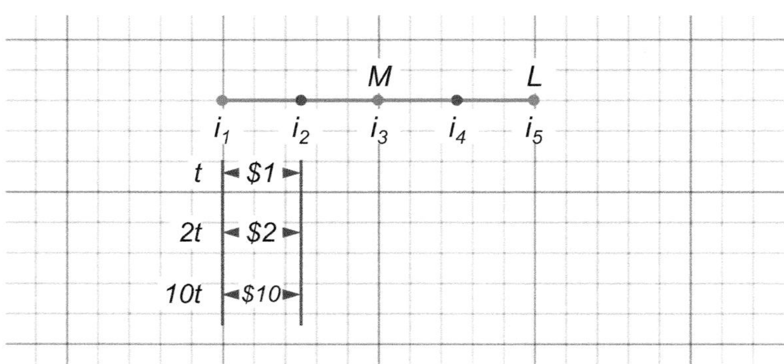

Figure 14.6
Intensity of consumer preference

can be created when $t = 0$, all consumers are indifferent between F_1 and F_2, regardless of where the two firms locate. Therefore, F_1 and F_2 end up with minimum product differentiation regardless. When $t = 0$, we also end up with $p_1 = p_2 = c$, and $\pi_1 = \pi_2 = 0$, the same conclusion as when $L = 0$. If t is infinite, all consumers will stick to their own locations, and will never compromise their preferences.

In fact, as long as $L = 0$ and/or $t = 0$, it does not matter where F_1 and F_2 choose to locate, because they are no longer able to differentiate their products on location. All locations end up with minimum product differentiation, whereby all consumers randomize over the two firms to patronize. This is because no consumer preference whatsoever can be created on location. Thus, differentiating products on location makes no sense to the firms. Suppose that consumers can buy the same airline tickets online from two travel agencies, other things being equal. Obviously, it does not matter where the two travel agencies locate geographically, because consumers have no preference on location in the first place. Thus, the two travel agencies' locations make no difference to their booking services from a consumer's point of view. In this case the geographical location should not be the attribute on which the two agencies aim to differentiate their booking services. Only when two products are differentiated on the attribute for which consumers have preference can product differentiation on that attribute be economically viable. Thus, consumer preference and product differentiation are the two sides of the same coin. On the one hand, it is consumer preference that leads to product differentiation on the supply side; and on the other hand, it is product differentiation that manifests consumer preference on the demand side.

14.4.3 Product differentiation beyond location

In the Hotelling model both the length of the street L and the average transportation cost t are instrumental in creating consumer preference on location, on which products can be differentiated. While location plays a pivotal role in setting up many hospitality businesses, such as hotels, restaurants, bars, and so on, it is by no means the only attribute on which products are differentiated. When the Hotelling model is extended from location to other attributes, such as color, size, and flavor of a product, to name a few, the length of the street metaphorically suggests the dispersion of consumer preference on any attribute concerned, and the average transportation cost is a metaphor of the degree to which consumers would compromise their preferences and be willing to change their preferences. For instance, L can be specified as a spectrum of color from white on the one end to black on the other with various evenly spaced colors in between, and t measures the degree to which consumers prefer each color against the less preferred one(s). As L extends, consumer preferences will spread on the color spectrum, and as t increases, consumer preference for a particular color will intensify, other things being equal. Of course, L and t are continuous for location, but might be discrete when applied to other attributes.

Therefore, firms can differentiate their products on any attribute for which consumers have preference, and the Hotelling model can provide compelling explanations. First, the extent to which products can be differentiated depends on the extent to which consumer preferences are dispersed in the market, measured by the length of the street L. Second, given a certain dispersion of consumer preference, the extent to which products are perceived as different depends on how intensive consumer preference is, measured by the average transportation cost t. Thus, not only the market power of firms but also their profits are ultimately derived from the dispersion of consumer preference in the market as well as the intensity of consumer preference. On the one hand, firms are inclined to imitate each other's products, ending up charging similar yet low prices, particularly when the dispersion and/or intensity of consumer preference are negligible. On the other hand, firms are enticed to differentiate their products drastically, which enables them to obtain tempting markups, particularly when the dispersion and/or intensity of consumer preference are substantial. If L and/or t increase, firms will always make their products as differentiated as possible because consumer preferences are increasingly dispersed and/or intensified.

14.5 Product differentiation and market efficiency

In minimum product differentiation in which F_1 and F_2 locate back to back halfway along the street, price competition ends up both charging $p_1 = p_2 = c$ and obtaining zero profits. Neither firm has market power over the other to raise or lower price, and thus the market price is equal to the marginal costs of the two firms. This conclusion is, in part, the same as what we obtained from perfect competition and Bertrand competition. In both perfect competition and Bertrand competition, firms are price takers, produce a quantity at which marginal revenue equals marginal cost equals market price, $P = MR = MC$, and earn zero profits in the short run. The fundamental difference is that both perfect competition and Bertrand competition are socially optimal whereas minimum product differentiation in the Hotelling model is not, because social surplus is not maximized. As long as two firms end up with minimum product differentiation in market equilibrium with positive L and t, social surplus is not maximized. In other words, social optimum in the Hotelling model entails a certain degree of product differentiation because consumer preference exists in the first place. Therefore, the two firms should locate differently: precisely one-quarter of the length of the street from both ends to reach social optimum (Figure 14.7). This ends up minimizing the distances between all consumers and the two firms. In other words, all consumer preferences are perfectly addressed by such product differentiation.

As we have discussed, minimum product differentiation will also arise as long as $L = 0$ and/or $t = 0$, regardless of where the two firms locate along the street. This ends up with the same conclusion, $p_1 = p_2 = c$ and $\pi_1 = \pi_2 = 0$, as in perfect competition and Bertrand competition. Nevertheless, in this case minimum product differentiation is indeed socially optimal because consumers have no preference on location in the first place, and therefore product differentiation on location becomes futile. Minimum product differentiation in the Hotelling model is thus

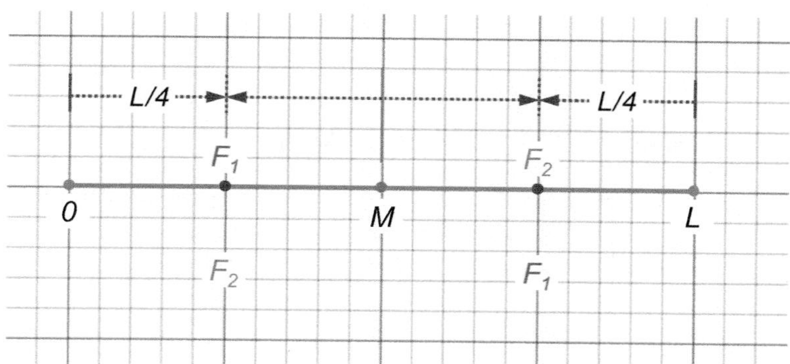

Figure 14.7
Social optimum and product differentiation

relegated to Bertrand competition in which duopolists compete only on price with homogenous products. It is also the same as firms in perfect competition which supply homogenous products, ending up with perfect market efficiency. This means that as long as consumer preference exists, that is, both $L > 0$ *and* $t > 0$, minimum product differentiation with two firms locating halfway along the street is in market equilibrium but not socially optimal. Nor is maximum product differentiation with two firms locating at the two ends of the street socially optimal, because it also fails to minimize transportation costs of consumers, and hence cannot adequately address consumer preference on location.

Summary

1. Product differentiation consists of horizontal product differentiation and vertical product differentiation. The former suggests relative consumer preference on a product attribute while the latter suggests absolute consumer preference.
2. Given two products, *A* and *B*, sold for the same price as assumed, they are horizontally differentiated if consumers have no consensus on which one is preferred, and vertically differentiated if otherwise.
3. The Hotelling model explains product differentiation in a way that two firms sell two products that are identical in all aspects but may differ in the locations that the two firms choose. The two products are differentiated on location as long as the two firms locate apart from each other along the street.
4. Regardless of whether the two firms compete for location and price successively or simultaneously, they end up locating back to back halfway along the street and charging the same price equal to their marginal costs. This is the market equilibrium in location and price, illustrating the law of minimum product differentiation.
5. In minimum product differentiation consumers have no preference whatsoever for the two products and thus randomize the two firms to patronize. The two firms equally split the market and earn zero economic profits in market equilibrium.

6. In the Hotelling model maximum product differentiation is manifested when the two firms locate at the two ends of the street. If they cannot change their locations, they will end up charging the same price above their marginal costs. Hence product differentiation endows firms with market power and markups.
7. In maximum product differentiation the two firms also equally split the market but consumers to the left of the center unanimously prefer the firm at the left end and those to the right of the center prefer the firm at the right end. The two firms end up charging the same price above their marginal costs and equally splitting the market profit.
8. The length of the street L suggests the dispersion of consumer preference and the average transportation cost t measures the intensity of consumer preference. Other things being equal, the longer the street, the more dispersed the consumer preferences; and the greater the average transportation cost, the more intensified the consumer preferences.
9. In both the Hotelling model and the Bertrand model two firms charge the same price equal to their marginal costs in market equilibrium, but the market equilibrium is perfectly efficient in the Bertrand model but not in the Hotelling model.
10. As long as consumer preference exists, both minimum and maximum product differentiation in the Hotelling model are not socially optimal. The reason is that they fail to address consumer preference adequately and equally.

REVIEW QUESTIONS

Each question has four options, and there is only one correct answer to each question.

1. In hotel classification there are six classes, luxury, upper upscale, upscale, upper midscale, midscale, and economy. Under each class there are a number of chains. For instance, major chains in luxury class include Marriott, Shangri-La, Ritz-Carlton, and so on, and major chains in economy class include Super 8, Days Inn, Motel 6, and so on. Suppose that all the hotel rooms are sold for the same price. Which of the following is correct?
   A) Luxury and economy classes are horizontal product differentiation.
   B) Upscale and midscale classes are vertical product differentiation.
   C) Marriott and Shangri-La are vertical product differentiation.
   D) Ritz-Carlton and Super 8 are horizontal product differentiation.
2. Which of the following is correct regarding the Hotelling model?
   A) It addresses competition stability of duopolists.
   B) It addresses location choice in the hotel industry.
   C) It addresses oligopoly with more than two firms.
   D) It addresses the effect of transportation on tourism demand.

3. Why do we need to assume a uniform distribution of consumers along the street in developing the Hotelling model?
   A) Equilibrium location would not be in the center of the street otherwise.
   B) Equilibrium price would not be equal to the marginal cost otherwise.
   C) Minimum product differentiation would not be possible otherwise.
   D) Competition between the two firms would not arise otherwise.
4. Two firms sell the same ice cream along a 2-mile long beach and do not collude. Suppose that they have the same marginal costs, and consumers are uniformly distributed along the beach with a positive transportation cost per mile. Which of the following is INCORRECT?
   A) They end up obtaining a zero profit each.
   B) They end up acquiring half of the consumers each.
   C) They end up differentiating their products horizontally.
   D) They end up charging the same price equal to the marginal costs.
5. Two restaurants locate at the two ends of a 5-mile long street selling the same products with the same constant marginal costs. Suppose that consumers are uniformly distributed along the street, incurring a positive transportation cost per mile. If the two restaurants cannot change their locations, which of the following is correct?
   A) They engage in minimum product differentiation.
   B) They charge different prices greater than their marginal costs.
   C) They are randomly patronized by the consumers.
   D) They obtain half of the consumers each.

Read the following to answer Questions 6 and 7.

Suppose that two vendors sell the same ice cream at the two ends of a 2-mile long beach, and they cannot change their locations. Suppose that the marginal cost of selling an ice cream is $5 for both vendors, and consumers are uniformly distributed along the beach.

6. Suppose that each consumer incurs a transportation cost of $0.5 per mile. Which of the following is correct?
   A) They end up charging an identical price below $6 per ice cream.
   B) They end up charging an identical price above $6 per ice cream.
   C) They end up charging an identical price equal to $6 per ice cream.
   D) All of the above.
7. Suppose that each consumer encounters a zero transportation cost per mile. Which of the following is correct regarding product differentiation?
   A) They will engage in minimum product differentiation.
   B) They will engage in maximum product differentiation.
   C) Each vendor will acquire half of the consumers adjacent to it.
   D) Each vendor will obtain the same positive profit.
8. Suppose that two car manufacturers produce an automobile that is identical in all aspects but color, and they incur the same marginal costs in production. Consumer

preference is uniformly distributed along a color spectrum from white to black. Assume that one manufacturer chooses black and the other chooses gray for their cars, and they cannot change the colors afterwards. Which of the following is correct if they charge the same price for their cars?

A) They will engage in minimum product differentiation.
B) They will engage in maximum product differentiation.
C) They will earn positive but different profits.
D) They will split the market equally.

9. Which of the following is correct regarding the economic meanings of the length of the street L and the average transportation cost t in the Hotelling model?

A) L suggests the intensity of consumer preference in the market.
B) t suggests the dispersion of consumer preference in the market.
C) $L = 0$ suggests maximum product differentiation in the market.
D) $t = 0$ suggests minimum product differentiation in the market.

10. Which of the following is INCORRECT regarding the market equilibria in the models of Hotelling competition, Bertrand competition, and perfect competition?

A) Firms in the three models earn zero profits in equilibrium.
B) Firms in the three models obtain zero markups in equilibrium.
C) Firms in the three models achieve social optimum in equilibrium.
D) Firms in the three models face perfectly elastic demand in equilibrium.

Problem solving

1. Suppose that two restaurants (F_1 and F_2) sell an identical burger with the same marginal costs of \$2.0 per burger and compete with each other. Consumers are uniformly distributed along a 6-mile long street, and each consumer encounters a transportation cost of \$0.50 per mile. We know that F_1 locates at one-third of the length of the street to the left end while F_2 is at the right end, and assume that they cannot change their locations. Suppose that F_1 charges \$5.0 per burger and will not change its price afterwards. If F_2 aims to acquire 50% of the market share, how much should F_2 charge?

2. McDonald's stresses the importance of location for consumers on its website: "McDonald's looks for the best locations within the marketplace to provide our customers with convenience. We build quality restaurants in neighborhoods as well as airports, malls, tollways and colleges at a value to our customers."[3] Suppose that consumers are uniformly distributed along a street with fixed length (L) miles and encounter a positive transportation cost (t) per mile, and there are no incumbent and potential competitors. If McDonald's plans to open two outlets along the street, what would be the best locations for the two outlets that can manifest its value proposition to customers?

3. Suppose that Coca-Cola and Pepsi decide to sell a cola which is homogenous except for sweetness, and assume that their brands have no influence on consumer choice. According to market research, consumer preference for sweetness is uniformly distributed along a spectrum from 0 to 10 degrees, with 0 indicating unsweetened and 10 indicating the highest degree of sweetness that consumers can accept. Each consumer is willing to compromise his preference to accept lower or higher degrees of sweetness, provided that a certain price discount per degree is offered. Suppose that Coca-Cola and Pepsi have the same marginal costs of selling the cola, and no additional cost is incurred in changing sweetness. If they do not collude, what will the sweetness of the cola be in the market?

Solutions to all review questions and problem solving tasks are included in the Support Material for this book, which can be accessed at www.routledge.com/9780367897352.

Notes

1 We use the two notations F_1 and F_2 to refer to the two firms in duopoly as well as their products.
2 We shall illustrate that the absolute number of consumers is irrelevant to the analysis.
3 McDonald's. U.S. real estate. Accessed on September 2, 2020 from https://www.mcdonalds.com/us/en-us/about-us/franchising/real-estate.html.

Bibliography

Harold, H. (1929). Stability in competition. *Economic Journal, 39*(153), 41–57.

d'Aspremont, C., Gabszewicz, J. J., & Thisse, J. F. (1979). On Hotelling's "Stability in competition". *Econometrica: Journal of the Econometric Society*, 1145–1150.

15 McDonald's versus Burger King in product differentiation[1]

This chapter is an application and also an extension of the standard Hotelling model. In this case study we focus on the location choice of two asymmetric firms, McDonald's and Burger King. This means that the two firms differ in their marginal costs among other things that will affect their location choices, and hence product differentiation on location. Drawing from simulation and empirical evidence, we first present the results of the price and profit responses of McDonald's and Burger King as one locates apart from the other and vice versa. Second, we examine the location response of McDonald's to the location of Burger King and vice versa, which demonstrates an asymmetric location pattern that differs from what the standard Hotelling model would predict. Third, we conclude that the location choices of McDonald's and Burger King vary by firm asymmetry, market size, and the distribution of consumers, all of which are not taken into account in the standard Hotelling model.

AFTER STUDYING THIS CHAPTER, YOU SHOULD BE ABLE TO:

- Understand and explain the causes of firm asymmetry between McDonald's and Burger King;
- Understand and explain the differences in firm profits and pricing of McDonald's and Burger King as they locate apart from each other;
- Analyze the location responses of McDonald's and Burger King as one locates apart from the other and vice versa; and
- Understand and explain the effects of firm asymmetry, market size, and consumer distribution on the location choice of firms.

15.1 Firms in the fast food industry

The fast food industry is dominated by a few large restaurant franchisors, such as McDonald's, Burger King, Kentucky Fried Chicken (KFC), and Subway to name a few.

They compete globally through increasing consumer awareness of and loyalty to their brands. The fast food industry in the United States alone generated a revenue of US$273 billion in 2019, accounting for 31.6% of the total revenue in the U.S. restaurant industry.[2] McDonald's has been the leading chain not only in the U.S. but worldwide. In 2019 McDonald's reaped a revenue of US$21.08 billion worldwide versus US$1.78 billion by Burger King,[3] its closest rival in terms of a comparable range of products. As a matter of fact, the competition between restaurant franchisors is manifested by their numerous franchisees vying for consumers in localized markets under the brands of franchisors. In a local market, say a city or even a county, franchisee outlets under different brands compete ferociously with each other for acquiring customers. A study in the U.S. shows that McDonald's and Burger King are the closest competitors within a distance of two miles.[4] This by and large conforms to our everyday experience as consumers in deciding which one to patronize as they usually locate next to each other in shopping malls and business centers.

One of the major reasons that the fast food franchising has been so successful is the universal standard of products and experience set by each franchisor. The universal standard applies not only to the food but to a wide range of peripherals, such as uniform signage of outlets, similar menu boards, and consistent layouts of dining space, all of which make consumers' dining experience across outlets almost identical. Obviously, the brands of franchisors matter to consumers, and there is no doubt, for instance, that McDonald's and Burger King have their own loyal customers who are lukewarm about the availability of the other. Yet the locations of franchisee outlets are arguably more crucial in affecting consumer choice and in the success of the fast food businesses as a whole. To the vast majority of consumers fast and casual dining is of low-involvement and high-frequency. Statistics show that as many as 83% of U.S. consumers patronize fast food restaurants at least once a week.[5] This suggests that location proximity would dominate over brand in consumer choice when it comes to local markets, for it renders a great deal of convenience to consumers. Table 15.1 shows that consumers see distance as the primary obstacle to their choice of McDonald's versus Burger King. Not surprisingly, transportation cost also has pronounced effects on consumer choice. Therefore, it is crucial for the outlets of McDonald's and Burger King to occupy prime locations that consumers prefer in order to succeed in market competition.

Note that McDonald's and Burger King are not the same as the duopolists in the standard Hotelling model addressed in Chapter 14. In addition to their different brand attractiveness, there are two issues worth noting which would affect consumer choice of one over the other. First, McDonald's provides a higher level of baseline utility (6.53) to consumers than Burger King (4.07) does (Table 15.1). This might be because consumers are more satisfied with the burgers or the dining environment that McDonald's provides. Hence consumers would prefer McDonald's, other things being equal. Second, McDonald's marginal cost of producing burgers ($1.45) is lower than Burger King's ($2.03). This is probably because McDonald's has higher labor efficiency and better management of its outlets.[6] Thus McDonald's obtains a cost advantage over Burger King, and hence market power. Intuitively, if McDonald's and Burger King located back to back, and thus engage in minimum

Table 15.1 McDonald's versus Burger King in fast food dining

Variables	Definitions	Parameters
Industry specific		
Distance disutility	Decrease in utility when traveling farther	2.58
Implied transportation cost	Coefficient of distance divided by coefficient of price	2.84
Price elasticity	Price elasticity of demand for burgers	0.91
Firm specific		
McDonald's baseline utility	Utility obtained from purchase at McDonald's	6.53
Burger King's baseline utility	Utility obtained from purchase at Burger King	4.07
McDonald's marginal cost	Marginal cost of burgers produced by McDonald's	1.45
Burger King's marginal cost	Marginal cost of burgers produced by Burger King	2.03

Note: The values in the last column are the parameters of the variables in the simulation models. We interpret the parameters as the values of the variables for expository simplicity.

Source: Thomadsen (2007), p. 796.

product differentiation, McDonald's would, in theory, drive Burger King out of the market through price competition. The dominant position of McDonald's over Burger King would in turn affect their decisions of location and price. For this reason, McDonald's and Burger King are referred to as asymmetric firms, as opposed to symmetric firms in the standard Hotelling model that are identical in all aspects except for their possible locations.

Thomadsen (2007) modeled the location choices of McDonald's versus Burger King through a series of numerical simulations. In order to make the simulations as realistic as possible, he estimated the parameters of the model based on real-world data collected from McDonald's and Burger King franchisees. The conclusions and insights are empirically relevant despite the study results having been theoretical. In what follows we demonstrate how the two firms' prices and profits would vary by letting their outlets gradually locate up to 5 miles apart. We shall see that McDonald's and Burger King adopt unparalleled strategies in pricing and location choice due to the asymmetries in their baseline utility and marginal costs shown in Table 15.1. It would not be surprising that the dominance of McDonald's over Burger King will reflect the asymmetries in their location choices, pricing, and profits. As we shall see below, the different strategies pursued by the two firms can be predicted from, but do not align with, the Hotelling model. In theory, McDonald's would be able to drive Burger King out of the market by mimicking the location of Burger King. In practice though, as the market becomes geographically large, McDonald's will also increasingly differentiate its product by locating apart from Burger King.

15.2 Location affecting price and profit

15.2.1 McDonald's price and profit

Figure 15.1 shows the distance that a McDonald's outlet locates apart from its Burger King counterpart on the *x*-axis and McDonald's outlet price on the left *y*-axis and profit on the right *y*-axis. Note that McDonald's profit is measured as the proportion in the monopoly profit which would otherwise be reaped if there were no competitors in the market. Figure 15.1 shows the changes in McDonald's price and profit as McDonald's outlet gradually locates apart from its Burger King counterpart. In other words, we assess the extent to which McDonald's price and profit will change as McDonald's differentiates its product by locating apart from Burger King. First, as McDonald's locates up to 2 miles apart from Burger King, McDonald's price increases monotonically from \$3.55 to \$3.70, which is the monopoly price that McDonald's would otherwise charge without Burger King in the market. This means that McDonald's product differentiation by locating 2 miles away from Burger King translates into an increase of 4.2% in price. Second, as McDonald's outlet locates between 2 and 3 miles apart from Burger King, McDonald's price bounces up a bit and then levels off to the monopoly price insofar as the two outlets are at least 3 miles apart.

Due to product differentiation, McDonald's profit by and large resembles the pattern of its price response which we discussed earlier. Figure 15.1 shows that McDonald's profit

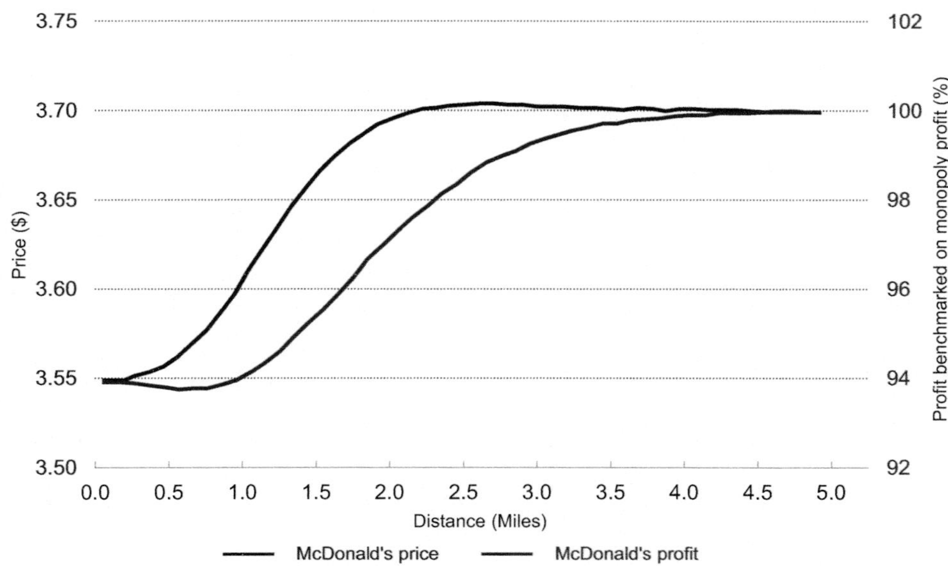

Figure 15.1
McDonald's price and profit with varying distances

Note: Price is the price that McDonald's is able to charge in the simulation, and profit is McDonald's profit benchmarked against its monopoly profit.

Source: Reproduced from Thomadsen (2007), p. 797.

increases as McDonald's outlet locates up to 4 miles apart from Burger King. As long as McDonald's locates next to Burger King, executing minimum product differentiation, it can reap 94% of its monopoly profit. Counterintuitively, McDonald's profit slightly declines as it locates up to 1 mile apart from Burger King. This is perhaps because consumers who are geographically closer to Burger King but prefer McDonald's start patronizing Burger King when both locate at the same place. Thus, as McDonald's locates apart from Burger King, not only can both firms better address the preferences of consumers who are closer to them, but the weaker firm ends up being better off from product differentiation. As McDonald's is between 1 and 4 miles farther apart from Burger King, its profit monotonically increases to the monopoly profit, which is precisely due to a high degree of product differentiation. As McDonald's locates more than 4 miles apart from Burger King, its profit is approximately fixed at the monopoly profit. This implies that when McDonald's is substantially differentiated from Burger King, it morphs into a monopolist despite the presence of Burger King in the market.

15.2.2 Burger King's price and profit

Now we examine the responses of Burger King's price and profit as Burger King outlet locates apart from McDonald's. Figure 15.2 shows the distance between Burger King and McDonald's on the *x*-axis and Burger King's price on the left *y*-axis and profit on the right *y*-axis. In the same vein, Burger King's profit is measured as the proportion of its monopoly profit which would otherwise be reaped if there were no McDonald's. Figure 15.2 shows that Burger King's price increases monotonically from around $3.18 to the monopoly price of $3.50 as Burger King locates up to 2.5 miles apart from McDonald's. The price will stick at $3.50 as Burger King continues to locate farther apart up to 5 miles from McDonald's (Figure 15.2). Burger King's price increases by approximately 10% in contrast to the increase of 4.2% for McDonald's in maximum product differentiation under investigation (Figures 15.1 and 15.2). Other things being equal, we can see that product differentiation actually benefits more to Burger King than to McDonald's. On the other hand, McDonald's price ends up being 11.6% higher than Burger King's when they locate next to each other, but only 5.7% higher when they locate farthest apart (Figures 15.1 and 15.2). Therefore, regardless of how McDonald's acts, the dominant strategy for Burger King is to differentiate its product.

Figure 15.2 shows that Burger King's profit pattern resembles its price response pattern. It is worth noting that Burger King reaps less than 40% of its monopoly profit when locating next to McDonald's as opposed to McDonald's 94% of the monopoly profit when locating next to Burger King (Figures 15.1 and 15.2). This provides further evidence for Burger King's dominant strategy mentioned above, namely that Burger King has a strong incentive to differentiate its product from McDonald's regardless of how McDonald's acts. As long as a certain degree of product differentiation is achieved by Burger King, that is, locating a distance of at least 2.5 miles apart from McDonald's (Figure 15.2), Burger King will be able to obtain the monopoly profit, which is 150% higher than its profit without product differentiation. By contrast, McDonald's profit in maximum product differentiation, equal to its monopoly profit, is only 6.4% higher

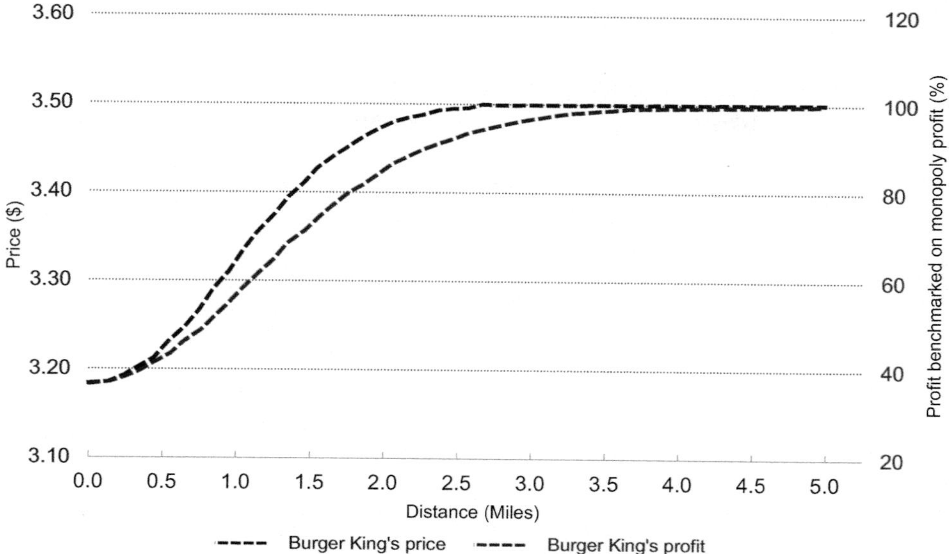

Figure 15.2
Burger King's price and profit with varying distances

Note: Price is the price that Burger King is able to charge in the simulation, and profit is Burger King's profit benchmarked against its monopoly profit.

Source: Reproduced from Thomadsen (2007), p. 797.

than its profit in minimum product differentiation (Figure 15.1). Even without product differentiation McDonald's can still by and large maintain its monopoly position in the market. Therefore, Burger King's overriding strategy must be product differentiation, regardless of whether it is executed directly by itself or indirectly by McDonald's.

15.2.3 McDonald's versus Burger King in pricing

Since location choice is supposed to occur in the long run, it is not realistic that McDonald's and Burger King outlets keep changing their locations. As long as McDonald's and Burger King are not differentiated, they will wage ferocious price competition as the Hotelling model suggests. However, if two products are increasingly differentiated, price competition will ease and both firms end up charging a price above their marginal costs. Yet the price response of one firm to the other would be different because McDonald's, in theory, could drive Burger King out of the market by undercutting Burger King. This is due to McDonald's lower marginal cost. To examine price competition, we define the price-response elasticity of the two outlets as the percentage change in one firm's price to a 1% change in the other's price. Figure 15.3 shows McDonald's and Burger King's price-response elasticities associated with the degree of product differentiation. Not surprisingly the two price-response elasticities are not parallel due to the asymmetries of the two firms in the market. On the one hand, McDonald's price-response elasticity monotonically decreases as the two outlets locate up to 2.5 miles apart. On the other hand, as long as the two outlets locate farther than 2.5 miles apart,

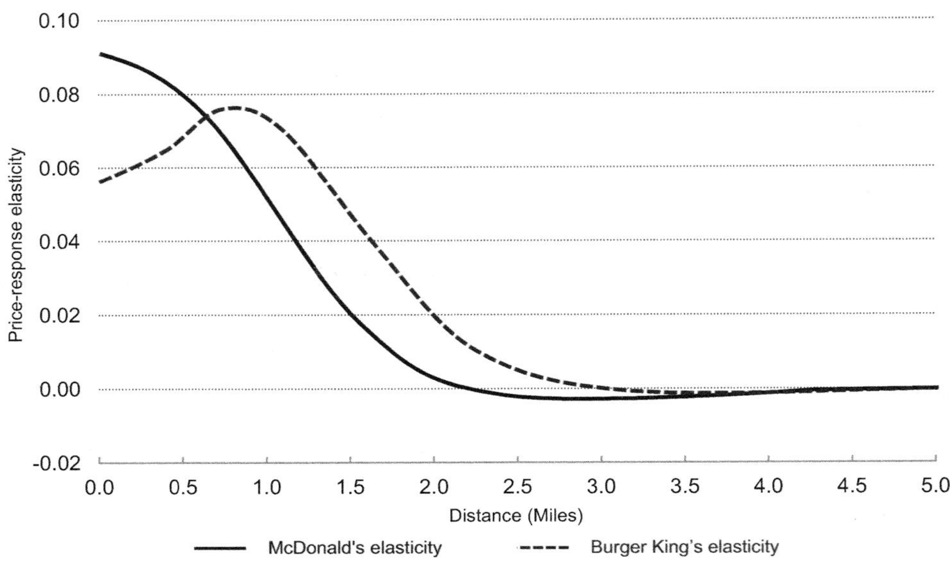

Figure 15.3
Price-response elasticity of McDonald's versus Burger King

Note: Price-response elasticity is defined as the percentage change in one firm's price to a 1% change in the other firm's price.

Source: Reproduced from Thomadsen (2007), p. 798.

McDonald's price will barely respond to Burger King's. The implication is that as the products of McDonald's and Burger King are sufficiently differentiated, McDonald's is less willing to compete with Burger King on price.

Interestingly, Burger King's price-response elasticity first increases as the two outlets locate up to 1 mile apart, and then monotonically decreases as they locate up to 3 miles apart (Figure 15.3). Obviously, when both outlets locate next to each other, Burger King's price will not respond as much as McDonald's does, because it has no market power over McDonald's in the first place. Yet as long as their products are increasingly differentiated, yet not substantially, Burger King starts responding positively to McDonald's price, because product differentiation brings about market power. Burger King can thus still retain and attract consumers despite raising price a bit. Similar to McDonald's, Burger King's price-response elasticity decreases when they locate at least 1 mile apart, which indicates increasingly differentiated products of the two outlets. This means that product differentiation alleviates price competition between the two firms despite the fact that Burger King is still more responsive than McDonald's in setting price. This price pattern is consistent with the preceding result that Burger King would raise price by approximately 10% in contrast to the increase of 4.2% by McDonald's in maximum product differentiation. As long as McDonald's and Burger King locate more than 3 miles apart, they will no longer respond to the price of each other. As shown in Figures 15.1 and 15.2, both end up charging their monopoly prices.

15.3 Competition and location choice

We proceed to analyze the location choices of McDonald's and Burger King, which help explain the differences in their prices and profits addressed above. Instead of resorting to the one-dimensional linear street in the Hotelling model, we place the two outlets of McDonald's and Burger King on a two-dimensional plane with varying sizes, 2×2 miles, 3×3 miles, 5×5 miles, 6×6 miles, and 8×8 miles, in order to simulate different markets. For expository simplicity we can still regard the two-dimensional market as the one-dimensional Hotelling street without loss of generality. Note that as the acting firm locates away from the center of the street, the responding firm can locate either on the same side as the acting firm or the opposite side. Given the location of the acting firm, we denote the location of the responding firm on the same side as a positive response (+) while on the opposite side as a negative response (–). We can thus take full account of the location responses of the two firms: how far the responding firm locates away from the center and in what direction. Besides, we can examine whether and how the two firms will change their locations across various lengths of the street, namely by the dispersion of consumer preference.

15.3.1 McDonald's responds to Burger King's location

Figure 15.4 shows how McDonald's responds to Burger King's location in the market with varying sizes. Burger King's location is placed on the x-axis starting from the center of the street, and McDonald's response is on the y-axis, which is a function of Burger King's location. Figure 15.4 shows that McDonald's response to Burger King's location varies drastically by the size of the market. In small markets (2×2 miles and 3×3 miles), McDonald's barely responds to Burger King's location. Specifically, McDonald's always occupies the center of the street irrespective of where Burger King has located in the first place. In a medium market (5×5 miles), McDonald's responds by first locating slightly away from the center but on the same side of Burger King, as Burger King locates up to 0.5 miles away from the center. Then, McDonald's gradually locates up to 0.5 miles away from the center on the opposite side, as Burger King continues to locate up to 1 mile away from the center. Eventually, McDonald's responds by locating slightly toward the center within around 0.25 miles as Burger King locates at least 1 mile away from the center.

There is an abrupt change in McDonald's location response in a medium market (6×6 miles). Similar to the 5×5 miles market, McDonald's wedges between the center and Burger King as Burger King locates up to 0.5 miles away from the center (Figure 15.4). As Burger King further locates away from the center, McDonald's switches to the opposite side, locating slightly less than 1 mile away from the center. From this location McDonald's starts to systematically respond to Burger King's location. That is, McDonald's consistently locates toward the center on the opposite side, as Burger King locates farther away from the center. McDonald's eventually ends up locating around 0.4 miles away from the center, as Burger King is at the end of the street. Figure 15.4 shows that such systematic location pattern becomes more pronounced in large markets (e.g., 8×8 miles). McDonald's will locate nearly 2 miles away

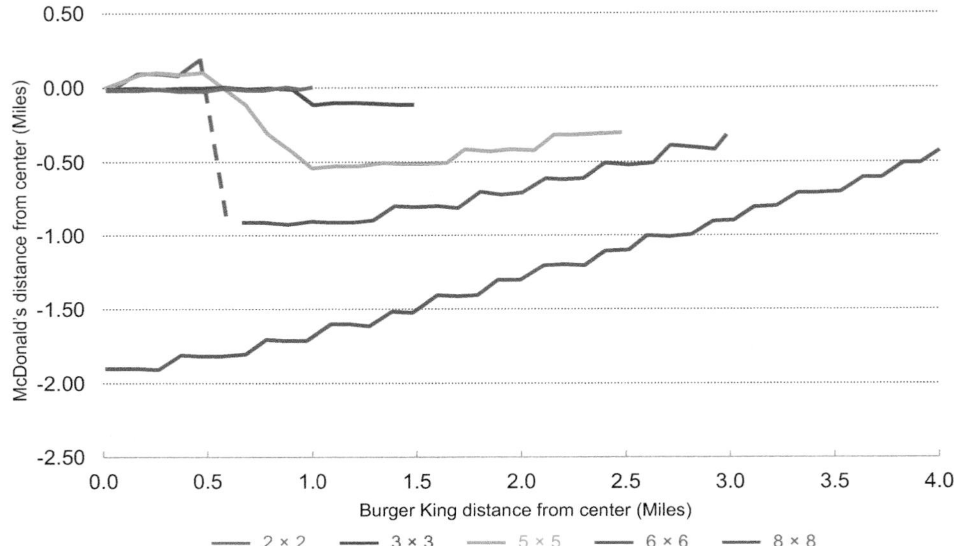

Figure 15.4
McDonald's responds to Burger King's location

Note: Positive figures on the *y*-axis indicate that McDonald's locates on the same side of Burger King from the center; negative figures indicate that McDonald's locates on the opposite side, and zero is the center.

Source: Reproduced from Thomadsen (2007), p. 798.

from the center on the opposite side, when Burger King occupies the center in the first place. However, as Burger King locates away from the center, McDonald's will gradually locate toward the center within 0.5 miles. Note that McDonald's does not occupy the center of the street, despite Burger King being at the end of the street, ending up with a distance of 4.5 miles between them.

15.3.2 Burger King responds to McDonald's location

Figure 15.5 shows Burger King's response to McDonald's location. We place the distance of McDonald's from the center on the *x*-axis and Burger King's response on the *y*-axis. While Burger King's response also varies by market size, it exhibits a great deal of consistency and regularity in all markets under investigation. First, Burger King will respond by persistently choosing to locate on the opposite side and keeping a distance of at least 0.5 miles away from the center, despite the fact that the center is ceded by McDonald's. Second, Burger King will monotonically locate toward the center on the opposite side, as long as McDonald's locates away from the center. In small markets (e.g., 2×2 miles), Burger King persistently keeps a distance of 0.5 miles away from the center, despite McDonald's locating away from the center toward the end of the street. As long as McDonald's occupies the center, Burger King will maintain a distance of around 0.8 miles away from the center on the opposite side in a small market (3×3 miles), 1.7 miles and 2 miles away from the center in medium

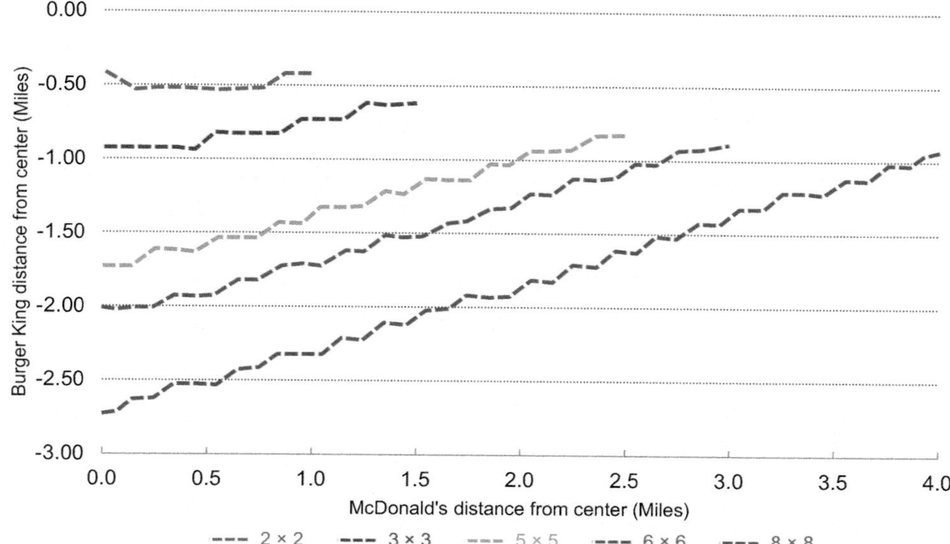

Figure 15.5
Burger King responds to McDonald's location

Note: Negative figures on the *y*-axis indicate that Burger King locates on the opposite side of McDonald's, and zero is the center.

Source: Reproduced from Thomadsen (2007), p. 799.

markets (5×5 miles and 6×6 miles), and 2.7 miles away from the center in a large market (8×8 miles). As long as McDonald's locates away from the center, Burger King consistently locates toward the center on the opposite side (Figure 15.5).

15.4 What affects location equilibrium

15.4.1 Firm asymmetry and location choice

The above analysis has shown that McDonald's and Burger King's location responses to each other are not paralleled. McDonald's exhibits a strong propensity to locate toward the center and even to occupy the center in small markets irrespective of whether Burger King moves first or not and where Burger King is located. By contrast, Burger King is inclined to locate apart from McDonald's, thereby proactively differentiating from McDonald's in the first place. In fact, Burger King tends to cede the center to McDonald's even if it moves first. This is because anticipated price competition from McDonald's, due to both locating at the center, would certainly be detrimental to Burger King. Only when the market is large enough would McDonald's be willing to differentiate from Burger King, each ending up monopolizing half of the market. The unparalleled location patterns are due to the asymmetries between McDonald's and Burger King, namely that McDonald's low marginal cost and high baseline utility provide it with a competitive advantage. Hence McDonald's incentive to differentiate products is not as strong as Burger King's, especially in small markets where consumer preferences are much less dispersed.

In fact, it is in McDonald's best interest not to differentiate its product from Burger King's in small markets, because the central location enables McDonald's to address consumer preference evenly. Even though a dominant firm can, in theory, choose to locate anywhere along the street, the prime location is always the center as long as consumers are uniformly distributed. This is why McDonald's is inclined to occupy the center in small markets regardless of where Burger King has located or will locate. Only when the market is large enough would McDonald's start to locate away from the center, but not between the center and Burger King. The conclusion that McDonald's takes better locations can be verified in a simulation by letting McDonald's and Burger King outlets swap locations with each other. If Burger King were able to earn more profits when operating at McDonald's locations whereas McDonald's were earning less when operating at Burger King's, the locations taken by McDonald's would certainly be more tempting. According to the simulation in Santa Clara County of California, out of the 38 Burger King outlets, 21 (55%) would earn more profits if swapping locations with the nearest McDonald's; by contrast, 26 out of the 62 McDonald's (42%) would earn more profits if swapping locations with the nearest Burger King.[7]

15.4.2 Market size, the "center," and location choice

The size of the market has significant impacts on the location choices of McDonald's and Burger King. On the one hand, the standard Hotelling model predicts that the length of the street does not matter to the location choice of symmetric firms because two firms would eventually end up locating in the center of the street. On the other hand, if both firms locate at the two ends of the street engaging in maximum product differentiation, they will split total profit in the market, which increases quadratically with the length of the street. This is an important conclusion which we obtained in Chapter 14, implying that differentiating products is more beneficial to firms in larger markets than in smaller ones. Therefore, even though McDonald's has less incentive to differentiate its product due to its market dominance, it proactively chooses to locate apart from Burger King in large markets as opposed to its strategy of occupying the center in small markets. A larger market in the Hotelling model suggests that consumer preferences are more dispersed on location, and hence more profits will be generated when products are differentiated. Thus, McDonald's location choice in large markets can be regarded as not only an immediate reaction to Burger King as a competitor, but also a strategic response to the increasingly dispersed consumer preferences.

However, there are no monotonic relationships between either price or profit and the degree of product differentiation for McDonald's and Burger King. Figures 15.1 and 15.2 show that both McDonald's and Burger King's prices converge to their monopoly prices when they locate around 2 miles and 2.5 miles apart from each other, respectively. Further product differentiation by locating up to 5 miles apart has no impact on their prices nor on their profits. This pattern is not aligned with what the standard Hotelling model would predict. In developing the Hotelling model we assumed that consumers' willingness to pay is higher than or equal to the market price(s), and the two firms have unlimited production capacities to serve the whole market. In practice though, there exists what is known as the edge-of-market effect, meaning that the number of consumers that a firm can attract will diminish as the firm locates closer to the edges of a market, especially in small markets. It takes more time and hence higher transportation costs for consumers to purchase from firms on the edges of the market. Hence firm profit declines on market edges. When a market is sufficiently large, firms tend to locate away from the center in both directions because the edge-of-market effects are not as significant as they are in small markets. Locating apart allows each firm to monopolize half of the market with their limited production capacities. Therefore, the edge-of-market effects limit how far apart two firms choose to locate, and hence reduce product differentiation.

In both symmetric and asymmetric cases the predilection of two firms to locate toward the center in small markets and far apart in large markets will not be held if consumers are concentrated somewhere other than the center of the street. This means that consumer preference for a particular location is more intensified than for others. Depending on how dense consumer demand is, McDonald's and Burger King would gravitate toward wherever the demand is concentrated, regardless of whether it is the geographic center or not. In essence, the center in the Hotelling street is more than the center in the geographic sense. It is the uniform distribution of consumer preference that leads to the overlap of the center of consumer preference and the geographic center of the street. For example, if there is a large mall or downtown along a street, both firms, regardless of symmetric or asymmetric, would choose to locate at the vicinity of the mall or downtown even though it may not be the geographic center of the street. This is because consumers are no longer uniformly distributed in the market but concentrated at the mall or downtown, and so are their preferences. A slight difference though for asymmetric firms, such as McDonald's and Burger King, is that McDonald's would locate much closer to the area than would Burger King. This explains why McDonald's and Burger King are often adjacent to each other in high-demand areas.

Summary

1. The fast food industry is dominated by large restaurant franchisors with strong brand influences in the global market, but the competition is manifested by numerous franchisee outlets vying for consumers in localized markets.
2. McDonald's and Burger King are asymmetric firms, because McDonald's has a lower marginal cost among other things that will affect its competition with Burger King on location and price. Thus, the competition between McDonald's and Burger King is similar, but not equivalent, to the competition of symmetric firms in the standard Hotelling model.
3. When McDonald's and Burger King execute minimum product differentiation, the former can reap 94% of its monopoly profit while the latter only obtains less than 40% of its monopoly profit. When their products are sufficiently differentiated, both are able to obtain a profit equal to their respective monopoly profits.

4. When McDonald's and Burger King are sufficiently differentiated, Burger King is able to raise price by approximately 10% in contrast to an increase of 4.2% for McDonald's compared to their prices in minimum product differentiation, respectively. Both are able to charge a price equal to their respective monopoly prices with sufficiently differentiated products.
5. McDonald's exhibits a strong propensity to locate toward the center of the street and even to occupy the center in small markets, irrespective of where Burger King has located or will locate. McDonald's starts to locate apart from the center and differentiate from Burger King as the size of the market increases.
6. By contrast, Burger King is inclined to locate apart from McDonald's and cede the center to McDonald's even though it moves first. Burger King proactively differentiates its product from McDonald's in the first place.
7. In practice there are no monotonic relationships between either price or profit of McDonald's and Burger King and the degree of product differentiation between them. The edge-of-market effects limit how far apart the two firms choose to locate, and hence reduce their product differentiation.
8. If consumers are not uniformly distributed along the street, two firms in both symmetric and asymmetric cases would gravitate toward wherever consumer demand is concentrated, regardless of whether it is the geographic center of the street or not.

Problem solving

1. We know that two firms in the standard Hotelling model are able to obtain increasingly greater market power as they locate apart from each other. This means that the prices they are able to charge monotonically increase as their products are increasingly differentiated. However, in practice McDonald's and Burger King are able to monopolize their respective market segments and charge the monopoly prices even though their products are not sufficiently differentiated as shown in Figures 15.1 and 15.2. How would you reconcile the contradiction between theory and practice?
2. Suppose that McDonald's and Burger King sell the same cheeseburger along a 10-mile long street, and assume that their brands have no influence on consumer choice. The marginal cost of producing and selling cheeseburgers by McDonald's is $2.50 per cheeseburger and by Burger King is $3.50 per cheeseburger. Suppose that there are 500 consumers uniformly distributed along the street, and each consumer has the same transportation cost of $0.5 per mile, and will buy only one cheeseburger. Suppose further that Burger King sets up its outlet first, locating halfway along the street, and sells each cheeseburger for $5.5, and it will not change its location and price afterwards. If McDonald's enters the market and is able to acquire 150 consumers, what would be the location of McDonald's and the price of its cheeseburgers?
3. Suppose that McDonald's and Burger King decide to sell an iced tea which is homogenous except for sweetness, and assume that their brands have no influence on consumer choice. According to market research, consumer preference for

sweetness is uniformly distributed along a spectrum from 0 to 10 degrees, with 0 indicating unsweetened and 10 indicating the highest degree of sweetness that consumers can accept. Each consumer is willing to compromise his preference to accept lower or higher degrees of sweetness, provided that a discount of $0.125 per degree is offered by the firms. Suppose that McDonald's marginal cost of selling the iced tea is $1.50 per bottle and Burger King's is $2.50 per bottle, and no additional cost is incurred in changing sweetness. If McDonald's enters the market first and sells the iced tea with the medium degree of sweetness for $2.00 per bottle (assume that McDonald's will not change the sweetness and price afterwards), should Burger King enter the market? If so, what degree of sweetness should Burger King sell, and what would the price be for its iced tea?

Solutions to all review questions and problem solving tasks are included in the Support Material for this book, which can be accessed at www.routledge.com/9780367897352.

Notes

1 This chapter is based on Thomadsen (2007). I am grateful to Professor Raphael Thomadsen at Olin Business School of Washington University in St. Louis for granting me the permission to use his study results.
2 *Statista*. Revenue of quick service restaurants in the U.S. 2002–2019. October 10, 2019.
3 *Statista*. Revenue of McDonald's 2005–2019. February 27, 2020. *Statista*. Revenue of Burger King worldwide 2004–2019. February 24, 2020.
4 Thomadsen (2005).
5 *Statista*. Most valuable QSR brands worldwide in 2020. July 1, 2020.
6 Thomadsen (2005), p. 917.
7 Thomadsen (2007), p. 800.

Bibliography

Harold, H. (1929). Stability in competition. *Economic Journal, 39*(153), 41–57.

Thomadsen, R. (2005). The effect of ownership structure on prices in geographically differentiated industries. *RAND Journal of Economics, 36*(4), 908–929.

Thomadsen, R. (2007). Product positioning and competition: The role of location in the fast food industry. *Marketing Science, 26*(6), 792–804.

MODULE 5

Transaction and institution

16 Intermediation and the bid-ask spread

From this chapter on we shift our focus from production and consumption to market transaction. This chapter addresses the fundamental role of intermediaries grounded on transaction costs in executing transactions between buyers and sellers. In essence, an intermediary is an institutional arrangement of market transaction to reduce transaction costs between buyers and sellers. We first discuss how transactions are made between buyers and sellers with and without transaction costs by comparing an intermediary and the Walrasian auctioneer. Second, we present a model of intermediation, known as the bid-ask model, in which buyers and sellers can either trade directly with each other or through an intermediary. In the model the intermediary is endogenously determined by transaction costs in the market, and so is its market power. Third, we draw implications of the bid-ask model to travel intermediaries and analyze the choice of intermediation versus disintermediation in the tourism market which depends on the existence and magnitude of transaction costs.

AFTER STUDYING THIS CHAPTER, YOU SHOULD BE ABLE TO:

- **Understand the concept of transaction costs and the role of intermediaries in reducing transaction costs;**
- **Understand and explain the difference between bilateral search and intermediation in relation to transaction costs;**
- **Analyze the behavior of the intermediary and figure out the optimal bid-ask spread in the intermediary's pricing; and**
- **Understand the sources of transaction costs in the tourism market and the emergence of intermediation versus disintermediation.**

16.1 Transaction costs and the firm

16.1.1 Walrasian auction and transaction costs

In conventional economic models we postulate an ideal market in which buyers and sellers transact with each other at a zero cost. Through searching for a trading partner in the market, each buyer and seller proceeds to bargain and concludes a deal only if it is mutually beneficial. Nevertheless, by no means is there no cost in the real world for each buyer and seller to search for a trading partner and eventually strike a bargain that is mutually acceptable. This means that a trade, despite being reciprocal, could be delayed, broken down, or even not executed due to the fact that the searching and bargaining process is time-consuming and even interminable. Hence a market equilibrium may not exist at all. To resolve this theoretical predicament, we postulate that there exists an impartial and omnipotent auctioneer outside the economic system who knows all buyers' and sellers' willingness to pay and sell for a good and can thus coordinate all transactions by matching all buyers and sellers who are able and willing to trade with each other. This presumed auctioneer is known as the Walrasian auctioneer, named after French economist Léon Walras (1834–1910) who proposed this idea. Since the Walrasian auctioneer is exogenous to the economic system and can auction the good for a price at which demand equals supply, the market eventually clears in equilibrium.

In the market equilibrium, which can now be called the Walrasian equilibrium, any buyer whose willingness to pay is higher than or equal to the equilibrium price will be able to buy the good and any seller whose willingness to sell is lower than or equal to the equilibrium price will be able to sell. Yet in the real world a buyer whose willingness to pay is higher than the market price may end up with no trade at all because he could not find a seller to trade with. Even if he could meet with a seller, they may dispute on the price of the good, leading to a delay or even a breakdown of trade. Hence executing market transactions is not without cost. The costs associated with using the price mechanism to execute market transactions are called transaction costs. The idea of transaction costs was formulated by British economist Ronald Coase (1910–2013) to justify the emergence of the *firm* as an institutional arrangement as opposed to the Walrasian market. As Coase states explicitly,

> [i]n order to carry out a market transaction it is necessary to discover who it is that one wishes to deal with, to inform people that one wishes to deal and on what terms, to conduct negotiations leading up to a bargain, to draw up the contract, to undertake the inspection needed to make sure that the terms of the contract are being observed, and so on. These operations are often extremely costly, sufficiently costly at any rate to prevent many transactions that would be carried out in a world in which the pricing system worked without cost.[1]

16.1.2 The firm and the intermediary

In a market with insuperable transaction costs, no transactions can be executed because no seller is able to trade with the buyer or vice versa. In a market without transaction costs the firm is synonymous with the producer or the seller on the supply side as opposed to the consumer or the buyer on the demand side. The market is the only institutional arrangement for executing transactions through the Walrasian auctioneer. Thus, the firm is nothing but a production function that maximizes profit and the consumer is nothing but a utility function that maximizes utility. This is how the word *firm* is used in preceding chapters and neoclassical economics in general. It is taken for granted that transactions between buyers and sellers can be fulfilled frictionlessly. As far as transaction costs are concerned, we need to make a canonical distinction between three types of market agents, the seller, the buyer, and the firm. The role that the *firm* plays, among other things, is to reduce transaction costs between the seller and the buyer, and hence the firm primarily functions as a middleman as opposed to sellers on the supply side and buyers on the demand side. The firm becomes an alternative institution to the market mechanism dictated by the Walrasian auctioneer. In contrast to the Walrasian auctioneer, the firm arises endogenously from, and hence is affected by, transaction costs. If transaction costs were zero, the firm would be negated in the market, leaving only the seller performing production and the buyer performing consumption.

We shall focus on the role of the firm in reducing transaction costs externally between buyers and sellers. This is the intermediating function of the firm in creating transactions in the market, and hence the firm is referred to as an *intermediary*. In principle, an intermediary is defined as an economic agent that purchases from sellers for resale to buyers or helps buyers and sellers meet and transact.[2] Insofar as transaction costs involved in direct trade between buyers and sellers are higher than the cost of intermediation, the intermediary obtains its legitimacy in executing market transactions and acquires market power as well. This explains why intermediaries tend to flourish in markets, such as a bazaar, real estate, finance and insurance, and tourism, that are characterized by considerable information search costs. In these markets the intermediary functions as an information broker, specialist, or an agent which furnishes traders on both sides with the information and expertise to facilitate transactions. Despite the importance of intermediaries, it was not until the late 1980s that economists started to model the behavior of the intermediary and highlight the intermediating function of the firm among other things.[3] This is perhaps due to the fact that the economy, in particular the U.S. economy, had been dominated by production sectors, particularly manufacturing. However, by 1993 wholesale and retail trade, which are the two major types of intermediates, accounted for 15.8% of the U.S. GDP and amassed 1,452,967 firms,[4] underscoring the increasing significance of intermediaries.

To execute transactions an intermediary plays two major functions in reducing transaction costs in the market. One is pricing in which the intermediary acts as an information broker to identify buyers and sellers and post prices to both at which transactions are fulfilled. This is also known as the retailing model, highlighting the role of the intermediary in reducing search and bargaining costs of traders. In this sense, the intermediary is precisely a market maker similar to the role that the Walrasian auctioneer performs. For instance, travel and real estate agents in essence perform the pricing function. The other one is inventorying in which the intermediary purchases a good from sellers and resells it to buyers simultaneously or in a different place and/or a different time. This is known as the merchandizing model, which suggests a transfer of ownership of the good from sellers to the intermediary which will eventually be passed on to buyers as end consumers. In this case the intermediary does not only reduce search and bargaining costs between buyers and sellers but also increases liquidity of the market. For instance, supermarkets and department stores have an inventory function besides retailing. Apart from pricing and inventorying, the intermediary needs to coordinate and monitor transactions by defining terms and conditions of transactions and manage payments as well. It also needs to make sure that transactions will be honored and enforced properly by punishing those who renege on their agreements.

16.2 Bilateral search versus intermediation

16.2.1 Buyers and sellers

After incorporating the intermediary in the market, market transactions between buyers and sellers can be executed through two institutional arrangements. One is the market mechanism in which buyers and sellers search and bargain with each other to reach a deal at a mutually agreed price. The other is intermediation in which an intermediary bids a lower price to purchase a good from sellers and quotes a higher price to resell it to buyers, thereby executing transactions indirectly. The model of intermediation we expound here was developed by German American economist Thomas Gehrig (1960–) who postulates a market in which buyers and sellers can trade off bilateral search against intermediation. Suppose that buyers' willingness to pay for a good is r, which, for expository simplicity, is assumed to be uniformly distributed in $[0,1]$. The market price of the good can be bargained by buyers and sellers directly in the market, or quoted and bid by an intermediary when buyers and sellers choose to transact with the intermediary, respectively. We shall discuss later how the market price p is determined when buyers choose between bargaining with sellers and trading with the intermediary. We can readily obtain the demand curve of buyers, which is linear with both the x- and y-intercept at 1 for the market price $p \in [0,1]$ (Figure 16.1). In a similar vein, suppose that sellers' willingness to sell the good is s, which is also uniformly distributed in $[0,1]$. If sellers can sell the good at the market price p as well, we can readily obtain sellers' supply curve in the market, which is a 45-degree ray from the origin for the market price $p \in [0,1]$ (Figure 16.1).

From the above assumptions exhibited in Figure 16.1, we can write out the demand function of buyers for the good $D(p)$:

$$D(p) = -p + 1. \tag{16.1}$$

As we assumed, function (16.1) suggests that buyers' willingness to pay is uniformly distributed in $[0,1]$ and the marginal demand is -1. Likewise, we can obtain sellers' supply function of the good $S(p)$:

$$S(p) = p. \tag{16.2}$$

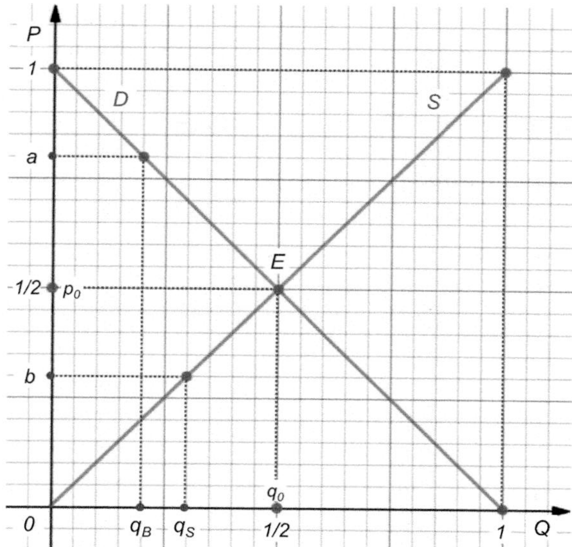

Figure 16.1
Walrasian equilibrium and intermediation

Function (16.2) suggests that sellers' willingness to sell is also uniformly distributed in [0,1], and the marginal supply is 1, which by definition is the change in quantity supplied divided by the change in price.

16.2.2 Bilateral search

If there were no transaction costs, in a perfectly competitive market buyers and sellers would end up trading in market equilibrium through the Walrasian auctioneer. The market equilibrium is the Walrasian equilibrium, which is the same as the market equilibrium we have discussed in preceding chapters in which transaction costs between buyers and sellers are assumed away. Figure 16.1 shows that the market clears in the Walrasian equilibrium *E* at which buyers' demand equals sellers' supply. Let buyers' demand in function (16.1) equal sellers' supply in function (16.2): $-p+1=p$, we obtain the equilibrium price, $p_0 = 1/2$, and the equilibrium quantity, $q_0 = 1/2$, known as the Walrasian price and quantity, respectively. All buyers whose willingness to pay is higher than or equal to 1/2 and all sellers whose willingness to sell is lower than or equal to 1/2 are able to trade at the equilibrium price. This is the typical, orthodox equilibrium analysis we have addressed so far. Assuming that buyers and sellers can search and bargain endlessly and costlessly, we will eventually end up with a perfectly efficient market in which demand equals supply. The market is made by the Walrasian auctioneer that perfectly coordinates buyers and sellers.

In the real world buyers and sellers trade with each other through search and bargaining, known as bilateral search. This is because buyers and sellers do not know each other's willingness to pay and sell in the market. It is through bilateral search and bargaining that buyers and sellers can grope for their respective willingness to pay and sell, thereby executing market transactions. In the search stage each buyer and seller enters the market to search for a trading partner. Obviously, not every buyer or seller can always find a trading partner because the number of buyers in search may not be equal to the number of sellers, and hence the ones on the short side will be rationed. Transaction costs arise in search because the searching process that matches buyers and sellers is time-consuming, costly, and uncertain. Even after a buyer successfully meets a seller or vice versa, they must bargain over prices for the good based on their respective willingness to pay and sell. For the buyer, the lower the price, the more consumer surplus will be; and for the seller, the higher the price, the more producer surplus will be. Thus, each trader aims to bid or quote a price that not only maximizes his own surplus but can also be accepted by the other to conclude a transaction. If the buyer's willingness to pay is lower than the seller's willingness to sell, the transaction cannot be executed. Hence, they have to continue to search for other trading partners and bargain again or choose to leave the market.

16.2.3 Intermediation

As transaction costs in bilateral search mount, market transactions could be delayed or even broken down. In contrast to bilateral search, intermediaries provide the immediacy of trade by standing ready to buy a good from sellers and resell it to buyers upon request. It follows that an intermediary bids a low price to buy the good from sellers, called bid price, and quotes a high price to sell it to buyers, referred to as ask price. In other words, the role that the intermediary plays is to price the good. Since bid and ask prices are publicly available, sellers and buyers can immediately decide whether to accept a bid price and an ask price, respectively, in exchange for the immediacy. Obviously, the decision is based on whether the cost of immediacy outweighs transaction costs in bilateral search. A transaction is intermediated as long as a seller accepts a bid price and/or a buyer accepts an ask price. Note that sellers and buyers do not have to accept a pair of the bid and ask prices at the same time. The discrepancy between a pair of the bid and ask prices is known as the bid-ask spread, which accrues to the intermediary as the profit for each intermediated transaction. Due to transaction costs, the intermediary will be economically viable in the market despite the fact that the ask price denoted as a is higher than the Walrasian price and the bid price denoted as b is lower than the Walrasian price (Figure 16.1). In fact, the bid-ask spread, $a-b$, is the reward to the intermediary for reducing transaction costs that would otherwise arise in bilateral search for each transaction.

In the first place, whether a buyer is *able to* accept an ask price depends on whether his willingness to pay is higher than, or at least equal to, the ask price. Likewise, whether a seller is *able to* accept a bid price depends on whether his willingness to sell is lower than, or at least equal to, the bid price. Figure 16.1 shows that the number of buyers and sellers who are able to trade with the intermediary is q_B and q_S, respectively. In other words, buyers to the right of q_B whose willingness to pay is lower than a and sellers to the right of q_S whose willingness to sell is higher than b have no choice but to engage in bilateral search. In the second place, whether a buyer or a seller is *willing to* trade with the intermediary depends on whether his surplus from intermediation is greater than the surplus from bilateral search. Some buyers or sellers who are able to trade with the intermediary may end up searching due to the surplus from bilateral search being greater than the surplus from intermediation. Therefore, there exists a market equilibrium in which the surplus that buyers and sellers obtain from bilateral search ends up being equal to the surplus from intermediation given the bid and ask prices charged by the intermediary. The market equilibrium suggests an optimal bid-ask spread that maximizes the intermediary's profit on the one hand, and on the other hand renders buyers and sellers indifferent between engaging in bilateral search and trading with the intermediary.

16.3 Determining the bid-ask spread

16.3.1 Search costs and intermediary profit

In the Walrasian auction only sellers whose willingness to sell is lower than or equal to the equilibrium price are coordinated with buyers whose willingness to pay is higher than or equal to the equilibrium price. Figure 16.1 shows that sellers are matched with buyers systematically by the Walrasian auctioneer from the 1st to q_0th in the market. Hence the matching probability is always 100% in the Walrasian auction. In a search market with transaction costs, we introduce parameter λ to indicate the matching probability between buyers and sellers when bilateral search is costly compared to the Walrasian auction. The parameter λ takes value between 0 and 1. When $\lambda = 0$, buyers and sellers are simply unable or unwilling to meet with each other in the market due to insurmountable search costs. Hence all buyers and sellers have no choice but to trade with the intermediary, and the search market becomes completely inactive. When $\lambda = 1$, all buyers and sellers are able to engage in bilateral search, and each buyer and seller can secure a trading partner with a probability of 100% because search costs are zero. In other words, each buyer and seller can search infinitely until he meets with a trading partner. Therefore, the parameter λ can be seen as a measure of search costs in the whole market. Other things being equal, the higher the λ, the lower the search costs, and the more searches buyers and sellers will undertake; and the lower the λ, the higher the search costs, and the fewer searches they will undertake.

In the search market since each buyer and seller only knows his own willingness to pay and sell, searching for a trading partner is random in contrast to the Walrasian auction. Note that $\lambda = 1$ does not mean that each pair of buyers and sellers in the search market can end up with a successful trade. Mismatch would arise when, for instance, a buyer, having met a seller, is willing to pay a price which is lower than the seller's willingness to sell. This leads to no trade between them. Therefore, both would continue to search or simply leave the market. Mismatch could also arise when a buyer whose willingness to pay is higher than the Walrasian price meets with a seller who would otherwise be negated in the Walrasian auction because his willingness to sell is also higher than the Walrasian price. Even though the trade could take place, the buyer's consumer surplus would not be maximized, leading him to terminate the trade and search for another seller. For each buyer and seller the probability of identifying a trading partner that maximizes his surplus in bilateral search is the same regardless of his willingness to pay and sell. If the intermediary is available, buyers with higher willingness to pay and sellers with lower willingness to sell will be more likely to trade with the intermediary for the sake of immediacy. Since bid and ask prices are immediately available, trading with the intermediary can save the costs of bargaining even though the matching probability is 100%. However, buyers and sellers trading with the intermediary may end up obtaining less surplus than they otherwise could in bilateral search.

Therefore, whether each buyer and seller decides to search or trade with the intermediary depends on the surplus from search and from intermediation given the bid and ask prices of the intermediary. This means that search and intermediation are interdependent yet mutually exclusive to each other. Since the intermediated market faces direct competition from the search market, an increase in search will drive down the ask price while pushing up the bid price. As long as $\lambda > 0$, the search market remains active and coexists with the intermediated market. Suppose that the intermediary sets bid price b and ask price a, and thus is able to attract the number of sellers q_S whose willingness to sell is lower than or equal to b and the number of buyers q_B whose willingness to pay is higher than or equal to a (Figure 16.1). If $q_B = q_S$, the intermediary can match each buyer with each seller perfectly, as does the Walrasian auctioneer, ending up with the number of transactions intermediated equal to $q_B = q_S = q$. In case $q_B \neq q_S$, the short side will be rationed by the intermediary, and hence the number of transactions intermediated is $min(q_B, q_S)$. For expository convenience, assuming that the cost of intermediating each transaction is zero without loss of generality, we obtain the profit function of the intermediary based on the bid and ask prices:

$$\pi = \min(q_B, q_S)(a - b). \tag{16.3}$$

Figure 16.2a shows that the intermediary sets bid and ask prices (a_1, b_1) that attract an equal number of buyers and sellers in the market, q_1. Hence the matching probability between buyers and sellers is 100%. The intermediary ends up obtaining a profit, $\pi_1 = q_1(a_1 - b_1)$, as shown in Figure 16.2a. On the other hand, Figure 16.2b shows that the intermediary sets bid and ask prices (a_2, b_2) that attract the number of buyers q_B and the number of sellers q_S. Since $q_B < q_S$ as indicated in Figure 16.2b, the buyers are rationed with the probability of q_B / q_S, that is, only a proportion q_B / q_S of the sellers who are able to trade with the intermediary can be matched with the buyers. Then the matching probability is smaller than 100%. Therefore, the number of transactions intermediated depends entirely on the number of buyers on the short side of the market. The intermediary ends up obtaining a profit, $\pi_2 = q_B(a_2 - b_2)$, as shown in Figure 16.2b. This is a special case of the intermediary's profit in function (16.3). Likewise, if the number of sellers attracted is smaller than the number of buyers, the sellers will be rationed. The intermediary ends up with a profit depending entirely on the number of sellers, which will be similar to Figure 16.2b. Those buyers or sellers that are not intermediated will then engage in bilateral search.

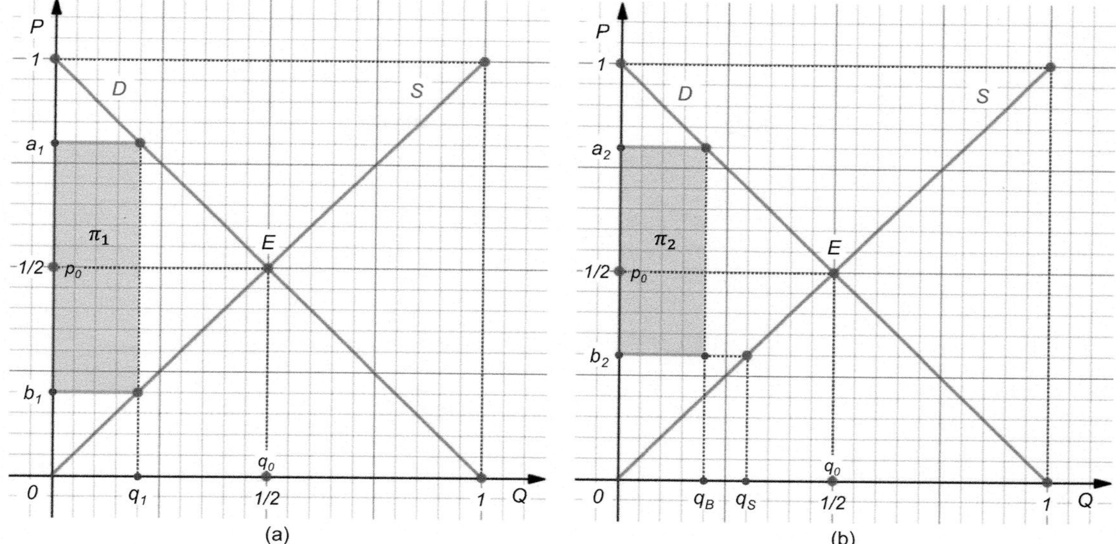

Figure 16.2
The bid-ask spread and intermediary profit

16.3.2 Bid-ask spread without search

We examine the polar case $\lambda = 0$ first, meaning that there is no search market. This could be a case where search costs are insurmountable, rendering buyers and sellers unable or unwilling to search at all. Thus, the intermediary's decision on bid and ask prices is independent of bilateral search while only dependent on the demand of buyers and the supply of sellers. Suppose that bid price b and ask price a are the optimal prices that enable the intermediary to maximize profit as shown in Figure 16.3. A geometric solution to the profit-maximizing problem is that a and b must maximize the area of the inscribed rectangle in the triangle bounded by the demand curve of buyers, the supply curve of sellers, and the y-axis. First of all, the precondition for maximizing the intermediary's profit is that the rectangle determined by the bid-ask spread (a,b) and the quantity q must be inscribed in the triangle. Any rectangle such as the one in Figure 16.2b that is not inscribed in the triangle is not maximized in area. As far as Figure 16.2b is concerned, the intermediary can simply lower the bid price b_2 precisely to the sellers' willingness to sell at q_B, and therefore increase its profit without changing the ask price a_2 on the demand side and the number of transactions intermediated in the market. This means that the number of buyers and sellers intermediated must be equal in order for the intermediary to maximize profit. Namely, a necessary condition for profit maximization of the intermediary is that the bid-ask spread (a,b) satisfies $q_B = q_S$.

Second, the profit-maximizing problem thus turns out to be an optimization problem in geometry of identifying the exact position of the inscribed rectangle in the triangle. As long as the position of the inscribed rectangle is determined, the bid price b and ask price a are determined in the market. Suppose that the number of

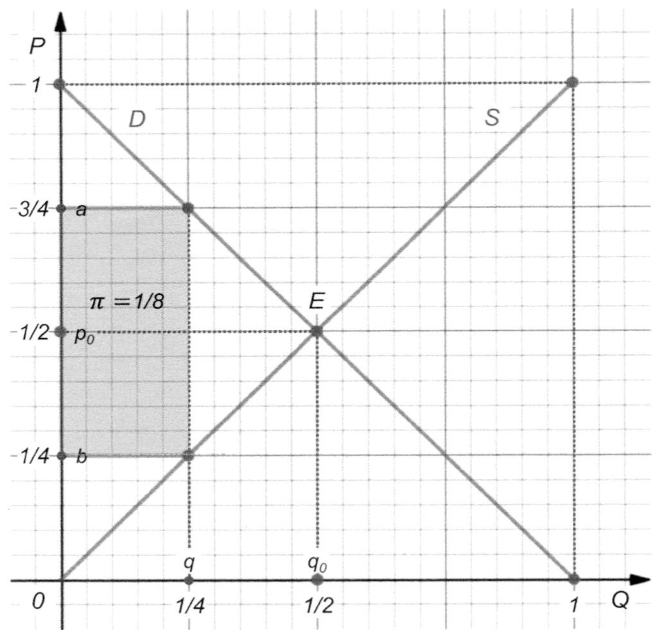

Figure 16.3
Optimal bid-ask spread without bilateral search

intermediated transactions that maximizes the intermediary's profit is q. Given the demand function of buyers (16.1) and the supply function of sellers (16.2), we obtain the ask price a as a function of q from the demand function and the bid price b as a function of q from the supply function:

$$\begin{cases} a = -q + 1, \\ b = q. \end{cases} \tag{16.4}$$

Plugging a and b in equations (16.4) into the intermediary's profit function (16.3), we obtain the intermediary's profit as a function of the quantity q:

$$\pi = q(a - b) = -2q^2 + q. \tag{16.5}$$

Function (16.5) suggests that the intermediary's profit ultimately depends on the number of transactions it can intermediate between buyers and sellers. Let the marginal profit ($M\pi$) with respect to q be zero for profit maximization, we have

$$M\pi = \frac{d\pi}{dq} = -4q + 1 = 0. \tag{16.6}$$

Solving equation (16.6) we obtain $q = 1/4$ at which the intermediary maximizes profit with the bid-ask spread (a,b). Plugging $q = 1/4$ into equations (16.4) we obtain the ask price $a = 3/4$ and the bid price $b = 1/4$, which are the optimal prices that the intermediary charges buyers and sellers, respectively. Thus, the intermediary sets the bid-ask spread, $a - b = 1/2$, and obtains the maximized profit, $\pi = 1/8$ (Figure 16.3). Since the above analysis is the case where buyers and sellers have no choice but to trade with the intermediary, the profit $\pi = 1/8$ is the maximum of the profit that the intermediary can obtain in the whole market for all $\lambda \in [0,1]$. In other words, the intermediary is not able to obtain a profit greater than 1/8 regardless of whether the search market is active or not. Intuitively, we also know that the ask price $a = 3/4$ is the maximum of ask price, and the bid price $b = 1/4$ is the minimum of bid price. As long as buyers and sellers are active in the search market ($\lambda > 0$), the ask price will be lower than 3/4 while the bid price will be higher than 1/4, thereby narrowing down the bid-ask spread. As the bid-ask spread shrinks, so does the intermediary's profit in the market.

16.3.3 Bid-ask spread with search

Given the bid-ask spread (a,b) of the intermediary and the matching probability $\lambda > 0$ in the search market, first of all, the marginal buyer whose willingness to pay equal to the ask price and the marginal seller whose willingness to sell equal to the bid price will certainly search. This is because the surplus obtained by trading with the intermediary for both is zero while bilateral search could at least bring about a positive surplus. Second, the marginal buyer whose willingness to pay is slightly higher than the ask price and the marginal seller whose willingness to sell is slightly lower than the bid price may also choose to search as long as the surplus from search outweighs the surplus from intermediation, and so on. Bilateral search thus becomes an alternative to intermediation for some buyers and sellers, which in turn forces the intermediary to lower the ask price and raise the bid price, thereby increasing surplus to the marginal buyers and marginal sellers, respectively. There exists an equilibrium in which the surplus obtained by the marginal buyers and marginal sellers from intermediation is equal to what they each would otherwise obtain from bilateral search. In the other polar case in which $\lambda = 1$, since the matching probability is 100%, all buyers and sellers can choose between bilateral search and intermediation depending on which option brings about more surplus.

As illustrated earlier, the precondition for the intermediary to maximize profit is that the bid and ask prices end up intermediating the same number of buyers and sellers. Any discrepancy between the two enables the intermediary to either raise the ask price or lower the bid price to increase the bid-ask spread while maintaining the same number of intermediated transactions. Due to complete competition in the search market ($\lambda = 1$), the intermediary is no longer able to intermediate more transactions than it does in the polar case of $\lambda = 0$ through reducing the bid-ask spread. This means that the maximum transactions intermediated will not exceed 1/4 as long as $\lambda > 0$. While the intermediary is able to intermediate more transactions by reducing the bid-ask spread if the search market is inactive ($\lambda = 0$), it is unwilling to do so because its profit will decrease. Hence the strategy of the intermediary in facing competition from the search market is to reduce the bid-ask spread based on the same optimal quantity $q = 1/4$ until both marginal sellers' producer surplus obtained from the higher bid price and marginal buyers' consumer surplus from the lower ask price each are equal to what they would otherwise obtain from bilateral search. Any discrepancy of the surplus between bilateral search and intermediation will lead the marginal buyers and marginal sellers to switch back and forth between search and intermediation.

Suppose that the intermediary lowers the ask price from $a = 3/4$ to a' and raises the bid price from $b = 1/4$ to b' as shown in Figure 16.4. This new bid-ask spread generates a profit, $\pi' = \frac{1}{4}(a' - b')$, to the intermediary when facing competition from bilateral search. Since now the marginal buyer i whose willingness to pay is equal to 3/4 would switch to search for the reason explained above, it follows that all buyers whose willingness to pay is lower than 3/4 will search. By the same token, the marginal seller j whose willingness to sell is equal to 1/4 would switch to search as well, and hence all sellers whose willingness to sell is higher than 1/4 will search. On the other hand, buyers whose willingness to pay is higher than 3/4 may also search until the incremental consumer surplus they obtain from intermediation due to the lower ask price a' is equal to the consumer surplus from search. Intuitively, buyer $i-1$ whose willingness to pay is just above that of buyer i would search if the ask price $a' = a = 3/4$, because he may be able to obtain more surplus through search, and so would buyers $i-2$, $i-3$, and so on with increasingly higher willingness to pay. In recognizing the imminent risk of losing buyers $i-1$, $i-2$, and so on, the intermediary must lower the ask price from a to a' at

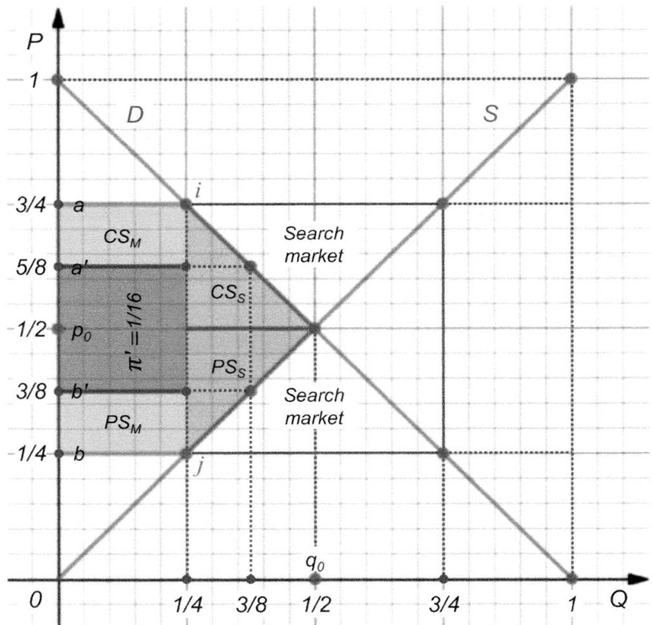

Figure 16.4
Optimal bid-ask spread with bilateral search

which the increase in consumer surplus to all the marginal buyers is equal to what they would otherwise obtain from search.

Figure 16.4 shows that the increased consumer surplus of the buyers in the intermediated market is represented by the rectangle bounded by $a = 3/4$ and a' on the y-axis and 0 and 1/4 on the x-axis, denoted as CS_M, due to the decrease in the ask price from $a = 3/4$ to a'. On the other hand, the maximum consumer surplus that the buyers would obtain in the search market is the triangle between the demand curve and the equilibrium price bounded by 1/4 and 1/2 on the x-axis, which is denoted as CS_S in Figure 16.4. The optimal ask price a' is thus determined when the two streams of consumer surplus are equal, $CS_M = CS_S$. We thus obtain the equation to equalize the consumer surplus of the buyers from intermediation and search:

$$\frac{1}{4}(a-a') = \frac{1}{2} \times \frac{1}{4}\left(a - \frac{1}{2}\right), \tag{16.7}$$

where $a = 3/4$. Solving equation (16.7) we obtain the optimal ask price $a' = 5/8$, which is the minimum of ask price that the intermediary is able and willing to charge buyers if $\lambda = 1$. The intermediary is not willing to lower the ask price below 5/8 because this will reduce its profit, nor is it willing to raise the ask price above 5/8 because this will end up losing the marginal buyers to the search market.

By the same token, sellers whose willingness to sell is lower than or equal to 1/4 may also search until the incremental producer surplus they obtain from a higher bid price is equal to the producer surplus from search. Intuitively, the seller $j-1$ whose willingness to sell is just lower than that of the marginal seller j would also search if the bid price $b' = b = 1/4$, because he could increase his producer surplus in the search market (Figure 16.4), and so would sellers $j-2$, $j-3$, and so on whose willingness to sell is increasingly lower. This again forces the intermediary to raise the bid price from b to b' in order to increase producer surplus to the sellers. Thus, the bid price b' is determined when the increase in producer surplus for the marginal sellers arising from b', denoted as PS_M, is equal to the producer surplus that the sellers would obtain in the search market, denoted as PS_S: $PS_M = PS_S$ (Figure 16.4). Thus, we obtain the equation to equalize the two streams of producer surplus of the sellers from intermediation and search:

$$\frac{1}{4}(b'-b) = \frac{1}{2} \times \frac{1}{4}\left(\frac{1}{2} - b\right), \tag{16.8}$$

where $b = 1/4$. Solving equation (16.8) yields the optimal bid price $b' = 3/8$, which is the maximum of bid price that the intermediary is able and willing to charge sellers if $\lambda = 1$. Thus, the intermediary's profit is maximized at $\pi' = \frac{1}{4}(a' - b') = 1/16$ when the search market is completely active ($\lambda = 1$) as opposed to $\pi = 1/8$ when the search market is inactive ($\lambda = 0$). Note that the profit $\pi' = 1/16$ is the minimum of the profit that the intermediary can obtain in the whole market for all $\lambda \in [0,1]$.

Therefore, when $0 \le \lambda \le 1$, we can readily infer that the ask price a that the intermediary charges will fall in the interval $\left[\frac{5}{8}, \frac{3}{4}\right]$ and the bid price b will fall in $\left[\frac{1}{4}, \frac{3}{8}\right]$. Figure 16.4 shows that the optimal bid-ask spreads straddle symmetrically the Walrasian price $p_0 = 1/2$ with the optimal quantity of transactions intermediated at $q = 1/4$. Figure 16.4 also shows that the bid and ask prices partition the market into three portions. First is the intermediated market in which buyers whose willingness to pay $r > \frac{3}{4}$ and sellers whose willingness to sell $s < \frac{1}{4}$ exclusively trade with the intermediary. Second is the search market in which buyers whose willingness to pay $\frac{1}{4} \le r \le \frac{3}{4}$ and sellers whose willingness to sell $\frac{1}{4} \le s \le \frac{3}{4}$ exclusively search. Third is buyers whose willingness to pay $r < \frac{1}{4}$ and sellers whose willingness to sell $s > \frac{3}{4}$ remain inactive in the market because they have no trading partners to trade with. Compared with the Walrasian auction, the intermediary along with the search market ends up increasing the number of active buyers and sellers each from 1/2 to 3/4. Buyers whose willingness to pay $\frac{1}{4} \le r < \frac{1}{2}$ and sellers whose willingness to sell $\frac{1}{2} < s \le \frac{3}{4}$ who are not coordinated in the Walrasian auction remain active in the search market (Figure 16.4).

16.4 Intermediation versus disintermediation

16.4.1 The emergence of intermediaries

While transaction costs are ubiquitous, they are arguably more severe in the tourism market than in markets for tangible commodities. There are three sources of transaction costs specific to the tourism market. First of all, the demand and supply in tourism are separated between two geographical locations. Firms rendering products and services to tourists are clustered at destinations while tourists could be hundreds or even thousands of miles away. Thus, search costs between tourists and service providers are substantial as long distances make communication extremely difficult and costly. As a consequence, a transaction may not occur at all because search costs could prevent a prospective tourist from identifying suitable suppliers and trading with them, or vice versa. Second, the tourism product is a conglomerate of all sorts of products and services in a wide range of sectors. Even after identifying the suppliers, tourists need to bargain with each of the suppliers to settle every single deal. This is not only time consuming but was impossible in the early days of modern tourism. Third, in addition to dealing with numerous suppliers, tourists need to make a series of reservations for tourism products and services in advance which are promised to be delivered by suppliers as soon as tourists arrive at destinations. However, monitoring the consistency between what is purchased in advance and what is delivered afterwards and enforcing a series of contracts between suppliers and tourists complicate the whole transactions.

Therefore, travel intermediaries have been instrumental in the development of modern tourism since the mid-nineteenth century. The pivotal role that Thomas Cook played was being an information broker between tourists and various suppliers, particularly in the accommodation and the transportation sectors. In 1855 Thomas Cook started to offer an all-inclusive package that incorporated travel, accommodation, and food in one single fare for the tour to the Great Exhibition in Paris.[5] Tourists would no longer need to contact individual service providers because a package tour incorporated all goods and services at their discretion. In the late nineteenth century when the telegraph and telephones were still decades away from being widely used by consumers, it was simply impossible for the masses to take independent trips to destinations far afield by cutting deals with various service providers. Thomas Cook economized on all transaction costs in the tourism market with a single fare for package tours. Tourists purchasing a package tour from a travel agency is as if they contract with the travel agency instead of numerous service providers for the products and services they need. Obviously, the contract will be enforced by the travel agency on behalf of both tourists and various service providers. Since a huge number of direct transactions between tourists and service providers are drastically reduced or even eliminated once for all, a breach of contract would less likely to occur.

16.4.2 Disintermediation

In the Internet age travel agencies that are adjacent to consumer markets have become less relevant than ever in selling tourism products and services. Hence conventional travel intermediaries such as Thomas Cook have been gradually supplanted by online travel agencies (OTA) as a superior institutional arrangement to further reduce transaction costs in the tourism market.[6] Apart from furnishing tourists with price and product information, OTAs can better assure the quality of products and services delivered by service providers through online customer reviews, leading to their predominance in the market. In the U.S. hotel market the direct-to-indirect booking ratio, a measure of the number of direct bookings from hotels for every indirect booking through travel intermediaries, decreased from 4.3 in 2011 to 2.7 in 2015.[7] A series of surveys in Switzerland also shows that hoteliers reported around 27% of their bookings from intermediaries in 2002, which peaked at 42.5% in 2014 before slightly decreasing ever since (Figure 16.5). The increased market share of indirect booking suggests that hotels rely heavily on intermediaries in selling hotel rooms despite technology also reducing the costs of direct booking in the meantime. Instead of rendering travel intermediaries obsolete, the Internet and mobile technology consolidate the market power of OTAs. This means that transaction costs between tourists and service providers cannot be eliminated due to the complexity of transactions in tourism and hospitality.

Nevertheless, there is an increasing concern about the escalating costs of OTAs in hotel distribution among others. These costs are, in essence, the bid-ask spread taking the form of commissions passed on by service providers to travel intermediaries. Yet it is not uncommon in other businesses, such as in the real estate market, that commissions are charged to buyers instead of to sellers. Figure 16.6 shows that in the U.S. hotel industry the growth of commissions was twice as fast as the growth of room revenue over the period 2011–2015. A survey in Switzerland found that nearly one-third of surveyed hotels (27%) paid as much as 15% of their room revenue as commissions

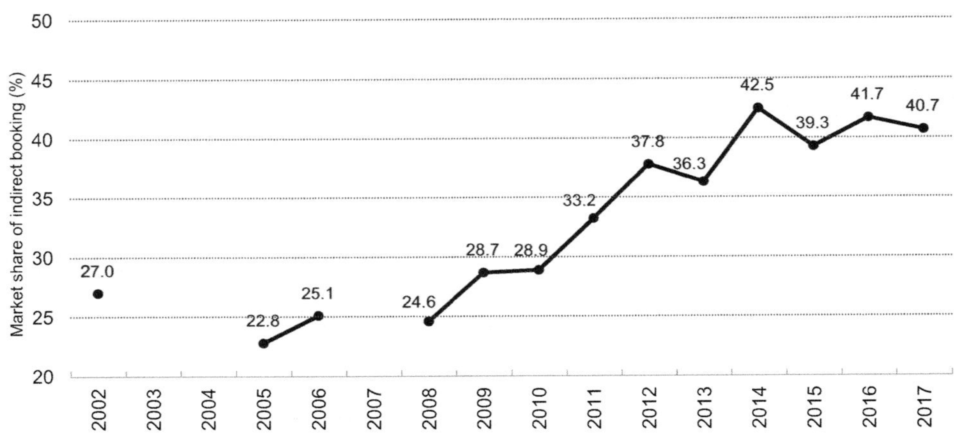

Figure 16.5
Market share of indirect booking in Swiss hotel industry

Note: Data in 2003, 2004, and 2007 are not available. Market shares of indirect booking in total bookings were recorded for 2002, 2005–2006, 2008–2012, and 2014; market shares of room nights from indirect booking in total room nights were recorded for 2013 and 2015. All data were collected from hoteliers in Switzerland.

Source: Roland Schegg. European Hotel Distribution Study 2018, p. 55.

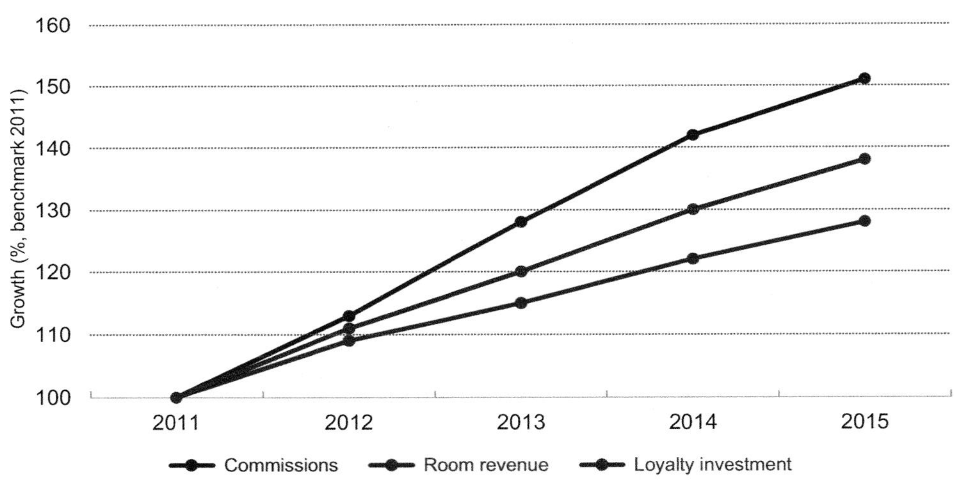

Figure 16.6
Commission growth in the U.S. hotel industry

Note: Commissions are the proportion of room revenue paid by hotels to travel intermediaries. Room revenue, or ADR, is the revenue obtained by hotels through room sales. Loyalty investment includes the fees paid by hotel franchisees to hotel chains in connection with hotel chains' loyalty programs designed to support franchisees in their efforts to acquire and retain guests. The year 2011 was the baseline year to calculate the growth rate as an index through 2015 in the U.S. hotel industry.

Source: Reproduced from Kalibri Labs. Outlook for Accommodations 2016, presentation slide 13.

to intermediaries in 2016.[8] This also means that transaction costs in the Internet age become more complicated, hence entailing new institutional arrangements, such as blockchain, which is a decentralized peer-to-peer ledger that records and enforces transactions. As tourists and consumers at large crave flexibility and efficiency more than accessibility and affordability, disintermediation would sooner or later substitute for intermediation, or both could coexist and grapple with each other in acquiring customers. This does not change the fundamental principle in market transaction that institutions emerged to reduce transaction costs, and those prevailing in the market are the ones which reduce transaction costs more efficiently than others.

Summary

1. In conventional economic models we postulate that market transactions are executed by the Walrasian auctioneer who knows all buyers' and sellers' willingness to pay and sell and can thus match all buyers and sellers who are able and willing to trade with each other. The Walrasian equilibrium is the market equilibrium.
2. Transaction costs are all sorts of costs associated with the fulfillment of market transactions between buyers and sellers. Transaction costs primarily include search costs in discovering and identifying trading partners, bargaining costs in reaching market prices and settling deals, and the costs of enforcing contracts, among others.
3. An intermediary is an economic agent that purchases from sellers for resale to buyers or helps buyers and sellers meet and transact with each other. Therefore, intermediaries arise from transaction costs and execute transactions, which sets them apart from sellers performing production and buyers performing consumption.
4. Bilateral search is a process where buyers and sellers meet with each other and grope for their willingness to pay and sell, and trade directly. Intermediation is trade intermediated by an intermediary between buyers and sellers.
5. In intermediation bid price is a low price that an intermediary buys a good from sellers whereas ask price is a high price that the intermediary quotes to buyers for resale. The bid-ask spread is the profit that the intermediary reaps from each transaction.
6. When transaction costs are insurmountable, the search market will become inactive and hence the intermediary monopolizes the market. Buyers and sellers have no choice but to trade through the intermediary, and hence the optimal bid-ask spread is maximized.
7. As long as the search market is active, the optimal bid-ask spread is determined in market equilibrium in which buyers' consumer surplus and sellers' producer surplus from intermediation each are equal to what they would otherwise obtain from search.
8. In market equilibrium the optimal ask price that the intermediary charges falls in the interval $\left[\frac{5}{8}, \frac{3}{4}\right]$ and the optimal bid price b falls in $\left[\frac{1}{4}, \frac{3}{8}\right]$. Compared with the Walrasian auction, intermediation increases the number of active buyers and sellers in the market.
9. Transaction costs in tourism can be attributed to the geographical separation of supply and demand, the tourism product as a conglomerate, and the asynchrony in purchase and delivery of tourism products and services.

10. The existence of transaction costs explains the emergence of travel agencies in the early days of modern tourism as well as online travel agencies in the Internet era. The advent of disintermediation, such as blockchain, suggests that new institutional arrangements are more efficient in reducing transaction costs in the market.

REVIEW QUESTIONS

Each question has four options, and there is only one correct answer to each question.

1. Which of the following aspects in market transaction gives rise to transaction costs in booking a hotel?
   A) Searching for various hotel information on Booking.com.
   B) Bargaining a room rate with a receptionist over the phone.
   C) Making a hotel reservation using a VISA credit card.
   D) All of the above.
2. As far as transaction costs are concerned, which of the following can be regarded as a *firm* as opposed to a producer?
   A) A travel agency
   B) An airline company
   C) A restaurant
   D) A railway company
3. Which of the following is the function of travel intermediaries?
   A) Purchasing room nights from hotels.
   B) Handling hotel reservations of guests.
   C) Facilitating payment between guests and hotels.
   D) All of the above.
4. Which of the following is the immediate reason that buyers and sellers choose to trade with an intermediary even though the matching probability in bilateral search is 100%?
   A) Marginal costs are considerable.
   B) Search costs are considerable.
   C) Bargaining costs are considerable.
   D) Contract enforcement costs are considerable.
5. Which of the following is correct regarding the bid and ask prices that an intermediary charges when the matching probability is zero in the search market?
   A) The bid price is the maximum.
   B) The ask price is the maximum.
   C) The bid price is higher than the Walrasian price.
   D) The ask price is lower than the Walrasian price.

6. Suppose that there are 100 buyers and 100 sellers in the market, and their willingness to pay and sell are uniformly distributed and standardized in the interval [0, 1]. If the matching probability is 100% ($\lambda = 1$) in the search market, how many buyers and sellers will engage in bilateral search, respectively, on the condition that the intermediary maximizes profit?
   A) 0; 0
   B) 25; 25
   C) 50; 50
   D) 75; 75
7. In Question 6 suppose that the maximum of buyers' willingness to pay is $40, which is equal to the maximum of sellers' willingness to sell. What would be the optimal bid-ask spread?
   A) $6
   B) $8
   C) $10
   D) $20
8. According to a study by Kalibri Labs in 2016, the direct-to-indirect booking ratio decreased from 4.3 in 2011 to 2.7 in 2015 in the U.S. hotel industry. Which of the following is correct?
   A) The volume of intermediated transactions increased.
   B) The volume of intermediated transactions decreased.
   C) Intermediated transactions increased relative to bilateral search.
   D) Intermediated transactions decreased relative to bilateral search.
9. Which of the following is NOT related to transaction costs in the hotel industry?
   A) Commissions
   B) Loyalty investment
   C) Room revenue
   D) Advertising
10. What would be the fundamental reason that traditional travel agencies, such as Thomas Cook, are gradually supplanted by online travel agencies (OTAs), such as Booking.com and TripAdvisor?
   A) OTAs would be more efficient in reducing transaction costs in the market.
   B) OTAs would have eliminated transaction costs in the market.
   C) OTAs would incur very few variable costs in operation.
   D) OTAs would incur very few fixed costs in operation.

Problem solving

1. Thomas Cook AG used to be the largest tour operator in the United Kingdom and the second largest in Europe before bankruptcy in 2019. In its 178 years of history since the foundation of Thomas Cook & Son, Thomas Cook acquired and merged with various travel agencies and airlines. As early as the 2000s, Thomas Cook acquired Condor Airlines, a Lufthansa subsidiary, to expand its airline

business and tour operating business in general.[9] In 2007, Thomas Cook merged with MyTravel, a UK tour operator with a stock market value of £1.1 billion, and this merger could cut operating costs by an estimated £75 million a year.[10] In 2011 Thomas Cook merged with one of the UK's largest tour operators, Co-operative Travel, which could save the company another £75 million a year.[11] Explain why Thomas Cook sought mergers and acquisitions.

2. According to market research on both travelers and its airline partners, a travel agency estimates that the demand function of travelers for the airline tickets on a particular route is $Q = -P + 500$, and the supply function of the airlines is $Q = P - 60$. Travelers' willingness to pay and airlines' willingness to sell are both uniformly distributed in the market. Suppose that the tickets can be sold either through the travel agency or through travelers' direct booking from the airlines. If the travel agency's intermediating cost is \$20 per ticket with travelers and \$40 per ticket with the airlines, will the intermediation be economically viable for the travel agency? If so, what would be the minimum and maximum profits of the travel agency, respectively, and on what conditions?
3. *Rate parity* is a legal agreement between hotels and online travel agencies (OTA) that stipulates that hotels must guarantee the same rate for the same room on all distribution channels, including their own websites. This means that hotels must provide the same room rate to OTAs, regardless of commissions, as they sell on their own websites or through any other direct booking channels, provided that the rooms and other relevant conditions that would affect consumer choice are the same. Rate parity has been gradually outlawed in many European countries including France, Austria, Italy, and Belgium since 2015, and many other countries are following the lead, including Switzerland.[12] How would rate parity affect economic surplus in the search and intermediated markets?

Solutions to all review questions and problem solving tasks are included in the Support Material for this book, which can be accessed at www.routledge.com/9780367897352.

Notes

1 Coase (1960), p. 15.

2 Spulber (1996b), p. 135.

3 Probably the first study that formally modeled the intermediary was Rubinstein's and Wolinsky's paper "Middlemen" published in the *Quarterly Journal of Economics* in 1987.

4 Spulber (1996b), p. 138.

5 CNN. Thomas Cook: A history of one of the world's oldest travel firms. September 23, 2019.

6 Thomas Cook declared a sudden bankruptcy on September 23, 2019, concluding its 178 years of splendid yet checkered history in tour operation. According to *Business Insider*, this bankruptcy left some 600,000 tourists stranded at destinations across the world, leading to the largest peacetime repatriation in British history.

7 The direct-to-indirect booking ratio was calculated for hotels with ADR greater than $100 in the U.S. Source: Green, C. E., and Lomanno, M. V. (2016). Demystifying the digital marketplace: Spotlight on the hospitality industry. (Part 1, p. 10.) Rockville, MD: Kalibri Labs.

8 A total number of 295 hotels were surveyed in Switzerland in 2016. Source: Roland Schegg. Strong growth of online travel agencies (OTA) in the Swiss hotel industry in 2016, p. 36.

9 eTurboNews. Is Condor Airlines still flying after Thomas Cook bankruptcy? September 23, 2019.

10 *The Independent*. MyTravel and Thomas Cook merge. February 12, 2007.

11 BBC. Thomas Cook and Co-Op Travel merger gets final approval. August 16, 2011.

12 The trivago Business Blog. What's happening with rate parity in the hotel industry? March 14, 2019.

Bibliography

Coase, R. H. (1937). The nature of the firm. *Economica (new series), 4*(16), 386–405.

Coase, R. H. (1960). The problem of social cost. *Journal of Law & Economics, 3*, 1–44.

Commons, J. R. (1931). Institutional economics. *American Economic Review, 21*(4), 648–657.

Gehrig, T. (1993). Intermediation in search markets. *Journal of Economics & Management Strategy, 2*(1), 97–120.

Rubinstein, A., & Wolinsky, A. (1987). Middlemen. *Quarterly Journal of Economics, 102*(3), 581–593.

Spulber, D. F. (1996a). Market making by price-setting firms. *Review of Economic Studies, 63*(4), 559–580.

Spulber, D. F. (1996b). Market microstructure and intermediation. *Journal of Economic Perspectives, 10*(3), 135–152.

Walras, L. (2014). *Leon Walras's elements of theoretical economics* (Translated and edited by D. A. Walker and J. van Daal). London, UK: Cambridge University Press.

17 The two-sided market and price structure

This chapter analyzes the behavior of platforms as the second type of institutional arrangement besides intermediaries. Platforms are grounded on and arise from the existence of externality between users on two sides of a market. We first present the stylized facts of the two-sided market in which cross-side network externality is instrumental in its function. Second, we provide a canonical definition of two-sidedness based on recent economic literature in order to articulate the essence of the market and to set it apart from other seemingly similar yet fundamentally distinct institutions, such as intermediaries, among others. Third, we analyze the pricing behavior of platforms which consists of setting an implicit price for interactions as a prerequisite and structuring the price on the two sides of the market as a manifestation. Finally, we draw implications from the Coase theorem to discuss why cross-side network externality cannot be internalized by users but by the platform as an institution in the market.

AFTER STUDYING THIS CHAPTER, YOU SHOULD BE ABLE TO:

- **Understand three market participants in the two-sided market and illustrate the cross-side network externality;**
- **Understand the market for interactions and how the market is made up of the demands from buyers and sellers on two sides;**
- **Analyze the behavior of platforms including pricing the interactions and structuring the price on the two sides in the market; and**
- **Understand the Coase theorem and explain the implications of the Coase theorem to the emergence of platforms.**

17.1 Externality and the platform

17.1.1 A descriptive framework

Over the past decade or so we have seen a number of enterprises, such as Uber, Airbnb, and OpenTable to name a few, operating as platforms through which users on one side interact with their counterparts on the other side. The interactions between users on two sides require them to get access to a platform equally and synchronically in the first place. In other words, the platform plays a central role in coordinating two sides of users, thereby enabling and facilitating interactions between them. Such an institutional arrangement is known as the two-sided market. Figure 17.1 describes a typical two-sided market exemplified by Uber.[1] On one side of Uber are riders purchasing riding services from drivers on the other side.[2] The transactions between riders and drivers are mediated by Uber as a platform in matching and coordinating riders' demand and drivers' supply in the market. On the one hand, riders rely on Uber to make ride requests which are served by drivers, and on the other hand drivers need to lure riders through Uber. Therefore, Uber needs to court both riders and drivers at the same time in order to mediate transactions between them. Insofar as riders and drivers circumvent Uber and transact directly by themselves, no transactions will be mediated by Uber as the platform but the transactions between them may be executed nonetheless.

Likewise, Airbnb is a platform in the two-sided market that coordinates transactions between guests on one side and hosts on the other, and so is OpenTable connecting diners on one side and restaurants on the other. Yet businesses featured by the two-sided market not only incorporate what are colloquially known as sharing economy businesses, but also relate to conventional products, enterprises, and institutions. For instance, a console of video games is a platform that links game developers on one side and gamers on the other. Thus a console company, such as Nintendo, needs to court both developers and gamers whereby an interaction is mediated when a gamer buys and plays a game that is designed by a developer for the console. A credit card is a platform which needs to court merchants who accept the card and cardholders who use the card for payment. An interaction is mediated when a cardholder uses the card to make a payment that is accepted by a merchant. A newspaper mediates interactions between readers and advertisers once a reader reads an advertisement posted by an advertiser in the newspaper. This is the same as Facebook, YouTube, Twitter, and the like, mediating interactions between viewers and advertisers. Therefore, a platform may

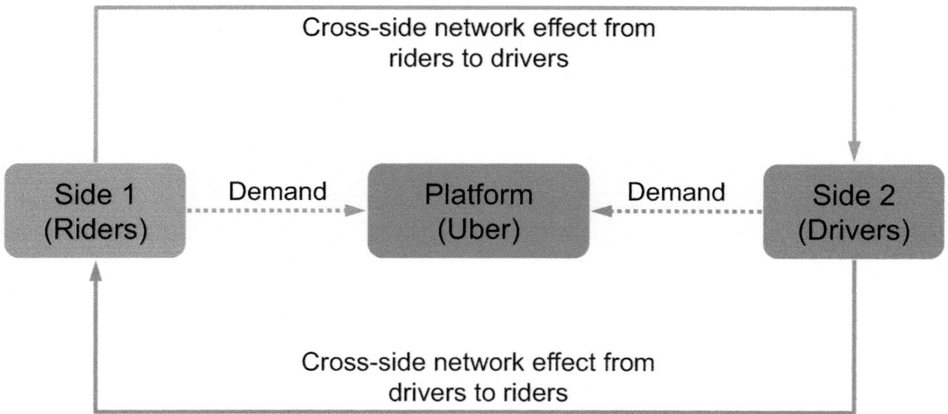

Figure 17.1
Uber in the two-sided market

not be a specific corporate entity, or a product thereof, but in essence an institutional arrangement that mediates interactions between two sides of users in the market.

17.1.2 Cross-side network externality

With very few exceptions, the more users are on one side, the more valuable a platform will become to users on the other side, and vice versa. This means that an increase in user base on one side of the platform generates an externality to users on the other side, and vice versa. This is known as cross-side network externality. As far as transactions are concerned, the cross-side network externality suggests the interdependence of buyers and sellers in using the platform, and is thus different from network externality generated on the same side. For Uber, the more drivers register on Uber, the more riders will be willing to use Uber and make ride requests. As drivers increase on Uber, Uber brings about more benefits to riders, thereby increasing the use of Uber by riders. Hence the cross-side network effect running from drivers to riders is positive (Figure 17.1).[3] On the other hand, drivers' use of Uber depends on the number of riders subscribing to Uber. The more riders register on Uber, the more drivers will be willing to use Uber to reach riders, because they can access more riders on Uber. If no riders were using Uber, it would make no sense for drivers to use Uber at all. Therefore, the cross-side network effect running from riders to drivers is also positive.

However, the cross-side network externality may not be reciprocal and symmetric. It is not reciprocal insofar as an increase of users on one side is detrimental to a platform for attracting users on the other side. For a newspaper, there is a positive cross-side network effect from readers to advertisers, meaning that the more readers subscribe to or read the newspaper, the more valuable the newspaper will become to advertisers for posting ads. However, the more ads are in the newspaper, the less attractive it will become to readers whose goal after all is to retrieve newsworthy information instead of reading ads. Thus, the cross-side network effect from advertisers to readers is negative. In order to mediate sufficient interactions between readers and advertisers, there is a tradeoff between increasing advertisers who generate revenue for the newspaper and captivating readers who entice advertisers to post ads. For dating clubs courting both bachelorettes and bachelors, the cross-side network effects are reciprocal yet perhaps asymmetric. In most cases dating clubs rest on females to attract males, not the other way around, and hence females are offered a discount or free entry while males are overcharged. Probably in some societies where males are in shortage, the cross-side network effect might be reversed, and hence the value of dating clubs lies in the number of males that are being attracted in the first place.

17.2 What makes a two-sided market?

17.2.1 The implicit market for interactions

The fundamental role that a platform plays is to create an implicit market for interactions between two sides of users engaging in some sort of transaction or exchange. This is the tenet of the two-sided market model developed by French economists Jean-Charles

Rochet (1958–) and Jean Tirole (1953–).[4] If the market for interactions were explicit, there would be a price for each interaction mediated by a platform that both sides would jointly be willing to pay. The interactions mediated by platforms can be market transactions between buyers and sellers in trading goods and services or simply interactions that have no bearing on trade. As for transactions, Uber matches riders and drivers in a way that riding services are transacted between the two sides through the platform of Uber. In this case, Uber resembles an intermediary, yet the difference is that a platform, by definition, does not resell riding services but only facilitates transactions between riders and drivers. Thus, platforms' profits depend on the price of each transaction they mediate instead of the bid-ask spread as in intermediation. From a platform's point of view, it does not matter whether market transactions can be ultimately fulfilled between users. What matters is the quantity and quality of interactions that platforms mediate which eventually lead to market transactions.

In the case of newspapers, transactions between readers and advertisers are not the same as interactions mediated by newspapers. As stated above, an interaction between two sides occurs when a reader reads an ad placed by an advertiser in a newspaper. Note that it is not the case in which the reader sees the ad and proceeds to transact with the advertiser for the product being advertised. The interaction comes with no market transactions between the reader and the advertiser, but with the visibility that the newspaper generates to the advertiser which in turn depends on the reader base. That said, it does not mean that the quality of interactions is immaterial, namely whether the reader reads the ad spontaneously or purposefully and whether he would proceed to purchase the product from the advertiser. It is true that those who read the ad purposefully are presumably prospective customers of the advertiser, and thus businesses can be channeled by the newspaper to the advertiser. Since the quantity and quality of interactions are difficult to measure, the advertiser would choose a newspaper that has a robust reader base on the one hand and on the other the readers' profile must be well aligned with what the advertiser's product appeals. Other things being equal, the more readers and advertisers affiliate to a newspaper, the more interactions the newspaper can mediate, and the more valuable it will become.

17.2.2 Demands for the platform

As long as interactions can be well defined and properly measured by a platform, it is plausible that the platform can sell the interactions to users. For instance, Uber could sell interactions between riders and drivers in a way that both sides share a fee for each ride request executed on its platform. The same is true for Airbnb and OpenTable, which can sell each interaction by charging a reservation fee that is shared by both sides of users. For some platforms such as newspapers and Facebook where the interactions are neither observable nor can be properly measured, selling interactions is no longer feasible. Obviously, interactions between readers and advertisers cannot be monitored and measured by a newspaper enterprise and hence cannot be sold as a separate good or service. Instead, the newspaper could charge readers a once-for-all subscription fee allowing them to get access to the platform irrespective of whether they read the ads spontaneously or purposefully while charging advertisers a fee for each ad posted in the newspaper. No matter what the industry contexts are, we would expect that the more users are on both sides of a platform, the more interactions the platform can mediate between them.

Therefore, the implicit market for interactions is manifested by the demands of users on both sides of a platform. If there are no or very few users on either side, the number of interactions mediated by the platform will be zero or negligible, regardless of the number of users on the other side. Thus platform companies aim to amass users on both sides simultaneously. Other things being equal, the number of users on either side is determined by the price that the platform charges on that side. Here we focus on a platform as a monopolist to simplify the analysis. Suppose that the platform charges buyers p_B and sellers p_S to entitle them to get access to and use the platform.[5] Thus, buyers' demand for using the platform is a function of price p_B: $D_B(p_B)$, which denotes the number of buyers willing to use the platform depending on the utility that they obtain from the platform. Note that the utility buyers obtain is not the benefit obtained when interacting with sellers but from the platform per se. For example, the utility that readers obtain from a newspaper is the newsworthy information instead of a product purchased from an advertiser. Likewise, sellers' demand for using the platform is a function of price p_S: $D_S(p_S)$, which denotes the number of sellers willing to use the platform depending on the utility they obtain from the platform per se. Thus, the number of potential interactions mediated by the platform is the number of buyers multiplied by the number of sellers who use the platform simultaneously:

$$N = D_B(p_B)D_S(p_S). \tag{17.1}$$

First of all, function (17.1) suggests that the number of interactions mediated by the platform depends on both the number of buyers and the number of sellers using the platform, which in turn depend on p_B and p_S, respectively. There are two ways to interpret the demands of buyers and sellers depending on whether their interactions involve market transactions or not. In the newspaper case without transactions, $D_B(p_B)$ can be interpreted as the number of readers who subscribe to a newspaper through paying a subscription fee p_B; $D_S(p_S)$ can be interpreted as the number of advertisers who place ads in the newspaper through paying an advertising fee p_S. In the Uber case with transactions, $D_B(p_B)$ can be interpreted as the number of riders who pay a reservation fee p_B in order to make a ride request on Uber, and $D_S(p_S)$ can be interpreted as the number of drivers who also pay a reservation fee p_S to be entitled to serve a ride request channeled by Uber. In both cases the lower p_B and p_S are, according to the law of demand, the greater $D_B(p_B)$ and $D_S(p_S)$ will be and hence the more interactions the platform can mediate between the two sides.

Second, function (17.1) suggests that the platform works as if it courts buyers and sellers separately with no regard to the cross-side network externality. As we have explained in great detail, the number of buyers $D_B(p_B)$ subscribing to a platform also depends on the number of sellers $D_S(p_S)$ using the platform, and vice versa.

Simply because the interaction is *the* product created by the platform after courting buyers and sellers, the number of interactions depends, in the first place, on the value of interactions to users on either side or both sides of the platform. In the case of newspapers, obviously the interaction is valued by advertisers instead of readers because the cross-side network effect running from readers to advertisers is positive. In the case of Uber, the interaction is valued by both sides because the cross-side network effects from riders to drivers and from drivers to riders are both positive, and hence reciprocal. Therefore, the greater the cross-side network externalities are, the more valuable the interactions will be, and the higher price the interactions can command. Thus, we can rewrite function (17.1) by incorporating the price of interactions in order to reflect the value of the cross-side network externality between the two sides of users:

$$N = f(p, p_B, p_S) = D_B(p_B)D_S(p_S), \tag{17.2}$$

where p is the price of interactions, which is implicit in the market and unobservable. This is because the platform does not charge the price p but instead allocates it to buyers and sellers in the form of $p = p_B + p_S$. Function (17.2) shows that the number of interactions mediated by the platform depends on three prices in two stages. In the first stage, the platform needs to set price for the interactions that are not taken into account by buyers and sellers when deciding to use the platform separately. If neither side valued the interactions, the price of interactions p would be zero, and then the platform is negated in the market. Hence there is no need to discuss p_B and p_S. In the second stage, given the price of interactions, p, the platform needs to structure p on the two sides, thereby determining the optimal prices p_B and p_S that will maximize the number of interactions, N. This is because N is the product of $D_B(p_B)$ and $D_S(p_S)$ which in turn are interdependent due to the cross-side network externality. Hence the allocation of p to buyers and sellers is by no means arbitrary. The optimal prices p_B and p_S constrained by p must maximize the number of interactions through coordinating the number of buyers and sellers participating on the platform. Therefore, p_B and p_S depend not only on buyers' and sellers' respective demands for using the platform but also on the extent to which they affect each other on using the platform.

17.2.3 Defining two-sidedness

Based on the two-sided market described in Figure 17.1, any institution that links two sides of trading partners may be seen as being in the two-sided market. For instance, an intermediary may mistakenly be regarded as a platform in linking sellers on one side and buyers on the other, and the bid and ask prices may thus be misinterpreted as p_S and p_B, respectively. According to Rochet and Tirole's model, a market is two-sided if and only if the number of interactions varies by the allocation of the implicit price p between buyers and sellers. This means that the number of interactions must be accounted for by the proportion of p_B versus p_S given the implicit price p rather than by the level of the implicit price as a whole. This definition allows us to model the cross-side network externalities that are peculiar to, and also a defining element of, two-sidedness. In other words, if the number of interactions mediated by a platform does not vary by the price structure of p_B and p_S holding the implicit price p constant, the market is still one-sided despite seemingly having two sides of users. Thus, an intermediary is one-sided because what matters to the intermediary is the bid-ask spread rather than how the bid and ask prices are allocated to sellers and buyers. For intermediaries, buyers' demand and sellers' supply are independent, and so are the ask and bid prices.

To illustrate the idea of two-sidedness, suppose that the implicit price of each interaction mediated by Uber is \$1 which maximizes Uber's profit. This implicit price can be interpreted as the price that Uber would charge for each ride request made and fulfilled on its platform. Obviously, there are numerous ways as to how the \$1 is shared by riders and drivers, and is thus manifested as p_B charged to riders and p_S to drivers. For instance, Uber could simply allow each rider and driver to split the \$1, and hence $p_B = p_S = \$0.5$, or charge more on one side while less on the other, say $p_B = \$0.6$ for riders and $p_S = \$0.4$ for drivers, and so on. If riders and drivers were independent in using Uber, what matters to Uber is not the allocation of p_B and p_S on the two sides but the implicit price of interactions that is maximized only when p_B and p_S are charged as two monopoly prices to riders and drivers, separately. However, holding the implicit price of interactions constant, if the number of interactions varies from one allocation of 50% versus 50% to another of 60% versus 40% or to any other allocations between riders and drivers, the market is two-sided. Thus, there exists an optimal allocation of p_B and p_S that maximizes the number of interactions, and hence the profit of the platform. If so, Uber can increase the number of interactions by simply structuring the implicit price of interactions without changing the price per se. It is the cross-side network externalities that make the price structure matter.

17.3 Price decision of the platform

17.3.1 Profit maximization

According to the definition of two-sidedness, a platform's profit-maximizing problem is two-fold. First, it needs to figure out the optimal implicit price of interactions p that maximizes its profit. Second, the platform needs to identify the optimal price structure by allocating the implicit price p on two sides to maximize the number of interactions and hence its profit. In other words, the platform needs to identify the optimal price p_B charged to buyers and p_S to sellers. Only when p_B and p_S are determined can the implicit price of interactions be manifested in the market. Suppose that the marginal cost of interactions mediated by the platform is c, then we can write out the profit function of the platform by factoring in the number of interactions determined in function (17.2):

$$\pi = (p - c)D_B D_S = (p_B + p_S - c)D_B D_S, \qquad (17.3)$$

where D_B is $D_B(p_B)$ and D_S is $D_S(p_S)$ for short, which are used from now on to simplify the notations throughout the analysis that follows. Function (17.3) suggests that the platform's profit depends on the implicit price of interactions, p, as well as on the price structure, namely how p is allocated on two sides. Once the implicit price p is determined, it reflects the value of interactions mediated by the platform on the one hand and, on the other hand, a constraint that the platform imposes on the two sides of users. Therefore, p_B and p_S are not monopoly prices that the platform will charge on both sides when the two sides are independent in their demand. This is why the platform needs to coordinate p_B and p_S under the constraint of the implicit price in order to maximize profit through maximizing the number of interactions in the first place. Based on two-sidedness as defined above, the profit-maximizing problem is, given the implicit price, how the platform allocates p on the two sides in order to maximize the number of interactions, and hence its profit.

17.3.2 Implicit price of interactions

Determining the implicit price of interactions is the prerequisite to identifying p_B and p_S. The platform's profit-maximizing price for interactions is straightforward. The optimal price of interactions is determined by referring to the Lerner index defined in formula (10.9) in Chapter 10. The Lerner index suggests that the price of interactions is determined by the marginal cost of interactions and the price elasticity of demand for interactions. Note that the demand for interactions is interpreted as if either buyers, sellers, or both sides would value an interaction mediated by the platform and are therefore willing to pay for it. In the case of newspapers, an interaction is arguably valued by advertisers, and hence they are willing to pay for it. In the case of Uber, an interaction is simply a ride request mediated by Uber that is valued by both riders and drivers as long as they engage in a trade. Suppose that the price elasticity of demand for interactions in the market is η, so the Lerner index is given as

$$\frac{p-c}{p}=-\frac{1}{\eta}, \tag{17.4}$$

where $\eta=(dN/dp)(p/N)$. Since $c>0$, we have $\eta<-1$. From formula (17.4) we derive the price of interactions $p=\frac{\eta}{\eta+1}c$ in the market. Thus, as long as we know the price elasticity of demand for interactions η and the platform's marginal cost c in mediating interactions between two sides, we can determine the implicit price of interactions. It is worth mentioning that the implicit price is a theoretical imperative for us to further determine p_B and p_S, because the platform after all does not charge the price of interactions in the market. We shall see shortly that the implicit price will be fully accounted for by p_B and p_S on the two sides of the platform, and hence it is indeed mute in the market. The reason is that there is usually no such market existing in the real world in which a platform could sell interactions to buyers, sellers, or both.

Nevertheless, the implicit price is the constraint imposed on the two sides that reflects the value of interactions to the two sides of users and suggests the size of the cross-side network externalities. Thus, p_B and p_S are not determined separately by the platform but are constrained by the value of interactions to the two sides of users.

17.3.3 Price structure on two sides

Given the implicit price of interactions solved from formula (17.4), we proceed to identify the optimal price structure that maximizes the number of interactions and hence the profit of the platform. Referring to the platform's profit function (17.3) which depends on both p_B and p_S, we know that the platform's profit is maximized when the marginal profits of the platform with respect to p_B and p_S are zero, respectively. If otherwise, the platform can always change its profit through altering the allocation of the implicit price on both sides. Hence only when the marginal profits with respect to p_B and p_S are both zero can the platform's profit be maximized. Thus, the partial derivatives of the profit with respect to p_B and p_S must be zero:

$$\begin{cases} \dfrac{\partial \pi}{\partial p_B} = D_B D_S + (p_B + p_S - c)(D_B)' D_S = 0, \\ \dfrac{\partial \pi}{\partial p_S} = D_B D_S + (p_B + p_S - c) D_B (D_S)' = 0, \end{cases} \tag{17.5}$$

where $(D_B)'$ is the derivative of D_B with respect to p_B, and hence it is the marginal demand of buyers for using the platform with no regard to sellers on the other side, other things being equal; $(D_S)'$ is the derivative of D_S with respect to p_S, indicating the marginal demand of sellers for using the platform with no regard to buyers. Solving equations (17.5) and simplifying the procedure, we obtain

$$(D_B)' D_S = D_B (D_S)', \tag{17.6}$$

where $(D_B)' D_S$ denotes the marginal change in the number of interactions with respect to p_B on buyers' side, and $D_B (D_S)'$ is the marginal change in the number of interactions with respect to p_S on sellers' side, other things being equal. The economic intuition of equation (17.6) is that only when the marginal changes in interactions with respect to p_B and p_S are equal can the total number of interactions be maximized, and hence the platform's profit is maximized. Otherwise, given the implicit price p, the platform can always manipulate p_B and p_S in order to alter the number of interactions mediated, thereby changing its profit. For instance, holding D_S constant, the platform can increase D_B by lowering p_B, thereby increasing the number of interactions $D_B D_S$. Obviously, if sellers' demand D_S does not respond to p_S at all, the platform can maximize the number of interactions $D_B D_S$ by only maximizing D_B, which entails minimizing p_B only. Yet this presumption is not compatible with the two-sided market as we shall see shortly. In fact, as p_B falls, the platform has to shift the price burden to sellers by increasing p_S, which will in turn diminish D_S, and hence the number of interactions $D_B D_S$ falls. Therefore, only if the marginal changes in $D_B D_S$ with respect to p_B and p_S are equal can the number of interactions be maximized, and also the platform's profit.

Referring to the relationship between marginal demand and the price elasticity of demand illustrated in formula (5.10) in Chapter 5, we are able to articulate the relationship between the marginal demand for using the platform on the two sides and their corresponding price elasticities of demand for using the platform. Suppose that buyers' demand elasticity for using the platform is η_B and sellers' demand elasticity for using the platform is η_S. By definition we have

$$\eta_B = (D_B)' \frac{p_B}{D_B}, \tag{17.7}$$

$$\eta_S = (D_S)' \frac{p_S}{D_S}. \tag{17.8}$$

Note that $\eta_B < 0$ and $\eta_S < 0$. Plugging equation (17.6) into η_B (or η_S) in formula (17.7) or (17.8) we obtain η_B (or η_S):

$$\eta_B = (D_B)' \frac{p_B}{D_B} = \frac{D_B (D_S)'}{D_S} \frac{p_B}{D_B} = \frac{\eta_S p_B}{p_S}. \tag{17.9}$$

Rearranging equation (17.9) we obtain the relationship between p_B and p_S and their corresponding price elasticities of demand for using the platform:

$$\frac{p_B}{\eta_B} = \frac{p_S}{\eta_S}. \tag{17.10}$$

Equation (17.10) articulates that p_B and p_S depend on, and are proportional to, buyers' and sellers' elasticities of demand for using the platform, respectively. At first glance, it seems counterintuitive that equation (17.10) implies that the platform must charge a higher price to the side with more elastic demand and a lower price to the side with less elastic demand in order to equalize the two ratios. Mathematically, this must be true because equation (17.10) would otherwise be invalid. As far as the economic intuition is concerned, in the two-sided market the platform does not aim to increase either buyers or sellers but to increase both at the same time, and hence p_B and p_S are related to, but are not determined by, buyers' and sellers' demand elasticities for using the platform. This counterintuitive conclusion would not arise if the two sides were independent in demand for using the platform. Namely, two monopoly prices would be charged on both sides instead, a lower price on the more elastic side and a higher price on the less elastic side. Because of the cross-side network externalities, the demand of the more elastic side for the platform is largely attributed to users on the other side. Therefore, the platform needs to increase users on the less elastic side by lowering the price in order to captivate users whose demand is more elastic. The price burden of interactions is shifted to the more elastic side, simply because it is locked in by the less elastic side in the first place.

For instance, if riders' demand for using Uber is more elastic while drivers' demand is less elastic, what matters to riders is no longer the price charged by the platform but the number of drivers on the other side. In this case, riders would crave interactions more than drivers do. Of course, lowering price for riders can increase their demand for using the platform, but this entails increasing price for drivers, ending up diminishing drivers. Since increasing drivers is instrumental in generating interactions, cutting price for drivers can increase the number of drivers, thereby attracting riders. Even though cutting price leads to a disproportionately smaller increase in the number of drivers, the cross-side network effect from drivers to riders is substantial. This can explain why Uber and Airbnb subsidize drivers and hosts in one way or another especially in their early days. For instance, Uber provides drivers with access to private health plans and helps them increase their tax deductions.[6] Airbnb used to provide free photography services to hosts in order for them to better present their listings and therefore attract guests.[7] Raising price on the more elastic side will lead to a decrease in demand, but this decrease can be largely offset by the positive cross-side network externality. Once riders become crucial in generating interactions, the price burden will be shifted to drivers because drivers' demand would become more elastic, holding the number of riders constant.

Having articulated the relationship between the price structure and buyers' and sellers' respective demand elasticities for using the platform, we proceed to identify the shares of p_B and p_S in the implicit price p. Plugging equations (17.7) and (17.8) into equation (17.5) to spell out the demand elasticities of buyers and sellers, we obtain

$$p_B + p_S - c = -\frac{p_B}{\eta_B} = -\frac{p_S}{\eta_S}. \tag{17.11}$$

Plugging equation (17.4) into equation (17.11) to link the implicit price of interactions and the demand elasticity for interactions, we obtain

$$\frac{p_B}{\eta_B} = \frac{p_S}{\eta_S} = \frac{p}{\eta}. \tag{17.12}$$

From equation (17.12) we obtain the ratio of the implicit price of interactions p to the price elasticity of demand for interactions we derived earlier. By referring to the implicit price p, equation (17.12) suggests that the two ratios in equation (17.10) are constrained by the ratio of the price of interactions to the price elasticity of demand for interactions in the first place. Along with equation (17.10), equation (17.12) suggests

that the three demands cannot be perfectly inelastic, that is, $\eta_B \neq 0$, $\eta_S \neq 0$, and $\eta \neq 0$. The three prices, p_B, p_S, and p, are proportional to their respective elasticities of demand. From equation (17.12) we can also prove[8]

$$\eta = \eta_B + \eta_S. \tag{17.13}$$

Equation (17.13) suggests that given the elasticity of demand for interactions, there is a tradeoff between the elasticities of demand of buyers and sellers for using the platform. Other things being equal, when the demand of one side becomes more elastic, the demand of the other side must be less elastic to hold the elasticity of demand for interactions constant. The economic intuition is that once the demand of, say, buyers becomes more elastic, the fact that buyers gravitate toward the platform is because of sellers in the first place. Sellers' demand is less elastic because sellers care more about the value of the platform per se and less about the interactions with buyers. For instance, readers' demand for a newspaper could be less elastic as they focus on the newsworthy value of the newspaper per se whereas advertisers' demand for using the newspaper could be more elastic because their demand depends more on the presence of readers. Holding the cross-side network effect from readers to advertisers constant across different newspapers, advertisers would be more likely to switch to an alternative newspaper provided that it charges a lower price for advertising. Note that the elasticities of demand on both sides can be inelastic, and thus the demand for interactions as a whole becomes less elastic. In this case, the cross-side network effects are reciprocal and robust. Each side gravitates to the platform largely because of the presence of the other side.

Based on formula (17.4) and equations (17.12) and (17.13), we obtain p_B and p_S:

$$p_B = \frac{\eta_B}{\eta_B + \eta_S} p = \frac{\eta_B}{\eta_B + \eta_S + 1} c, \tag{17.14}$$

$$p_S = \frac{\eta_S}{\eta_B + \eta_S} p = \frac{\eta_S}{\eta_B + \eta_S + 1} c. \tag{17.15}$$

Equations (17.14) and (17.15) further show that the implicit price is allocated according to the proportion of each side's demand elasticity in the price elasticity of demand for interactions. Ultimately, p_B and p_S are determined by the demand elasticities of the two sides and the marginal cost of interactions. Note that the two equations imply $\eta_B + \eta_S < -1$, because the platform as a monopolist charges the price of interactions in the elastic portion of demand for profit maximization as long as the marginal cost $c > 0$. Given the number of buyers and sellers on the two sides, if their demand elasticities are equal, $\eta_B = \eta_S = \frac{1}{2}\eta$, buyers and sellers will split the implicit price equally, each paying

$p_B = p_S = \frac{\eta}{2(\eta+1)}c$. This is the case in which the cross-side network effects are not only reciprocal but also symmetric. If buyers' demand is more elastic, $\eta_B > \eta_S$, the price burden will be on buyers' side, and sellers are subsidized in the sense that they are charged a price lower than buyers are for each interaction. If sellers' demand is more elastic, $\eta_S > \eta_B$, the price burden will be on sellers' side, and buyers are subsidized in the sense that they are charged a price lower than sellers are for each interaction. The fundamental reason is that users on one side have more elastic demand for using the platform due to the positive cross-side network externality generated by users on the other side. Since $\eta_B \neq 0$, $\eta_S \neq 0$, and $\eta \neq 0$ as stated above, equations (17.14) and (17.15) rule out the possibility that one side bears the whole price burden while the other side is fully subsidized, that is, $p_B = p$ and $p_S = 0$, or $p_S = p$ and $p_B = 0$.[9]

17.4 The Coase theorem and platformization

17.4.1 The failure of the Coase theorem

The existence of cross-side network externalities is a necessary yet not sufficient condition for platforms to function as an institution. If buyers and sellers can internalize the benefits and/or costs derived from the cross-side network externalities, platforms will be negated in the market. This idea can be traced back to Ronald Coase. According to what is widely known as the Coase theorem, if property rights are well defined and transaction costs are negligible, buyers and sellers can bargain with each other, which will lead to a socially efficient amount of outcome despite the existence of externality and irrespective of the initial allocation of property rights. In the two-sided market, the property rights may be interpreted as the use of a platform that can be granted to either buyers, sellers, or both. The number of interactions mediated in the market would be independent of who has the right to use the platform in the first place. If a buyer's use of the platform has a positive externality on a seller, they can negotiate a price for the externality that is paid by the seller to the buyer for inducing the buyer's use of the platform. In the Coasian bargaining of this sort, if a reader and an advertiser know precisely that the reader's subscription to a newspaper generates publicity for the advertiser worth $1, the advertiser should be willing to pay $1 to induce the reader's subscription. On the other hand, if the reader's benefit from having an ad-free newspaper is greater than or equal to $1 and the advertiser's loss of not posting ads is smaller than or equal to $1, the reader should be willing to pay $1 to the advertiser for inducing him not to post ads. This will end up with an optimal number of interactions that are socially desirable by users on both sides.

Nevertheless, the Coase theorem does not work in the two-sided market for reasons that are either general to real-world transactions or particular to platforms. First of all, due to asymmetric information, users on one side are perhaps unaware that their use of a platform affects the well-being of the other side, or both sides are unaware of the externalities on each other. For instance, Facebook users are usually unaware of the positive externality they generate to advertisers, nor can they claim the benefits generated, and hence tend to underuse Facebook from a social perspective. Second, it is hard for either side to verify and measure cross-side network externalities even though both are aware of the externalities. For instance, it is cumbersome and even impossible for an advertiser to know whether a Facebook user reads an ad or not and, if so, whether he reads it accidentally or purposefully. Since the user's viewing behavior is unobservable, negotiating a price for the externality that can be agreed upon by both the user and the advertiser becomes infeasible. Third, even if the externality can be measured and appraised, the advertiser will find it extremely difficult to transfer the remuneration of the externalities under various viewing conditions to an astronomical number of Facebook users. If at all, the transaction costs would be insuperable and end up exceeding the remuneration to users.

17.4.2 Internalization of externality

Similar to intermediaries that arise to reduce transaction costs, platforms internalize cross-side network externalities that cannot be dissolved in the Coasian bargaining. When both buyers and sellers make their decisions to use a platform, what matters to them is the price charged by the platform rather than the effect of their use of the platform on the other side. If cross-side network externalities are positive and there is no way to claim the benefits, users on both sides tend to underuse the platform, leading to fewer socially desired interactions. If cross-side network externalities are negative, they tend to overuse the platform because they do not bear the external cost of their use on the well-being of the other side. This will end up with more socially undesired interactions. The social optimal number of interactions is determined by the joint willingness to pay of buyers and sellers for each interaction, provided that they have perfect information of the cross-side network externalities and can trade the externalities with each other at a zero transaction cost. Due to the failure of the Coase theorem, platforms arise as an institutional arrangement to facilitate the trade of cross-side externalities in the market. The structure of the implicit price of interactions reflects the values of cross-side network externalities that are either overlooked by users when deciding whether to join a platform or cannot be properly measured by users themselves.

Strictly speaking, platforms do not coordinate transactions between users but mediate interactions between them despite the fact that transactions and interactions sometimes overlap. For example, what matters to a newspaper is the quantity and quality of interactions mediated between readers and advertisers rather than the transactions between readers and advertisers in exchange for goods and services that are being advertised. Since two sides of users are interdependent, which determines the quantity of interactions, platforms cannot simply charge a monopoly price on one side without taking into account the effect on the demand of the other side. In practice, platforms usually make profits only on one side through charging a price higher than they would otherwise charge, while intentionally losing money on the other side. For example, Facebook and YouTube allow individual users to get free access to their platforms while charging heftily for advertisers to post ads. The prices charged for using the platforms are entirely burdened by advertisers while users are subsidized, because courting users is the prerequisite to luring advertisers. Similar examples include what is known as "freemium" in selling information products, in which users on one side are furnished with free software and those on the other side are charged hefty usage fees.[10]

Summary

1. The two-sided market consists of three economic agents, buyers and sellers on the two sides of the market and a platform which mediates interactions between the two sides. The platform is the focus of the two-sided market.
2. The cross-side network effects suggest interdependence of users on the two sides of a platform, which is the key to the two-sided market. To make the two-sided market function, at least one cross-side network externality must be positive.
3. The fundamental role that a platform plays is to create an implicit market for interactions between two sides of users whose interdependence can be transaction-based or simply interaction-based. The market for interactions depends on the number of users that the platform can court simultaneously on both sides.
4. A market is defined as two-sided if and only if the number of interactions varies by the allocation of the implicit price of interactions between two sides. The market is one-sided if the number of interactions only depends on the implicit price of interactions.
5. The profit-maximizing problem of a platform is two-fold. First, the platform determines the optimal implicit price of interactions. Second, given the implicit price of interactions, it identifies the optimal price structure by allocating the implicit price on the two sides.
6. The price for interactions is determined based on the Lerner index. As long as we know the price elasticity of demand for interactions, we can calculate the implicit price of interactions that buyers and sellers would jointly be willing to pay.
7. The price structure is determined when the marginal demands for interactions with respect to the prices of both sides are equal. This conclusion suggests that the price of each side of users is proportional to the price elasticity of their demand for using the platform.
8. The optimal price structure suggests that the more elastic the demand is on one side, the higher the price burden will be; and the less elastic the demand is on one side, the lower the price burden will be. The fundamental reason is that one side with more elastic demand is due to a positive cross-side network externality generated by the other side.
9. The Coase theorem states that if property rights are well defined and transaction costs are negligible, both trading parties can end up producing a market efficient outcome in the presence of externality, which is independent of the distribution of property rights.

10. The Coase theorem provides a theoretical justification for the emergence of platforms as an institutional arrangement in internalizing cross-side externalities. Simply because the Coase theorem does not apply, the Coasian bargaining is supplanted by platformization in the two-sided market.

REVIEW QUESTIONS

Each question has four options, and there is only one correct answer to each question.

1. Which of the following is an example of the positive cross-side network externality in the two-sided market?
   A) Drivers using Uber attract other drivers to use Uber.
   B) Guests booking Airbnb attract other guests to book Airbnb.
   C) Users using Facebook attract advertisers to post ads on Facebook.
   D) Firms advertising on newspapers deter readers from subscription to newspapers.
2. Facebook is a platform in the two-sided market for social networking services. Which of the following is correct regarding the cross-side network effects?
   A) Both cross-side network effects are positive.
   B) Both cross-side network effects are reciprocal.
   C) The cross-side network effect from users to advertisers is negative.
   D) The cross-side network effect from advertisers to users is negative.
3. Which of the following is regarded as the occurrence of an interaction between a reader and an advertiser insofar as a newspaper is concerned?
   A) A reader subscribes to the newspaper.
   B) A reader reads an ad in the newspaper.
   C) An advertiser reads the newspaper.
   D) An advertiser posts an ad in the newspaper.
4. Suppose that the number of buyers affiliated to a platform is n, and the number of sellers affiliated to the same platform is m. If buyers increase by 20% whereas sellers remain unchanged on the platform, how many interactions can the platform mediate?
   A) $n \times m$
   B) $1.2n \times m$
   C) $1.2n + m$
   D) $1.2n/m$
5. Suppose that the implicit price of each interaction mediated by a platform is \$10. If the market is two-sided, which of the following price structures is improbable?
   A) \$5 and \$5
   B) \$4 and \$6
   C) \$2 and \$8
   D) \$0 and \$10

6. If a platform cuts price on buyers' side by $1, the number of interactions mediated by the platform will increase by 25,000, other things being equal; if it cuts price by $1 on sellers' side, the number of interactions mediated will also increase by 25,000, other things being equal. Which of the following is correct?
   A) The platform should cut prices by $1 on both sides.
   B) The platform should raise prices by $1 on both sides.
   C) The platform should cut price by $1 for buyers while raising price by $1 for sellers.
   D) The platform should raise price by $1 for buyers while cutting price by $1 for sellers.
7. Suppose that the price elasticity of demand for transactions between riders and drivers on Uber is –1.5. Which of the following is INCORRECT?
   A) The demand of riders for using Uber could be elastic.
   B) The demand of drivers for using Uber could be inelastic.
   C) The demands of both riders and drivers for using Uber could be elastic.
   D) The demands of both riders and drivers for using Uber could be inelastic.
8. Suppose that the demand of gentlemen for joining a dating club is elastic while the demand of ladies for joining the same dating club is inelastic. If the dating club operates in the two-sided market, which of the following is correct regarding the price charged to gentlemen, p_G, and the price charged to ladies, p_L?
   A) $p_G = p_L$
   B) $p_G < p_L$
   C) $p_G > p_L$
   D) All of the above.
9. Which of the following is one of the reasons that the Coase theorem does not apply in the two-sided market?
   A) Transaction costs in the two-sided market are negligible.
   B) The cross-side network externalities are asymmetric.
   C) The cross-side network externalities cannot be measured by users.
   D) Users on both sides are aware of cross-side network externalities.
10. Which of the following is INCORRECT regarding intermediaries and platforms in the market?
    A) Intermediaries reduce transaction costs in the market.
    B) Platforms internalize cross-side network externalities in the market.
    C) Intermediaries include traditional travel agencies and OTAs.
    D) Platforms include only sharing economy enterprises.

Problem solving

1. Since Uber riders and drivers do not always equally split the price of transactions mediated by the platform of Uber, why isn't Uber's pricing strategy third-degree price discrimination? Since the demands of riders and drivers for using Uber are not the same, why isn't the two-sided market an example of product differentiation?

2. Some people argue that Booking.com is a platform because it connects hoteliers and travelers in exchange for hotel room services. Booking.com needs to court both hoteliers and travelers to use its website at the same time. The more hoteliers use Booking.com for selling hotel rooms, the more valuable Booking.com will become to travelers, and thus entices travelers to book hotels via Booking.com, and vice versa. Others argue that Booking.com is not a platform but an intermediary that makes profit through maximizing the bid-ask spread in hotel distribution. What do you think of the business model of Booking.com, and why?
3. American Express issues a wide range of credit cards that allow travelers to pay for their hotels, flights, public transport tickets, and taxis as conveniently as possible. For many of its credit cards, American Express does not charge cardholders a per-usage fee but an annual subscription fee. The annual subscription fee, which could amount to hundreds of dollars depending on the type of credit cards, is usually waived for the first year of subscription. For instance, American Express waives an annual subscription fee of CHF 140 for its Classic credit card for the first year in the Swiss market.[11] On the other hand, American Express opposes a card surcharge imposed by merchants, which is a fee that merchants charge cardholders when making a purchase using its credit cards.[12] Explain why American Express waives the annual fee while opposing the surcharge. Why wouldn't American Express charge a per-usage fee for its credit cards?

Solutions to all review questions and problem solving tasks are included in the Support Material for this book, which can be accessed at www.routledge.com/9780367897352.

Notes

1 The Uber case in this chapter focuses on the role of Uber as an institution in internalizing cross-side network externalities in market transactions. Note that this focus is fundamentally different from the focus of the free market and price signal exemplified by Uber's surge pricing in Chapter 3.

2 In the two-sided market, the dichotomy of buyers versus sellers is one special case of two sides of users that are courted by platforms. In other words, two sides of users of a platform are not necessarily buyers and sellers in exchange for goods and services in the market.

3 We use "network externality" and "network effect" interchangeably in this chapter. In general, when referring to a specific externality, we use network effect to better illustrate the idea that one side initiates an act which has an externality on the other. This is the same principle as we adopted in Chapter 6.

4 Readers can refer to two alternative models of the two-sided market developed by Parker and Van Alstyne (2005) and Armstrong (2006), respectively. Parker and Van Alstyne's model is built upon an explicit market in which a platform sells two separate goods to two sides of users whose demands are interdependent. Rochet and Tirole's model, which we introduced in this chapter, can be dubbed as implicit interaction-based while Parker and Van Alstyne's model is explicit transaction-based. Armstrong's

model is consistent with Rochet and Tirole's theorization in principle, but does not explicitly address two-sidedness. Armstrong's model provides a more straightforward interpretation of the price structure.

5 For expository simplicity, we use "buyers" and "sellers" to represent users on the two sides of a platform. As mentioned in Note 2, users may not engage in market transactions for some platforms, and are thus not necessarily buyers versus sellers, for example, Facebook users versus advertisers.

6 *Time*. Why Uber is trying to make nice with its drivers. August 31, 2016.

7 Airbnb. Airbnb free photography: Celebrating 13,000 verified properties & worldwide launch. October 6, 2011.

8 The proof of equation (17.13) is as follows. From equation (17.12), we have

$$\begin{cases} \dfrac{p}{\eta} = \dfrac{p_B}{\eta_B} \\ \dfrac{p}{\eta} = \dfrac{p_S}{\eta_S} \end{cases} \Rightarrow \quad 2\frac{p}{\eta} = \frac{p_B}{\eta_B} + \frac{p_S}{\eta_S} \quad \Rightarrow 2p\eta_B\eta_S = \eta(p_B\eta_S + p_S\eta_B). \tag{1}$$

Replacing p in (1) with $p = p_B + p_S$, we obtain $2(p_B + p_S)\eta_B\eta_S = \eta(p_B\eta_S + p_S\eta_B)$, and then we have

$$\eta_S p_B(2\eta_B - \eta) = \eta_B p_S(\eta - 2\eta_S). \tag{2}$$

Given $\frac{p_B}{\eta_B} = \frac{p_S}{\eta_S}$, if $p_B = 0$, then $p_S = 0$ and $p = 0$; the market for interactions will no longer exist. We thus conclude $p_B \neq 0$ and $p_S \neq 0$, and hence $\eta_S p_B = \eta_B p_S \neq 0$. Equation (2) can thus be simplified as $2\eta_B - \eta = \eta - 2\eta_S$, and hence $\eta = \eta_B + \eta_S$.

9 In practice though, either p_B or p_S can be zero or even negative, provided that a platform can pass on a loss from one side to the other side through charging a higher price to compensate for the loss. In theory, Parker and Van Alstyne (2005) and Armstrong (2006) allow a zero and even a negative price to occur on one side.

10 Adobe PDF is a notable example. Adobe provides PDF in both a reader version (Acrobat Reader DC) with limited functions for free and a professional version by charging an annual subscription fee of US$179.88 in the United States as of August 2020. Note that the offer of the two versions of PDF software and the corresponding pricing strategy should not be interpreted as product differentiation or price discrimination.

11 American Express. The original: The American Express credit card. Accessed on September 13, 2020.

12 American Express. What is Credit Card surcharging? Accessed on September 13, 2020.

Bibliography

Armstrong, M. (2006). Competition in two-sided markets. *RAND Journal of Economics*, 37(3), 668–691.

Coase, R. H. (1937). The nature of the firm. *Economica (new series)*, *4*(16), 386–405.

Coase, R. H. (1960). The problem of social cost. *Journal of Law & Economics*, *3*, 1–44.

Parker, G. G., & Van Alstyne, M. W. (2005). Two-sided network effects: A theory of information product design. *Management Science*, *51*(10), 1494–1504.

Rochet, J. C., & Tirole, J. (2003). Platform competition in two-sided markets. *Journal of the European Economic Association*, *1*(4), 990–1029.

Rochet, J. C., & Tirole, J. (2004). Defining two-sided markets. *Toulouse, France: IDEI, mimeo, January*. Retrieved from http://citeseerx.ist.psu.edu/viewdoc/download?doi=10.1.1.191.787&rep=rep1&type=pdf

Rochet, J. C., & Tirole, J. (2004). Two-sided markets: An overview. *Institut d'Economie Industrielle working paper*. Retrieved from https://web.mit.edu/14.271/www/rochet_tirole.pdf

Rochet, J. C., & Tirole, J. (2006). Two-sided markets: A progress report. *RAND Journal of Economics, 37*(3), 645–667.

18 The platformization of OpenTable[1]

This chapter applies the two-sided market model to explore how OpenTable has evolved from a merchant of vending electronic reservation systems to a platform that courts both restaurants and diners. In addition to cross-side network externalities, we illustrate the same-side network externalities, particularly on diners' side, that are pivotal to consolidate the diner base. As OpenTable morphs into a platform, acquiring diners to entice restaurants becomes increasingly important, which is reflected in its pricing strategy to favor diners. Diners are provided with free booking services and all sorts of perks while restaurants bear the cost. Restaurants are discouraged by hefty monthly subscription fees especially when they are not able to discern how many incremental reservations are contributed by OpenTable. Hence competition arises as more and more alternative platforms are available providing lower rates while furnishing restaurants with more information to manage their guests than OpenTable does. Competing platforms allow users to multi-home on different platforms.

AFTER STUDYING THIS CHAPTER, YOU SHOULD BE ABLE TO:

- Understand how OpenTable exhibits four types of network externalities and discern the directions of the network effects;
- Understand why the transformation from the merchant model to a platform is imperative to OpenTable's success;
- Analyze how OpenTable's platform strategy is revealed by its previous and current pricing plans; and
- Understand the phenomenon of multi-homing and how it would challenge OpenTable's market dominance.

18.1 What is OpenTable?

The restaurant industry by and large is fragmented as it serves a vast majority of localized clientele. Even for global fast-food chains such as McDonald's and Burger King, competition between them is waged locally through thousands of outlets vying for local customers. This perhaps explains why the restaurant industry lagged far behind the airline and hotel sectors in embracing electronic reservation solutions. For instance, global distribution systems and online travel agencies have been widely adopted by the airline and hotel sectors since the 1980s and 1990s, respectively. The leading role of airlines and hotels in embracing technology is not accidental, for both render products and services to global customers, particularly tourists as opposed to locals. Thus, reducing transaction costs through technology along with new business models is more pressing for the airline and hotel sectors than for other hospitality sectors which have a local clientele base. In fact, a globalized distribution network may not be as effective for restaurants as it is for airlines and hotels. For many small and independent restaurants, the traditional paper-and-pencil book had been, for decades, not only effective but was also a norm in handling reservations. Fine-dining restaurants may not bother to innovate their reservation management because the cuisine and amenities are delicate enough to captivate customers who pursue gastronomic experience instead of scouring for a vacant seat.

Therefore, it is no wonder that a nation-wide restaurant reservation system, which could house and centralize a variety of restaurants across a country, did not emerge until the founding of OpenTable in San Francisco in 1998. Like innovations behind most startups over the past decade, such as Airbnb and Uber, the idea of OpenTable originated from desperate needs of users accidentally rather than long-awaited entrepreneurial aspirations. It came to Chuck Templeton, a former U.S. Army Ranger, one day in 1998 when seeing his wife spending hours on the phone trying to book a suitable restaurant for his father-in-law visiting them in town.[2] Since most restaurants in the United States at that time did not have computers, it was not surprising why reserving a restaurant for the Templetons turned out to be cumbersome and spectacularly inefficient. This unsatisfying experience led him to contemplate why an easier alternative was not available to make diners like him and his wife find a suitable restaurant and secure a reservation more efficiently. In the meantime, an easy solution, if any, could help restaurants to better manage and assign vacant seats, thereby increasing reservations and boosting management efficiency.

His website, later known as OpenTable.com, was launched the same year which marked the beginning of his business. However, the platform strategy that OpenTable has been pursuing since 2009 did not come without a painstaking groping process. In the first five years or so of operation, OpenTable aimed at superseding the paper-and-pencil book by its electronic reservation book (ERB), which is a computerized reservation system that allows restaurants to manage reservations and assign tables electronically.[3] The ERB was sold for a monthly subscription fee of $199 to restaurants, which suggests that the merchant model, according to OpenTable, was implemented long before most diners had even discovered OpenTable.com.[4] By 2001 OpenTable operated in 50 cities in the United States but was losing around US$900,000 each month;[5] by 2004 it had partnered only 2,423 restaurants since its foundation in 1998,[6] far below the expectation of its investors. Before its initial public offering (IPO) on the Nasdaq in 2009, *Fortune* reported that OpenTable was on the verge of bankruptcy because it could not identify a profitable business model to restore the confidence of venture capitalists to continue injecting money.[7] According to *Fortune*, it was not until the new management steered OpenTable toward building a consumer brand on the one hand and forging relationships with restaurateurs on the other that eventually success was achieved.[8]

18.2 OpenTable as a platform

18.2.1 The platform

OpenTable did not identify a platform strategy sooner probably because mobile technology, in particular smartphones, did not burgeon until 2008. In fact, OpenTable predated many mainstream platform companies such as Twitter, Instagram, and YouTube for almost a decade and even Facebook for five years, all of which resorted to mobile technology to amass users. It was not until 2010 that OpenTable explicitly stated in a note to restaurants that it helped connect diners with more than 15,000 restaurants worldwide at that time.[9] This suggests a shift in OpenTable's business model from a merchant of vending the ERB to a platform of acquiring users. The diner-oriented strategy has been corroborated since it launched the OpenTable mobile app in 2008, which allowed diners not only to make reservations more conveniently but also to interact with one another more frequently by sharing dining experience and posting reviews the same way as they use, for instance, Facebook and Instagram.[10] As soon as OpenTable morphed into a platform that connects restaurants on one side and diners on the other, its strategy was distinguished strikingly from the merchant model of selling the ERB. The role that OpenTable plays is not only to create interactions between restaurants and diners but to facilitate transactions between them. Besides courting restaurants and diners, OpenTable relies on the volume of transactions between the two, which sets it apart from Facebook, for instance, which mediates no transactions between users and advertisers.

18.2.2 Cross-side network effects

As discussed in Chapter 17, the prerequisite for the two-sided market to work is the existence of cross-side network externalities that cannot be internalized by the two sides of users themselves. Above all else, the positive cross-side network effect is not only instrumental in the functioning of a platform, but is also the very definition of the two-sided market. As far as OpenTable is concerned, the cross-side network effect from restaurants to diners suggests that diners' use of OpenTable to make reservations will increase as participating restaurants increase on OpenTable. It would not be worthwhile for diners to make reservations via OpenTable if there were not sufficient restaurants participating in the first place. Since the ERB simplifies the painstakingly slow and tedious booking procedure and enables restaurants to effectively manage reservations, restaurant seats can be freed up in a timely way to accommodate and entice diners. In its early days, OpenTable aimed to attract high-end restaurants to adopt the ERB because their visibility on the platform would lure more diners. OpenTable still features acclaimed business partners, such as luxury hotels and Michelin-starred restaurants, on the front page of its website to lure not only diners but also other restaurants. This is why OpenTable has been focusing on acquiring restaurants in metropolises such as San Francisco, New York City, and London with dense consumer bases.

On the other hand, the cross-side network effect from diners to restaurants suggests that restaurants' use of OpenTable will increase as the diner base expands. This cross-side network effect was overlooked by OpenTable in its early operation, which perhaps explains why participating restaurants had grown so slowly before 2009 to make it break even. As a matter of fact, it might not be worthwhile for restaurants to subscribe to OpenTable if it cannot channel sufficient reservations besides those that restaurants can secure by themselves anyway. This is also an issue raised by many restaurateurs regarding the number of incremental reservations which would not be made if there were no OpenTable. For instance, Anjan Mitra of Dosa, a fine-dining Indian restaurant in the U.S., told the *New York Times* in 2017 that "I don't mind paying OpenTable for new customers, but OpenTable was charging me for customers I already had and knew well."[11] Of course, OpenTable is aware of the importance of channeling valuable diners to restaurants in order to retain its restaurant partners. According to its policy, OpenTable will suspend a diner's account if the account accumulates no-shows for four times within a 12-month period, aiming to provide assurance of reservation to restaurants.[12] When considering switching to other reservation platforms, restaurateurs are also worried about losing their diners who are locked in by OpenTable and hence cannot readily discover their restaurants on new platforms.[13]

18.2.3 Same-side network effects

Similar to other platform companies such as Facebook, OpenTable will become more valuable to prospective diners as more diners use OpenTable to make reservations. This is referred to as a same-side network effect, an example of the bandwagon effect manifested on diners' side. While same-side network effects are not a prerequisite for the two-sided market to function, they explain the expansion of user base that would make a platform more valuable to other users on the same side. First of all, the expansion of diners using OpenTable would make it trendy and thus attract other diners, similar to how social networks such as Facebook and Instagram amass users. This bandwagon has been largely driven by mobile technology since 2008, which is why OpenTable not only developed its own mobile app as early as 2008 but has ever since partnered with other platform giants such as Facebook, Google, Instagram, and Snapchat, to name a few. This provides diners with a wide range of choices to make reservations on these third-party platforms, which contributed 17% of diners seated each month in the fourth quarter of 2019.[14] Second, the notable benefits that diners can obtain are customer reviews posted on OpenTable by their predecessors, which help newcomers to discern and select good restaurants. Since the introduction of the review program in 2008, diners contributed more than 1.3 million reviews on OpenTable each month.[15]

The same-side network effect on restaurants' side suggests that restaurants' use of OpenTable is affected by other restaurants. Presumably at the initial stage, as restaurant subscriptions to OpenTable increased, the platform would become more appealing to prospective restaurants as well. OpenTable's strategy of courting acclaimed restaurants as we mentioned earlier not only attracts diners but also other restaurants. This generates a bandwagon on the restaurants' side in which scrapping the paper-and-pencil book especially for restaurant chains would have become a trend. As more and more restaurants are equipped with the ERB, the switching cost to other platforms also increases. After all, the subscription fee of the ERB, which we shall address shortly, is an appreciable fixed cost. Like diners, restaurants can also be locked in by OpenTable. Only after OpenTable amasses considerable restaurant partners will it be able to reduce costs to serve its restaurant clientele. For instance, OpenTable has gradually waived the installation fees of the ERB and shifted to a cloud-based ERB. However, as the number of restaurants on OpenTable increases, it might become less appealing to other restaurants because an imminent fear of competition on the same platform may discourage followers. This can in part explain why some fine-dining restaurants unsubscribe from OpenTable as soon as alternative platforms become available.[16]

18.3 Structure of fees and user response

18.3.1 Structure of fees

Probably nothing could better articulate the metamorphosis of OpenTable from a merchant to a platform than its pricing strategy did. First of all, OpenTable allowed diners to make reservations for free because, as we mentioned earlier, it did not regard diners as its customers in its early operation. Second, as soon as it adopted a platform strategy, free reservation turned out to be a subsidy to diners while the profits were generated from restaurants, resembling the business model of Facebook and many other platform companies. For OpenTable, the price burden is entirely on restaurants. Table 18.1 shows fees charged to restaurants in two major categories. One is a flat monthly subscription fee of \$199–\$249 for using the ERB, irrespective of the number of reservations made via OpenTable. Along with the subscription fee, OpenTable used to charge a one-time ERB installation and training fee ranging from \$200 to \$700. The other category is the transaction fee based on the volume of transactions between restaurants and diners mediated by OpenTable. OpenTable charges \$1 per seated diner for reservations directly made on its website and app and \$0.25 for each walk-in or reservation made on the websites of restaurants or its business partners, such as Facebook, Instagram, TripAdvisor, and so on.

While OpenTable has largely adhered to the structure of the fixed subscription fee and the variable reservation fee shown in Table 18.1, its current pricing plan is customized to the needs of different types of restaurants. Table 18.2 shows the current pricing plan in three versions, basic, core, and professional. The basic version contains all reservation and marketing functions charged for a flat monthly fee of \$29. Besides including all functions of the basic version, the core version contains table management, waitlist management, and availability control charged for \$249 per month. The professional version, also the most expensive one, is expanded to incorporate advanced functions, such as relationship management and guest profiling, charged for \$449 per month. Yet the basic version is accompanied with the highest reservation fee, $1.5 per seated diner, as opposed to $1 per seated diner for the core and professional versions. In addition, OpenTable provides a booking widget which allows restaurants to enjoy discounted covers for reservations from their own websites, Facebook pages, and blogs. This widget is charged for either an additional flat fee of $49 per month or $0.25 per seated diner to restaurants signed up for the basic version, but is provided for free in the core and professional versions. Obviously, there is a heavy fixed-cost burden on restaurants subscribing to the core and professional versions and a heavy variable-cost burden on those signing up for the basic version.

Table 18.1 Previous fee structure of OpenTable

Category	Unit	Price (US$)	Current status
Fixed costs			
ERB subscription	Monthly	$199–$249	Cloud-based
ERB installation	Once for all	$200–$700	Phased out
Variable costs			
Booking from OpenTable	Per seated diner	$1	Available
Booking from restaurants	Per seated diner	$0.25	Available
Off-peak "1,000-point program"	Per seated diner	$7.5	Phased out

Note: The fees were charged in the U.S. market.

Source: OpenTable. How OpenTable works for restaurants. November 19, 2010. *Business Insider*. OpenTable explained: Here's how the company makes money. October 26, 2011.

Table 18.2 Current pricing plan of OpenTable

Category	Unit	Price (US$)		
		Basic	Core	Professional
Fixed costs				
Subscription fee	Monthly	$29 ($39 month-to-month)	$249	$449
Fixed/variable costs				
Network cover fee	Per cover	$1.50	$1	$1
Booking widget	Once for all or per cover	$49 flat fee or $0.25 per cover	Free	Free

Note: The fees are charged in the U.S. market.

Source: OpenTable, retrieved on August 22, 2020.

18.3.2 Restaurants' response

Restaurants could have responded differently to the fee structure in Table 18.1, which is in part reflected in the growth of restaurant subscriptions. Figure 18.1 shows that the number of participating restaurants increased from 7,861 in 2007 to 31,583 in the first quarter of 2014, an average increase of 5.7% on a quarterly basis. The majority of the participating restaurants were from the U.S., which made up nearly 80% of all participating restaurants in this period. However, the growth of international restaurants outpaced that of U.S. restaurants, with a quarterly growth rate of 13.9% versus 4.7% on average. Probably due to the effect of IPO in 2009, international restaurants surged from 2,221 in the third quarter of 2010 to 6,254 in the fourth quarter, and have since maintained an average quarterly growth of 18.7%. In terms of the price range of restaurants, obviously low- and medium-priced restaurants rely more on OpenTable for securing a steady flow of diners than high-priced restaurants do. This perhaps explains why OpenTable is now offering three versions of subscription (Table 18.2). Given the fact that high-priced restaurants are usually fine-dining restaurants which can fill their seats much easier, thanks to their loyal customers and repeat patronages, they may rely less on OpenTable for channeling reservations. However, OpenTable relies on marquee restaurants, many of which are high-priced, to substantiate its attractiveness to diners. This is reflected in OpenTable's current pricing plan for not only providing the booking widget for free to its core and professional subscribers but also charging them a lower reservation fee.

Despite the fact that restaurants can factor the subscription fee of $449 into their operating costs, the question is whether the subscription is worth paying. This depends

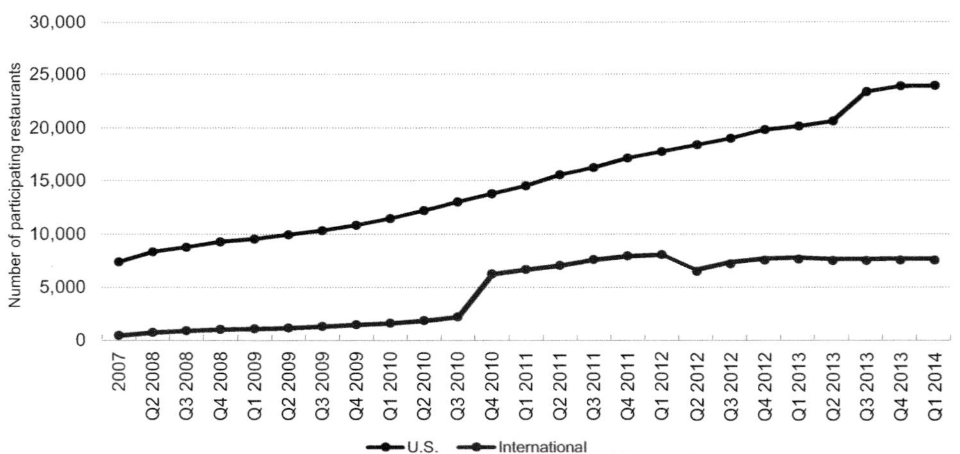

Figure 18.1
Growth of participating restaurants on OpenTable

Note: The number of participating restaurants is the accumulated number of restaurants at the end of each quarter. All the figures are on a quarterly basis except for 2007.

Source: Trefis Team.

very much on the number of incremental diners OpenTable can generate especially in off-peak periods as well as the number of repeat customers who would consistently use OpenTable to make reservations. How to accurately measure incremental diners has been a concern of many restaurateurs, such as Anjan Mitra of Dosa, who has no information at all about how many reservations can be exclusively attributed to OpenTable. For low-priced restaurants which make up the largest proportion of the restaurant industry, a low monthly subscription fee would entice them to use OpenTable, yet a high reservation fee per head will accumulate as reservations increase, thereby squeezing their already thin profit margins. Thus, this will discourage them from using OpenTable, thereby shrinking the user base of restaurants. For both medium- and high-priced restaurants though, the hefty monthly subscription fee could only be justified by a large number of incremental reservations solicited by OpenTable on the one hand and the number of seats that can be freed up to accommodate additional diners on the other. Unfortunately, the data that would allow us to dig deeper and examine these effects thoroughly are not yet accessible from OpenTable or its restaurant partners.

18.3.3 Diners' response

In addition to free reservation, OpenTable provides diners with various benefits to entice them to make reservations via its website or apps. To name a few, OpenTable implements a points reward scheme which allows diners to accumulate points for each completed reservation. These points can be used for future reservations or redeemed for Amazon gift cards. OpenTable also launched fast-check services, allowing diners to pay checks straight on their mobile app in order to save time for diners. These perks not only entice diners to use OpenTable as much as they can but also increase their dining frequency at selected restaurants. Subsidizing users by offering free products and services is the orthodox pricing strategy of platform companies to consolidate the user base in the first place. Figure 18.2 shows that seated diners increased from 8.5 million recorded in the first quarter of 2008 to 46.7 million recorded in the first quarter of 2014. The U.S. was and still is the major source of seated diners, accounting for 94.5% of seated diners on quarterly average between 2008 and 2014. This is largely due to large diner bases in many U.S. metropolises, such as New York City, Chicago, and San Francisco, where OpenTable has a predominant presence. Last but not least, the cost of acquiring diners is much lower than acquiring restaurant subscribers. Obviously, acquiring diners would incur a fixed cost primarily in marketing and promotion, which decreases sharply per head as long as diner numbers are scaled up.

Nevertheless, it is a misconception that OpenTable only courts diners by providing them with free booking among other things. In fact, it is infeasible for many platforms to charge a usage fee based on the volume of transactions, as the interactions between the two sides cannot be properly measured. Even if they could be, transaction costs involving millions of users would be insurmountable and thus negate the efficacy of any usage fee that is based on trade volume. Thus fixed subscription fees prevail in the market, granting users access to platform regardless of the quantity of interactions. For instance, YouTube launched a premium monthly subscription of US$11.99 in

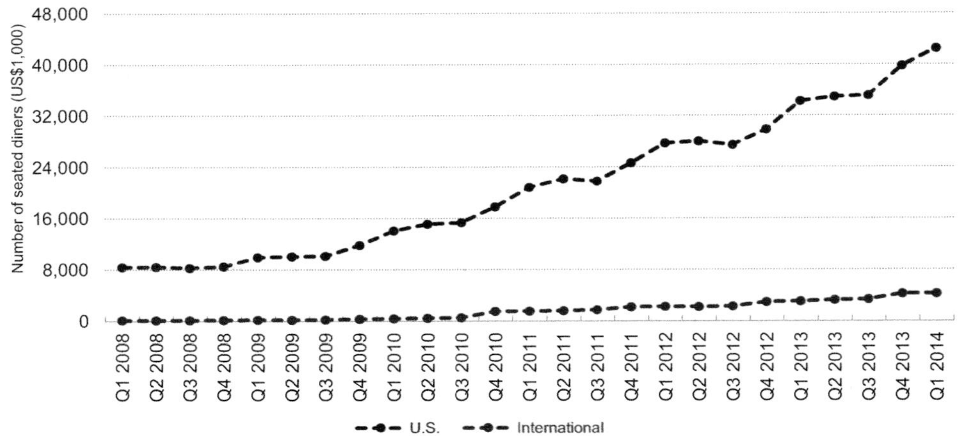

Figure 18.2
Growth of seated diners on OpenTable

Note: The number of diners is the number of seated diners in each quarter.

Source: Trefis Team.

2018 granting viewers ad-free access to its content and download options.[17] Different from YouTube though, OpenTable is able to charge diners a reservation fee or allows restaurants and diners to share the reservation fee because interactions between the two are reservations which can be identified and measured. In 2015 OpenTable did trial a premium reservation service in some U.S. cities, charging diners a premium reservation price for last-minute or prime-time reservations at popular restaurants.[18] Yet this strategy did not work out for diners or for restaurateurs. As the Coase theorem suggests, a reservation fee on diners' side, if any, can be internalized through restaurants compensating diners with an equivalent price discount. It thus does not matter whether the reservation fee is borne by diners or by restaurants, provided that the transaction costs between both sides in negotiating the fee are negligible.

18.4 Firm revenue and growth

Unfortunately, comprehensive statistics are sparse with regard to the relationship between OpenTable's financial performance and its pricing strategy. An article in *Business Insider* in 2011 stated that the majority of OpenTable's profit was from selling reservation tools, primarily the ERB, to its participating restaurants.[19] However, subscription and installation fees of the ERB, which would amount to thousands of dollars per restaurant per year, did not bring about a financial success for OpenTable in its early days. This is because scaling up the number of restaurants is far more difficult than increasing the number of diners. Figure 18.3 shows that reservation fees make up an increasingly large proportion of OpenTable's revenue, which grew from 44% in the first quarter of 2008 to nearly 64% in the first quarter of 2014, or US$34.3 million. There has been a noticeably high growth in reservation-based revenue since its IPO in 2009 (Figure 18.3). In contrast to subscription fees generated from participating restaurants, revenue from reservation fees accrues because robust network effects increase dining frequency. By the first quarter of 2014, revenue from diner reservations was twice as much as the revenue from restaurant subscriptions, a striking contrast to 52% of the revenue from restaurant subscriptions in the first quarter of 2008. OpenTable will no doubt continue to rely on reservation fees to generate profits as the number of restaurants is relatively stable in a certain period of time.

Besides analyzing OpenTable's pricing strategy, we can trace the platformization of OpenTable by exploring how its revenue changes with the growth of users. Figure 18.4 shows that the growth of OpenTable's revenue is closely associated with the growth of seated diners rather than the growth of participating restaurants. On the one hand, both diners and revenue experienced seasonal fluctuations in growth, which increased in the fourth and the following first quarters but declined in the second and third quarters each year. Such a seasonal growth was not evident for participating restaurants. On the other hand, the growth rate of diners outpaced revenue growth on average during the whole period 2008–2014. In particular, diner growth outpaced revenue growth by four percentage points in peak seasons, the third and fourth quarters. Figure 18.4 further shows that the 2009 IPO could be a tipping point for the growth of OpenTable. On the one hand, the growth of diners had been increasing faster than the revenue growth in the post-IPO period, and on the other the growth pattern of revenue resembled the growth of diners. Also worth noting is the surge in restaurant growth in 2010, probably because the 2009 IPO generated substantial publicity for OpenTable,

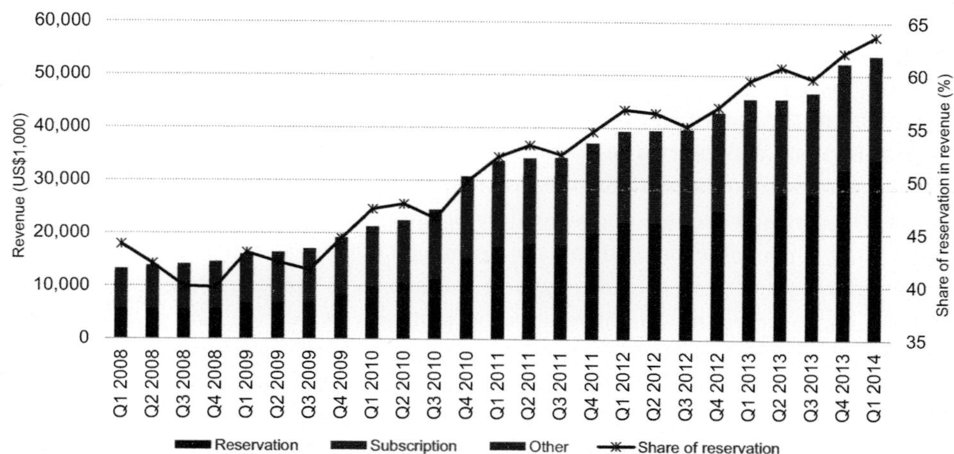

Figure 18.3
Revenue composition of OpenTable

Note: "Reservation" indicates the revenue obtained from reservation fees. "Subscription" indicates the revenue obtained from restaurants subscribing to the ERB. "Other" includes all other revenues. "Share of reservation" is the proportion of reservation-based revenue in total revenue of OpenTable.

Source: Trefis Team.

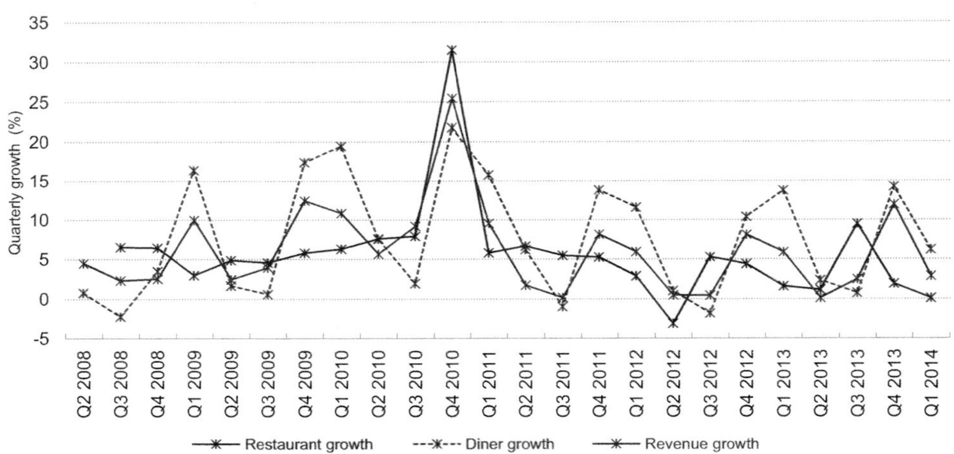

Figure 18.4
Growths of restaurants, diners, and revenue

Note: Restaurant growth is the growth of participating restaurants. Diner growth is the growth of seated diners. Revenue growth is the growth of total revenue.

Source: Trefis Team.

thereby attracting restaurants to join the platform. Yet the marketing effect of the IPO was short lived, as the growth of restaurants decreased sharply after 2010.

18.5 Platform competition and multi-homing

As an American company, OpenTable has its dominant presence in dozens of U.S. metropolises. In 2014, OpenTable was acquired by Priceline for US$2.6 billion to complement the parent company's incumbent hospitality and travel booking services, such as Booking.com, Agoda, and Kayak, aiming for international expansion. It has also collaborated with over 600 business partners, including Amazon, Facebook, Google, and so on,[20] which provide a great variety of options for diners to make reservations. As of 2019, OpenTable claimed to have homed 60,000 restaurants, bars, wineries, and other catering units in 80 countries, and seated over 31 million diners each month, making it the largest restaurant reservation platform worldwide. Since its foundation in 1998 OpenTable has seated more than 2 billion diners who spent US$91 billion at its partner restaurants and contributed 97 million customer reviews.[21] Behind the stellar growth of OpenTable is the power of network effects, which turn out to be an obstacle for competitors to challenge its market dominance. Moreover, network effects would have led to a drastic decrease in OpenTable's costs of serving a large number of restaurant partners and diners, making it a natural monopoly similar to Facebook, Twitter, and many other platform giants.

Because of OpenTable's hefty subscription fees, restaurateurs become less motivated to use OpenTable especially when alternatives are available. The competition that OpenTable faces could date back to 2011 outside the U.S. market, and it now faces competition from Resy, Yelp, Bookatable, and so on, which provide quite similar services to restaurants yet at lower rates. The Priceline acquisition in 2014 did not seem to fuel the international expansion of OpenTable beyond North America. There are a couple of reasons worth mentioning. First, as stated above the restaurant industry is far different from the hotel and airline sectors due to the localized clientele. Therefore, it is difficult, if not impossible, for one reservation platform to monopolize the global market. This could explain why the global expansion of OpenTable is far slower than that of Airbnb and Uber which were founded almost a decade later than OpenTable. Second, OpenTable's complex fee structure will impede its growth as long as better rates are provided by its competitors. For high-priced restaurants relying less on reservations from OpenTable, exorbitant monthly subscription fees would backfire when a lack of information hinders restaurateurs from discerning incremental reservations generated from OpenTable. For low-priced restaurants depending more on reservations mediated by OpenTable, high reservation fees would shrink their profit margins.

For restaurants and particularly for diners, it would be beneficial to use both OpenTable and alternative platforms at the same time. This is known as multi-homing in which a user affiliates to more than one platform simultaneously. A restaurant may choose to multi-home, for instance, on OpenTable and Resy, and can therefore reap reservations from both platforms. The exorbitant subscription fees may have led some restaurants to decouple from OpenTable completely. In September 2018, Danny Meyer's Union Square Hospitality Group (USHG) diverted all of its restaurants from OpenTable to Resy.[22] Danny Meyer's exclusive partnership with Resy is not only due to low subscription fees but also because Resy can provide a trove of information about diner profile and behavior.[23] While OpenTable can still secure incumbent restaurants and diners, acquiring new users would become more difficult and costly due to multi-homing and platform competition. Also, if an increasing number of bookings were made on a competitor's platform, OpenTable's revenue would shrink drastically because over 90% of its revenue is from monthly subscription and reservation fees. For diners, multi-homing is even more appealing because it allows diners to scoop more benefits at a negligible cost as a consequence of competition between platforms.

Summary

1. Prior to the foundation of OpenTable, the restaurant industry had lagged far behind the airline and hotel sectors in embracing electronic reservation solutions, largely because it serves a vast majority of localized clientele.
2. OpenTable did not adopt a platform strategy in the first place. It transformed from a merchant of vending the electronic reservation book to a platform that courts both restaurants and diners. A robust diner base is imperative to attract restaurants.
3. There are four network effects exhibited on OpenTable: two cross-side network effects between restaurants and diners and two same-side network effects on restaurants' and diners' sides, respectively. The same-side network effect on diners' side renders OpenTable similar to other social networks in sharing experiences.

4. OpenTable provides diners with free reservation along with a wide range of perks, such as point rewarding and redeeming for gifts while charging restaurants hefty subscription fees in various forms. The price burden is exclusively on restaurants' side.
5. In general, OpenTable charges restaurants a fixed monthly subscription fee for using its ERB and a variable reservation fee based on the volume of transactions between restaurants and diners. OpenTable now tailors its pricing plan to different restaurants.
6. Low monthly subscription fees entice low-priced restaurants, yet high reservation fees squeeze their profit margins. For medium- and high-priced restaurants, high monthly subscription fees could only be justified by incremental reservations solicited by OpenTable and the number of seats that can be freed up to accommodate diners.
7. OpenTable relies on reservation fees as the major source of its revenue as the number of restaurants is relatively stable in a certain period of time. OpenTable's revenue is largely driven by diner reservations as the growth of diners outpaces revenue growth.
8. Because of OpenTable's fee structure, restaurateurs are less motivated to use OpenTable especially when alternatives are available. For restaurants and particularly for diners, it would be beneficial to multi-home on different platforms.

Problem solving

1. Explain why OpenTable did not operate in the two-sided market at its initial stage. What would be the factors contributing to the platformization of OpenTable?
2. In Chapter 17 we did not take same-side network effects into account when modeling the behavior of the platform. Suppose that the same-side network effect on diners' side is positive while on restaurants' side is negative, other things being equal. How would the two same-side network effects affect the pricing strategy of OpenTable?
3. Consider three situations of multi-homing: (1) diners multi-home while restaurants single-home on OpenTable, (2) restaurants multi-home while diners single-home on OpenTable, and (3) both diners and restaurants multi-home. Explain the impact of each of the three situations on the pricing strategy and profits of OpenTable.

Solutions to all review questions and problem solving tasks are included in the Support Material for this book, which can be accessed at www.routledge.com/9780367897352.

Notes

1 I would like to thank Mr. Doug Nathman and Mr. Edward T. Rose from Trefis for furnishing me with the data of OpenTable as well as for granting me the permission to use the data in this chapter.
2 *Chicago Tribune*. New website helps neighbors share stuff, be green. May 26, 2011.
3 OpenTable. How OpenTable works for restaurants. November 19, 2010.
4 See Note 3.
5 *Fortune*. OpenTable—The hottest spot in town. August 14, 2009.
6 Software Platform Consulting. The OpenTable flywheel. October 31, 2011.
7 See Note 3.
8 See Note 3.
9 See Note 2.
10 OpenTable. OpenTable announces free iPhone application now available on Apple App Store. November 17, 2008.
11 *The New York Times*. OpenTable began a revolution. Now it's a power under siege. August 29, 2017.
12 OpenTable. OpenTable terms of use. Revision date: September 25, 2017.
13 Eater. The quest to topple OpenTable. September 24, 2018.
14 OpenTable. Global fast facts. Q4 2019.
15 See Note 14.
16 Skift. Union Square Hospitality Group to move all reservations to Resy. September 4, 2018.
17 Informa PLC. YouTube rebrands Red to Premium, announces European launches. May 17, 2018.
18 OpenTable. Now testing: Premium reservations in NYC. September 25, 2015.
19 *Business Insider*. OpenTable explained: Here's how the company makes money. October 26, 2011.
20 OpenTable. Global fast facts. Q4 2019.
21 OpenTable. Global fast facts. Q4 2019.
22 Resy. Resy launches exclusive partnership with Danny Meyer's Union Square Hospitality Group. September 4, 2018.
23 See Note 16.

Bibliography

Barton, T. L., & MacArthur, J. B. (2016). A teaching case on the benefits and costs of restaurants using OpenTable online restaurant reservations. *Journal of Business and Accounting*, *9*(1), 126–135.

Evans, D. S., & Schmalensee, R. (2016). *Matchmakers: The new economics of multisided platforms*. Boston, MA: Harvard Business Review Press.

AUTHOR INDEX

Note: Page numbers followed by "n" denote endnotes.

SUBJECT INDEX

Note: *Italic* page numbers refer to figures and page numbers followed by "n" denote endnotes.